KNIGHTS IN WHITES, MAJOR MEN

and preachers and teachers

THE DEFINITIVE WHO'S WHO OF NORFOLK CCC 1876-2011

Mike Davage

First published in Great Britain by
Colchester Print Group
© CPG, 2011

Mike Davage has asserted his right under the Copyright,
Designs and Patents Act 1988 to be identified as the author
of this work.

British Library Cataloguing-in-Publication Data.
A catalogue record for this book is available from the British
Library.

ISBN: 978-0-9570400-0-7
Typeset by Colchester Print Group

Introduction

In my youth I watched Hampshire CCC at the County Ground, Southampton and saw the County Championship clinched at Dean Park, Bournemouth on 1 September 1961 when my hero Derek Shackleton (24-10-39-6) bowled them to victory with his second innings performance. I even saw the legendary Bill Edrich play for Norfolk in a 1965 Gillette Cup match.

To explain the methodology of this book. The players are arranged by year of debut rather than alphabetically. The Players Yearly Appearance Section holds the key to finding a player. For Example JH Edrich only played 1954 and 1979 so to show just first and last date is misleading. I have departed from putting HS and BB in the Averages section as I needed columns for OW (other wickets) and Balls (NCCC were involved with 4,5,6 and 8 ball over games). One can now see in the biographies where and when the individual highest score and best bowling took place.

Re HS, BB and FF in bold print throughout the book.

HS & BB in Bold represents Minor County matches; *Italics* are for Cup games and Normal Type for Friendlies and the theme is continued in the Averages section. FF is for further/family facts. I have treated a Friendly as a first team affair if seven or more county players were involved (I used the same formula for the Norwich City book 'Canary Citizens').

I have thanked various individuals as you read the book. I have written 50% more than I budgeted for so a preface, acknowledgements and bibliography have fallen by the wayside due to lack of space. I would additionally however thank Stephen Skinner (NCCC's Club Secretary) for his support and access to Handbooks and his collection of 'Scores & Biographies'. The latter publication explains the (?) in the Averages – in olden days they showed balls and runs and not maidens/dots for bowling. Thanks also to Philip Bailey (Cricket Archive) for the database of NCCC players. He can now correct and update the website where necessary. David Cuffley (Archant Newspapers) found Bryan Steven's ledger which gave me another valuable cross referencing point. Undying gratitude to my darling wife Val (42 years married) for enduring my insatiable madness for facts and figures.

1876

BIRKBECK, Henry
(b) Stoke Holy Cross 12 May 1853
(d) West Acre, Norfolk 11 February 1930
Educ. – Eton College
Cricket. – Eton College; I Zingari; Ipswich & East Suffolk; Gurney's Bank; H.Birkbeck's X1; The Herons; Norfolk & Norwich; East Norfolk.
HS. 89 no v MCC July 1885 @ Lord's
'Scores & Biographies' quote, " Capital batsman, fast underarm bowler and fields at long leg and cover point "
103 for I Zingari v Gunton August 1875
Father of Gervase (q.v)
F.F. – West Acre High House in the Birkbeck family since 1897 until recently sold to 'Angel of the North' sculptor Anthony Gormley. Ancestors were Staplers,Merchants and Bankers who moved to King's Lynn in the 18th century and established a formidable banking partnership with the Gurney family. Henry also a Banker and Patron of Three Livings per 'Who Was Who'.

CHAMBERLAIN, Alfred Cranfield
(b) Sheringham, Norfolk 12 December 1842
(d) Wisbech OND 1891
Cricket. – Norfolk & Norwich; Yarmouth
HS. 9 v MCC August 1876 @ East Dereham
A pre 1876 NCCC player (ie 1866 & 1870)
F.F. – In 1861census listed as a Billiard Marker and living in Wisbech with his Innkeeper Grandfather. In unemployment after a spell as a Hotel Keeper he became an Accountant. (m) Elizabeth Hives and had a son plus 5 daughters.

COOMBER, Dr Francis, MRCS LRCP
(b) Wednesbury, Staffs 16 November 1849
(d) Chiswick 17 January 1913
Cricket. – Fakenham; West Norfolk; Dereham; JJ Miller's X1; Hempton.
HS. 51 v Suffolk August 1876 @ East Dereham
BB. 2/15 v MCC August 1876 @ East Dereham
Carried bat 147 no (232) for JJ Miller's X1 in June 1902.
F.F. – Brother of Richard (NCCC 1869) – an Inland Revenue Surveyor of Taxes. Francis at Royal College of Surgeons passing preliminary exams in anatomy and physiology on 8 April 1868 and licensed in 1871. Became a Medical Practitioner @ 6 St. Andrews Mansions, Fulham.

COOPER, T
Cricket. – West Norfolk; D. Spurrell's X1
HS. 25 v Essex (2) July 1876 @ Brentwood
BB. 3/? v Essex (2) July 1876 @ Brentwood

DAVIES, Revd Arthur Charles
(b) Prahran, Melbourne, Australia 21 April 1854
(d) Norwich 18 February 1929
Came to England age 8.
Educ. – Norwich GS; Leamington College; Cambridge University (St.John's College – BA)
Cricket. – Overstrand; Gunton; East Norfolk; CEYMS; Norfolk & Norwich; Aldborough; Reigate Priory.
HS. 12 v Cambridgeshire August 1895 @ Lakenham
HS. 143 v Herts August 1888 @ Hitchin
BB. 8/50 v Suffolk July 1878 @ Stowmarket (best NCCC debut v Suffolk)
Brother of Fairfax (q.v)
Fastish round arm (level with shoulder). NCCC Captain 1893-95. In 1883 match he was one of 6 Clergyman in NCCC team. 143 for East Norfolk v West Norfolk July 1877. In a match at Gunton he once scored 252.
F.F. – Deacon and Priest 1880. Curate Morley St. Botolph with St. Peter 1879. Curate Caston (Norfolk) 1880-82. Rector Aldborough 1882-89. Antingham St. Mary with Thorpe Market 1889-1919. Gave assistance in Parishes Cringleford and Eaton.
Probated will Norwich 8 April 1929 and one of the recipients was FR Bell (q.v) as he left £4,880-19-3.

FULCHER, William Popplewell
(b) Walton, Suffolk 22 October 1854
(d) Wimbledon 31 December 1934
Cricket. – Suffolk; Norfolk & Norwich; Yarmouth
HS. 26 v Essex July 1886 @ Brentwood
Played in derby game for both Norfolk and Suffolk. In a Suffolk v Norfolk match in 1880 on his side were men who also played for 'us' being TS Curteis, WS Gurney and CP Skerrett. 58 for Suffolk v Incogniti August 1880
F.F. – son of William (a Farmer) and Rosabella Popplewell. William was an Annuitant living on his own means in St. Helier, Jersey in 1901. Probated will London 8 March 1935 to his widow Alice Elizabeth Hines and his Dock Superintendent brother Victor Popplewell Fulcher. Left £13,688-14-3.

GURDON, His Honour Judge Charles
(b) Barnham Broom, Norfolk 3 December 1855
(d) Royal Free Hospital, West London 26 June 1931
Educ. – Haileybury College (Trevelyan 1869.1 – 1874.2); Cambridge University (Jesus College Oct 1874 – BA 1878 MA 1885)
Cricket. – Haileybury College; I Zingari; Cambridge University Long Vacation Club; MCC.
HS. 34 v I Zingari August 1877 @ Garboldisham
152 no for Haileybury College v Wellington College July 1874 – opposition scored just 62 & 46

Rugby Union. – England (14 caps); Cambridge University Blue 1877; Richmond Park.
Rowing. – Cambridge University – rowed Boat Race 1876-79 incl.

F.F. – 2nd son of Revd Edward & Catherine Margaret Frere - she the (d) of Canon of Westminster Temple Frere. Charles admitted at Inner Temple 16 November 1877, Called to the Bar 17 November 1881. Bencher & County Court Judge Circuit (Cornwall). President Old Haileyburian Society and an Equity Draughtsman & Conveyancer. A sporting family – his brothers ET & F debuted in 1879 for NCCC. His father Edward and Uncles Philip & William B played for NCCC pre 1876.
Left £30,934-4-2 to Robert Gurdon (also NCCC 1866-70) – he the 1st Baron Cranworth.

GURNEY, Walter Somerville

(b) Valley Field House, Middleton, Norfolk 8 June 1858
(d) King's Lynn 1 July 1942
Educ. – Haileybury College (Lawrence 1872.1 – 1876.2)
Cricket. – Haileybury College; Haileybury Wanderers; Suffolk; Ipswich & East Suffolk; MCC; West Norfolk; Gurney's Bank Club; Gentlemen of Norfolk
HS. 96 no v Hampshire July 1889 @ Southampton – batting at no 5 he ran out of partners as side dismissed for 197.
F.F. – A Barclays Bank Director and the son of Sir Arthur Somerville Gurney. A brother-in-law to Adair Craigie (NCCC 1862-66)

HARE, John Hugh Montague

(b) Docking Hall, Norfolk 31 May 1857
(d) Docking Hall, Norfolk Hall 1 August 1935
Educ. – Uppingham School; Oxford University (Exeter College 14 October 1876 – being captain of their fives, cricket & football teams. BA 1880 MA 1883)
Cricket. – Uppingham School; Uppingham Rovers; Eton Masters; Oxford University – Blue 1879; MCC; Harlequins; A. Pearson's X1; Gentlemen of Norfolk; Oxford University Undergraduates .
HS. 53 v Gentlemen of Nottingham August 1884 @ Lakenham
BB. 1/15 v MCC August 1882 @ Lakenham
1st class cricket - 8 matches 126 runs 6 catches 1 wkt
As an opener carried bat 37 no (62) Uppingham School v MCC August 1876 @ Lord's.
F.F. – Assistant Master Eton College 1885 – 1923. Member of Oxford Harlequins. His son Hugh became the Vicar of Docking and John left £957-11-10 to his widow Margaret and unmarried sister Anna.

JACKSON, J

The most worrying of all entries. There was a J. Jackson who played for NCCC 1867-71 and 1876, 1877, 1881, 1882, 1884. The 1877 man was reportedly a 'professional' from the XI of All England. This would appear to be ex-England man John Jackson (b. Bungay, Suffolk 21 May 1833; d. Liverpool Workhouse Infirmary 4 November 1901).
Unfortunately and surprisingly the cricket press and the local papers do not pick up on 'Foghorn' and make him the feature of an article –someone that famous would have been mentioned. He reportedly did not play much after 1866 due to a serious leg injury sustained whilst playing against Yorkshire. In 1870-74 he was at Lisburn in Ireland so he is not even NCCC's pre 1876 man. From 1875 he worked in a Liverpool warehouse.
The EDP 29 July 1886 stated categorically that John & James Jackson were brothers in the reported Cup match. It is not known if this refers to John the 'pro' or to another John or if James is the unknown player. John the 'pro' had a son named James (born 1861). In the averages section I have amalgamated seasons as mentioned. I have purposely not put in the resulting averages of the amalgamation as it is accepted that J. Jackson could be at least two men.

McLAREN, Lt Col William Henry

(b) York 23 November 1850
(d) College Gate, St. Andrews, Scotland 31 March 1911
Educ. – University of St Andrews
Cricket. – Gentlemen of Yorkshire; Cheshire; 1st Royal Volunteers
HS. 4 v MCC August 1876 @ East Dereham
BB. 6/34 v MCC August 1876 @ East Dereham- at the time this represented the best NCCC bowling analysis in an innings. (This is at odds with Norfolk papers who give him a 5 wicket haul and add a victim to F. Coomber (q.v). The website Cricket Archive show my figures).
F.F. - 1st Royal Dragoon Guards as Lieut 1874 rising to Lt. Colonel 1896. Son of Henry (a Merchant) and Elizabeth, he endured carcinoma of the colon for 15 months.

PAGE, A C

Cricket. – Gunton; Norfolk & Norwich
HS. 36 no v Essex July 1876 @ Brentwood

PATTESON, James Carlos

(b) London 24 December 1851
(d) Limpsfield, Surrey 30 June 1902
Educ. – Uppingham School; Cambridge University (Trinity College 24 February 1870 - BA1874)
Cricket. – Uppingham School; Rest of Uppingham School; Norfolk & Norwich
HS. 33 no v I Zingari August 1878 @ Garboldisham Brother Frank (q.v) in 1879
F.F. – Admitted Solicitor December 1877 working in

London and Limpsfield. Probated will London 9 September 1902 with one of two beneficiaries being his younger brother Frank. Left £16,062-11-6.

PIGOT . Sir George (5th Baronet of Patshull, Staffs)
(b) Moulton, Newmarket 15 December 1850
(d) Windsor 25 May 1934
Educ. – Thorpe GS
Cricket. – Thorpe GS; Norwich Union; Old Catton; MCC; Esher.
HS. 20 v Essex July 1876 @ Brentwood
F.F. – In 1891 living on his own means in Sunninghall with his father having a racing stable in Berkshire.
(m) Alice Louisa Raynsford McKenzie with 2 (s) 2 (d), a governess plus 10 servants. Received money from AK Tharp's (q.v) will. A very religious man and an associate of Edward V11. His father Robert was a Brigadier General and his wife the daughter of 1st Baronet of Glen Muir.

RHODES, Col Francis William, CB DSO
(b) Bishop's Stortford, Hertfordshire 9 April 1850
(d) Groote Schuur, Rondlelbosch, Cape Colony, South Africa 21 September 1905
Educ. – Eton College; RMC Sandhurst
Cricket. – Eton College; 1st Royal Volunteers; Harlequins; Eton Ramblers; MCC; Norfolk & Norwich; Grantham; Harrow; Winchester; 1st Royals; I Zingari; Gunton; East Norfolk; Gentlemen of Lincolnshire; Europeans
HS. 7 v MCC August 1876 @ East Dereham
1st class cricket – 1 match 22 runs for Europeans in Bombay alongside EB Raikes (q.v)
100 for I Zingari v Norfolk August 1879 and 40 plus 60 for I Zingari v Norfolk August 1885.
F.F. – 2nd Lt 1873, Col 1889 fighting in Egypt, Sudan and South Africa. Awarded Venus General Service medal, Khedive's bronze star, British S.A. Company medal; Order of the Bath and survived being shot and severely wounded. Several horses were shot from under him in engagements. In battles amongst others of El Teb and Khartoum. Also Relief of Mafeking and Siege of Ladysmith. He died of blackwater fever. Military Secretary to Governor of Bombay. Governor of Mashonaland and Matabeleland. Had a leading part in Jameson Raid and sentenced to death following a guilty plea to high treason. Sentence commuted to 15 years imprisonment. In June 1896 released on payment of a heavy fine with the British Army retiring him. The Times War Correspondent and he was the Managing Director of African Trans – Continental Telegraph Co to his demise. His brother Cecil was a founder of Rhodesia

RIVETT – CARNAC, Revd Sir George Clennell
(b) Harrow 23 October 1851

(d) Brighton 13 March 1932
Educ. – Harrow School (Rendalls House 9 July 1870 – 1874.3); Bradfield; Cambridge University (Trinity College – Michs 1870 BA 1874)
Cricket. – Harrow School; Priory Park; T.Meyrick's X1; Hingham; Rockland; Morley; Norfolk & Norwich; Windsor Home Park; East Norfolk; Shropshire – with his two brothers EH & WT.
HS. 12 no v Suffolk August 1876 @ East Dereham
BB. 4/48 v Suffolk July 1877 @ Lakenham
12 games for Shropshire scoring 110 runs and taking 39 wickets.
For Priory Park in 1875 he clean bowled WG and GF Grace in the same over.
Curate of Caston (Norfolk) 1875-78. Curate of Kew (Surrey) 1878-82. Vicar of Tong (Yalop) 1882-90. Vicar of Thorpe (Surrey) 1890-94. Rector of Graveley (Herts) 1894-98. Rector of Sweffling (Suffolk) 1898-1913. Rector of Woldingham (Surrey) 1913-1930
F.F. – 3rd son of William (Bengal Civil Service).
(m) 1. Emily Crabbe & 2. Eva Orr. His son James was a Vice Admiral.

STOCKS, Edward William
(b) Norwich 27 May 1856
(d) Norwich 26 October 1876
Educ. – Clergy Orphan School (Canterbury); Cambridge University (St. Catharine's College 12 October 1874)
Cricket. – Cambridge University; Cambridge University Long Vacation Club; Gunton; East Norfolk
HS. 10 v Essex July 1876 @ Brentwood
BB. 4/69 v Suffolk August 1876 @ Bury St. Edmunds
Brother of GA (q.v)
1st class cricket – 4 matches 18 runs 1 wicket
115 for CULVC v Bury & Suffolk August 1875
Athletics. – Cambridge University – Blue 1875/76 (Long Jump)
F.F. – son of Revd Edward – a Vice Master of King's College GS (Norwich)

STOCKS, George Alfred
(b) Eaton, Norwich 1 August 1858
(d) Shanklin, Isle of Wight 21 May 1934
Educ. – Clergy Orphan School (Canterbury); Cambridge University (Pembroke College 5 October 1876 – BA 1880 MA 1883)
Cricket. – Norfolk & Norwich; A.Lyttleton's X1; Cambridge University Next XV1; Cambridge University Long Vacation Club
HS. 1 no v Suffolk August 1876 @ East Dereham
Brother of EW (q.v)
Assistant Master Lancaster GS 1880-88. Headmaster Barrow High School 1889-1893. Headmaster Lancaster GS 1893-1903. Headmaster Blackburn GS 1903-1919

F.F. – Probated will Liverpool 21 July 1934 bequeathing £667-11-8 to widow Constance

THARP, Lt Arthur Keane

(b) Chippenham Park, Cambridge 15 September 1848

(d) Bitterne Park, Midanbury, Southampton 17 November 1928

Educ. – Haileybury College (Trevelyan & Edmonstone 1862.3 – 1867.1). Cambridge University (Gonville & Caius College 25 June 1867 & Trinity Hall 1 September 1867 but did not reside at the latter)

Cricket. – Suffolk; Cambridgeshire; Assyrians; Gentlemen of Norfolk; Gentlemen of Suffolk

HS. 55 v Essex July 1876 @ Brentwood – the first NCCC half century in the period covered by this book.

1st class cricket – 3 matches 37 runs 3 catches

F.F. –Third son of Revd Augustus Tharp. In Derbyshire Yeomanry. Secretary of Army & Navy Club. Member of Royal Yacht Squadron. Deputy Chairman Mutual Life Assurance Company. Chairman Messrs Bullers Ltd

THOMPSON, Benjamin

(b) Aldeburgh, Suffolk 21 July 1841

(d) Norwich 26 March 1914

Cricket. – clubs unknown

HS. 25 no v Suffolk August 1876 @ Bury St. Edmunds

Barclays Bank Clerkship 1865 and Bank Manager from 1895. Worked St. Mary's Baptist Church and his two marriages produced 3 (s) and 3(d).

F.F. – Left £5,786-13-4 to be shared by his widow Emily and 2nd daughter Elle.

TILLARD, Charles

(b) Wimbledon 18 April 1851

(d) Bathford, Somerset 7 March 1944

Educ. – Repton; Norwich GS; Cambridge University (Clare College 13 October 1870 – BA 1874 MA 1885)

Cricket. – Repton; Cheltenham; East Gloucestershire; Holt; Huntingdonshire; Surrey; Cambridge University – Blue 1871-74; Oxford & Cambridge Past & Present; MCC; Worcester; Gunton; Norwich; Quidnuncs; Fakenham; Cambridge Town Club; Oxford & Cambridge Universities; Free Foresters; Gentlemen of Norfolk

HS. 28 v Oxfordshire August 1895 @ Hertford

BB. 1/9 v Cambridgeshire August 1895 @ Fenner's

HS. 51 v Essex August 1887 @ Lakenham

BB. 8/24 v Essex August 1877 @ Lakenham – 15/60 in the match off 197 balls (4 ball overs)

1st class cricket – 16 matches 328 runs 54 wickets

A cricketing family – brother John (q.v), father-in-law Elliott Dowell (Somerset and NCCC pre 1876), brother-in-law AT Scott (C.U and NCCC 1870) plus four cousins with RM of the four

being a Gentlemen of Norfolk player pre 1876)

In 1870 for Repton v Uppingham he took 17 wickets in the match (15 bowled).

'Scores & Biographies' for his 6/42 for C.U in 1873 said "frequently whipping balls back from the pitch with his round arm fast medium bowling"

He 4 times progressively held NCCC bowling anaylsis record for an innings.

F.F. – Assistant Master Cheltenham College 1875-1907 and a Housemaster for over 20 years. Probated will Bristol 21 June 1944 leaving £26,489-19-11 to family members.

TILLARD, John

(b) Blakeney, Norfolk 4 February 1855

(d) Bath, Somerset 25 March 1914

Educ. – Brighton College; Cambridge University (St. John's College 24 May 1873 – BA 1877 MA 1880)

Cricket. – Brighton College; Gentlemen of Shropshire

HS. 0 (x 2) v Suffolk August 1876 @ Bury St. Edmunds – the first 'pair' in the period covered.

Brother of Charles (q.v)

Assistant Master Cowbridge School 1877. Assistant Master Shrewsbury School 1878-79. HM Inspector of Schools in Yorkshire, Norfolk & Somerset.

TURNER, Revd Henry Whitelock

(b) Barford, Norfolk 31 August 1852

(d) Stonely Grange, Kimbolton 19 January 1937

Educ. – Beccles School; Cambridge University (Gonville & Caius College 1 October 1870 – BA 1873 MA 1877)

Cricket. – Norfolk & Norwich; East Norfolk; Gentlemen of Norfolk; Gunton; MCC

HS. 32 no v Lincolnshire September 1880 @ Lakenham

BB. 3/42 v Suffolk July 1877 @ Lakenham

Deacon 1875, Priest (Norwich) 1876. Curate of Barford 1875-77. Curate of Colton 1877-92. Rector of North Runcton with Hardwicke & Setchey Diocese 1892 –1910.

F.F.- Left £597-11s in his will to his widow Blanche – she the daughter of JB Turner (NCCC pre 1876)

WILLETT, Ernest Henry

(b) Norwich 8 April 1850

(d) Tasburgh, Norfolk 4 November 1880

Educ. – Radley College

Cricket. – Radley College; Carrow; Norfolk & Norwich; East Norfolk; Gentlemen of Norfolk

HS. 26 v Suffolk August 1876 @ Bury St. Edmunds

BB. 4/18 v MCC August 1876 @ East Dereham

Ernest was a pre 1876 NCCC appearance maker.

F.F. – At 21 he was a student at law living in Isleworth with his Physician uncle. His personal estate was under £500 and sadly willed to his father Henry.

1877

ASH, Edward Philip
(b) Brisley, Norfolk 25 December 1842
(d) Downton, Petersfield 25 May 1909
Educ. – Rugby School; Cambridge University (Gonville & Caius College 30 September 1861- BA 1866 MA 1869)
Cricket. – Rugby School; Suffolk; Hertfordshire; Eastbourne; Free Foresters; Cheshire; Norfolk & Norwich; Gunton; Cambridge University – Blue 1865; Gentlemen of Warwickshire; Gentlemen of Norfolk
HS. 2 v Essex August 1877 @ Norwich
1st class cricket – 5 matches 126 runs 3 catches
Edward had played for NCCC pre 1876
130 (253) for Gentlemen of Norfolk v I Zingari July 1866
4/15 & 5/40 for Free Foresters v Staffordshire August 1872
86 & 56 for Cheshire v Staffordshire Borderers August 1876
59 no (103) for Gunton v Holbeach August 1877
112 no for Gunton v Ipswich GS Past & Present August 1877
Played in the same team with his brother Philip for Cheshire
School Assistant Master Haileybury College 1865-1902
Thomason House Housemaster 1868.3 – 1873.3
Hailey Housemaster 1883.3 – 1902.3
F.F. – Probated will London 24 June 1909 leaving £9,500-12-5 to his widow Emily

ATMORE, Edward Alfred
(b) King's Lynn JFM 1855 – baptism/christening 28 March 1855
(d) King's Lynn 8 October 1930
Cricket. – Lynn Cricket Club; Hingham; East Norfolk; Rocklands
HS. 0 (x2) v MCC August 1877 @ Norwich – one of five NCCC men to get a 'pair' in his only match
A Chemist & Druggist living in King's Lynn
His brother Robert played for NCCC in 1850 – some sources as Attmore.
His father George & uncle Edward played cricket for King's Lynn.
F.F. – Left £82 in his probated will to his 2nd wife Margaret.

BANKS, Charles James
(b) Sholden, Kent JFM 1851– baptism/christening 22 March 1851
(d) Norwich 15 June 1911
Cricket. – Norwich; East Norfolk; Norfolk & Norwich; Revd RA Law's X1
HS. 16 v Essex July 1877 @ Brentwood
Son of a Landowning Welsh JP with Charles listed as living on his own means. Cause of death were malignant glands in his neck

BARKER, C J
Cricket. – Gentlemen East Norfolk; Norfolk & Norwich

HS. 0 no v Essex August 1877 @ Norwich
A depressing set of information and statistics!

BARTON, Revd Alfred John
(b) Thexton House, Thetford 13 May 1850
(d) Felixtowe 19 September 1926
Educ. – Bury St. Edmunds School; Cambridge University (Peterhouse College 30 September 1868 – BA 1872)
Cricket. – Chelmsford; Melton Constable
HS. 63 v Essex July 1877 @ Brentwood – held the NCCC highest innings score record for 4 years for the period covered.
BB. 7/? v I Zingari August 1878 @ Garboldisham
Assistant Master Felsted School 1873-74. Assistant Master Cheltenham College 1876-78. Ordained 1880 Priest (Hereford) 1881. Curate of Hentland (Herefordshire) 1880-84. Vicar of Guestwick 1884-91. Rector of Strumpshaw with Braydeston 1891-1914.
F.F. -His 3 sons died in far flung places namely Deville Wood, Ypres and Canada. Left £1,950-16-3 in his Ipswich probated will

BARTON, Dr George Henry
(b) Market Rasen, Lincolnshire 30 July 1855
(d) The Grange, Market Rasen 31 March 1936
Cricket. – clubs unknown
HS. 16 v Essex July 1877 @ Brentwood
A Physician and Surgeon qualified 24 July 1878. A General Practitioner. He is also shown in some cricket records as GH Burton.
F.F. – (m) Florence Holdsworth and had 4 issue.
Probated will Norwich 20 July 1936 leaving £13,637-18-2

BUXTON, Major Geoffrey Fowell, CB JP DL TD VD
(b) London 21 June 1852
(d) Hoveton Hall, Norfolk 11 April 1929
Educ. – Uppingham School; Cambridge University (Trinity College 23 February 1871 – BA 1875)
Cricket. – Gurney's Bank Club; MCC; Gunton; East Norfolk
HS. 5 no v The Herons September 1879 @ Lakenham
Father of B (q.v)
On staff of Gurney, Birkbeck, Barclay & Buxton 1875, partner 1887. Director of Barclay & Co Ltd 1896-1929. High Sheriff 1890 & Mayor Norwich 1903-04. Vice President Norfolk Agrig. Society. Vice President CEYMS Society. Major 1st Volunteer Batt. Norfolk Regiment 1888-1895. Major & Hon. Lt. Col Norfolk Imperial Yeomanry.
F.F. – Governor of Norfolk & Norwich Hospital & Lowestoft Convalescent Home. Governor of Norwich GS. Promoted the establishment of Master of Dunston Harriers for 8 years. Left £278,836-8-2 in his London probated will

CAMPBELL, D

HS. 4 v Essex July 1877 @ Brentwood
Despite Charles Tillard (q.v) taking 10 wickets in the match referred to NCCC were easily beaten by 6 wickets.

CIRCUITT, Revd Richard William Perry

(b) Woburn, Berkshire 3 October 1846
(d) Totnes, Devon 26 September 1920
Educ. – King's College (London)
HS. 4 v Essex July 1877 @ Brentwood
Ordained 1869 Priest (Winchester) 1871. Curate of Ringwood & Harbridge 1869-71. Curate of Aylsham (Norfolk) 1871-76. Curate of Holy Trinity Halstead 1876-77. Curate of South Weald (Essex) 1877-78. Vicar of Cholsey (Berks) 1878-85. Chaplain Berks Co. Asylum 1879-85. Rector of St. Luke's Diocese (Heywood, Manchester) 1885-1919.
F.F. – Left £1,006-4-10 in his London probated will.

CRESSWELL, Cresswell Augustus

(b) Griskan Square, London 27 November 1856
(d) London 19 September 1935
Educ. – Radley College; Oxford University (Magdalen College 16 October 1875 - BA 1879 MA 1884)
Cricket. – West Norfolk
HS. 26 v Lincolnshire July 1881 @ Lincoln
Brother-in-Law of GB Gurney (q.v) plus the other relation MH Gurney played for Durham (pre county).
A Stock & Share Dealer. Memorial plaque in North Runcton Church. Probated will with Cresswell of 58 Connaught Square, Middlesex of Stock Exchange leaving £111,877-5-9.

DAVIES, Fairfax

(b) Kew, Melbourne, Australia 15 December 1855
(d) North Walsham 15 September 1927
Educ. – Norwich GS
Cricket. – CEYMS; North Walsham; Revd AJ Berwick's X1; Gunton; Aldborough; East Norfolk; Cambridgeshire (as a sub holding a catch for both sides); Norfolk & Norwich Brother of AC (q.v)
HS. 94 v Oxfordshire August 1895 @ Hertford
HS. 142 no v Essex July 1885 @ Lakenham
BB. 5/54 v Suffolk July 1877 @ Norwich
246 no for North Walsham v CEYMS 1888
165 no for North Walsham v Buxton Lammas July 1893
195 for Gunton v Fakenham July 1897
Articled Solicitor 1878 working at Wilkinson & Davies law firm. Clerk to Smallburgh Board of Guardians 1884-1926. Registrar North Walsham. Clerk of Governors of Paston School.
F.F.- Having a cup of tea and had a fatal stroke. Interred in North Walsham Cemetery.

DRAPER, Very Revd William Henry

(b) Chichester, Sussex 24 July 1836
(d) Haywards Heath, Sussex 24 January 1926
Educ. – Oxford University (Worcester College 14 November 1855 – BA 1859 MA 1862)
Cricket. – Priory Park; Oxford University; Old Oxonians; Bicester; Buckinghamshire; Hertfordshire; Oxfordshire; Gentlemen of Buckinghamshire
HS. 22 in both innings v I Zingari August 1877 @ Garboldisham
BB. 1/? v I Zingari August 1877 @ Garboldisham – he clean bowled Maj. Gen. Hon. Arthur Henniker – Major, CB.
94 for Bucks v Hunts August 1869.
Played for Oxfordshire when age 58.
Ordained 1860 and Priest 1861. Chaplain of Bromyard 1860-68. Rector of Edgcott (Bucks) 1868-74. Rector of Middleton Stoney 1874-1924. Rural Dean of Bicester 1895-1911.
F.F. – Probated will London 15 April 1926 leaving £2,059-16-8 to his unmarried sister Evelyn.

FLYNN, William

(b) Norwood, Surrey 1856
Cricket. – Dereham; Holkham; Norfolk & Norwich; Melton; Fakenham
HS. 13 v I Zingari August 1877 @ Garboldisham
BB. 5/49 v MCC August 1877 @ Norwich
The Norfolk and Holkham professional player.
F.F. -1871 census he was visiting his grandfather in North Elmham. 1881 census he was in Holt with an uncle with a listed occupation of Painter & Decorator. Latterly a Painter living in Yarmouth with wife Louisa and five children.

HANKINSON, Robert Scott, JP

(b) Derby 20 May 1857
(d) Bassett, Southampton 6 July 1914
Educ. – Winchester School; Cambridge University (Trinity College 25 May 1875 – BA 1879 MA 1883)
Cricket. – Gunton
HS. 4 v MCC August 1877 @ Norwich
F.F. – a Southampton Banker
Son of Robert Chatfield Hankinson & Louisa Anne Scott
In his probated will he left £24,045-12-3 to members of his family.

JARVIS, Major Lewis Kerrison

(b) Middleton Tower, King's Lynn 3 August 1857
(d) Kensington, London 16 May 1938
Educ. - St. James House (Lynn); Harrow School (The Park 1871.1 – 1876.2); Cambridge University (Trinity College – 7 June 1876)
Cricket. – Harrow School; Cambridge University – Blue 1887-89; MCC; Gentlemen of England; 1st Royal Volunteers;

Cheveley Park; Athenaeum; West Norfolk; LK Jarvis' X1; Undergraduates of Cambridge; Cambridge University Past & Present; Eton & Harrow X1; Quidnuncs; Old Harrovians; Gentlemen of Norfolk; I Zingari – everybody wanted him to play for them.

HS. 181 v MCC July 1885 @ Lord's

BB. 5/24 v Suffolk July 1881 @ Portman Rd, Ipswich

Brother of AW, CJE, FW (q.v)

1st class cricket – 23 matches 504 runs 7 catches 4 wickets
Bowled slow underhand lobs.
6' 1" & 12st per 'Scores & Biographies'
114 (207) for Athenaeum v I Zingari June 1879
142 for Cleveley Park v Lordswood Commons June 1899
For NCCC in 1882 he carried his bat for 75 no (130) v Bedfordshire and got 50 (109) in the 2nd innings.
Hurdles – Cambridge University – Triple Blue 1878-80
Football. – King's Lynn; Cambridge University – Blue 1879; Harrow School; Norfolk County 1881-82 (apps 2-0)
With H.E. Meek won Public Schools Rackets Challenge Cup in 1876.

F.F. -2nd son of Sir Lewis Whincop Jarvis - a Banker. Employed at Private Banking firm Jarvis & Jarvis of King's Lynn. Local Director of Barclays Bank Ltd @ 54, Lombard Street, London. Major in 3rd County of London Yeomanry (Sharpshooter) – with 4 medals held at Hever Castle. Served in Egypt and Sinai Peninsula; awarded 1914-15 Star.

KEMP, Sir Kenneth Hagar, CBE Bart JP DL (12th Baronet of Gissing)

(b) Erpingham, Norfolk 21 April 1853

(d) Sheringham, Norfolk 22 April 1936

Educ. – Clergy Orphan School (Canterbury); Canterbury School (when Fuller Pilch was coach); RMC Sandhurst: Cambridge University (Jesus College 1 October 1871- BA 1875)

Cricket. – Cambridge University; England X1; Norfolk 22 Colts; East Norfolk; Botesdale; St. Lawrence; Norfolk & Norwich; Players; MCC

HS. 45 v Gentlemen of Nottingham August 1884 @ Lakenham

1st class cricket – 4 matches 105 runs 1 catch
He received bat in 1866 inscribed 'with Fuller Pilch's love'.
Present at NCCC meeting in 1876. NCCC Hon Sec to 1889 – succeeding M. Birkbeck. Captained the RMC Sandhurst cricket team at Lord's. Contested North Norfolk 1895 & 1899. JP & DL of Norfolk and Mayor in 1894. Lt 7th Dragoon Guards. Lt. Col commanding 3rd Norfolk Regiment Batt (Militia) & then commanded 2nd (Garrison) Batt. Suffolk Regiment. Called to the Bar 26 January 1880 & Inner Temple 22 June 1880. Barrister & Banker. Formerly partner in Lacons,Yowell & Kemp (Bankers). Author of ' A Treatise on the Law of Allotments'.

F.F. – Owner & took up license Royal Hotel, Norwich. In fact he was one of those responsible for pulling it down on the Walk and building the Royal Arcade on the site. Left 4 daughters at death as Lady Kemp died 15 May 1931.

KENNAWAY, Revd Charles Lewis

(b) Brighton, Sussex 3 July 1847

(d) Spetisbury, Blandford, Dorset 23 April 1940

Educ. – Harrow School; Oxford University (University College 13 October 1866 – BA 1870 MA 1873)

Cricket. – Harrow School; Gentlemen of Worcestershire; Gentlemen of Warwickshire; Gentlemen of Dorset; Gentlemen of Norfolk; Harlequins; Old Harrovians; Dorset; Garboldisham; Quidenham Parsonage; Elmham Hall; GRH Wilson's X1.

HS. 147 v Free Foresters August 1882 @ Lakenham – this NCCC 1st century in the period covered by this book. His score was to be surpassed by LK Jarvis three seasons later.

BB. 1/10 v Suffolk July 1878 @ Stowmarket

Father of AL (q.v)

52 & 75 for Gentlemen of Worcestershire v Gentlemen of Herefordshire July 1870
45 no for Garboldisham in July 1897 at age 50.
Ordained 1872 Priest (Salisbury) 1872. Chaplain of Canford Magna (Dorset) 1871-76. Rural Dean of N & S Rockland 1898-1914. Rector of Garboldisham 1876-94. Perpetual Curate of Tarrant Crawford 1914 -1937.

F.F. – His father Revd Charles Edward Kennaway rose to be the Canon of Gloucester. £22,498-18-1 was lodged with his solicitor on the occasion of his demise.

KETTON, Robert William, JP

(b) Norwich 6 February 1856

(d) Maidstone, Kent 4 March 1935

Cricket. – Gunton; Coltishall; Aldborough; Norfolk Club & Ground; Aylsham; Melton Constable; East Norfolk

HS. 34 v Suffolk August 1878 @ East Dereham

BB. 2/21 v Suffolk July 1878 @ Stowmarket

102 no (171) carrying bat for Aylsham v Coltishall July 1877
70 for Gunton v Suffolk Borderers August 1899
He is the FW Ketton (1885) shown in the Norfolk papers.
North Norfolk Association (Liberal). A Magistrate who was for several years Chairman of North Erpingham Justices (Cromer). Landowner of Fellbrigg Hall for almost 30 years. High Sheriff of Norwich. Founder Royal Cromer Golf Club and its Captain.

LAW, George

(b) Rochdale 17 April 1846

(d) Marylebone, London 30 July 1911

Educ. – St. Peter's College; Radley College

Cricket. – Radley College; MCC; Middlesex; Southgate; Gentlemen of England; Gentlemen of Essex; Gentlemen of West Kent; Orleans Club; CI Thornton's X1

HS. 4 v Essex July 1877 @ Brentwood – absent for 1st innings.
1st class cricket – 11 matches 160 runs 6 catches
F.F. – His brother Revd William Law played cricket for Yorkshire. Left £40,981-3-6 in his probated London will.

MOORE, Lt. Col Richard St. Ledger, CB DL JP
(b) Kilbride Manor, Co. Wicklow 12 July 1848
(d) Naas, Co. Kildare, Ireland 18 October 1921
Educ. – Harrow School
Cricket. – 5th Lancers; Harrow School; Norfolk & Norwich; East Norfolk
HS. 16 v Suffolk July 1877 @ Norwich
President Irish Amateur Athletic Association
Master of the Kildare Foxhounds 1883-1897
Served 9th, 12th & 15th Lancers – a Cornet in the 9th, the third and lowest grade of commissioned officer in a British cavalry troop. He rose to Major 13 June 1896, Hon Lt. Col 1 August 1901.
Commanded Dublin Imperial Yeomanry and sent to Bulawayo as part of the British Boer War campaign. High Sheriff 1899.
F.F. – Lived as a country gentleman as owned 2,500 acres. His 4 large scrap albums, half morocco with gilt stamped spine were auctioned for £2,300

MORRICE, Capt Cuthbert Henry
(b) Hamswell House, Bath 25 March 1858
(d) Marks Tey, Essex 31 May 1917
Educ. – Harrow School (The Grove 1872.2 – 1875.2); Cambridge University (Trinity Hall College 29 January 1876)
Cricket. – Harrow School; Halifax; MCC; Waveney Valley; East Norfolk
HS. 104 v Essex July 1884 @ Brentwood
BB. 2/? v Suffolk August 1879 @ Lakenham
Brother of FLH (q.v)
Holds record 6th highest NCCC percentage, namely 60.7 %, of individual innings score in a completed innings total having scored 54 no (89) v Essex June 1884.
2nd Lt. W. Yorkshire Militia 1879. 2nd Lt. 7th Fusiliers 23 October 1880. Captain Royal Fusiliers 20 March 1888 retiring 2 April 1898
F.F. – Inspector of Survey Signalling in Egypt. Brigade Signaller, Poona 1889. Son of Frederick (of Ditchingham Hall, Bungay) and Georgiana Brown. (w) Nelly Maud Money was (d) of Sir Alonzo Money.

ROBINS, George Frederick
(b) Isleham, Cambridge 31 January 1848
(d) Isleham, Cambridge 16 January 1929 (age 81)
Cricket. – Fakenham; West Norfolk
HS. 13 v Essex August 1877 @ Norwich
F.F. – His father a Landowner / Farmer and Merchant.

Probated will London 4 September 1929 to his two farming sons Richard and Allan. He bequeathed £34,521-14-9 and they later sold the land.

SCOTT– CHAD, Charles, JP (name changed from Charles Scott Chad)
(b) Thursford Hall, East Dereham, Norfolk 23 March 1857
(d) Kensington, London 25 February 1926
Educ. – Eton College; Cambridge University (Trinity College 7 June 1876 – BA 1880 MA 1883)
Cricket. – Cambridge University; Thursford; West Norfolk; C. Scott –Chad's X1
HS. 27 v Essex July 1883 @ Brentwood
BB. 2/18 v Essex June 1883 @ Lakenham
Father of GN (q.v)
Football. – Wanderers; Norfolk County 1883-85 (apps 5-0)
Athletics. – Cambridge University – Blue 1880
Admitted Inner Temple 25 January 1881. Called to the Bar 7 May 1884. Became a Barrister –at –Law.
F.F. – His daughter Cecilia married Gerald Duckworth and one of his mothers ancestors was a Page to Marie Antoinette. Charles' mother married twice and a daughter of the second union wrote 'Virginia Woolf '.
Charles left £150,781-13-6 to his son G.N and Lt Gerald de L'Etam Duckworth.

1878

COLVIN, Sir Elliott Graham, KSCI CSI JP
(b) India 18 July 1861
(d) Bourne, Andover 2 August 1940
Educ. – Charterhouse School; Cambridge University (King's College 9 October 1880 – alumni incorrectly as Elliot)
Cricket. – Charterhouse School; Thetford; Thursford; Melton; Iceni; Old Carthusians; GB Studd's X1 (Freshman's trial)
HS. 29 v MCC August 1878 @ East Dereham
55 for Charterhouse School v Westminster School July 1876
Football. – Cambridge University – Blue 1881 & 1882; Norfolk County 1880 (apps 3-0)
Entered the Indian Civil Service 1882 – his father Bazett Wetenhal plus 3 uncles all had distinguished careers in India. Assistant Magistrate, Alipore. Political Assistant Private Secretary to the Lt.- Governor of Bengal 1887. Settlement Officer, North Behar 1891-95. Magistrate & Collector in Bengal 1895. Further postings in Alwar, Bharatpur, Eastern Rajputana States and Ajmer Merwara rising to the position of Chief Commissioner. British delegate on Bulgarian Reparation Commission 1921-24.
F.F. – Three pictures of him are in the National Portrait Gallery. Probated will Llandudno 23 January 1941 leaving £5,268-16-1 to his Army Captain brother

JARVIS, Sir Alexander Weston, KCMG MVO TD MP JP

(b) Middleton Tower, King's Lynn 26 December 1855
(d) Hobart Place, London 31 October 1939
Educ. – Harrow School (Small Houses & The Park leaving 1874.3)
Cricket. – Harrow; West Norfolk; I Zingari; Ipswich & East Suffolk; Lords & Commons; Middleton Towers
HS. 28 v Suffolk June 1881 @ Lakenham
Brother of CJE, LK & F W(q.v)
Football. – Harrow
Knighted 26 February 1931 for work as Chairman of Royal Empire Society. Formerly a Banker at Lynn. Conservative M.P. Lynn 25 August 1886 - July 1992. Commanded Imperial Yeomanry (Rhodesia) with various commissions, rising to Major. In Rhodesia when the Matabele Rebellion broke out and wounded during the Boer War.
Member of firm Partridge & Jarvis – being actively interested in the formation and control of a large number of Rhodesian undertakings. When the partnership was terminated by the effluxion of time he supervised the business of the Willoughby group of companies
In November 1902 proceeded to the Delhi Durbar on the staff of HRH the Duke of Connaught.
F.F. – Has an entry in the Anglo African Who's Who. An author with his published title 'Jottings from an Active Life 1928'. SA medal and four clasps, and KSA and two clasps. Director of the India Rubber, Gutta Percha & Telegraph Works.

JARVIS, Charles James Ernest

(b) Middleton Tower, King's Lynn 14 August 1859
(d) Norwich 5 July 1893
Educ. – St. James House (Lynn); Harrow School (The Park 1874.1-1878.2)
Cricket. - St. James House; Harrow; West Norfolk; Gentlemen of Norfolk; Middleton Towers
HS. 130 v MCC July 1885 @ Lord's – opening partnership of 241 with his brother LK
BB. 7/90 v I Zingari July 1885 @ Garboldisham
Brother of AW, LK & FW (q.v)
In 1880 he took match figures of 10/45 v Incogniti
In 1881 he carried his bat 84 no (156) for NCCC v Lincolnshire – making him and LK the only brothers to carry their bat for NCCC.
LK and CJE were the first brothers to achieve the feat of scoring more in their own individual first innings than the oppositions first innings total. LK (3 times) and CJE (2 times).
NCCC captain for many years and Joint Secretary 1881-1890.
'Scores & Biographies' quote – "steady and effective batsman, fast round arm, fields well at mid wicket ".
Football. – Harrow; Norfolk County 1881 (app 1-0)
F.F. – Probated will London 27 October 1893 leaving £1,904 -9-7 to be shared by his brothers AW and LK.

LEATHAM, Claude, DL

(b) Hemsworth, Yorkshire 18 April 1856
(d) York 25 April 1913
Cricket. – Wakefield; Incogniti; Gentlemen of Yorkshire
HS. 4 v I Zingari August 1878 @ Garboldisham
8/64 & 7/36 for Gentlemen of Yorkshire v Durham July 1876 – his brother GAB (a wicketkeeper) helped with five of the dismissals.
The youngest of 6 brothers who all played cricket to a decent standard (eg Barnsley, MCC, Gentlemen of Yorkshire and Shropshire)
A Magistrates' Clerk in Pontefract who became a Legal Solicitor with 5 servants in 1901.
F.F. – He opened Pontefract & District Golf Club (as their captain) 3 November 1904. A keen follower of the Badsworth Hunt. A Banking family whose business was taken into the Barclays Group. He married Mary Elizabeth Gurney Barclay and bequeathed a sum total of £12,817-2-4 between his widow and his second oldest brother Charles.

LEGGATT, Owen

(b) Belgravia, Middlesex 14 August 1854
(d) San Jose, California, USA 8 November 1886 – MURDERED.
Educ. – Rugby School; Cambridge University (Trinity Hall 16 April 1872)
Cricket. – East Dereham
HS. 3 v Suffolk August 1878 @ East Dereham
Admitted Inner Temple 4 May 1875
His father was Lt. Gen Edward Owen Leggatt (Indian Staff Corps 1825-1902)
Charting his short life –
Whilst in England he was living with his grandfather for a period and was a boarder and lodger at various premises until he left for USA in 1884.
For two years he visited various ports on the Pacific Coast. An Artist by profession – landscape drawings. He was living at the St. James Hotel, San Jose. He spoke nicely to a 12 year old girl and his murderer John Clark became jealous and knifed him inflicting a severe wound to the arm. The assailant was committed to an Insane Asylum in Stockton but was discharged after just 3 months.
Meanwhile Owen gained an interest in some Monterey mines and he submitted samples for assayers testing at Santa Clare College. Clark blamed him for his asylum spell and waited to kill him before finding him working at McKenzies Foundry. He shot him four times on First Street/Eldorado Street outside of Cavallaro's Barber shop – in the back; left arm; centre of breastbone and below the right nipple passing through the lungs and heart.

MONTGOMERIE, Cecil Thomas Crisp Molyneux, DL JP
(b) Marylebone, London 20 May 1864
(d) Basseterre, St. Kitts, West Indies 17 April 1901
Educ. – Eton College; Cambridge University (Trinity College 16 December 1863)
Cricket. – Gentlemen of Suffolk; East Norfolk; I Zingari; Suffolk; MCC
HS. 21 v The Herons September 1879 @ Lakenham
'Scores & Biographies' quote – " hard hitter, fields well mid wicket or long slip)."
In Grenadier Guards. County Alderman / Magistrate and Freemason. One of chief landowners East Harling (Kellys 1883) Lord of Manor of Fakenham – in – Garboldisham & Uphall – in – Garboldisham. Chairman Co. Justices Guiltcross & Shropham.
Member County Lunatic Asylum. Chairman Board of Mid-Anglian Light Railway. The 3 matches between I Zingari & NCCC (1877-79) were played at Montgomerie's family seat.
F.F. – Symptons of heart trouble so on his West Indies estate for a couple of weeks. Left £59,907-8-11 in his London probated will to his widow Eleanor.

MORRICE, Frederick Launcelot Hamilton
(b) Hamswell House, Bath, Somerset 5 February 1855
(d) Aosta, Italy 3 October 1915
Educ. – Harrow School (The Grove 1869.1 – 1874.2); Cambridge University (Trinity Hall College 13 October 1874)
Cricket. – Harrow School; Trinity Hall; Waveney Valley Club; MCC
HS. 26 v MCC August 1878 @ East Dereham
Brother of CH (q.v)
Inner Temple 20 June 1876. Called to the Bar 17 November 1879
F.F. – One of his sons was the advisor on irrigation and drainage to the Colonial Office and he was responsible for calculating the Nile water flow so the series of dams could be sited yet giving sufficient water flow for Egypt. Bequeathed £45,579-17-8 in his will

POLLARD, E
Cricket. – Norfolk & Norwich; Norwich District; East Dereham
HS. 29 v S.E. Circuit August 1881 @ Norwich

PONTIFEX, Revd Alfred
(b) London 17 March 1842
(d) Weston, Bath, Somerset 25 August 1930
Educ. – Bath School; Cambridge University (Trinity College 6 May 1861 – BA 1865 MA 1868)
Cricket. – Harleston; Norfolk & Norwich; Gloucestershire; Suffolk; Somerset (pre first class)
HS. 28 v I.Zingari August 1879 @ Garboldisham

1st class cricket – 1 match 12 runs 1 catch
Ordained 1865 Priest (Sarum) 1867. Chaplain Cheverel Parva (Wiltshire) 1865-67. Chaplain Allington (Wiltshire) 1868-69. Rector of Yate (Gloster) 1869-96.
F.F. – Probated will Bristol to the tune of £28,743-11-7 to be shared by his widow Julia and two others.

RYE, George Joseph
(b) Bracondale, Norwich 2 November 1856
(d) Acle, Norfolk 6 January 1943
Educ. – Princes Street (Norwich); Norwich GS
Cricket. – Princes Street; Carrow; Ipswich & East Suffolk; Norwich; East Norfolk; GJ Rye's X1; Norfolk News; Durham (took a catch as a sub fielder); Norwich Typographical
HS. 87 v MCC May 1893 @ Lakenham
BB. 8/34 v Lincolnshire August 1891 @ Lakenham
40 years at Norwich GS as cricket coach
Minor Counties Umpire 1895-1932 and officiated in many local Norfolk matches.
Landlord Lily Tavern 10 October 1882 – 21 January 1885
Landlord Freemasons Arms 17 November 1885 – 7 May 1912
He died at his daughter's house.

1879

CLARKE, Edward William Routh, JP
(b) Wymondham, Norfolk 23 May 1859
(d) Wattlefield House, East Norfolk 15 March 1907
Cricket. – Wymondham; Norwich District; East Norfolk; Norfolk & Norwich
HS. 76 v Hampshire July 1886 @ Southampton
BB. 4/17 v Suffolk June 1881 @ Lakenham
NCCC Committee 1905
His 48 for NCCC v Incogniti August 1881 exceeded the opposition's first innings total of just 41.
Son of William Robert (a Brewer & Merchant) and Elizabeth Clarke Routh. On 1871 census as a pupil boarder in Beccles. Elevated to being a Landowner and Magistrate with servants and a governess.

FORTESCUE, Revd Arthur Trosse
(b) Fallapit, Devon 7 April 1848
(d) Uxbridge, Middlesex 21 November 1899
Educ. - Marlborough College; Oxford University (Christchurch 18 October 1867 – BA 1875)
Cricket. – Marlborough College; Gentlemen of England; Gentlemen of Devon; Essex; JB Gilmore's House; Harlequins; Oxford University – Blue 1868-71; Lincolnshire; Gentlemen of Warwickshire; Lindum; I Zingari; EJ Sanders' X1
HS. 17 v Suffolk August 1879 @ Lakenham
BB. 3/3 v Suffolk August 1879 @ Lakenham
1st class cricket – 19 matches 480 runs 12 catches 16 wickets

104 for I Zingari v Devon August 1885
86 no for Marlborough College v Royal Ag. Coll. Cirencester
May 1866
58 no for EJ Sanders' XI v Ontario Association September 1886
– playing matches on tour in Montreal, New York, Philadelphia
and Toronto.
Ordained 1876 Priest 1882. Chaplain of Nantmel Radnors
1876-79. Chaplain of Denton (Norfolk) 1879-81. Chaplain of
Riventhall (Essex) 1881-82. Chaplain of Buntisford 1882-83.
Vicar of Hainton with Six Hills Dioceses 1883.
F.F. – Third son of William Blundell Fortescue. (m) Clara
Harriet Pease. Probated will Canterbury 16 May 1900
leaving £439-11-4

GURDON, Edward Temple

(b) Barnham Broom, Norfolk 25 January 1854
(d) Grosvenor Square, London 12 June 1929
Educ. – Haileybury College (Trevelyan House 1868.1 –
1873.2); Cambridge University (Trinity College 11 August
1873 – BA 1878 MA 1888)
Cricket. – Haileybury College; Norfolk Club & Ground;
Cambridge University Long Vacation Club: MCC
HS. 2 v The Herons September 1879 @ Lakenham
Brother of C & F (q.v)
His father and an uncle played for NCCC in the 1820s but were
not directly related to another set of brothers namely RT (NCCC
1862-1870) and WB (NCCC 1862).
The uncle Philip Gurdon was a founder member (and treasurer)
of the original Norfolk Club in 1827.
Rugby Union. – Cambridge University – Blue; Richmond;
England (16 caps & captain 1883-86)
President of Rugby Union 1890/91; President of Middlesex CFU
F.F. – Worked Public Record Office 1877-79. Admitted
Solicitor 1883 of Frere, Cholmely & Co. Founder Old
Haileyburian Society and their Hon. Sec. 1895-1929.
Left £75,155-3-7 to Hon. Judge Charles Gurdon

GURDON, Canon Francis

(b) Barnham Broom, Norfolk 11 April 1861
(d) Minster Yard, York 23 December 1929
Educ. – Haileybury College (Trevelyan 1874.2 – 1880.2);
Cambridge University (Trinity College 1 June 1880 – BA
1884 MA 1888)
Cricket. – Haileybury College
HS. 7 v Mr. Tapling's X1 August 1880 @ Lakenham
Brother of C & ET (q.v) and of course the family comment in
the previous entry also applies.
Ordained 1885 Priest 1886 Hon DD 1914. Chaplain of Isleworth
(Middx) 1885. Chaplain of St. Dunstan's (Stepney) 1888-94.
Rector of Limehouses 1894-1906. Vicar of Christchurch
(Lancaster Gate) 1906-13. Rector of Paddington 1907-13. Preb
of St. Pauls Cathedral 1908-13. Vicar of Hessle (Yorks) 1913-17.

Bishop Suffragen of Hull 1913-29. Canon of York 1917-29.
F.F. – Died suddenly after officiating at Evensong. President
of Old Haileyburian Society 1923-24. Bequeathed £17,283-
8-1 in his administered London will

GURNEY, Gerald Boileau

(b) North Runcton, Norfolk 12 March 1856
(d) Ipswich 4 December 1902
Educ. – Haileybury College (Lawrence House 1868.3 –
1872.3)
Cricket. – Haileybury College; West Norfolk; Queensland
(Australia)
HS. 21 v I Zingari August 1879 @ Garboldisham
34 for West Norfolk v East Norfolk July 1879
2 brothers-in-law and a nephew played cricket for Radley
College.
His brother Mortimer Hay Gurney played cricket for West
Norfolk (1877)
F.F. – 2 of 9 children to William Hay Gurney and Anna Maria
Boileau – she the daughter of Sir John Peter Boileau. So
not directly related to H (q.v) or WS (q.v). His sister Kathleen
Laura Alice married CA Cresswell (q.v). Gerald emigrated to
Australia but thankfully returned home.

HUMPHREY, William

(b) Low Mitcham, Surrey 15 September 1843
(d) Norwich 24 February 1918
Cricket. – Surrey; Hampshire; All England X1; Carrow; East
Hants Club; New All England; Players of the South; Players
of Hampshire; East Norfolk; Norwich District; United South
England; Southampton Union
HS. 31 v Suffolk August 1880 @ Bury St. Edmunds
BB. 3/? v Lincolnshire July 1880 @ Lincoln
A pre 1876 NCCC player who took a best 4/27 in 1865 v MCC @
East Dereham
1st class cricket 8 matches 99 runs 6 wickets 1 catch
On the Umpiring circuit with GJ Rye (q.v)
His 3 brothers J, R & T played cricket with the last two scoring
first class centuries for Surrey.
F.F. – On the 1881 census shown as a Cricketer living at 2,
Chester Place, Norwich. Latterly his occupation was as a
Mustard Miller worker.

LUDDINGTON, Henry Tansley, MBE JP

(b) Littleport, Ely, Cambridge 9 December 1854
(d) Waltons Park, Ashdon, Essex 14 April 1922
Educ. – King's School (Ely); Uppingham School; Cambridge
University (Jesus College October 1873 – BA 1878 MA 1881)
Cricket. - Uppingham School; Cambridge University –
Blue 1876 & 1877; Undergraduates of Cambridge; Anchor
Club; Gentlemen of England; Cambridge University
Long Vacation Club; Uppingham Rovers; Littleport;

Cambridgeshire
HS. 17 v Essex June 1883 @ Lakenham
BB. 7/? v Suffolk August 1879 @ Lakenhem
'Scores & Biographies' quote – "Average bat and fast round arm"
5/91 for Uppingham Rovers v Free Foresters July 1876
1st class cricket 11 matches 65 runs 42 wickets 4 catches
JP and Alderman County Co. for Isle of Ely. Governor Bedford Level Corp. Brass Plate recognising him in Ely Cathedral. Sheriff of Queen's Bench Division of High Court of Justice on the Morrow of Saint Martin. Acquired Waltons Park in 1917 Left £106,820-15-1 in his will to include as a beneficiary his widow Lily Bate.

MORTON, Capt.
Cricket. – East Norfolk; Norwich District
HS. 19 v I Zingari August 1879 @ Garboldisham
He bowled lobs.
45 no (110) for East Norfolk v West Norfolk July 1879
No clues have emerged to say which branch of the services he was in so no progress made to discover his name !

PATTESON, Frank Eugene, JP
(b) Chelsea 28 May 1854
(d) YMCA Hospital, Brighton, Sussex 24 October 1919
Educ. – Uppingham School and private tuition; Cambridge University (Gonville & Caius College 1 October 1972)
Cricket. – Uppingham School;Norfolk & Norwich;
HS. 81 v Suffolk July 1881 @ Ipswich – held for a time the highest NCCC innings score in the period covered by this book.
Brother of JC (q.v)
F.F.- Son of Revd John Patteson and Elizabeth Hoare. Worked at family firm Hoare, Miller & Co. Frank latterly was a Merchant in Calcutta, India. His administered will was resworn to the value of £89,344-16-7

1880

BUCKLE, Lt. Frederick Ainger
(b) Hoogley, India 13 December 1858
Educ. – King's Collegiate School (Windsor); Brighton College (Lent 1870 – Easter 1876); Cambridge University (Trinity Hall College January 1878 – BA 1882)
Cricket. – Brighton College; Coltishall; Norwich District; Gentlemen of Devon; Devon
HS. 52 v Suffolk July 1880 @ Norwich
BB. 2/20 v Suffolk August 1880 @ Bury St. Edmunds
54 & 3/22 for Brighton College v Lancing College June 1875
Lt. Late 37th Native Infantry in Calcutta.
Son of William Boyd Buckle of Bengal Civil Service.
F.F. – Frederick a Private Schoolmaster married a Belgian

Helen Jenkins and even had a stepbrother Ernest who was born Old Catton, Norwich (where the author presently lives). I am searching for his demise in Canada.

COLLISON, Revd Henry
(b) Bilney Hall, Litcham, Norfolk 2 July 1838
(d) Manor House, Coltishall, Norfolk 26 March 1911
Educ. – Cambridge University (Pembroke College 11 August 1857 – BA 1861 MA 1867)
Cricket. – clubs unknown
HS. 22 v Suffolk August 1880 @ Bury St. Edmunds
BB. 1/33 v Suffolk August 1880 @ Bury St. Edmunds
Ordained 1862 and Priest (Durham) 1864. Chaplain of Heworth (Durham) 1862-70. Chaplain of Nantwich (Cheshire) 1870-73. Rector of Wistason 1873-82. Rector of East Bilney (Norfolk) 1882-1908.
F.F. – He outlived his son Henry who spent the last 12 years of his life big game shooting in Mashonaland.

COLLYER, William Robert, ISO JP
(b) Camberwell, London 11 January 1842
(d) Hackford nr Reepham, Norfolk 27 October 1928
Educ. – Rugby School; Cambridge University (Gonville & Caius College 27 March 1861 – BA 1865 MA 1874)
Cricket. – Rugby School; Cambridge University; Cambridge University Long Vacation Club; Gentlemen of Norfolk; Norfolk & Suffolk; Norfolk & Norwich; MCC
HS. 11 v Lincolnshire July 1880 @ Lincolnshire
William played for NCCC pre 1876 – in fact as far back as 1862.
His brother Revd Daniel also played for NCCC (1869)
Have not yet found a family connection to F (NCCC 1863,1865) nor R (NCCC 1863)
1st class cricket – 1 match 2 runs 2 catches
110 for CULVC v Players engaged at Cambridge University July 1863
160 for Gentlemen of Norfolk v Gentlemen of Lincolnshire August 1866
0 for MCC v NCCC June 1895 – bowled by GJ Rye (q.v) when the batter was aged 53.
Assistant Master Clifton College 1865-67. Inner Temple 23 November 1866 & Barrister 1869. Acting Chief Justice (Sierra Leone) 1879. Acting Puisne Judge (Gold Coast Colony) 1880. Queen's Advocate (Cyprus) 1882-1892. Puisne Judge (Straits Settlement) 1892. Acting Attorney General (Gold Coast) 7 November 1893 – 4 February 1906.
F.F. – Second son of John & Georgina Frances Amy Johnston – she (d) of Sir William (7th Bt).

CURRIE, Lt. Col Frederick Alexander
(b) Ferozepore, Punjab, India 23 September 1851
(d) Aldeburgh, Suffolk 13 June 1902

Educ. – Harrow School (Rendalls House 1869.2); RMC Sandhurst

Cricket. – Harrow School; Eton & Harrow; RMC Sandhurst; Gentlemen of MCC; Overstrand; I Zingari; East Norfolk; Madras Cricket Club

HS. 100 v Free Foresters August 1887 @ Lakenham

BB. 1/13 v Surrey C& G July 1885 @ The Oval

57 no for Harrow School v Old Harrovians July 1869

NCCC career ended in 1887 but returned to play in a friendly in 1901 against Cambridge Quidnuncs – he did not bat nor bowl. Twice for NCCC his individual first innings total exceeded the total made by the opposition in their first innings.

His 86 for NCCC v Incogniti August 1881 was the highest score achieved to that point in the period covered by this book. Played for NCCC as Captain and Major Currie.

1st class cricket – 1 match 10 runs 1 catch

4 Brothers - in -law (Bateman-Chaplain) all played cricket for Gloucestershire. Also had cousins and uncles that played first class cricket.

F.F. – Son of Major Mark Edward Currie & Jane Upwood. He served in Jowaki Campaign 1877-80 and Afghan War 1878-79. Awarded N.W. Frontier & Afghan Medals

CURRIE, Rivers Grenfell

(b) Kingston, Surrey 8 June 1857

(d) Shrewsbury 3 May 1934

Educ. – Uppingham School

Cricket. – Uppingham School

HS. 4 no v Cambridge University Long Vacation Club July 1880 @ Norwich

His eldest brother Maj Gen Fendal Currie played cricket for Gentlemen of Kent. 5 nephews played County Cricket (four of them with Gloucestershire).

F.F. -Son of Sir Frederick (1st Baronet – 3 times married) – there is another Currie (NCCC 1850/1) who might be related given Sir Frederick's propensity for marriage ! Rivers' eldest son was Major Disney Rivers Currie (1894-1964).

Probated will Shrewsbury 21 August 1934 for £39,904- 2s to his widow Alice Theresa Disney Dunne and his eldest son Disney.

FELLOWES, Revd Henry Cecil

(b) Beighton, Norfolk 22 November 1851

(d) A Peerage website says died 1915. In Crockford's Clerical Directory 1902 but not in the1904 edition.

Lived 5 Eaton Terrace, Regents Park, London

Educ. – Fauconberg; Marlborough; Lichfield College

Cricket. – Staffordshire; Lichfield; Royal Navy; AE Fellowes' X1; HC Fellowes' X1

HS. 29 v Incogniti August 1880 @ Norwich

Originally played for NCCC in 1870

Brother of EL (NCCC 1863-1871) & EN (q.v)

Ordained 1875 Priest (Lichfield) 1876. Chaplain of Alrewas 1875-76. Chaplain of Chalfont St. Giles 1876. Rector of Framlingham Hall with Bixley 1876-78. Rector of Beighton 1878-84. Vicar of Kings Walden (Hertford) 1884-89. Diocesan Inspector of Schools (Norwich) 1884-86. Councillor Co. Didcote 1890.

F.F. – An 1883 Directory said – Has a pleasant rectory house (built 1846). A yearly rent of £420, in lieu of tithes.

HART - DAVIS, Sydney Osborne (name changed by deed poll 13 December 1880 to Hart – Davis from SOH Davis)

(b) Frognal, Hampstead 8 December 1859

(d) Cato Ridge, Kwazulu-Natal, South Africa 17 April 1934

Educ. – Wellington College; Cambridge University (Trinity Hall College 4 March 1878)

Cricket. – Gunton; Catton; Pietermaritzburg (S.A)

HS. 17 v Suffolk August 1880 @ Bury St. Edmunds

On 1881 census his occupation listed as in the banking service. Emigrated to the Cape, South Africa in 1887.

F.F. – Son of Richard (Commissioner of Board of Audit) and Anne (a registered blind Mauritian lady). Probated will Norwich 30 September 1934 leaving £21,093.45 with one of the beneficiaries being his widow Ruby.

HAWES, William George

(b) Middlesex 7 October 1855

(d) Norwich 1 May 1909 (age 53)

Cricket. – clubs unknown

HS. 6 v Suffolk August 1880 @ Bury St. Edmunds

On 1881 census – a Clerk and boarder in Lakenham. 10 years later listed as a Merchant Clerk. At death he had the occupation of Gardener with a cause of death as cardiac syncope

MORTON, Cecil Howard

(b) Tatterford Rectory, Norfolk 27 December 1858

(d) Colchester, Essex 3 April 1945

Educ. – Rossall School

Cricket. – Fakenham; Iceni; Free Foresters; MCC; Melton; Ipswich & East Suffolk; Gentlemen of MCC; South Eastern Circuit; Gentlemen of Norfolk; East Norfolk

HS. 0 v Hertfordshire July 1900 @ Bishop's Stortford

HS. 39 v Gentlemen of Suffolk August 1890 @ Hintlesham Park

BB. 8/13 v Suffolk August 1890 @ Hintlesham Park – the best innings analysis for NCCC to this point in the period covered.

Brother of PH (q.v)

5/23 for MCC v Hampshire June 1897

The last survivor of 1885 match @ Lord's between NCCC v MCC when NCCC scored a then record 695 in an innings.

The third NCCC player to take 8 wicket in an innings twice behind (C Tillard & EB Raikes) Seven other players have achieved the feat since.

MORTON, Philip Howard

(b) Tatterford Rectory, Norfolk 20 June 1857
(d) Boscombe, Bournemouth 13 May 1925
Educ. – Rossall School; Cambridge University (Trinity College 7 June 1876 – BA 1881 MA 1884)
Cricket. – Rossall School; Rossall Rangers; Quidnuncs; Cambridge University – Blue 1878-80; Elstree Masters; Undergraduates of Cambridge; Silwood Park; Hastings; Middleton Towers; Surrey; Gentlemen; Gentlemen of England; Cambridge University Past & Present; Scotland X1; MCC; Gentlemen of MCC
HS. 57 v MCC August 1883 @ Lakenham
BB. 7/15 v MCC August 1881 @ Lakenham
Brother of CH (q.v)
1st class cricket – 31 matches 346 runs 139 wickets 14 catches
Rossall School match 1876 v Masters he bowled all 11 in a 12 a-side game.
Played in C.U. trial match in 1879 after having just recovered from a broken arm.
7/45 & 5/25 for Cambridge University v Australia July 1878 @ Lord's
6/45 incl hat-trick in the Varsity match June 1880
Started Northern Nomads CC and the Secretary for 8 years
'Scores & Biographies' quote – " a bat above the average, fields well short leg or slip and fine fast right arm bowler"
Assistant Master Elstree School 1880-89. Headmaster Bracewell Hall (Skipton) 1889-96. Headmaster Scaitcliffe School (Englefield Green) 1896-1903. Headmaster Wixenfield School (Wokingham) 1903.
F.F. – Son of Revd Edward & Isabella Bushman. A mathematical tutor at Elstree School. Latterly lived Hoe Farm, Hascombe, Godalming

PERRY, Major

A wicketkeeper is all that has been found so far.
HS. 1 v Suffolk July 1880 @ Norwich in his one innings

PLATTEN, George

(b) Fakenham 26 April 1831
(d) Hunstanton 19 April 1917
Cricket. – King's Lynn; Gentlemen of Norfolk; Hunstanton; Fakenham; Holkham; West Norfolk
HS. 6 v Lincolnshire September 1880 @ Lakenham
BB. 7/49 v Suffolk August 1880 @ Bury St. Edmunds
He equals the best NCCC match analysis against Suffolk of 13/95
George first played for NCCC as far back as 1867
Slow bowler who took 41 wickets in one 8 innings spell being

28 for NCCC and 13 for West Norfolk in 1880.
Hunstanton CC Secretary. Father Robert in 1851 had a farm of 236 acres. George taking over the farming business in Sedgford saw it grow to 400 acres employing 9 men & 5 boys.
F.F. -George a Churchwarden in Sedgford. Hunt with Fitzroy's Harriers and member of Hunstanton Bowling Club. Left £8,125 –2s to his Dairyman son George in his probated Norwich will dated 21 July 1917. He died as Ella Fitzgerald was being born.

1881

CURTEIS, Revd Thomas Spencer

(b) Shelton, Norfolk 10 March 1843
(d) Brampton Rectory, Suffolk 5 June 1914
Educ. – Felsted School; Bury St. Edmunds; Cambridge University (Trinity College 14 March 1862 – BA 1866)
Cricket. – Cambridge University – Blue 1864-65; Gentlemen of Norfolk; Cheshire; Gentlemen of Cheshire; Suffolk; Gentlemen of Suffolk; Norfolk & Norwich Club; Halesworth; Ipswich & East Suffolk; CJE Jarvis' X1
HS. 16 v S.E. Circuit August 1881 @ Norwich
1st class cricket – 7 matches 65 runs 24 wickets 6 catches
Played for NCCC in 1860's
9/14 & 4/61 and 32 for NCCC (22 on side) v United South of England August 1869. NCCC won by 13 wickets (although 7 of the team left early) when they reached 24/8. United South of England 33 all out in their 1st innings.
4/56 & 6/58 for NCCC v Cambridge University May 1865
10 matches for Cheshire capturing two 10 wicket hauls amongst his 39 captures.
Ordained 1865 Priest 1867. Chaplain of Rostherne (Cheshire) 1866-68. Chaplain of Ben-acre with Covehithe 1868-70. Chaplain of Caston (Norfolk) 1871-73. Rector of Brampton (Suffolk) 1873-1914. Vicar of Stoven 1903-1914.
F.F. – Probated will 23 July 1914 to his widow Mary for £1,204-17-5.

ELWES, Gervase Paget

(b) Helhoughton, Suffolk 4 November 1855
(d) St. Andrews, Scotland 10 September 1925
Educ. – Radley College
Cricket. – Radley College; MCC
HS. 51 v Suffolk July 1881 @ Ipswich
BB. 1/7 v Lincolnshire July 1881 @ Lincoln
32 no (65) – batting at 3 for Radley College v Bradfield College June 1872
On 1881 census shown as a farm pupil on a 1,350 acre estate. He became a Landed Proprietor of 10 Murray Place, St. Andrews
F.F. – Cause of death was exhaustion after 2 years suffering with a malignant disease of the stomach

FELLOWES, Ailwyn Edward KCVO KBE PC MP DL JP (1st Bt Ailwyn of Honingham)

(b) Haverland Hall, Norfolk 10 November 1855
(d) Norwich 23 September 1924
Educ.- Eton College; Cambridge University (Trinity Hall College 20 September 1874 – BA 1878)
Cricket. – Eton College; MCC; Solicitors; Huntingdonshire; AE Fellowes' X1; Melton Constable; East Norfolk; House of Commons
HS. 4 v MCC August 1881 @ Lakenham
Father of RT (q.v)
46 for Solicitors v Articled Clerks (all out 25) May 1879
Middle Temple 17 November 1880 training as a Barrister, but never qualified, turning instead to Agriculture and Politics. Conservative MP North Huntingdonshire.
County Alderman for Huntingdonshire 1887-1906. JP Norfolk & Huntingdonshire. Capt & Hon Major 3rd Batt. Norfolk Regiment. Officer of Auxillary Force. Vice-Chamberlain of Queen Victoria's Household 10 July 1895 – 3 December 1900. Junior Lord of Treasury 1900-1905 (under Prime Ministers -The Marquess of Salisbury & Arthur Balfour) with a seat in the Cabinet until December 1905. President of Board of Agriculture 14 March 1905 – 4 December 1905. Whip of 1911 Government. Deputy President of the Royal Agricultural Show to the King and appointed a Knight Commander of the Royal Victorian Order (KCVO) in 1911 as per his Times Obituary. Chairman Agricultural Wages Board and Deputy Director of Food Production 1917-1919. Chairman Norfolk County Council from 1921. Director of London & N.E Railway, Norwich Union and the National Provident Association. Deputy Chairman of the Great Eastern Railway.
F.F. – In official Royal circles he was described as – 'One who has walked with Kings and yet has not lost the common touch'.
Son of Edward Fellowes (later Baron de Ramsey) and Hon Mary Julia Milles, (d) of 4th Baron Sondes. Inherited 4,500 acre estate in Honingham from his aunt Lady Bayning. Secretary of Unionist Agric Comm in House of Commons. Hansard 12 April 1888 – 17 August 1921 – 190 debates in the chamber as opposed to Michael Falcon (q.v). who spoke on just 22 occasions (1918-1923).

HANSELL, Capt Walter Edward

(b) St. Georges, Tombland, Norwich 15 November 1860
(d) Heigham Hall, Norwich 25 May 1938
Educ. – Crespigny Honour; Aldborough; Charterhouse School (Weekites – Verites Long Qtr 1873 –Oration Qtr 1878)
Cricket. – East Norfolk; Thorpe; Cromer; 22 Norfolk Colts
HS. 5 v Cambridge University Long Vacation Club August 1889 @ Fenner's
BB. 1/24 v Lincolnshire July 1881 @ Lincolnshire

He is the player 'Halsell' shown in the Norfolk press of 1881.
NCCC President 1927 – Hon Sec (3 yrs) and on Committee (20 yrs)
Football. – Old Carthusians – on a winning FA Cup side; Wanderers; Thorpe; Norfolk County 1880-1890 (apps 33 –11 goals)
Norfolk County Football hat-trick v Suffolk 27 December 1881. Solicitor qualified 1886 and partner in firm Hansell & Hales. Notary Public. 5 years Lt 1st Norfolk Rifle Volunteers. 2 years Capt 3rd Norfolk Regiment.
F.F. – Committee Member of N & N Musical Festival. Norwich Philharmonic Society. Chairman CEYMS Settlement House.
Clerk to Governors King Edward V11 GS
Probated will Norwich 3 October 1938 in the sum of £9,144 –7s to Solicitors Edward Morgan Hansell & John Baseley Hales.

MACK, Major Hugh Paston, JP

(b) Paston, Norfolk 22 March 1857
(d) Grove Nursing Home, Norwich 18 May 1933
Lived Old Hall, Woodbastwick.
Educ. – Bradfield College; Cambridge University (Trinity College 9 March 1876 – doubtful if resided)
Cricket. – Bradfield College; Trinity College; East Suffolk; Gunton; Felixstowe
HS. 0 v Suffolk June 1881 @ Lakenham
BB. 4/43 v Suffolk June 1881 @ Lakenham
Brother of Thomas (NCCC 1867-1870) and ESP (q.v)
Capt 4th Batt. Norfolk Regiment. WW1 – Royal Defence Corp – gazetted Major 1916. JP Blofield Bench. Lived on his own means with Governess and 4 servants.
F.F. - Family of 6 brothers and 6 sisters (he was the 7th) born to John (of Paston Hall & Tunstead Hall) and Susannah Margaret Shepheard. Probated will Norwich 10 July 1933 leaving £3,977-14-9

THURGAR, William Augustus

(b) Lakenham, Norwich 6 September 1856
(d) Lowestoft 22 April 1947
Educ. – Princes Street (Norwich); Bracondale School
Cricket. – Princes Street; Bracondale School; Norfolk Club & Ground; Veterans; Blofield; Thorpe; Carrow; Kingsley
HS. 29 v Free Foresters August 1882 @ Lakenham
BB. 1/12 v MCC June 1892 @ Lakenham
Father of RW (q.v)
88 no (218) for Carrow v Dereham (ao 85) in 1889 Senior Cup game
59 for Blofield v Thorpe Asylum July 1893
57 for Veterans v Youths August 1899 when almost age 43. Captain of Princes Street when they won Norfolk Senior Cup. Partner in firm Clowes & Nash (Auctioneers) retiring in 1917.

Assistant Master Bracondale School

F.F. – Son of William Thomas Thurgar (an Artist) and Maria Thompson Lanham. At death was of Saxlingham Hall, Nethergate and he left £25,086-14-7 to Auctioneer/Estate Agent Horace Marshall Thurgar.

WICKHAM, Revd Prebendary Archdale Palmer

(b) South Holmwood, Surrey 7 November 1855

(d) East Brent, Highbridge, Somerset 13 October 1935

Educ. – Marlborough College; Temple Grove; Rugby; Oxford University (New College 13 October 1874 - BA 1879); Leeds Clergy School

Cricket. – Rugby; Marlborough; Harlequins; Oxford University Past & Present; Gentlemen of Somerset; South of England; Gentlemen; Gentlemen of Norfolk; Undergraduates of Oxford; Catton Hall; JH Leslie's X1; VT Hill's X1; Oxford University – Blue 1878.

HS. 77 v Free Foresters August 1882 @ Lakenham

Best wicket keeping season for victims 1882 (15/9)

1st class cricket. – 93 matches 760 runs 150 victims (90/60)

Wore brown pads and Harlequins Cap whilst at Somerset. For his batting ability his name cruelly changed by some from Wickham to Snickham.

Uncle of BNB Smith (Middlesex, MCC etc). President of Somerset CCC. Curate of St. Stephens (Norwich) 1880-83. Curate of Rickinghall Superior (Suffolk) 1883-86. Curate of Buxton (Norfolk) 1886-88. Vicar of Martock (Somerset) 1888-1911. Surrogate for the Dioceses of Bath & Wells 1896. Rural Dean of Ilchester 1900-1911. Rural Dean of Axbridge & Burnham 1912. Prebendary of E.Haptree in Wells Cathedral 1904. Prebendary of Wells Cathedral 1911-1927

F.F. – His extensive collection of butterflies and moths are in the British Museum. Stained glass window and main gates St. Mary's Church (East Brent) dedicated to him. Known as 'The Bishop' he drove ducks along the main street in Martock. He once lost heavily at cards and quick-wittedly offered his ducks instead as a suitable sacrifice. Married twice – (1) Emily Helena Baldwin (2) Harriet Elizabeth Amy Strong

Probated will Bristol 20 December 1935 leaving £6,880-0-11 to Schoolmaster Archdale Kenneth Wickham

1882

BLYTH, Revd Alan Gwyn

(b) Fincham, Norfolk 14 July 1856

(d) Northrepps, Norfolk 27 September 1930

Educ. – Uppingham School; Cambridge University (Christ's College 3 March 1875 – BA 1879 MA 1888)

Cricket. – Uppingham School; Norfolk & Norwich; Gentlemen of Norfolk; CEYMS; Northrepps; West Norfolk

HS 13 v Worcestershire August 1896 @ Worcester

HS. 64 v Bedfordshire August 1882 @ Lakenham

Son of William Blyth (Rector of Fincham)

Ordained 1879 and Priest (Norwich) 1880. Curate of Feltwell 1879-1884. Curate of St. Phil. Heigham 1884-88. Vicar of St. Phil. Heigham 1888-1904. Rector of Northrepps Diocese Norwich from 1904

F.F. – Probated will London 23 October 1930 to Revd Ernest Wiliam Blyth and his widow Edith Mary Moule, bequeathing £3,978-12s

FELLOWES, Evelyn Napier

(b) Beighton, Norfolk 3 June 1862

(d) Richmond, Surrey 2 September 1936

Educ. – Oxford University (Trinity College 15 October 1881-BA 1884)

Cricket. – Free Foresters

HS. 39 v Bedfordshie August 1882 @ Lakenham

Brother of HC (q.v) and EL (q.v)

His brother Revd Edward Lyon Fellowes (23/04/1845 – 23/07/1896) played for NCCC (1863-71).

73 for Free Foresters v NCCC August 1882 @ Lakenham (batting at no 10)

Evelyn, a Solicitor at 4 Union Court Road, Broad Street, London, was in 1896 accused (falsely) with three other Solicitors of slander of title against one Joshua Jones re land at Mokaupro Province, Taranaki, New Zealand. The plaintiff at the Central Criminal Court withdrew the allegation and the Jury found a general verdict of guilty and he was discharged on his own recognizance of £500 to come up for judgement if called upon.

HARBOUR

HS. 2 and 1/18 v Leicestershire August 1882 @ Grace Road. A crushing 10 wicket defeat.

Cannot prove that he was the William who played for Lincolnshire in 1879.

JOHNSON, E G

HS. 0 (x2) v Leicestershire August 1882 @ Grace Road.

The 3rd NCCC player to get a pair in his only match.

Two of 7 ducks by the team in the match

The website Cricket Archive has him as ES Johnson with no substance. Cannot find either choice after trawling newspapers

MANSFIELD, The Hon James William

(b) Bombay, India 12 February 1862

(d) Westminster Hospital, London 17 June 1932

Lived 23 Pall Mall, London.

Educ. – Winchester College; Cambridge University (Trinity College 13 June 1881 – BA 1884)

Cricket. – Winchester College; Cambridge University – Blue 1883-84); England X1; Cambridge University Next XV1; GB Studd's X1; MCC.

HS. 2 v Free Foresters August 1882 @ Lakenham
1st class cricket – 17 matches 437 runs 10 catches
117 for Cambridge University v Orleans Club June 1883
49 (131) for Winchester College v Eton College June 1880
A Wine Merchant for Hatch, Mansfield & Co.
Lt. 4th Batt Middlesex Regiment 1886-89
4(s) of William Rose Mansfield (1st Baron Sandhurst) therefore did not succeed to the title.
F.F. – In the family were Commander-in-Chief Bombay Army; Lord Chamberlain of the Household and bemeddalled individuals. Also related to the Upcher family by marriage with many of the last named playing cricket for NCCC pre 1876. Left £18,539-4-2 in his probated London will dated 3 October 1932.

MARSHALL, Lawton Parry
(b) Llanidloes, Montgomeryshire AMJ 1858
(d) The Green, Llanidloes, Montgomeryshire 1 November 1899 age 43
Educ. – Shrewsbury GS
Cricket. – Shrewsbury GS; Free Foresters; Norfolk Club & Ground; Corporation Officials CC; S.E. Circuit; Carrow; Builth Wells
HS. 2 v Bedfordshire July 1882 @ Bedford
7 no (39) & 18 (44) for Builth Wells v Llandovery August 1890.
His Free Foresters appearance was against NCCC in August 1882.
His occupations were Bank Cashier, Auctioneer & Valuer and lastly an Hotelier of the Trewython Arms.
F.F. – His obituary in the Montgomery Express and Radnor Times dated 3 November 1899.

RAIKES, Ernest Barkley, OBE KC JP
(b) Carleton, Forehoe, Norfolk 18 November 1863
(d) Ham Common, Surrey 7 December 1931
Lived Oak Lodge, Kingston-on-Thames, Surrey
Educ. – Haileybury College (Trevelyan 1877.1- 1882.2); Oxford University (Keble College 17 October 1882 – BA 1887)
Cricket. – Haileybury College; Bombay; Bombay Gymkhana; Bombay Presidency; Europeans; Harleston; Drayton & Taverham; Bungay; Gentlemen of Norfolk; Brain's Team; MCC;
New University
HS. 27 no v Cambridgeshire August 1897 @ Fenner's
BB. 6/6 v Cambridgeshire August 1897 @ Lakenham
HS. 21 v Bedfordshire August 1882 @ Lakenham
BB. 9/44 v Hertfordshire August 1888 @ Lakenham – the best innings analysis to this point in the period covered by the book. 17/91 in this tied match which total still stands as the NCCC best record haul in a match.
Brother of GB (q.v) and Father of TB (q.v)

Chairman NCCC Committee to his death. 1926 he managed NCCC Colts and probably in other years as well.
1st class cricket – 9 matches 51 runs 49 wickets 1 catch – all in India.
In 1881 & 1882 season he took a combined 117 wickets for Haileybury College with his puzzling action.
89 for Brain's Team v Palairet's Team in May 1893
74 no for Drayton & Taverham v Fulthorpe July 1912 –when he was just short of his 50th birthday
8/26 for Bungay v Lowestoft College May 1910
8/22 for Europeans v Parsees September 1894
7/34 & 3/45 for Europeans v Parsees September 1892
Inner Temple 1888 and career at the India Bar in Bombay before Judicial Court of Privy Council (commercial cases in High Court).
At one time on staff of Lord Harris in Poona.
F.F. -Co. Sec. Norfolk Branch British Red Cross Society 1915-1920. East Norfolk Chairman of Quarter Sessions
Son of Revd Francis Raikes and Martha Barkley
Also in Haileybury College Rugby Union XV

SKERRETT, Charles Percival
(b) Mayo, Ireland 1853
(d) Burgess Hill, Sussex 14 April 1888 at age 35
Cricket. – Norfolk & Norwich; Norwich District; Suffolk
HS. 10 v Leicestershire August 1882 @ Grace Road
A Civil Engineer.
F.F. – On 1881 census he was visiting his Irish family in Marine Parade, Lowestoft. At the time of playing for NCCC his address was Pinarva House, Thorpe Hamlet. Probated will Norwich leaving £294 to his widow Ada Mildred Sperling.

WEIGHELL, Revd William Bartholomew
(b) Cheddington, Buckinghamshire 20 June 1846
(d) Shilton Vicarage, Burford, Oxfordshire 29 October 1905
Educ. – Bedford GS; Clergy Orphan School (Canterbury); Cambridge University (Jesus College 1 December 1864 – BA 1871)
Cricket. – Bedford GS; Cambridge University – Blue 1866,1868/69; Sussex; Bedfordshire; Quidnuncs; Gentlemen of Sussex; Veteran Gentlemen of Sussex; United South of England
HS. 23 v Suffolk May 1883 @ Lakenham
BB. 4/48 v Suffolk June 1883 @ Ipswich
1st class cricket – 26 matches 388 runs 25 wickets 15 catches
40 for Cambridge University v Old Cambridge Men May 1866
50 for Quidnuncs v Gentlemen of Sussex August 1866
128 for Gentlemen of Sussex v Royal Artillery May 1867
101 for Gentlemen of Sussex v Gentlemen of Hampshire July 1867
11 wickets in match for Gentlemen of Sussex v Gentlemen of

Hampshire August 1868
68 for United South of England v Broughton August 1877 – his one innings surpassing that of WG & GF Grace in the match as they made just 15 in their combined four efforts.
Ordained 1879 and Priest 1880. Curate of Leadgate (Co. Durham) 1879-81. Curate of St. Margaret's (King's Lynn) 1881-83. Vicar of Roughton 1883-91. Rector of Oxhill (Warwick) 1891-94. Rector of Amberley (Sussex) 1895-96. Vicar of Chiltington 1896-98. Vicar of Shilton (Oxon) 1898-1905
F.F. – Son of a Preacher man namely John. Surname is pronounced 'Weel' Administered will London 13 November 1905 to widow Catherine for £56.

WILSON, Charles Plumpton
(b) Roydon, Norfolk 12 May 1859
(d) Eckling Grange, East Dereham, Norfolk 9 March 1938
Educ. – Uppingham School; Marlborough College; Cambridge University (Trinity College 11 October 1877 – BA 1881 MA 1887)
Cricket. – Uppingham School; Marlborough College; Cambridge University – Blue 1880,1881; United South of England; Lincolnshire; Clifton; Herefordshire; Elstree Masters; Catton Hall
HS. 77 v Gentlemen of Nottingham August 1884 @ Lakenham
BB. 6/7 v Hertfordshire June 1882 @ St Albans
Brother of KP (q.v)
His 56 for NCCC v Leicestershire August 1883 surpassed the opposition's first innings total of 43.
1st class cricket – 10 matches 157 runs 22 wickets 6 catches
Rugby Union. – Cambridge University – Blue 1877-80; England 1881 (1 cap)
Football. – Hendon; Corinthians; England 1881 (2 caps)
His brother George also represented England at football.
Represented C.U v O.U 1879 in 25 mile bicycle race
Assistant Master Elstree School 1881-1896. Private Tutor of Mr Gurney Buxton of Catton Hall, Norwich. Headmaster Sandroyds School (Cobham) 1898-1920.

1883

ARNOLD, Revd Henry Abel
(b) London 5 April 1861
(d) The Rectory, Wolsingham, County Durham 29 December 1934
Educ. – Haileybury School (Hailey & Lawrence 1874.2 – 1878.3); Cambridge University (Jesus College 1 October 1882 – BA 1885 MA 1893)
Cricket. – Haileybury School
HS. 46 no v Suffolk May 1883 @ Lakenham
BB. 5/20 v Suffolk May 1883 @ Lakenham
Took 13 wickets in the match for Haileybury School v

Uppingham School June 1878
Ordained 1886 and Priest 1887. Curate of St. Michael's (Toxteth Park) 1886-87. Curate of St. Helen's 1887-90. Rector of Barrow 1890-97. Vicar of Alsager 1907-13. Vicar of Wolsingham 1913-34.
F.F. – Times Obituary dated 31 December 1934.
Not a relative of RM (q.v)

COZENS – HARDY, Ferneley (birth registered as F. Hardy)
(b) Cley Hall, Cley, Norfolk 16 August 1862
(d) Norwich 8 June 1918
Educ. – Amersham Hall; University of London – June 1879, a London degree in Arts)
Cricket. – Thorpe; Norwich District; Norfolk & Norwich; Sprowston; Carrow
HS. 16 no v MCC June 1887 @ Lakenham
BB. 2/24 v Essex June 1885 @ Brentwood
8/22 for Norfolk & Norwich v Reepham June 1886
Football. – Teachers; Carrow; Norfolk County 1885-89 (apps 5-0)
A Solicitor – working for 30 years for Messrs JO Taylor & Sons. Norwich Union Fire Insurance Legal Advisor
F.F. – Second son of Clement William Hardy Cozens-Hardy : Lord of the Manor). Father a Brewer Maltster who owned most of Letheringsett.

DINES, Ebenezer
(b) South Lynn 28 March 1855
(d) Lewisham 22 July 1917
Cricket. – Lynn; West Norfolk
HS. 7 v MCC June 1883 @ Lord's
BB. 7/40 v Suffolk May 1883 @ Lakenham
His occupations through life were as a Clerk in the coal trade; a Solicitor's Clerk to finally a Clerk to a Surveyor of Taxes at death.
F.F. – He married an Australian namely Clementina Sarah Jane Culley in Dalston, Hackney, London. He wasn't christened until he was aged twelve. He endured a dilation of his heart for three years before reaching the batting crease in the sky.

GROOM, Revd Arthur John
(b) Congham, Norfolk 23 January 1853
(d) Ashwicken Rectory, Norfolk 18 October 1937
Educ.- Rugby School; Cambridge University (Trinity College 8 July 1871 – BA 1874 MA 1878)
Cricket. – Huntingdonshire; West Norfolk
HS. 5 v Northamptonshire August 1883 @ Lakenham
Brother Horace Alfred played cricket for West Norfolk
Brother of JE (NCCC 1869)
Ordained 1876 and Priest (Norwich) 1877. Chaplain of Halifax 1876-77. Rector of Ashwicken with Leziate & Bawsey 1877-1937. Diocesan Inspector (Norwich) 1888-1905

MORRIS, Edward John
(b) Slough, Buckinghamshire 1 June 1859
(d) Heigham, Norwich 14 December 1902
Cricket. – Carrow; CEYMS; Prince's Street; Norfolk & Norwich; Norwich District; St. Philip's; Kingsley
HS. 46 v Essex July 1883 @ Brentwood
Referred to as 'The Norfolk Midget' in the local press.
53 for CEYMS v Kingsley August 1893
Occupations of Ironmonger; Licensed Victualler at The Angel, North Walsham and Mercantile Clerk at demise.

RUDD, Alfred
(b) Briston nr East Dereham, Norfolk 15 October 1856
(d) Ormesby St. Margaret, Norfolk 11 August 1934
Cricket. – Melton Constable; Norfolk Club & Ground; Midland Railway CC; Holt; Eastern & Midlands District, Lord Hastings' X1; Melton Constable Railways
HS. 19 v MCC July 1885 @ Lord's
BB. 7/38 v Staffordshire August 1886 @ Lakenham
He was stumped for 19 leaving H.Birkbeck (q.v) stranded on 89 no as NCCC's innings finally ended at 695 v MCC in 1885.
Always referred to as Fred in the Norfolk papers.
Possible relationship to T.Rudd with whom he played much of his club cricket.
A retired Railway Gateman whose stepson came down from Nantwich, Cheshire to comfort him and to be present at his passing.

SMITH, Jeffrey J
Educ. – King Edward V11 GS
Cricket. – CEYMS; East Dereham; Norfolk & Norwich; Norwich County Asylum; Thorpe; Carrow; Kingsley; Norwich District
HS. 8 no v Cambridgeshire August 1898 @ Fenner's
HS. 21 no v Quidnuncs June 1894 @ Lakenham
BB. 2/50 v I Zingari August 1893 @ Lakenham
He played in the Norfolk Senior Cup Final 1899 for CEYMS v Carrow with match figures of 20 (96) & 5/42.
7/12 for CEYMS v St. Marks September 1893
73 for CEYMS v Kingsley July 1894
A local stalwart who was rewarded with a Minor Counties Championship game after starting his NCCC career with an 1883 friendly.

WILSON, Kenneth Plumpton
(b) Ringstead, Norfolk 31 May 1861
(d) Moorcroft House, Hillingdon 18 May 1949
Lived Heatherdene, Crowthorne, Berkshire
Educ. – Rossall School; Marlborough College; Cambridge University (Pembroke College 11 October 1880 –BA 1884 MA 1890)
Cricket. – Cambridge University Long Vacation Club

HS. 15 v Essex July 1883 @ Brentwood AND 15 v Leicestershire August 1884 @ Grace Road
Brother of CP (q.v)
Football. – Cambridge University – Blue 1882-84. He preferred football to cricket. Assistant Master Fettes College 1884-1925.
His father was Revd Roger Plumpton Wilson – Lord Bishop of Wakefield.

1884

HANSELL, John
(b) North Elmham, Norfolk 20 July 1849
(d) North Elmham, Norfolk 19 January 1900
Cricket. – Elmham; East Dereham; Batley; Holbeck; Melton Constable; Dewsbury
HS. 136 v MCC July 1885 @ Lord's in 3 hours with 17 fours
BB. 7/25 v Suffolk May 1884 @ Bury St. Edmunds
Equal 2nd NCCC v Suffolk with 4 five in an innings returns against them.
WG Grace tried a number of times to dismiss him without success during his United South of England matches against Batley.
He has a (7) recorded as a scoring stroke in his 43 for NCCC v MCC in July 1886.
He batted left and bowled right arm fast medium.
8/11 for Elmham v Billingham August 1899
The NCCC Annual 1889 stated that he was engaged at Fenner's Ground, Cambridge.
F.F. – Listed on Census return as a professional Cricketer and a Warrener which meant that he followed in his father's footsteps in maintaining rabbit warrens to trap and kill them

JONES
HS. 6 no v Surrey Club & Ground July 1885 @ Oval
BB. 1/5 v Essex June 1884 @ Lakenham
Can anyone help with information about this untraced gentleman?

LUCAS, Percival Montague
(b) Filby, Norfolk 1 December 1860
(d) Sandwich Bay, Kent 20 April 1927
Educ. – Haileybury College (Hailey 1875.3 – 1876.2); Cambridge University (Jesus College 1 October 1880 – BA 1884)
Cricket.- Norfolk & Norwich; Melton Constable; Gunton; AG Steel's X1; GB Studd's X1
HS. 36 v Hampshire July 1886 @ Southampton
Played in University Freshman trial and a University Seniors trial.
Rugby Union – Cambridge University – Blue 1882.
Employed by NW Coal & Navigation Co. in Canada.

An undergraduate student living on his own means in his early days. Secretary of Princes Golf Club (Sandwich) – he helped put up most of the capital for the course. In 1914 he cut most of the greens and was involved with the billeting of Argyll & Sutherland Highlanders.

F.F. – Father of Wing Commander 'Laddie' Lucas CBE DSO DFC MP – a 1940's fighter ace and Walker Cup golfer.

MACK, Revd Edgar Shepheard Paston

(b) Paston, Norfolk 13 August 1861

(d) Bishop's Waltham, Hampshire 15 March 1944

Educ. – Bradfield College; Cambridge University (Pembroke College); Chichester Theological College

Cricket. – Gunton; Buxton Lammas; Norfolk & Norwich;

HS. 17 v Cambridgeshire August 1896 @ Lakenham.

BB. 5/19 v Hertfordshire July 1896 @ Bishop's Stortford

HS. 43 v I Zingari August 1894 @ Lakenham

BB. 4/40 v I Zingari July 1895 @ Lakenham

He took NCCC's first hat - trick in a Minor Counties match v Hertfordshire July 1896 in the analysis above of 5/19

Brother HP (q.v) and Thomas (NCCC 1867-1870)

8/32 (inc hat – trick) for Gunton v Club & Ground July 1893

79 no for Buxton Lammas v Coltishall June 1895

Football. - Norwich Wanderers; Norfolk County (1882-85 apps 10-0)

Ordained 1891 and Priest (Truro) 1892. Curate of Penkerd (Cornwall) 1892-93. Rector of Lammas 1893-1901. Vicar of Runham 1901-1902. Curate of Lound 1902-04. Rector of Lound 1904-08 .

MIDDLETON, Sir John Page

(b) Hindringham, Norfolk 8 June 1851

(d) Southsea,Portsmouth 17 June 1932

Educ. – Uppingham School; Cambridge University (Trinity Hall College 21 February 1869 – BA 1872)

Cricket. – Gentlemen of Norfolk

HS. 12 v Staffordshire June 1886 @ Stoke-on-Trent

BB. 2/8 v Suffolk May 1884 @ Bury St. Edmunds

Eldest of 3 brothers and 4 sisters with 5 servants and a governess in his childhood. Admitted Inner Temple 2 November 1871 and Called to the Bar 6 June 1874. On Norfolk & S. Eastern Circuits 1874-82. Acting Queen's Advocate (Gold Coast Colony) 1882. President District Court of Limassol (Cyprus) 1882-92. Puisne Judge (Cyprus) 1892-1902. Puisne Judge Supreme Court (Ceylon) 1902-12.

F.F. – JP for West Riding & Liberty of Ripon.

Author of 3 books including ' Cyprus under British Rule'

RUDD, T

Cricket. – Melton Constable; Holt; Norfolk Club & Ground

HS. 21 v Suffolk May 1884 @ Bury St. Edmunds

106 for Melton Constable v Cromer Visitors 1888.

He played for the same teams as Alfred known as Fred Rudd (q.v) but have been unable to prove if related.

STEWART, Revd Alexander Lamont

(b) Port of Spain, Trinidad 2 June 1858

(d) Marylebone, Middlesex 17 February 1904

Educ.- Clifton College; Oxford University (St. Edmund Hall 25 October 1888 – BA 1883); a commoner Magdalene College (as per Oxford Alumni)

Cricket. – Middlesex; HW Cave's X1; Oxford University Freshmen; Oxford University Next XV1; Kensington Park

HS. 11 v Gentlemen of Nottingham August 1884 @ Lakenham

BB. 3/24 v Gentlemen of Nottingham August 1884 @ Lakenham

1st class cricket – 4 matches 27 runs 6 wickets 5 catches

Scottish born Brother James played cricket for Middlesex

Scottish born Uncle Randolph played cricket for Gentlemen of England and succeeded to title 11th Earl of Galloway.

6/20 & 3/21 for HW Cave's X1 v LML Owen's X1 May 1882

A Student of Theology leading to –

Curate of Matlock (Somerset) 1886-88

Rector of Aisholt (Bridgwater) 1888

F.F. – Probated London will leaving £1,556-7-10 to his widow Charlotte.

1885

BECTON, F

Cricket. – West Norfolk

HS. 8 v Surrey Club & Ground July 1885 @ Oval

BB. 1/10 v Surrey Club & Ground July 1885 @ Oval

This was a game where John Hansell (q.v) took 7/66 and had a second innings knock of 134.

Have also seen surname given as Beckton and Beeton so the man is still a mystery.

de MOLEYNS, Lt. Col Frederick Rossmore Wauchope Eveleigh DSO DL (5th Baron Ventry)

(b) Niddrie House, Midlothian, Scotland 11 December 1861

(d) Hove, Sussex 22 September 1923

Educ. – Harrow School

Cricket. – Harrow School

HS. 8 v Essex July 1885 @ Lakenham

48 for Harrow School v Harrow Town July 1879

Football. – Harrow School

Army career with 4th Hussars – entered 1882 and made Captain 1890. Served in South Africa 1896/97 – twice mentioned in despatches. Commissioner of Police in Mashonaland. Deputy Lieutenant of County Kerry whilst living at Burnham House, Dingle.

F.F. – Family Estates in 1883 of 93,629 acres. Family history name change from Mullins later de Moleyns later Eveleigh de Moleyns. Family motto of *Vivere Sat Vincere* – To conquer is to live enough. Left £92,644-5-2 in his will (bequeathing £1,500 of it to Mary Lilian Skelmerdine – his nurse)

GWILLIM, James Herbert

(b) Marlborough, Wiltshire 6 January 1856
(d) Southampton 8 April 1911
Educ. – Marlborough GS; Cambridge University (St. John's College 23 January 1874 – BA 1878 MA 1881)
Cricket. – Marlborough GS
HS. 10 v I Zingari July 1885 @ Garboldisham
On 1881 census he was a lodger in Cooks Lane, Tombland, Norwich. Mathematical Master at King's School, Bruton. Assistant Master Norwich GS 1903-1911.
F.F. – Probated will London 19 July 1911 leaving £1,969-5-3 to his two unmarried sisters Katherine and Margaret.

HILDYARD, C

HS. 19 v I Zingari July 1885 @ Garboldisham
A disparaging press comment (EDP) of "not up to county form". I would settle for his one game match total of 23 runs ! The website Cricket Archive give his initials as an unproven C.H but I am still struggling to find out more about the gentleman.

JEE, Alfred Morland

(b) Worthing, Sussex 2 September 1858
(d) Colkirk, Fakenham, Norfolk 12 January 1932
Educ. – Worthing; Scarborough; Cambridge University (Trinity College 31 May 1887)
Cricket. – Colkirk; Fakenham; Gentlemen of Norfolk; East Dereham; Baynham; Melton Constable JJ Miller's X1; Norfolk Club & Ground; Lord Grey de Wilton's X1
HS. 27 v Hampshire May 1887 @ Southampton
BB. 5/? v Gentlemen of Suffolk August 1889 @ Hintlesham Park
Joint Hon. Sec NCCC in the 1890s and 1900s plus involved in arranging Norfolk Colts games.
61 for Fakenham v Rudham September 1895
4/23 for Baynham v Hampton September 1895
5/17 for Fakenham v Knighton May 1910 when age 51.
Member of West Norfolk Hunt & Hon. Sec. to the West Norfolk Hunt Club.
President of the Colkirk Conservative & Unionist Association
F.F. – Left £2,109-9-3 to his widow Augusta Vera Kepper

MOWER, Harry William

(b) Old Buckenham, Norfolk JFM 1863
(d) Norwich 15 January 1928
Lived Wakefield Lodge, Ipswich Road, Norwich
Cricket. – Carrow; Norfolk Colts; Norfolk & Norwich

HS. 6 v Suffolk June 1885 @ Bury St. Edmunds
Father of GH (q.v)
Football. - Carrow
A Foreman at a Flour Mill under his father Henry.
A Corn Buyer for J & J Colman being promoted to the Managership of the Flour & Oatmeal Departments to retirement 31 December 1927. A devastating retirement of only 15 days !

1886

DEWING, Revd Arthur May

(b) Beyton, Suffolk 24 January 1860
(d) Felixtowe 20 July 1935
Educ. - Beyton School; Bury St. Edmunds GS; Wells Theological College; Cambridge University (Gonville & Caius College 1 October 1879 – BA 1883 MA 1886)
Cricket. – Bury St. Edmunds GS; Norwich District; Norfolk & Norwich
HS. 26 v Hampshire June 1886 @ Southampton
His brothers RH & M played cricket for Suffolk.
His father EM played for NCCC (1845 and 47).
Ordained 1884 and Priest (Glos & Bristol) 1885. Chaplain of St. George Brandon Hill (Bristol) 1884-89. Chaplain of St. Margaret Redcliffe (Bristol) 1889-92. Vicar of St. George Brandon Hill (Bristol) 1892-1928. Chaplain of St. Mark's (Lord Mayors Chaplain) 1894-95. Rector of Camerton (Somerset) 1898-1918 Rector of Ottley (Suffolk) 1918-1926.
F.F. – Left £4,301-19-9 in his resworn will with one of the beneficiaries being his sister Edith

DUNN, Arthur Tempest Blakiston

(b) Whitby 12 August 1860
(d) Monken Hadley, Hertfordshire 20 February 1902
Educ. – Eton College; Cambridge University (Trinity College 1 June 1878)
Cricket. – Cambridge University Long Vacation Club; North Wales; I Zingari; Hertfordshire; MCC; Free Foresters; Elstree Masters; Eton Ramblers; Bryn-y-Neuadd; Caernarvonshire; Ludgrove School; Lord Glamis' X1; FGH Clayton's X1
HS. 54 v MCC August 1899 @ Lakenham
BB. 1/23 v Hampshire August 1887 @ Lakenham
202 no for Lord Glamis' X1 v TF Harrison's X1 July 1896
52 & 3/31 for CULVC v Gentlemen of Norfolk August 1889
5/23 for FGH Clayton's X1 v Northumberland September 1894
73 for Eton Ramblers v Henley May 1896
Between 1887-1902 he took 96 wickets for Eton Ramblers at an average of just 11.23 per wicket.
Football. - England 1883 – 1892 (4 caps); Cambridge University – Blue 1883/84; Eton; Granta; Old Etonians; Cambridgeshire; Corinthians; Amateurs South; Lynn Town; Norfolk County 1883/84 (apps 5 – 2goals).

Old Etonians FA Cup Winner 1882 and Finalist 1883.
The Arthur Dunn Cup – old boys of public schools trophy.
Founder & Schoolmaster Ludgrove School
F.F. – An Author of 'Corinthians & Cricketers Chapter V'. The best quote of him was 'He taught football as honourably as the game of life and he recited Kings of Judah and Israel. He also maintained that one had to love God and hate Harrow' Probated will London 30 April 1902 leaving £24,807-13-3.

FFOLKES, Revd Sir Francis Arthur Stanley MVO JP (5th Baron of Hillington)
(b) Hillington 8 December 1863
(d) The Rectory, Hillington 18 October 1938
Educ. – Stoke Poges; Honiton; Oakham; Durham University
Cricket. – Worcestershire Club & Ground; Worcestershire St. John's; Gunton; Hunstanton & District; Hingham; Norfolk 22 Colts
HS. 17 v Northamptonshire August 1886 @ Northampton
His ancestor the 3rd Baron played cricket for Gentlemen of Norfolk (1867)
Rugby Union. – Durham
Curate of Barnham Broom with Kimberley. Curate of Hingham & Hillington. Chaplain of Hillside School (Malvern). Chaplain attached to Norfolk Yeomanry King's Own Regiment. Rector of Anmer (Norfolk), Scoulton (Norfolk) & Wolferton (Norfolk). Hon. Chaplain to Queen Victoria (1900-01). Chaplain-in-Ordinary Edward V11 (1901-03). Chaplain-in-Ordinary to King George V1 (1937). SCF to 74th Division Egyptian Expeditionary Forces SCF to Kantara Canal Zone. Governor King Edward V11 School & High School Lynn.
F.F. – Medals – Jubilee, Coronation Edward V11, Coronation George V, Victory 1915, General Service medals, despatches 1917. Left £1,972-0-3 to his unmarried sister Phillipa Frances Boschelli Ffolkes

GOODLIFF, Frank
(b) Conington, Huntingdonshire JAS 1867
(d) Montague House, Huntingdon 18 December 1938
Cricket. – Norfolk & Norwich; Huntingdonshire
HS. 38 v Hampshire July 1886 @ Southampton
His brothers R & W played with him in the same Hunts team.
93 for Huntingdonshire v Oundle Rovers August 1885
Son of John (Hotel Keeper and Farmer) and Elizabeth Jenkins. One of 11 children with 9 servants to help look after them all. He learnt his trade as a Brewer Maltster to become a Wine and Spirit Merchant.
F.F. – Probated London will dated 2 March 1929 saw him bequeath £51,918 –11-9 to an assortment of people.

JARVIS, Lt. Col Frederick William
(b) King's Lynn 5 May 1866
(d) Finsbury, London 1 October 1934

Educ. – Harrow School (The Park, left 1884)
Cricket. – Gentlemen of Norfolk; Norfolk 22 Colts; Norfolk Club & Ground
HS. 40 v Free Foresters August 1888 Lakenham
Brother of AW, CJE and LK (q.v. for all three)
Served Hussars Boer War (despatches)
Commandant South Africa Constabulary 1903-07
Lt. Col Suffolk Yeomanry in Gallipoli, France & Egypt.
F.F. – At death he listed two addresses being – Boodle's Club, St. James Street, London SW1 together with 4 Stafford Mansions, Buckingham Gate, Middlesex.
Death Certificate gave cause of death as a result of Myocarditis and Bronchitis

MORLEY, Thomas
(b) Sutton-in-Ashfield 10 March 1863
(d) Thorpe St. Andrew, Norwich 28 October 1919
Cricket. – Gentlemen of Norfolk; Norfolk Club & Ground; Nottinghamshire; Ipswich & East Suffolk; Leeds Albion; Hastings; Lasswade; Blofield & District; Easton Park; Easton Ramblers; Thorpe; Belle Vue; Carrow; Sandringham; Revd W Francis' X1
HS. 74 no v Cambridgeshire August 1896 @ Fenners
BB. 6/27 v Hertfordshire August 1895 @ Lakenham
AND 6/27 v Northumberland July 1898 @ Gt. Yarmouth
HS. 52 v Hertfordshire August 1892 @ Lakenham
BB. 8/36 v Lincolnshire August 1894 @ Lakenham
1st class cricket – 1 match 17 runs
RH bat & right arm fast bowler plus an occasional wicket keeper.
Cousin of England Cricketer Fred Morley.
10/13 for Revd W Francis' X1 v Tenterden August 1887
107 for Norfolk v Fifteen Colts June 1890
7/21 for Thorpe v Bury & West Suffolk June 1893
52 for Sandringham v King's Lynn May 1893
101 for Easton Park v Bredfield & Charlsfield July 1914 age 51
Engaged by Duke of Hamilton at Easton Park which is why he appeared for them. Minor Counties Umpire plus officiated in local friendlies. Football. – Thorpe; Norfolk County (1889-93 apps 10-0). A Carpenter by trade and a Licensed Victualler. Before the Norwich Courts in 1902 as a fellow accused of selling stolen rabbits at Tom's pub.

WILSON, Frank M
(b) Calcutta, India 1865
(d) Elphinstone, St. Regina, Saskatchewan, Canada 1935 age 70
Cricket. – clubs unknown
HS. 20 v Hampshire May 1888 @ Southampton
44 & 2/17 for Norfolk v 22 Colts in 1887
Son of John (an Irish naval Officer) and Elizabeth (an Annuitant) in a family of 10 children. Lived in Newmarket

Terrace, Norwich. Frank married Blanche Linnington Symonds in N.W. Territories, Canada on 17 May 1896.

WILTSHIRE, Lt. Col Charles Jennings
(b) Gravesend, Kent 13 November 1862
(d) Stalham, Norfolk 19 July 1945
Educ. – Gt Yarmouth GS; Bury St. Edmunds; Dedham
Cricket. – Gt. Yarmouth; Yarmouth Etceteras; Norwich Teachers
HS. 3 v Free Foresters August 1888 @ Lakenham
Brother of FHC (q.v)
Football. – Thorpe; Yarmouth; Norfolk County 1887-93 (apps 19 – 10 goals)
Rtd Lt. Col 2nd Vol Batt Norfolk Regiment. Articled Clerk (admitted 1884). Solicitor of Wiltshire, Sons & Tunbridge at Quay, Yarmouth.
F.F. – His clubs were – Gt. Yarmouth Conservatives and Royal Norfolk & Suffolk Yacht Club. Left £1,110-16-6 in his probated Llandudno will dated 15 November 1945.

1887

BUXTON, Edward Gurney, JP
(b) West Ham, London 4 August 1865
(d) Barclays Bank, Bank Plain, Norwich 19 April 1929
Educ. – Dereham GS; Elstree School; Harrow School (Mr. Watson's – he left 1888); Cambridge University (Trinity College 21 June 1883 – BA 1887)
Cricket. – Dereham GS; Norwich Banks; Norfolk Club & Ground; Old Catton; EG Buxton's X1; Gurney's Bank; Free Foresters; Catton Hall; Gentlemen of Norfolk; MCC; I Zingari
HS. 24 v Gentlemen of Suffolk August 1890 @ Hintlesham Park
Son of SG (NCCC pre 1876) and Brother of HG (q.v) and Cousin AR (q.v)
Hon Sec NCCC from 1891 –1908.He dropped Sir FE Lacey (Hampshire) at 7 during his knock of 323 no in 1887 against NCCC.1st Vice President of Barclays Bank 1896. Norfolk JP and also the High Sheriff and Mayor. He taught the then Prince of Wales to shoot in Sheringham.
F.F. – He had 9 children with Laura Gurney with his father SG marrying twice, (1) Louisa Caroline Hoare and (2) Mary Anne Birkbeck so a complicated family tree to research the 5 Buxton's who played pre 1876

HOARE, Major Walter Robertson
(b) Great Marlow, Buckinghamshire 27 October 1867
(d) Lychpit, Glamorgan 1 July 1941
Educ.– Eton College
Cricket.– Eton College; Eton Ramblers; Gentlemen of Norfolk; Norfolk Club & Ground; Cambridge University Long Vacation Club; Old Etonians; FGH Clayton's XI; MCC;

Glamorgan; Fakenham; AJ Webb's X1; Easton Ramblers.
HS. 8 v Hertfordshire July 1896 @ Bishop's Stortford
BB. 1/13 v Hertfordshire July 1896 @ Bishop's Stortford
HS. 50 v Hertfordshire August 1891 @ Lakenham
BB. 2/53 v Derbyshire August 1890 @ Lakenham
Brother of AR (q.v) and VR (q.v)
3 brothers-in-law and 2 nephews played county cricket
100 for Old Etonians v Old Harrovians July 1891
54 for FGH Clayton's X1 v Northumberland September 1894
52 for MCC v Monmouthshire June 1901
Eton Ramblers Hon. Sec 1890-1921 – the 8th longest servant. He scored 2,470 runs and took 250 wickets for the club. At Eton College in 1st XIs for cricket, field hockey and fives. Captained NCCC at least once in 1892. By 1901 a Brewery Director so the three brothers were known as 'Bung' 'Bishop' and 'Bank'.

MASTER, Dr. Henry Hugh, LRCP LRCS
(b) Norwich JFM 1852 – baptism/christening 23 June 1852
Cricket.– Melton Constable; Demerara CC (Bridgetown, WI)
HS. 5 v Free Foresters August 1887 @ Lakenham
Father of HC (q.v)
1st class cricket – 3 matches 36 runs 16 wickets 1 catch
6/10 for Demerara v Trinidad September 1891
Practised medicine in Ixworth, Suffolk. Qualified as a Doctor in Edinburgh 22 October 1880.
Surgeon & Physician in Melbourne, Australia
F.F. – His 1st son Bertram died in POW camp 2 May 1917. His 2nd son Dudley (also a Surgeon & Physician) died Kawambwa, Northern Rhodesia on 27 June 1913 but I cannot find the whereabouts of their father.

1888

BARNES, Alfred
Cricket.– Norwich Union; Norwich Iron Works; Catton; St. Philip's CC
HS. 24 v MCC June 1888 @ Lakenham AND 24 v MCC July 1889 @ Lord's
BB. 1/37 v Cambridgeshire July 1893 @ Fenner's
Known as 'Slogger' the only clue discovered so far was the christian name above stated in the Eastern Daily Press production of 10 Jul 1902. In the NCCC 1889 Handbook he was living at 118, Dereham Road, Norwich

BARWELL, Charles Sedley William
(b) Norwich 4 May 1869
(d) Vancouver, Canada 29 September 1950
Educ. – Westminster School – 12 June 1884 to July 1888; Oxford University (Hertford College - Michaelmas 1888)
Cricket. – Westminster School; Gentlemen of Norfolk
HS. 3 v Parsees August 1888 @ Norwich

Uncle G.H played for NCCC pre 1876
84 for Westminster School v Charterhouse School July 1887
Football. – Thorpe; Norfolk County 1886-88 (apps 4-0): Oxford
University – February 1889.
Inter University Sports – Long Jump 1889. His brothers Francis
and Major Wilfred Thomas de Berdewelle Barwell both played
football for Norfolk County.
He sailed from Liverpool to Montreal 1890. A Dominion Land
Surveyor in the Yukon Territory.
Yukon Infantry Company 1915 – a Sgt of the Canadian
Machine Gunners serving in France 1918.
Officer of the Surveyor General of Alaska. Involved in the
Discovery of Klondike through his work whilst living in Dawson
City, Yukon. After returning to the UK (lived 49 Ogden Street,
London) he sailed on 'Ascania' from Southampton to Montreal
bound for Quebec on 25 May 1925. The ship's manifest showed
his occupation as Engineer.
F.F. – His family were in the Wine Merchant business as far
back as 1755. They sold their London Street Branch in 1921
and the building currently houses NatWest.

BUXTON, Major Abbot Redmond, JP
(b) Middlesex 31 August 1868
(d) Fritton Hall, Norfolk 7 March 1944
Educ. – Eldon Road School; Elstree School; Harrow School
(Mr. Cruikshank's - he left 1886); Cambridge University
(Trinity College 30 May 1887 – BA 1890)
Cricket. – I Zingari; EF Penn's X1; Thorpe; Taverham Hall;
Yarmouth
HS. 56 v Hertfordshire July 1898 @ Bishop's Stortford
HS. 95 v MCC July 1894 @ Gt Yarmouth
Cousin EG (q.v)
111 for I Zingari v NCCC July 1902
Kept wicket for NCCC in August 1895 when the regular minder
damaged a thumb. Captain of NCCC 1895-96 and also for
some games in 1894 and one match in 1903.
He and W. Thompson (q.v) are the only NCCC players with a
highest score in the nineties – to succumb twice at that mark.
Known by his second christian name.
Local Director of Barclay & Co, Bankers in Halesworth & Gt
Yarmouth. Major in the Norfolk Yeomanry – fighting in the
Boer War. JP for Norfolk & Suffolk . Mayor of Gt Yarmouth 1896
and the High Sheriff of Suffolk 1902.

COZENS-HARDY, Archibald, CBE JP
(b) Sprowston, Norwich 11 November 1869
(d) Norwich 19 March 1957
Educ. – Belle Vue House School; Amersham Hall School.
Cricket. – Carrow; Sprowston; Holt; Daily Press; Belle Vue
House; Norfolk 22 Colts.
HS. 7 v MCC June 1888 @ Lakenham
49 & 6/10 for Belle Vue House v Kingsley August 1886

65 for Carrow v Wymondham 1889
Left school and had a brief apprenticeship with Norfolk News
Co. In Fleet Street 1890-97 on the 'Star' newspaper. Editor
of Eastern Daily Press 1897 to July 1937 and he took up the
appointment a few days before the Diamond Jubilee of Queen
Victoria and he retired a few weeks after the Coronation of her
grandson. The newspaper's longest serving editor. President of
Newspaper Society. On the 'E.D.P' Board of Directors until his
death. An Alderman 1915 – January 1929. Chairman County
Library Committee for 17 years
Chairman Norwich Finance & General Purposes Committee,
retiring July 1948. Hon. VP of British Legion and the Norfolk
County Council Member for Sprowston from May 1915.
Governor at King Edward V1 GS, Gresham School and Paston
GS. Also a Magistrate on Holt Bench
F.F. – A Bachelor he was out shooting and collapsed.

HASTINGS, Revd Hugh Francis
(b) Gressenhall 6 February 1861
(d) Knighton, Shropshire 27 December 1928
Lived Brampton Road Rectory in Herefordshire.
Educ. – Norwich GS; Cambridge University (Queen's
College – BA 1884 MA 1887)
Cricket. – Norwich GS; Gentlemen of Norfolk; East Norfolk;
Shropshire; Worcestershire; Ludlow.
HS. 36 v Hampshire May 1888 @ Southampton
72 for Shropshire v Herefordshire August 1895
Assistant Master at Bingdon School 2/3 years. Assistant Master
at Portsmouth GS 10 years.
Headmaster Ludlow GS 1894-1912. Ordained 1895 and Priest
1896. Chaplain of Ludlow 1895-97.
Clergyman and Schoolmaster Dinham Hall. Rector Brampton
Bryan (Hereford) 1912-28.
F.F. – Probated London will leaving £10,534-5-10 to his
sister Penelope.

MARSH, Revd Theodore Henry
(b) Havelock, New Zealand 13 May 1863
(d) Grange-Over-Sands, Cumbria 14 October 1941
Lived West Runton, Cromer.
Educ. – Bishop's Stortford College; Cambridge University
(Pembroke College 2 October 1882 – BA 1885 MA 1905)
Cricket. – clubs unknown
HS. 26 v Hampshire July 1889 @ Southampton
BB. 6/85 v MCC June 1888 @ Lakenham
Football – Cambridge University – Blue 1885
Athletics. – Cambridge University – Blue 1886 (High Jump)
Ordained 1886 and Priest (Norwich) 1887. Curate of
Woodbridge 1886-88. Curate of St. Mark's Lakenham 1888-89.
Curate of St. Luke's (Southampton) 1889-93. Curate of St. Paul's
(Southampton) 1893-94.Vicar of Moordown 1894-1905. Rector
of Cawston 1905-1932

F.F.- Son of Octavius John Blake Marsh (165th Regiment in New Zealand)
Probated will 9 January 1942 for £13,627-12-5 with the beneficiaries being his two sisters and his solicitor.

MARSH, W
HS. 5 no v Hampshire May 1888 @ Southampton
BB. 3/35 v Hampshire May 1888 @ Southampton
Just two friendly matches with no clues surfacing as to who he was or from where he came.

RIX, William Arthur
(b) Paddington, London 9 October 1865
(d) St. Charles Hospital, London W10 27 October 1945
Lived 22 Molyneux Street, Bryanston Square, London W1.
Educ. – Wellington Hall (Lincoln); Cambridge University (St. John's College 29 August 1895 – BA 1899 MA 1903)
Cricket. – CEYMS; Norwich Teachers; Norfolk 22 Colts; Gentlemen of Norfolk; Beccles College; GL Jessop's XI; CJE Jarvis' XI.
HS. 2 v Worcestershire August 1896 @ Worcester
HS. 8 no v Parsees August 1888 @ Norwich
BB. 3/11 v Parsees August 1888 @ Norwich
74 for Norwich Teachers v Kingsley May 1888
7/18 for CEYMS v Thorpe Asylum August 1893
Football. – Thorpe; Norwich Teachers ; Norfolk County 1887-96 (apps 10-1goal).
An Army School Tutor leaving just £545-0-3 in his will

TIPPLE, Frederick Albert
(b) Toronto, Canada 1861
(d) Portsmouth 29 May 1929 age 68
Cricket. – Halesworth; Diss; East Dereham
HS. 5 no v Hertfordshire July 1895 @ Bishop's Stortford
BB. 1/2 v Hertfordshire July 1895 @ Bishop's Stortford
HS. 8 v Hertfordshire August 1888 @ Lakenham
BB. 1/39 v Hertfordshire August 1888 @ Lakenham
15/20 (being 7/8 & 8/12) for Diss v Beccles College June 1893
Hat-trick for Halesworth v Beccles College June 1899
9/42 for Halesworth v Benacre Park June 1899
8/18 for Halesworth v Fressingfield August 1899
Diss Football & Cycle Clubs. London & Provisional Bank Cashier (Downham).
London & Provisional Bank Manager (Portsmouth)
F.F. – Cause of Death attributed to malignant disease of oesophagus.

....

1889

BUXTON, Capt Harry Gurney, DL
(b) Catton Hall, Norwich 23 June 1871
(d) Hitchin 6 August 1936

Educ. – Harrow School; Cambridge University (Trinity College 25 June 1889 - BA 1892)
Cricket. – Gentlemen of Norfolk; CJE Jarvis' XI; Quidnuncs; MCC
HS. 10 v Gentlemen of Suffolk August 1889 @ Hintlesham Park
Son of SG (NCCC 1865-1870
Brother of EG (q.v) and Cousin of AR (q.v). (See EG for family thoughts)
Temp Capt 9th Batt Norfolks. Capt Norfolk Regiment & Bedfordshire Regiment. Served in South African War. A Dept. Lieut of Norfolk and a Farmer at Cokesford Farm, Tittleshall. His death as a result of a motorcycle accident.
F.F. – His widow Evelyn Musgrave Harvey and two other family members shared £18,591-3-7 from his probated will

DAVY, Major John Davy Wright
(b) Kilverstone Hall, Thetford 5 July 1865
(d) Mill House, Dersingham, Norfolk 24 January 1927
Educ. – Haileybury College (Bartle Frere 1879.2 – 1883.3); RMC Sandhurst
Cricket. – Gunton; YMCA; European; Bombay; Bangalore.
HS. 58 v Gentlemen of Suffolk August 1889 @ Hintlesham Park
1st class cricket - 2 matches 23 runs 2 catches with these games in India.
177 for Bangalore v Madras December 1888
In the 52nd Oxford Light Infantry.
F.F. – Probated London will dated 19 May 1927 leaving £16,454-11-7.

GURNEY, Edward Hay
(b) Thorpe, Norwich 12 October 1866
(d) Founereau Road Nursing Home, Ipswich 25 July 1935
Educ. – Marks House (Berkshire)
Cricket. – Gentlemen of Norfolk; Thorpe; Norfolk Club & Ground; Catton Hall
HS. 17 no v Gentlemen of Suffolk August 1889 @ Hintlesham Park
A direct descendant of Banking Company Gurney & Co. He did Bank Service in Norwich before to Ipswich as a Local Director until his demise. His funeral at St. Marys Church, Belstead where he worshipped for 30 years. A sudden death after an operation leaving £5,710-3-10 to his widow Isabel Louisa Buxton.
F.F.- Son of Francis Hay (of Thickthorn, Norwich) and Margaret Charlotte Folkes. Edward married Isabel Louisa Buxton so the families are intertwined.

GURNEY, Hugh
(b) Middleton , Norfolk 30 November 1867
(d) Valleyfield House, North Runcton, Norfolk 29 September 1913

Lived in Shropshire at time of demise.
Cricket. – Gentlemen of Norfolk
HS. 43 v Gentlemen of Suffolk August 1891 @ Hintlesham Park.
Brother of WS (q.v)
Son of Banker Sir Arthur Sommerville Gurney, KCVO DL JP.
Hugh was a Law Articled Clerk and the 1901 census has him as an Army Officer in the Shropshire Imperial Yeomanry but I have been unable to find his rank.
F.F. – Left £9,968-9-6 in his will dated 26 May 1914.

HOLLEY, Edward

(b) Sydney, New South Wales, Australia 20 July 1870
(d) Pietermaritzburg, Natal, South Africa 4 May 1929
He was christened EH Holley but he dropped his middle initial.
Educ. – Norwich GS; Haileybury College (Edmonstone 1884.2 –1887.2)
Cricket. – Haileybury College; I Zingari (catch as a sub fielder); Thorpe; Billingford Incapables; Norwich Union; Norfolk Club & Ground; Gentlemen of Norfolk; Norwich GS.
HS. 18 v MCC May 1893 @ Lakenham
BB. 5/36 v Hertfordshire August 1889 @ Hertford
Son of EF Holley and not related to H Holley (pre NCCC 1876 player)
54 no for Norwich Union v Old Catton May 1893 – also taking 8/26 and catching the other two men to be dismissed.
Played Rugby Union for Richmond. A Solicitor in partnership with TW Purdy to become Purdy & Holley. He sailed on 'City of Karachi' from London to Durban on 4 September 1925

HORNE, George Lazarus

(b) Norwich AMJ 1863
(d) Norwich 15 October 1949 at age 86
Cricket. – Barnham Broom; Norwich Teachers; Carrow; Riverside Ramblers.
HS. 0 v Hampshire July 1889 @ Southampton
54 for Norwich Teachers v CEYMS July 1893
102 for Barnham Broom v Wymondham August 1899
72 no for Carrow v Acle June 1894
Football. – Carrow; Norwich Teachers; CEYMS; Norfolk County 1884-96 (apps 27 – 6 goals).
A Merchant Clerk.

JONES, Arthur Morgan Bulkeley

(b) Loxley, Warwickshire 26 December 1861
(d) Mortlake, Surrey 20 March 1946
Lived Westminster, London
Cricket. – Norfolk Club & Ground
HS. 1 v Gentlemen of Suffolk August 1889 @ Hintlesham Park

A Captain in the 20th Hussars. A Landed Proprietor whose administered Oxford will revealed that he had no surviving family.

ORAMS, Major Edward

(b) Norwich 10 October 1869
(d) Mundesley, Norfolk 16 October 1927
Educ. – Clifton College
Cricket. – Clifton College; CJE Jarvis' X1; Norfolk Club & Ground; CEYMS; Thorpe.
HS. 20 no v Cambridgeshire July 1899 @ Fenner's
HS. 108 v Suffolk August 1902 @ Lakenham – in 135 minutes and he gave a chance on 91.
This being the first ton against Suffolk in the period covered by this book.
44 for Clifton College v Cheltenham College June 1888
76 for CEYMS v Thorpe July 1890
NCCC Committee Member 1905
Football. – Thorpe; Norfolk County 1890-99 (apps 20 -9 goals) ; CEYMS – also their Club Chairman.
He netted goals against such notable teams as Royal Arsenal and Old Etonians.
In the 9th Batt Norfolk Regiment – invalided out 1916 and thereafter worked service depot until Armistice. President Mundesley Branch of British Legion. Head of family firm Orams & Tyce (Ironmongers)
F.F. – His eldest daughter married Sir Alfred Appleby –an HM Coroner.

SHORE, Charles

(b) Sutton-in-Ashfield 21 November 1858
(d) Sutton-in-Ashfield 5 June 1912
Cricket. – Nottinghamshire; Lancashire; Liverpool & District; 22 Colts of England; Sefton; Colne; Gentlemen of Norfolk; CJE Jarvis's XI; Norfolk Club & Ground; Anchor Club; Huyton Club; Herefordshire; Hunstanton & District; Colts North; Sedgewick Park; Carrow; Trinity College CC (Dublin); Norwich Travellers; CEYMS Thursday XI.
HS. 31 v Cambridgeshire August 1897 @ Fenner's
BB. 10/50 v Durham July 1897 @ Lakenham – still the best ever innings analysis for NCCC and at the time the best ever in the Minor Counties Championship. His 16/72 match analysis in this game is also a NCCC record performance.
HS. 18 v Bedfordshire July 1891 @ Lakenham
BB. 9/26 v Eton Ramblers August 1891@ Lakenham- plus 7/58 in the other innings of the match.
1st class cricket – 13 matches 159 runs 41 wickets 9 catches as a Left hand bat and spin bowler.
Below is a brief selection of his litany of achievements on the cricket field – the only thing he did not do was take wickets at Manor Park !
86 and 7/15 for Carrow v Wymondham 1889

8/16 for Norfolk Club & Ground v London Ramblers July 1890 (analysis 24-15-16-8)
7/44 for Norfolk Club & Ground v London Ramblers August 1891
In 1891 for NCCC he took 69 wickets in a 7 match spell with only Michael Falcon 72 wickets in 1922 taking more but that was over 14 matches.
He took 8 or more in an innings for NCCC a remarkable six times
For Sefton CC he once took 10/8 in about 3 overs
In 9 seasons for Sefton CC from 1879 he took 850 wickets with a best annual return of 134 in 1883.
By June 1904 he was in charge of the ground in Sutton-in-Ashfield.
His death was attributable to chronic kidney problems.

STAFFORD, Brig. General William Francis Howard, CB
(b) Bengal, India 19 December 1854
(d) Crowthorne, Berkshire 8 August 1942
Educ. – Wellington College
Cricket. – Wellington College; Royal Military Academy Woolwich; Royal Engineers; Free Foresters
HS. 43 v Cambridge University Long Vacation Club August 1889 @ Fenner's – listed on the scorecard as just a lowly Captain.
43 no for Wellington College v Bradfield College September 1870
86 for Royal Engineers v Gentlemen of England June 1875
Football .– Royal Engineers (1875 FA Cup Final)
Rugby Union. – England (1 cap 1874)
Lieut 29 Apri1 1873; Capt 8 January 1885; Major 5 November 1892.
War Service – Afghanistan 1878-80, Mahsud Waziri Campaign 1881, S.Africa 1899-1901.
Awarded the Victory Medal, British Medal, Queen's Medal with 3 clasps - mentioned in despatches and King's Medal with 2 clasps.
F.F. – Probated Llandudno will dated 8 January 1943 in the sum of £13,349-8-10

TAYLOR, Charles Fisher
(b) Eaton, Norwich 19 September 1854
(d) Sunnyside Nursing Home, Norwich 4 April 1919
Lived 26 College Road, Norwich and he endured a painful illness for several weeks.
Educ. – Norwich GS
Cricket. – Norwich GS; Norfolk Club & Ground; CEYMS; Norfolk 22 Colts; East Norfolk; CF Taylor's XI; CJE Jarvis' XI.
HS. 33 v Hertfordshire August 1889 @ Hertford
NCCC Assistant Secretary from 1891 for nearly 20 years. He also prepared the cricket pitch at Earlham Road. Admitted Solicitor 1880 and Articled 1886. An Associate of legal firm

Messrs Overbury, Steward & Eaton (Norwich). Sgt Special Constabulary during WW1. When not on police duty he managed the canteen at St. Andrews Hall (Norwich) early evenings. Involved YMCA Soldier Club from 1915 to his death
F.F. – He was interred at Eaton with Fairfax Davies (q.v) and RG Pilch (q.v) in attendance

TREVOR, Capt Lionel Garrick
(b) Richmond, Surrey 16 June 1865
(d) Richmond, Surrey 27 November 1927
Educ. – Marlborough College
Cricket. – MCC; Gentlemen of Norfolk; Norfolk Club & Ground.
HS. 16 v Gentlemen of Suffolk August 1891 @ Hintlesham Park
BB. 6/10 v MCC July 1889 @ Lord's
Brother of PCW (q.v)
F.F.- His father Frederick George Brunton Trevor played one first class match for MCC. Lionel was a Capt 3rd Norfolk Regiment. Probated London will dated 30 January 1928 leaving £1,537-5-10 to his sister Margaret

1890

BARRATT, Legh
(b) Altrincham 10 December 1870
(d) Sheringham 14 December 1950
Cricket. – RS Lucas' XI; A Priestley's XI; Rossall School; Old Rossallians; Yarmouth; Norfolk Club & Ground; Eastern Ramblers; Overstrand; Aylsham; WHR Long's XI; Blofield & District; Gunton.
HS. 166 v Bedfordshire July 1908 @ Bedford School
BB. 5/53 v Durham August 1900 @ Lakenham
HS. 56 v MCC August 1901 @ Lakenham
BB. 4/101 v Yorkshire (2) July 1900 @ Leeds
Brother of G (q.v) and WP (q.v)
1st class cricket – 15 matches 253 runs 9 wickets 12 catches- no first class games in England.
96 for A. Priestley's X1 v Antigua January 1897
159 no for Norfolk Club & Ground v Yarmouth June 1899
4/0 off 3 completed overs v Northumberland in Minor Counties game August 1899
169 no for Gunton v Paston GS July 1900
Member of the first English Team to tour West Indies.
NCCC Captain 1904 & 1907/08 and he stood in as skipper in 1902/03/05/06.He missed a NCCC match in July 1893 as the club secretary sent the wrong date of the game by postcard.
Golf – Norfolk County; Yarmouth; Royal Norwich; Bungay
F.F. – Formed Norwich Stockbrokers Barratt & Cooke having earlier been a Farmer at Felmingham.
Served as a 1st Lt in the RASC during WW1.

BLAKE, Gerard Frederic

(b) Cathedral Close, Norwich 21 October 1863
(d) Waltham Lodge, Norwich 28 February 1921
Educ. – Haileybury College (Bartle Frere 1877.3–1881.2);
Cambridge University (Corpus Christi College 1 October
1881 – BA 1884 MA 1888)
Cricket. – Haileybury College; Blofield Norwich Banks; P
Oversheds' XI; Norfolk & Norwich; Norwich District; Thorpe;
Norfolk Club & Ground; Yarmouth Mechanics; Norwich
Union ; Eastern Ramblers; Carrow; Hunstanton & District;
County Asylum; Gentlemen of Norfolk; MCC.
**HS. 46 V Northumberland July 1897 @ Jesmond AND
46 v Northumberland August 1899 @ Jesmond AND 46
v Buckinghamshire August 1901 @ Aylesbury
BB 2/24 v Hertfordshire July 1897 @ Bishop's Stortford**
HS. 53 v Cambridgeshire August 1892 @ Fenner's
BB. 1/1 v Gentlemen of Suffolk August 1890 @ Hintlesham
Park
158 no for Blofield v Gunton July 1901
*He had spells as Captain of NCCC and he was a wicket keeper
with many stumpings to his credit.*
*Green Lilywhite's 1884 quote – "a hitting bat, driving hard and
well and a fair stumper."*
*An innings of 122 for Thorpe v CEYMS saw him get 21 (4s) and
1 (8)!*
*The eldest son of Henry Blake, a junior partner in a Solicitor's
practice. Gerard admitted Solicitor in 1888 subsequently
joining the firm of Keith, Blake & Co. Apart from his role as
Under Sheriff under Capt GW Taylor & HF Smith he was never
by choice prominent in public nor official life. He was however
acting as deputy returning officer when Michael Falcon was
first elected to be MP for East Norfolk in 1918.*

FRYER, Philip Algernon

(b) Blowick Hall, Wymondham 26 June 1870
(d) Ancaster House, Wilby, Northampton 4 November 1950
Educ. – Wymondham School; Wellingborough GS;
Cambridge University (Jesus College –1889 BA 1892 MA
1896)
Cricket. – Norfolk Club & Ground; Gentlemen of Norfolk;
Northamptonshire; Sudbury; Wellingborough Masters.
HS. 130 v Northumberland August 1899 @ Jesmond
HS. 94 v Cambridgeshire July 1893 @ Fenner's
Brother of EH (q.v.). Uncle of PWJ (q.v)
1st class cricket – 2 matches 83 runs 3 wickets 1 catch
306 for Wellingborough Masters v E.Scriven's XI June 1897
239 for Wellingborough Masters v Bedford Town June 1897
*274 for Wellingborough Masters v Leics Rosslyn July 1897 – he
therefore at the time had scored 1,086 runs in just 10 innings.*
119 for Sudbury v Grammar School Past & Present August 1899
NCCC 1895 – 6 victims to include 5 stumpings.
The first NCCC Minor Counties century partnership with AR

Buxton in 1895.
160 for Norfolk Club & Ground v Fakenham August 1899
*'Scores & Biographies Vol 15' stated that he had scored over
50 tons.*
*Football. – Wellingborough GS; Wymondham; Norfolk County
encompassing period 1888-96 (apps 5 –1goal); Corinthians;
Casuals; Swifts; Cambridge University – no Blue, missed chance
through being injured.*
*Assistant Master Wellingborough GS 1892-1907. Headmaster &
Chairman of Governors of Wellingborough GS 1907-1933*
F.F. – Father William Goodwin Fryer an Estate Agent &
Farmer (owning 1,543 acres and employing
35 men, 33 boys, 8 women and 2 children). He left £35,200-
19-11 in his probated will

HEASMAN, Dr. William Gratwicke, MRCS LRCP

(b) Angmering, Sussex 9 December 1862
(d) Upperton, Eastbourne, Sussex 25 January 1934
Educ. – Hurstpeirpoint College
Cricket. – Hurstpeirpoint College; Sussex; Gentlemen of
Sussex; United Hospitals; Aldeburgh; Arundel; Gunton;
Sussex Martlets; Richmond; Berkshire; Littlehampton;
Philadelphia CC; All Philadelphia; Eastern Ramblers.
HS. 58 v Hertfordshire August 1890 @ Lakenham
BB. 2/41 v Derbyshire August 1890 @ Lakenham
1st class cricket – 15 matches 566 runs 7 catches
*Grandfather of MRG Earls-Davis who played first class cricket
for Somerset and Cambridge University. KS Duleepsinhji lived
with the Doctor in order to qualify to play for Sussex.*
207 for United Hospitals v Chiswick Park 1887
*236 no for Aldeburgh v Gunton Park 1890 – one of 6 occasions
that saw him carry his bat in the season.*
59 no (100) for Richmond v Parsees August 1888
151 for Eastern Ramblers v Havant August 1891
*67(122) for Philadelphia v Germantown CC June 1906 –
touring with them to Bermuda.*
*I have frustratingly mislaid my 1910 photograph of the Doctor
with Archie MacLaren, WG Grace & Ranji – he moved in those
kind of circles. He served on the Sussex CC Committee.*
*Prior to the Eastbourne Foxhounds being amalgamated with
the East Sussex Hunt he officiated as Master of the Pack. For
many years he was one of the early morning bathers at the Pier
Head.*
F.F. – His probated will was re sworn to £29,001-6-8

HOARE, Revd Arthur Robertson

(b) Stibbard, Norfolk 17 October 1871
(d) Ashill Rectory, Norfolk 18 March 1941
Educ. – Eton College; Cambridge University (Trinity College
17 June 1890 - BA 1893); Wells Theological College.
Cricket. – Eton College; Eton Ramblers; EC Streatfeild's XI
(Freshman's trial); Norfolk Club & Ground; Old Etonians;

Gentlemen of Norfolk; MCC; Marquis of Graham's XI.

HS. 89 v Hertfordshire July 1904 @ Watford
BB. 5/30 v Hertfordshire July 1904 @ Watford
HS. 82 v Eton Ramblers August 1892 @ Lakenham
BB. 5/40 v Hertfordshire August 1891 @ Bishop's Stortford
Brother of VR (q.v) and WR(q.v)
*Had an Uncle, Father-in-Law and Brother-in-Law who all
played first class cricket*
1st class cricket – 1 match 46 runs 2 catches
Illness ruined his chance of gaining a Cricket Blue.
*For Eton Ramblers – 66 innings for 2,381 runs (ave 42.51) plus
120 wickets*
*Football.- Cambridge University – Blue 1893; Norfolk County.
Ordained 1894 and Priest 1896. Chaplain of Kettering 1894-98.
Missionary Chaplain Diocese Cape Town 1898-1900 – hence
the gap in his NCCC career. Acting Chaplain to Forces 1900-
1901, then Chaplain 1901-1909. At RMA Woolwich 1902-07
and Colchester 1907-09. Rector of Easton 1909-12. Temporary
Chaplain Forces 1916-19. Rector of Colkirk with Oxwick 1912-
1930. Rural Dean of Brisley 1921-1930. Rector of Ashill 1930-41*

HOARE, Major Vincent Robertson
(b) Colkirk, Norfolk 18 March 1873
(d) Ypres, France 15 February 1915
Educ. – Eton College
Cricket. – Eton College; Eton Ramblers; Fakenham; St.
James House (Lynn).
**HS. 17 v Buckinghamshire August 1904 @ Aylesbury
AND 17 v Suffolk July 1905 @ Lakenham**
BB. 1/15 v Suffolk July 1905 @ Lakenham
HS. 100 v Eton Ramblers July 1892 @ Lakenham
BB. 4/40 v Free Foresters July 1904 @ Lakenham
Brother of AR (q.v) and WR (q.v)
*Member of the MCC from 1893. At Eton he won the School
Fives and he scored the greatest aggregate total of runs for
Eton Ramblers being 5,592 as well as securing 273 wickets.
Like many others he bowled in the era of 5 ball and 6 ball overs.
A fast medium bowler who switched to leg breaks later in his
career.*
9/31 for Fakenham v Lynn Town June 1893
149 & 14-8-9-6 for Fakenham v King's Lynn May 1894
142 and 7/20 for St. James House v Dereham June 1894
*Eton College remarked on his cricket prowess in his last
year there of quote, " Heads the averages (29.38); a fine,
commanding bat, at times too eager to score, especially off
the leg-stump; has been exceedingly useful; a steady medium
bowler and an excellent field." The College wrote tough reports!
He worked for Hoare's Bank and he was a Director of North
British & Mercantile Insurance Co.
Served with The Rangers (12th Co. London Regiment) as well
as serving in South Africa as a trooper in Suffolk Yeomanry,
afterwards gaining a commission.*

F.F. – A residence of 37 Fleet Street, London his probated
will had him bequeathing £15,842-8-6

RAIKES, Revd George Barkley
(b) Carlton Forehoe, Norfolk 14 March 1873
(d) Lamyat, Shepton Mallet 18 December 1966
Educ. – Shrewsbury School; Oxford University (Magdalene
College – MA 1899)
Cricket. – Shrewsbury School; Oxford University – Blue
1894-95; Hampshire; Oxford University Past & Present;
England XI; CJE Jarvis' XI; MCC; Norfolk Club & Ground;
Thorpe; Gentlemen of Norfolk; Suffolk Borderers; Bergh
Apton; Portsea Clergy; Portsea Vicarage.
HS. 145 v Suffolk July 1904 @ Lakenham
BB. 9/24 (incl hat-trick) v Suffolk July 1910 @ Lakenham
HS. 123 v MCC August 1905 @ Lakenham
BB. 6/50 v Free Foresters July 1904 @ Lakenham
Brother of EB (q.v) and Uncle of TB (q.v)
*1st class cricket – 30 matches 816 runs 71 wickets 30 catches
Invited to play for Nottinghamshire but he declined as he was
the Norfolk Captain.
Participated in 11 century partnerships for NCCC involving 10
different players.
NCCC Captain 1905,1906,1910,1911 and he skippered the odd
game in other years plus being a Committee Member 1925. In
1910 he skippered NCCC to the title scoring 679 runs in 8 games
and taking 57 wickets.
84 for Portsea Vicarage v RMA June 1899
185 for Portsea Clergy v Sherborne School
9/19 (incl hat-trick) for Bergh Apton v Woodton May 1922
Football. – England 1895/96 (4 caps); Oxford University - Blue
1893-96; Corinthians; Shrewsbury School; Wymondham Town;
Thorpe; Norfolk County 1892 /93(2apps- 0 goals).
With height in his favour 6' 2 ", he had a great physical
advantage for goal keeping as he was very quick with his
hands and feet.
Ordained 1898 and Priest (Diocese of Winchester) 1899. Curate
of Portsea 1898-1905. Chaplain to Duke of Portland 1905-20.
Rector of Bergh Apton 1920-1936*
F.F. – Known as 'Ginger Beer'

SANDWITH, Revd William Fitzgerald Gambier
(b) Baroch, India 18 July 1861
(d) Littlestone-on-Sea, Kent 25 November 1949
Educ. – Twyford School; Westminster School – Queen's
Scholar; Oxford University (Christchurch College 24 January
1881 BA 1884 MA 1904)
Cricket. – Westminster School; T Meyrick's XI; MCC; Enville;
Worcestershire; Radnorshire; Norfolk Club & Ground;
Walsingham; Melton Constable; East Dereham; Fakenham;
Holkham Village and Hertfordshire (catch as a sub fielder)
HS. 99 v Northumberland August 1899 @ Jesmond –

the first NCCC player dismissed on 99 in the period covered by the book.

HS. 123 v Bedfordshire July 1891 @ Lakenham
Brother of ER (q.v)
5/23 for Westminster School v Charterhouse School July 1880
83 no for Holkham Village v Little Walsingham July 1895
53 (batting at 7) for Norfolk Club & Ground v Essex Club & Ground July 1892
NCCC Joint Hon. Sec with WE Hansell 1891 and EG Buxton 1892. NCCC Captain 1897-98 and stand in skipper on three other occasions
Football. – Westminster School; Oxford University – Blue 1882/03.
Ordained 1884 and Priest (London) 1885. Curate of St. Margaret's (Westminster) 1884-86.
Curate in charge of Enville (Staffs) 1886-87.Vicar of Holkham with Egmere and Waterlen 1887-1900.
Vicar of St. Barnabas with St. Silsa (S.Kensington) 1900-07.
Rector of St. Bartholomew (Greater London) 1907-1929
F.F. – Left £7,499-2-5 to Surveyor & Agent George Sebastian Sandwith

SUGDEN, A
Cricket. – Norfolk Club & Ground
HS. 14 v Eton Ramblers August 1890 @ Lakenham

TREVOR, Col Philip Christian William, CBE
(b) Richmond, Surrey 27 April 1863
(d) Barnet 14 November 1932
Educ. – Marlborough College; RMC Sandhurst
Cricket. – Marlborough College; MCC; Incogniti; Authors
HS. 0 (x2) Gentlemen of Suffolk August 1890 @ Hintlesham Park - keeping wicket in his only game.
Brother of LG (q.v)
Rank of Major when playing for NCCC.
49 no for Incogniti v Sherborne School June 1901
44 for Authors (alongside Arthur Conan Doyle & PG Wodehouse) v Actors June 1905
Cricket & Rugby Correspondent for The Daily Telegraph. He also worked for the Sportsman and the Daily Mail. Promoted in the Horse Guards to Colonel. Served in Burma Field Force 1888-90. Served in Boer War 1899-1902. For the European War he was the Assistant Director of Ordnance Services London District
F.F. – His publications are – 'The Lighter Side of Cricket'; 'The Problems of Cricket'; 'With the MCC in Australia'; 'Cricket and Cricketers'; 'Rugby Union Football'.
His Novel – 'The Prince of the People'. A number of serials, articles and stories to various magazines.
His Children's Plays – 'Under the Greenwood Tree' and 'The Looking Glass'

1891

COWLES, Sewell Robert Burton
(b) Cromer, Norfolk 25 February 1870
(d) Thorpe St. Andrew, Norwich 8 April 1938
Cricket. – Overstrand Royal Navy Hospital; South Heigham; Caley & Sons; CEYMS; Norwich Union Fire Office; Norfolk County Asylum; Sutton Valence; Norwich & London; Norwich Banks; Yarmouth Fifteen
HS. 82 no v Durham August 1900 @ Darlington
BB. 7/55 v Northumberland August 1900 @ Jesmond
HS. 45 no v MCC August 1896 @ Lakenham
BB. 6/52 v MCC June 1895 @ Lakenham
He played for NCCC as an Amateur (1891,93,98 & 1900-02) and as a Professional (1895-97)
7/25 for CEYMS v Fakenham July 1893
71 no for Sutton Valence v Hollingborne July 1896
102 no & 6/38 for CEYMS v Yarmouth July 1899
5/9 for Norwich & London v Thorpe Asylum July 1902
118 no for Norwich & London v Acle May 1904
8/12 for Norwich & London v Norwich Union June 1908
Football. – Caley & Sons; CEYMS; YMCA
Hon. Sec Norfolk County FA – had represented local football from 1905 being the Hon. Treasurer 1906 and Hon. Sec 1912 –1936. Also on Football Association Council for 20 years being awarded their long service medal on 28 April 1933. Head of Plate Glass Department at AJ Caley & Sons.
Also worked for Norwich & London Accident Insurance Office.
F.F. – Left £1,818-17-2 to his widow Ellen.

COZENS-HARDY, Edgar Wrigley, CMG
(b) Oak Lodge, Sprowston, Norwich 28 June 1872
(d) Oak Lodge, Sprowston, Norwich 1 April 1945
Lived in same house all his life but suffered increasing deafness as time went by.
Educ.– Belle Vue House; Amersham Hall
Cricket. – Norfolk Club & Ground; Carrow; Sprowston; Gold Coast
HS. 22 no v Bedfordshire July 1891 @ Lakenham
47 for Norfolk Club & Ground v Essex Club & Ground July 1891
8/48 for Sprowston v Carrow Seconds August 1899
In 1901 to Gold Coast as Assistant Surveyor of Roads. For 20 years an Assistant Railways Engineer out there and just before retirement he was the Governor & Commander-in-Chief of Gold Coast Colony. He returned to England and was an elected member of St. Faiths & Aylsham Rural District Council. Captain of Royal Norwich Golf Club. Kenneth Horne's (Round the Horne, BBC Radio show) mother Katherine was a member of this Cozens-Hardy family.
F.F. – Probated Llandudno will dated 16 June 1945 for £31,011-10-2

DRAKE, George Cyril

(b) Sedgebrook, Lincolnshire OND 1869
(d) Hampstead, London 7 October 1952
Educ. – Blair Lodge School (Scotland)
Cricket. – Norfolk Club & Ground
HS. 44 v Cambridgeshire August 1892 @ Fenner's
54 for Norfolk Club & Ground v London Ramblers August 1891.
Son of Hon. Canon of Worcester who was also Chaplain-in-Ordinary to the Queen 1862-96.
He came down from Scotland for a short stay in Norfolk. A Class Clerk in the Office of the Masters in Lunacy (Royal Court of Justice, London)

NEWBY, Edwin William

(b) Norwich OND 1870
(d) Norwich 2 July 1934
Cricket. – Norfolk Club & Ground; South Heigham
HS. 7 v Bedfordshire August 1891 @ Luton
6/11 for South Heigham v Lowestoft August 1899
Football. – Norfolk County 1890-95 (apps17- 5goals) – including a hat-trick v Essex 10 November 1892
An Umbrella Maker in the family workshop. Latterly a Travelling Salesmen and a Cork Merchant.

NORTH, Capt Marjoribanks Keppel

(b) Mitford, Northumberland 17 November 1865
(d) Amersham, Buckinghamshire 27 March 1949
Educ. – Marlborough College
Cricket. – Marlborough College; Demerara; British Guiana (South America); Norfolk Club & Ground.
HS. 15 v I Zingari August 1891 @ Diddington Park
1st class cricket – 7 matches 128 runs 2 catches- but the matches were not played in England
Son of Charles North and Augusta Keppel. A Civil Engineer working principally in Barbados and South Africa.

SANDWITH, Evelyn Rothe

(b) Ammabad, India 5 September 1868
(d) Southsea Nursing Home, Portsmouth 12 September 1942
Lived North Holmwood, Dorking, Surrey
Educ. – Westminster School; Cambridge University (Magdalene College 16 July 1887 – BA 1890)
Cricket. – clubs unknown
HS. 2 v Hertfordshire August 1891 @ Bishop's Stortford
Brother of WFG (q.v)
In the Army Pay Dept 1914-18 being the son of Scottish father William (retired Bombay Civil Service).
F.F. – He left £1,506-13-1 in his probated Llandudno will

SMITH, Sgt

Cricket. – Yarmouth; Royal Artillery ; Norfolk Club & Ground

HS. 14 v Lincolnshire August 1891 @ Lakenham
Also seen in the local press as S. Myth ?
A Yarmouth Newspaper dated 20 May 1891 said, "So Sgt Smith is going to be tried in a county match. I trust he may prove himself worthy of the honour, although there is not much fear of him not doing so. He deserves to be a successor to the illustrious wicket keeper Wickham".

WALTER, Capt Cyril Harry, DL JP

(b) Hellesdon, Norwich OND 1874
(d) Talconeston Hall, Norfolk 3 May 1953
Cricket. – Gentlemen of Norfolk
HS. 5 v I. Zingari August 1891 @ Diddington Park
Son of JHF who played for East Norfolk and who was a NCCC President.
Partnership of Delane, Magnay & Co. Ltd of Taverham Mills (Paper Manufacturers).Captain South African War in Service Company of Norfolk Artillery Militia . Served as Member of Claims Company Committee. Worked for firm of Palgrave, Brown & Co. Ltd (Timber Merchants).Chairman of Taverham Bench of Magistrates 1934-53. Chairman of Taverham Juvenile Court to 1952.Member of Standing Joint Committee of Norfolk County Council. A member of his past family was the original founder of The Times Newspaper.

1892

MASSINGHAM, Ernest Arthur

(b) East Dereham, Norfolk 27 September 1870
(d) Manchester 18 September 1938
Cricket. – East Dereham; Field Dalling
HS. 6 v Lincolnshire June 1895 @ Spalding
BB. 1/17 v Lincolnshire June 1895 @ Spalding
HS. 60 v I Zingari August 1893 @ Lakenham
BB. 2/16 v Lincolnshire June 1892 @ Lincoln
4-3-1-5 for Field Dalling v Upper Sheringham May 1893
In 1891 the East Dereham CC Treasurer with a press summation of his batting being – a stonewaller.
Formerly a Theatrical Manager
F.F. – Cause of Death attributed to a malignant bowel growth.

MORNEMENT, Surgeon Rear-Admiral Robert Harry, OBE MRCS LRCP

(b) Roudham Hall, Thetford, Norfolk 15 August 1873
(d) Royal Naval Hospital, Chatham 16 April 1948
Educ. – Middlesex Hospital
Cricket. – Hampshire; Royal Navy; MCC; Army & Navy; Fleet; Middlesex Hospital; Diss.
HS. 14 no v Hertfordshire July 1896 @ Bishop's Stortford
BB. 1/15 v Hertfordshire July 1895 @ Bishop's Stortford

HS. 11 v Hertfordshire August 1893 @ Bishop's Stortford
BB. 3/31 v Cambridgeshire July 1894 @ Fenner's
1st class cricket – 5 matches 121 runs 9 wickets 4 catches
132 for Diss v Martham 1892
66 no for Middlesex Hospital v Christ's College June 1893
52 and 6/19 for Fleet v Mr. Watling's X1 June 1905
Assistant Medical Officer London County Asylum. RN 1908 as
Staff Surgeon on Ship 'Commonwealth' (Channel Fleet)

PAGE, Capt Sydney Durrant
(b) Norwich 17 February 1873
(d) Gaza, Palestine 19 April 1917
Lived Elms, Heigham Grove, Norwich
Educ. – Belle Vue House School; Tettenham College
Cricket. – Belle Vue House; CEYMS; Norwich Union; WJ
Blake's XI; HL Horsfall's XI; YMCA.
HS. 96 no v Hertfordshire August 1899 @ Lakenham
– left stranded by C. Shore even though he offered him a
sovereign for every ball survived.
BB. 1/6 v Northumberland August 1898 @ Jesmond
HS. 34 v MCC August 1899 @ Lakenham
NCCC Committee Member 1905. He captained NCCC for one
game in 1909.
90 no for CEYMS v Dereham 1899
In 2nd Gaza Battle with 1st/4th Batt. Norfolks. Wounded
Gallipoli August 1915 and returned to duty 27 April 1916. One
of the Founders of the Boys Brigade & Soldiers Institute. Vice
President Boys Brigade and on the YMCA Committee. A portrait
of him was unveiled at Norwich YMCA by the Lord Mayor in
September 1918
F.F. – Unfortunately I cannot link him as a relative of AC
Page (q.v)

1893

BARTLETT, Venerable Donald Mackenzie Maynard
(b) Barnham Broom, Norfolk 25 August 1873
(d) Ripon 16 October 1969
Educ. – Haileybury College (Batten 1887.2 – 1892.2);
Cambridge University (Clare College 10 October 1892);
Wells Theological College.
Cricket. – Haileybury College; CJE Jarvis' XI.
HS. 28 v Hertfordshire June 1901 @ Bishop's Stortford
HS. 4 no v Hertfordshire August 1893 @ Bishop's Stortford
Rugby. – Haileybury College; Wymondham
Ordained 1896 and Priest 1897. Assistant Priest @ St. Matthew's
(Bethnal Green) 1896-99.
Curate of Ashill 1899-1900. Curate of Leeds Parish Church 1900-
1904. Vicar of St. Mark's Woodhouse (Leeds) 1904-1919. TCF
1914-16 Dardanelles Expeditionary Force. Vicar of St. Wilfred's
Church (Harrogate) 1919-1940. Hon. Canon & Librarian of
Ripon Cathedral 1929-1938.

Archdeacon of Leeds 1937-40. Canon Residentiary of Ripon
Cathedral 1940-61.Canon Ameritus from 1966

DOWSON, Harold
(b) Southdown, Suffolk JAS 1871
(d) Nyeri, Kenya Colony 1 June 1936
Cricket. – East Dereham; Scarning; Norfolk Club & Ground;
Fakenham; Diss.
HS. 2 v Lincolnshire June 1893 @ Spalding
9-4-9-6 for Dereham v Colne School June 1893
114 no for Scarning v Shipdham July 1893
An occupation of a Maltsters Assistant
His brother Richard also played cricket for Dereham.
F.F. – Probated London will dated 20 April 1937 with him
leaving £564-3s to his widow Moira Frances Lee

HOPKINS, Dr Charles Leighton, MB BCh
(b) Littleport, Cambridge 31 July 1869
(d) St. Leonards-on-Sea, Sussex 16 March 1926
Educ. – Haileybury College (Edmonstone 1883.3 – 1887.2);
Cambridge University (Gonville & Caius College 1 October
1888 – BA 1891)
Cricket. – clubs unknown
HS. 0 (x2) v Hertfordshire August 1893 @ Bishop's Stortford
The fourth NCCC player to record a 'pair' in his only appearance
for the County.
Assistant Medical Officer Kent County Lunatic Asylum. Medical
Superintendent of York City Asylum (Fulford). Guy's Hospital
Chemical Assistant and resident Obstetrician

SMITH, Charles George
(b) Gt. Ryburgh, Norfolk 31 March 1876
(d) Hammersmith 21 February 1941
Educ. – Brighton College; Cambridge University (Clare
College 25 April 1896)
Cricket. – Brighton College; Surrey 2nd X1; Little
Massingham; Little Massingham Rectory.
HS. 2 no v Lincolnshire June 1895 @ Spalding
BB. 2/23 v Lincolnshire June 1895 @ Spalding
HS. 11 no v I Zingari July 1896 @ Lakenham
BB. 3/12 v Quidnuncs June 1894 @ Lakenham
Brother of HJ (q.v)
6/10 for Dereham v Thorpe July 1893
In 1892 season for Brighton College he bagged 52 wickets (ave
9.25). By 1901 he was living on his own means. Lillywhite's Red
Book quote," A juvenile looking colt. A really good bowler with
nice easy action. Breaks both ways and able to keep a very
good length."

SMITH, Harry Jacob
(b) Gt. Ryburgh, Norfolk 11 February 1875
(d) Wroxham 24 October 1942

Educ. – Brighton College
Cricket. – Brighton College; Kingsley
HS. 5 v I Zingari August 1893 @ Lakenham
BB. 3/76 v I Zingari August 1893 @ Lakenham
Brother of CG (q.v)
7/27 for Kingsley v Norwich Teachers June 1893
A Police Constable living in Yarmouth in 1901. Latterly a retired Estate Handyman

1894

ARNOLD, Robert Marston
(b) Norwich 6 January 1870
(d) Norwich 11 December 1940
Educ. – Norwich Middle School
Cricket. – Norwich Middle School; Carrow; Norwich & London; Kingsley; Norwich Banks; Blofield & District; Barclays Bank; Diss.
HS. 1 v Worcestershire August 1896 @ Worcester
HS. 13 v Lincolnshire June 1894 @ Grantham
90 no (carried bat) for Middle School v Norwich & London May 1893
103 for Norwich & London v Yarmouth Temple June 1899
102 no for Carrow v Haveland August 1904
A NCCC trial as far back as 1888. Water Polo for Norwich Swans. A Norwich Corporation Rate Collector. His father ran St. Margaret's Brewery so Robert is not a relation of HA (q.v)

BARRATT, Gordon
(b) Altrincham, Cheshire 13 April 1869
(d) Bungay, Suffolk 23 December 1954
Cricket. – Gunton; Thorpe; Royal Navy Hospital; Bungay; Yarmouth Fifteen
HS. 20 v Lincolnshire June 1894 @ Grantham
Brother of L and WP (both q.v)
89 for Gunton v Paston GS July 1894
6/9 for Bungay v Brooke June 1899
9/27 for Bungay v Lowestoft July 1900
A Wine Merchant living with his brother Legh in Felmingham per the 1901 Census.
F.F. – Probated will bequeathing £6,289-18s to his widow Judith

CAMPBELL, Christian Armstrong
(b) Hampstead, London JAS 1865 – baptism/christening 24 September 1865
(d) Cookham Rise, Berkshire 1 September 1939
Cricket. – Diss; Harleston; Norfolk Club & Ground; East Norfolk; West Norfolk; Yarmouth.
HS. 16 v Lincolnshire June 1894 @ Grantham
55 for Harleston v Norwich Union Fire Office July 1895
8/35 and 6/24 for Harleston v Fressingfield August 1899

5/47 for Yarmouth v Ipswich & East Suffolk July 1900
An Insurance District Manager

CUTHBERTSON, Major Norman William
(b) Shanghai 21 October 1861
(d) London 12 February 1915
Educ. – Trinity College (Glenalmond, Perthshire); Staff College Sandhurst
Cricket. – I Zingari; MCC; Staff College Sandhurst; Wymondham
HS. 13 v I Zingari August 1894 @ Lakenham
100 for I Zingari v Charterhouse School May 1895
His father Gilmour Cuthbertson was Manager of Bank of Australia in Adelaide.
In the Royal Highlanders – as a Lt 9 September 1882, Captain 7 December 1888, Major 3 July 1898.
Instructor Royal Military College 25 August 1897 to 21 October 1899. Served in Egyptian campaign (Medal & Bronze Star) and took part in advance of Kimberley. Severely wounded at Magersfontein – mentioned in despatches (Queen's Medal with 5 clasps). On outbreak of European War he was appointed as a General Staff Officer and died in office with his home being in Plymouth.

DARNELL, Alfred Frederick
(b) St. Giles, Northampton 28 October 1866
(d) Northampton 14 August 1951
Cricket. – Diss; Norfolk Club & Ground; Primitives
HS. 16 no v Lincolnshire June 1895 @ Spalding
HS. 16 v MCC July 1894 @ Gt. Yarmouth
BB. 1/8 v MCC June 1895 @ Lakenham
8/13 for Primitives v Bracondale July 1890
54 and 5/13 for Diss v Wymondham June 1894
Occupations of a Merchant's Clerk, a Cricket Coach and a retired Leather Dresser. His father Joseph a Solicitor's Clerk and his brother Albert was the Northampton Coroner.

FRERE, Lionel Robert Temple
(b) Marylebone, London 10 December 1870
(d) Kensington, London 15 March 1936
Educ. – Kidbroke House School; Haileybury College (Trevelyan 1884.3–1889.3); Cambridge University (Trinity College 27 May 1889 – BA 1892)
Cricket. – Cambridge University – no Blue; Norfolk Club & Ground; Norfolk 22 Colts; Gryphons.
HS. 21 v Northumberland June 1897 @ Lakenham
HS. 16 no v Cambridgeshire August 1894 @ Lakenham
1st class cricket – 1 match 3 runs 2 catches
For NCCC he had 9 matches and he made stumpings in six of them.
Rugby Union. – Haileybury College; President Richmond RFC. President of Old Haileyburians Society 1928-29. Wine

Merchant for Chaile Richards & Co.
An illustrious family with his grandfather Temple being the Canon of Westminster plus his father Robert was admitted to the Royal College of Surgeons in 1841.

PATEY, Ernest
(b) Blackheath, Kent 20 November 1875
(d) Mundesley, Norfolk 17 May 1907
Educ. – Norwich GS
Cricket. – Norwich GS; CEYMS
HS. 9 v I Zingari August 1894 @ Lakenham
89 for Norwich GS v 1st King's Dragoon Guards June 1894
His great grandfather was a RN Commander; his grandfather was an Admiral and his father Charles a Solicitor. His brother Edward was a Rifle Brigade Captain who was killed in action in 1917.
In 1901 Ernest was an Insurance Clerk who bequeathed £5,921-10-7 to be held by his own Solicitor until distribution.

SEWELL, Archibald Percival
(b) Swaffham, Norfolk 15 October 1868
(d) Tankerton, Kent 19 March 1947
Cricket. – Swaffham
HS 0 no v Hertfordshire August 1895 @ Lakenham AND 0 v Cambridgeshire August 1895 @ Lakenham AND 0 v Oxfordshire August 1895 @ Lakenham
BB. 2/9 v Hertfordshire August 1895 @ Lakenham
HS. 21 no v Lincolnshire August 1894 @ Lakenham
BB. 3/16 v MCC July 1894 @ Gt. Yarmouth
61 for Swaffham v Holt August 1893
7/21 for Swaffham v Lynn GS July 1896
In 1901 'Bob' as he preferred to be known was a Gentlemen's Secretary and Companion.
He married Lizzie Anne Kettelwell when he was aged 53. His father Robert was an Attorney-at-Law.

SKRIMSHIRE, Dr John Fenwick, MB B.Chir
(b) Holt, Norfolk 18 October 1872
(d) Dorset Square, Middlesex 11 November 1919
Died in a Nursing Home after 4 major operations
Educ. – Gresham's School; Cambridge University (St. John's College 10 October 1891)
Cricket. – Upper Sheringham; Melton Constable Estate; MCC; Gunton; HL Horsfall's XI; J Astley's XI; Holt; Cromer; DAW Willson's XI; Holiday Hittites; Overstrand; St. John's College; St. Mary's Hospital; Fakenham; Gresham Masters.
HS. 83 v Lincolnshire June 1895 @ Spalding
BB. 4/15 v Worcestershire August 1896 @ Worcester
HS. 47 v I Zingari July 1895 @ Lakenham
Brother of HF (q.v)
95 for Holt v Norwich Union June 1894
106 no for Melton Constable Estate v Cromer July 1900

200 no for Holiday Hittites v CEYMS 1908
'Jack' had a medical practice in Melton Constable. Medical Officer Health for Melton Constable.
Member of Melton Parish Council and School management.
On Melton Railway Institute Committee
F.F. – One of the beneficiaries of his will was Basil Cozens-Hardy (q.v)

SNELLING, Thomas
(b) Norwich 17 December 1871
(d) Norwich 28 August 1945
Educ. – Norwich St. James School
Cricket. – St. Mark's Avenue; Riverside Ramblers; CEYMS; Norwich Teachers; Caley's XI; Norwich & London; Rose Lane CC; Hertfordshire (a catch as a substitute fielder)
HS. 3 no v Cambridgeshire August 1901 @ Lakenham
HS. 9 no v Lincolnshire June 1894 @ Grantham
BB. 1/20 v Lincolnshire June 1894 @ Grantham
He helped with the nets at Lakenham in his time with the County.
7/15 for Rose Lane v Carrow Juniors June 1893
8-6-4-6 for Rose Lane v Yarmouth North Hospital August 1893
66 and 4/17 for Rose Lane v Coltishall July 1894
10/13 for Riverside Ramblers v RNH July 1901
Football. – YMCA; CEYMS; Norfolk County 1894-1901 (apps 7–2 goals)
Also Norwich City FC Trainer. Bowls for Carrow Jubilee (won 9 NBA titles).
A Fishmonger in 1911. Before his health failed he was the Mine Host of 'True Comrades' from 1934 to 1942

....

1895
....

ASTLEY, Major Delaval Graham L'Estrange, CB DL JP
(b) Aylsham, Norfolk 7 December 1868
(d) Norwich 17 May 1951
Educ. – Rugby School
Cricket. – Rugby School; Ishmaelites; MCC
HS. 14 v I Zingari July 1895 @ Lakenham (12 a side match)
Lieut. in the Welsh Regiment rising to Major in the North Somerset Yeomanry.
County Alderman for Norfolk plus a DL and JP (Norfolk)
F.F. – Son of Frederic Bernard and Emma Augusta Schreiber
His uncle was Revd HD Astley – a renowned Zoologist.
His daughter Betty married Lord Muirshiel (Secretary State of Scotland 1957-1962)

BIRKBECK, Major Gen Sir William Henry, MC KCB CMG
(b) Sutton, Yorkshire 8 April 1863
(d) Dinard, France 16 April 1929
Educ. – Wellington College; RMC Sandhurst
Cricket. – clubs unknown

HS. 22 v Lincolnshire June 1895 @ Spalding
Served Hazare, Chin Lushai and South Africa between 1888 and 1902 (despatches, medals and clasps in all his engagements). Attached to Japanese 3rd Army in Manchuria 1905. Order of Rising Sun (3rd class) in 1st Dragoon Guards. Commandant of the Cavalry School at Netheraron 1906-11. Director of Remounts at Army HQ 1912-1920

COCKBURN, Maurice Kean

(b) Burdwan, West Bengal, India 11 April 1871
Cricket. – Guild; King's Royal Dragoon Guards
HS. 4 v Hertfordshire July 1895 @ Bishop's Stortford
102 no for Guild v Kingsley Seconds in September 1893 (in 60 minutes)
61 for King's Royal Dragoon Guards v Diss May 1894
NCCC had by all accounts an undesirable playing for them.
He came to England when aged 19 as the son of an Inspector General of the Bengal Police.
For starters he lied about his name, age, army rank and marital status. He was arrested (long after his one NCCC game) and appeared in court as Major James Cockburn (aka 'Jack') being accused of –
(1) feloniously marrying Caroline Buck, his wife then being alive.
(2) stealing silver goods; obtaining a legacy from Ellen Jacobs by false pretences.
(3) obtaining a diamond ring, a gold chain and a gold cross (all of which he pawned) from Jane Upham. He pleaded guilty to the bigamy indictment. He claimed to many young women to be rich and heir to his uncle in India. Also claimed that he heavily invested in Canadian Sun Insurance Company and to be insured with them to the tune of several thousands. He never invested nor insured but for a while he was a sub agent of Sun Life Assurance Company in Sheffield in 1904. A true statement –he was in the King's Royal Dragoon Guards and by 1901 he attained the position of Riding Master, with a commission and rank of Lieutenant. Drafted to the 21st Lancers in Dublin and again in trouble by passing dishonoured cheques. A further proven charge against him of having lodged a Government horse in payment of a private debt. Court marshalled and cashiered in July 1903. On 6th February 1908 he was given two terms of 5 years penal servitude – the sentences to run concurrently. I have read the Court papers and did my own independent research so that no libel can be attached to these comments. I have been unable to find his demise.

FRYER, Ernest Henry

(b) Wymondham, Norfolk 13 September 1871
(d) Henley-upon-Thames 11 October 1903
Educ. – Wellingborough School
Cricket. – Wellingborough School

HS. 32 no v Cambridgeshire August 1895 @ Fenner's
Brother of PA (q.v) but not related to PWJ (q.v)
Football for Wymondham and Norfolk County (between 1886 to1896 – 5 apps).
Son of William Goodwin (a Farmer) and Caroline Howes
F.F. – Probated London will dated 18 November 1905 leaving £134-2-6 to his eldest brother.

HESLOP, Gerald Gwydyr

(b) Ditton Marsh, Thames Ditton 17 April 1879
(d) Cringleford, Norwich 28 November 1913
Educ. – Norwich GS; Paston GS; Cambridge University (Clare College 12 October 1897 – BA 1901)
Cricket. – Norwich GS; Cambridge University; CEYMS; Royal Navy Hospital; R Scott Holmes' XI; Blofield & District; Clare College; Blofield; CEM Wilson's X1.
HS. 68 v Durham August 1900 @ Darlington
BB. 5/36 v Cambridgeshire July 1899 @ Fenner's
HS. 132 no v Yorkshire (2) July 1900 @ Headingley
BB. 3/60 v Yorkshire (2) July 1900 @ Headingley
1st class cricket – 2 matches 19 runs 1 catch
He scored 57.1% of innings total ie 36(63) for NCCC v Northumberland June 1900
The fifth youngest NCCC man to make a NCCC Minor County Championship debut. At age 16 he was getting tons in club and college cricket
83 (146) for Norwich GS v Ipswich School July 1897.
104 no for Clare College v Magdalene College June 1899.
5/25 for RNH v Bury July 1899
146 no for Blofield v Norwich Union July 1899.
Red Lillywhite of 1898 said – "described as the most promising bat Norfolk have had for years".
F.F. – Assistant Master Fonthill Prep School (East Grinstead)1903. He retired early through ill health and he tried to build up his weakened constitution by visiting South Africa for the warmer climate.

LAKE, Edward Arthur

(b) Swainsthorpe, Norfolk 15 September 1867
(d) Norwich OND 1940 at age 73
Cricket. – St. Marks
HS. 10 v I Zingari July 1895 @ Lakenham (12 a side match)
BB. 2/17 v I Zingari July 1895 @ Lakenham (12 a side match)
13-6-7-9 (including 4 in 4) for St. Marks v Belle Vue 1895
F.F. – Son of William and Hannah Long Cannell. In 1891 Census he was living in New Lakenham with an occupation of a Baker. He was latterly a Confectioner's Assistant.

TONGE, Lt. Col William Corrie, DSO

(b) Starborough, Dormans Land, Surrey 14 April 1862
(d) Fulmer Grange, Buckinghamshire 2 May 1943

Lived 69 Courtfield Gardens, Kingston and he endured a long illness before his passing.
'The Who's Who of Cricket 1984' incorrectly gives his birthplace as in Kent.
Educ. – Brighton School; Tonbridge School; Cheltenham College; RMC Sandhurst.
Cricket. – Cheltenham College; Gloucestershire; MCC; RMC Sandhurst; Gunton; Thorpe Asylum.
HS. 17 v Hertfordshire July 1896 @ Bishop's Stortford
HS. 16 v I Zingari July 1896 @ Lakenham
1st class cricket – 2 matches 8 runs
55 for Thorpe Asylum v King's Royal Dragoon Guards September 1893
108 for Gunton v Lord Battersea's X1 August 1899.
A Barrister-at-Law 1939. A Captain in the 3rd Norfolk Regiment when debuting for NCCC and he latterly served in the South African War being twice mentioned in despatches. A Lt. Col commanding 3rd Battallion in 1910.

WILSON, Revd James Clunes
(b) Denton, Norfolk 11 February 1862
(d) The Peebles Nursing Home, Hunstanton, Norfolk 30 March 1943
Lived The Feathers Hotel, Dersingham
Educ. – Mawston School; Cambridge University (Corpus Christi College 1 October 1881 – BA 1884 MA 1888)
Cricket. – CEYMS; Holkham; Rev JC Wilson's XI; Billingford Incapables; Norfolk 22 Colts.
HS. 23 v Cambridgeshire August 1895 @ Cambridge
HS. 5 v MCC August 1898 @ Lakenham
5/18 for Billingford Incapables v F Kerrison's XI June 1899
Ordained 1890 and Priest 1891. Assistant Master Sutton Valence School 1884-1888. 2nd Master Sutton Valence School 1888-1897. Rector of Billingford (Norfolk) 1897-1899. Rector of Longford (Derby) 1899-1918. Rector of Cranwich with Didlington and Colveston 1918-1924. Rector of Belton (Suffolk) 1924-1927. Vicar of Holkham with Egmere and Waterden 1928-1932. Vicar of Dalby-on-the-Wolds (Leicester) 1932-1937.

1896

BATHURST, Lt Lawrence Charles Villebois
(b) Gressenhall, Norfolk 4 June 1871
(d) Bonechurch, Isle of Wight 22 February 1939
Educ. – Radley College (MA Hussey's House); Oxford University (Trinity College)
Cricket. – Radley College; Oxford University – Blue 1893/94; Trinity College; I Zingari; Lord Hawke's XI; MCC Anchor Club; JA Berners' XI; Middlesex; HD Astley's XI; Gentlemen; AJ Webbe's XI; T Westray's XI; HDG Leveson-Gower's XI.
HS. 67 v Cambridgeshire Aug 1898 @ Fenner's
BB. 6/43 v Durham August 1898 @ Lakenham

HS. 53 v MCC August 1899 @ Lakenham
BB. 6/44 v MCC August 1899 @ Lakenham
1st class cricket – 33 matches 671 runs 96 wickets 19 catches
A NCCC Captain in 1899. Right hand bat, slow left arm medium with spin. A lob bowler.
He was reckoned to be by far the most reliable trundler at either Varsity (June 1894).
8/40 for Oxford University v Colonials June 1894 (his opening spell was 9-6-5-5)
90 for HD Astley's X1 v Rougham September 1895
108 for I Zingari v Shorncliffe Garrison June 1899
Football. – Radley College; Oxford University – Blue 1893
Rackets.- Radley College
With the 62nd Co. Imperial Yeomanry and also the 30th Regiment Imperial Yeomanry serving in Cape Colony and the Wittenbergen.
F.F. – Probated London will dated 4 April 1939 leaving £1,498-10-8 to his widow Alice.

LOMAS, H
Cricket. – Gunton; SH Wood's XI
HS. 27 v Hertfordshire July 1897 @ Bishop's Stortford
HS. 5 v I Zingari July 1896 @ Lakenenham
154 no for Gunton v Fakenham July 1897 (with F.Davies (q.v) scoring 195)
He played in the match where Charlie Shore (q.v) took 10/50 in an innings for NCCC.
It is rumoured that he was the Lancashire 2nd X1 player of 1894-97 but I have been unable to prove the case.

WILSON, Brereton Knyvet
(b) Fritton, Long Stratton, Norfolk 9 May 1868
(d) Saxlingham, Nethergate, Norfolk 15 October 1939
Educ. – Felsted School; Oxford University (Magdalene College – solo choir boy 1877-84)
Cricket. – Felsted School; Pulham; Nothumberland; CEYMS; Gunton.
HS. 76 v Cambridgeshire August 1906 @ Fenner's
BB. 2/7 v Cambridgeshire August 1898 @ Lakenham
HS. 83 v Free Foresters July 1907 @ Lakenham – a stand-in skipper for this game.
BB. 1/9 v Yorkshire (2) August 1900 @ Lakenham
Captain of NCCC 1909
106 no for Gunton v Cromer Visitors August 1893
107 for CEYMS v Overstrand August 1899
NCCC Hon. Sec 1901-03 and Joint Sec 1910 with CBL Prior (q.v).
Admitted Solicitor 1891 and a joint partnership in Bignold, Pollard and Wilson. Royal Norwich Golf captain 1926-28

WILSON, T E
HS. 4 no v Cambridgeshire August 1896 @ Fenner's
This man still remains a mystery despite extensive research

1897

BERWICK, Revd Theodore Francis Hartley
(b) Erchfont, Wiltshire 12 September 1872
(d) Guisborough, North Riding 22 July 1931
Educ. – Guisborough GS; Cambridge University (St.
Catharine's College 15 October 1891 – BA 1894 MA 1919)
Cricket. – Yarmouth; Yarmouth Fifteen; MCC
HS. 31 v Cambridgeshire August 1897 @ Fenner's
108 for Yarmouth v Aldeburgh July 1897
*Ordained 1897 (Norwich) and Priest 1898 (Hereford). Curate of
Burgh Castle (Norfolk) 1897-98.*
Curate of Hereford Cathedral and Curate of Tupsley 1898-99.
*Assistant Master S.F. College (Ramsgate) 1899. Assistant Master
Gt. Yarmouth GS 1900. Chaplain Wadhurst Hill 1902-04.*
*Assistant Master and Chaplain St. John's School (Leatherhead)
1904-05. Headmaster Guisborough School (Yorkshire) 1905-
1931*
F.F. – His father Joseph was a Cleric who married a
Yarmouth lass, namely Emma Cowl.
The family were constantly on the move around the UK.

GOODE, William Frederick
(b) Tiffield, Northampton 29 August 1866
(d) Gt. Yarmouth, Norfolk 12 January 1961
Cricket. – Yarmouth; Yarmouth Fifteen
HS. 10 no v Cambridgeshire August 1897 @ Lakenham
*In 1891 census he was a Teacher living in Gorleston. In 1901
census he was a Teacher of Dancing and a Caterer. The local
Norfolk Press give him the forename initials WFG which do not
appear on his death certificate.*

SKRIMSHIRE, Dr. Henry Finch, MRCS LRCP
(b) Holt, Norfolk 8 March 1874
(d) Hill House, Holt, Norfolk 2 March 1953
Educ. – Gresham's School; Cambridge University (Trinity
College October 1895 – BA 1898); Durham College of
Science
Cricket. – Gresham's School; Holt
HS. 9 v Cambridgeshire August 1897 @ Fenner's
Brother of JF (q.v)
70 no for Holt v Norwich Union 1895
*At University School Charing Cross Hospital 1899-1905. In 1902
the Resident Medical Officer at St. Mary's Hospital for Women
and Children (Plaistow). Assistant House Physician Worcester
General Hospital. Trustee of Prosperity Lodge & Forester's Friendly
Society. Member of Holt's Literary Institute. Vice President of
Letheringsett Bowls Club. The Medical Officer for Bramblewood
Sanitorium.*
*Practised at Holt for nearly 50 years after his mentioned
Charing Cross stint.*

SMITH, Dr. Major Reginald, MRCS LRCP TD
(b) Warrington 1 May 1868
(d) Scarborough 5 October 1943
His will has his surname as Starkey-Smith
Educ. – Owens College; Royal Institution of Liverpool
Cricket. – Lynn; Lancashire
HS. 13 v Northumberland June 1897 @ Lakenham
*1st class cricket – 1 match 6 runs as a fast bowler and a mid-off
fielder*
8/29 for Lynn v Carrow in Norfolk Senior Cup Final 1896
*A Major in R.A.M.C.Honorary Surgeon Manchester Royal
Infirmary. Honorary Surgeon West Norfolk Hospital*
F.F. – Author of 'Case of Oesophageal Pouch'.
His Solicitor held the residue of his will being just £148-17s

WORMAN, James Nicholls
(b) Midhurst, Sussex 16 June 1875
(d) Newmarket 15 June 1950
Lived Grafton House, Brandon, Suffolk
Educ. – King's Lynn GS; Donnington GS
Cricket. – King's Lynn GS; Lincolnshire; Minor Counties;
Spalding; Gosberton; Hunstanton & District
HS. 72 v Hertfordshire August 1905 @ Lakenham
(batting at 8)
BB. 8/53 v Suffolk July 1906 @ Lakenham
HS. 70 v I Zingari July 1902 @ Lakenham
BB. 4/21 v MCC August 1903 @ Lakenham
*About 3,000 spectators went to Lakenham in 1903 to see WG
Grace bat for London County – Worman bowled him for a
duck and the umpire allowed it to stand. His son Paul also
played for Lincolnshire and they were in the same team v NCCC
in an August 1930 clash at Lakenham. They both took a wicket,
held a catch and each made a 'pair'!*
109 no for King's Lynn GS v Wisbech June 1894
9/6 for King's Lynn GS v Town June 1899
102 no for Spalding v Lynn June 1908
*A Teacher at King's Lynn GS. A 1905 Press summation of – "he
was never mastered, splendid accuracy, variation of pace and
an ability to make the ball get up quickly". To prove a point his
bowling in 1905 was instrumental in NCCC winning the Minor
Counties Championship.*

1898

BURRELL, Canon Herbert John Edwin
(b) Newmarket 15 November 1866
(d) Trumpington, Cambridge 22 May 1949
Educ. – Charterhouse School; Cuddeston College; Oxford
University (Magdalene College 23 October 1885 – BA 1889
MA 1892)
Cricket. – Charterhouse School; Oundle; Thetford Town;
Sidestrand; Essex; MCC; Hertfordshire; Oxford University –

no Blue

HS. 12 v Northumberland June 1900 @ Lakenham
HS. 4 v Yorkshire (2) July 1898 @ Lakenham
1st class cricket – 3 matches 15 runs 2 wickets
The HG Burrell (NCCC 1898) is this gentleman and his Brother
RJ also played for Essex and MCC. Secretary of Thetford Golf
Club. Lawn Tennis – Doubles for O.U. v C.U. 1886/87. Chaplain
of Hillingdon 1890-94. Domestic Chaplain to Bishop of St.
Albans 1894-99. Vicar of Wiggington (Herts) 1899-1910. Rector
of Balsham 1910-1934. Rural Dean of Camps 1929-1934. Hon.
Canon of Ely from 1927

COOKSON, Lt. Geoffrey
(b) Newborough Hall, Chollerton, Northumberland 12
March 1882
(d) Jubbulpore, India 25 August 1907
Lived in Trelissick, Truro
Educ. – Garboldisham School; Harrow School (Druries
House Easter 1896 – 1900.2)
Cricket. – Harrow School; Garboldisham; Cornwall; Punjab
(India).
HS. 12 v Cambridgeshire August 1898 @ Fenner's
BB. 1/6 v Cambridgeshire August 1898 @ Lakenham
HS. 8 v MCC August 1898 @ Lakenham
BB. 1/13 v MCC August 1898 @ Lakenham
85 for Harrow School v Quidnuncs June 1899
28 for Punjab v Oxford University Authentics January 1903.
He joined 2nd Batt. K.R.R.C. in 1901
Football. – Harrow School
F.F. – Led a merry dance trying to trace this fellow. The 1891
Census listed him as Jeffrey !
The 'Eastern Daily Press' of June 1899 said he was Gerald
Cookson! Found him as an Army 2nd Lt. living in Chelsea.
His father George died in Truro which reasonably explained
Geoffrey's appearances for Cornwall.

FISHER, Dr. Herbert Wortley, MRCS LRCP
(b) Queensferry, Linlithgow 26 June 1876
(d) Gilvan, Plymstock 10 January 1936
Cricket. – Fakenham
HS. 47 v Durham August 1898 @ West Hartlepool
HS. 18 no v Yorkshire (2) August 1898 @ Scarborough
A registered Doctor 22 June 1900 yet referred to as such in 1898.
The Medical Register (1927) showed his address as East Cowes,
Isle of Wight
F.F. – His father John was a Royal Naval Surgeon and an
Inspector General of His Majesty's Hospitals and Fleets.
Five generations on Herbert's paternal side produced 39
children. A recent visit to Fakenham to watch the Norfolk
Development team in action afforded the opportunity
to prove that the Dr. Fisher Cup was not named after this
Norfolk cricketer.

NICHOLS, John Ernest
(b) Norwich 20 April 1878
(d) Thorpe, Norwich 29 February 1952
Cricket. – Worcestershire; Staffordshire; Minor Counties;
Uttoxeter; Oldfields; West Bromwich Dartmouth; Stoke;
Norwich Wanderers; JE Nichols' X1
HS. 127 v Staffordshire June 1925 @ Wolverhampton
BB. 7/14 v Leicester (2) July 1927 @ Leicester
HS. 53 (111) v New Zealand August 1927 @ Lakenham
BB. 2/7 v West Indies August 1923 @ Lakenham
1st class cricket - 6 matches 45 runs 3 catches
In 1898 NCCC had no finances to enable them to retain him.
For Staffordshire he took 81 wickets and scored 2,061 runs.
Holds the 2nd highest individual percentage (66.5%) of
personal runs in a completed Norfolk innings being 127 (191) –
see above for more match detail.
In 1930 he had the remarkable figures of 14.2-10-8-6 for NCCC
v Hertfordshire
Has a NCCC stumping to his name (1931) – it was stated that
there was not a NCCC qualified keeper capable of dealing
with Michael Falcon's fast bowling. From 1932-38 'Jack' was
the NCCC Cricket Coach and afterwards he coached schools
including Norwich School, Bracondale School and Bishop's
Stortford College. Wounded during WW1 when with the Kings
Liverpool Regiment
WW2 – Constabulary Service
Football for Loughborough Town

PARTRIDGE, Edward Richard Walter
(b) Upper Rickinghall, Suffolk 7 October 1875
(d) Malaya 1 December 1958
Educ. – Haileybury College (Trevelyan 1890.1 – 1893.2)
Cricket. – Haileybury College; JC Wilson's XI; R Scott-
Holmes' XI
Brother of PW (q.v)
HS. 18 v Northumberland July 1898 @ Gt. Yarmouth
75 for JC Wilson's X1 v Holkham August 1899
Originally a Nurseryman living in Oxford being the son of
Walter the Curate of Holywell.
He sailed from London to Penang in 1953 and in the Fed. Malay
States he managed various Rubber Estates.

PARTRIDGE, Percival Walter
(b) Witney, Oxfordshire 27 August 1879
(d) Esher, Surrey 12 July 1964
Educ. – Felsted School
Cricket. – JS Holmes' XI; Madras CC; R Scott-Holmes' XI; CF
Taylor's XI; Europeans; Madras Presidency
HS. 82 v Hertfordshire July 1900 @ Bishop's Stortford
HS. 28 v Yorkshire (2) August 1898 @ Scarborough
Brother of ERW (q.v)
1st class cricket – 3 matches 85 runs 2 catches- all these games

were in India
The first NCCC player to feature in two Minor Counties ton partnerships for the period covered by this book.
122 for CF Taylor's XI v Gunton July 1900
Football. – CEYMS; Norfolk County 1899/1900 (2 apps– 0 goals)
Solicitor at King & Partridge (Madras) being firstly a Partner then Head Director followed by an appointment of being the first elected President of the Company.

PEARSE, Charles, JP

(b) Rookery, Carlton Colville, Suffolk 24 December 1867
(d) Downing Court Nursing Home, Sheringham, Norfolk 1 May 1936
Educ. – Bedford GS; Wellington College; Cambridge University (Christ's College 27 April 1886)
Cricket. – Bedford GS; Wellington College; Dereham; RG Pilch's XI; Hertfordshire; F Marshall's XI.
HS. 8 no v Durham August 1898 @ West Hartlepool
HS. 16 v Yorkshire (2) August 1898 @ Scarborough
50 for Dereham v Blofield July 1899
JP for Norfolk. His widowed mother became in her own right a Landowner with 700 acres. Charles studied Brewing in Rickmansworth and he acquired Messrs Cooper, Brown & Co's Brewery at East Dereham. The business was remodelled and was later taken over by Steward & Patteson
F.F. – He left £3,019-7-10 in his Probated will.

RELF, Albert Edward

(b) Burwash, Sussex 26 June 1874
(d) The Pavilion, Wellington College, Crowthorne 26 March 1937
Lived Kia Ora, Ravenswood Avenue, Crowthorne
Cricket. – Gt. Bircham; MCC; Sussex; London County; England XI; Auckland; Kent & Sussex; Rest of England; CB Fry's XI; Lord Londesborough's XI; Berkshire; Players of the South; South of England; Lord Grey de Witton's XI; England (13 Tests).
HS. 103 v Northumberland July 1899 @ Lakenham
BB. 6/78 v Durham August 1899 @ Durham
HS. 40 v Yorkshire (2) July 1898 @ Lakenham
BB. 4/55 v MCC August 1899 @ Lakenham
Brother of EH and RR (both were Sussex cricketers)
A fabulous career playing in 13 Tests for 416 runs, 14 catches and 25 wickets. He toured with the MCC to Australia and the West Indies.
1st class cricket – 565 matches 22,238 runs (with 26 tons) and took 537 catches plus the small matter of 1,897 wickets. He did the 'double' of 1,000 runs and 100 wickets in a season a mere 8 times.
He had a 4 year engagement from Lord Grey de Witton at Holkham Hall which contract terminated in October 1899.
He coached at Wellington School after WW1 – succeeding

his father in the task. He was one of Wisden's Five Cricketers of the Year in 1914. A Wisden eulogy of – " Few bowlers were so difficult to play on a wicket the least bit crumbled. Taking a short run with an easy, natural delivery, he possessed perfect command of length and never showed fatigue. His style of batting gave rather a false idea of his powers. He let the ball hit the bat in a way not impressive to the eye but season after season he made as many runs as men who looked greatly his superior. Also a brilliant fieldsman in the slips."
He shot himself with the sad act being attributed to poor health and depression due to the at the time serious illness of his wife Agnes. He died a reasonably wealthy man as his widow Agnes had a share of £20,880-14-9 from the London Probated will

ROBERSON, Frank

(b) Spore-with-Palgrave, Norfolk 19 August 1864
(d) Ely, Cambridgeshire 30 March 1949
Educ. – Oundle School
Cricket. – Oundle Rovers; Ely; Cambridgeshire; F Marshall's XI
HS. 2 v Hertfordshire July 1898 @ Bishop's Stortford
HS. 0 (x2) v Yorkshire (2) July 1898 @ Lakenham
27 matches for Cambridgeshire with a highest score of 190 for Cambridgeshire v NCCC July 1893 @ Fenner's – after his side were all out for 39 in the 1st innings. He did well to prolong his cricket career to 1910 as in June 1899 he was having serious trouble with an eye

1899

BARRATT, William Percy

(b) Altrincham 31 December 1866
(d) Ormesby St. Margaret, Norfolk 5 February 1934
Cricket. – Blofield; Eastern Ramblers
HS. 8 v Cambridgeshire July 1899 @ Fenner's
Brother of L (q.v) and G (q.v)
A wicket keeper and the eldest of the three NCCC cricketing brothers.A Farmer late of Burlingham Lodge, Norwich
F.F. – His re sworn will dated 11 April 1934 saw him leave £6,574-13-7 to his widow Annie (nee Ravenscroft)

GARNIER, Edward Thomas

(b) Apsley Guise, Bedfordshire 5 July 1876
(d) Gorgate Hall, Hoe, Swanton Morley 11 December 1924
Educ. – Marlborough School; Oxford University (Oriel College)
Cricket. – Marlborough School; Hertfordshire; Quidenham Parsonage; Authentics; I Zingari; Dereham; Holkham.
HS. 90 v Cambridgeshire August 1907 @ Lakenham
BB. 1/21 v Hertfordshire August 1899 @ Lakenham
HS. 44 v MCC August 1903 @ Lakenham

Father of EHC (q.v)

One of 10 NCCC men with a HS in the 90s. In June 1899 he amassed 968 runs in 8 matches for Quidenham Parsonage with 1(100) and 5(50). Athletics for Oxford University Hurdler – Blue 1896-98

Many of his family played cricket to a useful standard being his other brothers, grandfather, father,

great uncle and uncles. Edward was the eldest son of a Canon who himself was the son of a Dean. I know my place! After WW1 he was a private Tutor coaching pupils for Oxford University.

F.F. – Left £6,723-16s to his widow Dorothy (nee Hemsworth)

McCORMICK, Dean Joseph Gough

(b) New Cross, London 19 February 1874
(d) Broughton, Salford, Manchester 30 August 1924
Lived The Deanery, Manchester
Educ. – Exeter School; Choir School (Hull); Cambridge University (St. John's College 20 June 1893 – BA 1896 MA 1900)
Cricket. – Kent (2); MCC; London Clergy; Yarmouth; Yarmouth Etecteras; CF Taylor's XI ; Liverpool & District; Yarmouth Etonians
HS. 141 v Oxfordshire August 1905 @ Oxford – batting at no. 7 and run out
BB. 1/13 v Cambridgeshire August 1904 @ Lakenham
HS. 63 v London County August 1904 @ Lakenham
He took part in 4 NCCC ton partnerships.
107 for Yarmouth Etecteras v RMS Albatross June 1901
Vice President of Lancashire CCC 1924. His brother and father reached first class cricket level.
Ordained 1897 and Priest 1898. Curate of Gt. Yarmouth 1897-1901. Vicar of St. Paul's (Princes Place, Liverpool) 1901-09. Vicar of St. Michael's (Chester Square) 1909-1920. Hon. Chaplain to King George V 1915-18. Chaplain to King George V 1918-20. Proctor in Convocation for the Diocese of London 1919. Dean of Manchester from 1920
F.F. – An author of 'Plain Words on Vexed Questions' and 'Christ and Common Topics'.
Left £6,812-6-9 in his Probated will to his widow Alison (nee Conybeare)

PENN, Capt Eric Frank

(b) Westminster, London 17 April 1878
(d) Hoz Hohenzollern near Loos, France 18 October 1915
Lived 42 Gloucester Square, Hyde Park, London
Educ. – Eton College; Cambridge University (Trinity College 25 June 1897)
Cricket. – Eton College; MCC; I Zingari; AJ Webbe's XI; Eton Ramblers; PF Warner's XI; Cambridge University – Blue 1899,1902); JH Stogdon's XI

HS. 133 v Hertfordshire June 1905 @ Watford
BB. 4/48 v Hertfordshire June 1905 @ Watford
HS. 81 v Suffolk August 1902 @ Lakenham
BB. 5/50 v MCC August 1903 @ Lakenham
1st class cricket – 22 matches 449 runs 13 catches 34 wickets and his father, certain uncles and brothers-in-law all played first class cricket. Eric toured with Warner's team to North America.
With LH Leman (q.v) he still shares the NCCC sixth wicket partnership record of 200 v Hertfordshire at Watford in 1905
80 for I Zingari v NCCC July 1902
In 4th Green Guards serving in South Africa 1900/01. Lieut. 3rd Royal Scots. WW1 – 2nd Lt Norfolk Yeomanry. Capt 4th Grenadier Guards 1915 (mentioned in despatches).
F.F. – He left £12,010-14-4 in his will which stated rather starkly KIA Flanders with his Times obituary being dated 25 October 1915. The University War List erroneously gives his death as February 11th. His son Lt. Col Sir Eric Charles William Mackenzie Penn was awarded the MC. Sir Eric was an extra Equerry to Queen Elizabeth and he organized / planned the weddings of the Princesses Margaret and Anne as well as the funeral of Earl Mountbatten.

PILCH, Robert George

(b) Holt, Norfolk 12 October 1877
(d) Norwich 1 November 1957
Known in the family as 'Old George' to distinguish him from his son 'Young George'.
Cricket. – CF Taylor's X1; HL Horsfall's XI; CEYMS; L Robinson's XI; Holiday Hittites; Norfolk Club & Ground; Yarmouth XI
HS. 88 v Cambridgeshire August 1905 @ Lakenham
BB. 4/61 v Cambridgeshire August 1901 @ Fenner's
HS. 75 v L. Robinson's XI May 1912 @ Old Buckenham Hall
BB. 2/30 v Cambridgeshire August 1902 @ Fenner's
Grandfather of DG (q.v) and Father of GE (q.v) and a distant ancestor of Fuller Pilch.
With AK Watson (q.v) he still shares the NCCC eighth wicket partnership record of 152 v Cambridgeshire @ Lakenham in 1905
He Umpired the first class game between L Robinson's XI & Australian Imperial Forces in 1919 at Old Buckenham.
7/9 for CEYMS v Aubyns July 1899
62 for Holiday Hittites v Overstrand August 1911
A former NCCC Committee Member. Norwich Wanderers CC President and Chairman
Chairman Club and Ground (a Newspaper article June 1946)
Football. – Melton Constable; Caleys' 3rds; CEYMS; Tottenham Hotspur FC; Everton FC; Norfolk County 1895-1913 (apps 37–10 goals); Norwich City FC.
A Norwich City FC Director 1923 – 21 August 1953 and the Vice-Chairman 1930-1947.

Norfolk County FA Life Member and awarded their long service medal. The CEYMS President / Secretary / Chairman. Worked at the Melton Constable Hall Gardens. Earlham Recreation Groundsman 1895-1906 . Founded the Pilch's Sports Outfitters in Brigg Street, Norwich in 1906.

Golf. - Norfolk County; Eaton; Royal Norwich; West Norfolk
He also represented Norfolk County at Bowls
F.F. – A Freemason and Rotarian. President Norwich Grasshoppers Hockey Club. He lived and breathed sport for over 60 years and just listing his litany of achievements makes one humble.

STAPLES, S
Cricket. – Houghton Hall; Gt. Bircham; Norfolk Colts
HS. 57 v Durham August 1899 @ Durham
BB. 3/10 v Durham August 1899 @ Durham
HS. 3 v MCC August 1899 @ Lakenham
In June 1899 he was assisting Gt. Bircham with AE Relf. In July 1899 the local press stated that he had showed promise in the previous years Colts match. He was the Houghton Hall professional but no further clues have been forthcoming despite my asking their Archivist.

1900

CHURCH, Percy
Cricket. – Yarmouth Town
HS. 0 v Yorkshire (2) August 1900 @ Lakenham
BB. 5/25 v Yorkshire (2) August 1900 @ Lakenham
His one County match,a friendly above, saw him bowl unchanged with Charlie Shore (q.v) in the first innings of the game. After 6 overs he had taken 2 wickets for no runs and he finished the day with an analysis of 10-7-11-4.
174 and 6/40 for Yarmouth v Ipswich & Suffolk July 1900.
He was in the Yarmouth team alongside NCCC players Backhouse, Leman , McCormick and Watling.
My favourite newspaper find was his dismissal in a Yarmouth match of – 'Church out to Steeples'.

COMPTON, John James
(b) Deane, Northampton 7 January 1870
(d) Trowell, Northampton 1 February 1945
Cricket. – Overstrand; Tudor House; North Norfolk District
HS. 54 no v Hertfordshire July 1900 @ Bishop's Stortford
BB. 2/8 v Northumberland June 1900 @ Lakenham
HS. 40 v Essex (2) June 1910 @ Lakenham
BB. 3/51 v Old Buckenham Hall July 1911 @ Old Buckenham Hall
He Captained NCCC in 3 games in 1910.
111 no and 5/28 for Overstrand v Mr. Corballis' XI August 1899
150 for Overstrand v West Wanstead June 1908

69 no (109) for Overstrand v Carrow August 1911
In 1901 Census he was listed as a Domestic Valet living in Overstrand. Latterly a Greyhound Racing Manager
F.F. – He bequeathed £673-16-11 to his widow Gertrude. His father James (a Coachman) married May Underhill

GARNETT, Cecil Frederick
(b) East Lodge, Easton, Norfolk 10 April 1868
(d) France 27 November 1934
Cricket. – Overstrand
HS. 70 v Durham August 1900 @ Darlington
BB. 3/19 v Cambridgeshire August 1901 @ Lakenham
HS. 13 v Yorkshire (2) July 1900 @ Leeds
BB. 2/30 v West Indies August 1900 @ Lakenham
128 for Overstrand v Gresham's School July 1900
110 for Overstrand v Trunch July 1900 – these two scores came in successive innings.
With PW Partridge he once held NCCC's 7th wicket partnership record of 103 in 1900 for the period covered by this book.
F.F. – His father was a retired Major who married into French aristocracy and Cecil also took a French wife to continue the lineage and he lived with servants and a Coachman.

HAYTER, Walter Louis Bazaine
(b) Middlesex, London 11 October 1864
(d) Addenbrooke's Hospital, Cambridge 11 February 1950
Educ. – Highgate School; Fitzroy College; Cambridge University (Queens' College 1884 – BA 1887 MA 1891)
Cricket. – West Wratting Park; Hunstanton & District; Cambridgeshire; Rev W Boyce's XI; King's Lynn; Hunstanton
HS. 81 no v Surrey (2) Aug 1901 @ The Oval
BB. 2/28 v Surrey (2) July 1901 @ Lakenham
HS. 38 v I Zingari July 1902 @ Lakenham
8/20 for Hunstanton v Lynn YMCA July 1899
71 no (115) for Hunstanton v Glebe House June 1901 –an opener so he carried his bat.
By 1901 he was a private Tutor to the Army and University. He coached cricket at West Wratting Park.
He played four times for Cambridgeshire v NCCC scoring 97 runs in total. Secretary of the newly formed Hunstanton CC.
Football. – Hunstanton; Norfolk County 1900 (1 app)
F.F. – Son of Angelo who was the Chief Reviewer of Wills at Somerset House.
Walter left £6,930-15-4 to his widow Harriette

HOWLETT, Albert Edward
(b) Lakenham, Norwich 13 October 1866
(d) Norfolk & Norwich Hospital 3 June 1942
Lived 232 Denmark Road, Lowestoft
Educ. – Commercial School
Cricket. – Commercial School; Carrow; St. Marks; Catton;

Riverside Ramblers; Caistor

HS. 10 no v Buckinghamshire August 1901 @ Aylesbury

BB. 5/106 v Surrey (2) August 1901 @ The Oval

60 no for St. Marks v Catton May 1893

9/32 for Carrow v Acle June 1894

8/8 for Carrow v Yarmouth Temple August 1896

The 'EDP' of August 1904 stated that he was fast approaching the veteran stage. The 1889 NCCC Handbook confirmed his address at the time in Lakenham and a Census search showed that he was a General Labourer.

IRELAND, Lt. Maurice William

(b) Guestwick Hall, Norfolk JFM 1876

(d) Norwich 26 February 1921

Educ. – Norwich GS

Cricket. – Norwich GS; Norwich GS Old Boys; EG Buxton's XI; Carrow; 1st V.B. Norfolk Regiment; MW Ireland's XI; R Scott-Holmes' XI; RG Pilch's XI; CEYMS; Diss; Holiday Hittites; WHR Long's XI; Easton Ramblers; Marquis of Grahams' XI; S Hill-Wood's XI; HL Horsfall's XI; Norwich Wanderers.

HS. 38 no v Hertfordshire June 1901 @ Bishop's Stortford

BB. 7/68 v Buckinghamshire May 1901 @ Lakenham

HS. 55 no v Free Foresters July 1905 @ Lakenham

BB. 8/38 v Suffolk July 1903 @ Ipswich

He Captained NCCC in 2 games in 1908

80 for Carrow v Overstrand August 1907

He took all 10 wickets in an innings for HL Horsfall's XI v S Hill-Wood's XI in August 1909

Worked for the family firm namely Ireland's –the Auctioneers and Valuers. In days of yore they used to auction 1,000 cattle a day.

F.F. – The 1891 Census listed him as Morice. In the 1st Batt. Norfolk Regiment

LEMAN, Leonard Henry

(b) Loddon, Norfolk 19 February 1872

(d) Haverfordwest, Pembroke 28 July 1932

Cricket. – Royal Navy Hospital; Loddon; Yarmouth; Durham County Asylum.

HS. 72 no v Hertfordshire June 1905 @ Watford

BB. 3/86 v Bedfordshire July 1908 @ Bedford

HS. 45 v Free Foresters July 1907 @ Lakenham

BB. 1/12 v Free Foresters July 1907 @ Lakenham

7/23 for RNH v Ormesby July 1900

100 no for RNH v Mechanics July 1904

He carried his bat for 44 no (152) for NCCC v Suffolk in August 1906 - it wasn't his fault that NCCC batted one short due to the absence of Owen Dunell.

He played in one friendly for NCCC under the pseudonym WB Louis!

He had century partnerships for NCCC for the 3rd, 6th and 7th

wicket with AK Watson, EF Penn and G Starling respectively

F.F. – A Navy Hospital Keeper and latterly in Wales he was a Domestic Chauffeur. His family have sent me glowing testimonials that were written by the Gt. Yarmouth CC Hon Sec and the DCA Assistant Medical Officer with reference to his cricket performances.

PEACHMENT, Edward

(b) Billingford, Norfolk 5 September 1874

(d) Watton, Norfolk 23 April 1952

Cricket. – Dereham; Billingford; Rev F Marshall's XI; Great Eastern Railways; Holkham.

HS. 11 v Buckinghamshire August 1901 @ Aylesbury

BB. 4/58 v Surrey (2) July 1901 @ Lakenham

5/6 for Billingford v Mattishall July 1893

7/5 for GER v Salhouse July 1900

150 no for Holkham v Sandringham July 1902

He followed in his father's footsteps (tracks!) and became an Engine Driver based in Bawdeswell.

The local newspapers gave him an extra middle initial of (A)

F.F. – His Probated Norwich will saw him leave £246-19s to his widow Pleasance

RAVEN, Revd Charles Olive

(b) Gt. Yarmouth, Norfolk 28 September 1869

(d) The Homes of St. Barnabas Dormans, Surrey 5 May 1963

Lived in Oxford and otherwise known as Charles Oliver.

Educ. – Gt. Yarmouth GS; Cambridge University (St. John's College 8 October 1889 – BA 1892 MA 1923)

Cricket. – Harleston CC

HS. 108 no v Northumberland August 1900 @ Jesmond

BB. 1/4 v Durham August 1900 @ Darlington

HS. 3 v Yorkshire (2) July 1900 @ Headingley

Just review his Minor County Championship Batting Average – the one that got away!

Assistant Master Colchester GS 1888-89. Assistant Master Framlingham College 1892-93.

Assistant Master Chiselhurst Prep School 1894. Assistant Master Harrogate College (Yorkshire) 1895-1901. He was residing with his Uncle and studying history before the clergy came calling. Ordained (St. Albans) 1907 and Priest 1908. Assistant Chaplain Bancroft's School (Woodford, Essex) 1907-29. Rector of Souldern (Oxon) 1929-36. Licentiate to Diocese of Oxford, Coventry and Peterborough 1936-51

1901

BERESFORD, Richard Augustus Agincourt

(b) Castor Rectory near Peterborough 12 August 1869

(d) Derby Royal Infirmary Hospital 12 July 1941

Educ. – Oundle School; School House; Cambridge University (Selwyn College 1 October 1888 – BA 1891 MA 1895)

Cricket. – Oundle School; Oundle Rovers; Northamptonshire; Hunstanton; Houghton Hall; West Norfolk; Cambridge University – no Blue; Thetford; GL Parker's X1.

HS. 63 v Cambridgeshire August 1909 @ King's Lynn

HS. 58 v MCC August 1903 @ Lakenham

Father of RM (q.v)

1st class cricket – 7 matches 177 runs 2 catches
307 no for School House v Layton House May 1888 and in the next match he amassed 225 no.
7/11 for Hunstanton v King Edward VI School July 1911
Took the first 9 wickets for GL Parker's XI @ Sandringham at the age of 55.
Athletics – Cambridge University Shot Putt – Blue 1891/92
Rugby Union – Lennox; Surrey County. Playing Member of Hustanton Golf Club.
7 years experience of teaching in a Prep School in Norwich. Assistant Master Dulwich Prep School 1891-98. Headmaster Lydgate House Prep School (Hunstanton) 1899 –1932

F.F. - The London Gazette 31 October 1941 carried a notice Pursuant to the 1925 Trustee Act for all persons having claims against his estate. The executors were the widow Lilian and his Schoolmaster son RM (q.v)

COLLINSON, Robert Whiteley, BSc

(b) Halifax 6 November 1875

(d) Norwich 26 December 1963

Educ. – Ackworth School; Owen's College

Cricket. - Yorkshire; Keighley; North & East Riding; Carrow; Yarmouth Temple; Dr. Prior's XI; New City CC; Norwich .

HS. 139 v Northumberland August 1911 @ Lakenham

HS. 29 v Cambridgeshire August 1902 @ Lakenham

BB. 8/77 v MCC August 1901 @ Lakenham

1st class cricket – 2 matches 58 runs
In season 1909 he hit 9 tons in the Norwich League ending with a batting average of over 100.
152 for Carrow v Cannon Street June 1908
7/11 for Carrow v Norwich Teachers July 1911
Football.- Ackworth School; Owen's College; Mytholmroyd; Anglo American Club (Switzerland); CEYMS; Norfolk County 1900-1904 (apps 12-14 goals); Norwich City FC 20 September 1902 retired 1905.
Voted into Norwich City FC's Hall of Fame 13 November 2009. When NCFC turned professional 'Bob' turned his considerable talent to cricket. Rugby Union for Mytholmroyd - 55 tries in his last year leading to his being selected for Yorkshire XV. He joined J & J Colman as an Analytical Chemist and from 1912-1938 he was the Manager of the Carrow Works Starch Dept.

F.F. – When born 'Bob' fell out of bed with charisma and he was one of the finest amateur sportsmen with a professional attitude. He married an American woman namely Blanche Hoover of Pennsylvania

FINCH, Capt Alfred

(b) Honingtoft, Norfolk 11 October 1870

(d) Honingham, Norfolk 13 May 1943

Educ. – Twyford School; Haileybury College (Lawrence House 1885.1- 1889.2); Cambridge University (Jesus College October 1890- BA 1894)

Cricket. – Haileybury College; EG Buxton's XI; Norfolk Club & Ground; Billingford.

HS. – Did not bat in his one game v Cambridgeshire August 1901 @ Fenner's

Rugby Union for Haileybury College. Captain of the Royal Norwich Golf Club 1903/04. Captain in the Norfolk Regiment, R.E (wounded in Great War). A Director of Steward & Patterson's Brewery

F.F. – His Probated will revealed that he had an Estate worth £119,634-1-3.

FRASER, H B

Cricket. – EG Buxton's XI; Gunton; CEYMS; Reedham; Norfolk Club & Ground; Catton Hall

HS. 34 v Hertfordshire June 1901 @ Bishop's Stortford

The only seemingly valid clue as to this mystery gentlemen was a Press note that he was the Stepson of Mr. Thomson of Weston. I am still toying with possible initials GH and HG such is the nature of this beast!

MANN. Major Edward John (2nd Bt of Thelveton Hall)

(b) Bawdeswell, Norfolk 26 January 1883

(d) Saxlingham Hall, Norfolk 17 September 1971

Educ. – Marlborough College

Cricket. – Marlborough College; Middlesex 2nds

HS. 18 v Cambridgeshire August 1901 @ Fenner's

A former NCCC President and the Norwich High Sheriff 1936. Chairman of the London Hospital.
Director of Mann, Crossman & Paulin Co (London Brewery Co). WW1 – Captain and Adjutant 4th Batt. Royal Norfolks. Also a senior District Home Guard Officer

MASON, Major Hubert Dempster, MRCS

(b) Solihull, Warwickshire 21 May 1863

(d) Suez Canal 9 April 1905

Cricket. – Warwickshire; Warwickshire Club & Ground; Norfolk Club & Ground; CEYMS

HS. 22 v Hertfordshire June 1901 @ Bishop's Stortford

A Captain in 1901 he rose to the position of Major on 31 January 1904. Appointed Surgeon on 31 January 1891 and he served in the South African War 1899-1900 being awarded the Queen's Medal with Clasp. The 'British Medical Journal' informed that he died on board the Italian Hospital Ship 'Sicilia'. As a student of Maritime matters I know that the troop carrying ship was launched in 1900 for P & O's immediate services to India, Australia and the Far East. No relation to PL (q.v)

F.F. – His Probated London will 15 July 1905 saw his widow receive £1,112-18-11

ROBERTSON, Walter Knyvet
(b) Hazarybaugh, Madras, India 17 October 1868
(d) Bratton Fleming, North Devon 12 March 1941
Orphaned by 1872, he lived with an Aunt in Colkirk having been a wandering soul residing in a short space of time in Brighton, Oundle and Enfield.
Educ. – Oundle School; Cambridge University (Pembroke College 1 October 1887 – BA 1890 MA 1900)
Cricket. – Oundle Rovers; Fakenham; Elstree Masters
HS. 19 v Hertfordshire August 1901 @ Lakenham
BB. 3/45 v Cambridgeshire August 1901 @ Lakenham
HS. 5 v MCC August 1901 @ Lakenham AND Essex (2) August 1903 @ Lakenham
6/12 for Fakenham v CEYMS July 1893
He played for Elstree Masters alongside CP Wilson (q.v.).
Assistant Master Elstree Prep School 1892-1900. Headmaster South Lodge Prep School (Enfield Chase) 1900-1931. His late father Vincent was in the 2nd Dragoon Guards

SCOTT, Revd George Arbuthnot
(b) Wimbledon 12 April 1879
(d) Sandrock Hall, Hastings, Sussex 8 June 1927
Educ. – Tonbridge School; Cambridge University (Emmanuel College October 1898 – BA 1901 MA 1907)
Cricket. – Tonbridge School; Cambridge University; Kent 2nds; WP Robertson's XI ; Elstree Masters
HS. 9 v Hertfordshire June 1901 @ Bishop's Stortford
BB. 2/58 v Hertfordshire June 1901 @ Bishop's Stortford
Son of AT (NCCC 1870) with a brother who played first class cricket for the Royal Navy.
1st class cricket – 5 matches 40 runs 8 wickets
He qualified to play for NCCC by occasional residence at his father's house in Blakeney.
Ordained (Southwark) 1905 and Priest (Chichester) 1906. Curate of Limpsfield (Sussex) 1905/06. Curate of St. John's Evangelist and St. Leonard's 1906-08. Assistant Master (and Partner) Elstree School 1908-10. School Headmaster in Bexhill-on-Sea 1910-20. Headmaster of Sandrock Hall.
F.F. – £18,026-16-5 was left in his will to his widow Mary

1902

ALLEN, George
Cricket. – Norfolk Club & Ground
HS. 34 no v Cambridgeshire August 1905 @ Fenner's
HS. 8 v MCC August 1902 @ Lakenham
Best wicket keeping season in the Championship (13c 3 s) in 1905, with another 2 catches in other games.The 'Eastern Daily Press' only offered the following clue – "An unknown stumper

from the Berkshire area." It is not known if he was born there or just lived in the area nor if he just played cricket for a team in the location?

COZENS-HARDY, Basil
(b) Bracondale, Norwich 4 February 1885
(d) Norfolk & Norwich Hospital 13 January 1976
Educ. – Norwich GS; Rugby School; Oxford University (Trinity College – MA)
Cricket. – Rugby School; Public Schools; Holiday Hittites; Carrow
HS. 102 v Bedfordshire August 1908 @ Lakenham
BB. 1/9 v Hertfordshire August 1906 @ Lakenham
HS. 48 v West Indies August 1906 @ Lakenham
BB. 6/39 v Cambridgeshire August 1902 @ Fenner's
He Captained NCCC once in each of the seasons 1908 and 1909.
52 and 3/32 for Rugby School v Magdalene College July 1902 @ Lord's
106 no for Carrow v CEYMS July 1911
Wisden 1915 credited him with scoring a century in both innings of a minor match?
He shared the NCCC 4th wicket record stand of 139 with L Barratt v Bedfordshire in 1908.
Rugby Union for Harlequins; Norfolk County and Oxford University – Blue 1904-06
He qualified as a Solicitor in 1911. Norwich Sheriff in 1938. Clerk for Norwich Town Close Estate Charity plus Norwich Consolidated Charities Ltd. He sat as a Liberal on the Norwich City Council.
Director of Norwich Union Societies. The Norfolk & Norwich Society Secretary and Hon. Fellowship after Membership for 50 years.
F.F. – Injured at St. Quentin with his right leg being amputated in 1918.
Cozens-Hardy Road in Norwich is named after his father.

GIBSON, Edward
(b) Warrington 16 November 1883
(d) Darwen 4 October 1958
Cricket. – Lancashire Club & Ground; Norfolk Club & Ground
HS. 48 no v Cambridgeshire August 1907 @ Fenner's
BB. 8/46 v Hertfordshire July 1908 @ St. Alban's
HS. 45 v Suffolk August 1902 @ Lakenham
BB. 7/35 v London County August 1903 @ Lakenham
NCCC hat-trick v Hertfordshire 1908. Left hand bat and slow left arm bowler.
Only M Falcon, RC Rought-Rought, T Moore and C Shore grabbed more wickets then him in the Norfolk cause. He also umpired some NCCC matches after WW1. Holds the record for the most NCCC wickets v Suffolk being 101.

The 'EDP' stated that in June 1922 that he was Mine Host of Blackburn Arms in Warrington

JAMES
Cricket. – clubs unknown
HS. 2 v Quidnuncs June 1902 @ Lakenham
His one game above was even abandoned without a result with the highlight being Legh Barratt's 52.
There are no clues as to if he was a Cowboy (Jesse) or even a Comedian (Sid)!

SCOBELL, 2nd Lt. George Barton, JP
(b) Kensington, London 15 October 1875
(d) High Littleton, Somerset 19 April 1920
Educ. – Exeter College; Radley College
Cricket. – Exeter College; Radley College; Lansdown; MCC
HS. 1 v Suffolk July 1902 @ Ipswich
He played for Lansdown against DGL Astley (q.v) – the latter being in the Ishmaelites team.
JP for Somerset and a 2nd Lt. in Royal Fusiliers and the eldest son of Major Barton Scobell.
A Landed Proprieter with the family home Kingwell Hall becoming a Prep School in 1921.
The Hall was built in 1840 and inherited on George's death by his younger brother Walter who lost a leg in the Great War, was a bachelor and running a market garden at the time. He admitted that it was not suitable for his way of life.
F.F. – Probated Llandudno will bequeathed £1,821-12-7 to his widow Catharine (nee Knapp)

SHELFORD, Percy William
(b) Eveniley, Northampton OND 1877
(d) Alnwick, Northumberland 24 January 1956
Educ. – Banham GS
Cricket. – Banham GS; Quidenham Park
HS. 34 v Essex (2) June 1903 @ Leyton
BB. 1/16 v Suffolk July 1902 @ Ipswich
5/30 for Banham GS v Aldrich Bros July 1902
The 1901 Census lists him as an Assistant Schoolmaster in a Private Grammar School in Banham.
Schoolmaster at Thetford GS. Headmaster at Duke School (Alnwick)
F.F. – He left £2,775-5-8 to his widow Ethel

SHINGLER, Albert
(b) Leicester 23 November 1875
(d) Norwich 27 February 1957
Cricket.- CEYMS; Norwich Wanderers; CF Taylor's XI; Commercial Travellers; Norfolk Club & Ground; CEYMS Thursday XI
HS. 59 v Suffolk July 1904 @ Lakenham – as part of NCCC's record (at the time) 7th wicket partnership (with

Rev GB Raikes)
BB. 3/17 v Suffolk July 1908 @ Lakenham
HS. 102 v I Zingari July 1902 @ Lakenham – AR Buxton (q.v) dropped him on 26.
BB. 2/32 v Suffolk August 1902 @ Lakenham
8/43 for CEYMS v Overstrand August 1907
127 for Commercial Travellers v Old Buckenham July 1911
8/9 for CEYMS v Norwich Teachers July 1912
A Trade Shoe Designer in Leicester who came to Norwich in 1901. He joined James Southall & Co Ltd in Norwich. After WW1 he founded Shingler & Thetford Ltd – Shoe Manufacturers in Pottergate. A Member of Perseverance (Mason's Lodge)

SMITH, Edgar William
(b) Crockenhill, Kent 27 October 1876
(d) Warwick Hospital 8 August 1942
Lived 68, Gerald Avenue, Canley, Coventry
Cricket. – Norwich & London; Yarmouth
HS. 47 v Bedfordshire August 1908 @ Lakenham
BB. 9/63 v Lincolnshire August 1909 @ Lakenham
HS. 15 v London County August 1904 @ Lakenham
BB. 9/28 v London County August 1904 @ Lakenham – he conceded 9 runs before he took a wicket and took the last 7 for just 4 runs to include 6 victims in 11 balls – including the wicket of WG Grace and he earned a collection from the gathered crowd.
An habitual no 11 batsman who was difficult to dismiss based on the number of his undefeated knocks. He missed out on being in the NCCC Championship winning side in 1910 as his Norfolk career ended in 1909.
16.3-9-25-10 and 40 no (171) for Norwich & London v CEYMS
The youngest of 5 children of Richard (an Engine Driver) and Joanna. By 1911 he was a Coal Miner Hewer in Foleshill with 6 children. He became a Publican and added another 3 children to his brood with his wife Alice tragically dying during her 9th childbirth.
His eldest son Frederick gave notice of his father's demise whilst he working as a Night Watchman

1903

HOARE, Oliver Vaughan Gurney
(b) London 18 July 1882
(d) Chelsea 6 May 1957
Educ. – Harrow School (Small Houses and The Head Master's – Monitor 1899 left 1900.2); Oxford University (New College)
Cricket. – Harrow School; Sidestrand; Overstrand
HS. 19 no v Suffolk July 1903 @ Ipswich
100 no for Overstrand v Sandringham Estate August 1900
2nd son of Sir Samuel Hoare (1841-1915) and younger brother of Sir Samuel John Gurney Hoare (1st Viscount Templewood)

Rackets for Harrow School and Lawn Tennis for Oxford University (Doubles 1904).
F.F. – Oliver was a Partner of Messrs Cox & Co (Bankers)

KEYWORTH, Frederick M
(b) Calcutta, India 1884
(d) Merguy, Bengal, India 13 October 1926
On 21 April 1893 he landed on these shores with his Missionary parents having sailed from Calcutta.
Cricket. – Straits Settlement
HS. 10 v Free Foresters July 1903 @ Lakenham
His second NCCC match versus the Free Foresters was when he happened to be on the ground, so a 12-a-side match was agreed upon with EG Buxton (NCCC Secretary) playing for the opposition. His father Edwin died 7 February 1920 in Palamcottah, Madras, India.

SALISBURY W E
Cricket. – Ryburgh Reserves; Royal Naval Hospital
HS. 12 v Cambridgeshire August 1904 @ Lakenham
HS. 2 no v MCC August 1903 @ Lakenham
The NCCC oracle Dr. Stephen Musk (q.v in Curio Corner) has opted for WE as above in his copious Averages Sheets. Philip Yaxley's book 'Looking Back at Norfolk Cricket' has reproduced the scorecard from his game of a dozen runs in an innings – it has the lone initial W.
Other confusing instances are –
Sgt Salisbury for Yarmouth RA in June 1894.
P.Salisbury for Fakenham in June 1908.
E. Salisbury for RNH in August 1911.

TURNER, Revd James Frederick
(b) Enmore, Somerset 1 January 1871
(d) Cheltenham, Gloucester 11 July 1967
Lived Norton Fitzwarren, Taunton, Somerset
Educ. – Trinity School (Cavendish House); Cambridge University (Downing College – BA 1890 MA 1895)
Cricket. – Norfolk Club & Ground; Shouldham; Thorpe
HS. 9 v Essex (2) August 1903 @ Lakenham
Assistant Master King's Lynn GS 1892. Assistant Master All Saints School (Bloxham) 1892-97.
Assistant Master Ashby-de-la-Zouch School (Leicester)1897. Assistant Master Royal GS (Stroud) 1898. Ordained 1909 & Priest 1910 .Curate of St. Cuthbert's (Wells) 1909-12 . Curate of Blagdon with Charterhouse-on-Mendip 1912-14. Rector of Chelwood 1915-16. Perpetual Curate of Mark Diocese (Bath & Wells) 1916-31. Rector of Puckington with Stocklynch 1931-46
F.F. – Son of William - a Farmer with 633 acres in Denver, Norfolk

WALSH, Lt. Col Charles Herbert, DSO MC
(b) Lincoln 15 September 1882

(d) Wroxall, Isle of Wight 29 May 1965
Educ. – Wellington College (Bluchar Boarding House)
Cricket. – Norfolk Club & Ground
HS. 20 v Suffolk July 1904 @ Lakenham
BB. 1/0 v Hertfordshire August 1906 @ Lakenham
HS. 20 v London County August 1904 @ Lakenham
The 'EDP' July 1904 stated that he was studying for the Army. It was some study as his subsequent Commissions and Medals were –2nd Lt. 20 March 1907; Full Lt. 6 October 1909; Lt. Col 17 December 1914; DSO 3 June 1916 and a Military Cross 3 June 1919.
In 1st Connaught Rangers attached to Signal Service Royal Engineers – in Ireland. Commanding Officer 32nd Div. Sig. Coy in Dublin.
F.F. – He left £9,368 to his three unmarried sisters. The fate and resting place for his Medals was not declared.

WATSON, Arthur Kenelm
(b) Harrow 23 March 1867
(d) Harrow-on-The-Hill 2 January 1947
Educ. – Harrow School; Oxford University (Balliol College)
Cricket. – Harrow School; Gentlemen of England; Suffolk; Oxford University – Blue 1889; Middlesex; Oxford University Past & Present
HS. 105 v Hertfordshire August 1907 @ Lakenham
HS. 35 v London County August 1904 @ Lakenham
Father of CP (q.v) and not a relation to AC (q.v)
1st class cricket – 34 matches 847 runs 13 catches 1 wicket
His brother HD and two uncles also played first class cricket.
135 for Harrow School v Eton College July 1885 in a 2nd wicket stand of 235 with E Crawley.
61 for Oxford University in Trial Match May 1898
128 for Suffolk v Cambridgeshire August 1911
In the Suffolk side v NCCC August 1912 when his team were dismissed for 39 and 40.
He still shares the NCCC 8th wicket partnership record with RG Pilch of 152 as per the 2011 NCCC Handbook. Involved in five NCCC century partnerships.
Assistant Master Rugby School 1891-1906. Headmaster Queen Elizabeth School (Ipswich) 1906-18.
Principal of Darululum School (Bombay) 1920-27. Before 1939 he had exhibited daffodils at the Royal Horticultural Society Shows. In later life he was the Joint Secretary of the Norfolk Branch of National Playing Fields Association.
F.F. – He left £32,097-13-7 to be shared by his Schoolmaster son Charles and sister Barbara.

1904

BARTON, Major Walter John
(b) East Dereham, Norfolk 12 June 1875
(d) East Dereham, Norfolk 18 September 1948

Educ. – Haileybury College (Edmonstone 1888.2-1893.2); Cambridge University (Clare College 7 October 1893 – BA 1896)
Cricket. – Haileybury College; East Dereham
HS. 12 (x2) v Hertfordshire July 1904 @ Watford
BB. 1/23 v Hertfordshire July 1904 @ Watford
HS. 17 v Free Foresters July 1904 @ Lakenham
Father of AW (q.v)
Partner of Barton & Sons (Solicitors). A Lt. 2nd Vol. Serv. Co Norfolk Regiment in South African War.
Made Captain 5 August 1914 of 1/5 Batt. Norfolk Regiment and promoted November 1914 to Major serving in Gallipoli, Egypt and Sinai Peninsula. Latterly a Church Warden, a Coroner and Clerk to Magistrates. He married a Norwegian girl Karin Leverin in 1910

FELLOWES, The Hon. Reginald Ailwyn, JP
(b) Marylebone, London 20 January 1884
(d) Donnington Grove, Newbury, Berkshire 19 March 1953
Lived 69 Rue de Lille, Paris
Educ. – Eton College
Cricket. – Eton College; AE Fellowes' XI; East Dereham
HS. 5 v Suffolk July 1904 @ Felixstowe
HS. 15 no v Free Foresters July 1904 @ Lakenham
F.F. – Son of Lord de Ramsay he married Daisy Marguerite Severine Phillippine Decazes de Glucksberg – the heiress to the Singer Sewing Machine fortune. She was a 20th Century fashion icon and society figure who was additionally the Editor-in-Chief of the French 'Harper's Bazaar'. RA was a Banker cousin of Sir Winston Churchill

GARNIER, Revd George Ronald
(b) Titsey, Oxted, Surrey 8 March 1880
(d) Shropham Hall, Norfolk 9 March 1948
Educ. – Sherborne School; Oxford University (Oriel College – BA 1902 MA 1906); Wells Theological College
Cricket. – Sherborne School; Oxford University (Freshman's match 1900); Quidenham Parsonage.
HS. 36 v Hertfordshire July 1904 @ Watford
Brother of ET (q.v) and Uncle of EHC (q.v)
His Father ES and Grandfather TP both played first class cricket and gained cricket blues from Oxford. Athletics for Oxford University as a Hurdler – Blue 1900-02
WW1 – RASC Driver who was invalided out 1st battle of Somme. WW1 Pensions has him in the Army Reserve in Attleborough. Ordained 1904 & Priest 1905. Curate of Benfield 1904-09. Vicar of Lenham 1909-14. Rector of Garboldisham 1914-19.

HOSKEN, John Fayrer
(b) Islington, London 25 November 1877
(d) St. George's Hospital, London 6 February 1962

Lived 27 South Eaton Place, London SW1
Educ. – Warren Hill Prep School
Cricket. – Gunton; Overstrand
HS. 3 v Hertfordshire July 1904 @ Watford
90 for Overstrand v RG Pilch's X1 August 1911
Son of Richard (Clergyman) and Ann Caroline Fayrer. His brother CCF is listed on the Cricket Archive website as playing cricket for Highgate School.
F.F. – He left £7,270-16-8 to his married sister Jacqueline and her husband Raymond Brett-Holt.

KENNAWAY, 2nd Lt. Arthur Lewis
(b) Garboldisham, Norfolk 16 June 1881
(d) On the Heights above Suvla Bay, Turkey 21 August 1915
Lived Sherborne, Dorset with his will giving his death as at Gallipoli.
Educ. – Eton College (Rev Sydney Rhodes James's and Herbert Francis William Tatham's Houses); Oxford University (Oriel College – BA 1903); Wells Theological College
Cricket. – Norfolk Club & Ground; MCC; Garboldisham Manor; Eton Ramblers
HS. 7 v Buckinghamshire August 1904 @ Aylesbury
Son of CL (q,v)
At Wells Theological College where he studied before deciding to take holy orders. He later decided that the Church was not his true vocation and therefore entered upon the study of Land Agency.
His first experience in this business was on the Culford Estate of the Earl of Cadogan followed by working for RH Eden of Sherborne, Dorset. He became a Partner in Eden, Baines and Kennaway (Land Agents)
F.F. – At the outbreak of the European War he held a commission in the Dorset Yeomanry

WILTSHIRE, Sir Frank Herbert Cafande, MC
(b) Bradwell, Gt Yarmouth, Norfolk 27 November 1881
(d) Surrey 19 March 1949
Educ. – Yarmouth GS; Felsted School
Cricket. – Yarmouth GS; Felsted School; Public Schools; Lowestoft; Yarmouth Fifteen
HS. 1 v Hertfordshire July 1904 @ Watford
Brother of CJ (q.v)
6/9 for Yarmouth GS v Winchester House June 1894
7/11 for Lowestoft v Norwich Teachers July 1899
Admitted Solicitor 1908 and working in Yarmouth to 1918
The Birmingham Town Clerk October 1919 to November 1946 and the Clerk of Peace 1937-46.
Solicitor to Birmingham (Tame & Rea District) Drainage Board 1919-46. Hon. Freeman City of Birmingham 18 October 1947.
Vice President Institute of Public Administration. Judge in Alderney from November 1947 and involved with the States of Alderney and Guernsey being linked.

1905

BROWN, Harold Ethelwald
(b) Brixworth, Northampton 19 June 1882
(d) Heath Road Wing, Ipswich & East Suffolk Hospital 26 June 1960
Lived Swan Meadow, Westerfield, Suffolk
Educ. – Wellingborough GS
Cricket. – clubs unknown
HS. 0 v Suffolk July 1905 @ Lakenham
Son of Jacob (Schoolmaster) and Marion Cole (Schoolmistress).
Vice-President Geographical & Scientific Society at Framlingham College. Schoolmaster of the Upper Fourth at Framlingham College. He was unorthodox to the point of eccentricity as he scorned text-books, and all his Geography lessons resolved into a detailed study, with diagrams, of Fenner's Cricket Ground. Long after his teaching days were over he joined the Choir in the annual Carol Service. He was well known for his pre-calculator management of the Tuck Shop.

CHARLES, Lt. Col Stephen Flockton
(b) Romford, Essex 17 August 1858
(d) Wroxham House, Norfolk 24 June 1950
Lived in Wroxham House for over 40 years
Educ. – Harrow School (The Headmaster's 1872.2 –1876.2); RMC Sandhurst
Cricket. – Harrow School; MCC; Gentlemen; Army; CEYMS; Westminster Wanderers; Cheshire; Western; Gentlemen of MCC.
HS. 54 v Oxfordshire August 1906 @ Oxford
HS. 31 v Free Foresters July 1906 @ Lakenham
1st class cricket – 8 matches 43 runs 10 victims (5c 5s)
Captained NCCC in 4 matches.
43 for Westminster Wanderers v MCC August 1877
34 (76) for Cheshire v Staffordshire May 1881
A wicket keeper with his best NCCC season being 1906 (12c 7s) in all matches.
Adjutant to Auxiliary Forces 1890. Commanded the 20th Lancashire Fusiliers (1st Batt) in the West Indies. He had a private funeral with no flowers, no letters nor mourners as per his wish.

DUNELL, 2nd Lt. Owen Henry Christian
(b) Paddington, London 20 October 1886
(d) West Malling, Kent 13 September 1950
Educ. – Eton College; Trinity College
Cricket. – Eton College; Garboldisham Manor; Eastern Province; Suffolk Borderers; Eton Ramblers.
HS. 75 v Bedfordshire July 1908 @ Bedford
BB. 5/27 v Bedfordshire August 1909 @ Lakenham – his

only wickets for NCCC
HS.11 v Harrow Wanderers August 1907 @ Lakenham
His father Owen (1856-1929) played Test cricket for South Africa.
A 2nd Lt. RGA in France & Italy being awarded the Croce di Guerra (an Italian decoration for military valour). He had business interests in Port Elizabeth, South Africa

DUNNING, Cyril Edward
(b) Colby, Norfolk 20 February 1888
(d) Paston, Norfolk 11 January 1962
Educ. – Bracondale School; Mundesley
Cricket. – North Walsham; Norfolk Club & Ground; Overstrand
HS. 99 v Cambridgeshire August 1908 @ Lakenham
BB. 1/13 v Bedfordshire July 1908 @ Bedford
HS. 76 no v Free Foresters July 1908 @ Lakenham
BB. 1/19 v Essex (2) June 1910 @ Norwich CEYMS
The second of three NCCC players to be dismissed for 99.
140 no for North Walsham v Norfolk County Asylum July 1908
His batting average for North Walsham in one season was 383 as he was not dismissed in 10 innings.
He featured in five century partnerships in 1908, a record to this point.
Football. – Bracondale School; Mundesley; Cromer; Norwich City FC; Tulse Hill; Chelmsford; Norfolk County 1906-09 (5 apps –5 goals); Peterborough; England Amateur International – 5 caps
His first job was in a London Stockbroking firm.
F.F. – *His father Edward specialised in breaking and training horses one of which, it was said, was sold to the then Shah of Persia for £750 in the early 1900's. A Farming Family with Cyril taking up Poultry Farming at River Mount, Knapton and until his death in 1962 he had spent the last forty years farming at Paston.*

FELLOWES, Lt. Col Ronald Townshend, DSO MC DL (2nd Baron Ailwyn)
(b) Stratton Street, Piccadilly, London 7 December 1886
(d) Norwich 30 August 1936
Died of wounds received during WW1 and buried 2 September 1936 in Ipswich.
Educ. – Eton College; RMC Sandhurst
Cricket. – Eton College; RMC Sandhurst; Free Foresters; Norfolk Club & Ground; RT Fellowes' XI.
HS. 33 v Free Foresters July 1905 @ Lakenham
Son of AE (q.v)
Gained the rank of officer in 1907 in the service of The Rifle Brigade (his headstone bears the inscription Rifle Brigade 1886-1936). Gentleman Cadet Ian Fleming (creator of James Bond) served under the Major the Lord Ailwyn in No. 5 Company at Newport Pagnell. He was gazetted MC on 22 June 1915;

appointed Deputy Assistant Adjutant and Quartermaster-General with effect from 22 September 1915; acting Major while commanding a Battalion with effect from 17 August 1916; in March 1920 he was appointed to the War Office as a General Staff Officer. Deputy Assistant Adjutant – General Southern Command 1924 rising to Lt. Col in 1928

MASTER, Humphrey Claude
(b) Thingoe, Suffolk 3 October 1880
(d) Norwich 7 May 1943
Educ. – Haileybury College (Hailey House 1894.3-1898.2)
Cricket. – Hailey House; Norwich Old Public School Boys; Langham; CMG Heslop's XI; CF Taylor's XI; CEYMS; Norfolk Club & Ground; Elmham Hall; Easton Ramblers; Marquis of Graham's XI; S Hill-Wood's XI; Norwich Wanderers; Carrow; Holliday Hittites; Cpt Long's XI ; Commercial Travellers; Wensum CC; WJ Blake's XI.
HS. 16 no v Hertfordshire August 1905 @ Lakenham
HS. 43 v L. Robinson's XI June 1911 @ Norwich CEYMS
Son of HH (q.v)
150 for CEYMS v Blofield August 1901
5/13 for CEYMS v Norfolk County Asylum May 1908
209 no for CEYMS v Wensum CC June 1908
Chairman NCCC Committee 1925-39. Chairman & Managing Director of Ranson's Ltd (Timber Merchants). A Press summation of him – "a free batsman and a very good field."
F.F. – Probated Norwich will bequeathing £9,637-8-1 to his widow Violet

STARLING, George
(b) Norwich 24 July 1880
(d) Lowestoft, Suffolk 2 January 1951
Cricket. – HL Horsfall's XI; CEYMS; Norwich GPO
HS. 74 v Suffolk July 1906 @ Felixtowe – sharing a 101 run partnership for the 7th wicket with LH Leman
BB. 5/39 v Cambridgeshire August 1905 @ Lakenham
HS. 1 v MCC August 1905 @ Lakenham
BB. 2/24 v MCC August 1905 @ Lakenham
115 for CEYMS v Gunton August 1899
9/14 for CEYMS v Harleston August 1904
5/0 for CEYMS v Commercial Travellers July 1912
Captain in the Norfolk Regiment 1914-18

STEVENS, George
(b) South Bersted, Bognor, Sussex 20 December 1867
(d) Gaywood, King's Lynn 28 March 1957
Educ. – King's Lynn GS
Cricket. – King's Lynn; Alton; Norfolk Club & Ground ; Bath; Gloucester; Alnwick; Duke's School (Alnwick).
HS. 58 v Bedfordshire July 1907 @ Bedford
BB. 6/56 v Suffolk July 1909 @ Lakenham
HS. 36 v Free Foresters July 1906 @ Lakenham

BB. 2/67 v Harrow Wanderers July 1909 @ Lakenham
Shared, at the time, a record 117 run partnership v Bedfordshire in 1907 with the unrelated GA Stevens
10/28 (9 bowled) for Alnwick v Northumberland County & Ground August 1903
King Edward VII Groundsman for 41 years
Dr EM Grace once wrote of George – "no one knows better to prepare a first class pitch."
F.F. – His Probated will saw his widow Melita receive £1,055-12s

STEVENS, Major Norman Walter, MB ChB
(b) Norwich 7 October 1887
(d) Colaba Military Hospital, Bombay, India 27 July 1919
Lived 104 Thorpe Road, Norwich. Died of Enteric Fever
Educ. – Norwich GS; Edinburgh University
Cricket. – Norwich GS; CEYMS; Old Norvicensians
HS. 57 v Berkshire August 1910 @ Lakenham
HS. 3 v Free Foresters July 1905 @ Lakenham AND 3 v Harrow Wanderers July 1909 @ Lakenham
Brother of GA (q.v) and GS (q.v)
68 for Norwich GS v Ipswich School June 1903
In Royal Army Medical Corp with successive promotions of Lt. 26 July 1912, Captain 30 March 1915 to Brevet Major 3 June 1917

1906

BIRKBECK, Capt Gervase William
(b) Bixley 20 April 1886
(d) Gaza, Palestine 19 April 1917
In 1912 at Wood Farm, Sprowston, Norfolk
Educ. – Ludgrove School; Eton College; Cambridge University (Trinity College)
Cricket. – Eton College; Trinity College
HS. 118 v Bedfordshire July 1912 @ Bedford
BB. 2/11 v Cambridgeshire August 1911 @ King's Lynn
HS. 38 no v Essex (2) June 1910 @ Colchester
BB. 3/13 v Free Foresters July 1908 @ Lakenham
Son of H (q.v)
He was taken prisoner by the Turks April 1917 and was thought to have been shot.
Part of Gurney's, Birkbeck, Barclay & Buxton Banking Family. He was in the Banking business at their Peterborough Branch. In 1/5th Norfolks (the vanished Battalion). In December 1916 he was the only remaining officer of the original 1/5ths He left England on the 'Aquitania' and he was detailed for duty as the Embarkation Officer until the final evacuation to rejoin the Battalion.
F.F. – Did you know that related to the Birkbeck family are – Robert Hobart – Hobart, Tasmania named after him. He is an 8th cousin, 4 times removed.
Robert Le Roy Parker (aka Butch Cassidy). He is a 6th cousin,

9 times removed

George Orwell. He is a 12th cousin, once removed

CAMPBELL, Gerald Vincent

(b) Kensington, London 29 April 1884

(d) Delmere House, Lymington, Hampshire 26 March 1950

Educ. – Eton College

Cricket. – Eton College; Europeans; Surrey; MCC; House of Commons South; Sussex Martlets; Suffolk Borderers; South London.

HS. 9 v Hertfordshire June 1906 @ Watford – after a first ball dismissal in his opening innings

BB. 1/35 v Hertfordshire June 1906 @ Watford

1st class cricket – 2 matches 16 runs

50 no for Suffolk Borderers v Scots Greys August 1904

His brother HG played first class cricket for the Royal Navy.

CATOR, Christopher Arthur Mohun

(b) Coates, Gloucester 25 January 1881

(d) Landguard Manor, Shanklin, Isle of Wight 6 December 1923

Educ. – Eton College (Easter 1894 – Election 1898)

Cricket. – Norfolk Club & Ground; Woodbastwick; Elmham Hall

Son of Edward Cator (NCCC 1869-1871)

HS. 0 v Free Foresters July 1906 @ Lakenham

'The Montreal Gazette' dated 10 December 1923 revealed the following –

"A Stockbroker out of Vancouver (he sailed to Halifax, Canada on 18 February 1920 with the Ship's Register disclosing that he was a Financial Gentleman). He was back in England staying with his brother and he went out shooting but did not return. His brother found the body with a head wound with the gun lying on the body. The Coroner ruled the cause of death to be as a result of an accidental discharge of the gun. The body was found on rough ground in a covert and the brother thought that he must have stumbled."

FALCON, Michael, LLB MP JP

(b) Horstead Hall, Norfolk 21 July 1888

(d) Cathedral Close, Norwich 27 February 1976

Educ. – Suffield Park Prep School; Harrow School (Mr Rendall's House); Cambridge University (Pembroke College 21 October 1907 - BA 1910)

Cricket. – Cambridge University – Blue 1908-11; MCC; Oxford & Cambridge Universities; Free Foresters; England XI; L Robinson's XI; CI Thornton's XI; PF Warner's XI; HDG Leveson-Gower's XI; Harrow School; Harrow Wanderers; Old Harrovians; Incogniti; I Zingari; House of Commons North; M Falcon's XI (1907 when the 3 brothers played together for the only time); Perambulators; Gentlemen; GL Pilch's XI; Old Buckenham Hall; Minor Counties; Minor Counties

North; Norwich Union; Yarmouth; FG Mann's XI; RT Fellowes' XI; Overstrand; East Norfolk; CEYMS; Norfolk Club & Ground; Gidea Park; RA Young's XI.

HS. 205 v Hertfordshire July 1920 @ Cheshunt

BB. 8/41 v Bedfordshire August 1923 @ King's Lynn

HS. 102 no v Harrow Wanderers August 1907 @ Lakenham

BB. 7/37 v Eton Ramblers August 1922 @ Lakenham

Brother of JH (q.v) and Son-in-law of CGO Gascoigne (q.v)

1st class cricket – 89 matches 3,282 runs 44 catches and 231 wickets

The man is a Legend and those in the know reckon that he could have played in Test Matches but he chose to stay with NCCC. A look at the Averages Section shows that there are too many games and feats to cover. There is enough material for a book – and one has been published. See 'Lives in Cricket. Michael Falcon Norfolk's Gentleman Cricketer' (2010) by Stephen Musk.

Horning & District CC President. In November 1911 called to the Bar by the Inner Temple. Barrister at Law. NCCC Captain for a 1910 Friendly and from 1912-46; Chairman 1950-69, President 1969-71. NCCC Hon Life Vice President. The High Sheriff of Norfolk 1943-44 and JP for the County and also Essex. Unionist MP for East Norfolk 1918-23. Norfolk Territorial Artillery serving in France, Egypt and Palestine. Director of the Yarmouth Brewery firm E. Lacon & Co. Ltd and its Chairman 1941-63. Director of the Life Insurance Society 1935 and of the Fire Society 1936. Vice-President of the Life Society 1948 and of the Fire Society 1958. He also played Football & Rugby Union for Harrow School

JACKSON, Geoffrey Russell

(b) Kensington, London 9 May 1887

(d) Barberton, Transvaal, South Africa 4 December 1940

Educ. – Haileybury College (Lawrence House 1902.3 – 1906.2)

Cricket. – Haileybury College

HS. 16 v Cambridgeshire August 1907 @ Fenner's

HS. 4 v West Indies August 1906 @ Lakenham

69 for Haileybury College v Cheltenham College August 1906 @ Lord's

A School Prefect and Captain at Cricket, Rugby Union, Rackets and Fives.

Just like his Australian father he was a wanderer turning up in Geldeston, Sussex, Oxford and Ceylon.

F.F. – He left just £230-15-3 in his Probated will.

PRIOR, Capt Charles Bolingbroke Leathes, JP

(b) Bury St. Edmunds 28 January 1883

(d) Norwich 5 January 1964

Educ. – Felsted School; Haileybury College (Bartle Frere & Lawrence I louse 1897.1-1900.2)

Cricket. – Felsted School; Haileybury College; Dr. Prior's

XI; CEYMS; Eastern Counties; TW Breed's XI; CF Taylor's XI; Norwich Old Public Schoolboys; Langham; CMG Heslop's XI.
HS. 20 v Old Buckenham Hall July 1911 @ Old Buckenham Hall
BB. 1/14 v Old Buckenham Hall July 1911 @ Old Buckenham Hall
NCCC Member from 1893, Committee 1906, Hon. Sec 1910, Committee Chairman 1937- 1954,
NCCC Chairman 1946-49 and President 1956 – so connected to the club for over 60 years . Editor of 'The Norfolk Cricket Annual' 1909/10 & 1910/11. JP for the period 1940-1957 and the Official Receiver in Bankruptcy 1922 to 15 July 1937 dealing with 849 cases. Norwich City FC Chairman. The Chairman of F. Lambert & Sons Ltd 1930-37. Vice-Chairman of Norwich Branch of Discharged Prisoners. He bought and became the Chairman of the firm Girling & Ransome (Tea & Tobacco Merchant).
F.F. – The Beneficiaries of his £12,281 will were his son James and a Reverend.

STEVENS, Geoffrey Alden, AICE
(b) Norwich 25 October 1890
(d) Norwich 24 March 1963
Educ. – Norwich GS
Cricket. – Norwich GS; Old Norvicensians; Minor Counties; L. Robinson's XI; GA Stevens' XI; Norwich Wanderers; Commercial Travellers; Holiday Hittites; Cpt Long's XI.
HS. 222 v Bedfordshire August 1920 @ Lakenham – this was more than the opposition's total in the game (84 & 109)
BB. 1/15 v Hertfordshire July 1911 @ St. Albans
HS. 1 v Free Foresters July 1908 @ Lakenham
Father of BGW (q.v) . Brother of GS (q.v) and NW (q.v)
1st class cricket – 3 matches 56 runs 6 catches
Coached by GJ Rye (q.v) who declared that GA was the best school prospect that he had seen.
256 for Norwich GS v Ipswich School June 1908 and as a 17 year old he scored 2,831 runs in the season.
201 for NCCC v Berkshire in 1910 Challenge Match.
202 no for Commercial Travellers v Yarmouth Conservatives July 1911
He did not play in 1919 when his brother NW died. Involved in 14 Century partnerships for NCCC.
The first NCCC player to score 2 double hundreds (feat equalled later by DF Walker).
One of 6 NCCC men to have been dismissed in the 90s more than twice .In the two Minor County matches v Buckinghamshire in 1927 NCCC completed innings' totals were 94,48,36 and 61. In the latter total GA scored an incredible 41(61) to represent 67.2% of the runs – no one has bettered that feat since for NCCC. He was also the NCCC Secretary 1952-61.
Served in France with the Royal Engineers. Qualified Associate Institute of Civil Engineers. Retired his position as Senior

Engineers Assistant in Norwich City Engineers Office on 30 October 1951. His last job being his involvement on the Yare Valley Main Drainage System.
F.F. – His Probated Norwich will 26 June 1963 left £22,582-18-7 to be divided between his widow Mabel, his Journalist son BGW and Thomas Stevenson (Sport's Outfitter)

WATLING, Ralph George
(b) Yarmouth, Norfolk 12 September 1872
(d) Ormesby St. Margaret, Norfolk 10 May 1951
Educ. – Harrow School
Cricket. – Yarmouth; Hethersett; Royal Naval Hospital; Morley Hall; South Norfolk
HS. 33 v Hertfordshire June 1906 @ Watford
HS. 15 v Free Foresters July 1906 @ Lakenham
6/8 for Hethersett v Norman & Beards May 1895
Joined his father's firm RA Watling's (Corn Merchants) at age 16. During 1914-18 in defiance of the law he replaced the men who had been called up by women to keep the Maltings open. The Home Office changed the law as a result of his actions. An outstanding Yachtsman at Acle Regatta winning the Yarmouth Gold Cup (3 times) and the Bezor Cup outright. In 1902 and 1903 he won the All England Badminton Singles Championship and he was the losing finalist in 1901 and 1905
F.F. – His business acumen enabled him to leave £137,875-1-5 to various interested parties.

WATSON, Col Arthur Campbell, DSO
(b) Henfold, Surrey 17 March 1884
(d) Shermanbury , Horsham, Sussex 16 January 1952
Educ. – Uppingham School
Cricket. – Uppingham School; Essex; Sussex
HS. 68 v Free Foresters July 1906 @ Lakenham
1st class cricket – 106 matches 2,724 runs 37 catches 5 wickets His highest career score of 111 for Sussex v Northants in June 1922 was achieved from a no.10 batting position as he helped add 73 and 95 for the last two wickets.

1907

ALLSOPP, Sgt Thomas Charlesworth
(b) Leicester 18 December 1880
(d) Norwich 7 March 1919
Cricket. – Leicestershire; CEYMS; Caley's; HL Horsfall's XI; Norfolk Club & Ground; MCC.
HS. 69 no v Bedfordshire August 1910 @ Lakenham
BB. 6/43 v Durham July 1910 @ King's Lynn
HS. 52 v Harrow Wanderers August 1907 @ Lakenham
BB. 4/45 v Free Foresters July 1907 @ Lakenham
1st class cricket – 37 matches 347 runs 10 catches 88 wickets Took 55 wickets for NCCC in 1910 season
106 (152) for Caley's v Carrow August 1907

79 for Norfolk Club & Ground v Harrow Wanderers July 1908
Football. – Leicester Fosse; Luton Town; Brighton & Hove Albion;
Norwich City FC 1 June 1907 to 1911
The only man to play football and cricket for Leicester/Norwich
and Leicestershire /Norfolk
He joined the Royal Garrison Artillery in 1916 winning
his stripes with the 126th Labour Battalion and he was
demobilized from France. He caught influenza on the boat
coming home and in less than a week had died at the City
Arms, Redwell Street, Norwich where he was the Landlord. His
second wife Edith took over the licensee and shame to say that
she had a conviction on 20 April 1927 for failing to admit the
police to the premises.

BUXTON, RN Commander Bernard, DSO
(b) Blofield, Norfolk 21 October 1882
(d) Hoveton Hall, Norwich 29 December 1923
Educ. – Cheam School; Naval Staff College
Cricket. – MCC
HS. 35 no v Cambridgeshire August 1907 @ Lakenham
Son of Lt. Col Geoffrey Fowell Buxton and Lady Hermione
Grimston – she the daughter of the 3rd Earl of Verulam.
He rose dramatically from being just a Midshipman in 1901
serving on the 'HMS Britannia' in Crete, Greece. Mentioned in
despatches in WW1 and he was also decorated with the award
of Order of the Sacred Treasure of Japan and he joined the
Admiralty in 1918
F.F. – Sadly his 4 children had died by 1979

STEPHENS, Vivian
(b) Finchley, London November 1888
(d) Kelowna, British Columbia, Canada 16 June 1914
Educ. – Uppingham School (Lorne House September 1903
– April 1906)
Cricket. – Uppingham School; CEYMS; Norfolk Club &
Ground
HS. 25 v Suffolk June 1908 @ Ipswich
HS. 14 v Free Foresters July 1907 @ Lakenham
A wicket keeper he was picked for his third game but he injured
himself before the start.
40 for Uppingham School v Haileybury College July 1905.
In the 1911 Census he was a visitor at the Waldorf Hotel
in London with his occupation listed as a Herring Fishing
Employer.

THURGAR, Capt Ralph William, MC
(b) Brundall, Norfolk 28 September 1890
(d) Gaza 19 April 1917
Educ. – Norwich GS
Cricket. – Norwich GS; Old Norvensians; CEYMS; Norwich
Union; Old Buckenham Hall; Suffolk (as a substitute fielder);
Sir Blake's XI

HS. 155 v Cambridgeshire August 1913 @ Fenner's
HS. 68 v Essex (2) June 1910 @ Lakenham
Son of WA (q.v)
A fine wicket keeper with his best season for dismissals being in
1911 (14 c 13 s)
He featured in three NCCC century partnerships and was
reckoned to never be a rapid scorer but he had a good defence
106 for Sir Blake's XI v Norwich GS July 1911
67 for Norwich Union v Norfolk County Asylum July 1912
Wisden 1917 stated that he was reported wounded and
missing.
Football. – CEYMS; Norfolk County 1909-14 (26 apps) –
awarded a Silver medal in 1913 for his service. A Capt 1st/4th
Batt. Norfolk Regiment

1908

FOWLER, Sir Ralph Howard, OBE FRS
(b) Fedsden, Roydon, Essex 17 January 1889
(d) Trumpington, Cambridgeshire 28 July 1944
Educ. – Evans Prep School; Winchester College; Cambridge
University (Trinity College – BA 1911 MA 1915)
Cricket. – Winchester College; Holiday Hittites
HS. 53 v Lincolnshire August 1909 @ Lakenham
His father and two uncles played first class cricket.His sister
Dorothy was a Champion Golfer.
WW1 in Royal Marine Artillery being wounded in the shoulder
in Gallipoli. He studied Thermodynamics, Statistical Mechanics
and Ballistics being in the Experimental Department of HMS
Excellent on Whale Island in Portsmouth Harbour. Assistant
Director Anti-Aircraft Experimental Society Munitions. He
transferred from being a Pure Mathematician prior to WW1
to Physicist & Engineer visiting Professorships at Princeton and
the University of Wisconsin. On the Ordnance Board and he
became a College Lecturer in Mathematics in 1920. Proctor
at Cambridge in 1922 producing papers on Spectroscopy.
A Plummer Professor of Applied Maths in University of
Cambridge from 1932 and a Director of National Physics Lab
in 1938
F.F. – He published – 'Differential Geometry of Plane
Curves'. He married Eileen the daughter of Lord Rutherford.
Where was he when I needed help with the Batting &
Bowling Averages!

GASCOIGNE, Capt Clifton Charles Orby
(b) Middlesex, London 7 March 1870
(d) Ipswich 30 June 1940
Died following an operation
Educ. – Windlesham School; MCC
Cricket. – Yarmouth; Catton Village; Ipswich & East Suffolk
HS. 0 v Bedfordshire July 1908 @ Bedford
HS. 5 v Free Foresters July 1908 @ Lakenham

Father-in-Law of M Falcon (q.v)
MCC v NCCC August 1912 @ Gt. Yarmouth saw Michael Falcon clean bowl his future Father-in-Law.
He married Sybil Mary Clive the daughter of General Edward Henry Clive and he bequeathed her £3,561-15-3. A Captain in the Seaforth Highlanders. Secretary of Norfolk Territorial Forces Association

MAYES, Arthur Robert
(b) King's Lynn 26 October 1885
(d) Norwich 7 March 1911
Educ. – King's Lynn GS
Cricket. – King's Lynn GS; Mid Norfolk; East Dereham; Billingford; Norfolk Club & Ground
HS. 21 v Suffolk June 1908 @ Ipswich
128 for King's Lynn GS v YMCA July 1901
From a family of seven children he was latterly a Billingford Farmer

STEVENS, George Southall
(b) Norwich 21 August 1883
(d) Norwich 10 February 1956
Cricket. – CEYMS; Evershed's XI
HS. 18 v Suffolk June 1909 @ Woodbridge
HS. 20 v Free Foresters July 1908 @ Lakenham
Brother of GA (q.v) and NW (q.v)
64 for Evershed's XI v Gresham's School in 1905
Football. – CEYMS; Norfolk County 1904-10 (9 apps)
Died after working for 50 years as a Solicitor. Worked for his father's firm Stevens, Miller & Jones.
The Norwich City Coroner for one year being 1941. In 1942 he joined Messers Rackham & Robinson to his demise

WHARTON, Corp Thomas Henry
(b) Gt. Bircham, Norfolk 10 June 1889
(d) Gommecourt, France 3 July 1916
Lived Bircham, King's Lynn
Educ. – Norwich Middle School; King's Lynn GS; Wellingborough GS
Cricket. – King's Lynn GS; Wellingborough GS; Gt. Bircham; West Norfolk; Hunstanton; Norfolk Club & Ground
HS. 46 v Hertfordshire August 1908 @ Lakenham – in a 3rd wicket stand of 129 with GA Stevens
BB. 2/38 v Hertfordshire August 1908 @ Lakenham
HS. 17 v Essex (2) June 1910 @ Colchester
110 no for Wellingborough GS v Bedford Modern School June 1905
93 & 48 for Norfolk Club & Ground v Harrow Wanderers 1908
A Farmer in Ringstead. In the 9th Batt. Essex Regiment
F.F. – His Probated London will dated 25 July 1917 saw him leave £900-11-8 to his sister Annie.

1909

DURRANT, Charles Edward
(b) King's Lynn 28 February 1888
(d) Upwell, Cambridgeshire 24 October 1932
Cricket. – Hunstanton; West Norfolk
HS. 26 V Cambridgeshire August 1909 @ King's Lynn
His father was a Steam Engine Driver
F.F. – Probated Will left £3,207-8-1.

FARMER, George Adderley Herbert
(b) Paddington, London 27 September 1889
(d) Porterville, Tulare County, California, U.S.A 21 August 1932
Educ. – St. Paul's School
Cricket. – St. Paul's School; MCC
HS. 1 v Cambridgeshire July 1909 @ Newmarket
HS. 26 v Harrow Wanderers July 1909 @ Lakenham
54 for St. Paul's School v Bedford GS June 1908
He made 3 sailings from the UK to New York with the last arrival 24 August 1928.
F.F. – His father James was a Scottish born Solicitor who married a Bahamian. George was on a Ship's Manifest as being in Real Estate

HORSFALL, Thomas Harry Stewart
(b) Chevening, Kent 4 April 1890
(d) West Suffolk Hospital, Bury St. Edmunds 24 August 1967
Cricket. – clubs unknown
HS. 6 (x 2) v Hertfordshire August 1909 @ Lakenham – his score in both innings
HS. 33 v Harrow Wanderers July 1909 @ Lakenham
BB. 1/15 v Harrow Wanderers July 1909 @ Lakenham
Even at his birth his father Henry Leake Horsfall was a man of independent means. Thomas' death was attributed to Carcinomatosis and he was a Farmer living at Hinderclay Hall, Thedwastre

LORD, E
Cricket. – CEYMS; Norwich & London; YMCA; RG Pilch's XI.
HS. 3 no v Suffolk July 1909 @ Lakenham
BB. 1/8 v Suffolk July 1909 @ Lakenham
18 no (56) for YMCA v CEYMS July 1908 – carrying his bat as GA Stevens scored 122 not out for the opposition.
23 (41) for YMCA v Carrow August 1911
More information is needed for this gentleman – does any reader know of him?

MEYRICK-JONES, Revd Frederic (September 1893 changed his name to Frederic Meyrick Meyrick-Jones)
(b) Blackheath, Kent 14 January 1867
(d) Shaftesbury, Dorset 25 October 1950

Educ. – Marlborough College; Cambridge University (Trinity College 8 October 1885 – BA 1889)

Cricket. – Marlborough College; Cambridge University – Blue 1888); Hampshire; Home Place; FM Meyrick-Jones XI; Elstree Masters; Kent; Eton Ramblers; WG Grace's XI; WC Bridgeman's XI; Cambridge University Next XVI; Gentlemen of Hampshire

HS. 46 no v Suffolk June 1909 @ Woodbridge

1st class cricket – 18 matches 512 runs 2 wickets also an occasional wicket keeper – (9c 2s)

137 for Home Place v Gresham's School July 1911

142 recorded matches for Eton Ramblers.

160 no for Elstree Masters v Eton Ramblers June 1890 – 3 small boys spent many hot, but undoubtedly healthy, hours in retrieving the ball from the abutting shrubberies, hayfields and outhouses, whither M-J smote it at will and with impartial nonchalance.

Ordained 1890 & Priest 1892. Curate Elstree 1890-93. Assistant Master Elstree School 1894-96.

Curate of St. Agnes (Bristol) 1896-9. Headmaster Rugby School Mission 1898-1905.

Latterly a Head of a Private School in Holt. An Antiquarian of some note per his Wisden Obituary 1951

MITCHELL, Lewis George
(b) Kirby Bredon, Norfolk 29 April 1882

(d) Cringleford, Norwich 3 February 1969

Cricket. – Norwich Union; Norwich Union Fire Office

HS. Did not Bat nor Bowl v Bedfordshire June 1909 @ Bedford – play only lasted for 41 overs

HS. 7 (x2) v Essex (2) June 1910 @ Colchester

BB. 1/11 v Essex (2) June 1910 @ Colchester

Father of G (q.v)

5/25 for Norwich Union v Norwich United July 1900

Athletics for Norfolk County being a Half Mile & Mile Champion in 1904

Son of a London born Dairy Farmer

SMITH, Lt Cuthbert Bede
(b) Lewisham, London 5 October 1879

(d) Little Common, Bexhill-on-Sea, East Sussex 22 August 1963

Educ. – Haileybury College (Batten House 1892.3 – 1898.2)

Cricket. – Haileybury College; CF Taylor's XI; F Keppel's XI; JB Gillam's XI; Kent XV; Rest XV; Kent 2nds; CEYMS

HS. 41 v Suffolk August 1911 @ Lakenham

HS. 14 v L Robinson's XI June 1911 @ Norwich CEYMS

79 no (164) for Haileybury College v Uppingham College June 1898 – as an opener carrying his bat

100 no for Haileybury College v Cheltenham College July 1898

90 no for CEYMS v Lowestoft July 1911

The 'Haileybury and Imperial Service College Register Vol 1'

(1862-1911) states that he was selected for England but he was unable to play through his illness!

Lt in Norfolk Regiment. Worked at the Trunch Brewery

F.F. – He left £36,381-1s in his will.

TAYLOR, 2nd Lt Ronald Francis
(b) Harleston, Norfolk 29 February 1888

(d) Suvla Bay, Turkey 8 August 1915

Lived in Parish of Starston where is father Alfred was a Landowner

Educ. – St. Andrews (Eastbourne); Malvern College; RMC Sandhurst

Cricket. – Malvern College; Aliens

HS. 8 v Suffolk June 1909 @ Woodbridge

49 no (106) for Aliens v Malvern College June 1913

Assistant Master at St. Andrews (Eastbourne). He joined the firm Osler's in Birmingham prior to WW1

In 5th Batt. King's Shropshire Light Infantry and he was killed by a bursting shell.

TREGLOWN, Lt. Col Claude Jesse Helby, MC
(b) Herne Bay, Kent 13 February 1893

(d) Worthing, Sussex 7 May 1980

Educ. – Norwich GS

Cricket. – Norwich GS; Morley Hall; Essex; Sussex 2nds

HS. 55 v Cambridgeshire August 1910 @ Fenner's

HS. 28 no v Essex (2) June 1910 @ Lakenham

1st class cricket – 34 matches 792 runs 11 catches

161 for Norwich GS v Bury School July 1911

In Norfolk Regiment and he was awarded the Military Cross 7 February 1919

Football. – Norwich GS; Norfolk County 1910-11 (1 app –2 goals)

1910

BAKER, Lt. Col Sidney Ellis
(b) Roughton, Norfolk 1 October 1890

(d) Coney Weston Hall, Coney Weston, Bury St. Edmunds 17 July 1956

Cricket. – Overstrand; North Norfolk; Drayton & Taverham; Morley Hall

HS. 7 v Suffolk August 1910 @ Portman Road, Ipswich

90 for Overstrand v North Middlesex 1909

Son of Sam (a Roughton Schoolmaster) and Elizabeth Brown. His death certificate has him as a Lt. Colonel of the Duke of Wellington's Regiment (Retired)

BEVAN, Revd John Stacey
(b) Hampstead, London JAS 1888

(d) Frenchay Hospital, Bristol 5 November 1964

Lived 21 Forest Avenue, Bristol

Educ. – Yarmouth GS; University of Durham
Cricket. – Conservative Club; Yarmouth; Yarmouth
Old Boys; Rest of Norfolk; Lydgate House; Yarmouth
Conservatives; Royal Naval Hospital; JS Bevan's XI
HS. 25 v MCC August 1910 @ Gt. Yarmouth
100 for Conservative Club v Norwich & London July 1911
6/26 for Yarmouth Old Boys v Yarmouth GS July 1911
Ordained 1913 & Priest 1919. Curate of St. Julian (Shrewsbury)
1913-16. Assistant Master Henley-on-Thames GS 1919-25.
Curate of St. Barn (Holloway) 1926-28 & St. Paul 1928-30.
Rector of Pulverbatch and Vicar of Rattinghope 1930-31.Vicar
of St. Luke, Barton Hill (Bristol) 1932-5. Curate-in-Charge of
Christchurch (Barton Hill) 1946-58

FALCON, Major Joseph Henry
(b) Horstead House, Norfolk 9 April 1892
(d) Lowestoft 11 February 1950
Educ. – Harrow School (Small Houses & West Acre);
Cambridge University (Pembroke College)
Cricket. – Harrow School; Harrow Wanderers; Free
Foresters; Old Harrovians; Cambridge University – trial
match SH Saville's XI); Vancouver; Sir AD McAlpine's XI; MCC;
Norfolk Club & Ground
HS. 103 no v Essex (2) July 1920 @ Witham
BB. 3/19 v Cambridgeshire August 1913 @ Lakenham
HS. 8 v MCC August 1910 @ Gt. Yarmouth
BB. 1/28 v MCC August 1919 @ Lakenham
Brother of M (q.v)
1st class cricket – 2 matches 3 runs 5 wickets
4/59 for Harrow School v MC Kemp's X1 May 1911
61 for Norfolk Club & Ground v Fakenham & District August
1919
Captain RFA – 1st East Anglian & 266th Brigade. Member of
London Stock Exchange.
Preferred to be called 'Harry' and he took (not literally) a Danish
wife Greta.

FULCHER, Capt Eric Jesser, MC
(b) Bearstead, Kent 12 March 1890
(d) Pilstone Farm, Llandogo, Monmouth 12 February 1923
Died in a Gun accident
Educ. – Radley College
Cricket. – Radley College; MCC; Kent; L Robinson's XI; South
Wales; Aylsham; Norwich Wanderers; Old Buckenham
Hall; Norfolk Club & Ground; Rest of Norfolk; North Norfolk
District
HS. 83 v Nottinghamshire (2) July 1910 @ Trent Bridge
– his 6th NCCC innings with 83 out of 105 in 35 minutes
BB. 5/26 v Glamorgan September 1913 @ Lakenham
HS. 126 v MCC June 1914 @ Lord's
BB. 7/74 v L Robinson's X1 June 1911 @ Norwich CEYMS
1st class cricket – 10 matches 329 runs 9 catches 4 wickets

126 for Aylsham v Marsham July 1912
Father Arthur played first class cricket for Kent (1878-87)
The world of Agriculture and Estate Agency attracted him
so much so he spent two years on the Walsingham Estate
followed by a period on the Blickling Estate. Football. – Watton;
Aylsham; Attleborough; Old Buckenham and he became a
Norwich City FC Director. 2nd Lt 3rd Batt. Queens Own Royal
West Kent Regiment 3 June 1915. Awarded the Military Cross
2 December 1918 for conspicuous gallantry and devotion
to duty during an attack. He pushed up a platoon from his
support company when the attack was wavering, and by his
action the objective was gained and consolidated.
F.F. – Left £918-10s in his Probated London will
The 'London Gazette' 17 March 1919 advised that he
relinquished the acting rank of captain on 1 February 1919
and further on 16 December 1920 retained the same rank
with the 4th Batt. Norfolk Regiment

POPHAM, 2nd Lt Reginald Francis
(b) Kensington, London 8 January 1892
(d) Old Manor, Warham, Sussex 9 September 1975
Educ. – Repton School; Oxford University
Cricket. – Repton School; MCC; Norfolk Club & Ground;
Suffolk Borderers; Repton Pilgrims
HS. 117 v Bedfordshire August 1914 @ Lakenham
HS. 34 v MCC August 1919 @ Lakenham
Brother of CH (q.v)
1st class cricket – 5 matches 151 runs
226 at Old Buckenham Hall v Harrow Blues X1 August 1912
partnering RV Minnett in 2nd wicket stand of 463
Shared with GA Stevens the record 2nd wicket stand of 147 in
1913 – it stood for a further 10 years
Football. – Repton School; Hertford; Oxford University – Blue &
captain; 6th Norfolks; England amateur International – 3 caps;
Norwich City FC 21 February 1914 & 21 April 1919; Corinthians.
Entered the London Stock Exchange in May 1915
F.F. – His family heritage include Sir John who was a
Speaker in the House of Commons and an Attorney
General who sentenced Mary, Queen of Scots for treason
plus Home Riggs Popham a Navy Admiral in the times of
Admiral Horatio Nelson

TAYLOR, A P
Cricket. – CEYMS; RG Pilch's XI
HS. 0 (x2) v Suffolk July 1910 @ Lakenham
HS. 19 v Essex (2) June 1910 @ Norwich CEYMS
50 no for CEYMS v Norfolk News August 1899
81 no for CEYMS v Knighton (Leicester) May 1910
Thought I had his death namely Aubrey Percival Taylor
in Ringwood, Hampshire on 8 September 1912 at age
38. However the 'EDP' of 22 May 1904 said that he was a
youngster!

THURSBY, Walter

(b) Holne, Breconshire 29 July 1890
(d) Moorside, Farnham Common 3 December 1953
Lived Oakmead Lodge, Copthorne, Sussex
Educ. – Sedbergh School; Cambridge Univeristy (Queens' College)
Cricket. – Sedbergh School; Rest of Norfolk; Castle Rising; West Norfolk
HS. 74 v Nottinghamshire (2) July 1910 @ Trent Bridge
BB. 1/18 v Cambridgeshire August 1911 @ King's Lynn
Brother of MH (q.v)
72 for Sedbergh School v Merchiston Castle School July 1909
134 for West Norfolk v Stow & District July 1912
Went to Canada in 1912 hence his ten year gap in appearances. A former Schoolteacher and the Greyhound Manager at Brighton & Hove Albion Stadium
F.F. – He died of an aneurysm on the evening of his sister's daughter's wedding.
WW2 – with the Royal Observer Corps in Scotland

WATSON, Harold

(b) Gooderstone, Norfolk 5 March 1888
(d) Hauxton near Cambridge 14 March 1969
Educ. – Thetford GS
Cricket. – Thetford GS; Lord's Groundstaff; MCC; Norfolk Ramblers; Minor Counties; Minor Counties North
HS. 68 v Hertfordshire August 1921 @ Lakenham – batting at no. 11
BB. 7/27 v Hertfordshire July 1920 @ Cheshunt
HS. 31 no v Eton Ramblers May 1923 @ Lakenham
BB. 6/38 v L Robinson's X1 May 1912 @ Old Buckenham Hall
1st class cricket – 13 matches 189 runs 5 catches 37 wickets
At Thetford GS with RW Cant (q.v) and GER Neville (q.v)
Cricket Coach for RNC Dartmouth; Bishop's Stortford College and Perse School.
Head Porter at Trinity College, Cambridge
F.F. – The NCCC 1999 Handbook (Page 5) advised that in the past 12 months the Club received a legacy of £10,000 from the Estate of the late Miss Vera Watson in memory of her father Harold

WILLIAMS, Gomer

(b) Lampeter, Cardiganshire JAS 1883
(d) New Dock, Llanelly 29 November 1951 age 68
Educ. – St John's Foundation School (Leatherhead); Yarmouth GS
Cricket. – Yarmouth GS; Yarmouth Conservatives; Rest of Norfolk
HS. 38 v Cambridgeshire August 1910 @ Lakenham
BB. 1/9 v Cambridgeshire August 1911 @ King's Lynn
HS. 10 v MCC August 1910 @ Gt. Yarmouth

BB. 6/47 v MCC August 1912 @ Gt. Yarmouth
9/4 for Yarmouth GS v RNH July 1911
Schoolmaster at Yarmouth GS teaching Latin. Latterly a Rollerman in a Tinplate Works.
F.F. – Achos Marwolaeth (Cause of Death) was Toxaemia and Intra Nasal Carcinoma – well it was a Welsh death certificate.

1911

AMES, Stuart Stone

(b) Norwich 26 January 1890
(d) Norwich 23 December 1980
Educ. – Belle Vue Road School
Cricket. – Belle Vue Road School; Norwich YMCA; CEYMS; Norfolk Club & Ground; RG Pilch's XI; CEYMS Thursday XI; Norwich Banks
HS. 22 v Suffolk August 1911 @ Bury St. Edmunds
BB. 2/39 v Cambridgeshire August 1911 @ Fenner's
HS. 32 v Old Buckenham Hall July 1911 @ Old Buckenham Hall
In June 1923 there were 6 NCCC players in the CEYMS side, the others being Dann, Greenwell, Holmes, Read and Theobald.
7/36 for Norfolk Club & Ground v 5th Norfolks May 1911
7/25 for CEYMS Thursday X1 v Depot Norfolk Regiment July 1924 – included 4 in 4 balls and 5 in 7 balls for 0 runs

COLMAN, Capt Geoffrey Russell Rees, JP

(b) Bracondale Woods, Norwich 14 March 1892
(d) Framlingham, Norwich 18 March 1935
Educ. – Suffield Park School; Sedbergh School; Evelyns (West Drayton); Eton College (the Rev Raymond Coxe Radcliffe's and Clarence Henry Kennett Marten's Houses); Oxford University (Christ Church College)
Cricket. – Norfolk Club & Ground; Eton Ramblers; Minor Counties Incogniti; Oxford University – Blue 1913-14; Old Etonians; MCC; L Robinson's XI; Oxford University Authentics
HS. 126 v Surrey (2) July 1925 @ Hunstanton
BB. 5/59 v Kent (2) August 1924 @ Lakenham
HS. 40 no (85) v West Indies August 1923 @ Lakenham
Father of DWJ (q.v) and Brother of AR (q.v)
Unsure about CS Colman (q.v) being a possible relation
1st class cricket – 23 matches 958 runs 17 catches 1 wicket
Jointly held in 1923 with M Falcon the NCCC 2nd wicket record of 158 for 10 years
90 for Eton Ramblers v NCCC June 1923
NCCC Committee Member 1925 and Oxford University Hon Sec 1914. He went on the Incogniti tour to North America with Michael Falcon in 1913 and captained his Varsity side in 1915. Norwich High Sheriff 1934 and a JP from 1919. Lt in the 7th Batt (Service) of the Rifle Brigade and a Captain in Machine Gun Corps – hit by a bullet 19 January 1916 (mentioned in

despatches), illness for several months with blood poisoning affecting an already overstrained heart. This condition continued to hamper his availability for NCCC for the rest of his career.
Of Colman's the Mustard Empire – had his own goat carriage. Directorships of Norwich Union Life and Fire Insurance Societies, J & J Colman Ltd and Norfolk News
F.F. – Geoffrey Road in Norwich was named after him. At age 6 he laid the foundation stone of the Jenny Lind Infirmary on land given by his grandfather.

CUBITT, Temp. Lt. Bryan Barton
(b) Witton, Norfolk AMJ 1892 – baptism/christening 8 June 1892
(d) France & Flanders 26 September 1915
Cricket. – Overstrand; Norfolk Club & Ground
HS. 16 v Old Buckenham Hall July 1911 @ Old Buckenham Hall
47 no for Overstrand v Dereham July 1911 – with JJ Compton (q.v) making 70 not out.
In the East Yorkshire Regiment (8th Batt)
The family were tenant Farmers of Abbey Farm for several generations.
F.F. – He left a widow Helen, a daughter and two grand children

GEMMELL, George
(b) King's Lynn 9 August 1889
(d) Rutland Nursing Home, Langham, Rutland 25 January 1965
Lived 234 Eastfield Road, Peterborough
Educ. – King's Lynn GS
Cricket. – King's Lynn GS; Hunstanton; Rest of Norfolk; Rhodesia
HS. 26 v Bedfordshire July 1911 @ Bedford
HS. 29 v Old Buckenham Hall July 1911 @ Old Buckenham Hall
1st class cricket – 3 matches 45 runs 1 catch 1 wicket and these games were played in Rhodesia.
77 for Hunstanton v West Norfolk August 1911
F.F. – Fourth child of Scottish born George (Draper & Outfitter) and Annie Little.
Left £10,399 in his will

THURSBY, Miles Herbert
(b) Castle Rising, Norfolk 17 August 1893
(d) Hamilton Nursing Home, Hunstanton, Norfolk 27 March 1991
Educ. – Glebe House School; Sedbergh School
Cricket. – Sedbergh School; GH Mowers' XI
HS. 51 v Cambridgeshire August 1911 @ Fenner's
HS. 16 no v MCC August 1912 @ Gt. Yarmouth

Brother of W (q.v)
159 no (281) for Sedbergh School v Giggleswick School July 1911 – as an opener carrying his bat
In Canada from 1912 to 1927 working for the Canadian Bank of Commerce. A retired Estate Manager upon his return to the UK.
F.F. – The family advise that he was Shipwrecked on one voyage. He died as a result of a chest infection and ventricular failure

WAKEFIELD, Capt Herbert Russell
(b) Sandgate, Kent 9 May 1888
(d) Kensington, London 2 August 1964
Educ. – Marlborough College; Oxford University (University College)
Cricket. – Old Buckenham Hall; Marlborough College
HS. 71 v Bedfordshire July 1911 @ Bedford
BB. 3/62 v Hertfordshire July 1911 @ St Albans
50 and 44 for Marlborough College v Cheltenham College June 1906
89 for Old Buckenham Hall v Eton Ramblers July 1911.
He also played golf, hockey and football to a decent college standard. Served in France & Balkans with the Royal Scots Fusiliers. By 1930 he was a full time Writer – with his final output being short stories (50), novels (4), publisher and as per John Betjeman – " he rivalled M R James as a ghost writer (28)." Editor at Philip Alan Publishers (London) to 1930. Chief Editor Wm Collins (Book Publisher). In WW2 he was an Air Raid Warden
F.F. – He became a recluse, hurt and embittered by the neglect from his countrymen. He subsequently destroyed his files, manuscripts and photos of himself. I lost my First Edition of his 1935 book 'A Ghostly Company' – one of the regrets of my life.

1912

BAGNALL, Reginald St Vincent
(b) East Dereham 10 April 1891
(d) Hockham Lodge, Thetford, Norfolk 10 June 1984
Educ. – Aldenham School
Cricket. – Aldenham School; East Dereham; Norfolk Club & Ground; Gressenhall; Mid Norfolk; Cowichan; British Columbia Colts; Yarmouth Conservatives; Victoria XXII
HS. 37 v Staffordshire July 1925 @ Lakenham
BB. 2/11 v Hertfordshire August 1924 @ Lakenham
HS. 36 v Eton Ramblers May 1923 @ Lakenham
BB. 4/65 v Eton Ramblers May 1923 @ Lakenham
He played in a NCCC friendly in 1912 and reappeared in 1923.
9/24 for Yarmouth Conservatives v CEYMS May 1910
3/68 for Victoria XX11 v Australians September 1913 –

including the wicket of Arthur Mailey who was destined to become a Test Player with his 'leggies.'
50 for Victoria XX11 v Australians September 1913
Occupation of a Solicitor
F.F. – His WW1 Attestation Paper described him thus – In 80th Highland of Canada signing up 7 November 1916. Height 5ft 6 inches, dark complexion, brown eyes, dark brown hair and listed as a Farmer.

BARTON, Charles Thomas

(b) East Dereham, Norfolk 26 December 1878
(d) Otford near Seven Oaks, Kent 30 May 1965
Educ. – Bradfield College
Cricket. – Bradfield College; Dereham; Mid Norfolk; Rev JC Wilson's XI; East Dereham
HS. 2 v Hertfordshire July 1912 @ St Albans
Father of MR (q.v), Uncle of AW (q.v), Brother of WJ (q.v)
102 (226) for Mid Norfolk v West Norfolk May 1910
Son of Walter (Solicitor) and Edith Pilling. On 1901 Census as an Articled Solicitor's Clerk.
Severely wounded in Gaza 19 April 1917. He was appointed Clerk to Liverpool City Justice on 25 February 1918

FALCONER, Roderick

(b) Scole, Suffolk 10 November 1886
(d) Malvern, Worcestershire 8 March 1966
Cricket. – Northamptonshire ; Minor Counties
HS. 52 no v Cambridgeshire August 1912 @ Lakenham – batting at no. 9
BB. 7/32 v Cambridgeshire August 1913 @ Lakenham
HS. 2 v MCC June 1914 @ Lord's
BB. 3/35 v MCC June 1914 @ Lord's
1st class cricket – 7 matches 29 runs 1 catch 9 wickets
He equals the best NCCC v Suffolk match analysis of 13/95. He took 130 wickets in his three NCCC seasons leading up to WW1. In his debut season he took 65 Championship wickets – a record for Norfolk which still stands. He had three 10 wicket match hauls and nine 5 wickets performances that season.

FREDERICK, Lt Thomas Henry, MC

(b) Moulton St Mary near Acle, Norfolk 7 March 1893
(d) Lady Murray's (No. 10 Red Cross) Hospital, Le Treport, France 14 December 1917
Lived Burgh Hall, Burgh Castle, Norfolk
Educ. – Aldenham School; Cambridge University (St. John's College)
Cricket. – Aldenham School
HS. 7 no v MCC August 1912 @ Gt. Yarmouth
He studied for the Bar in Cambridge but he obeyed the King's call. His father Henry was a London born Solicitor. Tom joined 9th Norfolks in Norwich 9 September 1914 and trained at Shoreham before moving to Blackdown Camp in Aldershot.

He was part of the 24th Division in France and was wounded at Lonely Tree Hill (south of La Bassee Canal) on 26 September 1915. Awarded the Military Cross on 5 June 1916 and again wounded (by a rifle bullet) two days later in the trenches. The Battalion were transferred to the 6th Division after the debacle at Loos. He contracted septic pneumonia and was reported by the War Office as buried somewhere in France. This was amended to wounded and reported missing in action. His father persevered in the belief that his son was alive and he found him and crossed to France to be at his bedside.

HILL, Sidney Dennis

(b) Wymondham, Norfolk 17 May 1877
(d) Norwich 26 September 1947
Educ. – Wymondham Commercial School
Cricket. – Wymondham Commercial School; Wellingborough; Norwich Wanderers; Norwich Travellers; Commercial Travellers
HS. 33 v Cambridgeshire August 1914 @ Fenner's
HS. 13 v L Robinson's X1 May 1912 @ Old Buckenham Hall
102 no for Wymondham Commercial School v YMCA August 1895
102 no for Norwich Travellers v Stratton Strawless June 1908
NCCC Committee Member with the responsibity for many years of arranging the Lakenham Tents.
Also serving on the Entertainments and Ground Committee. On 1901 Census as a Provision Commission Agent. Hon Life Member of Norwich Wanderers CC (formed 1913 from Commercial Travellers) after being a player, captain and Committee Chairman to retirement in 1935. Member Earlham Tennis Club. Rep. and later Director of the London Provision House firm of I. Beer & Sons
F.F. – Left £2,662-15-10 with a recipient being his widow Evelyn

PRIOR, Sir Henry Carlos , KCIE CSI

(b) Cambridge 6 January 1890
(d) Weymouth, Dorset 29 March 1967
Lived Lynchets, Bridport, Dorset
Educ. – Rottingdean School; Eton College; Cambridge University (King's College)
Cricket. – Eton College; Eton Ramblers
HS. 63 v Suffolk August 1912 @ Bury St Edmunds
HS. 21 v Old Buckenham Hall July 1911 @ Old Buckenham Hall
In Indian Civil Service 1914 and the Indian Army Reserve of Officers 1915-19. Knight Commander of the Order Indian Empire (KCIE) on 23 June 1936. Continuing to work abroad he was subsequently the Secretary to Government of Bihar (in Finance Dept), Secretary of the Labour Dept 1941, Secretary of Dept Works, Mines and Power. Minister of Housing and Local Government 1951-64

ROUSE, Capt Arthur William
(b) Wacton, Norfolk – baptism/christening 12 April 1885
(d) West End, Costessey, Norfolk 7 March 1944 age 59
Educ. – Yarmouth GS
Cricket. – Yarmouth GS; Yarmouth Conservatives; Yarmouth Town
HS. 8 v Eton Ramblers August 1922 @ Lakenham
By the time that he took his 1,000th wicket for Yarmouth Town they were at the rate of one every 4 overs for an average of 7.6 per wicket.
In the Cadet Corps 1915 and firstly affiliated to RFA followed by being in the Norfolk Regiment.
From 1921-31 he was the Yarmouth GS Music & Mathematics Teacher .

WYNNE-WILLSON, Major Linton Frederick
(b) Winchester, Hampshire 5 April 1879
(d) Bristol 14 July 1937
Suffered a heart attack walking back to the pavilion after scoring 19 for Men o' Mendip v Gloster Regiment.
Lived High Littleton House, Somerset
Educ. – Holt School
Cricket. – Holt School; Hunstanton; West Norfolk; Holiday Hittites; LF Wynne –Wilson's XI; Home Place; North Norfolk District; Men o' Mendip
HS. 33 v Hertfordshire August 1912 @ Lakenham
BB. 2/36 v Hertfordshire August 1912 @ Lakenham
1901 Census as LFW Wilson – a 2nd Lt India Regiment.
163 for Holiday Hittites v Sheringham Visitors August 1911
8/43 for LF Wynne-Willson's XI v DA Wynne-Willson's XI July 1912
157 for Home Place v Gresham's Masters June 1914
F.F. – His will did not have his name hyphenated

1913

CARTER, 2nd Lt George Thomas
(b) Magdalen, Norfolk 10 July 1896
(d) Um-Al-Hannah, Mesopotamia 10 March 1916
Lived Holley House, Wiggenhill St Mary Magdalen, Norfolk
Cricket. – Wellingborough GS; Wellingborough School
HS. 48 v Cambridgeshire August 1914 @ Fenner's
BB. 1/5 v Cambridgeshire August 1914 @ Fenner's
HS. 32 v MCC June 1914 @ Lord's
Brother of RD (q.v) and Uncle of DD (q.v)
200 no for Wellingborough School v Bedford Modern School June 1914
Also in their football team, a high jumper and once threw a cricket ball 127 yards 2 feet.
In the 2nd Lt Norfolk Regiment attached to the Black Watch

HUDSON, Alexander Robert
(b) Billingford, Norfolk 23 October 1892

(d) Bylaugh, East Dereham, Norfolk 20 March 1928
Educ. – Aldenham School; Edinburgh University
Cricket. – Dereham
HS. 39 v Hertfordshire August 1913 @ King's Lynn
BB. 4/15 v Cambridgeshire August 1913 @ Lakenham
HS. 31 no v MCC June 1914 @ Lord's
Brother of RC (q.v)
In the same school side as RStV Bagnall (q.v)
F.F. – His administered London will saw him leave £149-12-5 to his brother Roland

PEDDER, Capt Guy Richard
(b) Brandiston Hall, Norfolk 7 July 1892
(d) Park House, Hoxne, Suffolk 6 April 1964
Educ. – Repton School
Cricket. – Repton School; Repton Pilgrims; MCC; Minor Counties; Gloucestershire; Army; Catterick Garrison; Aldershot; Royal Tank Corps; Free Foresters; Trinity College
HS. 47 v Hertfordshire July 1914 @ Bushey
Best wicket keeping season 1931 (10c 4s) plus another catch in a friendly match.
HS. 26 v MCC June 1914 @ Lord's
1st class cricket – 5 matches 120 runs and 9 victims (7c 2s.)
His Brother-in-Law HSR Critchley-Salmonson played first class cricket. Guy served in the Gloucester Yeomanry with the 'Wisden' Obituary showing him as a Major?

TRAFFORD, Major Sigismund William Joseph, DL JP
(b) St George's Square, London 15 March 1883
(d) Wroxham Hall, Norfolk 8 September 1953
He was in ill health for about 10 months
Educ. – Oratory School (Birmingham)
Cricket. – Green Jackets; Norfolk County Asylum
HS. 10 no v Bedfordshire July 1913 @ Bedford
Served with the Norfolk Militia, Rifle Brigade and the Green Jackets. Presiding Magistrate from 1917 on the Taverham Bench and he sat as late as the Saturday before his death. President of the British Order of Knight of Malta (a Catholic Order of Chivalry). Member of Norfolk County Council serving St. Faith's and Aylsham RDC from 1918-53. Chairmanships of Wroxham Parish Council and the Broads Advisory Committee. President and Hon. Life Member of the Norfolk Broads Yacht Club
F.F. – He owned Estates in Norfolk, Lincolnshire and the Midlands and also land in Norwich.
His London Probated will saw him leave £105,936-19-9 – a considerable sum of money in 1953.
He is shown in some cricket sources as Captain RS Trafford.

WINGFIELD, Ralph Arthur
(b) Streatham, London 2 January 1895
(d) Donnington Hayes, Newbury, Berkshire 2 April 1982

Educ. – Bedford Harper Trust School; St. Paul's School
Cricket. – CEYMS; Commercial Travellers
HS. 7 v Bedfordshire July 1913 @ Bedford
151 no for Commercial Travellers v Morley Hall July 1911
His surname incorrectly shown as Winfield in some match
scorecards.

He was in the Heavy Artillery Co, Royal Irish Fusiliers and the
Royal Flying Corps progressing to be a Test Pilot. His traced
family advised that his successive occupations were that he
trained as a Master Printer – he had his own business; a North
Devon Farmer and a Market Gardener in Berkshire

1914

HADLEY, Capt Isaac Peyton Sheldon, MC
(b) Cambridge 27 March 1895
(d) Eastbourne, Sussex 25 October 1918
He died after being caught in the Flu Epidemic of the time.
Educ. – Charterhouse School; Perse School
Cricket. – Charterhouse School
HS. 4 v Cambridgeshire August 1914 @ Fenner's
BB. 1/25 v Cambridgeshire August 1914 @ Fenner's
In 7th Batt. Northampton Regiment. Universally known as
Peyton.
His father William was a Pembroke College Schoolmaster.
F.F. – He left £287-16-6 to his brother and he is buried in
NW part of St. Mary's Churchyard in Heacham. One of 7
known Perse School pupils to receive the Military Cross.

HALE, Frank William
(b) Norwich 22 August 1893
(d) Frimley Park Hospital, Frimley, Surrey 20 January 1980
Lived Cowley Cottage, Dora Green, Farnham, Surrey
Cricket. – CEYMS
HS. 21 v Bedfordshire July 1914 @ Bedford
His father was a Wholesale Boot & Shoe Manufacturer married
to Sarah Tofts. Frank was a Retired Bank Manager

JESSOPP, 2nd Lt Neville Augustus
(b) South Leasingham House, Sleaford, Lincolnshire 31 July
1898
(d) Claremont, Cape Province, South Africa 13 July 1977
Educ. – Harrow School (Druries House)
Cricket. – MCC; Harrow School; Old Harrovians; JHP Brain's
XI; Lord's Schools; Norfolk Club & Ground; Fakenham &
District
HS. 44 v Essex (2) July 1920 @ Witham
BB. 2/16 v Cambridgeshire August 1914 @ Lakenham
HS. 15 no v FB Baker's Cambridge X1 August 1919 @
Lakenham
BB. 3/14 v FB Baker's Cambridge X1 August 1919 @
Lakenham

1st class cricket – 2 matches 2 runs 2 catches 7 wickets
The second youngest NCCC player on debut being aged 16 years
and 37 days but the youngest catcher of all time for Norfolk.
7/47 for Harrow School v RMC Sandhurst June 1916
9/12 for Harrow School v Winchester College July 1916
5/47 for Lord's Schools v The Rest August 1916
5/49, 5/100, 3 catches, 20 & 23 for Fakenham & District v
Norfolk Club & Ground August 1919
He was a Farmer who sailed from London to Mombassa on
17 December 1920. He farmed extensively in British East Africa.
Neville was a 2nd Lt. Royal Horse Guards. Also a footballer for
Harrow School

PRETHEROE, Edward Owen, AG MC QC
(b) Bury St. Edmunds 26 March 1896
(d) University College Hospital, London 4 August 1962
Educ. – Thetford GS; Cambridge University (St John's
College)
Cricket. – Thetford GS; Yarmouth Town; Yarmouth
Wanderers; Clergy XI; Nigeria; FB Baker's Cambridge XI.
HS. 10 v Cambridgeshire August 1914 @ Fenner's
7/19 for Clergy X1 v Yarmouth July 1923
An Attorney General in British Guyana and Malaya. Latterly in
Colonial Legal service in Nigeria, British Guyana and Malaya
F.F. – Death Notice incorrectly given as Protheroe in many
Consulate sources.
His Lewes Administered will dated 20 March 1963 to his
Schoolmaster brother Thomas in the amount of £17,949-4s.
The papers were resealed in the Supreme Court of Fed of
Malay on 6 September 1963 – I did not understand this either!

STEPHENSON, Edward Keppel
(b) Beanfort Gardens, Kensington, London 22 March 1891
(d) Blyth, Suffolk 21 April 1969
Many sources show his death in Northumberland but his
demise was registered in Suffolk.
Educ. – Ludgrove Prep School; Eton College; Oxford
University (Merton College)
Cricket. – Oxford University Authentics; MCC; Bengal
Governor's XI
HS. 63 v Cambridgeshire August 1914 @ Fenner's – a
third wicket partnership with GA Stevens of 145 runs in his
only game.
1st class cricket 1 match 0 runs 1 catch and a 'pair' in his only
such game in India.
F.F. – Son of Major Keppel Stephenson and Helena
Greathead

THORNE, Lt. Col Gordon Calthrop, CMG DSO
(b) Chelsea 3 March 1897
(d) Indian Ocean 2 March 1942 – presumed drowned while
attempting to escape.

Educ. – Haileybury College (Melvill House 1911.3-1915.2); Hurst Court; RMC Sandhurst
Cricket. – Haileybury College; Army
HS. 61 v Surrey (2) July 1924 @ Hunstanton
59 for Haileybury College v Cheltenham College August 1914
Son of Major FG Thorne (NCCC President 1946)
Uncle of DC (q.v) and ME (q.v)
1st class cricket 1 match 24 runs
2nd Norfolks to France - wounded. In 1919 with the 2nd Battalion Expedition to NW Frontier and Adjutant 1927-29. 1934 the Garrison Adjutant at Bordon (Hampshire). 1936 to Ceylon as Staff Officer to the Ceylon Defence Force becoming the Commandant. 1941 – a Temporary Brigadier. Lastly with the 18th (East Anglian) Infantry Division commanding the 2nd Batt. Cambridgeshire Regiment
F.F. – His wife Pamela Meredyth (nee Colwell) survived both her husbands and she died in Manchester, Massachusetts, USA in 2001 aged 94 with 14 grandchildren and 17 great grandchildren

....

1919

....

BORTHWICK, Capt Cecil Hamilton
(b) Cambridge 3 July 1887
(d) Burgate, Diss, Norfolk 30 December 1977
Educ. – Blundell's School
Cricket. – Cambridgeshire; Kent 2nds
HS. 5 no v Surrey (2) August 1923 @ Richmond
HS. 10 v Eton Ramblers August 1922 @ Lakenham
A wicket keeper for NCCC with seven dismissals in 1923 (6c 1s). Just two games for Cambridgeshire with eleven runs to his name. WW1 – with the Royal Field Artillery

CANT, Reginald William
(b) Norwich 4 October 1897
(d) Thetford, Norfolk 13 January 1980
Educ. – Thetford GS
Cricket. – Thetford GS; Norwich Wanderers; GA Stevens' X1; FB Baker's Cambridge X1 (a NCCC player fielding as a substitute)
HS. 46 no v Kent (2) May 1928 @ Beckenham – batting at no. 10
BB. 4/58 v Kent (2) August 1928 @ Lakenham
HS. 19 no v Eton Ramblers August 1922 @ Lakenham
BB. 2/11 v MCC August 1920 @ Old Buckenham
The 22 March 1930 AGM of Norwich Wanderers had SD Hill (q.v) as club Chairman and recorded that Reg Cant's wickets were achieved at 12.8 per run (Third in their averages behind AG Utting (q.v) and WJ Lingwood (q.v))

COLMAN, Charles Stanley
(b) Rockland, Norfolk 2 December 1898

Educ. – Wellingborough School
Cricket. – Wellingborough School; Norfolk Club & Ground
HS. 49 v Hertfordshire July 1921 @ Watford
BB. 3/34 v Bedfordshire August 1920 @ Lakenham
HS. 42 no v FB Baker's Cambridge XI August 1919 @ Lakenham
101 for Norfolk Club & Ground v Hunstanton 1919.
F.F. – His demise should be a routine find but all I have proven so far is that he is not related to GRR Colman (q.v)

DOUGILL, Harold
(b) Bramley, West Yorkshire 23 August 1888
(d) Lymington, Hampshire 15 May 1963
Came to Norfolk in 1912
Cricket. – Norwich Wanderers; Norfolk Club & Ground; YMCA; RG Pilch's XI; Old Buckenham
HS. 43 v Buckinghamshire July 1928 @ Wing
BB. 2/54 v Leicestershire (2) August 1926 @ Lakenham
HS. 31 v MCC August 1920 @ Old Buckenham
7/8 for YMCA v Norwich & London July 1912
5/5 for Norwich Wanderers v Carrow May 1913
President of Norfolk Golf Union and a member at Eaton Golf Club

EDRICH, Edwin Harry
(b) Blofield, Norfolk 11 October 1891
(d) Low Farm, Blofield, Norfolk 22 November 1968
Educ. – Bracondale School
Cricket. – Blofield; Edrich XI; Norfolk Club & Ground
HS. 71 no v FB Baker's Cambridge XI August 1919 @ Lakenham
54 and 9/7 for Blofield v Lingwood May 1911
91 no for Blofield v Yarmouth Colts July 1911
An Umpire for South Walsham District and Thorpe Mental Hospital CC.
The forgotten Edrich who was the first one of the dynasty to play for NCCC – albeit only a friendly game.
'The Cricketing Family of Edrich' by Ralph Barker (1976) recounts the following story – "Bill Edrich (ie WA) and Edwin were invited to play as both were present at Lakenham. Shortly before the start WA was approached by Edward Gibson (NCCC) who asked if he could play as the side were a man short ? WA stated that he hadn't got his things so Edwin was asked and he responded by saying I'll play if you get me some gear." Edwin was a pacy bowler and an attacking bat.
One of 13 children of Harry Edrich and Elizabeth Barcham.

HEADING, Robert Brerson
(b) Thornham, Norfolk 15 February 1893
(d) Heacham, Norfolk 6 January 1947
Educ. – Wellingborough School
Cricket. – Wellingborough School; Fakenham & District; West Norfolk

HS. 33 v Hertfordshire July 1920 @ **Cheshunt**
HS. 30 v MCC August 1919 @ Lakenham
66 for Fakenham & District v Norfolk Club & Ground August 1919
104 no (183) for West Norfolk v March Town July 1927
F.F. – His younger brother Richard was left £5,428-12s in the will

HUDSON, Roland Cecil
(b) Billingford, Norfolk 28 March 1894
(d) Midhurst, Sussex 1 January 1970
Educ. – Aldenham School
Cricket. – Norfolk Club & Ground
HS. 22 v FB Baker's Cambridge XI August 1919 @ Lakenham
Brother of AR (q.v)
F.F. – His brother's will referred to RC as an Assistant Manager – there was no illumination as to the nature of his business.

NEVILLE, George Edgar Robertson
(b) Feltwell, Norfolk 20 June 1897
(d) Feltwell, Norfolk 7 October 1971
Educ. – Thetford GS
Cricket. – Thetford GS; Wisbech CC; Lexham; Houghton Hall; Lord Cholmondeley's XI; L Robinson's XI; North Runcton; Hunstanton; Castle Rising; Feltwell; South Norfolk; Norfolk Club & Ground.
HS. 13 v Leicestershire (2) June 1926 @ **Hinckley**
BB. 1/4 v Kent (2) August 1928 @ **Lakenham**
HS. 20 no v FB Baker's Cambridge XI August 1919 @ Lakenham
BB. 4/30 v FB Baker's Cambridge XI August 1919 @ Lakenham
5/9 for Thetford GS v Mundford July 1912
6/11 for Thetford GS v Quidenham July 1912
8/6 for Thetford GS v East Anglian School July 1912
Originally a Norfolk Farmer and he latterly worked for British Sugar.
His death certificate showed his occupation as Fieldsman (Sugar Factory)

POPHAM, Cyril Home
(b) Kensington, London 6 April 1896
(d) Horsham, Sussex 30 May 1962
Educ. – Repton School
Cricket. – Repton School; Repton Pilgrims; Norfolk Yeomanry; Incogniti
HS. 1 v Kent (2) August 1921 @ **Hythe**
HS. 0 v FB Baker's Cambridge X1 August 1919 @ Lakenham
BB. 2/9 v FB Baker's Cambridge X1 August 1919 @ Lakenham
Brother of RF (q.v)

Due to play for Norwich City FC with his elder brother in 1919. He worked in the family Stockbroking Firm Popham, Lisle and Smith.
F.F. – Probated London will dated 29 August 1962 leaving £5,065-18-5 to be shared by his widow Ivy (nee Gordon) and his aforesaid brother

RAIKES, Thomas Barkley
(b) Malabar Hill, Bombay, India 16 December 1902
(d) Rickinghall Superior, Suffolk 2 March 1984
Educ. –Winchester College; Oxford University (Trinity College)
Cricket. – Winchester College; Oxford University – Blue 1922-24; Public Schools; The Rest; Minor Counties North.
HS. 74 no v Cambridgeshire August 1921 @ Lakenham
BB. 5/21 v Bedfordshire July 1922 @ Luton
HS. 4 v MCC August 1919 @ Lakenham
Son of EB (q.v) and Nephew of GB (q.v)
1st class cricket – 38 matches 554 runs 24 catches 132 wickets
7/92 for Winchester College v Eton College June 1921
94 and 8/14 for Winchester College v Charterhouse School June 1921
9/38 for Oxford University v The Army June 1924 (13/80 in the match - this classified as a first class match. He took 5/5 in a non first class Freshman's match and he bowled 57 balls before a run was scored off him. Secretary of Oxford University 1924. Wisden quote – "Put on too much weight as pleasure of life at Oxford too alluring."

1920

BEADSMOORE, Walter Arthur
(b) Carlton, Basford, Nottingham 29 October 1891
(d) Watford, Hertfordshire 13 April 1964
Educ. – Mansfield School
Cricket. – Norfolk Club & Ground; MCC; Minor Counties; Minor Counties North; Sheffield Collegiate
HS. 36 no v Kent (2) August 1923 @ Lakenham
BB. 8/59 v Staffordshire August 1923 @ Lakenham
HS. 11 no v West Indies August 1923 @ Lakenham
BB. 5/37 v West Indies May 1928 @ Lakenham
1st class cricket – 1 match 10 runs 5 wickets in helping the Minor Counties beat the South African tourists in 1924
He took 294 NCCC Minor County wickets yet he did not have a Wisden Obituary.
He three times took 10 wickets in a match for NCCC being 10/58 (Kent (2) in 1921); 12/79 (Staffs in 1923) and 11/68 (Bucks in 1927)
F.F. – Distantly related family believe that he was a Policeman outside of cricket and they are still checking as we go to press.

CARTER, Richard Dring

(b) Hubbert's Bridge, Boston, Lincolnshire 19 July 1891
(d) Crabbe's Abbey, King's Lynn, Norfolk 24 August 1969
Many cricket sources give his demise as Norwich but the
death was registered in Downham, Norfolk.
Educ. – Wellingborough GS
Cricket. – Wellingborough GS; East of England; Rest of
Norfolk; Stow & District; Stow; Houghton Hall; West Norfolk
HS. 73 no v Bedfordshire July 1922 @ Lakenham
HS. 71 v Eton Ramblers May 1923 @ Lakenham
Father of DD (q.v), Brother of GT (q.v)
1st class cricket 1 match 1 run
73 no for Stow v Lynn July 1911
144 no for West Norfolk v FP Long's XI August 1911
He put on 171 for the sixth wicket v Kent (2) in August 1922
with GA Stevens – as they chased the record of 205 set in 1905.
NCCC President 1961 and 1962 when Michael Falcon was the
Chairman and Bill Edrich was the Captain

EDWARDS, Major Reginald Owen

(b) Gt. Yarmouth, Norfolk 17 October 1881
(d) Bishop's Stortford, Hertfordshire 15 November 1925
Educ. – Christ's Hospital
Cricket. – Cambridgeshire; MCC; Incogniti; Rest of England;
Surrey 2nds; Cambridgeshire Regiment
HS. 9 no v Bedfordshire July 1920 @ Biddenham
1st class cricket 1 match 1 run
In the Cambridgeshire Regiment. He played for the MCC in
Germany and for Incogniti in Holland. He spent a considerable
time in Africa and found solace during solitary days up country
reading 'Wisden' to which he frequently contributed. Gassed
badly during the war, and in a later expedition to Southern
Russia he lost all his baggage which accompanied him on all
his travels. He supported Yorkshire zealously without undue
prejudice and he never tired of retelling stories of first class
cricketers.

ENGLISH, Leslie Malcolm

(b) Brixton, London 7 August 1899
(d) East Dereham, Norfolk 17 October 1976
Lived Thynnes Place, Mattishall
Cricket. – clubs unknown
HS. 5 no v Bedfordshire July 1920 @ Biddenham
His Great Grandfather (a Farmer) raised 22 children. Before
WW2 he went back to London to take over one of his father's
businesses in Streatham. Leslie later lived in USA where he was
in Hotel Management for many years. He returned to Norfolk
to retire.
F.F. – A notable Bowls player he left a widow Ivy, a son, a
daughter, 7 grandchildren and 6 great grandchildren

GARLAND, Dr Thomas Ownsworth, MD MB BChir DPH MRCS LRCP

(b) Reigate, Surrey 30 December 1903
(d) Spyrie Hospital, Elgin, Scotland 8 February 1993
Lived 80 Divinty Road, Oxford
Educ. – Gresham's School (Sept 1917 –1922); Cambridge
University; Guy's Hospital (London)
Cricket. – Gresham's School
HS. 11 no v Kent (2) August 1921 @ Hythe
HS. 30 v Eton Ramblers August 1922 @ Lakenham
He is the 7th youngest NCCC Minor County player in the club's
history up to and including season 2011.
80 for Gresham's School v North West Norfolk Wanderers July
1920
Tennis for Cambridge University and Rugby Union for St Mary's
Hospital and he was a Reserve Fly-Half for England.
He is revered as the Father of New Zealand Occupational
Medicine. A qualified Doctor from Guy's Hospital October 1927.
His first House job saw him contract tuberculosis and confined
in Mundesley Sanitorium in September 1928 – he discharged
himself in 1929. A Ship's Doctor on 'SS Morton Bay' going to
Australia. A Diploma Public Health gained at the London
School of Hygiene. Worked at the Lawn Road Fever Hospital
and as the Rossall School Doctor . A Factory Doctor to Carreras
for 4 years. A District M.O.H to Kettering RDU. In 1947 a post
in New Zealand to be the country's first Industrial Hygienist
and he started the Clinic's revolution for countless factories.
Returning eventually to the UK he worked at London's Central
Middlesex Hospital

MacLAREN, Archibald Campbell

(b) Whalley Range, Manchester 1 December 1871
(d) Warfield Park, Bracknell 17 November 1944
Educ. – Elstree; Harrow School (Mr Hutton's House) leaving
1890.2
Cricket. – Lancashire; MCC; London County; Harrow
School; Liverpool & District; North of England; Gentlemen;
XI of Lancashire; AE Stoddart's XI; Rest of England; KS
Ranjitsinhji's XI; Lancashire & Yorkshire; CI Thornton's XI;
J Bamford's XI; L Robinson's XI; HDG Leveson-Gower's
XI; WG Grace's XI; AC MacLaren's XI; MC Kemp's XI; Old
Harrovarians; Army Service Corp; England – 35 Tests
HS. 21 v MCC August 1920 @ Old Buckenham Hall
1st class cricket – 424 matches 22,237 runs 452 catches 1
wicket with two brothers being first class cricketers.
'Wisden' Cricketer of the Year 1895 with their later quote of, "An
immaculate batsman possessing the grand manner, he would
have gained still higher renown on the playing field but for
periods of poor health and the calls of business."
424 (801) for Lancashire v Somerset July 1895 – the opposition's
wicket keeper was AP Wickham (q.v) and in Lancashire's
mammoth score he conceded but 9 byes.Captain of his School,

County and England (22 times).
A Journalist – Daily Chronicle, Cricketer and other magazines (1920s –1930s.)
A variety of jobs – Manchester & Liverpool District Bank, taught at a Harrow Prep School, in RASC but invalidated out and worked as a P.T. Instructor at Aldershot, bought and ran a Hotel (but was in the habit of being rude to the guests).
His only successes were in the cricket world – he toured Australia, USA, Argentina and New Zealand. Also the Lancashire CCC Coach plus he Managed S.B. Joel's X1 tour of South Africa; Secretary to Ranjitsinhji in India (1905-08) and employed by Lionel Robinson to manage the cricket and horse racing interests at his Estate in Old Buckenham. He also discovered the legendary Sydney Barnes.
Convicted of non - payment of rates (1908) – some 10 years after his wife Maud Power used her allowance to help keep him out of the debtors' court. He had a walk - on part in Alexander Korda's film 'The Four Feathers' as a monocled Crimean veteran.
In the mid 1930s, his wife inherited a large fortune and they built an estate on 150 acres near Bracknell.

MORSE, Capt Sydney Arthur, TD
(b) Norwich 24 July 1902
(d) Norwich 19 April 1969
Lived Bergh Apton Manor, South Norfolk
Educ. – Charterhouse School; Cambridge University (Trinity College)
Cricket. – Sherwood Rangers; Norfolk Yeomanry
HS. 10 v Cambridgeshire August 1921 @ Fenner's
HS. 1 v MCC August 1920 @ Old Buckenham Hall
Father of MH (q.v)
No relation of Charles (NCCC pre 1876). NCCC Committee & Secretary and their President 1966. Norfolk High Sheriff 1967. Former Director of Steward & Patteson Ltd and Watney Mann Ltd. At his death he was a Director of Norwich Union Life & Fire Insurance Co. He was captured in Crete in 1941 and was a POW until 1945.The widow of EJ Belton (q.v) sent me a copy of Hon. Sec. SA Morse's letter dated 2 June 1948 to her husband. It reads quote, " Dear Belton, I enclose 12 Clothing Coupons which I have received from the MCC and hope they will be a slight help to you during the coming season."

MOWER, Geoffrey Harry
(b) Norwich 26 January 1902
Educ. – Bradfield College
Cricket. – Bradfield College; GH Mower's XI; Norfolk Club & Ground; Carrow; Southern Schools; GA Rotherham's XI
HS. 28 no v Kent (2) August 1923 @ Lakenham
BB. 4/33 v Hertfordshire July 1927 @ Cokenach
HS. 15 v Eton Ramblers May 1923 @ Lakenham
BB. 1/56 v New Zealand August 1927 @ Lakenham

Son of HW (q.v)
7/31 for Bradfield College v Radley College June 1917
79 for Bradfield College v Radley College June 1920
Football & Fives for Bradfield College. He was a Grain Importer who sailed from London to Sydney, Australia in 1932 and it is reckoned that he died abroad.

NUGENT, Lt. Col Lord Terence Edmund Gascoigne, GCVO MC (1st Baron of West Harling)
(b) London 11 August 1895
(d) Midhurst, Sussex 27 April 1973
Educ. – Eton College; RMC Sandhurst
Cricket. – Eton College; Eton Ramblers; Army; The Butterflies; Free Foresters; Household Brigade.
HS. Did not Bat nor Bowl in his one MC match but he did hold a catch v Hertfordshire July 1920 @ Cheshunt
44 for Eton College v I Zingari July 1913
4/85 for Household Brigade v Green Jackets May 1925.
He gave the address at Sir Pelham Warner's memorial service. Generally known as Tim Nugent – but I know my place ! Awarded the Military Cross when with the Irish Guards (wounded and mentioned in despatches) and he was the Brigade Major of the British Guards 1929-33. Adjutant 1st Battalion Irish Guards employed as GSO3 War Office. Personal Assistant to the Chief of the Imperial General Staff and he accompanied the Duke and Duchess of York on their Australian and NZ tour 1924-26. Lt. Col Comptroller, Lord Chamberlain's Dept 1936. Equerry to HRH Duke of York. Extra Equerry to King George V1, 1937-52 and to the Queen from 1952. A Permanent Lord-in-Waiting to the Queen from 1960. President MCC 1962-63 and the President of Surrey CCC 1966-69

SCOTT-CHAD, Capt George Norman
(b) Kensington, London 1 November 1899
(d) St. Mary's Hospital, Paddington, London 4 July 1950
Educ. – Eton College
Cricket. – Eton College; Eton Ramblers; MCC; Army; Household Brigade; Eastern Counties; Lord Tennyson's XI.
HS. 76 v Bedfordshire July 1921 @ Bedford
BB. 3/7 v Buckinghamshire August 1930 @ Wing
HS. 14 v South Africans June 1929 @ Lakenham
BB. 3/13 v All India June 1932 @ Lakenham
Son of C (q.v)
1st class cricket – 3 matches 49 runs 4 catches 6 wickets and he toured Jamaica with Tennyson's team (1931-2) but did not play a first class game. He played for Eton Ramblers against Norfolk in 1922 (scored 60) and 1923. In the Coldstream Guards. An Army Fives and Squash Champion
F.F.- His Probated London will saw his Estate valued at £160,775-0-3

1921

FRYER, Philip William John, MBE
(b) Blowick Hall, Wymondham, Norfolk 24 October 1900
(d) Norwich 3 January 1974
Educ. – Wellingborough GS; Cambridge University (Jesus College)
Cricket. – Wellingborough GS
HS. 46 v Surrey (2) June 1925 @ Oval
BB. 3/26 v Leicestershire (2) August 1925 @ Lakenham
HS. 19 v Eton Ramblers May 1923 @ Lakenham
BB. 4/60 v Eton Ramblers May 1923 @ Lakenham
Nephew of EH (q.v) & PA (q.v)
NCCC Vice President but he gave up the post to run his father's Farm in 1926. Awarded the MBE for his Home Guard Service. Wymondham Church Warden for 40 years. Served Wymondham UDC as a Conservative. Chairman of Upper Yare and Tay River Boards

MAHON, Sir Gerald MacMahon
(b) Norwich 24 July 1904
(d) Bicester, Oxon 6 April 1982
Lived The Plough House, Stratton Audley, Oxfordshire
Educ. – Dulwich College; Oxford University (Brasenose College – BA)
Cricket. – Dulwich College; Norfolk Club & Ground; NC Tufnell's XI.
HS. 32 no v Bedfordshire July 1923 @ Luton
HS. 46 v Eton Ramblers May 1923 @ Lakenham
Called to the Bar (Inner Temple) 1926. Resident Magistrate Tanganyika 1936. Judge, HM High Court of Tanganyika Territory 1949-59. Chief Justice of Zanzibar 1959 to retirement 1964. Chairman Medical Appeal Tribunals under Industrial Acts 1964-76

MARTIN, George Harlow
(b) King's Lynn, Norfolk 21 July 1884
(d) Lynn General Hospital, Norfolk 5 February 1964
Educ. – Lynn Technical College; Peterborough Technical College
Cricket. – Hunstanton; West Norfolk; Norfolk Club & Ground
HS. 69 v Staffordshire July 1921 @ Walsall
Football. – Lynn Technical College; Peterborough Technical College; King's Lynn; Ilford; Norwich City FC; England Amateur International trials; Southern Counties; Norfolk County 1905-14 (26 apps 25 goals – to include a double hat-trick v Suffolk 30 December 1909.)
The Eastern Football News in February 1921 said that he had won 35 medals including three junior ones plus four each with Ilford and Peterborough and the rest with King's Lynn.

2nd Lt Norfolk Regiment and also in the Norfolk Fusiliers serving in France. Teacher All Saints Elementary School 1905. General Study Master King Edward VII GS 1910-49 – plus, of course, the Games Master and he also taught Woodwork.

ORTON, Major John Overton Cone, MC AFC
(b) Marylebone, London 30 August 1989
(d) St. Peters Hospital, Westminster, London 23 May 1962
Lived Endsleigh Court, Woburn Place, London WC1
Educ. – Imperial Service College; RMC Sandhurst
Cricket. – Lacey's; Bury St Edmunds; Free Foresters
HS. 3 v Staffordshire June 1921 @ Lakenham
In Royal Flying Corp and Royal Air Corp. The Military Cross won when after a set of 3 missions his plane had 20 bullet holes. In WW1 he flew for Serbian Royal Army and on 27 August 1916 he was awarded the Order of Karageorge. Gazetted Royal Norfolk Regiment 1909 and retired as Major in 1924.
Golf- The Australian Long Driver Champion and he played Hockey for Norfolk County.
Lawn Tennis – in 1924 he won the Norwich mixed doubles tournament with his wife.
A famous British Film Scriptwriter and Director. Formerly an Editor of 'Silents' (1925-44)
He wrote scripts for Comedians Will Hay and Arthur Askey. A Contract Writer to Alfred Hitchcock and a Staff Writer for Gainsborough Pictures (1930-48).
He gained a considerable measure of credit for forming the Anglo-Swedish Film Alliance.
An 'EDP' interview produced on 24 October 1928 revealed – He joined 9th Regiment (known as Holy Boys) and later served in the Home Defence Wing flying operations over the Eastern Counties. When with the Air Force his old Norfolk Regiment were besieged. He had the idea to drop 'scissor' cigarettes in parcels tied with the Norfolk Regiment colours. A wireless message told him not to favour one Corps at the expense of others but he ignored the request/order.
F.F. – *His 3x great grandfather Spencer Houghton Cone was a Chaplain for the Houses of Representatives in Washington. There are actors / actresses galore in their family tree*

1922

EVERETT, Richard Anthony Luntley
(b) Norwich 3 February 1902
(d) Blandford Forum, Dorset 7 August 1996
Educ. – Norwich GS; Cambridge University (Jesus College – BA 1923 MA 1930)
Cricket. – Norfolk Ramblers; GH Mower's XI; Norwich Wanderers
HS. 20 v Hertfordshire July 1924 @ Stevenage AND 20 no v Surrey (2) June 1928 @ The Oval

Athletics – Cambridge University Low Hurdler
Son of Ernest Everett (a Norwich Surgeon)

GODERSON, Richard
(b) Mileham, Norfolk 13 September 1902
(d) Mileham, Norfolk 24 October 1966
Educ. – Mileham School
Cricket. – Norfolk Club & Ground
He was a substitute Fielder for JE Nichols (off with a swollen knee) v Staffordshire August 1923 @ Lakenham. He held two catches in this minor counties game at mid off to help Walter Beadsmoore snag 8/59.
HS. 26 v Eton Ramblers August 1922 @ Lakenham
He was an Agricultural Labourer in his early days

HARVEY, George Edward Anthony
(b) Great Witchingham, Norfolk 18 November 1896
(d) West Norwich Hospital 10 June 1966
Lived 447 Earlham Road, Norwich
Cricket. – Trumpington
HS. 30 v Bedfordshire July 1922 @ Lakenham
HS. 22 v Eton Ramblers May 1923 @ Lakenham
The 'EDP' in 1923 said that he had leg hitting and driving power. A Norwich Union Fire Officer.
The Norwich Municipal Golf Club Captain in 1943
F.F.- He left £5,187 to the Norwich Union Life Insurance Society.
He just missed England winning the 1966 Football World Cup

WHITE, Karl
(b) Putney, London 27 September 1895
(d) Brentwood, Essex JFM 1972
Educ. – Wellingborough GS
Cricket. – Wellingborough GS; Old Wellingburians
HS. 62 v Eton Ramblers August 1922 @ Lakenham – scored in 42 minutes with 9 (4) and 1 (6).
A prolific scorer for his school evidenced the following examples – 110 v Bedford Modern School July 1911; 105 v Nottingham High School June 1912 and 102 v Bedford Modern School July 1913

WORMALD, Major John, MC DL JP
(b) Westminster, London 23 February 1882
(d) East Dereham, Norfolk 13 November 1957
Lived Gorgate Hall and was ill for some time
Educ. – Eton College
Cricket. – Eton College; Eton Ramblers; Gressenhall; Gentlemen of Surrey; Middlesex; MCC; I Zingari; Dereham
HS. 78 no v Surrey (2) June 1922 @ Lakenham
HS. 3 v West Indies August 1923 @ Lakenham

1st class cricket – 23 matches 548 runs 8 catches
A Deputy Lieutenant for Norfolk. Commissioned in the 60th Rifles (awarded Queens Medal and 2 clasps) retiring in 1911 but rejoined until 1919. In WW2 he was an A.R.P. sub contractor in Northampton and Norfolk. A Vicar's Warden at Hoe 1925-40 and the same role in Dereham 1945 to April 1957. Chairman of Governors of Dereham High School for Girls. Schoolmaster and School Manager of London Road and Toftwood School
F.F. – He married the widow of ET Garnier (q.v)

1923

EVANS, Noel Glyn
(b) Clydach, Glamorgan 20 September 1895
(d) Royal Infirmary, Bristol 7 January 1961
Lived 44 Redbrook Road, Newport
Cricket. – Yarmouth Town
HS. 3 v Kent (2) July 1923 @ Beckenham
One of 6 NCCC players at Yarmouth at the time (Aitken, Pretheroe, Rouse, Veale and Wyllys were the others). His fielding won him golden opinions

LONG, Edward Fortescue
(b) Swinderby, Lincolnshire 4 December 1876
(d) Grove House Nursing Home, Norwich 29 September 1955
Educ. – Haileybury College (Hailey House 1890.3-1895.2); Yorkshire College
Cricket. – Haileybury College; CEYMS; Lincolnshire; Barrow; Collingham; Norfolk Ramblers
HS. 51 v Hertfordshire August 1923 @ Lakenham – in his 46th year
BB. 4/25 v Surrey (2) August 1923 @ Lakenham
HS. 13 v West Indies August 1923 @ Lakenham
8/50 for Norfolk Ramblers v Yarmouth July 1924
He was the last man to be selected for his County (first class or Minor) as a specialist lob bowler.
The family came to Norfolk as his brother Walter was the Newton Flotman Rector in 1914. Occupation of shell making at Lawrence & Scotts (1915-18). Edward was an Electrical Engineer at Brush Electrical Engineering Co in Loughborough. Chief Electrical Engineer at Vickers (Barrow -in-Furness)
F.F. – He bequeathed £84,116-9-1 to his aforesaid brother in 1955

PEARSE, Arthur John
(b) Leicester 28 January 1902
(d) Saskatchewan, Canada 25 April 1995
Educ. – Oakham School
Cricket. – Norwich Wanderers
HS. 12 v Hertfordshire Jul 1923 @ Stevenage
HS. 61 v Eton Ramblers May 1923 @ Lakenham

On 3 April 1924 he sailed from Liverpool to St John, New Brunswick on 'Montlaurier'
No relation to Martin Pearse (Norfolk Over 50s and Over 60s)

RAYNER, George Robert
(b) Cambridge Barracks, Portsmouth Town 6 September 1880
(d) Diss, Norfolk 31 January 1947
Cricket. – Diss
HS. 4 v Bedfordshire July 1923 @ Luton AND 4 v Hertfordshire July 1923 @ Stevenage
He had a Brewery House in Diss when working for Youngs, Crayshay & Youngs (Brewers).
Licensee of 'Greyhound' in Diss 1922-25. Licensee 'Beehive' in Diss March 10 1926 – 14 April 1926 and 8 October 1930 – 1933.
F.F. – Son of John (Colour Sgt 69th Regiment) and Emma Hoare

STONE, George James
(b) East Dereham, Norfolk 1 June 1894
(d) Whittingham Hospital, Trowse, Norwich December 1960
Lived 54 Hughenden Road, Norwich
Cricket. – Carrow
HS. 23 v Surrey (2) August 1923 @ Lakenham
A Carrow Works Engineer
F.F. – His Norwich administered will saw him leave £632-10s to his widow Ivy (nee King)
I found his 83 year old son Geoffrey but unfortunately he has had a stroke and his memory took a turn for the worse.

TUFNELL, Neville Charsley
(b) Simla, Punjab. India 13 June 1887
(d) London Hospital, Mile End Road, London 3 August 1951
Lived Fairfield, Sunningdale, Berkshire
Educ. – Eton College; Cambridge University (Trinity College)
Cricket. – Eton College; NC Tufnell's XI; Cambridge University – Blue 1909-10 ;Public Schools; Stoke Edith; Surrey; I Zingari; Gentlemen; South of England; Army; Free Foresters; GJV Weigall's XI; HDG Leveson- Gower's XI; L Robinson's XI; PF Warner's XI; MCC; Eton Ramblers; England – 1 Test Match v South Africa (Cape Town) being the first ever substitute fielder to effect a stumping in such a match.
HS. 33 no v Surrey (2) June 1925 @ The Oval
HS. 9 v West Indies August 1923 @ Lakenham
1st class cricket – 70 matches 1,514 runs 1 wicket 99 victims (59c 40s)
125 for Eton Ramblers v NCCC May 1923
His father and father-in-law also played 1st class cricket.
Commissioned 1st Vol. Batt Queens Royal West Surrey Regiment. Captain Grenadier Guards. Appointed Lt. Col as a Group Commander in National Defence Corp and transferred

to King's Royal Rifle Corps. Gentleman Usher to George VI (1 March 1937 to 3 August 1951). An Insurance Broker and Lloyd's Underwriter
F.F. – His family inherited £79,455-2-4 from his will

....

1924
....

AITKEN, Sir Arthur Percival Hay
(b) Hereford 2 October 1905
(d) Aldeburgh, Suffolk 25 May 1984
Known as Sir Peter Aitken
Educ. – Norwich GS; Oxford University (Trinity College)
Cricket. – Yarmouth; Overstrand; NC Tufnell's XI; Gentlemen of Suffolk; Oxford Emeriti
HS. 24 v Surrey (2) July 1924 @ Hunstanton
Chairman of Norwich Union Ins. Group and other subsidiaries. Former Managing Director & Chairman Textile Machinery Makers Ltd to include the period 1949-1960. Deputy Chairman Stone-Platt Industries Ltd retiring 1975. Director of Norwich General Trust. Board Member Commonwealth Development Corp
F.F. – There is painting of him in London's Portrait Gallery. A 'Who Was Who' publication lists his clubs as Royal Thames Yacht Club and Aldeburgh Golf Club

BACKHOUSE, Jonathan
(b) Darlington 16 March 1907
(d) Gt. Horkesley, Essex 7 December 1993
Educ. – RNC Dartmouth
Cricket. – RNC Dartmouth; Yarmouth
HS. 11 v Hertfordshire August 1924 @ Lakenham
Grandson of GF Buxton (q.v)
Worked for a Merchant Bank from 1924-28 and 1950-70. On the Stock Exchange 1928-50. In Royal Artillery 1939-45

COLDHAM, John Maurice
(b) Forsbrook, Staffordshire 17 January 1901
(d) Woking, Surrey 25 July 1986
Died in Hospital after a long period of ill-health
Educ. – Repton School; Oxford University
Cricket. – Repton School; Yarmouth Town; Yarmouth Nomads; Oxford University – no Blue as his game was against the Army; Oxford University Authentics; Repton Pilgrims; AR Tanner's XI; Minor Counties.
HS. 111 v Hertfordshire August 1926 @ Lakenham
HS. 13 v New Zealand August 1931 @ Lakenham
1st class cricket – 2 matches 73 runs
61 no for Repton School v Uppingham School June 1917
75 no for Repton Pilgrims v Derbyshire Club & Ground August 1946
3/43 for Repton Pilgrims v Derbyshire Club & Ground August 1947

One of seven Norfolk players in the Minor Counties side that walloped the 1924 South Africans.
Wisden quoted of him ,"Tall and strong, he was a good, upstanding batsman, a fine slip and, if required, a competent wicket keeper. He faced with skill the quality bowling of Yorkshire's Rhodes and Hirst, Staffordshire's Barnes and South Africa's Pegler."
Games Master at Sedbergh running the cricket operation for 21 years

COLMAN, Major Alan Rees, JP

(b) Bracondale, Norwich 3 January 1901
(d) Sherburn, Yorkshire 17 January 1943
Lived Thickthorn Hall, Norwich
Killed in Action while ferrying aircraft to England when as a First Officer (Air Transport Auxillary) his Hurricane 1V looped on landing and tipped over into the water – he drowned. His duties included collecting new, factory-built aircraft and flying them to operational squadrons.
Educ. – Evelyns School; Eton College
Cricket. – Eton College; Eton Ramblers
HS. 2 v Surrey (2) July 1924 @ Hunstanton
Brother of GRR (q.v) and Uncle of DWJ (q.v)
NCCC Hon. Secretary 1923-1931 (everyone should read his 1928 Subscription Reminder for Norfolk Members reproduced on Page 22 of NCCC 1993 handbook – very witty and clever.) Director of family firm JJ Colman. Director of Pathe Co as per his seen Norfolk & Norwich Aero Club certificate when he was flying Gypsy Moths. He made Ocean crossings to Canada and USA as per Passenger Lists that are available to view on the World Wide Web. The Norfolk Record Office hold family papers including letters to his wife from Sierra Leone written the year before he was tragically killed

COVILL, Reginald John

(b) Cambridge 10 August 1905
(d) Colchester, Essex 18 March 2002
Educ. – St. Luke's School (left school at age 12)
Cricket. – Norfolk Club & Ground; East of England; MCC; MCC Young Professionals; Eastern Counties; Covill's XI; Cambridgeshire; Minor Counties; Clacton; College Servants.
HS. 33 v Leicestershire (2) June 1926 @ Hinckley
BB. 4/34 v Leicestershire (2) August 1927 @ Hunstanton
1st class cricket – 12 matches 322 runs 4 catches 23 wickets
He did everything in the Cambridgeshire v Lincolnshire match August 1933 at Fenner's – he hit 146 with 15 fours, a five and a six; took 6/33 to include a hat-trick; held a catch and took 2/47 in the second innings. His father and brother also played for Cambridgeshire. He had an offer to join Middlesex but war broke out. The St. John's College Groundsman for 21 years. Reg worked as a Landscape Gardener and for Green King Drays and tended Bowling Greens. His son visited me and brought

along some marvellous mementos of his father's cricketing career.

VEALE, Frank Henry

(b) Yarmouth, Norfolk 4 January 1894
(d) Yarmouth, Norfolk 23 January 1938
Educ. – Yarmouth GS
Cricket. – Yarmouth GS;Yarmouth Town; YMCA; Yarmouth Athletic; Yarmouth Old Boys
HS. 18 v Hertfordshire July 1924 @ Stevenage – played because GRR Colman was assisting Old Etonians
10/46 (in match) for Yarmouth Old Boys v Yarmouth GS July 1911
6/11 for YMCA v RNH July 1912
Football for Yarmouth and Gorleston Town. Secretary of YMCA Billiard's Club. The 1911 Census lists him as an Architect.
F.F. – He left £741-9-1 in his will to his family but unfortunately he was a widower due to the death of his wife Mildred (nee Felmingham).

1925

HOLMES, John Bridgman

(b) Norwich 25 January 1908
(d) Dunston, Norwich 17 March 1990
Educ. – Norwich GS
Cricket. – Norwich GS; CEYMS; Norfolk Club & Ground; South Norfolk
HS. 21 v Leicestershire (2) June 1928 @ Coalville
A right hand bat and right arm fast bowler.
He left at death his wife Beryl and two daughters Anne and Jane

OWENS, Dr Col John Herbert, MRCS LRCP TD

(b) Long Stratton, Norfolk 26 December 1886
(d) Norfolk & Norwich Hospital 22 May 1964
Lived Ipswich Road, Long Stratton
Cricket. – Norwich Wanderers
HS. 22 v Hertfordshire July 1928 @ Cokenach
Colonel Army Medical Services. British Medical Association Member. Examiner Med. Officer for Ministry of Pensions and National Insurance. Norfolk & Norwich Hon. Surgeon & Hon. Physician.
Hon. Surgeon Addenbrooke's Hospital (Cambridge)

WILLIAMSON, Ernest Clarke

(b) Murton Colliery, County Durham 24 May 1890
(d) West Norwich Hospital 30 April 1964
Cricket. – Morley; Norfolk Club & Ground; Norwich City CC; GH Mower's XI
HS. 24 no v Hertfordshire August 1925 @ Lakenham

HS. 4 v New Zealand August 1927 @ Lakenham
Best wicket keeping season 1925 with 18 victims (17c 1s)
Football. – Murton Red Star; Wingate Albion; Croydon
Common; Tottenham Hotspur; Footballer's Battalion (17th
Middlesex Batt); Woolwich Arsenal; Norwich City FC June
1923; Army; England – 2 caps
*A Professional Footballer at age 15 and a goalkeeper so he
obviously donned the gloves for NCCC.*
*His WW1 Attestation Papers (showing him to be a Sgt Major)
reveal that he asked for all his wages to be allotted to his wife
back in the UK. A Publican at 'Flower in Hand' from 22 July
1924 to 3 October 1927 – he could have stocked the Pavilion
Bar! His longest Publican spell was at the 'Mitre Tavern' from 4
October 1927 to 29 November 1958 where many an ex NCFC
player would seek his company over a pint.*

1926

GATHERGOOD, Dr Leslie Somerville, MD BCh
(b) Terrington St John, Norfolk 5 November 1892
(d) Birmingham 5 August 1968
Educ. – The Leys School; Cambridge University – MA;
University of London
Cricket. – The Leys School; Bishop's Stortford
HS. 14 v Hertfordshire July 1926 @ Cokenach
*He trained to be a Dentist and supposedly played in a
Cambridge University Freshman's Trial ?*
*He gained his Degree 18 February 1921 per the British Medical
Journal. Leslie Joined the Royal Flying Corp 31 August 1915
and he flew 75 different types of aeroplane in logging 695
hours (including air races). He was also a Barrister-at-Law. Part
of a threesome (Gathergood, Crombie & Green) who headed
a Working Party appointed by the College of Practitioners to
report on Family History of Diabetes.*

LOW, Harry Frederick
(b) Norwich 3 August 1903
(d) Norwich 6 March 1968
Educ. – Bracondale School
Cricket. – GA Stevens' XI; Norfolk Ramblers; Overstrand;
Norfolk Club & Ground; NC Tufnell's XI; HF Low's XI.
HS. 83 v Surrey (2) June 1928 @ The Oval
BB. 1/35 v Kent (2) July 1933 @ Tonbridge
HS. 63 v Suffolk July 1933 @ Lowestoft
BB. 2/75 v Suffolk July 1933 @ Lowestoft
*Took part in two NCCC century partnerships plus a double
century one with M. Falcon of 213 (3rd wicket) v Surrey (2) in
1928.*
*He worked for 21 years for A.E. Coe & Sons retiring in 1966
as a Director of the Company. An award winning National
Photographer with one of his photos 'Grace Space Pace' in
1954 becoming famous as a Jaguar Car advertisement.*

F.F. –Tragically a 70ft Elm tree crashed into his dark green
Hillman Minx Estate car in a snowstorm/gale killing him.

ROUGHT-ROUGHT, Basil William
(b) Brandon, Suffolk 15 September 1904
(d) Brandon, Suffolk 27 October 1995
1902 Deed Poll – Elizabeth Rought and Albert Rought Witta
became Rought-Rought
Cricket. – Heath House CC; GE Pilch's XI; GH Mower's XI;
HDG Leveson-Gower's XI; Minor Counties; South Norfolk;
Norfolk & Suffolk Nomads; 5th Norfolks
HS. 159 v Lincolnshire July 1937 @ Grimsby – hitting his
only three 6s for NCCC
HS. 57 v West Indies August 1933 @ Lakenham
Brother of DC (q.v) and RC (q.v)
1st class cricket – 4 matches 229 runs 3 catches
*Basil a left handed bat and not an all rounder like his two
younger brothers. He hit a substantial 757 Minor County runs
in 1937.The three of them played in the same NCCC side on 41
occasions with 37 being in a Minor County match.*
102 no for 5th Norfolks v CEYMS May 1927
*NCCC President 1967 and a former Club Captain.With the 7th
Norfolks in France and a Prisoner of War in Germany - David
Armstrong (q.v) relates the story that Basil escaped near the end
of the War and was sheltered by a French Farming woman. She
took a fancy to him and did not tell him when the War ended,
keeping him as a 'toy boy'. Basil was seriously injured in a car
crash in 1961.*

ROUGHT-ROUGHT, Rodney Charles
(b) Brandon, Suffolk 17 February 1908
(d) Chelsea, London 5 May 1979
He fell from the balcony of his second floor flat
Educ. – Educated privately; Cambridge University
(Emmanuel College)
Cricket. – Heath House CC; Cambridge University – Blue
1930,1932; Free Foresters; South Norfolk; HDG Leveson-
Gower's XI; 5th Norfolks.
HS. 84 v Buckinghamshire July 1928 @ Wing
BB. 8/24 v Hertfordshire July 1933 @ Broxbourne – at
one point his analysis read 8-6-2-5.
HS. 26 v New Zealand June 1937 @ Lakenham
BB. 6/31 v Cambridge Crusaders June 1934 @ Lakenham
– all bowled
Brother of BW (q.v) and DC (q.v)
*7/24 and 72 for 5th Norfolks v CEYMS May 1927 – to include a
hat-trick*
*6/15 for NCCC v Buckinghamshire July 1929 – to include a
hat-trick*
*5/102 for Cambridge University v Sussex June 1932 – to include
a hat-trick*
1st class cricket – 34 matches 457 runs 17 catches 122 wickets

He missed season 1936 (torn muscle) and 1938 (strained muscle).
The third leading wicket taker in Championship games for Norfolk.
In family Hatters & Furriers business – W. Rought Ltd of Brandon. He retired from a London firm of Furriers and continued to live in the Capital.

1927

BALLY, Capt John Harold
(b) Edmonton, London 31 August 1906
(d) Germany 25 April 1945
Buried at Becklingen War Cemetery, Soltau, Germany
Lived Kowai, 3 Summerhill Close, Haywards Heath, Sussex
Educ. – St John's School (Leatherhead)
Cricket. – St John's School; Needham; Harleston; Yarmouth Town; GA Stevens' XI; East Norfolk
HS. 107 v Leicestershire (2) July 1929 @ Hinckley
HS. 4 no v West Indies May 1928 @ Lakenham AND 4 v South Africa June 1929 @ Lakenham
Best wicket keeping season 1929 with 23 victims (20c 3s) plus a catch against the South African touring side. Solicitor for Yarmouth Town and a Partner in Waugh, Brumell & Bally and a Captain in the Royal Sussex Regiment (6th Batt).
F.F. – *The site of Becklingen was chosen for its position overlooking Luneburg Heath where on 4 May 1945 Field Marshall Montgomery accepted German surrender from Admiral Doenitz.*

CATTERMOULE, Kenneth Malcolm
(b) Norwich 13 May 1905
(d) Poole, Dorset 18 October 1999
Educ. – City of Norwich School
Cricket. – City of Norwich School; GH Mower's XI; Norfolk Club & Ground; Dean Park CC; Trident CC
HS. 15 no v Leicestershire (2) August 1927 @ Hunstanton
WW2 in Fire Service. Incorrectly shown in the Norfolk Papers as Cattermole. Manager at Norwich Union Office in Southampton. An Insurance Broker in Boscombe, Bournemouth. He played Hockey for Norwich. I have held the mounted ball that is in his family in recognition of his 10/44 in an innings on 9 August 1930 – to include a hat-trick.

CRAWSHAY, Frederick George Luke
(b) Murree, Bengal, India 18 October 1900
(d) Norwich 9 February 1973
He came to the UK when he was aged 3
Educ. – Imperial Service College (Windsor)
Cricket. – Norfolk Club & Ground; Oxfordshire
HS. 49 no v Surrey (2) August 1928 @ Lakenham

F.F. – *His Funeral was held in Chalfont St Peters in Buckinghamshire*

GLADDEN, Robert Hubert
(b) Crosswight Hall, Smallburgh, Norfolk 31 March 1910
(d) Fakenham, Norfolk 15 March 1988
Educ. – Sherborne School
Cricket. – Sherborne School; HF Low's XI; West Norfolk Colts
HS. 94 v Lincolnshire August 1935 @ Hunstanton
HS. 50 v South Africa June 1929 @ Lakenham
74 for Sherborne School v Downside School June 1928
A Poultry Farmer living in Taverham he was sentenced to 9 months imprisonment on 25 January 1940 at Norwich Assizes for dangerous driving. The Norwich Sheriff EJ Mann (q.v) delivered up the Court notes and precepts. Robert caused the death of a young soldier in Hellesdon at 10.30pm on 30 September 1939. He pleaded not guilty to manslaughter with it being revealed that the soldier was carried 108 feet by the car. The defendant had driven for 13 years with only one previous conviction. His license was suspended for 5 years.

LORD, Albert
(b) Barwell, Leicester 28 August 1888
(d) Barwell, Leicester 29 March 1969
His real name was Albert Callington. The story behind his pseudonym is that he arrived on the Leicestershire staff to find one cricketer named 'King' and another called 'Knight', so he thought he should also join the aristocracy. How bizzare!
Cricket. – Leicestershire Club & Ground; Leicestershire; CE de Trafford's XI; CEYMS
HS. 9 v West Indies May 1928 @ Lakenham
1st class cricket – 130 matches 3,864 runs 72 catches 39 wickets.
53 & 4/31 and 3/19 for Leicestershire (2) v NCCC June 1926
58 & 2/43 and 3/4 for Leicestershire (2) v NCCC August 1926

MACKENZIE, Rothsay Seaforth
(b) Umercarry, Bombay, India 11 May 1888
(d) Lezayre, Isle of Man 23 February 1983
Educ. – Repton School
Cricket. – Repton School; Norwich Wanderers; Norfolk Club & Ground
HS. 14 no v Leicestershire (2) July 1927 @ Leicester
Son of AG Mackenzie of Bombay, India and a good enough athlete as he won his Norfolk Lawn Tennis Colours in 1931. He married Hester Chase on 13 May 1916 in Hobart, Tasmania. He was in (First) Australian Imperial Force 1914-18 and listed as a Schoolteacher at Hutchings School.
Embarked from Melbourne, Australia on 21 October 1916 on board 'Star of Victoria's a member of the 4th Batt (NSW)

Infantry and saw service on the Western Front as well as previously in
India. On 26 June 1917 he was promoted from 2nd Lt to Lieut. On 14 February 1918 he had his left small toe amputated as a result of a gunshot wound. He left India to avoid ructions after working for his brother as an Accountant. Other occupations attributed to him are as a Property Developer in Holland Park, London; an Articled Clerk at Price Waterhouse and an Accounts Clerk at Norwich Mercury Newspaper. His wife could not cope with his supposedly 'Walter Mitty' lifestyle so she sailed back to Melbourne without her two children. She did eventually recover her health and she passed away peacefully in Sydenham, London in 1963.

F.F. – He was of dark complexion, brown eyes, black hair, a scar back part of ring finger and 71 inches tall plus weighing 136 pounds. In a letter dated 13 June 1939 he wrote from Glenview, Thorpe St Andrew, Norwich to the A.I.F Base Record Office about his war medals. He wrote again on 28 February 1966 (almost 27 years later) requesting recommendation which he believed was submitted for the award of a Military Cross. Not surprisingly no record of such an award nor recommendation existed.

READ, John Arthur
(b) Yarmouth, Norfolk 24 June 1898
(d) Norwich 8 April 1986
Educ. – Hethersett School
Cricket. – Hethersett; GH Mower's XI; Norwich Union
HS. 4 v Buckinghamshire August 1927 @ Lakenham
NCCC Club Secretary October 1961 to 1966. Michael Falcon in his 1962 Handbook Annual Report stated that John, accompanied by HE Theobald (q.v) visited Australia this winter to watch the Test series

WYLLYS, Gerard Hugh de Burgh
(b) Hampstead, London 29 June 1902
(d) Poole, Dorset 23 February 1986
Lived Tarrant, Launceston, Blandford
Educ. – Repton School (The Cross House); Oxford University (Wadham College – MA 1923)
Cricket. – Repton School;Yarmouth Town; RAF; Repton Pilgrims; Nomads; HF Low's XI; Dorset Rangers; NC Tufnell's XI; Oxford University Authentics; GA Stevens' XI
HS. 16 v Kent (2) May 1928 @ Beckenham
HS. 12 v Suffolk July 1933 @ Lowestoft
BB. 1/16 v Suffolk July 1933 @ Lowestoft
81 for GA Stevens' XI v GH Mower's XI in a Norfolk County trial match.
101 no for Yarmouth Town v CEYMS in 1934 – the opposition had Norfolk men Ames, Dann, Holmes & George Pilch in their side.
On NCCC Executive Committee and Norfolk Cricket Association

Committee. With Yarmouth Town CC from 1921, secretary from 1927 and captain from 1929. Solicitor at Lucas & Wyllys, a firm still operating in Norfolk. He left the Yarmouth district in 1936 for Bournemouth. A former F/Lt. and an Adjutant 1942 at RAF Cosford School of Physical Training and in RAF Legal Section until demob in 1945. Worked for Lacey & Sons (Solicitors) until retirement.
F.F. – He was known as Hugh with his son William Gerard known as Gerard. The latter like me has trawled 'The London Gazette' in order to find detail of DF Walker's (q.v) DFC award without success.
The award was hinted at by BGW Stevens in his ledger.

1928

BELL, Frederic Robinson
(b) Sunderland 21 October 1899
(d) North Walsham, Norfolk 30 July 1981
He was found dead on his kitchen floor by a Manservant
Educ. – Royal Grammar School (Newcastle-upon-Tyne)
Cricket. – Durham County; GH Mower's XI; Norfolk Ramblers; North Walsham
HS. 68 v Kent (2) July 1929 @ Canterbury
BB. 1/22 v Hertfordshire August 1930 @ Lakenham
HS. 69 v South Africa June 1929 @ Lakenham
BB. 2/13 v West Indies May 1928 @ Lakenham
A retired Solicitor (Wilkinson & Davies) and Coroner. He was a beneficiary in Rev AC Davies (q.v) will.
F.F. – His daughter-in-law Dorothy revealed that the cause of death was Heart and Artery disease.

1929

ABEL, Albert George
(b) Norwich 24 April 1902
(d) Norwich 1 December 1998
Cricket. – Norfolk Club & Ground; Yarmouth; Norwich Union Fire Office
HS. 11 v Leicestershire (2) July 1919 @ Hinckley
104 no for NUFO v Norwich Wanderers July 1925
F.F. – He died peacefully with his funeral in Aylsham and he left a widow Hilda (nee Melton).
His 'EDP' obituary dated 3 December 1998 mentioned that he was an Uncle to three boys and one girl as he had no children from his marriage.

BERESFORD, Major Richard Marcus
(b) Hunstanton, Norfolk 13 November 1912
(d) Oundle, Northamptonshire 19 August 1968
Educ. – Oundle School; Cambridge University
Cricket. – Oundle School; Cambridge University trials; Public Schools; Lord's XI; The Rest; West Norfolk.

HS. 72 v Suffolk August 1948 @ Lakenham
BB. 1/6 v Suffolk August 1948 @ Lakenham
HS. 42 no v West Indies June 1939 @ Lakenham
Son of RAA (q.v)
He played for NCCC while still at school and he is the 10th
youngest debutant in NCCC's Minor County history.
110 for Oundle School v Leys School June 1930 – the following
year he hit 686 runs for them at an average of 57.16.
Hockey for Oundle School and a Major in the Royal Signals.
Latterly an Oundle School Housemaster

DANN, Walter Edward
(b) Hethersett, Norwich 16 April 1906
(d) Hethersett, Norwich 1 March 1977
Educ. – Hethersett School: City of Norwich School
Cricket. – Hethersett; CEYMS; East Norfolk; South Norfolk;
Norfolk Bitterns
HS. 6 v Hertfordshire July 1934 @ Broxbourne
102 no (155-9) for CEYMS v Yarmouth Exiles (a.o 77) in Norfolk
Junior Cup at Lakenham 1929.
A Master Butcher – the family business from which he retired
in 1968. He played Lawn Bowls for Wymondham and Norfolk
County. A Wymondham Bowls Assistant Treasurer and Vice
President.
The Norfolk EBA Delegate

GREENWELL, John Wilfred
(b) Hamsterley, Co Durham 3 May 1901
(d) Birmingham AMJ 1974
Cricket. – CEYMS
HS. 8 v Leicestershire (2) July 1929 @ Hinckley
For those who have the Norwich City FC book 'Glorious
Canaries 1902-1994' the above b/d is a corrected update for
'Sticks' as he was known.
Football.- Stanhope; Crook Town; Ferryhill Athletic; Annfield
Plain; Norwich City FC 13 April 1928; Swindon Town; Bath City;
Western House
He was Mine Host of the 'Colman Arms' in Birmingham.
Such confusion in trying to trace him as the NCFC Handbook
1929/30 and T.W Pegg & Sons publication has him as
W.Greenwell; the Football League Ledger of Registrations
1931/32 has him as John W; the 1928 Athletic News has W and
the 1929 edition has J.W. His more famous brother Jack was at
FC Barcelona into the 1930s and became coach to the Spanish
national side before passing away in Santa Fe, Argentina in
1945.

UTTING, Alec George
(b) Norwich 13 June 1895
(d) Cringleford, Norwich 20 April 1960
Educ. – St Marks School
Cricket. – St Marks School; Norfolk Club & Ground; Norwich

Wanderers; GA Stevens' XI
HS. 11 v Buckinghamshire August 1929 @ Lakenham
BB. 5/24 v Buckinghamshire August 1931 @ Lakenham
HS. 2 v All India June 1932 @ Lakenham
BB. 4/34 v All India June 1932 @ Lakenham – had 8/95 in
the match
Son of William who was the scorer for NCCC for over 25
years.
F.F. – His Probated Norwich will dated 23 August 1960 saw
him leave £3,627-3-2

WATSON, Charles Philip, JP
(b) School House, Ipswich 13 April 1910
(d) Upton, Norfolk 28 January 1977
Educ. – Harrow School; Oxford University (Balliol College)
Cricket. – Harrow School; Upton
HS. 35 v Leicestershire (2) August 1929 @ Hunstanton
Son of AK (q.v)
Two Great Uncles and an Uncle all gained their Oxford
University Blues for cricket.
Football for Upton Athletic FC and he also taught football at
Upton School. A Teacher, Councillor and Magistrate during his
life. He represented Upton with Fishley on the old Blofield and
Flegg District Council and was the Plans Committee Chairman.
Governor at Acle Secondary Modern School

1930

DALEY, John Valiant
(b) Beccles, Suffolk 1 February 1906
(d) East Margate, Kent 14 June 1986
He moved to Norwich in 1914
Cricket. – Surrey; MW Tate's XI; British Empire XI; Army;
Suffolk; Eastern Command; Eastern Counties; Aldershot
District
HS. 22 no v Kent (2) July 1931 @ Beckenham
1st class cricket – 28 matches 75 runs 13 catches 67 wickets
8/86 for Suffolk v Lincolnshire June 1939
44 and 7/118 for Suffolk v Berkshire August 1939
49 and 6/67 & 4/98 for Suffolk v Bedfordshire August 1939
Football.- CEYMS; Norfolk County 1930-32 (apps 5-1 goal);
Kingstonian (appeared in FA Amateur Cup Final).
A leg break bowler who flourished after leaving Norfolk as
some of the figures above testify.

EAGLE, Walter George
(b) Haskerton, Suffolk 3 April 1903
(d) Littleport, Cambridgeshire 3 March 1994
Educ. – Ely GS
Cricket. – Heath House CC; Wisbech; South Norfolk; March;
Ely CC; Whittlesey; Eastern Counties; Cambridgeshire
HS. 23 no v Surrey (2) July 1930 @ The Oval AND 23 v

Lincolnshire August 1930 @ Lakenham
BB. 6/27 v Hertfordshire July 1931 @ Watford
BB. 4/63 v New Zealand August 1931 @ Lakenham
In 16 NCCC Minor County games he took a very healthy 66 wickets. An incredible 66.7% of his victims were his own work in that they were either bowled, lbw or caught & bowled. He latterly snapped up 34 wickets in nine matches for Cambridgeshire.

LINGWOOD, William John
(b) Peckham, London 13 January 1911
(d) West Norwich Hospital 13 November 1985
Lived 12 Sunnyside, New Costessey, Norwich
Cricket. – JE Nichols' XI; GH Mower's XI
HS. 27 v Cambridgeshire August 1934 @ Fenner's
BB. 8/24 and 8/50 v Lincolnshire June 1932 @ Gainsborough – and he caught one of the batsman he did not bowl out. His match analysis has only been bettered by Charlie Shore (16/72) in a NCCC Minor Counties game.
HS. 6 v Suffolk July 1933 @ Lowestoft
BB. 3/28 v All India June 1932 @ Lakenham
He took 55 wickets in 1932 (all matches). A Nurse at St Andrew's Hospital for 35 years and known as 'Jack' throughout his life.

THEOBALD, Harold Ernest
(b) Norwich 18 March 1896
(d) Norwich 20 July 1982
Educ. – Bracondale School; Taunton School
Cricket. – Taunton School; GE Pilch's XI; Norwich Wanderers; YMCA; East Norfolk; Bristol; Minor Counties; Norwich Union Fire Office; Norfolk & Suffolk Nomads.
HS.104 v Cambridgeshire August 1937 @ Fenner's
HS. 72 v Suffolk July 1933 @ Lowestoft
1st class cricket – 1 match 42 runs 1 catch
He held a share for 63 years of the record 1st wicket partnership of 323 with DF Walker v Northumberland in 1939 – his share being 93. In 1975 he was still involved with NCCC as he organised Norfolk Young Amateurs & Colts matches plus the Easter holiday coaching classes.
Norwich Wanderers CC Fixture Secretary 1946-68 and a Life Member.
Rugby Union for Taunton School and Hockey for Taunton School and Norwich Grasshoppers.
Football. - Gloucester; Norwich YMCA; Norfolk County for period encompassing 1927-31 (3apps-1 goal).
After 8 years in business in Bristol he came back to Norwich in 1926.He retired after 49 years at Norvic Shoe Co Ltd (Norwich) as a Sales Director having been an Overseas Department Manager in his time.
F.F. – The 'EDP' in July 1931 referred to him as Harved Theobald. The Norfolk Cricket Association Senior 20 Over KO Competition prize is for the Harold Theobald Shield.

THISTLETON-SMITH, John Cedric
(b) East Barsham, Fakenham, Norfolk 10 May 1910
(d) Fakenham, Norfolk 13 March 1998
Educ. – Glebe House School; Malvern College; Taunton School; Wye Agricultural College.
Cricket. – Malvern College; YMCA; 5th Norfolks; Old Malvernians; West Norfolk; Wye Agricultural College; Norfolk Club & Ground; Fakenham
HS. 174 v Cambridgeshire August 1933 @ Fenner's
HS. 34 v All India June 1932 @ Lakenham – top score in a total of 138.
Lawn Tennis – Norfolk Junior Champion. Golf – Norfolk Boys and Norwich Boys Champion.
Football – Gloucester County; Old Malvernians.
He helped found Fakenham CC, was an MCC Member and on the NCCC Executive Committee.
He was a Farmer at Althorpe Hall from the age of 21. A member of WW2 Resistance – the Army built a secret (not to him) bunker on his land and it housed fellow resistance members. He worked in the Wine Trade and also bred Suffolk Punch Horses.
F.F. – The 1999 NCCC Handbook revealed that the club had received a collection of cricketing memorabilia from 'Cedric's' Estate.

1931

FOSTER, Major General Norman Leslie, CB DSO
(b) Wimbledon 26 August 1909
(d) Farnham, Surrey 3 January 1995
Educ. – Westminster School; RMA Woolwich
Cricket. – Westminster School; Westminster XI; Army; Royal Artillery
HS. 5 v Buckinghamshire August 1931 @ Lakenham
HS. 28 v All India June 1932 @ Lakenham
54 no for Wellington School v Malvern College June 1926
2nd Lt in Royal Artillery during his appearances for NCCC. He married Joan Drury the daughter of a Canon. He served 1939-45 War in Egypt and Italy. Commanded Royal Artillery 11th Armoured Division 1955-56. Imperial Defence College and Deputy Military Secretary War Office 1958-59. General Officer Commanding Royal Nigerian Army 1959-62. President Regular Commissions Board 1962-65. Director of Security (Army) Ministry of Defence 1965-73. Colonel Commandant Royal Artillery Regiment 1966-74. President of Truman & Knightley Education Trust Ltd 1982-87 having been the Chairman 1976-80

ROGERSON, Major William Thomas Carroll, CBE TD
(b) Pateley Bridge, East Riding, Yorkshire 10 November 1912
(d) Orvieto, Italy 9 August 1963
Educ. – Haileybury College (Le Bas House 1926.2-1931.2);

Cambridge University (Sidney Sussex College)

Cricket. – Haileybury College; Young Amateurs (not a Norfolk side)

HS. 13 v Lincolnshire August 1931 @ Lakenham

70 for Haileybury College v Wellington College July 1930 – batting at no. 9.

114 for Haileybury College v Cheltenham College August 1930 – as an opener.

The son of a Reverend he married Maria Luisa Belviglieri – the knowledge of which helped considerably in finding the Major's final resting place . Hockey & Rugby Union for Haileybury College. In the Royal Artillery and for the 1939-45 War a Major with the 8th Army in the Western Desert. Director of British Aeroplane Co Ltd and other companies.

ROUGHT-ROUGHT, Desmond Charles

(b) Brandon, Suffolk 3 May 1912

(d) Cambridge 7 January 1970

Desmond and his wife were both killed in the same motor cycle accident

Educ. – Educated privately; Cambridge University (Emmanuel College)

Cricket. – Heath House CC; Cambridge University – Blue 1937; South Norfolk; Minor Counties; Free Foresters; HM Martineau's XI; Sir Pierce Lacy's XI

HS. 135 v Hertfordshire July 1934 @ Broxbourne

BB. 6/38 v Hertfordshire August 1933 @ Lakenham

HS. 38 v West Indies June 1939 @ Lakenham

BB. 3/23 v Cambridge Crusaders June 1934 @ Lakenham

Brother of BW (q.v) and RC (q.v)

5/40 for HM Martineau's XI v Gezira Sporting Club April 1938

45 for HM Martineau's XI v United Services April 1938 – the last man in.

He hit 10 (6) in his short NCCC Minor County career.

1st class cricket – 24 matches 739 runs 16 catches 74 wickets

'The Independent' Newspaper's article dated 11 August 2000 under the heading 'The final lament of Lakenham' by Henry Blofeld (q.v) carried the euology quote, " The three Rought-Rought brothers who played with great style before and after the war."

WALKER, Ft. Lt David Frank

(b) Aldeburgh Lodge, Ditchingham 31 May 1913

(d) Off Norwegian Coast 7 February 1942

His Lockheed Hudson was shot down (608 Squadron Coastal Command) and he is buried at Trondheim.

Lived Trinity House, Bungay and he married Monica Crush on 8 November 1941 and she lost him just 60 days later.

Educ. – Uppingham School; Oxford University (Brasenose College)

Cricket. – Uppingham School; Oxford University – Blue 1933-35; MCC; Sir PF Warner's XI; RAF; HM Martineau's XI;

Public Schools; Club Cricket Conference; Free Foresters

HS. 217 v Northumberland August 1939 @ Lakenham

BB. 2/13 v Lincolnshire August 1934 @ Lakenham

HS. 31 no v New Zealand August 1931 @ Lakenham

He went 63 consecutive NCCC innings without a duck and his final average is to be admired and envied. If only I had seen just one of his 472(4) and 29(6) in M.C matches!

1st class cricket – 37 matches 1,880 runs 18 catches 6 wickets

224 no for Uppingham School v Shrewsbury School (a.o 159 & 111) July 1932

101 for Free Foresters v Harrow School June 1937

85 for MCC v Ireland August 1938

Hockey for Oxford University – Blue 1933. History and Cricket Master at Harrow School 1936-39. In September 1939 he took up an Education Post with the Sudan Government. On the 3 week tour to Egypt with HM Martineau's XI in April 1939 he caressed the ball to achieve 4 (100s) and 3(50s). The 1943 'Wisden' gave a brilliant obituary for a non County player – one apt statement was 'a brilliant exponent of many strokes'

1932

BALLANCE, Major Tristan George Lance, MC

(b) Norwich 21 April 1916

(d) nr Naples, Italy 4 December 1943

Educ. – All Saints Green School; Uppingham School; Oxford University (Brasenose College)

Cricket. – All Saints Green School; Aldeburgh Lodge; Uppingham School; Marlborough CC; Public Schools; The Rest; Free Foresters; Oxford University – Blue 1935 &37; Ashford; Minor Counties; JE Nichols' XI; West Norfolk; Aldershot Command

HS. 107 v Buckinghamshire August 1937 @ Lakenham

BB. 9/32 v Buckinghamshire August 1936 @ High Wycombe

HS. 3 v West Indies August 1933 @ Lakenham

BB. 2/111 v West Indies August 1933 @ Lakenham

5/17 & 8/20 for NCCC v Hertfordshire June 1936 – with the 5 wickets taken for no runs off just 16 balls (was 0/17) and for the second achievement he stood at 10-7-4-4- before finally getting his 8/20.

6/25 for Uppingham School v Shrewsbury School July 1932

11/72 in match for Uppingham School v Shrewsbury School July 1933

5/56 & 4/60 for The Rest v Lord's Schools August 1934

He at times topped the NCCC batting and bowling averages, took 10 wickets in a match once, scored tons and featured in century partnerships. The 4th youngest NCCC Minor County player. A right hand bat and slow left arm bowler.

1st class cricket – 23 matches 190 runs 18 catches 51 wickets.

Military Cross awarded in 1943 serving in the Durham Light Infantry

F.F. – A Schoolmaster by profession. Son of Sir Hamilton Ballance (Consulting Surgeon Norfolk & Norwich Hospital)

BARTON, Lance Corporal Alexander Walter
(b) Dereham, Norfolk 18 June 1914
(d) Singapore 26 January 1942
Educ. – Haileybury College (Edmonstone House 1928.3-1933.2)
Cricket. – Haileybury College; Dereham
HS. 32 no v Kent (2) August 1932 @ Lakenham
BB. 3/21 v Kent (2) August 1932 @Lakenham
HS. 1 v Cambridge Crusaders June 1934 @ Lakenham
Son of WJ (q.v.). Cousin of MR (q.v.). Nephew of CT (q.v)
54 for Haileybury College v Uppingham School June 1933 (TGL Ballance the bowler dismissed him).
64 & 42 for Haileybury College v Wellington College July 1933. A slow right arm googly bowler who wore spectacles. Not a direct descendant of AJ or GH (both NCCC). In 6th Batt. Norfolk Regiment and rose to be a Lance Corp Royal Norfolk Regiment

CUNLIFFE, Frank
(b) Accrington, Lancashire 28 July 1906
(d) Norwich 28 November 1968
Match reports show him as FD but b/d records do not show a middle initial
Educ. – Accrington GS
Cricket. – Accrington GS; Norwich YMCA; Norfolk & Suffolk Nomads; Norwich Wanderers; Eye; Harleston; President's XI Suffolk (a catch for them as a NCCC substitute fielder)
HS. 68 v Kent (2) August 1933 @ Lakenham
HS. 55 no v South Africa July 1935 @ Lakenham – batting at no. 9
100 no for Norfolk & Suffolk Nomads v The Mote June 1955
The 1962 NCCC Handbook had him detailed to arrange fixtures and teams.
Football for Norwich YMCA and Norfolk County 1933/34 (3 apps). His family came to Norfolk in 1929 – it was said that he was an Amateur Footballer with Accrington Stanley & Blackburn Rovers but alas I have not found proof. He did become a local (Norfolk) Football Referee.
F.F. – A Freemason who was Clerk to Hartismere RDC for 41 years to his retirement in July 1968

EDRICH, William John, DFC
(b) Lingwood, Norfolk 26 March 1916
(d) Whitehill Court, Chesham, Buckinghamshire 24 April 1986
Educ. – Bracondale School; Derby Flying Training School
Cricket. – Bracondale School; Minor Counties; Upton; MCC; Middlesex; South of England; England XI; Lord Tennyson's XI; Players; Sir PF Warner's XI; RAF; HDG Leveson – Gower's XI; Rest of England; Gentlemen; Gentlemen & Players;

Edrich XI; TN Pearce's XI; CG Howard's XI; AP Freeman's XI; Middlesex & Essex; Lord's XI; MA Crouch's XI; DL Donnelly's XI; RAF South; WR Hammond's XI; Thomas Owen's XI; CS Marriott's XI; Lord's Taverners President's XI; JE Nichols' XI; England – 39 Tests
HS. 152 v Hertfordshire July 1935 @ Broxbourne
BB. 7/45 v Suffolk August 1962 @ Lakenham
HS. 111 v South Africa July 1935 @ Lakenham
BB. 2/51 v Fezela June 1961 @ Lakenham
HS. 36 v Middlesex April 1970 @ Lord's
BB. 2/76 v Cheshire May 1968 @ Macclesfield
Brother of EH and GA (q.v.). Cousin of JH (q.v.) and Brian (Kent & Glamorgan) – there are far too many cricketing Edrich's to cover them all
The 6th youngest NCCC Minor County debutant
10/18 for Bracondale School v Norwich High School June 1930 – all bowled in 49 balls
121 no & 8/20 for Bracondale School v Diss Secondary School June 1930
167 no (221/9) for Edrich X1 v Norfolk X1 September 1955
Football – Bracondale School; Norwich City FC August 1932; Tottenham Hotspur October 1934;
Northfleet October 1934 (loan) turning pro with Spurs August 1935; Chelmsford August 1939 and during WW2 played for Bournemouth and Lincoln City.
1st class cricket – 571 matches 36,965 runs 529 catches 1 stumping and 479 wickets and I would suggest for more detailed information about his fabulous career outside of Norfolk that one reads his biography (by Alan Hill) or even his own two publications 'Cricketing Heritage' and 'Cricketing Days'. He also co-authored 'Cricket and all That' with Denis Compton.
He scored 86 first class centuries against a total of 28 teams and featured in 136 century partnerships (38 of which with DS Compton). The ultimate accolade is the Edrich and Compton Stands at Lord's. NCCC Captain who left the team in 1936 and triumphantly returned in1959 and was made an Honorary Life Member. A Sportswriter once wrote of Bill, "He epitomised the particularly British breed of incurable scallywag. He lived life to the full (married five times) and like as not, he would be out on the tiles at close of play but ready to perform the next day." Wisden on reporting his death (He fell down the stairs at home around midnight. It was said that he was following the St. George's Day celebrations) reckoned that he would have been the answer to prayer in the troubled England sides of the day.
F.F. – A Pilot with 21 Squadron Coastal Command in Norfolk rising to Flight Lt to Acting Squadron Leader. His DFC awarded after a daylight attack on Cologne Power Stations on 12 August 1941 as he led a section of 107 Squadron. At Army Staff College (Camberley) to RAF Group Operations Room in preparation for D-Day

THOMPSON, Wilfrid Sydenham

(b) Holbeach, Lincolnshire 9 February 1912
(d) King's Lynn, Norfolk 17 December 1988
Educ. – Uppingham School
Cricket. – Uppingham School; LC Stevens' XI; MCC; Free Foresters; West Norfolk; Musketeers; Norfolk Club & Ground; GS Hoghton's XI
HS. 94 v Cambridgeshire August 1947 @ King's Lynn
BB. 6/27 for Hertfordshire July 1935 @ Broxbourne
HS. 44 v Cambridge Crusaders June 1934 @ Lakenham – batting at no. 9
BB. 4/42 v New Zealand June 1937 @ Lakenham
NCCC Captain 1947-50; President 1975 and 1976 and on the Executive Committee.
His daughter is the wife of RHG Hoff (q.v). An occupation outside of cricket of a Farmer.
A Major in Coldstream Guards, part of the Coates Mission charged with the task of guarding the Royal Family in the event of a German invasion.
Golf – A scratch golfer and a member at Royal & Ancient Golf Club; Royal West Norfolk; Royal Worlington & Newmarket . He played Rugby Union for West Norfolk and had Eastern Counties trials. He smote 103 (6) in the Norfolk cause and nobody else runs him close. His best season for them was in 1937 (14) and most in an innings were in his 84 (6) v Kent 2nds July 1949. He twice hit (5) and five times (4) amongst 51 knocks where he cleared the ropes. A team mate of the time says that Wilf once cleared the Canterbury Lime Tree – a prodigious hit not achieved by many plus he was an extremely fast bowler with over 200 NCCC wickets to his name.

TYLER, Arthur Wellesley

(b) Charlton, S.E.London 18 June 1907
(d) Farnham, Surrey 23 January 1985
Educ. – Cheltenham College
Cricket. – Cheltenham College; Public Schools; Royal Artillery; Army; HM Martineau's XI; Lord's Schools; Young Amateurs (not the Norfolk side)
HS. 8 v Leicestershire (2) August 1932 @ Lakenham
HS. 6 v All India June 1932 @ Lakenham
1st class cricket – 3 matches 77 runs 6 victims (4c 2s)
A wicket keeper with a fine record for stumpings at Cheltenham College.
79 for Royal Artillery v West Kent July 1929
52 for Army v Public Schools August 1932
Rugby Union for the Army.

1933

BARTON, Michael Richard

(b) Dereham, Norfolk 14 October 1914
(d) Sevenoaks, Kent 1 July 2006

Educ. – Winchester College; Oxford University (Oriel College)
Cricket. – Winchester College; Oxford University – Blue 1936-37; MCC; South of England; Surrey; Combined Services; Northern Command; Free Foresters; MR Barton's XI; Old Surrey.
HS. 141 v Middlesex (2) August 1937 @ Lakenham – he hit 25 (4s) in the match and featured in two century stands.
HS. 59 v South Africans July 1935 @ Lakenham
Son of CT (q.v). Cousin of AW (q.v). Nephew of WJ (q.v)
1st class cricket 147 matches 5,965 runs 117 catches – with 1,000 runs in a season three times.
192 for Oxford University v Gloucester May 1937 – with TGL Ballance on his side.
99 for Surrey v West Indians May 1950 – out LBW to Frank Worrell.
He played with and against the greats – Bradman, Weekes, Worrell, Walcott, May & Shackleton.
He held catches off of the bowling of Laker, Lock and Bedser as he Captained Surrey (1949-51).
'Wisden' records that he scored the boundary versus Leicestershire in 1950 that ensured a shared championship

BRIGHTON, Norman Arthur

(b) Norwich 20 September 1909
(d) Norwich 4 December 1999
Educ. – Bracondale School
Cricket. – Bracondale School; Wymondham; GE Pilch's XI; Evergreens
HS. 6 v Lincolnshire June 1933 @ Grantham
BB. 4/17 v Lincolnshire June 1933 @ Grantham
HS. 6 v Suffolk July 1933 @ Lowestoft
BB. 2/44 v Suffolk July 1933 @ Lowestoft
44 & 4/7 for Wymondham v JE Nichols' XI August 1932
In GE Pilch's XI alongside Norwich City FC's Reg Foulkes and Ken Nethercott.

CLOWES, Brigadier Frank Worts

(b) Coggleshall, Essex 26 June 1901
(d) Northampton 23 June 1991
Educ. – Oundle School; RMC Sandhurst
Cricket. – Oundle School; Aldeburgh; RMC Sandhurst; East Norfolk
HS. 5 v Suffolk July 1933 @ Lowestoft
Referred to as Brigadier 'Boy' Clowes in P. Yaxley's book 'Looking Back at Norfolk Cricket'.
Frank was involved in the Arakan campaign of 1944 and the ultimate capture of Port of Gwa.
In 1945 he was Acting Commanding Officer 1st West African Brigade in Burma and then the Commanding Officer of the 2nd West African Brigade.

WOOD, Bob John Holt
(b) Morston, Norfolk 8 March 1913
(d) King's Lynn, Norfolk 18 October 1995
Educ. – Worksop College
Cricket. – Norwich Union; GE Pilch's XI
HS. 50 v Hertfordshire August 1948 @ Lakenham
HS. 2 no v Suffolk July 1933 @ Lowestoft AND 2 v
Cambridge Crusaders June 1934 @ Lakenham AND 2 v
South Africa July 1935 @ Lakenham
*He has the third highest total of NCCC wicket keeping
dismissals in a season namely 32 (30c 2s) in 1933. Chosen as
the wicket keeper for the Norfolk team in the 'Minor Counties
2000' Handbook lists of all-time greats.*
*2nd Lt in the 7th Norfolks and captured at St Valery June 1940
and therefore a POW in Germany finally arriving home May
1945. His brother Peter was a National Hunt Jockey.*

1934

BURROWS, John Walter
(b) Holt, Norfolk 20 April 1914
(d) Downton, Salisbury, Wiltshire 29 May 2005
Educ. – Gresham's School
Cricket. – Gresham's School; Norwich Union
HS. 0 v Cambridge Crusaders June 1934 @ Lakenham – it
took 92 from M. Falcon and 44 from WS Thompson to
rescue NCCC in John's only appearance at no. 3 in the
batting line up as eight of the side scored four or less.

MOULTON, Allan Frederick
(b) Mileham, Norfolk 11 June 1909
(d) Chipstead, Surrey 23 February 1986
Educ. – City of Norwich School
Cricket. – City of Norwich School; Reepham; Spencers CC
HS. 16 no v Cambridgeshire August 1934 @ Fenner's
*A Radio Engineer with his own firm namely Metropolitan
Relays (Battersea)*

SELF, Frederick George
(b) Norwich 13 August 1916
(d) Norwich 19 March 2006
Educ. – Norwich GS; Cambridge University (St Catharine's
College- BA 1938 MA 1946)
Cricket. – Norwich GS; Norwich Wanderers; Perambulators;
JE Nichols' XI; Norfolk Colts; Old Norvicensians
HS. 69 v Hertfordshire August 1934 @ Lakenham –
including 1(7) off of Fred Appleyard's bowling
HS. 25 v New Zealand June 1937 @ Lakenham
*Hockey. – Norfolk County; England; East of England;
Cambridge University – Blue; Wanderers; Yorkshire*
*Only 635 runs for NCCC in Minor County games but he still
shared three century stands being two with DF Walker and one*

*with BW Rought-Rought. A Schoolmaster at Beverley then the
Deputy Headmaster at Norwich GS, teaching Geography. The
pupils referred to him as ' Freddie the Elf' being a reference to
his small stature.*

1935

BIRKBECK, Henry
(b) West Acre, Norfolk 15 November 1915
(d) Castle Acre, Norfolk 21 February 2003
Educ. – Eton College
Cricket. – Eton College; Eton Ramblers; MCC
HS. 42 no v Lincolnshire July 1935 @ Lincoln
BB. 4/52 v Surrey (2) July 1947 @ The Oval
*2/64 for Eton College v Winchester College – as MR Barton (q.v)
plundered 136 for the opposition.*
*Known as 'Harry' he was part of the Birkbeck Dynasty out of
West Acre. The 1965 NCCC President.*

EDRICH, Eric Harry
(b) Lingwood, Norfolk 27 March 1914
(d) Wiston, Cambridge 9 July 1993
Educ. – Bracondale School
Cricket. – Warboys CC; Minor Counties; North of England;
GOB Allen's XI; Edrich XI; Huntingdonshire; WJ Edrich's XI;
Heacham; Upton; HDG Leveson-Gower's XI; Lancashire;
Northamptonshire
HS. 170 no v Kent(2) August 1949 @ Lakenham
HS. 47 v West Indies June 1939 @ Lakenham
*Best wicket keeping season for dismissals 1939 (25c 8s) plus 2
catches as a substitute fielder*
Brother of GA and WJ (q.v). Cousin of JH (q.v) and Brian
(Kent & Glamorgan)
1st class cricket – 36 matches 949 runs 38c & 15s
*Many followers consider Eric to be the best wicket keeper to
play for NCCC – he even stumped Don Bradman (not of course
when playing for Norfolk) ! His 13 stumpings in 1950 equalled
the record of AP Wickham in 1887.*
*He shared 8 century partnerships for the County including two
in the same match and still holds with Michael Falcon the 5th
wicket record of 171 achieved versus Hertfordshire in 1937.*
*For NCCC he dealt mostly in boundaries with 277 (4) and 10
(6) in his Minor County career, twice reaching 20 (4) in one
innings. He coached at Stowe School, briefly emigrated to New
Zealand, then returned to Norfolk and Chicken Farming.*

PILCH, George Everett, JP
(b) Norwich 19 February 1912
(d) Cringleford, Norwich 12 September 1979
Educ. – Norwich GS
Cricket. – Norwich & District; GE Pilch's XI
HS. 31 v Middlesex (2) July 1937 @ Hornsey

BB. 4/29 v Hertfordshire June 1938 @ Sawbridgeworth
HS. 8 v New Zealand June 1937 @ Lakenham
BB. 1/20 v New Zealand June 1937 @ Lakenham
Father of DG (q.v) and Son of RG (q.v)
Bowls/Golf/Hockey/Football/Squash for Norfolk County
Norfolk Golf Captain 1951-55 and the Royal Norwich Golf
Club website recounts the story of Walter Hagen & George
winning by 1 hole against Walker Cup player Lister Hartley
and Roy Donald in July 1933. An RAF Flight Lieutenant. On the
NCCC Executive Committee 1975-77 and a former President
of Norfolk Cricket Association. 50 years in the Sports Trade for
Pilch's

PURDY, Major Robert John, CMG OBE
(b) Aylsham, Norfolk 2 March 1916
(d) Norwich 18 March 1988
Lived Spratt's Green, Aylsham
Educ. – Haileybury College (Battle Frere House 1930.1-
1935.2); Cambridge University (Jesus College - BA 1938)
Cricket. – Haileybury College
HS. 14 v Hertfordshire June 1936 @ Cokenach
71 for Haileybury College v Wellington College July 1933
Rugby Union. – Wanderers and Eastern Counties
N. Nigeria Colonial Civil Service 1938 and appointed to
Colonial Administrative Service a year later.
Promoted to Senior Resident Adamawa Province (1957),
Plateau Province (1958-61) and Sokoto Province (1961to
retirement 1963). He served 1940-46 with the Royal West
African Frontier Force. Bursar at Gresham's School 1965-1981.
F.F. – He left a widow Elizabeth, children Robert, Andrew
and Susanna and four grandchildren.

1936

ABBS, Graeme Renwick
(b) Lewisham, London 5 May 1917
Lives in Felixstowe and is recovering well after a month in
Hospital recently.
Educ. – Giggleswick School
Cricket. – Giggleswick School
**HS. 22 v Cambridgeshire July 1936 @ Lakenham AND
22 v Middlesex (2) August 1937 @ Lakenham
BB. 3/19 v Buckinghamshire August 1936 @ High
Wycombe**
HS. 8 no v New Zealand June 1937 @ Lakenham
BB. 1/25 v New Zealand June 1937 @ Lakenham
A right arm swing bowler who wore spectacles. A Captain
in Manchester Regiment. Worked on the Stock Exchange in
London but on the death of his father he returned to Norfolk to
run the Family Hotel in West Runton.

1937

EDRICH, Geoffrey Arthur
(b) Lingwood, Norfolk 13 July 1918
(d) Cheltenham, Gloucestershire 2 January 2004
Educ. – Bracondale School
Cricket. – Bracondale School; Heacham; Lancashire;
Rest of England; Edrich XI; North of England; Over 32s;
Commonwealth XI; Cumberland; JE Nichols' XI
**HS. 124 no v Cambridgeshire August 1939 @ Lakenham
BB. 5/19 v Buckinghamshire August 1938 @ Lakenham**
HS. 53 v West Indies June 1939 @ Lakenham
BB. 2/71 v West Indies June 1939 @ Lakenham
Brother of EH and WJ (q.v) and Cousin of JH (q.v) and Brian.
1st class cricket 339 matches 15,600 runs 333 catches 5 wickets
A former East Anglian Farm Worker. Sgt in Royal Norfolk
Regiment with his weight reduced to six stone after being set
to work on the Railroad of Death in Thailand following his
capture by the Japanese. A solid rather than stellar batsman
who held the pose after stroking the ball to the outfield.
He was close to signing for Hampshire (my County) but he
reached 1,000 runs in eight seasons for Lancashire with
Michael Falcon taking credit for getting him a chance to play
at first class county level. An occasional captain when Cyril
Washbrook was away, he always played to win; Cyril played
not to lose. He took a menial job in a steelworks in the winter
and latterly became a respected Groundsman /Coach at
Cheltenham College, presiding over Gloucestershire's annual
festival there until his retirement
F.F. – He was married to Olga (nee Quayle) for 64 years with
the fabulous partnership only ending at Geoff's demise.

JACKSON, 2nd Lt. James Bertram
(b) South Africa 17 November 1917
(d) Colchester Military Hospital 21 August 1940
His death was as a result of a motor cycle accident
He came to Norfolk at the age of 6 and he lived Red Dawn,
Heacham, Norfolk
Educ. – Eton College
Cricket. – Eton College
HS. 13 v Cambridgeshire August 1937 @ Fenner's
A 2nd Lt in 4/7 Royal Dragoon Guards
F.F. – His Lincoln Probated will dated 14 February 1941 saw
him bequeath £1,625-15s to his widow Kathleen.

PERKINS, Raymond William
(b) Yarmouth, Norfolk 9 February 1913
(d) Yarmouth, Norfolk 16 November 1991
Educ. – Priory School
Cricket. – Priory School; Yarmouth Town
**HS. 51 v Hertfordshire August 1950 @ Lakenham
BB. 3/26 v Hertfordshire July 1950 @ Hertford**

HS. 0 v West Indies June 1939 @ Lakenham
In the 1938 season for Yarmouth Town he reached 1,000 runs in 15 innings (to include 4 tons) using the nickname of 'Gilly'. Football for Yarmouth YMCA and Table Tennis for Yarmouth being at one time the singles & mixed doubles champion (with his wife). A Lineotype Operator with the newspaper 'Yarmouth Mercury'.
Teacher of remedial children at Hospital School and the Greenacre School.

STEVENS, Bryan Geoffrey Wills
(b) Norwich 17 October 1920
(d) Norwich 24 May 2002
Educ. – Norwich GS
Cricket. – Norwich GS; Norfolk Club & Ground; Royal Signals; Norwich Wanderers; GE Pilch's XI; Old Norvicensians
HS. 55 no v Kent (2) July 1952 @ Aylesford AND 55 v Suffolk August 1953 @ Felixstowe
HS. 24 v FG Mann's X1 June 1951 @ Lakenham
Son of GA (q.v) and Nephew of GS and NW (q.v)
He effected 5 stumpings in the M.C. match v Hertfordshire August 1954.
I have seen a printed scorecard for the game v Suffolk August 1967 with Bryan shown as the Scorer.
NCCC Executive Committee and Hon Team Secretary (1967-82, President 1985 and 1986.
With the Royal Signals in Cairo. He performed like his father with whole hearted thoughtfulness and modesty. An 'Eastern Daily Press' Sportswriter for 17 years missing just two NCCC matches and always writing with clarity and good English. He listed his favourite players as Ballance, Walker and Walmsley and it is to Bryan that I extend gratitude as I was granted access to one of his well maintained ledgers (lodged at Archant Newspapers) and it was 'my starter for ten' on this mammoth project.

1938

BARRETT, Laurence Ambrose
(b) King's Lynn, Norfolk 28 October 1915
(d) Norwich 16 December 1976
Lived The Lodge Cottage, Colney Lane, Norwich and he sadly endured a lengthy illness.
Educ. – Repton School; Cambridge University (St John's College)
Cricket. – Repton School; Norfolk Club & Ground; GE Pilch's XI
HS. 103 v Essex (2) July 1953 @ Mistley – with 13(4) and 3(6) at a run a minute.
HS. 25 no v Huntingdonshire June 1951 @ Lakenham
'Laurie' was a NCCC Captain 1951-54 & Fixture Secretary 1949-69; plus the role of Chairman from 1969 to August 1976. Also a

Norfolk Cricket Association Vice President.
Hockey – Cambridge University – a Blue; Essex; Norfolk County; Grasshoppers; England Trial.
His wife Evelyn Maingay played Lawn Tennis for Norfolk. Qualified as a Solicitor in 1947 (he left C.U. with a law degree) and he joined Francis & Back (Solicitors). A Territorial Officer with the Royal Norfolk Regiment serving in Singapore as a Platoon Commander. Trustee of CEYMS Club and closely associated with Cringleford Parish Church.

CLEMENTS, Bertram Arthur
(b) Attleborough, Norfolk 1 December 1913
(d) James Paget Hospital, Gorleston, Norfolk 9 July 2000
Lived Keens Lane, Reydon, Southwold and known as 'George'
Educ. – City of Norwich School
Cricket. – City of Norwich School
HS. 114 v Hertfordshire July 1947 @ St Albans
BB. 7/20 v Kent July 1949 @ Dartford – a wicket with balls 23, 46, 53, 64, 66, 73 and 88.
HS. 11 v FG Mann's XI June 1951 @ Norwich
BB. 3/12 v FG Mann's XI June 1951 @ Norwich
NCCC Captain for 4 games in 1950 and he hit for them 175(4), 2(5) and 6 (6).
Football – City of Norwich School; London University; Casuals; Essex County; Corinthians; England Amateur International – played in 1936 Olympic Games rather than make his debut for NCCC.
F.F. – A former School Headmaster. His cause of death was a Cerebro Vascular Accident

1939

BOSWELL, Cecil Stanley Reginald
(b) Enfield, Middlesex 19 January 1910
(d) Shields Court, Brundall, Norfolk 15 August 1985
Educ. – Clarke's College
Cricket. – High Wych CC; Bishop's Stortford; CEYMS; Essex Club & Ground; Essex; Northern Command; Army; Ingham
HS. 94 v Surrey (2) July 1955 @ The Oval – in his final NCCC season
BB. 9/90 v Hertfordshire August 1947 @ Lakenham – a wicket with his third ball and his figures for the innings in question climbed to 3/74 at one stage.
HS. 22 v FG Mann's XI June 1951 @ Lakenham
BB. 5/112 v FG Mann's XI June 1951 @ Lakenham
7/18 for CEYMS v Lowestoft August 1954
Father of BRD (q.v)
1st class cricket – 30 matches 406 runs 12 catches 36 wickets
In July 1939 he smashed 3 consecutive sixes off Albert Elsdon (Durham) and he progressed to 26 off 7 balls in the 8 ball over. He managed 31(6) in his NCCC career.

Coached at Britannia Barracks, Norwich in 1950s – a pupil was JH Edrich (q.v).
Involved with NCCC Coaching schemes, Committees and Norfolk Young Amateurs plus organising games for the Colts. Also made an Honorary NCCC Life Member. Equal 4th with the most wickets for Norfolk against Suffolk namely 62. Norwich School Groundsman for 21 years, retiring 1975

COLMAN, 2nd Lt David Wyndham James
(b) Bixley, Norfolk 4 September 1921
(d) El Alamein, Egypt 5 November 1942
Lt. Gen. Bernard Montgomery had a force of 195,000 men for the 2nd Battle of Alamein which total was ultimately reduced by 13,560 casualties. The Allied victory however turned the tide in the North African Campaign.
Educ. – Eton College
Cricket. – Eton College; Poringland
HS. 6 v Cambridgeshire August 1939 @ Lakenham
Son of GRR (q.v) and Nephew of AR (q.v)
92 for Eton College v Harrow School July 1940
In 2nd King's Royal Rifle Corps

GARNIER, Major Edward Hethersett Charles, MC
(b) Darlington 7 March 1920
(d) Norwich 26 March 1999
Educ. – Eton College
Cricket. – Eton College
HS. 0 no v Northumberland August 1939 @ Jesmond
BB. 1/17 v Durham July 1939 @ Consett – bowled at the time of 8 ball overs
Son of ET (q.v) and Stepson of John Wormald (q.v) but not a relation to GR (q.v)
His Grandfather, Great Grandfather plus two Great Uncles all played first class cricket.
3/45 for Eton College v Harrow School July 1938
He was wounded in 1942 as a Captain in the Rifle Brigade. Into the 1950s he was Commanding The Green Jackets and was heavily involved with their Adult Training Depot to assist affiliated TA and Cadet organisations.
F.F. – He left a widow Alice, two sons and two granddaughters.

LANGDALE, George Richmond, OBE
(b) Thornaby-on-Tees, Yorkshire 11 March 1916
(d) Holbeck, Nottingham 24 April 2002
Educ. – City of Norwich School; Nottingham University
Cricket. – City of Norwich School; Nottingham University; Derbyshire; Somerset; University Athletic Union; Anti Aircraft Command; Army; Berkshire; Club Cricket Conference; Minor Counties; Sandhurst Wanderers
HS. 44 v Buckinghamshire August 1939 @ Wing
BB. 4/17 v Hertfordshire August 1939 @ Lakenham

1st class cricket – 25 matches 709 runs 7 catches 23 wickets 19-7-25-10 for Berkshire v Dorset August 1953 – the 5th best innings analysis in Minor Counties history.
A Left Hand Bat and Right Arm Off Break Bowler who gained his Somerset Cap in 1946 and his Berkshire Cap in 1952. Schoolmaster at City of Norwich School from 1 September 1938 to 1 December 1946. He published papers on mathematical subjects. An Instructor at RMA Sandhurst and a Senior Lecturer at Welbeck College for the M.O.D.

LEGGETT, Rufus
(b) Dersingham, Norfolk 1 September 1920
(d) Ashwicken, King's Lynn, Norfolk 16 February 1988
Educ. – King's Lynn GS
Cricket. – King's Lynn GS; West Norfolk; RAF; Castle Rising
HS. 31 v Suffolk August 1950 @ Bury St Edmunds
BB. 2/28 v Essex (2) August 1953 @ Lakenham
54 for RAF v Nottinghamshire July 1953
114 no for RAF v Army August 1955 – with the 100 reached in 90 minutes.
In his RAF side were future England players Trevor Bailey, Martin Horton, Ray Illingworth, Alan Moss, John Murray, Jim Parks, Fred Titmus and Fred Trueman so he moved in good company. An RAF Pilot during the war and a permanent commission afterwards.

1946

COOKE, Neville Roy, BDS LDS RCS
(b) Brighton, Sussex 27 May 1929
He came to Norwich in 1933 and still lives locally
Educ. – Norwich GS; Guy's Hospital; St George's Hospital
Cricket. – Norwich GS; Old Norvicensians; London University; United Hospitals; Guy's Hospital; GE Pilch's XI; Norwich Wanderers
HS. 31 v Cambridgeshire August 1947 @ Fenner's
BB. 1/24 v Suffolk August 1949 @ Lakenham
No relation to FBR (q.v)
108 no for Norwich GS v West Norfolk 1947
A classmate of NH Moore (q.v) and they were both to the fore with their brilliant batting and bowling. Neville was described as "fastish, and can produce a cut leg break" They both benefited from being coached by 'Jack' Nichols (q.v) and they were regarded as the best two school products since GA Stevens (q.v). A NCCC debut in August 1946 as a substitute fielder who took a catch versus Cambridgeshire. He studied Dentistry at Guy's Hospital and became a Dental Surgeon in Norwich, retiring in 1985. Neville also played Rugby Union for Norwich GS. He is still the Chairman of the Barry Boswell (q.v) Trust Fund with JB Rolph (q.v) being the Treasurer. The NCCC Manager of the Young Cricketers for a five year spell.

JORY, Dr Harold Ian, MA LLB TD

(b) Marylebone, London 15 February 1926
(d) Mere, Wiltshire 15 February 2007
Educ. – Malvern College; Oxford University (Brasenose College)
Cricket. – Malvern College; Oxford University - wartime Blue if they existed (see below); Oxford University Authentics; Old Malvernians

HS. 78 v Kent (2) July 1948 @ Dartford

He also kept wicket for two matches
29 for Oxford University v Cambridge University June 1945
His National Service in Korea from 1951-52 as a company commander of 21 Field Ambulance Unit being awarded the Bronze Star by the US military. He then commanded a Territorial Army Parachute and Field Ambulance Unit and was an assistant director of medical services to the East Anglian Brigade.Chairman of Governors at Richard Hale School (Hertford) and Queenswood School (Hatfield) plus being a JP and a Hertford Borough Councillor. Master of the Worshipful Company of Salters (1976-77) – charitable work particulary for almhouses. A Consultant Radiologist at Hertford County Hospital and Queen Elizabeth 11 in Welwyn Garden City. A Medical Officer to Christ's Hospital Girls' School plus the same role at the Balls Park Teacher Training College. Completed a Law Degree at the University of Hertfordshire after he retired from his General Practice in October 1987

MACE, Alfred Frank Alwyn

(b) Sedgeford, Nr Hunstanton, Norfolk 17 April 1921
Alive in Sculthorpe but now partly blind
Educ. – Sedgeford School
Cricket. – Sedgeford School; Toftrees; Fakenham; Wisbech; March; West Norfolk
HS. 72 v Kent (2) July 1947 @ Dartford – bowled by Brian Edrich (the Edrich brother who did not play for NCCC).
BB. 1/7 v Cambridgeshire August 1946 @ Lakenham
As a schoolboy he was advised by the county coach 'Jack' Nichols, to practise in front of a large mirror. Lost years to the game because of the war as he worked as a Baker and in Agriculture as a Farm Worker. He was impressive in club cricket so much so that Leicestershire CCC invited him for a trial but the chance was lost when he broke his leg playing football. In the Mid Norfolk Sunday Cricket League is the Alf Mace Division 4 League. Alf was in the Insurance business in Cambridge.

MARSH, Frederick Thomas

(b) North Elmham, Norfolk 17 December 1913
(d) Norwich 16 February 1978
Cricket. – North Elmham; Dereham
HS. 4 no v Suffolk August 1948 @ Lakenham
BB. 2/10 v Hertfordshire August 1946 @ Lakenham
In the Bedfordshire and Hertfordshire Regiments and the Royal

Scots Fusiliers. Member of the Royal British Legion. He worked for R.J. Seaman & Sons Ltd (Agriculture Merchant) for 40 years. His 115 wickets for Dereham in season 1947 was finally surpassed in 1975 by E. Wright (q.v)

MAYHEW, Kenneth George

(b) Helmingham, Suffolk 1 January 1917
Ken is the oldest survivor by 125 days (see GR Abbs) and he has been in Norfolk since 1936.
Educ. – St Felix Prep School; Framlingham College
Cricket. – Framlingham College; Suffolk; President's XI; CEYMS; Norfolk Young Amateurs; Incogniti; East Norfolk; Norwich Wanderers; Army

HS. 13 v Suffolk August 1948 @ Felixstowe

In the President's X1 side with him were NCCC players namely Cunliffe, Mitchell, Walmsley and Witherden.
Hockey. – Grasshoppers; Norfolk County – a fabulous half back line of Self, Barrett and Mayhew.
Joined the Territorial Army in June 1939; 6th Royal Norfolks and he was a 1st Batt. Suffolk Regiment Major. Part of the Combined Operations in Normandy seeing action in Belgium and Holland and he was awarded the Dutch Medal. A Representative for Fison's Fertilizers and he had his own businesses being KG Mayhew Ltd (Grain & Agriculture Merchant) plus Mayhew Freight Limited.
A Member of Royal Norwich Golf Club and still participating in the sport at age 94.

MITCHELL, Gerald

(b) Poringland, South Norfolk 17 August 1928
(d) Norwich 21 October 2005
Educ. – Framlingham College
Cricket. – RAF; Dereham; Norwich Wanderers; West Norfolk; Norfolk Club & Ground; President's XI
HS. 139 v Kent (2) July 1950 @ Dartford – with 21(4) and 4 (6) and 48 scoring shots in all
BB. 3/23 v Essex (2) July 1950 @ Chelmsford
Son of LG (q.v)
He did his National Service in the RAF and outside of cricket he worked for an Agricultural Merchant.
His widow Alix has moved back to Swanton Morley, Dereham to live.
F.F. – His father was the Secretary to the Medical Board at Norwich Union

PEARSON, James Maurice

(b) Ripon, Yorkshire 5 September 1915
(d) Downham Market, Norfolk 9 November 1974
Educ. – Durham University
Cricket. – Durham University; WR Hammond's XI; RAF
HS. 56 v Kent (2) August 1949 @ Lakenham – the game when a cow came onto the field.

BB. 4/132 v Surrey (2) July 1949 @ Guildford – Surrey's
Bernard Constable hit 249 no in the match.
50 no for WR Hammond's X1 v RAF July 1945
5/56 for Durham University v Durham May 1956
Schoolmaster at Lynn Grammar School 20 June 1946 to 24
March 1948. He continued his career in Sedgeford and London
and preferred to be known by his second name.

POWELL, Peter George
(b) Norwich 30 October 1920
(d) Norfolk & Norwich Hospital 19 May 1999
Lived Mile End Road, Norwich and never married
Educ. – Unthank College
Cricket. – Norwich Wanderers; Ingham; Norfolk Club &
Ground
HS. 172 v Suffolk August 1950 @ Lakenham
BB. 5/39 v Hertfordshire August 1946 @ Lakenham
HS. 67 v FG Mann's XI June 1951 @ Lakenham
Flight Lt. RAF – ferrying aircraft from North Africa. He equals
the record of most NCCC centuries against Suffolk with CJ
Rogers – both have 3.
NCCC Captain (1955-58), Executive Committee, Honorary
Fixture Secretary and Vice President.
One of only 6 NCCC players to hold 100 catches (or more)
in Minor County matches. He also featured in 15 century
partnerships to include the 4th wicket record of 188 in 1950 – it
lasted as the best until 1998. A drinking partner with Boswell
and Walmsley (but only half pints!) and the latter remembers
Peter being chastised by his team mates for putting a towel
inside his trousers for protection (before the days of thigh pads).
He commenced his career as a specialist spinner (batting at no.
9 or 10), was not selected in 1947 or 1948, but then reappeared
as an opening bat who rarely bowled at all. He worked for
Stanton and Staveley (Pipe Manufacturers)

RICE, Dr David, MRCS LRCP
(b) Hellesdon, Norwich 8 April 1914
(d) Brighton, Sussex 13 September 1997
Educ. – Lancing College
Cricket. – LC Stevens' XI; Royal Navy; Sussex; Empire XI
HS. 12 v Cambridgeshire August 1946 @ March
1st class cricket – 2 matches 32 runs 2 catches 1 wicket
4/86 for Royal Navy v Army July 1942
41 for Royal Navy v Australian Services August 1945
A Lt. Cdr in the Royal Navy – the equivalent of Major (Army)
and Squadron Leader (RAF)
F.F. – His father David (1871-1935) was the Medical Officer
for 27 years at Hellesdon, Norwich being from November
1907 to his demise July 1935. The only thing that
survives of the David Rice Hospital is the plaque struck to
acknowledge his service there.

STANTON, John Charles Clifford
(b) Dersingham, Norfolk 10 July 1920
Educ. – Oundle School
Cricket. – Oundle School; Ingoldsthorpe; West Norfolk
HS. 3 v Hertfordshire August 1946 @ St Albans
No relation to TH nor W (q.v)
A Farmer now living in Walsingham

....

1947
....

BELTON, Edward John
(b) Skendleby, Lincolnshire 10 September 1930
(d) Polebrook Nursing Home, nr Oundle, Northamptonshire
27 February 2008
Lived Stibbington, Peterborough
Educ. – Lingfield School (Hunstanton); Wellingborough
School
Cricket. – Wellingborough School; North Runcton;
Northamptonshire 2nds; Castle Rising; Peterbrorough
Town; Northamptonshire Club & Ground; The Rest; Royal
Engineers
HS. 28 v Cambridgeshire August 1947 @ King's Lynn
BB. 2/16 v Cambridgeshire August 1947 @ King's Lynn
The 13th youngest NCCC Minor County debutant but the 8th
to this point.
In the May 1947 fixture against Hertfordshire there were 6 Bs
in the team namely Barrett, Barton, Belton, Beresford, Birkbeck
and Boswell.
He once opened the bowling in a Northants 2nd X1 match
with Frank 'Typhoon' Tyson.
Hockey. – Pelicans; Lincolnshire (96 Caps); Peterborough Town;
East of England
Football. – Wellingborough Old Boys; King's Lynn;
Peterborough United
Rugby Union for Wellingborough School
F.F. – His widow Pauline posted to me some marvellous
cuttings kept by Ted. His cricket career paled into
insignificance when compared to his Hockey exploits. He
even managed a double hat trick in one such game.

CARTER, David Dring
(b) Crabbe's Abbey, King's Lynn, Norfolk 27 August 1928
(d) Queen Elizabeth Hospital, King's Lynn, Norfolk 16
October 1986
Lived The Cottage, Stow, Bardolph
Educ. – Uppingham School
Cricket. – Uppingham School; Gentlemen of Leicester;
MCC; Frogs CC; Norfolk Club & Ground; Free Foresters; West
Norfolk; Northern Schools; GS Hoghton's XI; The Rest
HS. 76 v Kent (2) July 1952 @ Aylesford
BB. 6/65 v Hertfordshire July 1948 @ St Albans
HS. 46 no v FG Mann's XI June 1951 @ Lakenham

BB. 1/35 v FG Mann's XI June 1951 @ Lakenham
Son of RD (q.v) and Nephew of GT (q.v)
4/7 for Uppingham School v Repton School June 1946
96 no for Uppingham School v Shrewsbury School June 1946
President West Norfolk CC to his death. A medium pace bowler with an unorthodox action and a magnificent gully fielder. In 1986 his name was forwarded to be the NCCC President but he sadly passed away before taking office. Rugby Union for West Norfolk. A Farmer with his brother Arthur

HARE, Sir Thomas, ARICS (The 5th Baronet of Stow Hall)
(b) Westminster, London 27 July 1930
(d) King's Lynn Hospital, Norfolk 25 January 1993
Educ. – Ludgrove School; Eton College; Cambridge University (Magdalene College - MA)
Cricket. – Cambridge University – no Blue; Free Foresters; Southern Schools; I Zingari
HS. 22 v Cambridgeshire August 1947 @ Fenner's
BB. 1/20 v Cambridgeshire August 1947 @ Fenner's
1st class cricket – 10 matches 218 runs 5 catches 19 wickets
103 for Eton College v Harrow July 1947 – attending on the first days play were the King, Queen, 2 Princesses and Lord Mountbatten.
Highlights for C.U in early 1953 were as follows –
47 on debut v Sussex April 1953 (caught by England's Hubert Doggart).
Against Middlesex he dismissed Denis Compton and bowled to Bill Edrich. Took 4/73 v Australians May 1953 (Miller/Harvey/Davidson/Ring were his captures)
5/35 v Worcestershire May 1953
F.F. – A Farmer and son of Sir Ralph Leigh Hare who married the 9th Earl of Darnley's daughter

HAYLES, Col Basil Ratcliffe Marshall
(b) Andover, Hampshire 29 October 1916
(d) Aldeburgh, Suffolk 4 November 2007
Educ. – Haileybury College (Thomason House 1930.2-1934.3); RMA Woolwich
Cricket. – Haileybury College; Public Schools; Lord's Schools; Army; Combined Services; Hampshire Hogs
HS. 2 v Suffolk August 1947 @ Lakenham
Son-in-Law of CBL Prior (q.v)
72 for Haileybury College v Wellington College July 1934
72 for Army v RAF August 1947
He regularly performed at Lord's as a 9, 10, Jack batsman and a wicket keeper with quick reflexes. He kept to Tony Lock and was not knocked over by Fred Trueman during a fiery spell.
1st class cricket – 7 matches 69 runs wicket keeper dismissals 8 (6c 2s).
Married to his widow Jean for 64 years who kindly let me have access to her husband's magnificent scrapbook. In the Royal Signals with the 8th Army in Palestine and an Instructor Staff

College, Haifa and a career soldier who retired 1971. He had served with the British Expeditionary Force plus the Middle East Force

MOORE, Nigel Howard
(b) Norwich 20 April 1930
(d) Norwich 24 December 2003
He died just 4 months after his wife Ruth
Educ. – Town Close School (Norwich); Norwich GS; Cambridge University (Corpus Christi College BA 1952 MA 1956)
Cricket. – Norwich GS; Old Norvicensians; Norwich & District School ; Norfolk Club & Ground; Minor Counties; GE Pilch's XI; Cambridge University – no Blue; Perambulators; Cambridge Crusaders; Corpus Christi College; Norwich Wanderers – to President.
HS. 163 no v Buckinghamshire August 1957 @ Lakenham
BB. 5/27 v Hertfordshire August 1954 @ Croxley Green
HS. 25 v Huntingdonshire June 1954 @ Warboys
BB. 2/36 v Huntingdonshire June 1954 @ Warboys
Father of DS, GJ (q.v) – see Curio Corner for both.
1st class cricket – 4 matches 139 runs 2 catches
His NCCC 1957 batting average was 87.66.
In the 1952 Norwich Wanderers side were Bate, Fielding, N. Moore, P.Powell, Softley, Stannard, B.Stevens, Theobald and E. Ward.
Golf – Cambridge University –Blue 1951and 1952; Cambridge Stymies; Royal Norwich; Grasshoppers; Norfolk County
NCCC Executive Committee and President 1996 and 1997.
Thirteen NCCC Century partnerships to include holding the 3rd wicket record of an unbroken 261 with Ted Witherden in 1957 versus Buckinghamshire. It took until 1993 for the total to be passed. MCC Member until 1970.
National Service in RASC Intelligence Corps and posted to Klagenfort (Austria) as part of Field Security. Passed his Law Exam 5 August 1950 and a Partner in Solicitors Claude Stratford & Moore and it was for business reasons that he was not always available for selection.
F.F. – An Ornithologist who by 1967 had identified 100 species of bird. He even spent much of the NCCC tour to South Africa in the 1990s bird watching and he increased his sightings to a few below 3,000 – it is estimated that there are over 10,000 species in the world so Nigel's is a remarkable effort. His son Gregory made the trip to my home to lend me one of his father's magnificent binders of his sporting career and life.

PIERPOINT, Frederick George
(b) St George, Camberwell, London 24 April 1915
(d) Princes Royal Hospital, Telford 23 July 1997
Lived Summercroft, Tureff Avenue, Donnington

Cricket. – London Counties; Devon; Surrey; Glamorgan 2nds; Surrey & Kent; Reading; Allscott CC; Aldershot District; British Empire X1

HS. 20 no v Cambridgeshire August 1947 @ King's Lynn

BB. 6/66 v Hertfordshire August 1947 @ Lakenham

1st class cricket – 8 matches 15 runs 3 catches 13 wickets
6/33 for Aldershot District v RAF July 1942
8/21 & 4/32 for Aldershot District v Sir PF Warner's XI August 1942
Coached Cricket at Wrekin College with his daughter Marilyn stating that he lived and breathed sport.
The first NCCC player to have 10 not outs in a season (1947) since E. Gibson (1910). He was proud to tell everybody that he was born within the sound of Bow Bells. He originally trained to be a Waiter and latterly became a Weighbridge Clerk at Allscott's Sugar Beet Factory

SKINNER, Terence John McInnes

(b) Henstead, Suffolk 7 July 1929
(d) Melton Mowbray, Leicester 6 August 1995
Educ. – Rosehill Prep School; Harrow School (Elmfield House)
Cricket. – Harrow School

HS. 24 v Suffolk August 1947 @ Lakenham

Michael Falcon recommended him to the club and he was erroneously shown in some match reports as McInnes - Skinner. 49 no for Harrow School v Eton College July 1947
A Lt. in Seaforth Highlanders in Malaya. A Farmer at East Carlton Manor who subsequently moved to Leicester.

WARD, Eric Ernest

(b) Bedford 7 July 1914
(d) Two Acres Nursing Home, Taverham 19 January 2002
Educ. – Bedford Modern School
Cricket. – Bedford Modern School; Bedford Town; Norwich Wanderers; GE Pilch's XI; Norfolk Club & Ground

HS. 77 v Cambridgeshire August 1947 @ Fenner's

Worked for Bedford Council in the salaries/wages department. A Norfolk County Council Assistant Treasurer. For a list of his Wanderers team mates see Nigel Moore (q.v)
F.F. – His grand daughter was a school classmate of my daughter

1948

BRAYNE, Thomas Lugard

(b) Delhi, India 20 June 1921
(d) Birmingham 7 April 2009
Educ. – Sherborne School; Cambridge University (Pembroke College - BA 1949 MA 1965)
Cricket. – Norfolk Club & Ground

HS. 72 v Surrey (2) July 1949 @ Guildford

BB. 1/32 v Kent (2) July 1948 @ Lakenham

He was 78 inches in height (I don't do metric!) and the son of Frank who was appointed the Deputy Commissioner of Gurgaon District (Punjab).Thomas was in the Indian Army

RUSHFORTH, Tom

(b) Halifax 30 October 1910
(d) Norwich 23 December 2001
Lived in the Dereham Road area for 50 years
Cricket. – Norwich Wanderers

HS. 4 v Buckinghamshire August 1948 @ Slough

In the Wanderers team were NCCC men Falcon, Fielding, Powell, Self and Theobald so he was in great company. Tom had a Fire Extinguisher business
F.F. – He left a widow Ivy and four children

1949

COOKE, Frederick Bruce Rennie

(b) Wetherby,West Yorkshire 21 June 1922
(d) Fingringhoe, Essex 7 December 1987
Educ. – Aldeburgh School; Uppingham School (Meadhurst House); Cambridge University
Cricket. – Uppingham School; Aldeburgh; Meadhurst House; Cambridge University – 1942 no Blue.

HS. 13 v Buckinghamshire August 1949 @ Lakenham

Not a relation to NR (q.v)
51 for Uppingham School v Rugby School July 1941
2/9 for Cambridge University v Public Schools Wanderers Rugby Union & Fives for Uppingham School.
F.F. – An Engineer by profession

HANCOCK, William Draycott

(b) King's Lynn, Norfolk 23 February 1926
(d) King's Lynn, Norfolk 25 November 2003
Lived Church Farm, Lynn Road, Bawsey, Peterborough
Educ. – Repton School
Cricket. – Repton School; West Norfolk

HS. 26 v Suffolk August 1949 @ Felixstowe

BB. 5/72 v Suffolk August 1951 @ Lakenham

BB. 4/20 v Huntingdonshire June 1952 @ Warboys

HS. 3 no v Fezela June 1961 @ Lakenham

He hit 27 (4) and 2 (6) in his NCCC career
Football for Repton School and Corinthians
A Farmer on the Sandringham Estate and on his own farm from the 1980s. Master of West Norfolk Hunt and a Point to Point participant.

LAY, Leonard Charles

(b) Norwich 17 May 1925
(d) Stannington Hospital, Morpeth, Northumberland 31 July 1990

Educ. – City of Norwich School; Hull University
Cricket. – City of Norwich School; St Barnabas; Hull University
HS. 10 v Buckinghamshire August 1950 @ Slough
One of only 16 players used in 1949, the lowest roster back to and including 1876.
Football for Hull University and Hockey with City of Norwich School. A Headmaster in Livingstone, Zambia retiring 1973 with his specialist subject being History.

....

1950

....

HARRISON, Michael John
(b) Walsoken, Norfolk 29 May 1932
Educ. – Culford School (Bury St Edmunds)
Cricket. – Culford School; Cambridge Colts; Barleycorns; West Norfolk; North Devon; Devon Dumplings; Norwich Wanderers; Castle Rising; Norfolk Club & Ground
HS. 22 no v Buckinghamshire July 1953 @ Lakenham
BB. 4/13 v Kent (2) August 1950 @ Lakenham
He managed to strike 10 (4) and 1 (6) in his 12 match career for Norfolk County.
On the NCCC Executive Committee and Chairman of Promotion & Sponsorship Sub-Committee – the 1991 NCCC Handbook reflected on organised events such as the Lakenham Centenary Year work, new tracksuits for the County Squad, support for the marquees and providing funds for coaching, travel and accommodation. Worked for C.E. Heath as a Lloyds Insurance Broker.

O'BRIEN, Lt John Richard
(b) Calcutta, India 1928
(d) Korea 8 December 1950
Lived Hanborough,11 South Street, Sheringham
He tragically fell off the back of a jeep at age just 22.
Educ. – Oxford University (Brasenose College)
Cricket. – Norfolk Club & Ground
HS. 64 v Hertfordshire August 1950 @ Lakenham – he topped the batting averages in his only season.
The players called him 'Poona' in a light hearted manner and the 'madman' took great delight by the affectionate name. He was commissioned shortly before he completed his National Service. However after 6 months at home he entered Oxford University but he quit his studies to volunteer with the United Nations Force. A Lt. in the Royal Artillery
F.F. – In Korean Administration but Probated London will 15 June 1951 saw the sum left re sworn to £600-4-6d

WALMSLEY, Peter Gauntlett
(b) Dunbar, Scotland 5 January 1931
Educ. – Buxton College
Cricket. – Buxton College; President's XI; Norfolk & Suffolk

Nomads; Norwich Union; RAF (Hornchurch); Norfolk Club & Ground; West Norfolk; Barleycorns; Dereham; King's Lynn; Norwich Union Head Office
HS. 28 v Suffolk August 1952 @ Lowestoft – with 4 (6s) in 5 balls off the redoubtable Cyril Perkins
BB. 8/40 v Buckinghamshire August 1954 @ Slough
HS. 9 v Fezela June 1961 @ Lakenham
BB. 5/23 v Huntingdonshire June 1952 @ Warboys
9/35 for Norwich Union v Lowestoft July 1953 – including a hat trick
9/18 for Norfolk & Suffolk Nomads v Witham June 1955 –on the 3 week tour he took 51 wickets at a cost of 5.23 per strike. He took more NCCC wickets than the runs he scored with left arm very pacy bowling seeing him top the averages in 1953,1954 and 1958. His 67 wickets obtained against Suffolk is the 2nd best haul for NCCC against them. He is one of only 10 players to twice take 8 or more wickets in an innings.
An RAF Corporal during his National Service. A Norwich Union UK Fire Manager until retirement.
F.F. – Of the hundreds of ex-players contacted Peter has been truly outstanding with his knowledge of his former NCCC team mates.

....

1951

....

ATHERTON, Air Commodore David Anthony
(b) East Dereham, Norfolk 2 April 1931
Lives Cheltenham, Gloucester
Educ. – Norwich GS; Cranwell College
Cricket. – Norwich GS; RAF
HS. 5 v Buckinghamshire August 1951 @ High Wycombe
BB. 1/10 v Huntingdonshire June 1952 @ Warboys
Rugby Union – Norfolk County
Hockey for Norfolk County – he modestly states that he was in goal for one game because of a player shortage. RAF service 1949-1984. Cheltenham College Bursar retiring 1997 and also the Council Secretary.

DRINKWATER, Walter Lewis
(b) Elland, Leeds 17 December 1917
(d) La Tretoire nr Paris, France 26 December 1998
He died peacefully at his son's home and was universally known as 'Bill'.
Educ. – Elland GS; Oxford University (Keeble College)
Studying Maths at University but the war broke out.
Cricket. – CEYMS; Oxford University Authentics; Norfolk Club & Ground
HS. 85 v Essex (2) July 1953 @ Mistley
BB. 4/19 v Suffolk August 1951 @ Lakenham – magnificent figures of 24-14-19-4
HS. 49 v FG Mann's XI June 1951 @ Lakenham

BB. 2/39 v FG Mann's XI June 1951 @ Lakenham
He struck 76 (4) in his Minor County career.
He was at CEYMS with Lambert, Laws, R. Smith & Tilney (all q.v.). Royal Artillery Anti Aircraft – his boat sunk on landing and he remembered losing his treasured pipe. His employer was Rowntree's (Norwich) from 1951 to 1980 with the last 4 years as a General Manager. Also a member at Eaton Golf Club.

EDRICH, Peter George
(b) South Walsham, Norfolk 3 March 1927
Cricket. – Norfolk Club & Ground; South Walsham; Ingham
HS. 7 v Buckinghamshire August 1951 @ Bury
HS. 4 v Huntingdonshire June 1951 @ Lakenham
BB. 3/36 v Huntingdonshire June 1951 @ Lakenham
A cousin of the other Norfolk cricketers named Edrich – other cousins in the Edrich XI were AE, D, GC and GH.
9/31 for Ingham v Mallards May 1955 – he denied himself all 10 wickets as he held a diving slip catch.
6/26 for South Walsham v Lowestoft May 1955

HANWORTH, William Ronald, LDS BDS
(b) Cairo, Egypt 15 March 1923
Known as 'John' but alas now seriously ill with Parkinson's Disease in a Nursing Home.
Educ. – Brentwood School
Cricket. – Brentwood School; Brentwood; Barleycorns; United Hospital; Norfolk Club & Ground; Royal London Hospital
HS. 27 v Huntingdonshire June 1951 @ Lakenham
Captain in Royal Army Dental Corps with an Unthank Road, Norwich Practice.
Football for England Schoolboys
F.F. – His father was a Cairo Teacher, a Military Cross recipient, who died of cancer of the jaw in Basingstoke during WW2.

HOFF, Richard Henry Gibson
(b) Shouldham Thorpe, Norfolk 18 June 1923
Educ. – Glebe House Prep School; Aldenham School
Cricket. – Castle Rising; GS Hoghton's XI; West Norfolk; Frogs CC; Gentlemen of Leicester; LC Stevens' XI
HS. 118 v Hertfordshire August 1955 @ Lakenham – scored in 80 minutes with 12 (4) & 5 (6) and 44 scoring shots in all.
HS. 34 no v FG Mann's XI June 1951 @ Lakenham
He logged 36 (4) and 7(6) in his 1950s Minor County career.
101 for West Norfolk v Cambridge MA's July 1955
A right hand bat and wicket keeper. An occupation of Farmer. Henry Blofield's (q.v) foreward to David Armstrong's 'A Short History of Norfolk County Cricket' recounted his extraneous memory of the lift he was given in Dick's E-Type Jaguar to a match in Felixstowe.

SMITH, Ray
Cricket. – Norfolk Club & Ground ; CEYMS
HS. 46 v Huntingdonshire June 1951 @ Lakenham
His one innings saw two Yorkshire born men open the innings – he partnered 'Bill' Drinkwater to a 78 run stand.
40 for Norfolk Club & Ground v Cambridge Crusaders June 1951
A Morgan Brewery Mechanic with the 'EDP' newspaper describing him as,"Having a high backlift and nimble feet".

SOFTLEY, Peter Leslie Hayhoe
(b) Norwich 30 January 1921
(d) Ashfield Care Home, Norwich 7 August 2002
Educ. – City of Norwich School; St Mark & St John Teacher Training College (Exeter)
Cricket. – Norwich Wanderers
HS. 3 no v FG Mann's XI June 1951 @ Lakenham
BB. 1/13 v FG Mann's XI June 1951 @ Lakenham – his only Norfolk wicket and a highly prized one, that of Michael Falcon.
He had a 40 year career teaching Music at various Secondary Modern Schools to include Alderman Jex and Gurney Henderson.Hockey & Badminton for Norfolk County. The President of Norwich Sports Council and gained 1999 Civic Award for Voluntary service in Norwich. The Peter Softley Shield is awarded for the best annual sports team effort in Norwich. He took part in the World Veteran Orienteering Championships four times. Editor of St Mary's Baptist Church Magazine
F.F. – Hayhoe is his mothers' maiden name and his son Tim is Head of Chemistry at Oxford University.
He was married to his widow Joyce for 53 years.

STANNARD, Geoffrey Michael
(b) Horsham, Sussex 29 January 1930
For many years The Blakeney Hotel (which the family owns) ran a full page advert in the NCCC Handbook. He is still a NCCC Member.
Educ. – The Leys School
Cricket. – Barton Broad; Norwich Wanderers
HS. 6 v Buckinghamshire August 1951 @ High Wycombe
HS. 5 v Huntingdonshire June 1952 @ Warboys
In the Wanderers team with him were D. Drake, Grant, Richardson, BGW Stevens and Theobald.

1952

BATE, John Cunnington
(b) Frinton-on-Sea, Essex 4 April 1915
(d) Norwich 21 December 1984
Cricket. – Norfolk Club & Ground; Norwich Wanderers
HS. 139 v Kent (2) July 1957 @ Aylesford

HS. 35 v Huntingdonshire June 1952 @ Warboys
Four NCCC century partnerships with Peter Powell namely 104,111,126 and 164 at the top of the order. One of eight NCCC players to score 2 (50s) v Suffolk in one match.
Hockey – Grasshoppers; Norfolk County; Essex County; East; England Trial
Badminton – YMCA (Norwich); Norfolk County; Essex County
Lawn Tennis – Eaton (Norwich); Norfolk County
He was a Norwich Parks and Closed Tennis Champion and even a four handicapper at Golf.
He coached youngsters at Badminton and Tennis. He left Essex in 1951 and apart from a spell in Kent (1958-63) he was with the Norfolk County Council Highways Department to retirement.

BEARE, John Cumby
(b) Gorleston, Norfolk 3 March 1933
(d) Gorleston, Norfolk 3 January 1999
Cricket. – clubs unknown
HS. 2 no v Essex (2) July 1952 @ Clacton-on-Sea
BB. 2/46 v Essex (2) July 1952 @ Clacton-on-Sea
A medium pace bowler and still a work in progress as I am trying to trace his three married daughters.

FIELDING, John Lewis
(b) Norwich 20 September 1922
(d) Norwich 22 July 2004
Cricket. – Norfolk Club & Ground; Norwich Wanderers; Ingham; Norfolk & Suffolk Nomads
HS. 22 v Buckinghamshire July 1952 @ Lakenham
BB. 5/57 v Essex (2) August 1952 @ Lakenham – at one time his analysis was 5/24 (wickets with his 17, 41, 50, 55 & 57 balls)
HS. 8 no v Huntingdonshire June 1955 @ Lakenham
NCCC Membership & Home Matches Sub - Committee throughout the 1990s.
Articled as a Chartered Accountant but the prospect did not thrill him after WW2 so he became a Chartered Surveyor.
F.F. – John was part of 1 Troop B Squadron 1st Special Air-Service Regiment. He spent four years acquiring the skills needed to wage guerrilla warfare behind enemy lines. The Force named SAS Operation Bulbasket saw him parachuted into occupied France in a commando style operation in support of the Normandy Invasion. They operated in unison with local French resistance in wooded country between Poitiers and Limoges. 33 SAS men were captured and executed but John had left camp on 1 July 1944 in a successful attack on the Paris-Bordeaux railway line (south of Poitiers).
The Allies broke out of the Normandy Beachhead and John went on to serve the SAS during the advance through Holland and into Germany. He made many pilgrimages back to the area – if you had met him you would never

have known of his 'Murders in the Forest' ordeal.

LAWS, Brian Michael, BSc PhD
(b) Shotesham, South Norfolk 31 December 1935
Lives Chelmondiston, Ipswich
Educ. – Langley School; City College; Reading University
Cricket. – Langley School; Ingham; CEYMS; Norfolk Young Amateurs; Norfolk Club & Ground
HS. 12 v Buckinghamshire July 1952 @ Lakenham
HS. 46 v Huntingdonshire June 1952 @ Warboys
At CEYMS with Drinkwater, Lambert, R. Smith & Tilney. He quite looked forward to National Service but he failed the medical because of his knee problems. Gained 4 'A' Levels and chose Reading University as he felt it was less intimidating than Cambridge. Technical Director of Paul's Agriculture in Ipswich. The firm acquired in 1984 by Harrisons & Crosfield plc and Brian became a Director of IT Management there. He is just about to relinquish his role of Trustee of the Pensions Fund.

MASON, Peter Leonard
(b) East Dereham, Norfolk 22 April 1934
(d) King's Lynn, Norfolk 26 September 1995
Educ. – Felsted School
Cricket. – Felsted School; Norfolk Young Amateurs; West Norfolk
HS. 14 v Buckinghamshire August 1952 @ Slough
Father-in-Law of CD Adams (q.v)
68 no for Felsted School v Gentlemen of Essex 1952 – on his way to a School average for the year of 45.
An occupation of Farmer

MORSE, Michael Haig
(b) Bishop's Stortford, Hertfordshire 7 May 1934
(d) Chelsea, London 18 September 1987
Educ. – Winchester College
Cricket. – Winchester College; MCC; Norfolk Young Amateurs; Norfolk Club & Ground
HS. 3 v Suffolk August 1952 @ Lakenham
HS. 33 v Huntingdonshire June 1955 @ Lakenham
Son of SA (q.v)
A Jobber at W. Greenwell & Co (London Stockbroker)

THOMAS, William Owen
(b) Linthorpe, Middlesbrough 27 April 1921
(d) Sheringham, Norfolk 8 August 2000
He died just two days before the final NCCC match at Lakenham
Educ. – Dulwich College; Cambridge University (Pembroke College – BA 1948 MA 1964)
Cricket. – Dulwich College; Cambridge University – no Blue; West Norfolk; MCC; Norfolk Club & Ground; Castle Rising; Dulwich

HS. 113 v Buckinghamshire July 1955 @ Lakenham

BB. 4/20 v Middlesex (2) August 1956 @ Lakenham

HS. 144 v Huntingdonshire June 1952 @ Warboys – 100 in 122 minutes; 182 minutes altogether with 18(4) 1(5) & 3(6). The opponets all out for just 69.

BB. 1/11 v Huntingdonshire June 1955 @ Lakenham
Father-in-Law of FLQ Handley (q.v) and Brother-in-Law of DJM Armstrong (q.v. Curio Corner)

1st class cricket – 4 matches 44 runs 2 catches 3 wickets
Left arm spinner who 'Wisden' referred to as 'Spongey' and they also said that he could give the ball quite a tweak in his schooldays.
47 for Dulwich College v Brighton College June 1940
4/58 for Cambridge University v Essex May 1948 @ Fenner's
A Major in the Green Howards. Housemaster at Gresham's School to retirement in 1988

THORNTON, Godfrey Gervase

(b) Basford, Nottingham 18 June 1925
(d) Norwich 18 July 1980
Lived Church Farm, Trimmingham, Norfolk
Educ. – Winchester College
Cricket. – West Norfolk
HS. 15 v Kent (2) July 1952 @ Aylsford
BB. 1/61 v Kent (2) July 1952 @ Aylsford
5/23 for West Norfolk v Norwich Wanderers July 1955
A Farmer in Trimmingham

1953

CHAMBERLAIN, Derrick Harry

(b) Guist, Norfolk 2 July 1922
(d) Holt, Norfolk 28 August 2007
Educ. – Fakenham GS
Cricket. – Fakenham GS; Dereham; Castle Rising; Norfolk Club & Ground; Hindringham
HS. 59 no v Essex (2) August 1953 @ Lakenham
HS. 17 no v Huntingdonshire June 1953 @ Lakenham
A Farmer until retirement
F.F. – He was married to Eileen (nee Duffield) for 54 years

GRAINGE, Clifford Marshall

(b) Heckmondwike, Yorkshire 21 July 1927
(d) Leeds 26 May 1989
Educ. – Heckmondwike GS; Oxford University (Keble College BA 1951 MA 1954)
Cricket. – Heckmondwike GS; Oxford University –no Blue; Oxford University Authentics; LA Barrett's XI
HS. He did not bat nor bowl in his one friendly appearance v Huntingdonshire June 1953 @ Lakenham as there were only 77 minutes play due to persistent rain falling.
1st class cricket – 14 matches 47 runs 4 catches 25 wickets

Athletics for Heckmondwike GS. In the Oxford Society 1956-60 and an Assistant Master at Langley School. Senior Master Leeds GS from September 1953 to retirement 1987 – taught Geography .He served in the Royal Artillery
F.F. – Kept his first name quiet at school – known as 'Nick' or 'Charlie'

GREATREX, Edward John

(b) Nuneaton 18 November 1936
Still lives in Norfolk
Educ. – Albury Secondary Modern School
Cricket. – Birmingham & District Schoolboys; Warwickshire Club & Ground; Blacksheep CC; Norfolk Club & Ground; Yarmouth
HS. 39 v Cambridgeshire July 1969 @ Cambridge – a 7th wicket stand of 119 with Bill Edrich and constantly repelling former England bowler Johnny Wardle.
HS. 10 v Essex April 1970 @ Lakenham – out to paceman John Lever who was to graduate to the England Test team.
HS. *12 v Middlesex April 1970 @ Lord's*
Best wicket keeping season was 1969 with 30 victims (23c 7s) and, of course, a professional goalkeeper.
Football.- Coventry City Schoolboys; Norwich City FC 1953 (am), June 1954 (pro); Cambridge City; Chelmsford City; Clacton; Bury St Edmund; Yarmouth Town.
A debut v Huntingdonshire in a friendly on 11 June 1953 replacing BGW Stevens in a game that lasted just 77 minutes because of inclement weather. His Minor County debut was not until 1957. He represented Yarmouth against the Variety Artists in the 1954 annual charity match between the town and the showbiz stars in residence for the Summer season. He ran Holiday Flats on the East Coast and was an Inland Revenue Tax Officer. I spent a delightful lunch hour in his company at a NCCC Minor Championship match recently.

MILLS, Arthur

Cricket. – RAF; Norfolk Club & Ground; PG Powell's XI
HS. 32 no v Suffolk August 1953 @ Lakenham
31 & 22 for RAF v Royal Navy August 1950 @ Lord's – outscored his team mate Rufus Leggett (q.v).
It was announced on 13 June 1953 that he was one of 22 men invited for trials (he scored 40 not out).
He did deal in boundaries as 55.7% of his runs for NCCC came that way.
He was stationed at RAF Watton but I have been unable to find a quoted age or service rank so his trail has gone cold.

PARFITT, Peter Howard

(b) Billingford, Norfolk 8 December 1936
Educ. – Fakenham GS; King Edward VII GS
Cricket. – Fakenham GS; King Edward V II GS; Reepham; Norfolk Junior Colts; Norfolk Club & Ground; Norfolk Senior

Colts; Norfolk Young Amateurs; Norfolk Grammar School; Middlesex; MCC RAF; DH Robins' XI; RW Hooker's XI; TN Pearce's XI; AER Gilligan's XI; Combined Services; England – 37 Tests.

HS. 131 v Kent (2) August 1955 @ Lakenham
BB. 7/44 v Hertfordshire August 1955 @ St Albans
Brother of JH (q.v) and he received the wise counselling of GH Martin (q.v)
1st class cricket – 498 match 26,924 runs 564 catches 277 wickets. Went on many International Tours and he achieved 1,000 runs in a season 14 times.
Wisden Cricketer of the Year 1963 and an Honorary MCC member.
The first NCCC Schoolboy Cap since 1907 (GA Stevens) and he grew 7 inches in just a year when age 18. He was interviewed for entrance into Loughborough College as he took his A Levels (Geography & Zoology). He ran a Public House on the Lancashire/Yorkshire border. An Amateur on Norwich City FC's books and a Sports Teacher at Croyland Road Senior School. Peter sold his own Corporate Hospitality Business and he is in demand as an After Dinner Speaker.
'The stars for him were set in the right quarter from the very start' is a very apt description as he played with an almost impertinent fluency of stroke play.
National Service in RAF (Henlow) saw him once score 108 v Col Stevens' X1 in a slow 58 minutes!

ROBINSON, Michael Ian
(b) Rougham, Suffolk 5 March 1934
Educ. – Uppingham School
Cricket. – Uppingham School; West Norfolk; Norfolk Club & Ground
HS. 23 v Buckinghamshire August 1953 @ Wing
He played in the ill fated (only 77 minutes play) friendly game against Huntingdonshire but he didn't bat, bowl or take a catch.
He scored 561 runs for his school in 1952
F.F. – His father Claude was an Egg Merchant operating out of Basle in Switzerland and Michael joined the family business.

1954

CUSHION, John Colman
(b) Blofield Norfolk 20 April 1935
(d) Sheringham, Norfolk 21 October 1992
He retired from work through ill health in August 1992 and he endured illness for several years.
Educ. – Norwich GS
Cricket. – Norwich GS; Norfolk Schoolboys; CEYMS
HS. 16 v Huntingdonshire June 1954 @ Warboys
The press comment of his performance was, "A confident

display; drafted in as Bill Thomas was playing for the MCC."
Rugby Union for Eastern Counties Colts. A Royal Norwich Golfer and he won athletic medals at a 440 yard runner. Treasurer Tyneside Club in Sheringham. He worked for 36 years for Eastern Counties Newspapers as a Sport's Journalist covering Golf for the 'EDP' and Darts for the 'EEN'. Bryan Stevens (q.v) endorsed his talents by saying that John was a very fine Sport's Journalist.

DUFFIELD, Kenneth
(b) Coventry JAS 1932
Cricket. – Warwickshire; Midland Cricket Club Conference
HS. 0 v Huntingdonshire June 1954 @ Warboys
BB. 1/32 v Huntingdonshire June 1954 @ Warboys
2/51 for Midland Cricket Club Conference v Oxford University Authentics May 1962
No relation to PG (q.v)
The 'EDP' said that he played in top class Midlands cricket. I haven't found the teams nor have I found Ken's whereabouts

EDRICH, John Hugh, MBE
(b) Blofield, Norfolk 21 June 1937
It was announced in August 2000 that he has a rare form of leukaemia
Educ. – Bracondale School
Cricket. – Bracondale School; Blofield Village; South Walsham; Army XI; Norfolk Colts; Norfolk Club & Ground; CEYMS; Combined Services; Surrey; International Cavaliers; DH Robins' XI; International Wanderers; MCC; Players; All Edrich XI; England – 77 Tests (one as Captain - in Sydney)
HS. 56 no v Suffolk August 1979 @ Lakenham AND 56 v Buckinghamshire July 1954 @ Lakenham – an amazing 25 years apart. For posterity his first 56 runs for Norfolk consisted of 18 (1), 2 (2), 2 (3) 7(4)
HS. 6 v Huntingdonshire June 1954 @ Lakenham
Cousin of BR, EH, GA, WJ – the last three feature for NCCC. John became the 5th member of the dynasty to appear in County Cricket
310 no for England v New Zealand July 1965 @ Headingley
171 for All Edrich X1 v Norfolk X1 September 1960
In the early days he also kept wicket and he attended Easter coaching sessions at Britannia Barracks, Norwich under the tuition of CSR Boswell (q.v). Tours to Rhodesia, India, Australia, New Zealand, West Indies, Ceylon, Pakistan and South Africa – have broad bat, will travel. For 12 years he was the most dependable England opener – you had to prise him from the crease. Scored 1,000 runs in a season 21 times and in six of the seasons exceeded 2,000 runs.
1st class cricket – 564 matches 39,970 runs 311 catches 103 tons
Wisden Cricketer of the Year 1966 and England's batting coach 1995. 2006/07 President of Surrey CCC .The 4th man to get 100

Centuries for Surrey behind Hobbs, Sandham and Hayward . He broke the first finger of his left hand four times and claimed that he was the only batsman who could be out LBW when struck on the hand !

F.F. – His Book - 'Runs in the Family' is a good read. At Sotherby's Auction 11 July 1995 his bat with which he scored his 100th ton was sold for £400 – an absolute bargain.

GORROD, Michael Anthony
(b) Norwich 25 June 1933
Lives in Kettering
Educ. – City of Norwich School
Cricket. – City of Norwich School; CEYMS; West of Scotland CC; Rockingham Castle; Norfolk Club & Ground
HS. 15 v Buckinghamshire July 1954 @ Lakenham – stumped in both innings of the match.
BB. 3/34 v Buckinghamshire August 1955 @ Chesham
HS. 1 no v Huntingdonshire June 1954 @ Warboys
BB. 4/21 v Huntingdonshire June 1954 @ Warboys
In his NCCC Minor Counties career he managed 3(4) and 1(6). He worked for the Norwich Shoe Company.

GRANT, Cyril Butcher
(b) Stroud, Gloucestershire 24 June 1922
(d) Stroud, Gloucestershire 15 September 2002
Cricket. – Norfolk Club & Ground; Norwich Wanderers
HS. 29 v Hertfordshire August 1955 @ St Albans – out obstructing the field. My type of cricketer – give them nothing.
BB. 2/23 v Buckinghamshire August 1954 @ Slough
HS. 45 v RAF July 1955 @ Lakenham – batting at no. 9
BB. 1/21 v RAF July 1955 @ Lakenham
5/9 for Norfolk Club & Ground v Combined Schools June 1954
F.F. – Butcher was his mothers' maiden name and he was living Weybourne, Holt while turning out for NCCC.

LAMBERT, Derek Charles
(b) Marylebone, London 21 January 1931
(d) Norfolk & Norwich Hospital 13 July 2002
Cricket. – Lord's Groundstaff; Norfolk Club & Ground; CEYMS
HS. 1 v Huntingdonshire June 1954 @ Warboys
BB. 1/7 v RAF July 1955 @ Lakenham – taking the wicket of Rufus Leggett (q.v)
An Eastern Counties Bus Driver

THORNE, Major General Sir David Calthrop, KBE CVO
(b) Hertford 13 December 1933
(d) Framlingham, Suffolk 23 April 2000
He spent 5 years of his childhood in Tanganyika being the son of a Colonial Policeman.

Educ. – St Edward's School (Oxford)
Cricket. – St Edward's School; Army; Combined Services; Norfolk Club & Ground
HS. 36 no v Buckinghamshire August 1954 @ Slough
BB. 7/48 v Hertfordshire August 1960 @ Lakenham
HS. 24 v Fezela June 1961 @ Lakenham
BB. 2/126 v Fezela June 1961 @ Lakenham
Brother of ME (q.v) and Nephew of GC (q.v)
1st class cricket – 2 matches 98 runs 2 wickets
7/50 & 3/46 for Army v Cambridge University June 1958
NCCC Captain and President 1993-95
Squash for Army & Norfolk County
Royal Norfolks – Private 1952, Commissioned 1954, Service in Ceylon (Eoka Campaign).
Graduated Staff College (Camberley in 1963), Joint Services Staff College 1967, Defence Intelligence Staff for 3 years, Instructor at RAF College 1970-72, Col. General Staff Ministry of Defence 1975-77. (Sir) David took command in Cyprus of Battalion that he had joined 20 years earlier – now named 1st Batt. The Royal Anglian Regiment. To Ulster commanding the 3rd Infantry 1978-79 being on active border service. He was in Ulster when Lord Louis Mountbatten was murdered. In 1981 he was the Army's youngest Major General and he commanded the British Forces in the Falklands. He was dubbed 'The man with the spring loaded salute'. General-in-Command 1st Armoured Division in B.A.O.R 1983-85 and Director of Infantry 1986-88. Director General Commonwealth Trust and Secretary General of the Royal Commonwealth Society 1989-1997. Project Director of National Skills Festival 1998-2000.
He worked with Coutts (Queen's Bank) Consulting Group where I once attended a lecture by him.
A truly inspiring man whose NCCC playing career came second to his military life.

TILNEY, Neville John
(b) Frettenham, Norfolk 2 March 1936
Educ. – Coltishall School
Cricket. – Coltishall School; St Barnabas; CEYMS; Norfolk Club & Ground; Norwich Natives; Frettenham
HS. 26 no v Suffolk August 1955 @ Lowestoft
BB. 3/26 v Surrey July 1955 @ The Oval
HS. 35 v RAF July 1955 @ Lakenham
BB. 4/62 v Huntingdonshire July 1955 @ Lakenham
He lost both his parents early in his life so he continued Farming at Greenacres Game Farm in Hainford

WOODHOUSE, James Stephen
(b) Luton 21 May 1933
Son of the Bishop of Thetford and he is still living in Norfolk.
Educ. – St Edward's School (Oxford); Lancing College; Oxford University (St Catherines' College)
Cricket. – St Edward's School (Oxford); West Norfolk; Crusaders

HS. 11 no v Hertfordshire August 1954 @ Croxley Green
He played in the same school team as the twins DC & ME Thorne (q.v.)
Schoolteacher Westminster School (London) 1957 – teaching English and Drama and the Deputy Headmaster in 1963 being Master of Queen's Scholars and he ran the Cricket team. Headmaster Rugby School 1967. Former Chairman of Headmasters Conference. A Director of ISIS East plus a Trustee of AEGIS.

1955

CORRAN, Andrew John
(b) Eaton, Norwich 25 November 1936
Lives West Lulworth
Educ. – Gresham's School; Oxford University (Trinity College)
Cricket. – Oxford University – Blue 1958-60; Rest of Schools; Nottinghamshire ; Gentlemen; Gentlemen of East; JD Clay's XI ; ER Dexter's XI; RL Jowett's XI; AJ Corran's XI
HS. 113 v Hertfordshire August 1958 @ Lakenham
BB. 8/102 v Buckinghamshire July 1960 @ Lakenham
1st class cricket – 132 matches 2,476 runs 77 catches 410 wickets
The nineteenth Nottinghamshire player at the time to take over 100 wickets in a season (111 in 1965 at ave.20.31) – the list includes the likes of Larwood and Voce.
146 no for Gresham's School v Old Greshamians July 1955 6/48 & 6/70 for Oxford University v Cambridge University July 1960 – the best match figures in the Varsity game since 1930 (Peebles 13/237)
The first University Blue to make his debut for NCCC since 1937 and he averaged 3 wickets a match for NCCC.
Formerly a Schoolmaster. The Cranleigh School Cricket Coach and he coached in Denmark.
Hockey - Nottinghamshire; Oxfordshire; Oxford University – Blue
F.F. – *Son of John William (Chief Chemist of J & J Colman and a Delegate to United Nations). For a time (1945) he was the NCCC Secretary. His mother Edith was one of the first women in the country to gain a PhD.*

DRAKE, Desmond
(b) Kensington, London 16 November 1921
Still lives locally but suffers from deafness.
Cricket. – Old Oxonians; Norfolk Club & Ground; Norwich Wanderers
HS. 0 v Suffolk August 1955 @ Lakenham – he played due to absence of ME Thorne who had a sceptic hand
He was in the talented Wanderers side of 1955 that boasted players of the calibre of Fielding, Grant, N. Moore, P.Powell, Richardson, Stannard and Theobald.
He had an occupation of Civil Servant

FRANCIS, Jack Noel
(b) Reading 11 December 1920
(d) Gainsborough, Lincolnshire 11 August 1983
Lived Thorpe Road, Norwich when he played for NCCC
Cricket. – Norwich Natives
HS. 14 v Huntingdonshire June 1955 @ Lakenham
He worked for Willsmore & Tibbenham Ltd in Norwich

PARFITT, John Howard
(b) Billingford, Norfolk 29 July 1933
Still lives in Norfolk
Educ. – Billingford Primary School; King's Lynn GS
Cricket. – Dereham; Norfolk Club & Ground; Driffield; RAF XI
HS. 27 no v Kent (2) July 1955 @ Sevenoaks
HS. 10 v RAF July 1955 @ Lakenham
Brother of PH (q.v)
The family were Fruit Growers but for the last 10 years of his working life he was employed at Bernard Matthews as a Poultryman.

REYNOLDS, Ronald
(b) St John's Wood, London 13 March 1930
Cricket. – Lord's Groundstaff ; MCC; Gresham's School
HS. 74 no v Hertfordshire August 1957 @ Lakenham
HS. 15 v Huntingdonshire June 1955 @ Lakenham
BB. 1/28 v Huntingdonshire June 1955 @ Lakenham
He played for NCCC on a match by match basis as required. Gresham's School Cricket Professional July 1954 – July 1958. The Finchley CC Groundsman. I was loaned a glorious photo of him entering the field of play with Nigel Moore (q.v) but alas I am no further forward in finding Ron.

RICHARDSON, Michael E
Cricket. – Norwich Wanderers
BB. 1/15 v Huntingdonshire June 1955 @ Lakenham
A Flight Lt at RAF Coltishall is the only clue gleaned so far

SCHOFIELD, Roger, BSc DipEd
(b) Norwich 12 December 1935
Still lives locally and is a Norwich City season ticket holder
Educ. – City of Norwich School; Nottingham University
Cricket. – City of Norwich School; Nottingham University; CEYMS; Barleycorns; Norwich; Norfolk Club & Ground; Norfolk Young Amateurs; Mallards
HS. 15 no v Hertfordshire July 1958 @ Hertford AND 15 v Suffolk August 1957 @ Felixstowe
BB. 7/53 v Buckinghamshire August 1957 @ Lakenham
– in a match of 3 unbeaten tons. Roger also had two catches dropped off his bowling.
A right hand bat and leg break bowler with Michael Falcon's 1957 Annual Report saying quote. "We were however

encouraged by the bowling of two newcomers to the County side, R. Schofield and J.J.W. Tomlinson; both are young and with experience should be a great asset." A Teacher of Mathematics at Thorpe GS.

THORNE, Brigadier Michael Everard, CBE
(b) Hertford 13 December 1933
Still a NCCC Member at 2011
Educ. – St Edward's School (Oxford)
Cricket. – Free Foresters; Royal Norfolks; Royal Anglian Army; Norfolk Club & Ground
HS. 65 v Surrey (2) August 1955 @ Lakenham
Brother of DC (q.v) and Nephew of GC (q.v)
Commanded 2nd Batt. Royal Anglian Regiment in Germany and Northern Ireland . Role as Military Intelligence Coordinator for Ministry of Defence. Organiser Marie Curie Community Charity.
A Degree in Medieval History from Queen Mary University of London earned when he was a state pensioner.

1956

BLOFELD, Henry Calthorpe, OBE
(b) Hoveton Home Farm, Norfolk 23 September 1939
Still a NCCC Member from his base in London.
Educ. – Sunningdale School; Eton College (GW Nickson House & MN Forrest House); Cambridge University (King's College)
Cricket. – Sunningdale School; Eton College; Eton Ramblers; Southern Schools; Public Schools; Free Foresters; Norfolk Young Amateurs; Perambulators; Quidnuncs; I Zingari; MCC; Butterflies; Hoveton & Wroxham; Cambridge University – Blue 1959
HS. 76 v Nottinghamshire (2) August 1956 @Lakenham
BB. 1/19 v Buckinghamshire August 1965 @ High Wycombe
Best wicket keeping season for dismissals in 1958 (12c 7s) – he also took 16 catches for NCCC in his career as an outfielder.
HS. *60 v Hampshire May 1965 @ Southampton* – he was stumped off of the brilliant Peter Sainsbury (76 and 7/30) in this Gillette Cup match
Brother of JCC (q.v) and related to England player FSG Calthorpe
His first visit to Lakenham was at age seven and he commentated for Radio Norfolk for the last game there in 2000.
1st class cricket – 17 matches 758 runs 11 catches
104 no for Public Schools v Combined Services August 1956
85 for Perambulators v Etceteras April 1959
67 for Eton Ramblers v Radley Rangers July 1967 – to be outgunned by Ted Dexter's 78 not out.

Known affectionately as 'Blowers' his family were Landowners with his father going to Eton with author Ian Fleming who used the name Blofeld for one of his villains. The Cricket Society Promising Young Cricketer 1956. Henry was hit by a bus while riding a bicycle to Eton's cricket ground on 7 June 1957 and he was unconscious for 28 days.
He worked initially at a Merchant Bank and for The Times, The Guardian and The Observer and many varied publications since as a Sport's Journalist. An ITV Commentator on cricket from the 1960s and a Test Match Special Radio Commentator from 1973 in the great recording days of Brian Johnston.
An excellent read is his book 'Dear Old Thing: Talking Cricket' and he has returned to Norwich with his superb theatrical show an 'Evening with Blowers'.

BRAND, Walter George
(b) Brisley, Norfolk 29 September 1916
(d) Julian Hospital, Norwich 1 March 2002
Lived Weston Longville and known in the family as 'Dick'.
Cricket. – Dereham
HS. Did not bat in his one friendly game which is listed below
BB. 1/36 v Huntingdonshire June 1956 @ Ramsey
At Dereham CC with D.H.Chamberlain, G. Mitchell and J.H.Parfitt.
5/19 for Dereham v Yarmouth July 1955
My thanks go to the present NCCC Vice Chairman Ted Wright (q.v) who provided the necessary clues to finding this player.

COOMB, Arthur Grenfell
(b) Kempston, Bedfordshire 3 March 1929
Lives in Truro
Educ. – Bedford Modern School
Cricket. – Bedford Modern School; Bedfordshire; Minor Counties; Royal Navy; TH Clark's XI; Combined Services; Norwich Wanderers
HS. 69 v Buckinghamshire August 1962 @ High Wycombe
BB. 7/40 v Buckinghamshire August 1959 @ High Wycombe – bowling unchanged in the innings with Andy Corran.
1st class cricket – 5 matches 55 runs 1 catch 8 wickets
He captained NCCC on five occasions and he went to school with EE Ward (q.v).
6/117 for Royal Navy v Worcestershire June 1949
3/70 for Minor Counties v Indians September 1952 @ Lakenham and he also top scored with 40, batting at no. 9.
He took 147 wickets for Bedfordshire to go with his 120 for NCCC as a right arm medium fast bowler.
A former Marketing Executive for an International Agricultural Company.

FARRER, Richard John
(b) St Faiths, Norwich 17 October 1936
(d) Neath General Hospital 25 June 1994
Lived Glyncorrwg, Port Talbot
Educ. – Norwich GS
Cricket. – Norwich GS; Norwich Wanderers; Barleycorns; Norfolk Young Amateurs; CP Lemmon's XI
HS. 18 no v Suffolk August 1957 @ Lakenham
BB. 1/25 v Kent (2) July 1957 @ Aylesford
HS. Did not bat in his one friendly match which is mentioned below
BB. 5/72 v Huntingdonshire June 1956 @ Ramsey
7/55 for Norwich GS v Old Norvicensians May 1952
F.F. – His stepson Timothy Thomas advised that Richard was a retired Schoolteacher

FIDDLER, Geoffrey George
(b) Norwich 20 December 1935
Still lives locally
Educ. – Norwich GS
Cricket. – Norwich GS; Norwich Union; CEYMS; Barleycorns; Norfolk Club & Ground; Norfolk Young Amateurs; MCC
HS. 81 v Suffolk August 1962 @ Lakenham
BB. 3/12 v Hertfordshire August 1957 @ Lakenham
HS. 27 no v Huntingdonshire June 1956 @ Ramsey
99 for Norfolk Club & Ground v Suffolk Club & Ground 1964 – run out foolishly (his words) going for a second run.
One of eight NCCC players to score a 50 in both innings v Suffolk. He shared 4 century partnerships with PG Powell (112), EG Witherden (110), WJ Edrich (147no) and NH Moore (119) as he personally scored a 50 in 7 successive seasons (1958-64)
Rugby Union – Norwich Union; Crusaders; Eastern Counties; Norfolk County – and Chairman of their Selectors. Geoff worked at Norwich Union and he had the Norwich Sports Shop. He latterly opened Norwich Screen Sports Shop- a business that printed for example T Shirts.

HALL, Thomas Auckland
(b) Darlington 19 August 1930
(d) Arlesey, Bedfordshire 21 April 1984
Educ. – Uppingham School
Cricket. – Uppingham School; Public Schools; MCC; Free Foresters; Derbyshire Club & Ground; Derbyshire; Somerset; Combined Services; T.N. Pearce's XI; RAF; The Rest
HS. 4 v Suffolk August 1957 @ Lakenham
BB. 4/56 v Suffolk August 1957 @ Lakenham
52 (147) for Derbyshire v Surrey May 1950 – batting at 9 against Bedser, Laker and Lock
69 no for Somerset v Northamptonshire July 1953 – an unbroken 9th wicket stand of 130 in facing the almost indecipherable Australian George Tribe.
1st class cricket – 66 matches 892 runs 29 catches 183 wickets

A fine sportsman, he was a member of the crew of the original 'Crossbow', which broke the world sailing record

PHIPPS, Douglas David
(b) Edmonton, London 21 July 1934
Educ. – Mill Hill School; RMA Sandhurst
Cricket. – Mill Hill School; RMA Sandhurst; Buckinghamshire; Combined Services; Army; Essex 2nds; Essex Club & Ground; Sussex Club & Ground
HS. 8 no v Kent (2) August 1956 @ Lakenham AND 8 v Kent (2) July 1956 @ Tunbridge Wells
BB. 4/67 v Kent (2) July 1956 @ Tunbridge Wells
1st class cricket – 1 match 15 runs 1 catch 1 wicket
Schoolmaster at Langley School. A Car Photo Journalist with articles in Sporting Motorist.
Sport's Editor of Autocar

THAXTER, David William
(b) Cambridge 20 November 1934
(d) Hunstanton, Norfolk 14 May 2001
Missing on this day as he drowned and his body was never found
Cricket. – Hunstanton; Norfolk Club & Ground; West Norfolk
HS. 39 no v Middlesex (2) July 1956 @ Ealing
HS. 2 v Huntingdonshire June 1956 @ Ramsey

WATTS, Ivan Maurice
(b) Upton, Norfolk 7 March 1938
Still lives locally
Educ. – Acle School
Cricket. – Acle School; Upton; Norwich Wanderers; Barleycorns; CP Lemmon's XI; Norfolk Young Amateurs
HS. 64 v Buckinghamshire August 1963 @ Slough
HS. 5 no v Huntingdonshire June 1956 @ Ramsey
118 no for Norwich Wanderers v Papworth July 1969
A Nurse at Little Plumstead Hospital and then he ran a Farm as a tenant

WILSON, Michael Dunham
(b) Norwich 8 March 1940
Still lives locally
Educ. – Langley School; Nottingham Training College
Cricket. – Langley School; Ingham; Norfolk Young Amateurs; AJ Corran's X1
HS. 7 v Suffolk August 1960 @ Lowestoft
HS. 5 v Huntingdonshire June 1956 @ Ramsey
Rugby Union – Norwich; Norfolk County; Eastern Counties
Lawn Tennis – Norfolk County
Originally a Teacher in Upton he was the Norwich School PE Teacher for 36 years.

WITHERDEN, Edwin George
(b) Goudhurst, Kent 1 May 1922
Lives Bury St Edmunds
Cricket. – Kent; Lord Cornwallis' XI; Carrow; Ingham; EG
Witherden's XI
**HS. 134 no v Nottinghamshire (2) August 1959 @
Lakenham**
BB. 5/44 v Suffolk August 1954 @ Felixstowe
HS. 44 v Fezela June 1961 @ Lakenham
Father of N (q.v)
1st class cricket – 40 matches 1,380 runs 13 catches 9 wickets
Ingham CC Professional and Head Groundsman. The
Tonbridge School Groundsman for 9 years. Bishop's Stortford
Cricket Coach 1962 and Head Groundsman – he passed the
mower to his son Nigel.
Badminton for Norfolk County and Football for Lye FC (Kent)
'Ted' played with consummate ease and topped the NCCC
batting averages 4 times and he headed the bowling averages
once. He hammered 13 centuries for the County between
1957-62. He and Steve Plumb stand together having totalled 9
half centuries each against Suffolk. Also stands equal eleventh
having been involved in 16 century partnerships with seven
different partners. 'Ted' scored 1,031 runs in Championship
matches in 1959 – highest ever by a Norfolk player and the
eighth best by any player.
He passed 800 runs in four consecutive seasons (1957-60).
I liked the story from Henry Blofeld of Ted , "There were the daily
cataloguings of EGW's injuries and illnesses, each one of which
invariably guaranteed the owner a century."

1957

BLOFELD, Sir John Christopher Calthorpe
(b) Hoveton Home Farm, Norfolk 11 July 1932
Educ. – St Paul's School; Eton College (GW Nickson House);
Cambridge University (King's College – BA 1955 MA 1961)
Cricket. – Eton College; Eton Ramblers; Free Foresters;
MCC; I Zingari
HS. 36 v Kent (2) July 1957 @ Aylesford
Brother of HC (q.v)
Chancellor Diocese of St Edmund and Ipswich. Inspector for
Department of Trade 1979-1981.
A Circuit Judge 1982-1990 and Presiding Judge South Eastern
Circuit 1993-96. A Queen's Counsel from 1975 and the Queen's
Bench 1990-2001. Barrister and a retired High Court Judge.
A Recorder of Crown Court 1975-1982. Deputy Lieutenant
Norfolk 1991. Real Tennis for Cambridge University gaining a
Blue

BOWETT, Thomas David
(b) Gaywood Nursing Home, King's Lynn, Norfolk 9 May
1936

Still lives in Norfolk
Educ. – Glebe House School (Hunstanton); Repton School
(The Cross)
Cricket. – Repton School; North Runcton; West Norfolk;
Castle Rising; Georgetown CC
HS. 35 v Hertfordshire July 1958 @ Hertford
Known as David he is a Qualified Mechanical Engineer. He
lived in British Guyana and Trinidad dealing with conversion of
Sugar Estates. His National Service was with the Royal Norfolks
and latterly he was in the King's African Rifles. He still plays Golf
regularly with RHG Hoff (q.v) and RI Jefferson (q.v).

KENT, Eric Arthur
(b) Norwich 1 September 1934
Educ. – St Mark's School; City of Norwich School
Cricket. – City of Norwich School; Army; Brooke; Carrow; St
Giles; East Anglian Wanderers; Dereham
HS. Did not Bat in his two Minor County games
BB. 1/24 v Hertfordshire July 1957 @ Hertford
Born at Lakenham and a score card seller in the Len Hart
days. Eric remembers bowling to Harold Theobald (q.v) in the
Lakenham nets with the added incentive of a shilling being
placed on the stumps which was yours if the great man was
bowled.
He was in the Royal Army Pay Corp and was posted to the
West Indies with his C.O getting him a Test Match ticket
so he watched all the greats for free in the Caribbean –
Weekes,Worrell,Walcott and Sobers etc. A Carrow cricketer
for 25 years who was employed at Norvic Shoes and Anglian
Industrial Gases. He started his own business called Wensum
Welding Supplies and as I write he is recovering in hospital after
having a knee replacement.

TOMLINSON, Jeremy John William
(b) Wootton-under-Edge, Gloucestershire 6 March 1941
Lives in Cambridge
Educ. – Dragon School; Repton School (Brook House)
Cricket. – Repton School; Repton Pilgrims; South Walsham;
Free Foresters; Barleycorns; Loughton
**HS. 11 no v Buckinghamshire August 1957 @ Wing
AND 11 v Suffolk August 1963 @ Lowestoft
BB. 2/18 v Buckinghamshire August 1957 @ Wing**
63 for Repton Pilgrims v Old Tonbridgians June 1971
128 for Loughton v Buckhurst Hill 1976
A retired Corporate Pensions Consultant

WESLEY, Peter William
(b) Norwich 11 January 1937
Lives Salisbury, Wiltshire
Educ. – Avenue Road School ; City of Norwich School;
Bristol University
Cricket. – City of Norwich School; Norfolk Grammar

Schools; St Barnabas; CEYMS; Norwich Wanderers; Barleycorns; Bristol University

HS. 34 v Middlesex (2) July 1957 @ Ealing – with 2 (4) and 2 (6)

Not a relation of RJ (q.v)

Studied Mathematics at Bristol University. A Fellow of the Royal Institute of Chartered Surveyors. He worked extensively throughout Africa. A retired Deputy Director General of the Board of Ordnance Survey.

1958

CUNNINGHAM, Alan David

(b) Auckland, County Durham 26 March 1921

Lives Pitochry, Scotland

Educ. – Durham School; Durham University

Cricket. – Durham School; Durham University; County Club (Newcastle); Northumberland ; Castle Rising; Norfolk Club & Ground

HS. 80 v Suffolk August 1958 @ Felixstowe

35 for Durham School v Giggleswick School (all out 23) June 1939

41 for Durham School v Percy Main (all out 39) June 1940

103 no for County Club v Tynemouth July 1947

Flight Lt. Demobbed in 1946. Schoolmaster teaching English, PE and Games at Gresham's (1957-65) and latterly at Rannoch School in Scotland.

GIBSON, Joseph John Campbell

(b) Norwich 13 February 1933

(d) Norwich 30 January 2004

Always referred to in the press as Joe Campbell Gibson and his name was invariably hyphenated as Campbell-Gibson. Campbell was a family name.

Educ. – Douai School (Berkshire)

Cricket. – Barleycorns; St Andrews Hospital; Norfolk Club & Ground

HS. 64 not out v Staffordshire August 1961 @ Stoke-on-Trent

BB. 6/50 v Staffordshire July 1963 @ Lakenham

Brother-in-Law of BGW Stevens (q.v)

56 no & 5/27 for St. Andrews Hospital v Norwich Gas July 1980 – at age 47.

60 & 13 no & 6/81 & 3/32 for NCCC v Suffolk August 1962 Joe was an Export Manager for Edwards & Holmes (Shoe Manufacturer)

GODFREY, Derek Gordon

(b) Ware, Hertfordshire 31 January 1942

Educ. – City of Norwich School; Loughborough College

Cricket. – England Schools Cricket Association; Nottinghamshire 2nds – as a loaned substitute fielder;

Norfolk Young Amateurs; Horsford; Carrow; Barleycorns; Griquland Country District (Cape Province)

HS. 7 v Cambridgeshire July 1961 @ Wisbech

BB. 5/25 v Cambridgeshire July 1959 @ Fenner's

Uncle of RG Panter (q.v)

A Chartered Civil Engineer (BSc CEng FICE) with many positions in his working life such as Project Manager, Divisional Director and Executive Vice President of an American Company.

His father Gordon (1918-1987) was a Poultry Farmer and a Hellesdon Councillor for 27 years. Also a Broadland Council Vice Chairman and Gordon Godfrey Way is named after his father.

1959

ALLCOCK, Terence

(b) Leeds 10 December 1935

Educ. – St Anthony's School; Mount St Mary's School

Cricket. – Leeds Boys; Yorkshire Boys – with K. Taylor (q.v); Yorkshire Federation (Under 18) Blackpool CC; Ingham; Gresham Masters; Holbeck

HS. 82 v Cambridgeshire July 1973 @ Lakenham

Best wicket keeping season in 1959 with 15 victims (12c 3 s) to include seven dismissals in one match.

HS. 39 v South Africa June 1961 @ Lakenham – out of a team score of just 98.

HS. *24 v Hampshire May 1965 @ Southampton*

Coached cricket at Gresham's School for 8 years.

The Allcock Family Funeral services is based in Norwich and his wife Barbara swam for Lancashire and had Empire Games trials.

Football. - St Anthony's School; Mount St Mary's School; Leeds Boys; Yorkshire Schoolboys; National Schoolboys trials; Bolton Wanderers; Norwich City FC 15 March 1958, later youth team manager and chief coach; Manchester City coach and manager's assistant; also with Dereham and local village sides.

A fabulous Norwich City football career of 127 goals and a recommended read is 'Glorious Canaries' published in 1994 which details the NCFC Hall of Famer in this sport in far greater detail. His appearances for NCCC were limited by his commitments to the Canaries.

CAMPION-JONES, Peter

(b) Welshpool,Wales 31 July 1941

(d) Norwich October 2002

Educ. – Gresham's School (Old School House)

Cricket. – Gresham's School; Norfolk Young Amateurs; Norfolk Club & Ground; Norwich Wanderers

HS. 2 v Cambridgeshire July 1959 @ Fenner's

The late Bryan Stevens' (q.v) NCCC attempted bible of players has him as Peter Campion Jones but Tracey Moore (q.v) correctly revealed that his surname was hyphenated.

Peter in 1967 was residing in Peterborough and by 1971 in Blofield. He was a Rolls Royce Salesman for Mann Egerton and worked at the Gold Seal Garage on North Walsham Road, Norwich in the 1980s.

FELLOWES, The Right Honourable Lord Robert, GCB GCVO QSO PC
(b) Sandringham Estate, Norfolk 11 December 1941
Educ. – Eton College
Cricket. – clubs unknown
HS. 9 v Nottinghamshire (2) August 1959 @ Trent Bridge
Son of Scots Guards Major Sir William (the Queen's Land Agent at Sandringham), and of his wife Jane, daughter of Brigadier General AFH Ferguson (great-grandfather of Sarah, Duchess of York – which made her a first cousin once removed). Robert married Lady Jane Spencer, elder sister of Diana Princess of Wales at Westminster Abbey when he was an assistant Private Secretary to the Queen.
Joined the Scots Guards in 1960 on a short service commission to 1963. Entered the Banking industry, working for Allen Harvey and Ross Ltd, discount brokers and bankers (1964-77) and he was a Managing Director from 1968. He spent 1977-1997 in the Royal Household becoming the Queen's Private Secretary in 1990. A Life Peerage as Baron Fellowes of Shotesham and he took his seat in the House of Lords formally on 26 October 1999.
Chairman of Barclays Private Banking and a Company Director, and a Trustee, of the Rhodes Trust, the Mandela-Rhodes Foundation as well as the Winston Churchill Memorial Trust. A Vice Chairman of the Commonwealth Institute and he became Chair of the Prison Reform Trust in 2001. He remained Secretary and Registrar of the Order of Merit.

KENYON, Christopher Michael
(b) Luton 27 March 1938
Lives in Cheltenham
Educ. – Uppingham School; Cambridge University (Jesus College – BA 1961 MA 1965)
Cricket. – Uppingham School; Cambridge University Crusaders; Free Foresters; The Cryptics; Yorkshire Gentlemen; Gloucestershire Gypsies
HS. 22 v Nottinghamshire (2) August 1959 @ Trent Bridge
Best wicket keeping season in 1959 with 9 victims (8c 1s) Chris got an Honours Degree in Geography and Theology and he was a Schoolmaster at Dean Close School in Cheltenham for 36 years.

MOORE, Tracey Ian
(b) Ingham, Norfolk 16 December 1941
Still lives locally

Educ. – Stalham Secondary School
Cricket. – Ingham; Blacksheep CC; Minor Counties North; Minor Counties East; Cromer
HS. 55 v Hertfordshire August 1977 @ Lakenham
BB. 8/71 v Hertfordshire July 1967 @ Hertford
HS. 8 no v Cambridge University May 1976 @ Fenner's AND 8 v Cambridge University May 1977 @ Fenner's
BB. 2/97 v Fezela June 1961 @ Lakenham
HS. *2 v Yorkshire May 1969 @ Lakenham*
BB. *6/48 v Yorkshire May 1969 @ Lakenham*
He was at Ingham CC for an incredible 43 years.
NCCC Captain 1976-78 and on their Executive Committee until 1984. In 1975 he came out of retirement when the team were short of a bowler and he got his Norfolk County maiden half century in 153 minutes. Second only to Michael Falcon in the number of NCCC wickets secured in the M.C. Championship. Thirteen times he took 20 or more wickets in the season with his best haul being 53 (1969) and a fine 44 (1971) when the next highest capture that season was just 12 wickets by Billy Rose. His appearances for the Minor Counties were in the Benson & Hedges Cup.
Tracey was a Sales Representative for Waveney Fork Trucks and still has not retired from working for a living.

ROSSI, David Martin
(b) Northfield, Birmingham 19 April 1935
Lives locally and still a NCCC member in 2011
Cricket. – Norwich Wanderers; Norfolk Club & Ground; Wolverhampton CC; Barleycorns
HS. 79 no v Suffolk August 1959 @Lakenham – finishing second in that years averages behind Ted Witherden.
HS. 4 v Fezela June 1961 @ Lakenham
He was on the NCCC Executive Committee and also the Treasurer.

1960

DUFFIELD, Peter George
(b) Kelling Village, Norfolk 21 August 1936
Lives locally
Cricket. – Kelling; Holt; Army; Norwich Wanderers
HS. 1 v Cambridgeshire July 1960 @ Ely
BB. 5/45 v Nottinghamshire (2) July 1960 @ Newark-on-Trent (all bowled)
An Electrician, a trade he learnt in the Army.

EMONSON, Michael Robert
(b) Edmonton, London 16 October 1942
(d) Whipps Cross Hospital, Leytonstone 11 August 1996
Lived Woodford Green, Essex
Educ. – Gresham's School
Cricket. – Gresham's School; Norwich Wanderers

HS. 1 no (x2) v Nottinghamshire (2) July 1960 @ Newark-on-Trent – NCCC needed 8 off the last over, they lost 2 wickets and it took a six by Joe Gibson off the fifth ball in order to win.

His cricket coach at Gresham's was Terry Allcock but he missed playing with him in this match.

A wicket keeper with 7 victims in his first season as against the 13 that Allcock claimed and a Norfolk County Hockey Goalkeeper. A Law Clerk and his daughter Elizabeth advised that her father had end stage alcoholic liver disease.

WESLEY, Robert John
(b) Downham Market, Norfolk 27 November 1942
Lives SW London
Educ. – Repton School; Cambridge University (Fitzwilliam College)
Cricket. – Repton School; Downham Market; RJ Wesley's XI; Bourne Town; West Norfolk; Norfolk Young Amateurs; Castle Rising; Wimbledon; Cambridge University Crusaders; Cryptics; Repton Pilgrims; Penywren Taverners.
HS. 79 v Lincolnshire August 1961 @ Lincoln
BB. 3/40 v Lincolnshire August 1961 @ Lincoln
Not related to PW Wesley (q.v.).
3/27 for Repton School v Derbyshire Club & Ground June 1961. He studied Natural Sciences at University and latterly worked for the Hong Kong Trading Company.
An MCC Member he was involved in Commercial Projects in the Rubber Industry.

1961

GURNEY, William Stephen Claude
(b) London 26 December 1937
Lives in Foulsham as a semi retired Farmer.
Educ. – Fernden Prep School; Bradfield College (The Close); Oxford University (Trinity College).
Cricket. – Bradfield College; Trinity College; Norfolk Colts; Norfolk Club & Ground; MCC; West Norfolk; Bradfield Waifs
HS. 16 v Staffordshire August 1961 @ Stoke-on-Trent
He was selected to play for NCCC when he was in Libya doing his National Service with the Kings Royal Rifle Corps (60th), becoming the Green Jackets.
He latterly worked in London in Advertising and became a qualified Chartered Accountant (FCA) working at Lovewell Blake. The life of Fruit Farming became Arable Farming and I managed to interview him as he was about to disappear with the watering can – so dry is the earth!

HALL, Evan Raymond
(b) Reepham, Norfolk 6 August 1942
Lives locally
Educ. – Reepham School; Holt Hall School

Cricket. – Reepham School; MCC Groundstaff (1958-62); Dereham; Carrow; Ingham; Leicestershire (2); Middlesex (2)
HS. 66 v Cambridgeshire July 1961 @ Wisbech – his debut match with 56 in the first innings.
BB. 2/36 v Cambridgeshire July 1961 @ Wisbech
HS. 45 v Fezela June 1961 @ Lakenham
48 no for Middlesex v Surrey in a 2nd XI fixture May 1962
2 years coaching Rugby School. A Postman for 23 years.

MATTOCKS, Douglas Eric
(b) Costessey,Norwich 5 July 1944
(d) Norwich 7 October 1999
Educ. – Loddon School; Sir John Leman School; Suffolk GS; Loughborough College
Cricket. – Loddon School; Sir John Leman School; Loughborough College; Suffolk GS; Suffolk Young Amateurs; Nottinghamshire 2nds; Nottinghamshire Club & Ground; Universities Athletic Union; Minor Counties; Lowestoft; Cromer; Harleston.
HS. 104 v Suffolk August 1966 @ Lowestoft
Best wicket keeping season in terms of victims was 1977 (24c 4s), one of ten times he topped 20 dismissals and he has by far the most NCCC dismissals in such a role exceeding anybody else in M.C. Championship history.
HS. 2 no v Bedfordshire June 1982 @ Pinebanks AND 2 v Suffolk May 1978 @ Lakenham
HS. *48 no v Suffolk June 1986 @ Horsford*
1st class cricket 1 match 1 run 4 catches
73 for Universities Athletic Union v Warwickshire (2) June 1964 On the Norfolk Executive Committee and a former Captain. He is still on the records page for the last wicket stand of 101 with TM Wright v Hertfordshire @ Lakenham in 1963.
In 1974 he was one of 8 Schoolteachers on NCCC's playing roster. There are two trophies named after him namely the Doug Mattocks Wicket Keeping Award and the Doug Mattocks Handicap Trophy in Golf. He was one of Norfolk's most successful and respected sporting figures. He was first coached when he was aged 11 and he started keeping from the age of 13. Doug was playing in Ted Witherden's Benefit Match and Bill Edrich was impressed by him. A call from Team Secretary George Pilch followed and the rest is history. He said that he couldn't separate Bill Edrich and Phil Sharpe when it came to captaincy. Bill, per Doug, was the sort of fellow who led from the front and if he told you to do something, you went out and did it. And he could make a game out of nothing. 'Sharpie,' he further stated, was a totally different character, but a great organizer. The whole team believed in him and tactically he was brilliant.

OXBURY, Michael David
(b) Norwich 14 October 1942
Educ. – Norwich GS

Cricket. – Norwich GS; Norfolk Club & Ground; Ingham; Norfolk Young Amateurs; K. Lamming's XI; Norwich Union; Barleycorns

HS. 16 v Lincolnshire August 1962 @ Scunthorpe

BB. 4/68 v Hertfordshire July 1970 @ Hertford

HS. 11 v Essex May 1976 @ Chelmsford – Graham Gooch scored 99 as NCCC mustered just 96 all out.

BB. 2/87 v Essex May 1976 @ Chelmsford

His wife is the grand daughter of former Norwich City FC's Goalkeeper 'Dillo' Sparks (1879-1974)

PILCH, David George

(b) West Kirby, Cheshire 2 February 1943

Lives locally

Educ. – Repton School (The Orchard)

Cricket. – Repton School; Repton Pilgrims; Barleycorns; Norwich Wanderers; Minor Counties; Minor Counties North; RJ Wesley's XI; Norfolk & Suffolk XI

HS. 102 no v Cambridgeshire July 1976 @ Lakenham

BB. 7/35 v Suffolk August 1974 @ Bury St Edmunds

HS. 30 no v Cambridge University May 1976 @ Fenner's

BB. 3/60 v Essex May 1976 @ Chelmsford – he had Graham Gooch caught for 99 in the game

HS. *11 v Glamorgan June 1983 @ Lakenham*

BB. *3/15 v Glamorgan June 1983 @ Lakenham*

Son of GE (q.v) and Grandson of RE (q.v)

5/20 for Repton Pilgrims v Uppingham Rovers May 1970

8/12 for Norwich Wanderers v Carrow June 1984

Hockey. - Grasshoppers; Norfolk County; East of England

Squash. - Norfolk County (just once)

NCCC Captain (1972-75), Hon Team Secretary and on the Executive Committee.

His 50 innings for NCCC v Suffolk surpasses Doug Mattock's total by three. One of NCCC's great all rounders with over 6,000 runs and more than 200 wickets to his name. He did not look out of place either standing next to Phil Sharpe (q.v) in the slip cordon. An integral part for many decades of the family store RG Pilch (Sports Outfitters)

RADLEY, Clive Thornton, MBE

(b) Hertford 13 May 1944

Lives Rickmansworth

Educ. – Norwich GS

Cricket. – Norwich GS; Norfolk Club & Ground; Middlesex; MCC; MCC Young Cricketers; Auckland; England U25s; DH Robins' XI; Rest of England; DB Close's XI; Old England XI; TN Pearce's XI; LC Stevens' XI; Middlesex Club & Ground; Middlesex Past & Present; RW Hooker's Middlesex XI; International Cavaliers; New Zealand Universities; K Lamming's XI; Sir JP Getty's XI; Lavinia, Duchess of Norfolk's XI; England – 8 Tests - scoring two centuries.

HS. 59 no v Suffolk August 1961 @ Lakenham

BB. 1/15 v Suffolk August 1961 @ Lakenham

1st class cricket – 559 matches 26,441 runs 516 catches 8 wickets

He coached cricket in South Africa and Australia and was the MCC Head Coach 1991-2009.

Wisden Cricketer of the Year 1979 and he was voted a NCCC Life Member at the 2009 AGM.

In one season as he started out in Norfolk he had 1,640 runs by 26 June 1961- 542 for Norwich School, 341 in House Matches, 57 for Norwich Club & Ground and 700 in club games. The Lord's institution Archie Fowler coached Clive as a Norwich Schoolboy and Bill Edrich smoothed the way to Middlesex. He had a versatile cut and a powerful off drive as he put many a bowler to the sword and his quick running between the wickets secured many an extra run to his total. If only NCCC had him for more than the one season.

RUTTER, Rev Canon Allen Edward Henry

(b) Bickley, Kent 24 December 1928

Lives in Somerset and universally known as 'Claude' – a name from his schooldays that stuck with him.

Educ. – Monkton Combe; Dauntsey's School; Cambridge University (Queens' College & St John's College - BA 1952 MA 1956); Cranmer Hall; University of Durham.

Cricket. – Wiltshire Under 19s; Wiltshire Queries CC; Wiltshire; The Mote; Cambridge University Crusaders; Cambridge University; Free Foresters; Hastings and St Leonard's Priory; Bath CC; Dereham; Ingham; Norwich Diocesan CC; MCC; Compton House; Salisbury Diocesan

HS. 76 v Staffordshire July 1965 @ Bignall End

HS. *7 v Hampshire May 1965 @ Southampton- the only Clergyman to play in the Gillette Cup.*

His cricket career embraced 1946-1996 apart from a gap from 1970-72.

Hockey. – Cambridge University; Norwich Wanderers; Maidstone

Golf. – The Clergy Champion 1977 and 1991

Son of Rev Norman and Hilda Mason.

Scientific Liasion Officer East Malling Res Station 1953-56. Curate Bath Abbey 1959-60. Rector East Dereham 1960-64. Chaplain Cawston College 1964-69. Gingindhlovu Zululand 1969-73 (also Agric. Sec. Helwel Diocese of Zululand). Rural Dean Queen Thorne 1973-96. Rural Dean Sherborne 1976-87. Canon and Prebendary Salisbury Cathedral from 1986-96. Other Diocesan appointments to be followed by Consultant Archbishop's Commission on Rural Areas 1989-91. Vicar and RAF Chaplain Ascension Island 1996-97. Priest-in-Charge Thorncombe with Forde Abbey, Winsham and Cricket St Thomas 1998

1962

DONALDSON, James Andrew
(b) Castle Rising, Norfolk 27 August 1943
Lives in King's Lynn
Educ. – Wellingborough School
Cricket. – Wellingborough School; Castle Rising; West Norfolk; North Runcton; Gentlemen of Leicestershire; Swallows
HS. 77 no v Cambridgeshire June 1971 @ Wisbech
HS. 0 v Essex April 1968 @ Chelmsford
HS. *21 v Yorkshire May 1969 @ Lakenham*
One of 40 players to score 2(50s) in a match and he had a catalogue of hand and foot injuries spanning seasons 1962/63/67 & 68.
He owns and runs a Camping and Caravan Park in King's Lynn.

HEYWOOD, Brigadier Richard John, OBE DL
(b) Gayton, Norfolk 12 June 1944
Educ. – Radley College
Cricket. – Radley College; Radley Rangers; Norfolk Colts; I Zingari; Free Foresters; Coldstream Guards; Army; RJ Wesley's XI
HS. 20 no v Lincolnshire August 1962 @ Scunthorpe
In the Cricketer Cup Final of 1967 on his Radley Rangers side was Ted Dexter and against him for Repton Pilgrims were DG Pilch (q.v), Richard Hutton and Donald Carr.
At the Ministry of Defence and a 37 year career man with the Coldstream Guards (1963-99) involved with Trooping the Colour, Horse Guards Parade and the Queen's Birthday Pagentry. He has known Robert Fellowes (q.v) since their schooldays. Still regularly plays Golf with two former NCCC players namely DG Pilch and GW Goodley (q.v).

SWARBRICK, Squadron Leader Denys Leigh
(b) Saltash, Cornwall 17 May 1930
Living in Sidmouth he sadly he suffers from Dementia
Educ. – Saltash GS
Cricket. – Saltash GS; RAF Apprentices CC; RAF Cove CC; Devon
HS. 34 no v Hertfordshire July 1962 @ Hertford
As a cricketer he first surfaced on the radar as a Pilot Officer based at RAF Coltishall

WRIGHT, Thomas Martin
(b) Wombwell, Barnsley 16 October 1934
(d) Harrogate District Hospital 21 March 2002
Lived in Knaresborough
Educ. – St Joseph's Catholic School (Pudsey)
Cricket. – Pudsey St Lawrence; Norwich Wanderers; Barleycorns
HS. 48 v Hertfordshire August 1963 @ Lakenham – still

a record last wicket stand of 101 with Doug Mattocks.
BB. 6/45 v Lincolnshire August 1964 @ Lakenham – also took 4/48 in the same game
HS. *1 no v Hampshire May 1965 @ Southampton*
Second in the bowling averages to Bill Edrich in his debut season and also second in 1964 of the five men who took 20 or more wickets.
A Sales manager in the Knitwear Industry with Byford's plus he worked for Double Two Shirts. Martin then became his own boss as a Sales Textile Agent. His widow Barbara is due to visit the family friend DM Rossi (q.v) this summer.

1963

GOODLEY, Gerald William
(b) Tilney St Lawrence, Norfolk 16 October 1944
Lives locally and owns a Farm in West Norfolk.
Educ. – Gresham's School (Howson's House)
Cricket. – Gresham's School; Castle Rising Colts; Norfolk Young Amateurs; Ingham; West Norfolk; MCC; Free Foresters; Swallows; Gentlemen of Leicester
HS. 74 v Buckinghamshire August 1970 @ Beaconsfield
He played for Gentlemen of Leicester in the Channel Islands and for Swallows in America.
NCCC Executive Committee and Hon Fixture Secretary 1975/76. A Qualified Solicitor 1970 working at the firm CBL Prior (q.v). 'Crow', his nickname, had an unusual call up in the away match in July 1974 against Hertfordshire. There was no play on day one and with Robin Huggins injuring his back he was included in the side with Norfolk winning by 8 wickets in a single innings match

ROSE, William
(b) Gt Yarmouth 8 December 1934
Lives locally after returning to the area in 1944 following a spell in Staffordshire.
Educ. – Edward Worlledge Junior School; Gt Yarmouth Technical High School; Norwich City College; University of London - for his teaching qualification.
Cricket. – Gt Yarmouth Town; Ingham; Minor Counties; Black Sheep CC
HS. 47 v Hertfordshire June 1977 @ Watford – the NCCC top scorer that day
BB. 8/41 v Hertfordshire June 1977 @ Watford – he was on for a 9-for but the Herts captain declared at nine down.
HS. 18 v Essex April 1970 @ Lakenham
BB. 1/24 v Essex (2) June 1977 @ Lakenham
HS. *2 v Hampshire May 1965 @ Southampton* – the author was a spectator
NCCC Executive Committee 1975-77. He twice took over 40 wickets in a season (1964 & 1970); topped the bowling averages four times and he was unplayable in 1970, snaring 43 wickets at a minute cost of 12.9 for each wicket.

Football for Gorleston and like John Greatrex (q.v) he appeared in the fund raising cricket match between Yarmouth and the Variety Artists.

National Service in RAF in Air Radar as a Junior Technician . A Schoolteacher at Woolwich Polytechnic and at Gt Yarmouth School until retirement, specializing in Maths and Science.

SHARPE, Peter James

(b) Denver, Norfolk 4 April 1944

Lives in Lichfield

Educ. – King Edward VII School (King's Lynn)

Cricket. – King Edward VII School; Ingham; Norfolk Young Amateurs; Castle Rising; Norwich Union; Nottingham Forest CC; Lichfield; Kings Heath; K Lamming's XI

HS. 62 v Buckinghamshire July 1964 @ Lakenham

BB. 2/28 v Hertfordshire July 1964 @ Hertford

HS. *0 v Hampshire May 1965 @ Southampton*

BB. *1/38 v Hampshire May 1965 @ Southampton*

Brother of JM (q.v)

34 no & 4/49 for Norwich Union v Norwich Wanderers – in the 20 over Norfolk Cricket Association Championship Final. Hockey – Norfolk County; Nottinghamshire; Staffordshire; Midlands; Norwich Union; Cannock Grassiles; England 'B'; England Over 60s.

A superb Hockey career with some of his appointments being as follows – Chairman England Selectors, Member GB Olympic Committee and Chairman Cannock Club. His son Ben was in the GB Hockey Squad for the 2000 Sydney Olympics. Peter was the Chief Executive of the Police Mutual Association Society for fifteen years.

SHEPPERD, John

(b) Willesden, Middlesex 8 May 1937

Still lives locally

Educ. – Wykeham Secondary Modern School

Cricket. – MCC Groundstaff & Senior Staff; Middlesex; LC Stevens' XI; Barleycorns; Black Sheep CC; Norwich Union

HS. 59 v Lincolnshire August 1966 @ Lakenham

BB. 6/24 v Cambridgeshire June 1964 @ Wisbech

HS. 8 v Essex April 1968 @ Chelmsford

BB. 1/38 v Essex April 1968 @ Chelmsford

HS. *4 v Cheshire May 1968 @ Macclesfield*

BB. *3/23 v Cheshire May 1968 @ Macclesfield*

1st class cricket – 4 matches 32 runs 4 wickets

NCCC Hon Team Manager and Wymondham College Cricket Coach. Also a NCCC Scorer and a First Class/Minor Counties Umpire. As a Team Manager he invariably became a substitute fielder for NCCC. The 1962 NCCC Handbook stated that he had obtained the advanced diploma for coaching league cricket. Involved with the Nelson Barracks Easter Cricket Coaching Sessions.

He worked for Norwich Union.

1964

MERCER, Ian Pickford

(b) Oldham, Lancashire 30 May 1930

(d) North Walsham 22 May 2004

Cricket. – Sheringham; Norwich Wanderers; Cromer; Minor Counties

HS. 127 v Cambridgeshire July 1964 @ Lakenham – he batted 5 hours in an innings total of 209-9 declared off 115 overs. Also hit 5 half centuries in a great debut season.

BB. 1/8 v Buckinghamshire August 1965 @ High Wycombe

HS. 14 v Essex April 1968 @ Chelmsford

BB. 1/81 v Essex April 1968 @ Chelmsford

HS. *31 v Hampshire May 1965 @ Southampton*

1st class cricket – 1 match 1 run 1 wicket

NCCC Captain in 1970 and 1971. 'Manny' was a Physical Education Instructor in Sheringham.

The 23rd NCCC player to score 2 (50s) in the same match and involved in 6 century partnerships with such a stand in both innings v Hertfordshire August 1967 at Lakenham with James Donaldson and then Graham Saville.

1965

BLAND, Tony Gordon

(b) Ranworth, Norfolk 19 July 1941

Still lives locally and a NCCC Member at 2011.

Educ. – City of Norwich School; London University; Bradford University

Cricket. – City of Norwich School; CEYMS; Barleycorns; Ingham; Norfolk Young Amateurs; RJ Wesley's XI; Bradford Park Avenue CC.

HS. 36 no v Lincolnshire August 1967 @ Lakenham – in a last wicket stand of 61 with Tracey Moore. Tony thwarted Norman McVicker's attempt at a hat-trick.

BB. 4/59 v Lincolnshire August 1966 @ Lakenham

HS. 0 v Essex April 1968 @ Chelmsford

BB. 1/29 v Essex April 1968 @ Chelmsford

HS. *7 v Cheshire May 1968 @ Macclesfield*

BB. *1/29 v Cheshire May 1968 @ Macclesfield*

A Chartered Electrical Engineer with the qualifications BSc and PhD.

GOODWIN, Roger

(b) Fincham, Norfolk 18 October 1945

Lives Melbourne, Australia

Educ. – Fincham Primary Schol; Wymondham College

Cricket. – Wymondham College; M. Falcon's XI; Wimbledon CC; Barclaycards CC; Korakaia CC (NZ); Gardiner Ewing (Australia)

HS. 13 no v Lincolnshire August 1965 @ Lincoln

BB. 4/59 v Staffordshire July 1967 @ Stoke-on-Trent
A Quantity Surveyor (ARICS) who has lived in such diverse places as London, Middle East and New Zealand.

HUGGINS, Robin David Paul
(b) Coltishall, Norfolk 28 April 1947
Lives in Norfolk and has made the NCCC Man of the Match Award on a number of occasions.
The Colman's of Norwich Player of the Season himself in 1975
Educ. – City of Norwich School
Cricket. – Gothic; Barleycorns; Norwich Wanderers; Ingham; West Norfolk; North Runcton; Minor Counties ; Past Norfolk; Norfolk Over 50s.
HS.110 no v Lincolnshire July 1981 @ Lakenham AND 110 v Lincolnshire July 1987 @ Burghley Park
HS. 37 v Suffolk May 1978 @ Lakenham
HS. *96 v Lincolnshire June 1986 @ Swardeston* - a 251 run partnership for the second wicket with Steve Plumb. If it had been a Championship match it would have beaten a 52 year old NCCC record.
One of the many Schoolteachers of the 1970s NCCC side and only five men have scored more Championship runs than Robin. NCCC Committee Man for 11 years embracing roles such as Fixture Secretary and Chairman of Selectors with assistance from NCCC men to include Barry Battelley, Doug Mattocks, John Shepperd and Dave Thomas. His 1993 NCCC Handbook article on Page 3 succinctly sums up the difficulties in arranging fixtures/selecting players. At the conclusion of the Club's Annual General meeting (5/12/99) Robin quietly and deliberately – to avoid any risk of fuss – stood down from his Committee role to end almost 35 years' unbroken service.

RICE, Peter William Michael
(b) Drayton, Norwich 15 March 1946
Educ. – Uppingham School
Cricket. – Uppingham School; Uppingham Rovers; West Norfolk; MCC; Free Foresters; Gentlemen of Leicester; Gentlemen of Suffolk; South Hampstead; Falmouth; Cambridge Granta - and their President 1994-2006.
HS. 13 v Buckinghamshire August 1965 @ High Wycombe
44 for Uppingham School v Haileybury & Imperial Service College July 1962.
Peter has had a knee replacement and has a fund of stories about former cricketing colleagues which he kindly related when we met at the Cambridge Granta ground in July 2011. A retired Company Director of a Publishing House.

WOOLSTENCROFT, Michael Lee
(b) King's Lynn, Norfolk 30 October 1944
Lives in Eastbourne

Educ. – Beeston Hall School; Worksop College
Cricket. – Beeston Hall School; Worksop College; Castle Rising Colts; Nippers CC; DR Ellis' XI; Sandringham CC; Northamptonshire Young Amateurs; Castle Rising; Middlesex Club & Ground; Lord's Groundstaff; MCC; Haywards Heath
HS. 26 v Suffolk August 1965 @ Lowestoft AND 26 v Hertfordshire August 1966 @ Lakenham
His Uncle George had four games for Cambridgeshire in the 1930s.
Oratory School Cricket Coach and Muir College Cricket Coach (Cape Province).
Schoolteacher at Oratory School retiring 2004.

1966

ATKINS, John Phillipe
(b) Norwich 4 March 1946
Lives in Oxfordshire
Educ. – Norwich GS; London University (Imperial College)
Cricket. – Norwich GS; Norfolk Young Amateurs; North Under 19s; CEYMS; Barleycorns; Cavaliers; Aylesford Paper Mills; Marden CC; Wallingford; North of England; Hertfordshire – a substitute fielder when a player of theirs broke a finger.
HS. 37 v Nottinghamshire (2) July 1966 @ Trent Bridge
He was proud to play with his boyhood hero Bill Edrich. His 1967 appearance had Alan Halford in his place on the official scorecard and a 1968 selection for the away game against Lincolnshire was abandoned without a ball being bowled as thunder, gales and rain left the pitch waterlogged.

McMANUS, Colin Alan
(b) Norwich 19 September 1943
Lives in Kent
Educ. – Thorpe Hamlet Infants & Juniors; City of Norwich School; Loughborough College
Cricket. – City of Norwich School Old Boys; Barleycorns; Lowestoft; Acle; Loughborough; Minor Counties North; GH Wolstenholme's Norfolk PE Teachers XI
HS. 103 no v Hertfordshire August 1974 @ Lakenham – 186-6 declared as he hit 12 (4) & 1 (6)
HS. 19 v Essex April 1968 @ Chelmsford
HS. *16 v Cheshire May 1968 @ Macclesfield*
He played in the same Loughborough side as Doug Mattocks (q.v.) and he participated in three NCCC century partnerships with 3 different men for the 2nd, 3rd and 4th wickets.
Colin was one of the plethora of Schoolteachers in the NCCC side. He taught at Gt Yarmouth GS, Gorleston GS and Lynn Grove High School.
Also represented Norfolk County at Football and Athletics.

WATERS, Hugh William
(b) Bury St Edmunds 7 January 1940
Lives in Norfolk
Educ. – Sutherland House Prep School; Old Buckenham Hall School; Repton School (The Mitre)
Cricket. – Repton School; Repton Pilgrims; West Norfolk; Gentlemen of Norfolk; Gentlemen of Suffolk; Clare Wild Oats CC
HS. 6 v Staffordshire July 1966 @ Newcastle-under-Lyme
He married the second daughter of WS Thompson (q.v)
Hugh had availability problems in playing for NCCC as he was newly married, had a new job and he lived in Suffolk. A Corn Merchant.

1967

BELL, Ronald Victor
(b) Chelsea, London 7 January 1931
(d) Farnham, Surrey 26 October 1989
Cricket. – Middlesex; Sussex; MCC; LC Stevens' XI
HS. 26 v Staffordshire July 1967 @ Lakenham
BB. 8/46 v Buckinghamshire August 1967 @ Lakenham
A remarkable 74 wickets in just two NCCC seasons as he effectively took Billy Rose's place in the slow left arm bowling department.
1st class cricket – 189 matches 1,558 runs 150 catches 392 wickets
His 392 wickets were against 23 teams with 11 v Tourists; 48 against the Universites and 39 v Glamorgan. He took 5 or more wickets in an innings against 12 of the Counties.
Cricket Coach NCCC 1968 and to an Army X1 as well as being on RMA Sandhurst's staff.
At Football he was on Chelsea FC's retained list of players as at 3 May 1952 but he never made the first team.

BORRETT, Paul Clarke
(b) Martham, Norfolk 1 February 1944
Lives locally
Educ. – Norwich GS
Cricket. – Norwich GS; Ingham; Black Sheep CC; RJ Wesley's XI; Hertfordshire – a substitute fielder once on both sides in the NCCC fixture.
HS. 61 v Hertfordshire August 1970 @ Lakenham
BB. 1/24 v Cambridgeshire July 1968 @ Chatteris AND 1/24 v Buckinghamshire July 1973 @ Lakenham
HS. 17 v Essex (2) May 1975 @ Chelmsford
HS. *1 v Middlesex April 1970 @ Lord's*
Father of CR (q.v) and Andrew (NCCC Scorer)
Three of his Minor County catches were as a substitute fielder.
Norwich CC Chairman and Vice Chairman (2011). A Farmer.

BOSWELL, Barry Reginald David
(b) Falkirk, Scotland 9 October 1947
(d) Priscilla Bacon Lodge, Norwich 8 July 1983
Lived Old Catton, Norwich
Educ. – Norwich GS
Cricket. – Norwich GS; Norwich Wanderers
HS. 5 v Staffordshire July 1967 @ Great Chell
BB. 5/43 v Lincolnshire June 1974 @ Grimsby –
dismissing 5 of the top 7 batsmen to help NCCC to a 15 run win.
Son of CSR (q.v)
Tragically died at only age 35 and the Barry Boswell Fund provides grants for coaching the County's most promising cricketers.

GREEN, Geoffrey Gordon Blyth
(b) Guist, Norfolk 4 May 1949
(d) Peace Memorial Hospital, Watford, Hertfordshire 28 July 1984
Lived in Ampthill, Bedfordshire
Unbelievably another passing at just age 35 – he succumbed to a skull fracture with lacerations of the brain and his occupation was given as an Accounts Manager. The Coroner reported that it was an Accidental Death.
Educ. – Fakenham GS
Cricket. – Norfolk Colts; Norfolk Young Amateurs; English Schools Cricket Association; Dereham.
HS. 50 no v Lincolnshire May 1968 @ Lakenham
142 no for Norfolk Colts v Derbyshire Juniors August 1966

HALFORD, Alan John
(b) Leicester 1 November 1934
(d) Malaga, Spain 25 September 1984
Educ. – Alderman Newton's Boys GS
Cricket. – Norwich Wanderers; MCC; Midland Cricket Conference; HMS Sheffield; Leicestershire Young Amateurs; Bishop's Stortford; Norwich; Cromer; Leicester CC.
HS. 33 v Staffordshire July 1967 @ Stoke-on-Trent
BB. 5/23 v Lincolnshire August 1968 @ Lakenham
HS. 24 v Essex April 1970 @ Lakenham
BB. 2/34 v Essex April 1970 @ Lakenham
HS. *5 v Yorkshire May 1969 @ Lakenham* – one of Chris Old's three victims
BB. *1/34 v Yorkshire May 1969 @ Lakenham* – he had Phil Sharpe caught.
He played in the 150th Anniversary match for MCC against Norfolk at Lakenham in August 1977.
10/6 for Leicester CC v Nuneaton May 1960
National Service (1953-55) in the Royal Marines. In 1954 he appeared for HMS Sheffield versus Naval HQ in Ottawa, Canada with the Duke of Edinburgh a spectator. An Insurance Surveyor, a Commercial Traveller and also a Managing Director at Continental Insurance.

SAVILLE, Graham John

(b) Leytonstone, Essex 5 February 1944

Still a NCCC Member 2011

Educ. – St George Monoux GS; Essex GS

Cricket. – Essex GS; Colchester; E. Essex CC; Chingford; Essex; Minor Counties; Essex Young Amateurs; Essex Club & Ground

HS. 148 v Buckinghamshire September 1969 @ Beaconsfield – his 5th ton and the only man post war to get consecutively the last five scored for NCCC.

HS. 46 v Essex April 1968 @ Chelmsford

HS. 73 v Cheshire May 1968 @ Macclesfield

1st class cricket – 126 matches 4,476 runs 3 wickets 103 catches and a Cousin of Graham Gooch.

He topped the NCCC batting averages in the three seasons he played.

Cricket Coach at various times for Wymondham College, Cambridge University, Eastern Regional National and the National Cricket Association. Former England Under 19 Coach (5 years) and Manager for 9 years and a position as the ECB Development of Excellence Manager. Has also been the Essex Chairman of Cricket following his previous role as Assistant Secretary and he was with the Essex Development XI at Manor Park in August 2011.

STOCKINGS, David Charles

(b) Cambridge 22 July 1946

Lives locally

Educ. – Langley School

Cricket. – Langley School; Norwich Union; Barleycorns; CEYMS; Aldborough; D Lee -Warner's XI

HS. 81 v Buckinghamshire August 1967 @ Beaconsfield

HS. 9 v Essex April 1968 @ Chelmsford

HS. *3 v Cheshire May 1968 @ Macclesfield*

David worked for Norwich Union when he left school - in the days when they boastfully advertised that they had jobs for every school leaver in Norfolk. He was the Area Production Manager for Daylay (Chicken and Egg Production). A redundancy at 50 saw him be his own boss as a Gardener but back trouble ensued. Now kept busy with his allotment and looking after his Father (95) and Step-Mother (101).

....

1968

BATTELLEY, Ian Nicholas

(b) Dereham 19 January 1944

Still lives in Dereham

Educ. – London Road Infants; National Junior School; Crown Road Secondary School

Cricket. – Jentique CC; Dereham; Northamptonshire 2nds; Black Sheep CC; East Anglian Wanderers; Norfolk Over 50s & 60s; England Over 60s.

HS. 55 v Lincolnshire June 1975 @ Grimsby

BB. 1/20 v Cambridgeshire June 1977 @ Papworth

HS. 62 v Essex (2) June 1977 @ Lakenham

BB. 2/11 v Cambridge University May 1977 @ Fenner's

HS. *29 v Middlesex April 1970 @ Lord's*

Brother of BL (q.v)

Ian has been a Teaching Assistant for 17 years at the Fred Nicholson Special Needs School in Toftwood.

JEFFERSON, Richard Ingleby

(b) Frimley Green, Surrey 15 August 1941

Still lives in Norfolk

Educ. – Winchester School; Cambridge University (Corpus Christi College)

Cricket. – Cambridge University- Blue 1961; Surrey Young Amateurs; Surrey; MCC; Minor Counties; Minor Counties North; Southern Schools; Public Schools; LC Stevens' XI; MJ Stewart's XI; London New Zealand Club; International Cavaliers; Old Wykehamists; Free Foresters; AER Gilligan's XI; FR Brown's XI.

HS. 42 no v Hertfordshire July 1969 @ Hertford

BB. 6/22 v Hertfordshire August 1969 @ Lakenham – he took 4 wickets in 10 balls and had match analysis of 12/46.

HS. 39 v Essex April 1970 @ Lakenham

BB. 3/17 v Essex April 1970 @ Lakenham – dismissing Graham Saville (q.v), Keith Fletcher and Keith Boyce.

HS. *55 v Cheshire May 1968 @ Macclesfield*

BB. *2/15 v Yorkshire May 1969 @ Lakenham*

Father of WI (q.v) and son of Julian who also had first class matches to his name

1st class cricket 94 matches 2,094 runs 32 catches 263 wickets

An astounding 1969 season with 58 Minor Counties wickets for NCCC at the paltry average rate of 9.71 per wicket with 3(10s) and 6(5s). The most economical bowler (right arm fast medium from a great height) as he went for just 1.85 runs an over for NCCC.

In the 1960 Public Schools side with Mike Brearley and the 1963 LC Stevens' team with Clive Radley (q.v). As an amateur he could claim from Surrey expenses of 6d a mile and £1 a day for kit cleaning.

Batting at number nine in the July 1961 Varsity match he top scored with 54 as he stroked the ball with comfort to all parts of the field before the Hampshire man Dan Piachaud dismissed him. The University captain the Nawab of Pataudi had lost an eye in a motor accident at Hove crossroads just a week before.

8/24 & 53 no for Surrey Young Amateurs v Essex Young Amateurs September 1960

11.1-10-1-3 for MCC v Argentina January 1965 in Buenos Aires. John Arlott described Richard's bowling thus, "An off break at unusually high speed. Awkward lift off of a length and on a pitch which gave him any help he could be all but unplayable."

Football for Corinthian Casuals and also at one time the Dulwich College Cricket Coach

1969

BATTELLEY, Barry Linstead
(b) Dereham, Norfolk 30 March 1946
Still lives in Norfolk
Educ. – London Road Infants; National Junior School;
Crown Road Secondary School
Cricket. – Dereham; Norfolk Over 50s; Black Sheep CC;
Cromer; Norfolk Over 60s
HS. 37 v Suffolk August 1977 @ Lakenham
BB. 7/83 v Cambridgeshire June 1977 @ Papworth – his
brother caught two of his victims.
HS. 16 v Essex May 1976 @ Chelmsford
BB. 3/110 v Essex May 1976 @ Chelmsford - one of two
one day games. This one played the day after his 16 score
above.
Brother of IN (q.v)
Awarded his County Cap in 1976 and he formed part of the
NCCC Executive Committee. He was also the Norfolk Over 50s
President as he took 82 wickets for them.
The immensely jovial Sir Charles Mott-Radclyffe wrote in the
1978 Handbook as the NCCC Chairman,"The bowling, despite
the preponderance of left handers – five out of the six regular
bowlers – all enjoyed their triumphs with Barry obtaining his
NCCC career best."
Barry relates a story about his first game under 'Skip' Bill Edrich
of," I was wandering aimlessly not knowing where to field. Bill
never told me where to field so Terry Allcock said he wont be
find a hole (gap in the field) and go there."
Barry thoroughly enjoyed his job as Sales Manager for Readimix
Concrete Company despite takeovers by Mexicans and the
French.

GILLHAM, Christopher John
(b) Highams Park, Essex 26 March 1946
Still lives locally and a 2011 NCCC Member.
Educ. – St Edmund's College (Ware)
Cricket. – Bristol University; Letchworth; Richmond; West
Norfolk; Castle Rising; Ingham
HS. 27 v Suffolk August 1969 @ Lowestoft
NCCC Promotion and Sponsorship Committee throughout
the 1990s under the Chairmanships of Mike Harrison (q.v) and
Nigel Rudd (q.v Curio Corner). He attempted to start an ECB
Over 50s side in the early nineties.
A lengthy career with Ingham CC from 1975-1999. The Black
Sheep CC Chairman and Tour Organiser. Rugby Union for
Norwich and West Norfolk and also the Hon Solicitor for
Norfolk RF Union. He remembers clearly his second game away
to Buckinghamshire when Bill Edrich insisted he stayed for a
drink with him. Four hours had passed before he got to go to
bed and the moral was that where Bill could stay up all night
and get a ton the next day Chris said he couldn't.

HANDLEY, Frederick Lester Quorn
(b) Kampala, Uganda 11 August 1949
Still lives locally
Educ. – Yarmouth GS
Cricket. – Hemsby; Ingham; Leicestershire 2nds; Minor
Counties; Past Norfolk; Norfolk Over 50s; Minor Counties
North; MCC
HS. 122 v Lincolnshire August 1982 @ Lakenham – his
highest of 10 NCCC tons.
HS. 52 v Essex May 1975 @ Chelmsford
HS. *65 v Berkshire June 1983 @ Pinebanks*
Son-in-Law WO Thomas (q.v)
116 no for Minor Counties v Tanzania Cricket Association
Chairman's X1 October 1982 in Dar-es-Salaam. The target of
189 was reached in 34 overs without loss so Robin Huggins
was denied a batting opportunity.
Holds the 4th highest percentage of a completed innings with
his 88 (140) v Hertfordshire June 1976.
NCCC Captain 1983-86. Fred played many a whirlwind innings
evidenced his 101 no v Cumberland in 1983 in just 67 balls with
10(4) & 4(6). On four occasions he was dismissed for exactly
100.
Suffolk County never dismissed him for a duck in their 42
attempts.
Cricket Coaching - Gresham's School Under 14s; Hales CC
'Chance 2 Shine' Lead Coach and East District Lead Coach
through the Norfolk Cricket Board. Fred has had a myriad of
jobs but I remember him successfully selling me Cavity Wall
Insulation many years ago.

ROLPH, John Bernard
(b) Norwich 16 March 1944
Lives in Thetford
Educ. – Gresham's School
Cricket. – Gresham's School; Norfolk Young Amateurs;
Barleycorns; Norfolk & Suffolk Amateurs; K Lamming's XI;
Norwich Wanderers
HS. 3 no v Staffordshire June 1969 @ Cheadle
BB. 2/21 v Lincolnshire July 1969 @ Bourne
NCCC Finance Committee Chairman 1991-92 and Hon
Treasurer 1993-98 dealing with the results of sponsorship,
advertisers, fixed assets, depreciation, corporation tax,
overheads and commercial activities – a challenging role. He
worked for Cooper & Lybrand, B.D.O. Stoy Hayward and Baker
Tilly. A continuous involvement with the Barry Boswell Trust
Fund alongside Neville Cooke.

SHARPE, John Malcolm, FRICS
(b) The Nursing Home, Coltishall, Norfolk 13 October 1948
Lives in King's Lynn
Educ. – King Edward VII School (King's Lynn)
Cricket. – Norwich Union; West Norfolk; Kings Heath

HS. 5 v Hertfordshire July 1969 @ Hertford
BB. 2/23 v Cambridgeshire July 1969 @ Lakenham
Brother of Peter J (q.v)
Hockey. – Norfolk County; Gloucestershire; Southwell and Nottinghamshire.
An occupation of Land Agent.

WHITAKER, Mark Robin
(b) Walton-on-Thames, Surrey 20 September 1946
Educ. – Cambridge University
Cricket. – Cambridge University
HS. *2 no v Yorkshire May 1969 @ Lakenham*
1st class cricket – 12 matches 16 runs 2 catches 20 wickets Mark rarely troubled the scorers in his short career.
5/62 for Cambridge University v Middlesex May 1965 – clean bowling England Test players Mike Brearley, Eric Russell and Mike Smith
4/43 for Cambridge University v Quidnuncs May 1965 – disturbing the bails of Henry Blofeld for one of his successes

WRIGHT, Edward
(b) Shipdham 3 April 1945
Educ. – Galveston School; Swaffham GS
Cricket. – JJ Wrights; Dereham; Norwich Wanderers; Cromer
HS. 30 v Lincolnshire August 1976 @ Lakenham – adding 50 for the last wicket with Doug Mattocks.
BB. 7/39 v Cambridgeshire July 1980 @ Lakenham – with Alan Ponder scoring an incredible 111 (155) before Ted shattered his stumps.
HS. 6 v MCC August 1977 @ Lakenham
BB. 4/69 v MCC August 1977 @ Lakenham
He formed one of the best Minor County opening attacks with Terry Barnes but amazingly did not achieve a match haul of 10 wickets, a staggering statistic for someone with over 200 County wickets to his name. He claimed 20 or more wickets in seven successive seasons.
Right hand bat and Left arm fast with fine service to the NCCC cause with successful roles as President (2007-09) and Vice Chairman of the Executive Committee. He joined Bernard Matthews Ltd in 1965; became Production Director in 1982 and in 1990 worked closely on the company's overseas expansion, initially in South Africa and New Zealand before going to the Bernard Matthews subsidiary Saga Foods of Hungary in 1996 where he was Managing Director from 1998 to 2004. A former Chairman of the British Poultry Council handling legislation up to Ministerial level. Ted is the new Chairman of the Red Tractor Farm Assurance Poultry Sector and an Industry Ombudsman for the Food Standards Agency. In July 2011 he was made a Freeman of the City of London.

1970

BARRETT, John
(b) Norwich 12 November 1946
Lives in Norfolk
Educ. – King's Lynn GS
Cricket. – King's Lynn GS; Norfolk Over 50s
HS. 75 v Suffolk August 1976 @ Felixstowe
BB. 3/38 v Buckinghamshire July 1980 @ Lakenham
HS. 60 v Bedfordshire June 1982 @ Pinebanks
BB. 1/20 v MCC August 1977 @ Lakenham – the 150th Anniversary Match as he bowled Bill Edrich for just 5.
HS. *1 v Leicestershire July 1982 @ Grace Road*

ELLIOTT, Walter John
(b) Bessingham, Norfolk 1 April 1941
Educ. – Matlaske School; Aldborough School; Gresham's School
Cricket. – Aldborough; Overstrand; Black Sheep CC; Cromer – for 27 years
HS. 90 v Lincolnshire August 1971 @ Lakenham – the 30th NCCC player to be out in the nineties in the period covered by this book.
BB. 4/38 v Suffolk August 1972 @ Bury St Edmunds
HS. 115 v Essex May 1976 @ Chelmsford
BB. 5/85 v Cambridge University May 1976 @ Fenner's
The highest of his three century partnerships was 158 with David Pilch for the 4th wicket against Cambridgeshire in 1976.

KENNON, Neil Sandilands
(b) Regents Park nr Johannesburg, South Africa 26 November 1933
Lives locally
Educ. – Regents Park Junior & Senior School (Johannesburg); Robert Hick's (Pretoria)
Cricket. – Huddersfield FC at cricket; Dereham; Ingham
HS. 39 v Buckinghamshire July 1970
'Sandy' played rugby, baseball and football in his youth. A Scottish father and the youngest of 13 children. He was a Riveter and a Men's Clothing Salesman in South Africa before his goalkeeping talent was discovered. Football.- Umbilo FC; Berea Park; Queens Park FC; Rhodesia; Huddersfield Town; Norwich City FC 5 February 1959 – 255 appearances; Colchester United; Lowestoft Town.
'Sandy' modestly says he was not in the cricketing class of others in the side but he had a good eye which served him well. He owned two Betting Shops and went into partnership with Alan Bunney. He is a retired Sales Executive for Famous Grouse (Whisky) and indeed 'The Famous Grouse Trophy' was awarded to a NCCC player from 1993-98.

MINDHAM, Philip Roy

(b) Holme Hale, Norfolk 3 July 1941
Still lives in Norfolk
Educ. – Holme Hale Primary School; Hammond's GS (Swaffham); Bede College; Durham University
Cricket. – Holme Hale; Cromer; Black Sheep CC; Garboldisham; Swaffham; GH Wolstenholme's Norfolk PE Teachers XI; Carrow.
HS. 65 no v Buckinghamshire July 1970 @ Lakenham
192 no for Garboldisham v Merton 1979 – a Norfolk League Record at the time.
Phil is the current Vice President of Cromer CC and the Manager of Cromer Sports Centre. A former Cromer Schoolteacher spanning the Secondary Modern to High School days.

SMART, Anthony Leonard, MSc

(b) West Bridgford, Nottingham 8 March 1940
Lives in his home town
Educ. – West Bridgford GS; Loughborough University
Cricket. – West Bridgford Old Scholars; Lincoln Lindum; Lincolnshire; Nottinghamshire (Juniors/Youth/2nds); Notts Forest CC; Mitre CC
HS. 44 v Cambridgeshire July 1970 @ Spalding
BB. 3/35 v Hertfordshire July 1970 @ Hertford
3/13 & 26 for Nottinghamshire Youth v Derbyshire Juniors August 1959
A Professional Civil Engineer and Builder

WILD, David Kenneth

(b) Thorpe End, Norwich 4 May 1942
Still lives locally
Educ. – Frettenham School
Cricket. – CEYMS; Woodford Wells; Cavaliers
HS. 7 no v Hertfordshire July 1970 @ Hertford
HS. 1 no v Essex May 1975 @ Chelmsford
Right hand bat and wicket keeper with 11 Minor County dismissals in 5 such games.
NCCC Secretary 1986-87 and Chairman 1998 to 2002 as well as serving on the Executive Committee and Sub Committees. A former Norfolk County Squash Champion and subsequently the England Manager. Also the Squash Tournament Director of British Open Championships. A Freeman of the City of London and a Liveryman of the Worshipful Company of Glovers. Director of a Financial Consultantcy Company.

1971

COOK, Nigel Dennis

(b) Swanton Morley, Norfolk 10 May 1954
Lives in Norfolk
Educ. – Swanton Morley Primary School; Norwich GS
Cricket. – Norwich GS; Dereham; Norfolk Young Amateurs;

Nottinghamshire 2nds
HS. 100 v Suffolk August 1981 @ Felixstowe – in a 2nd wicket partnership with Parvez Mir.
BB. 1/24 v Northumberland June 1983 @ Jesmond
HS. 60 v Cambridge University 'A' May 1980 @ Fenner's
HS. *31 no v Leicestershire July 1982 @ Grace Road*
One of just 17 players with a ton against Suffolk but alas not many appearances for 18 playing seasons. Still good enough though to feature in four century partnerships in the 1980s with the best in terms of runs his unbeaten 149 partnership with Robin Huggins v Durham in 1983 in a match where 877 runs came in 276 overs .He played for Dereham CC from 1967-2003. The Family business is G D Cook & Son (Leathergoods and Footwear) in Dereham's Market Place.

FLOWER, John Ernest

(b) Chislehurst, Kent 7 November 1938
Lives in Paris, France
Cricket. – Berkshire; Reading
HS. 3 v Cambridgeshire June 1971 @ Wisbech
BB. 3/66 v Lincolnshire July 1971 @ Cleethorpes – a right arm medium pacer who went for over four runs an over during his short time at NCCC.
8/62 for Berkshire v Buckinghamshire July 1970

LAWES, Anthony Charles Hebron

(b) Padworth, Berkshire 2 March 1941
(d) Sheringham, Norfolk 31 July 2000
Cricket. – Gresham Village; Aldborough; Cromer
HS. 13 v Hertfordshire July 1973 @ Hertford
HS. 17 v Essex May 1975 @ Chelmsford
Tony was with Cromer CC for 40 years and their Full-time Groundsman.
F.F. – Married to Mary with four step children and four grandchildren.

RUDD, Raymond Keith

(b) Terrington St Clement, Norfolk 8 May 1946
Lives in Norfolk
Educ. – Terrington St Clement; King Edward VII GS
Cricket. – North Runcton; Minor Counties; Nottinghamshire Club & Ground and 2nds.
HS. 36 v Buckinghamshire August 1975 @ Amersham
BB. 4/56 v Cambridgeshire June 1979 @ Papworth – bowling left arm fast medium
HS. 14 no v Essex (2) June 1977 @ Lakenham
BB. 2/31 v Suffolk May 1978 @ Lakenham
BB. *1/25 v Bedfordshire June 1984 @ Pinebanks*
8-4-9-4 for Nottinghamshire Club & Ground v Pembrokeshire August 1972
11.2-7-12-4 for Nottinghamshire (2) v Glamorgan (2) July 1972
3/49 for Nottinghamshire (2) v Lancashire (2) July 1972 –

dismissing 'Bumble' David Lloyd.
A sporting career dominated by football with King's Lynn. Scorer of over 200 goals in 604 appearances for them netting 8 hat-tricks and latterly gaining a UEFA 'A' and 'B' License as well as being rewarded with an FA Loyalty Badge. Keith was their Player Manager May 1977 to May 1979 and from November 1979 to August 1984 together with three spells as Caretaker Manager between April 1988 and November 1997. One of the many Schoolteachers in the 1970s NCCC sides.

SHREEVE, Colin Maurice
(b) Drayton, Norwich 13 August 1945
Lives locally
Educ. – Cromer Juniors & Seniors; Wymondham College
Cricket. – Wymondham College; Cromer; Norfolk Over 50s; Bradfield
HS. 20 v Lincolnshire July 1971 @ Cleethorpes
BB. 1/39 v Lincolnshire July 1971 @ Cleethorpes
A qualified ECB cricket coach. A Landscaper and Stock Controller for Kettle Foods.

1972

BEACOCK, Gregory Neil
(b) Scunthorpe, Lincolnshire 23 December 1947
Lives locally
Educ. – John Legget GS; King Edward VI (Spilsby); Keswick Hall College of Education
Cricket. – John Legget GS; King Edward VI; Scunthorpe; Lincolnshire Colts; Norwich Wanderers; Norwich CC; Black Sheep CC.
HS. 63 v Cambridgeshire July 1974 @ Lakenham
BB. 5/22 v Buckinghamshire August 1974 @ Lakenham
– off 21 overs.
A proud day for Neil was his 3/40 and 5/47and his unbeaten 27 runs for NCCC against his home county in June 1974 at Grimsby. He recalled his rare feat of a hat-trick off the last three balls of the game to win the match for Norwich Wanderers versus Saffron Walden and the occasion when David Pilch (q.v) removed him from the bowling attack in order that the game did not become farcical seeing as Neil had 6 wickets for just 4 runs.
A Headmaster at just age 26 at Braconash Primary School – far too young as he had to be too sensible at such an early age. Followed by being the Headmaster of Stoke Holy Cross Primary School with progression and promotion to his Headmaster's role at Taverham Middle School up to retirement in 2006.

TAYLOR, Kenneth
(b) Primrose Hill, Huddersfield 21 August 1935
Lives in Melton Constable
Educ. – Stile Common Elementary School; Huddersfield School Fine Arts; Slade School of Fine Art

Cricket. – Stile Common Elementary School; Primrose Hill; Huddersfield Schools; Yorkshire Schoolboys; North of England; Auckland; Yorkshire; Minor Counties; EW Swanton's XI; MCC; England – 3 Test Matches
HS. 127 v Hertfordshire July 1972 @ Hertford
BB. 1/34 v Hertfordshire July 1972 @ Hertford
Father of NS (q.v)
1st class cricket – 313 matches 13,053 runs 150 catches 131 wickets
1,000 runs in a season six times and with Yorkshire he won the County Championship seven times.
8/0 for Stile Common v Netherton County School who were all out for just 9.
Football for Huddersfield Town; Bradford Park Avenue and England Under 23s.
South Africa National Cricket Coach 1968-70. For 15 years a Sports Master and Cricket Coach at Gresham's School. Ken taught Art in Norfolk for 30 years and produced his book 'Drawn to Sport' – an extremely talented artist who succeeded with three careers. He also taught part time at Beeston Hall Prep School where his wife Avril was the head and part time at Rondebosch High School in Cape Town. He rightly won the Wilfred Rhodes Trophy in his first NCCC season (1972). In 10 matches he hit 4 tons and 3 fifties – with a fabulous performance against Lincolnshire July 1972 when he remained undefeated on 99 as his last two partners were run out, and this achieved contending with Sonny Ramadhin. He hadn't picked up a bat in four years and with little practice he still proceeded to decimate attacks. A superb fielder he was a rare talent who could play majestically. His Huddersfield Town Manager Bill Shankly didn't like it when he was off playing cricket. He called it a lassie's game.
He Umpired in first class matches and in Warwickshire Pool games as well as for the two Universities.

1973

BLUNDELL, Mark Charles
(b) Hammersmith, London 16 January 1955
Lives in Radlett, Hertfordshire
Educ. – Berkhampstead School
Cricket. – Berkhampstead School; Brondesbury; Cromer; Buccaneers; Radlett; Free Foresters; Hertfordshire; National Association of Youth Clubs North; Lavinia Duchess of Norfolk's XI.
HS. 71 no v Buckinghamshire August 1973 @ Amersham – David Pilch declared at 195/7 thereby denying Mark a chance of getting a century in only his second game. He would have easily topped the batting averages if assessed on just 4 innings.
Despite a NCCC 'pair' versus Hertfordshire in August 1975 he amazingly turned out for the latter 23 years later.

LEIGH, Bryan John

(b) Harleston, Norfolk 14 September 1948
Lives in Norfolk
Educ. – Norwich GS
Cricket. – Norwich GS; Norwich Cavaliers; CEYMS; Norwich Wanderers; Royal Marines; Incogniti; Royal Navy; Norfolk Club & Ground; Norfolk Young Amateurs; United Services; Mount CC; Joint Services (Singapore); Norwich CC; Dorset.
HS. 57 v Lincolnshire June 1974 @ Grimsby
A Lieutenant in the Royal Marines. The Managing Director of the firm started by his father namely A C Leigh Ltd (Architectural Ironmongers). Bryan is now a Parish Clerk for six Parishes.

WILTON, Graeme Wren

(b) Sheringham, Norfolk 31 December 1947
Lives locally
Educ. – Paston GS; Borough Road College
Cricket. – Paston GS; Borough Road College; Cromer; Norfolk Over 50s
HS. 84 v Lincolnshire June 1975 @ Grimsby – topping the batting averages for the season
BB. 4/67 v Buckinghamshire July 1973 @ Lakenham
HS. 16 v Essex May 1976 @ Chelmsford
BB. 3/75 v Cambridge University May 1976 @ Fenners
148 for Cromer v Beccles May 1980 with his runs gathered in a record fourth wicket partnership of 285 in the Carter Cup. Graeme joined Cromer CC in 1961 and is now their Vice President.
He gave 30 years service to NCCC and was rightly made an Honorary Life Member in 2002. He took the NCCC Youth Development Chair plus the same role for the Norfolk Cricket Association and his farewell notes appeared in the 2003 Handbook. A Schoolteacher outside of his devotion to cricket with Graeme hoping that he had given back to the game through coaching, initiating new ideas and general administration in recompense for the enjoyment and satisfaction gained from his playing days. He taught PE at North Walsham High School and was also PE Advisor to County Hall.
Now the Captain of Royal Cromer Golf Club playing off a handicap of thirteen which is now too good for me.

1974

ROWE, Jeremy Conrad

(b) Watford 16 March 1955
Lives in Preston
Educ. – Thorpe GS
Cricket. – Thorpe GS; Norfolk Young Amateurs; Horsford; Bradfield; Ingham
HS. 10 v Suffolk August 1976 @ Felixstowe

HS. 39 v Cambridge University May 1976 @ Fenner's
He had a back operation a few years ago and has Umpired in the Southport & District League

1975

DODDS, Nigel David Patrick, LLB

(b) Nelson, Lancashire 17 March 1948
Lives King's Lynn
Educ. – City of Norwich School; King Edward VII School (King's Lynn); London University (Queen Mary College)
Cricket. – City of Norwich School; King Edward VII School; Norfolk Schoolboys; West Norfolk; Castle Rising
HS. 19 no v Buckinghamshire August 1975 @ Amersham
Laurie Barrett (q.v) in his 1976 Annual report said,"Dodds deputised for Mattocks and showed promise."
Norfolk Schoolboys – Hockey, Tennis and Rugby
Norfolk County – Hockey.
A Qualified Solicitor and a Senior Partner with Kenneth Bush based in King's Lynn. Member of the Personal Injury Panel since its onset in 1994. Held the position of Adjudicator for the LCS in respect of Costs Reviews and Nigel also specializes in Licensing Law

MEIGH, Brian Andrew

(b) Hastings, Sussex 30 November 1947
Lives in Australia and he came to Ted Wright's (q.v) player reunion during the 2009 Cricket Festival at Manor Park
Cricket. – Norwich Union; Barleycorns; Norwich Wanderers
HS. 27 no v Suffolk August 1981 @ Felixstowe
BB. 5/105 v Buckinghamshire August 1980 @ Amersham
HS. 9 no v MCC August 1977 @ Lakenham
BB. 3/64 v Essex May 1975 @ Chelmsford
A slow left arm bowler 'Bertie' developed the 'yips' but he held 18 catches in his total of 31 NCCC games. Employed by Norwich Union and he worked in IT.

ORMISTON, Ross William

(b) New Plymouth, Taranaki, New Zealand 19 October 1955
Lives in New Zealand
Cricket. – Central Districts; Wellington; New Zealand Under 23s; Eastern Suburbs; Rest of New Zealand; Barleycorns; CEYMS; Ingham; Bacup; Victoria University of Wellington; Taranaki CC
HS. 79 v Lincolnshire August 1976 @ Lakenham
BB. 4/65 v Lincolnshire August 1975 @ Lakenham
HS. 53 v Cambridge University May 1976 @ Fenner's
BB. 1/54 v Essex May 1976 @ Chelmsford
A disappointment in not turning fifties into centuries at NCCC in terms of batting performances (especially as he scored runs

everywhere else) but an outstanding 1976 season with 15 catches.

1st class cricket – 56 matches 2,166 runs 1 wicket 47 catches with his best score being his 179 for Wellington v Central Districts January 1983

He was sensational in his two season Lancashire League stint with Bacup amassing 13 (50s) – especially as they only played 34 overs a side. He was a Painter and Decorator in the UK but is a Manager of a Telecommunications, Distributor and Wholesaler in Wellington.

1976

RILEY, Jeremy Harold
(b) Pulham St Mary, Norfolk 21 May 1956
Lives in Norfolk
Educ. – Norwich Town House School; Denstone College (Staffs)
Cricket. – Norwich Wanderers
HS. 6 v Staffordshire July 1986 @ Leek
HS. 8 v Cambridge University May 1982 @ Fenner's
Jeremy played in the NCCC 150th Anniversary Match and among those he caught were Peter Parfitt and Mickey Stewart. A day he would like to forget was in 1986 against Hertfordshire at Stevenage when he was struck in the mouth as the ball was deflected off bat/pad. Paul Whittaker took the gloves but it is not known who subbed in the field for him. Jeremy never noticed as he had to have major dentistry work as a result.
Rugby Union for Norwich Crusaders
Managing Director of J. Riley Harvesters (UK) Ltd.
F.F. – I remember as skipper of my works side I played Jeremy as a 'ringer' in a cup tie at Eaton Park.
He only asked that the ball was pitched 'on' the lively square as he stood up to all the bowlers and proceeded to make stumpings seemingly before the ball had passed the stumps. Boy did the opposition complain.

1977

AGAR, Andrew Charles
(b) Sanderstead, Surrey 19 February 1956
Lives in Crawley
Educ. – Dell Primary School; Thorpe GS
Cricket. – Norwich Union; Norfolk Young Amateurs; CEYMS; Barleycorns; Sprowston; Watton (coach/professional)
HS. 35 v Suffolk August 1978 @ Fakenham
BB. 3/16 v Buckinghamshire August 1981 @ Lakenham
HS. 9 no v Cambridge University May 1982 @ Fenner's
BB. 3/49 v Essex (2) June 1977 @ Lakenham
HS. *10 no v Berkshire June 1983 @ Pinebanks*
BB. *2/44 v Hampshire July 1984 @ Lakenham*
Andy's Professional Qualifications are JO1(Personal Tax),

RO1(Financial services, regulation and ethics), Chartered Institute of Insurance – Certificate in Financial Planning (FPC/ Cert PFS) and presently studying for his Diploma in Financial Planning. Would he be able to handle the Duckworth/Lewis system though?
Inland Revenue Tax Consultant 1972-85. Norwich Union Product Manager 1986 to August 1988.
Legal & General Assurance Society September 1988 to October 2006 as the Head of Pensions Product Development. Now a self employed Wealth Management Financial Adviser.

BARNES, Terence Harold
(b) Grantham, Lincolnshire 22 October 1945
Lives in Portishead, Bristol
Educ. – Alma Park Juniors & Seniors; Kings School (Grantham)
Cricket. – Pudsey St Lawrence; Cleethorpes; Lincolnshire Colts; Ingham; Lincolnshire; Downend; Wiltshire; Minor Counties
HS. 14 no v Suffolk August 1978 @ Lakenham
BB. 8/45 v Buckinghamshire July 1977 @ Lakenham – side 157/8 declared so he had all eight (aided by superb catching by Phil Sharpe) but their skipper Brian Poll (who later apologised) denied Terry the chance of all ten wickets. His match analysis was 11/100.
HS. 1 no v Suffolk May 1978 @ Lakenham
BB. 3/70 v Cambridge University May 1977 @ Fenner's
BB. *1/34 v Leicestershire July 1982 @ Leicester*
10/5 for Kings School v Lincolnshire Gentlemen 1963.
9/11 for Kings School v Sheffield GS – just 3 days after the above performance and he took the first nine. An overall 19/16 haul made the National Press.
212 Minor Counties wickets in just six NCCC seasons culminating in his winning the 1982 Frank Edward Trophy as the leading M.C. bowler that year. The NCCC leading M.C. wicket taker in each of his six seasons. He also took over 200 wickets for Lincolnshire with 14 of them gained against Norfolk; he did however take 58 wickets for NCCC against his home county.
Terry turned down the chance of joining a County side choosing instead the Civil Service. An Inland Revenue Collector of Taxes he rose through the ranks to become a Deputy Director in charge of Special Investigations until his wanted early retirement. Now a Lay Inspector for the Health Care Commission.

DUNN, Marcus Julian
(b) Skegness 20 October 1958
Lives locally
Educ. – Blofield County Primary School; Wymondham College; Christ Church College (Canterbury)
Cricket. – Wymondham College; Christ Church College;

England Under 15s; British Colleges (in West Indies); Norfolk Young Amateurs; Vauxhall Mallards; Norwich Wanderers; Barleycorns; Swardeston; St Lawrence; Chestfield; St Albans; Potters Bar; Datchworth; Nottinghamshire Under 25s & 2nds; National Association of Young Cricketers North.

HS 22 no v Lincolnshire July 1977 @ Spalding

HS. 11 v Cambridge University May 1977 @ Fenner's

10/21 & 70 no for Wymondham College v Downham Market July 1972

10 & 33 for Nottinghamshire (2) v Northamptonshire (2) – one of Wayne Larkins' (q.v.) wickets as he took 7/31.

PE Teacher at Mount Grace High School (Potters Bar). Worked for Advertising Agencies in Hammersmith and Twickenham and for a Football Agency. Set up a sporting company Stumps and Studs and he now works for Travelex.

KILSHAW, Peter John

(b) Norwich 5 August 1947

Lives locally

Educ. – Avenue Junior School; Henderson Secondary Modern School; Hewett GS; Loughborough College; University College of Swansea

Cricket. – Carrow; Black Sheep CC; St Barnabas; Norwich CC; Sprowston; Loughborough College; GH Wolstenholme's PE Teachers XI; Norfolk Over 50s and Over 60s.

HS. 95 no v Cambridgeshire July 1977 @ Lakenham – denied his ton by a declaration at 268/7. After his first four M.C. innings his average stood at 143. Peter stands as one of 10 NCCC men with a highest score in the nineties.

BB. 1/44 v Hertfordshire August 1979 @ Lakenham

HS. 3 v MCC August 1977 @ Lakenham - stumped off the bowling of Peter Parfitt (q.v)

He taught PE at Homerton College / Bowthorpe and Heartsease Middle.

ROBERTS, Gregory J

(b) New Zealand 26 January 1953

Cricket. – Taranaki

HS. 19 no v Lincolnshire August 1977 @ Lakenham

HS. 57 v MCC August 1977 @ Lakenham – out of 151.

NCCC's Chairman (at the time) Sir Charles Mott-Radclyffe stated in the 1978 Handbook that Greg was 'a grave disappointment'. He was referring to the performances on the field.

SHARPE, Philip John

(b) Shipley, Yorkshire 27 December 1936

Educ. – Bradford GS; Worksop College- playing cricket, rugby, hockey, squash & tennis

Cricket. – Worksop College; Public Schools; The Rest; Yorkshire Federation Youth XI; Army; Combined Services; Yorkshire; Derbyshire; Minor Counties; Players; International

Cavaliers; TN Pearce's XI; MCC; MCC President's XI; Rest of England; England XI; Old England XI; Indian Board President's XI; Duke of Norfolk's XI; Gillette Invitation XI; England – 12 Tests

HS. 117 no v Hertfordshire June 1982 @ Watford

BB. 1/19 v Buckinghamshire August 1977 @ Amersham

HS. *0 v Leicestershire July 1982 @ Leicester*

He twice topped the NCCC batting averages with the best return being his 55.70 average in 1980.

An Hon NCCC Life member he featured in nine century partnerships for NCCC.

1st class cricket – 493 matches 22,530 runs 618 catches 3 wickets..

Generally regarded to be the best slip fieldsman of his era in the country (71catches in 1962 alone) and on Yorkshire's all time list in 4th spot in this category) and a sportsman far above average ability. Twenty first in appearances total for Yorkshire with 23 County tons plus he reached the magical 2,000 runs in a season (1962).

His father a Mill Executive sent him for coaching in the school holidays with a former Headmaster quoted as saying,"The boy will never play cricket, he is too small." Boy did he grow in stature.

Phil left school in September 1955 but not until after he had amassed 240 v Wrekin; 216 v Cryptics plus 200 v Notts as a Yorkshire Cricket Federation Youth player. Phil had a job learning wool sorting alongside Doug Padgett before he made the step up to County Cricket.

Hockey. – Ben Raydding Sports Club; Yorkshire; England Trials. He attends Ted Wright's (q.v) bi-annual reunion during Manor Park's Cricket Festival.

1978

BRADFORD, Robert Leslie

(b) Swardeston, Norfolk 29 April 1952

Lives Norfolk

Educ. – Swardeston Primary School; Wymondham College

Cricket. – Wymondham College; Mulbarton; Swardeston

HS. 111 no v Buckinghamshire August 1981 @ High Wycombe – an innings of 11(4) & 3 (6).

HS. 11 v Cambridge University 'A' May 1980 @ Fenner's

HS. *15 v Hertfordshire July 1974 @ Fenner's – in the Final of the English Estates Trophy*

He joined Eastern Gas from school. Worked in Peter Thomas' Garage for fifteen years. Rob has worked for many years for Castlegate Car Sales.

PLUMB, Stephen George

(b) Wimbush, Essex 17 January 1954

Lives in Essex

Educ. – Elmbridge Boarding School (Cranleigh); Saffron

Walden County High School; Writtle Agricultural College.
Cricket. – Saffron Walden; Chingford; Ilford; Essex; Minor Counties; Club Cricket Conference; Lincolnshire; Derbyshire 2nds; MCC; Bishop's Stortford; Minor Counties South.
HS. 204 no v Cumberland July 1988 @ Millom
BB. 6/58 v Suffolk August 1994 @ Copdock
HS. 93 v Pinelands March 1994 @ Cape Town (South Africa)
BB. 3/27 v Mick Horner's X1 February 1994 @ Constantia (South Africa)
HS. *164 v Lincolnshire June 1986 @ Swardeston – still the highest score by any batsman in the Minor Counties KO Cup.*
BB. *4/37 v Berkshire June 1983 @ Pinebanks*
1st class cricket – 5 matches 216 runs 2 catches 3 wickets
Steve did it all and with style and panache as for NCCC alone he took well over 300 wickets, held 90 catches and totalled over 11,500 runs with four years captaincy thrown in. His 18 hundreds in our cause does not tell the whole story as he was dismissed ten times in the nineties alone. A record getter and setter in that he is the only man to twice get a hundred in each innings of a Minor County match – 102 & 116 no v Bedfordshire in 1986 and 111 no & 120 no v Hertfordshire in 1991. He is the second highest compiler of runs (12,266) in M.C. history when his runs for Lincolnshire are included. Norfolk have not found a genuine all-rounder apart from David Thomas (q.v) and Steve Goldsmith (q.v) to replace Steve since he finished in 1995. A former Farmer and now a Tanker Driver which he combined with coaching at Saffron Walden.

1979

AYRES, Ian Martin
(b) Bromley, Kent 29 April 1957
Lives in Portsmouth
Educ. – Bancroft School; Leicester University
Cricket. – Bancroft School; Leicester University; Sprowston; Brentwood; Portsmouth & Southsea; South Woodford Colts
HS. 0 no v Cambridgeshire July 1979 @ Lakenham AND 0 no v Buckinghamshire August 1979 @ Lakenham
BB. 3/32 v Cambridgeshire July 1979 @ Lakenham
Left hand bat and right arm off break bowler who was only given four games.
A Business Development Director for Groundwork Solent

INNES, Richard Francis
(b) Aberdeen 31 August 1953
Lives locally
Educ. – Town Close House School; The Leys (Cambridge)
Cricket. – Norwich Wanderers; Hunstanton; Carrow; Norfolk Young Amateurs; Cavaliers; North Runcton; Cromer
HS. 32 no v Cambridgeshire June 1983 @ Wisbech
BB. 4/41 v Suffolk August 1982 @ Felixstowe
HS. 14 v UEA May 1982 @ Colney Lane, Norwich

BB. 1/10 v UEA May 1982 @ Colney Lane, Norwich
HS. *3 no v Berkshire June 1983 @ Pinebanks*
BB. *2/25 v Berkshire June 1983 @ Pinebanks*
Hockey. – *Norwich City; Pelicans; Norwich Wanderers; Norfolk County*
Richard was with Barclays Bank 1971-2004 and is now a Relationship Director with NatWest Bank.

STARLING, Simon John
(b) Wimbotsham, Norfolk 1 June 1959
Lives locally
Educ. – Wymondham College
Cricket. – Wymondham College; CEYMS; Barleycorns; Norwich Union; Vauxhall Mallards
HS. 9 v Cambridgeshire June 1979 @ Papworth Everard AND 9 v Cambridgeshire July 1979 @ Lakenham
BB. 4/79 v Buckinghamshire August 1979 @ High Wycombe
HS. 8 no v Cambridge University 'A' May 1980 @ Fenner's
BB. 6/38 v Cambridge University 'A' May 1980 @ Fenner's
He was coached at Wymondham College by John Shepperd (q.v) and in the 1980 season had the same bowling average as Ted Wright but he took 30 wickets less. Another employee of Norwich Union.

1980

WITHERDEN, Nigel
(b) Norwich 1 April 1959
Lives in Bishop's Stortford
Educ. – Hadham Hall School; Bishop's Stortford College
Cricket. – Hadham Hall School; Stansted Hall CC; Norfolk Club & Ground; Bishop's Stortford
HS. 53 no v Cambridge University 'A' May 1980 @ Fenner's
Son of EG (q.v)
A qualified Level 2 cricket coach and he was with Steve Plumb (q.v) at Bishop's Stortford.
The Head Groundsman at Bishop's Stortford College for 25 years – a position that he took over from his father.
F.F. – His daughters Lucy and Rebecca play cricket for Hertfordshire

1981

LAMBOURNE, Ian Richard
(b) Oxford 20 December 1954
Educ. – Lord Williams GS
Cricket. – Lord Williams GS; Aston Rowant; Aylesbury Town; Ingham; South Oxfordshire Amateurs CC; Lincolnshire – as a substitute fielder for Jonathan Munton (who broke a finger bone)
HS. 6 no v Cumberland July 1984 @ Kendal

BB. 4/65 v Northumberland August 1984 @ Lakenham
An eccentric bowling action as he stopped in his delivery stride and then he released the ball from a low height. A NatWest Bank Manager and now a self-employed Gardener after taking early retirement.

MIR, Parvez Jamil
(b) Sutrapur, Dacca, Pakistan 24 September 1953
Cricket. – Rawlpindi Blues; Lahore 'A''B''City''Blues' & 'Whites'; Pakistan Universities; Derbyshire; Habib Bank Limited; BCCP Patron's XI; North West Frontier Province Governor's XI; Punjab 'A'; Glamorgan; Norfolk; MCC; Norfolk & Suffolk; Lancashire 2nds; Walkden; Waltham; Horsford; Swardeston; Norfolk Over 50s; Pakistan
HS. 126 no v Durham June 1985 @ South Shields
BB. 7/36 v Durham August 1984 @ Lakenham
HS. 134 v Bedfordshire June 1982 @ Pinebanks
BB. 3/10 v Cambridge University May 1982 @ Fenner's
HS. *55 v Leicestershire July 1982 @ Grace Road*
BB. *3/43 v Glamorgan June 1983 @ Lakenham*
203 no & 80 for Glamorgan (2) v Gloucestershire (2) July 1979 – in a first innings score of 265/4 declared. This performance alerted people to his talent.
1st class cricket – 80 matches 3,983 runs 73 catches 192 wickets One Day Internationals for Pakistan – 3 matches 26 runs 2 catches 3 wickets
His NCCC 1984 Man-of-the-Season exploits best sum up his five seasons with the club – after which he was unable to serve the County following a change in the Registration regulations with regard to overseas players. He completed a rare double of 500 runs and 50 wickets for the two day matches, last achieved for Norfolk in 1923 by Michael Falcon. He won the Frank Edwards Trophy for his batting and picked up the Wilfred Rhodes Trophy the following year for his batting. These were trophies awarded for overall performances in the Minor Counties Championship. In 1984 he also easily topped the batting averages in the English Estate games. Only David Thomas and Steve Goldsmith since have become an effective all-rounder for Norfolk. The Cricket Archive website revealed that he moved to the U.S.A. and as a Director of the North American Cricket Authority, he arranged exhibition matches involving teams from England and the West Indies. He served as the Pakistan Media Manager and was also the Anchor man for a Political Talk Show on TV.

MOTUM, Paul Alvin
(b) Colchester, Essex 6 October 1955
Educ. – Langley School
Cricket. – Langley School; Beckenham; Staplehurst; Ingham; Norfolk Young Amateurs; Gore Court; MCC
HS. 40 v Cambridgeshire June 1981 @ Wisbech
BB. 2/18 v Suffolk August 1982 @ Lakenham

HS. 10 v UEA May 1982 @ Colney Lane, Norwich
112 for Norfolk Young Amateurs v Suffolk Colts August 1975
60 for Gore Court v Hartley Country Club August 2001 – his side boosted by the arrival of ex England player Martin McCague.
66 for Gore Court v Bickley Park June 2003
A Player and Sports Clothing Agent with one of his clients being Kent CCC. Latterly a Management Consultant.

1982

BACON, Sir Nicholas Hickman Ponsoby, OBE DL (14th and 15th Baronet)
(b) London Clinic 17 May 1953
A Premier Baronet of England – succeeded 1982, the Baronetcy dates back to 1611.
14th Baronet of Redgrave and 15th Baronet of Mildenhall
Educ. – Eton College (JDR McConnell); Dundee University – MA)
Cricket. – Eton College; Dundee University; I Zingari; Free Foresters; Eton Ramblers; Norfolk Young Amateurs; Norfolk Club & Ground
HS. 12 v Cambridge University May 1982 @ Fenner's
34 & 26 for Eton College v Harrow School July 1971
President of Hales Cricket Club. Council Member National Trust and RHS. Barrister at Law, Gray's Inn 1978. Page of Honour to the Queen (1966-69). Dept Lieutenant Norfolk 1998. Liveryman of Grocers' Company. Lord Warden of the Stannaries and Keeper of the Privy Seal, Duchy of Cornwall since 2006.
F.F. – A Norfolk Landowner with commercial interests principally in London. President of Norfolk Beekeepers Association

BAILEY, Francis Paul
(b) Norwich 8 January 1948
Lives locally
Educ. – Sir John Leman School, Borough Road College (Isleworth)
Cricket. – Sir John Leman School; Lowestoft; Suffolk Schools - captain; Norfolk Young Amateurs; Norwich Wanderers; Dereham; Hadleigh;
HS. 0 v Northumberland June 1985 @ Jesmond
HS. 0 v UEA May 1982 @ Colney Lane, Norwich
A right hand bat and wicket keeper who had the unenviable task of displacing Doug Mattocks in the side. Now a Director of a Civil Engineering Company

BELMONT, Richard James
(b) Dronfield, Derbyshire 17 May 1965
Lives in Oxford
Educ. – Wymondham College; Exeter University
Cricket. – Wymondham College; Norwich Schools Under 19s; CEYMS; Swardeston; Exeter University; Sidmouth; Club

Cricket Conference Under 25s; Sydney University (Australia); Cheshunt; Oxford Nondescripts; Hertfordshire; University Athletic Union CC.

HS. 29 v Hertfordshire August 1988 @ Letchworth
BB. 2/15 v Durham August 1988 @ Lakenham
HS. 2 v Cambridge University May 1988 @ Fenner's
BB. 3/55 v Cambridge University May 1988 @ Fenner's
HS. *29 no v Cambridgeshire June 1991 @ The Leys School, Cambridge*
BB. *1/53 v Gloucestershire June 1991 @ Bristol*
5/41 for Norwich Schools v Suffolk Schools July 1982
He played for the MCC in Buenos Aires and Santiago. He is the Coombe CC Coach and has been in the same team as his son Jack (played for Oxfordshire U14s)

DENTON, Colin Samuel
(b) Thorpe St Andrew, Norwich 4 June 1959
Lives in Scarborough
Educ. – Thorpe GS
Cricket. – Thorpe GS; Norfolk Schoolboys Under 15s; Norfolk Club & Ground; St Andrews Hospital; Norwich Wanderers; Exceteras; South Walsham; Norwich Cavaliers; Ingham; Swardeston; Norwich Natives; Hackness CC; Filey; Brompton-by-Sawdon; Cayton CC
HS. 11 no v UEA May 1982 @ Colney Lane, Norwich
BB. 2/47 v UEA May 1982 @ Colney Lane, Norwich
Colin has spent his working life in the Printing Trade with Clays/Fletchers/Jarrolds and Pinders.

FOX, Neil
(b) Norwich 10 February 1962
Lives in Norfolk
Educ. – Thorpe GS
Cricket. – CEYMS; Barleycorns; Swardeston; Norfolk Alliance; Martham; Norwich CC; Norfolk Young Amateurs; GG Fiddler's X1.
HS. 75 no v Bedfordshire July 1999 @ Lakenham
BB. 5/43 v Hertfordshire August 1993 @ Hertford
HS. 46 v Cape Town February 1997 @ Plumstead (South Africa)
BB. 4/26 v MCC Young Amateurs May 1994 @ North Runcton
HS. *68 v Hampshire June 1996 @ Southampton - the highest score by a Norfolk batsman in a limited over match against a first class county.*
BB. *2/25 v Suffolk May 1998 @ Framlingham College*
Holds the Minor County KO Cup record 7th wicket partnership with D.R.Thomas of 105 against Berkshire in 1993. Involved in two more NCCC century partnerships namely 122 with Carl Amos (1998) and an undefeated 118 with Paul Newman (1999).
Norfolk County at Basketball, Football and Tennis and he

was on Ipswich Town's books as a youngster. Neil has his own business Fox Insurance just north of Norwich.

POOLE, Julian Charles
(b) Sprowston, Norwich 21 October 1956
Lives locally
Educ. – Sprowston Infants & Juniors; Sprowston Secondary Modern
Cricket. – Sprowston School; Sprowston CC; Norfolk Club & Ground; Ingham (on tour)
HS. Did not bat v UEA May 1982 Colney Lane, Norwich - and only had 4 overs (see statistics section). A First X1 side that day that were missing Huggins and Plumb who were on Minor Counties playing duty.
Took 6/33 against Ingham in August 1980 who were dismissed for 97 despite having in their team Messrs Allcock, Borrett, Gillham, Moore, Motum and Rose (all q.v).
Football. – Newton Flotman; Busmen; Lakeford; Sprowston Wanderers.
He did his apprenticeship in the Motor Trade and is now a Transport Manager.

POWELL, Tyrone Lyndon
(b) Bargoed, Glamorgan 17 June 1953
He moved to New Zealand at an early age
Educ. – Fraser Crescent School; Hereatunga College (NZ)
Cricket. – Glamorgan; New Zealand Under 23s; Wellington Under 20s & 23s; Hutt Valley CC; NZ Brabin XI; Hawke's Bay; Acle CC
HS. 115 v Suffolk August 1982 @ Lakenham – the only time that he showed NCCC his worth as a batsman. The 1982 final order in the batting averages were Plumb, Powell, Mir, Sharpe, Huggins and Handley so there was quality in the side.
1st class cricket – 2 matches 24 runs
100 no for Wellington Under 20s v Auckland Under 20s December 1972
101 no for Hutt Valley v Fiji January 1978
He worked for Wright & Carmen Printing Ltd (Upper Hutt) and apart from a spell with Great Yarmouth Marina Centre he stayed in the print trade and is now working for Downey & Company in Yarmouth.

RINGWOOD, Philip John
(b) Narborough, Norfolk 7 August 1953
Lives in Norfolk
Educ. – Swaffham Secondary Modern School
Cricket. – Swaffham Secondary Modern School; Narborough; Represented South Lincolnshire League; North Runcton; Norfolk Developmennt Squad; Black Sheep CC; Norfolk Over 50s
HS. 89 v Cambridgeshire June 1983 @ Wisbech – his first innings score was instrumental in keeping NCCC in the

game as they eventually won by 4 wickets.

HS. 28 v Cambridge University May 1988 @ Fenner's
HS. *20 v Berkshire June 1983 @ Pinebanks*
Phil has his own Electrical Business

THOMAS, Peter Wynne
(b) Swardeston, Norfolk 11 April 1952
Lives in Norfolk
Educ. – Langley School
Cricket. – CEYMS; Cromer; Swardeston; Minor Counties;
Norfolk Alliance
HS. 13 v Buckinghamshire August 1982 @ Amersham
BB. 3/46 v Bedfordshire July 1983 @ Lakenham
HS. 16 v Cambridge University May 1982 @ Fenner's
HS. *8 no v Wiltshire August 1983 @ Marlborough College*
BB. *2/35 v Glamorgan June 1983 @ Lakenham*
Father of MW (q.v) and Brother of DR (q.v)
Peter served on the Norfolk Over 50s Committee and
he is presently the Norfolk Cricket Alliance Chairman. A
Schoolteacher at Norwich School with Rodney Bunting (q.v)

1983

BASSINGTHWAITE, David Norman
(b) Norwich 15 April 1947
Lives locally
Educ. – Foncett St Peter's Primary School; Long Stratton
Secondary Modern School
Cricket. – Long Stratton School; Braconash; Swardeston;
Norfolk Over 50s; Norfolk Over 60s – one game as an
underage player.
HS. 0 no & 0 v Suffolk August 1983 @ Lakenham
BB. 1/111 v Cumberland July 1983 @ Lakenham
A former Interior Trimmer for Lotus Cars

HODSON, Edward Robert
(b) Lincoln 16 August 1964
Lives in Coventry
Educ. – Toftwood Primary School; Hammond's GS; Warwick
University - studying Politics and International Studies.
Cricket. – Hammond's GS; Dereham; Norwich Schools;
Norfolk Young Cricketers and U15,16,18,19 & 25s; Warwick
University; English UAU; Stoneleigh; Coventry & North
Warwickshire; Past Norfolk XI
HS. 29 v Cumberland July 1983 @ Lakenham
BB. 1/27 V Cumberland July 1988 @ Millom
HS. *36 v Wiltshire August 1983 @ Marlborough College*
117 no for Dereham v Ingham in the 1982 Carter Cup Final –
the youngest ever centurion to that point.
43 & 3/51 for Past Norfolk XI v Past Suffolk XI July 2004 @
Woodbridge School with one of his victims being Derek Randall.
A Citizens Advice Bureau Advisor in Coventry

THOMAS, David Robert
(b) Swardeston, Norfolk 26 January 1963
Lives in Norfolk
Educ. – Langley Prep & Senior School; Wymondham
College
Cricket. – Swardeston; Minor Counties; Lavinia, Duchess of
Norfolk's XI; Norfolk Young Amateurs; MCC; Minor Counties
Under 25s in Kenya.
HS. 75 no v Cambridgeshire August 1984 @ Lakenham
BB. 7/63 v Cambridgeshire August 1998 @ Lakenham
HS. 52 no v MCC Young Cricketers April 1996 @ Dereham
BB. 3/12 v Alma Marist February 1997 @ Cape Town (South
Africa)
HS. *89 v Bedfordshire May 1993 @ Lakenham*
BB. *4/20 v Suffolk May 1984 @ Pinebanks*
Brother of PW (q.v) and Uncle of MW (q.v)
1st class cricket – 1 match 27 runs
7.1-4-3-4 for Minor Counties Under 25s v Coast Cricket
Association Under 25s February 1986 in Kenya.
He played for the Minor Counties versus Sri Lanka alongside
Steve Plumb (q.v)
David compiled 21 NCCC half centuries and as befits a fine
fielder he held 115 catches in all games for the County. I have
however noted two centuries for Swardeston in the East
Anglian Premier League. A sensational bowling season in 1989
saw him pick up 20 wickets for a miserly 11.05 per wicket to
win the Frank Edwards Trophy. Six Man-of-the- Match awards
and the Famous Grouse Trophy (1998) were also added to
his collection. In the mid 2000s he won the Local Community
Links Award for his cricket work with schools and voluntary
organisations and he set up and organised Swardeston
Schools' Coaching. Cricket Coach at Norwich School
Lawn Tennis. – Norfolk County; Great Britain Under 16s –
ranked number three at one time.
He worked in the family business – Electric Motor & Garage and
now runs his own Property Company.

WHITTAKER, Paul Kevin
(b) Oxford 7 August 1956
Educ. – Oxford GS; Nonington College
Cricket. – Oxford GS; Oxfordshire Colts; NatWest Bank CC;
Vauxhall Mallards; Lowestoft; Cheshunt; Welwyn Garden
City
HS. 22 v Northumberland June 1985 @ Jesmond
BB. 5/51 v Hertfordshire August 1984 @ Hertford
HS. *9 no v Bedfordshire May 1989 @ Swardeston*
BB. *3/23 v Cambridgeshire May 1986 @ Trinity College*
Paul was a talented sportsman as per the following
achievements:-
Football. – Oxfordshire
Lawn Tennis. – Kent
Basketball. – Norfolk County

Squash. – Hertfordshire Police
He worked for NatWest Bank for three years and latterly taught PE at Nonington College and Taverham Hall Prep School. Also the Hertfordshire Constabulary PE Adviser. A Teacher at the Sports and Science Gateshead College and a Director and Coach of Gateshead Golf Academy (he plays off 9)
F.F. – The Gateshead Golf website has him incorrectly shown as Whitaker!

1984

CARTER, John Ronald
(b) Brundall, Norfolk 9 August 1963
Lives in Norfolk
Educ. – Thorpe GS
Cricket. – Thorpe GS; Norfolk Young Amateurs; Norfolk Under 25s; Vauxhall Mallards; Horsford
HS. 120 v Bedfordshire June 1986 @ Dunstable
HS. *43 v Cambridgeshire May 1986 @ Trinity College*
John grew too big to be a jockey so he turned to cricket. An Author of two books being 'US Masters Golf' (for which I was happy to proof and offer advice) and the very glossy production 'Newmarket – a year at the home of Horseracing'
F.F. – The author occasionally captained John for our works side in local park cup ties.

TOPLEY, Thomas Donald
(b) Canterbury, Kent 25 February 1964
Educ. – St Peter's Primary School; Royal Hospital School
Cricket. – Essex; Surrey; Gloucestershire 2nds; MCC Groundstaff, Young Cricketers & Young Professionals; Kent 2nds; Carrow; Norwich Cavaliers; Loughton; South Hampstead; Harare Sports Club (Zimbabwe); Kimberley BH (S.A); Natal Midlands (S.A); Roodepoort CC (S.A); Noodsborg (S.A); Griqualand West (S.A); Colchester and East Essex; England – fielded as a 12th man
HS. 13 no v Durham August 1984 @ Lakenham
BB. 6/98 v Suffolk August 1984 @ Ipswich
HS. *9 v Hampshire July 1984 @ Lakenham*
BB. *2/26 v Northumberland July 1984 @ Lakenham*
1st class cricket – 120 matches 1,693 runs 70 catches 367 wickets with his brother Peter playing for Kent CCC. His son Reece is an Essex County player.
He worked as a Postman and once had a spring loaded letter box catch his fingers – not an ideal scenario for a cricketer. The 1988 Cricketer's Who's Who by Iain Sproat stated that he was an NCA coach and that he exported to the Gulf States.The Zimbabwe Cricket Coach 1989-92 including the 1992 World Cup.
F.F. – Always remembered for his dazzling one handed catch off Malcolm Marshall while fielding as a substitute for England v West Indies in 1984. He stepped over the

boundary so a six was given. In June 2009 his son Reece, then a 15 year old on the staff of Essex principally as a bowler, was struck on the head by a thunderous drive from Kevin Pietersen in the Loughborough University nets and he needed stitches as well as an overnight stay in hospital. Don did suggest to him that he might have dropped a catch and the reply was 'at least I stopped it going for a six.'

WHITEHEAD, John
(b) Oldham, Lancashire 2 July 1962
Lives locally
Educ. – Royton & Crompton Comprehensive School; Salford Polytechnic
Cricket. – Lancashire Schools; North England Schools; Swardeston; Lancashire Federation; Lancashire (2nds); Norden CC; Ingham; Norwich Wanderers; Norfolk up to Under 25s.
HS. 63 no v Cambridgeshire August 1984 @ Lakenham
HS. *33 v MCC August 1990 @ Lakenham*
HS. *29 v Hertfordshire June 1985 @ Potter's Bar*
43 for Lancashire (2) v Nottinghamshire (2) September 1983
Worked for NatWest in Manchester and moved to Equity & Law. Head of Financial Planning for Eversheds (1989-2002) and now Managing Director and Financial Adviser for the Alan Boswell Group.

1985

BUNTING, Rodney Alan
(b) East Winch, Norfolk 25 April 1965
Lives locally
Educ. – King Edward VII School (King's Lynn)
Cricket. – North Runcton; Ingham; Norfolk Under 16s; Norwich Wanderers; Sussex; Minor Counties; 2nds of Northamptonshire, Somerset and Gloucestershire; Norwich & Coltishall Wanderers.
HS. 49 no v Hertfordshire August 1992 @ Lakenham
BB. 6/35 v Northumberland July 1986 @ Lakenham
BB. *4/39 v Essex (2) May 1995 @ Lakenham*
HS. *22 no v Suffolk June 1986 @ Horsford – the first competitive county match at Manor Park*
BB. *4/33 v Bedfordshire June 1994 @ Lakenham*
Brother of SJ (q.v) and Uncle of KJ (q.v)
1st class cricket – 38 matches 366 runs 5 catches 80 wickets He took 243 wickets for Norfolk at an average of 20.83 and won three Man-of-the-Match awards.
His 41 wickets against Suffolk puts him in tenth place in this category.
A Schoolteacher of Cricket and Rugby Union at Norwich School.

JERVIS, Martin Michael
(b) King's Lynn 8 July 1963

Lives in Peterborough
Educ. – King Edward VII School (King's Lynn)
Cricket. – King Edward VII School; North Runcton; Norfolk Under 25s; Norfolk Young Amateurs; Grimston
HS. 14 no v Cambridgeshire August 1990 @ Lakenham AND 14 no v Cambridgeshire July 1992 @ Lakenham AND 14 v Suffolk August 1992 @ Copdock
A right handed wicket keeper who did not bat in friendly nor cup matches but took two catches in the Holt Cup KO game versus Suffolk in 1992 off of JCM Lewis' bowling.
An occupation of a Sales Manager.

RICE, Paul Christopher
(b) Exeter 22 February 1948
Lives in Norfolk
Educ. – Exeter Technical College; Birmingham University
Cricket. – Devon Schools; Suffolk; Mallards; Carrow; Old Buckenham; Norwich CC; Somerset 2nds; Warwickshire 2nds; Lowestoft; Exeter CC; Norfolk Over 50s & 60s; England Over 60s.
HS. 25 v Lincolnshire July 1985 @ Lincoln Lindum
Paul is remembered for skippering the Lowestoft side to Norfolk Alliance and Carter Cup success in the 1980s. A prolific and fast scorer for Norfolk Over 50s (1996-2009) with 2,248 runs at an average of 45.87 as he formed a formidable opening partnership with Martin Pearse.
He captained England Over 60s cricket team against Wales on 4 June 2009.
He played Football for Exeter City Reserves and he took up cycling before being tempted back into the cricket fold. A PE Teacher at Sir John Leman High School to 2006. A Sports Co-ordinator for one day a week in Schools such as those in Beccles and Brampton.

TATE, John Stephen
(b) Gt Yarmouth, Norfolk 23 May 1963
Lives in Norfolk
Educ. – Denes High School (Lowestoft)
Cricket. – Lowestoft; Barleycorns; Norwich & Coltishall Wanderers.
HS. 10 no v Staffordshire July 1986 @ Leek AND 10 no v Bedfordshire June 1988 @ Henlow
BB. 4/28 v Bedfordshire July 1987 @ Lakenham
HS. *1 v Cambridgeshire June 1988 @ Fenner's*
BB. *1/28 v Cambridgeshire June 1987 @ Pinebanks*
Steve is the Norwich & Coltishall Wanderers Treasurer and Child Welfare Officer

ZAIDI, Syed Mohammad Nasir
(b) Karachi, Pakistan 25 March 1961
Cricket. – Karachi; Lancashire; 2nds of Glamorgan and Nottinghamshire; Middlesex Under 25s; Gloucestershire

Under 25s; MCC Young Cricketers; Berkshire; Lavinia, Duchess of Norfolk's XI
HS. 11 v Staffordshire August 1985 @ Lakenham
BB. 6/46 v Hertfordshire August 1985 @ Lakenham – after not bowling in the 55 overs of the first innings.
HS. *4 Hertfordshire June 1985 @ Potter's Bar*
BB. *1/41 v Hertfordshire June 1985 @ Potter's Bar*
1st class cricket – 19 matches 313 runs 15 catches 19 wickets 6/50 & 3/32 for MCC Young Cricketers v Essex (2) August 1981 3/67 for Lancashire (2) v Derbyshire (2) July 1983 – with Paul Newman (q.v) being 61 not out.
74 for Lancashire (2) v Yorkshire (2) July 1984
An expensive (in terms of runs conceded) leg break bowler for NCCC

1986

COOPER, Kevin Peter
(b) Lowestoft, Suffolk 5 August 1962
Lives locally
Educ. – Kirkley High School; The Deans; N.E. London Polytechnic
Cricket. – Kirkley High School; Kirkley; Lowestoft; Suffolk Under 19s; Swardeston
HS. 20 v Cumberland June 1994 @ Barrow
BB. 1/3 v Cumberland June 1994 @ Barrow
HS. 47 no v D. Mackay's XI February 1994 @ Cape Town (South Africa)
HS. *31 v Cambridgeshire June 1987 @ Pinebanks*
BB. *2/26 v Cambridgeshire June 1994 @ Leys School*
102 no for Swardeston 'A' v Dereham 1st X1 June 2008
Kevin is on the Swardeston player committee and he is also their Under 11 Manager. He fulfilled the role of NCCC Under 10 Manager at one time and is presently shown on the Norfolk Cricket Board website as the County Youth Under 11 Manager. He gained a BSc (Hons) in Land Management and is a Qualified Chartered Surveyor working for Norwich Union.

DIXON, Stephen Brian
(b) Bolton, Lancashire 12 July 1958
Lives Leicestershire
Educ. – Peel Primary School; Hayward GS
Cricket. – Hayward GS; Lancashire Schoolboys; Little Hulton; Westhoughton; St Andrew's Methodists CC; Lancashire Federation Under 18s; Lancashire 2nds; Roegreen CC; Ingham; Bourne; Boston CC; Nuneaton; Lullington Park; Derbyshire Over 50s
HS. 79 v Northumberland August 1992 @ Lakenham
BB. 2/84 v Buckinghamshire August 1992 @ Beaconsfield
HS. 64 v MCC August 1990 @ Lakenham
HS. *36 v Devon June 1992 @ Lakenham*

4/42 & 65 for Nuneaton v Kenilworth June 2000
Between 1988-1992 he featured in seven NCCC century partnerships with Roger Finney (3), Steve Plumb (3) and Robin Huggins (1) for the 2nd,3rd and 4th wickets.
He is still playing for Lullington Park and is a Level 3 Coach serving Staffordshire as well as coaching Derbyshire Under 15s and their Academy. Steve worked for Coop Bank (Norwich) and for a Silicon Manufacturer until 2008 before becoming self-employed with his cricket coaching.

LEWIS, Patrick Charles Mansel
(b) Ditchingham, Norfolk 21 November 1965
Lived Northumberland but works in London and as we go to press he is in the throes of moving down there.
Educ. – Gresham's School; Beeston Hall School
Cricket. – Gresham's School; Ingham; Tynedale; Western Province CC (S.A); The Borderers CC – also a former Chairman of the latter side.
HS. *Did not bat in his one game*
BB. *1/52 v Lincolnshire June 1986 @ Swardeston - he started the ball rolling to a 99 run win by claiming the first wicket.*
Brother of JCM (q.v)
A former Gresham's cricket captain he amassed 1,093 runs and took 101 wickets for them.
'Paddy' is the UK Head of Investment Management for UBS Wealth Management. His previous roles were Investment Director at Laing & Cruickshank and a Vice President at Merrill Lynch

ROFF, Geoffrey Mark
(b) Norwich 14 September 1964
Lives locally
Educ. – Hillside Avenue Primary School; Thorpe St Andrew Secondary School
Cricket. – Sprowston; Barleycorns; Norwich; Norfolk Under 25s; Essex Under 25s & 2nds; Norfolk Alliance.
HS. 35 v Durham August 1986 @ Lakenham
BB. 4/43 v Durham August 1986 @ Lakenham
HS. *0 v Hertfordshire July 1986 @ St Albans AND 0 v Cambridgeshire June 1988 @ Fenner's*
BB. *3/50 v Lincolnshire June 1986 @ Swardeston*
60 no & 4/14 for Norfolk Under 25s v Cromer August 1985
3/15 for Essex (2) v Sussex (2) June 1986 – with Don Topley and Nasser Hussain in his side.
Geoff is still playing for Sprowston in the Alliance Premier League.Trained to be a Quantity Surveyor but moved into IT working in succession for HMSO, Eastern Electricity, Deutsche Bank and Banner Business Supplies.

WAYMOUTH, Simon Nicholas
(b) Welwyn Garden City, Hertfordshire 10 December 1966
Lives New Malden

Educ. – King Edward VII GS; Digby Stuart College; Roehampton Institute
Cricket. – North Runcton; Norfolk Young Amateurs; Castle Rising; Norfolk Under 25s; Wimbledon
HS. 40 no v Suffolk August 1987 @ Lakenham
BB. 4/93 v Lincolnshire August 1986 @ Lakenham
7/31 for Norfolk Young Amateurs v Nottinghamshire August 1984
6/25 for Norfolk Young Amateurs v Hunts & Peterborough August 1984
6/54 for Norfolk Under 25s v Loughborough College June 1986
The Group Risk Manager for Cadogan Tate Ltd (Fine Art storage/shipping & Office removals)

1987

ELLIS, Mark Thomas
(b) Castle Acre, Norfolk 19 May 1962
Lives in Norfolk
Educ. – Swaffham Secondary Modern School
Cricket. – Dereham; Castle Acre; Norfolk Young Amateurs; Sprowston; Swardeston
HS. 9 v Cumberland July 1988 @ Millom
BB. 6/60 v Bedfordshire July 1990 @ Southill Park – a late replacement for the unavailable Nick Taylor (q.v)
HS. *5 v Lincolnshire June 1990 @ Swardeston*
BB. *3/41 v Cambridgeshire June 1991 @ The Leys School*
A Car Salesman for Busseys for many years

KINGSHOTT, Raymond
(b) Merriwa, New South Wales, Australia 13 January 1957
He lived in the UK 1960-2006 until he returned home
Educ. – St David's Church of England School (Hornsey) - left at age 16 to work in London.
Cricket. – Alexandra Park; Cheshunt; Letchworth; Reed Tamworth; Alrewas; Newcastle City; Belmont; Middlesex County Under 17s; Hertfordshire Under 25s; Club Cricket Conference; Hertfordshire; England Amateur Squad; Past Norfolk
HS. 70 no v Northumberland June 1989 @ Jesmond
BB. 8/47 v Northumberland August 1990 @ Lakenham
HS. *20 v Koeberg February 1997 @ Koeberg (South Africa)*
BB. *4/74 v MCC August 1990 @ Lakenham*
HS. *23 v Hertfordshire June 1991 @ Hitchin*
BB. *2/16 v Cambridgeshire June 1990 @ The Leys School*
He topped the NCCC bowling averages in 1987 and 1991
9/41 for Cheshunt v Luton 1981
He scored 10,961 runs in his first eleven career with 3 tons –
101 for Cheshunt v Southgate September 1984
102 for Cheshunt v Wembley June 1986
107 no for Cheshunt v Hawkins June 2006
He additionally took 2,146 wickets for Cheshunt (1976-1997)

F.F. – Ray emailed me from Australia with a remarkable spreadsheet showing every analysis throughout his club cricket career. Nicknamed by his teammates 'Schnorbitz' and very cleverly as Bobby Charlton because of this former footballer's raking shot.

LEWIS, James Christopher Mansel
(b) Ditchingham, Norfolk 3 October 1967
Lives in Turkey
Educ. – Gresham's School; Beeston Hall School; Bedford Polytechnic
Cricket. – Gresham's School; Ingham; Minor Counties
HS. 88 v Lincolnshire August 1990 @ Lakenham – in 90 balls with 12 (4) & 1 (7)
BB. 6/62 v Suffolk July 1990 @ Bury St Edmunds
HS. 27 no v Western Province March 1994 @ Impala Park, Cape Town (South Africa)
BB. 5/43 v MCC August 1990 @ Lakenham – including the wicket of Parvez Mir (q.v)
HS. 19 no v Cambridgeshire June 1991 @ The Leys School
BB. 4/44 v Suffolk June 1992 @ Framlingham College
Brother of PCM (q.v)
9/19 for Gresham's School v Culford . For Gresham's (1983-86) he scored 1,316 runs and took 125 wickets. A Former Mathematics Teacher who now lives abroad working for a Publishing Company.

PAYNE, Andrew Norman
(b) Ely, Cambridge 15 April 1957
Lives in Norfolk
Educ. – Framlingham College
Cricket. – Lowestoft; Vauxhall Mallards; Horsford; Great Withchingham; Norfolk Under 15s, Under 19s, Under 25s; Norfolk Young Amateurs; Solihull; Midland Club
HS. 1 no v Lincolnshire July 1988 @ Lakenham
Best overall wicket keeping season was 18 dismissals in 1988 (16c 2s)
HS. *0 no v Cambridgeshire June 1988 @ Fenner's Chairperson (as per the club website) of Great Witchingham CC and Director of Sampson Leisure Ltd (Hotel, Leisure and Property Consultants)*

RAYNER, Marcus John
(b) Marks Tey, Colchester, Essex 17 December 1965
Lives in Norfolk
Educ. – Alleyn Court School; Sponne Comprehensive School
Cricket. – Essex Under 11 &13s; Northampton Schools Under 18 &19s; Swardeston; Norfolk Alliance
HS.13 v Cambridgeshire June 1987 @ Wisbech – a debut as Rodney Bunting had work commitments
BB. 5/48 v Lincolnshire July 1988 @ Lakenham – on a miserably damp, chilly and windy day.
BB. *1/19 v Cambridgeshire June 1990 @ Leys School*
A left hand bat and he bowled right arm seamers. Marcus worked for Barclays Bank and Lloyds Bank

SANDS, David William
(b) Cromer, Norfolk 15 December 1962
Lives in Norfolk
Educ. – Gresham's School; Easton College
Cricket. – Gresham's School; Aldborough; Cromer; Norfolk Under 12,14,16 & 18s;
HS. 15 v Hertfordshire August 1987 @ Lakenham
A Farmer in Melton Constable

SAVAGE, Darren Graham
(b) King's Lynn, Norfolk 24 December 1968
Lives in Norfolk
Cricket. – Thetford; Norfolk Young Amateurs; Old Buckenham; Norfolk Under 25s; Past Norfolk
HS. 45 v Staffordshire July 1988 @ Old Hill –the NCCC Handbook said that he shone plus he held an outstanding mid-wicket boundary catch.
BB. 1/34 v Northumberland August 1988 @ Lakenham
HS. 48 v Cambridge University May 1988 @ Fenner's
BB. 1/33 v Cambridge University May 1988 @ Fenner's
HS. *1 v Gloucestershire June 1991 @ Bristol*
7/47 & 42 for Norfolk Young Amateurs v Suffolk Young Amateurs August 1986
75 no for Norfolk Under 25s v Norfolk Schools July 1987
4/28 for Norfolk Under 25s v Suffolk Under 25s May 1991 @ Lakenham
He spent a few years on NCCC's Cricket Committee as an observer to try and find up and coming talent. He dismissed Justin Edrich in the 2004 Suffolk CCC Centenary match as a Past Norfolk player.

WILLIAMS, Daniel James
(b) West Runcton, Norfolk 14 November 1968
Educ. – Paston GS
Cricket. – Paston GS; Norfolk Schools; Cromer
HS. 37 v Staffordshire August 1987 @ Lakenham – in a stand of 105 with Doug Mattocks who was his senior by 24 years. Danny badly injured the inside of his knee and was therefore absent for the second innings. Despite displaying a pleasing array of strokes and a lot of commonsense it was to be his last County game.
74 for Norfolk Schools v Norfolk Under 25s July 1987

1988

COOTE, Peter
(b) Cleethorpes, Lincoln 28 October 1957

Lives in King's Lynn
Educ. – Skegness GS
Cricket. – Skegness; Burgh CC; Leicester University; North Runcton; Norfolk Over 50s - also a Committee member.
HS. 91 no v Hertfordshire August 1988 @ Letchford – Steve Plumb declared the innings saying to Peter, "You'll get plenty of other opportunites to get a ton." As it happened Hertfordshire had no intention of making a game of it as they set Norfolk 213 in 90 minutes plus 20 overs.
Just three Minor County games with a century partnership in each of them with Steve Plumb and a year end 49.60 average. A travesty not unlike Dave Stringer who ended his Norwich City FC career on 499 appearances.
HS. *38 v Bedfordshire May 1989 @ Swardeston*
85 no (112 balls) for Norfolk Over 50s v Northamptonshire Over 50s June 2011 – in a first wicket stand of 142 with Martin Pearce.
A classy left handed batsman wicket keeper who hit three tons in 10 innings for the Norfolk Over 50s for an average of 74.33.
A Schoolteacher at King's Lynn Academy (formerly Park High School)

STAMP, Daniel Malcolm
(b) Paddington, London 23 November 1966
Educ. – Pinewood Senior School; Felsted School
Cricket. – Felsted School; S.England Schools Under 13s; MCC Young Professionals; Munford; Dereham; Swardeston; Vauxhall Mallards; Norfolk Under 25s
HS. 81 v Durham July 1990 @ Lakenham – in the first match of the 100th Lakenham Cricket Festival
BB. 1/2 v Suffolk August 1989 @ Lakenham
HS. 27 no v MCC August 1990 @ Lakenham
HS. *73 v Lincolnshire June 1990 @ Swardeston*
The 1990 NCCC Handbook has a fine action shot of Danny on Page 38. He shared in three century partnerships with Roger Finney twice and Carl Rogers once.

TAYLOR, Stephen Kirby
(b) York 28 November 1963
Educ. – Archbishop Holgate's GS; Carnegie School of Physical Education – BA 1987
Cricket. – Archbishop Holgate's GS; Yorkshire Schools Under 15s; North Yorkshire Schools; York CC; Norwich Union; Swardeston; Barleycorns
HS. 77 v Bedfordshire July 1991 @ Lakenham
HS. 5 v MCC Young Professionals May 1993 @ Lakenham
HS. *0 v Leicestershire June 1992 @ Grace Road*
107 no for Norfolk Under 25s v Suffolk Under 25s July 1992 with 12 (4) in his only knock for them that season. His BA was in Leisure Studies and Steve is the Co-Founder of Fitness Express at Barnham Broom

TUCK, Evan Louis
(b) Fakenham, Norfolk 12 March 1944
Lives locally
Educ. – Stiffkey Village School; York St John's College
Cricket. – North Middlesex; Cromer; XL Club; Sheringham; Norfolk Over 50s; England Over 60s
HS. 0 (x2) v Lincolnshire July 1988 @ Lakenham AND v Suffolk August 1988 @ Bury St Edmunds
BB. 2/48 v Suffolk August 1988 @ Bury St Edmunds
Father of KSC (q.v)
Gresham's School Swimming Coach and an England Under 21 Gymnastics Coach. He owns Sports Spectrum Publishing Company.

1989

FINNEY, Roger John
(b) Darley Dale, Derby 2 August 1960
Lives locally
Educ. – Lady Manners School (Bakewell)
Cricket. – Derby Schools Under 13,15 & 19s; Chesterfield; MCC Groundstaff; MCC Young Professionals; North Runcton; National Association of Young Cricketers; Derbyshire; Vauxhall Mallards; Alexandrians (S.A)
HS. 125 v Durham June 1989 @ Stockton-on-Tees – awarded his county cap after an immaculate knock that followed his first inning 69. Featured in a century partnership in both innings.
BB. 5/59 v Buckinghamshire August 1992 @ Beaconsfield – he took 7 wickets in just 14 overs career wise for NCCC. These five were 'bought' off just seven overs in an attempt to force a declaration with the inclement weather winning the day.
HS. 49 v Essex (2) May 1992 @ Lakenham
HS. *53 v Devon June 1992 @ Lakenham*
Stepfather of SG Robinson (q.v)
1st class cricket – 114 matches 2,856 runs 26 catches 202 wickets
Not a heavy scorer with four tons but a compiler of sixteen fifties and only two ducks in 122 innings.
Roger had five years winter coaching in South Africa and was also the NCCC player coach during his time as well as other roles such as being the Commercial Manager. He had the cognomen 'Albert' after the famous actor. In the 1980s he was listed as being a Production Clerk and a Sports Salesman. A back injury from 1986 forced him to change from medium pace to left arm spin.

MACK, Andrew James
(b) Aylsham, Norfolk 14 January 1956
Cricket. – Surrey; Glamorgan; Skewen; Pontardawe; Metropolitan Police; Barleycorns; Minor Counties; Norfolk

Constabulary; Tas Valley; Tacolneston; Norfolk Over 50s
HS. 7 v Staffordshire August 1989 @ Lakenham
BB. 7/52 v Bedfordshire August 1989 @ Lakenham – his
left arm line and length medium pacers earned him his
County cap and his only Man-of-the-Match award.
HS. *7 no v Hertfordshire June 1991 @ Hitchin*
1st class cricket – 31 matches 102 runs 4 catches 44 wickets.
In 1978 he topped the first-class bowling averages taking 16
wickets at 12.18 each for Glamorgan.
No relation to ESP nor HP (q.v both)
4/35 for Surrey (2) v Middlesex (2) June 1976
7/39 for Glamorgan (2) v Hampshire (2) August 1979 –
claiming Mark Nicholas for a duck and adding Chris Tremlett's
dad Tim to the list. He got a wicket with his second ball for
NCCC against Northumberland in June 1989 at distant
Jesmond.

TAYLOR, Nicholas Simon
(b) Holmfirth, Yorkshire 2 June 1963
Lives California, U.S.A
Educ. – Gresham's School
Cricket. – Gresham's School; English Schools Cricket
Association; Yorkshire (Colts, Under 25s & 2nds); Surrey;
Somerset
HS. 46 v Staffordshire June 1990 @ Bignall End
BB.3/18 v Cambridgeshire August 1989 @ March
HS. *53 v Cambridgeshire June 1990 @ The Leys School - in Holt*
Cup with 4 (6) in a 31 ball knock
BB. *3/53 v Lincolnshire June 1990 @ Swardeston*
Son of K (q.v)
1st class cricket – 34 matches 180 runs 7 catches 79 wickets
6/49 for Yorkshire (2) v Surrey (2) June 1983 – including the
dismissal of Alec Stewart
46 for Yorkshire (2) v Lancashire (2) August 1983 – facing Nasir
Zaidi (q.v)
5/90 & 6/58 for Surrey (2) v Essex (2) May 1985 – with Steve
Waugh being a victim
3/38 & 5/58 & 45 for Surrey (2) v Sussex (2) September 1985
F.F. – His mother Avril is the daughter of a self employed
Textile Merchant. Nicholas experiments with abstract art
while earning his living as an interior decorator.

1990

GOODFELLOW, Professor Brian James
(b) London 31 October 1963
Educ. – Alexandra Park; York University
Cricket. – Vauxhall Mallards; Norfolk Under 25s; Oporto CC
(Portugal)
HS. 0 no (x2) v Lincolnshire August 1990 @ Lakenham
BB. 1/17 v Durham July 1990 @ Lakenham
3/44 for Norfolk Under 25s v Norwich Union Norfolk Alliance

XI May 1992 – claiming the wickets of Steve Harvey (q.v) and
Neil Fox (q.v)
He got a First in Chemistry at York University. A Professor at
Universidade de Aveiro (Portugal) and an Auxillary Professor at
CICECO (University of Aviero) with thanks for this information
to his London based parents.

ROGERS, Carl John
(b) Norwich 20 October 1970
Educ. – Reepham High School
Cricket. – Great Witchingham; Norwich CC; Swardeston;
Minor Counties; National Association Young Cricketers;
Australian Cricket Board Chairman's XI; MCC; MCC
Young Cricketers; Minor Counties Under 25s; Norfolk
Young Cricketers; Norfolk 2nds; Norfolk Select XI; 2nds of
Derbyshire, Essex, Middlesex and Sussex
HS 173 v Northumberland June 2011 @ Jesmond – 224
balls faced with 24 (4) and 4 (6)
BB. 4/23 v Suffolk August 1991 @ Lakenham – his first
bowl for Norfolk and he took two wickets with his first two
balls.
HS. 126 no v Huntingdonshire May 2005 @ Horsford
BB. 2/45 v An England XI May 1997 @ Swaffham
HS. *151 v Suffolk May 1998 @ Framlingham College*
BB. *5/30 v Devon July 2008 @ Horsford*
103 for Norfolk Young Cricketers v Suffolk August 1990
150 no for Norfolk Under 25s v Alliance XI May 1990
At club level he has scored many thousands of runs.
Awarded the Wilfred Rhodes Trophy (2005), Man-of-the-Match
seven times, Norfolk Young Player-of-the-Year (1990), Alan
Boswell Group Trophy (2005) and Clydesdale Bank Trophy
(2006). Six times dismissed in the 90s (equals Steve Goldsmith)
with Carl once being 99 not out. The most NCCC runs scored
against Suffolk with Steve Plumb a distant second – one of his
many records for the County.
How does one compare a decade or an era when bracketing
two NCCC captains to discover their relative worth or
importance? Carl has scored more runs for NCCC than the
legendary Michael Falcon in less innings and with more tons
and fifties and less ducks. His total includes a marvellous cup
tie record, which competitions were not available to MF; but
there were more Minor County matches in days gone by so
MF benefits there. MF however, most importantly, lost eleven
seasons to both World Wars. When an Oxfordshire player
queried if he had passed MF's Minor Counties total of runs he
was asked when he was going to make a start on claiming
wickets! Carl has taken a minor fraction of MF's total wickets
but has registered more catches. It has to be said that he
has had more opportunities in the slips given that MF was
constantly turning his arm. There is no comparison when it
comes to the all-rounder mantle but both men are in the top
echelons.

BUNTING, Steward James

(b) King's Lynn, Norfolk 30 August 1961

Lives King's Lynn

Educ. – King Edward VII School (King's Lynn)

Cricket. – King Edward VII School; North Runcton; Norfolk Under 25s

HS. 1 no v Durham August 1991 @ Durham

BB. 2/22 v Suffolk August 1991 @ Lakenham

Brother of RA (q.v) and Father of KJ (q.v)

44 (82) for North Runcton June 1990 batting at number 9 with 4 (6) as Mark Ellis (q.v) snapped up 8/24.

The NCCC 1988 Handbook article by Neville Cooke (q.v) on (Pages 34/ 35) lists OTHER MATCH being a Norfolk X I(Under 25s) v Leicestershire (2) with Stewart (as he is known – in his words 'among other things') taking 3/20 and scoring 31 no. Brother Rodney scored 12 and took 0/20 in the match.

The North Runcton Treasurer and Bursar at King Edward VII School and also the School's Business Manager.

ELLISON, Bruce Charles Aurelius, BSc MBA

(b) King's Lynn, Norfolk 10 December 1969

Lives Johannesburg, South Africa

Educ. – Rugby School; Durham University; Oxford University - no Blue; Dereham; University of Cape Town.

Cricket. – Oxford University; MCC Schools; Oxfordshire; Minor Counties Under 25s; Gloucestershire 2nds; Norfolk Young Amateurs; Rugby Meteors

HS 24 no v Northumberland August 1991 @ Jesmond

BB. 1/26 v Buckinghamshire August 1992 @ Beaconsfield

Cousin of England's Richard Ellison

1st class cricket – 1 match 0 runs 2 wickets

A heavy scorer at Oxfordshire evidenced a few examples below namely –

90 & 60 for Oxfordshire v Wiltshire July 1996

122 no for Oxfordshire v Cornwall July 1998

92 no for Oxfordshire v Devon July 1998

1/26 for Oxford University v Sir JP Getty's X1 May 1993 – he caught Tim Boon (q.v) and bowled England's Paul Downton. At Oxford he rescued a fellow undergraduate from the hands of a 'gun touting stalker' who had trapped his victim in her room just before Bruce wandered by and 'interceded' by taking the gun off the assailant. A Strategy Consultant with Bain & Company in London and Johannesburg. Also in the same line of work for Pyxis Capital Management and Decipher, before joining Taurus. Manager at STA (Specialist Transactions Advisors) with clients at the South African Revenue Services, as well as the broadcasting, motor manufacturing and banking industries.

FARROW, Richard Daniel Ellis

(b) Grays, Essex 31 August 1972

Lives in London

Educ. – Horsford Primary School; Hellesdon High School; Sussex University- BA (Hons) in History.

Cricket. – Horsford; Lewes CC; Sussex University; Derbyshire 2nds; Norfolk Cricket Board XI; Norfolk Young Cricketers; Dulwich; Queens Park CC (West Indies)

HS. 78 v Hertfordshire August 1992 @ Lakenham

HS. *162 v Elgin February 1994 @ Elgin nr Cape Town- no one remembers how many sixes he smote that day with many into the nearby dried up part of the lake.*

HS. *35 no v Suffolk June 1992 @ Framlingham Earl*

The Clerical Medical Investment Norfolk Young Cricketer of the Year for 1991 and 1992.

5/51 & 65 for Norfolk Young Cricketers v Hunts & Peterborough August 1990.

He continued this rich vein of form for them in 1991 with scores of 96, 92 and 99 run out.

55 for Derbyshire (2) v Lancashire (2) April 1992 with the first three batsmen on the scorecard being Carl Rogers (76), Richard and Steve Goldsmith (23).

74 no (139) for Dulwich v Sunbury August 2008 – carrying his bat.

He was part of three century Minor County partnerships in 1992 in three out of four successive matches. A superb colour picture of him adorns the cover of the NCCC 1993 Handbook. A Schoolteacher at Lyndhurst Primary School in London

GARNER, James Peter

(b) Tittleshall, Norfolk 27 January 1972

Lives in London and a 2011 NCCC Member

Educ. – Felsted School

Cricket. – Norwich CC; Horsford; Dereham; Felsted Robins; MCC (in Greece); Norfolk Young Cricketers; West Norfolk; Great Witchingham; Norfolk Under 25s

HS. 74 v Cambridgeshire June 2001 @ Saffron Walden

HS. *20 v MCC Young Cricketers April 2003 @ High Wycombe*

HS. *37 no v Northamptonshire May 2001 @ Raunds*

71 for Norwich CC v Maldon August 2002

A right handed wicket keeper with 75 NCCC career victims (56 c 19s) and who in 1991 was competing for the gloves with Doug Mattocks(q.v) and David Morrell (q.v).

LIVERMORE, Stephen John Berry

(b) Chippenham, Wiltshire 8 September 1970

Lives in Cambridge

Cricket. – Calthorpe Park; Hampshire Under 13-19s; Hampshire Club & Ground; Cove CC; Dereham; Ingham; Norwich CC; Sheffield Collegiate; Norfolk Under 25s; Derbyshire 2nds; MCC; Saffron Walden

HS. 62 no v Lincolnshire July 2000 @ Lakenham

HS. *79 v Essex Cricket Board June 1998 @ Lakenham*
89 for Norwich CC v Cambridge Granta May 2004 – with Tony Penberthy (q.v) 129 and Chris Borrett (q.v) with 61 also scoring heavily in the match for Norwich.
He played for Derbyshire 2nds at the same time as Richard Farrow (q.v). A former NCCC captain and an MCC area representative for East Anglia with him playing for the MCC in Japan (2005) and Croatia (2009). Steve had far more Cup games for Norfolk than Minor Counties matches.

MORRELL, David Mark

(b) Newport, Monmouthshire 8 October 1971
Lives in Bristol but lived in Germany for 10 years until the age of twelve.
Educ. – Prince Rupert School (Rinteln, Germany); Wayland High School; Nottingham Trent University – BA (Hons) in European Business
Cricket. – Wayland High School; Swardeston; Norfolk Under 25s
HS. 6 v Durham August 1991 @ Durham
HS. *6 v Leicestershire June 1992 @ Leicester*
An IT Programme Manager for Friends Life, who incidentally sponsor the Twenty20 Cup won by my county Hampshire in 2010.

1992

CAREY, Christopher Stephen

(b) Chelmsford, Essex 3 April 1973
Lives in Norfolk
Educ. – Aylsham High School; Paston College; De Montfort University (Bedford – BA (Hons) Business Studies with Sports Studies)
Cricket. – Cromer; Swardeston; Sheringham; Horsford; Norfolk Young Cricketers; Past Norfolk; Norfolk Cricket Board XI
HS. 72 no v Staffordshire August 2001 @ Walsall
BB. 4/60 v Staffordshire June 2000 @ Stone
HS. *50 v MCC Young Cricketers April 2003 @ High Wycombe*
BB. *1/7 v Essex (2) May 1992 @ Lakenham*
HS. *23 v Wales Minor County May 2001 @ Horsford*
BB. *2/14 v Cambridgeshire June 2000 @ Wisbech*
66 & 4/33 for Norfolk Young Cricketers v Cambridgeshire Young Cricketers July 1992
A Schoolteacher at Cromer High School taking multiple subjects.

READ, Christopher Carl

(b) East Dereham, Norfolk 13 January 1968
Lives in Norfolk
Educ. – Watton Juniors; Wymondham College

Cricket. – Watton Juniors; Wymondham College; Norfolk Schools Under 15 and 19s; Norfolk Under 25s; Norfolk Young Amateurs; Swardeston; Norfolk Alliance League XI
HS. 6 v Staffordshire July 1992 @ Norton
HS. *9 v Constantia February 1997 @ Constantia, Cape Town*
BB. *1/27 v Fish Hoek February 1997 @ Cape Town*
71 for Norfolk Young Amateurs v Cheshire Young Amateurs August 1985 - with the 1986 Handbook stating that Chris showed distinct promise as a batsman as he went on to play 22 years with Swardeston.
F.F. – A Barclays Bank Associate Director

ROWE, Stephen Arthur

(b) Norwich 28 June 1962
Lives in Norfolk
Educ. – Yarmouth GS; Norwich City College
Cricket. – Yarmouth GS; Acle; Norfolk Alliance League XI; Barleycorns; Norfolk Under 25s; Hales; Past Norfolk XI
HS. 22 v Cambridgeshire July 1992 @ Lakenham
BB. 2/31 v Bedfordshire June 1992 @ Bedford School
Steve was with Acle CC 1981-95 and spent five years with Hales as their captain and coach. He was also the Norfolk Under 16 Manager with Carl Rogers under his tutelage .He is a self-employed Oracle Database Administrator.

1993

ADAMS, David James

(b) Romford, Essex 22 September 1967
Cricket. – 2nds of Derbyshire, Somerset, Gloucestershire and Norfolk; National Association of Young Cricketers; MCC
HS. 3 no v Northumberland June 1993 @ Jesmond
BB. 2/26 v Northumberland July 1993 @ Jesmond – his only appearance saw him add valuable variety to the attack with his left-arm spin.
His brother Chris played for Derbyshire and England and his niece Georgia for Sussex.
5/103 & 40 for Gloucestershire (2) v Derbyshire (2) June 1988 – he bowled his brother on 88.
5/44 for Derby (2) v Surrey (2) June 1990
3/20 for MCC v Kenya Under 19s February 2008 in Kampala, Uganda

AMOS, Carl

(b) King's Lynn, Norfolk 30 March 1973
Lives in Norfolk
Educ. – Smithdon High School
Cricket. – Sandringham CC; North Runcton; Swardeston; Norfolk Under 25s and 2nds; Vauxhall Mallards; Norfolk Select XI; England & Wales Cricket Board; England Board XI; Minor Counties (selected but game rained off)
HS. 226 no v Lincolnshire July 1998 @ Lakenham - A

solid man who put in solid performances culminating in this NCCC record individual innings. The eighth time a double century has been achieved for the club. The score remains the highest individual innings in the Eastern Division of the M.C Championship.

BB. 1/67 v Lincolnshire July 2001 @ Horsford
HS. 107 v An International XI August 1997 @ Lakenham
HS. *130 no v Leicestershire Cricket Board June 2000 @ Oakham School*
151 no for Swardeston v Bury St Edmunds June 2004
He still jointly (of course) holds the Minor Counties record of 335 for the first wicket with Carl Rogers away to Hertfordshire set in 2002. To show his versatility he even kept wicket in an innings against Lincolnshire in July 1996. Not unnaturally he picked up the Famous Grouse Trophy (1997) and the Adnams Trophy (2000). The most potent opening partnership with Carl Rogers as they racked up 17 century stands with seven of them exceeding 150 runs. Four other lower order century stands with Carl as part of the overall 34 in which he participated. Not all success as four times he fell in the 90s. 'Ginga' is still plundering runs at club level and he works for the Biss family at the Vauxhall Holiday Park.

COLE, Adam Peter
(b) Norwich 4 May 1974
Lives in Lowestoft
Educ. – St Joseph's College (Ipswich)
Cricket. – Kirtley; Lowestoft; Barleycorns; Norfolk Under 25s; Norfolk Young Cricketers; Randwick (Australia); 2nds of Essex, Hampshire, Sussex and Worcestershire; MCC Young Cricketers; MCC; Buckinghamshire; High Wycombe; Esher
HS. 102 v Buckinghamshire August 1994 @ Marlow – as night watchman coming in at the loss of Carl Rogers for a duck and hitting 17 (4) and 1(6). Adam normally batted at nine or lower.
BB. 4/6 v Northumberland August 1994 @ Lakenham
HS. 14 no v Durban University February 1994 @ Durban, South Africa
BB. 5/29 v MCC Young Professionals May 1993 @ Lakenham
HS. *8 no v Worcestershire June 1994 @ Lakenham*
BB. *2/55 v Worcestershire June 1994 @ Lakenham*
102 for Norfolk Young Cricketers v Bedfordshire Young Cricketers July 1993- the captain leading from the front
6-5-2-6 for Buckinghamshire v Sussex Cricket Board June 1998.
6/77 for Buckinghamshire v Lincolnshire August 1998 – with Steve Plumb playing for the opposition.
Adam was the Clerical Medical Investment Group Norfolk Young Player of the Year (1993).
Table Tennis – Norfolk County Under 17s and the England no 8 at Under 14 level.
The Family Retail Business is his trade.

CROWLEY, Stephen Christopher
(b) Hillingdon, Middlesex 18 December 1961
Educ. – Thorpe GS
Cricket. – Old Catton CC; Barleycorns; Norfolk Young Amateurs; Norfolk Under 25s; CEYMS; England University Unicorns; British Police; National TSB; MCC; Norfolk Select XI
HS. 20 no v Hertfordshire June 1995 @ Hitchin
Held 7 catches and made 2 stumpings for a NCCC record on debut v Cambridgeshire June 1993 @ Wisbech. He is fourth equal with the most victims in a season with 30 (28c 2s) in 1994. 'Creepy' (his nickname) also holds the amazing record of not being dismissed in his last 13 Championship innings. He was not out in 75% of his innings for the County.
HS. 18 no v Wombats February 1994 @ Cape Town, South Africa
HS. *2 no v Bedfordshire June 1994 @ Lakenham AND 2 no v Lancashire June 1995 @ Old Trafford AND 2 v Hampshire June 1996 @ Southampton*
He worked for the TSB and is now in the Norfolk Constabulary as a Traffic Officer.

EARTHY, Mark Colin
(b) Chelmsford, Essex 15 January 1963
Lives in Norfolk
Educ. – St Martin's Comprehensive School (Brentwood)
Cricket. – St Martin's Comprehensive School; Essex Under 13,15, 19 and 2nds; Hutton CC; Parnell CC (Auckland); Ingham
HS. Did not bat in his two matches
BB. 2/0 v Buckinghamshire July 1993 @ Lakenham – wicket (stumping) with his first ball on debut; a missed stumping by James Garner off the second ball and a wicket with his fourth ball to end the innings.
3/63 & 23 for Essex (2) v Little Baddow July 1981 – with Mike Denness (England) and Neil Foster (q.v) on his side as well as the talented Paul Prichard (he hit 245 in a County Match).
Mark is a Director of a Fashion Agency.

GOLDSMITH, Stephen Clive
(b) Ashford, Kent 19 December 1964
Still lives locally
Educ. – Simon Langton GS (Canterbury)
Cricket. – Kent; Derbyshire; Minor Counties; Colne; Vauxhall Mallards; English Schools Cricket Association – to Zimbabwe; UK Upsetters – to Trinidad & Tobago; National Association of Young Cricketers; Norfolk Select XI; Lavinia, Duchess of Norfolk's XI; Essenden (Australia); Pirates CC (Durban); Culthorpe CC
HS. 200 no v Cumberland July 1993 @ Lakenham – 236 minutes, 214 balls, 31(4) 4(6) and the fifth man to reach this milestone for the County.

BB. 7/74 v Cumberland June 1998 @ Barrow-in-Furness
HS. 95 v MCC Young Cricketers April 1995 @ Postwick
BB. 5/23 v MCC Young Cricketers April 2003 @ High Wycombe
HS. *107 v Leicestershire Cricket Board June 2000 @ Oakham School*
BB. *5/42 v Shropshire August 1997 @ Lord's – in the M.C.C. Trophy Knockout Final*
1st class cricket – 75 matches 2,646 runs 37 catches 29 wickets
137 for Vauxhall Mallards v Cambridge Granta May 2004
Many roles at NCCC such as Manager, Captain and Coach and the holder of many club records. For example 'Goldy' has scored two 50s in a match on eleven occasions .Won a record 9 Man-of-the -Match awards plus the Famous Grouse Trophy (1993 & 1995) and Adnams Trophy (2002).
He still shares the NCCC record partnership for the 3rd and 4th wicket being in turn, an undefeated 290 with Roger Finney when he scored his 200 no and 195 with Carl Rogers against Hertfordshire at Lakenham in 1998. From his first wicket in County Cricket (David Gower 1987) to the present date Steve has been an effective partnership breaker and an economic asphyxiater when called upon . His aggressive wielding of the willow has put many a fielding side to the sword as the ball disappeared over the boundary ropes. An ECB Level 3 Coach with the Norfolk Cricket Board website listing Steve as Manager of the Under 15 and 17s.
F.F. – A 1988 insight into his life said that his jobs outside cricket were Bar Steward, Waiter and an Undertaker's Assistant. It was a quality publication!

HARVEY, Stephen Robert
(b) Little Snoring, Norfolk 12 July 1964
Educ. – Fakenham High School
Cricket. – Fakenham High School; Fakenham CC; Cromer; Dereham; Barleycorns; Norwich Union; Norfolk Young Cricketers; Norfolk Alliance XI; Norfolk Under 25s
HS. 46 v Northumberland August 1996 @ Jesmond
HS. 48 v MCC Young Cricketers April 1995 @ Postwick
HS. *39 v Lancashire June 1995 @ Old Trafford*
Father of BL (q.v)
83 for Norfolk Under 25s v Suffolk Under 25s May 1992 – helping the side recover from a precarious 24/4 as he topped that seasons batting averages.

LOGAN, Donald John Campbell
(b) Liverpool 2 May 1966
Lives in King's Lynn
Cricket. – North Runcton; Norfolk Under 25s; Bury St Edmunds; Norfolk 2nd XI
HS. 16 no v Hertfordshire August 1993 @ Hertford
BB. 1/30 v Bedfordshire August 1993 @ Lakenham
A right hander and a fast medium bowler who played in only

three NCCC matches at first team level.
4/39 for Norfolk Under 25s v Suffolk Under 25s June 1991.
He played for Bury St Edmunds in the East Anglian Premier League against Swardeston in 1999, the latter side fielding 8 NCCC players.

MAYNARD, John Carl
(b) Hanleys Road,Gingerland, Nevis, West Indies 18 May 1969
Cricket. – Leeward Isles; St Kitts and Nevis; Nevis Pro Team; 2nds of Derbyshire, Hampshire and Leicestershire; Camden
HS. *0 v Worcestershire June 1994 @ Fakenham* – a first ball duck caught by Graeme Hick
BB. *1/52 v Worcestershire June 1994 @ Fakenham* – he nabbed Graeme Hick's wicket.
1st class cricket – 13 matches 79 runs 4 catches 35 wickets.
There were selection problems for the pre-season 1993 friendly matches against Essex 2nds and MCC Young Professionals as Bunting and Payne reported ill and then Carey suffered a footballing injury. Their misfortune led to the inclusion of Leeward Islands opening bowler John Maynard.
4/9 for Nevis Pro Team v St Kitts July 2006 – in the Stanford Twenty20. Man-of-the-Match winning $25,000.
Nicknamed the 'Dentist' after Antiguan Zorah Barthley hooked the ball into his teeth, shattering them.
An annoyed Maynard reckoned it was the quickest ball he had ever bowled as the player nicked the one before and never walked. Probably the most famous W.I. bowler never to have played a Test missing selection to the likes of Ottis Gibson, Vasbert Drakes and Nixon McLean. Has even been a guest summariser on 2007 Test Match Special.

TIPPING, Mark Robert
(b) Norwich 27 October 1963
Lives in Norfolk
Educ. – Sprowston High School
Cricket. – Sprowston High School; Sprowston School; Barleycorns; Norwich CC; Norfolk Under 16s and 25s; Norfolk Alliance XI; Norfolk Select XI
HS. 59 v Bedfordshire July 1999 @ Lakenham
HS. 21 v Mid Norfolk Sunday Cricket League XI September 1998 @ Lakenham
HS. *36 v Dorset July 1997 @ Dean Park*
118 no for Norfolk Alliance XI v Norfolk Under 25s May 1993
58 for Norwich CC v Leicester Taverners July 2002 – with his son Jake on the same side as his father.
The 2011 Norwich CC Fixture Secretary

1994

ADAMS, Clive David
(b) King's Lynn, Norfolk 22 November 1956

Lives in North Runcton
Educ. – Alderman Catleugh High School; King's Lynn Technical School
Cricket. – Alderman Catleugh High School; Norfolk Alliance XI; Norfolk Under 15 and 19s; Midlands Under 15s; North Runcton; Norfolk Over 50s
HS. 24 no v D. Mackay's XI February 1994 @ Constantia Uitsig, South Africa
Son-in-Law to PL Mason (q.v)
Football.- King's Lynn – with Keith Rudd (q.v); Corby City; London City (Canada).
The General Manager of Foster Sports Social Club and Clive is in the Property Renting Business.
He is also the North Runcton CC Website Co-ordinator.

BLANCHETT, Ian Neale
(b) Melbourne, Australia 2 October 1975
Raised in Norfolk
Educ. – Feltwell Primary School; Downham Market High School; Methwold High School; Luton University- after 8 GSCE & 2 'A' Levels.
Cricket. – Norfolk Young Cricketers; Norfolk Under 25s; Mundford; 2nds of Essex, Middlesex, Kent and Somerset; Middlesex; Cambridgeshire; Cambridge & Godmanchester; Middlesex County Cricket League; Minor Counties Under 25s; Ealing; Sir JP Getty's XI; St Albans CC (New Zealand)
HS. 4 no v Suffolk August 1994 @ Copdock
BB. 1/10 v Bedfordshire July 1994 @ Bedford
BB. 2/41 v Essex (2) May 1995 @ Lakenham
1st class cricket – 5 matches 36 runs 2 catches 7 wickets
6/75 for Norfolk Young Cricketers v Bedfordshire Young Cricketers July 1993
5/61 & 40 for Norfolk Young Cricketers v Yorkshire Young Cricketers August 1993.
54 no for Norfolk (2) v Cambridgeshire (2) May 1994 as he topped the bowling averages.
Right arm fast medium from a height of 6' 4" he was voted Norfolk's Young Player-of-the-Year 1994.
He was doing a Health Science/Leisure Degree and was last spotted playing in the Victorian Turf Association League. Ian has also undertaken Cricket Coaching in Australia and New Zealand as well as being a player/coach for Ealing when in the UK.

GREEN, Cameron Rufus Frederick
(b) Harpley, Norfolk 25 October 1968
Lives in Stratford-upon-Avon
Educ. – Ipswich GS; University of London
Cricket. – Camden; Cambridgeshire
HS.22 v Cambridgeshire August 1994 @ Lakenham
BB. 1/28 v Northumberland August 1994 @ Lakenham
He was good enough to claim 64 wickets for Cambridgeshire

including the analysis 12-9-7-2 v Norfolk June 1987. He was stumped off the occasional bowling of Mike Atherton in 1989 playing for Cambridgeshire against Cambridge University.

HARWOOD, Paul James
(b) King's Lynn, Norfolk 16 February 1977
Lives in Norfolk
Educ. – Smithdon High School (King's Lynn)
Cricket. – Hunstanton; North Runcton; Dersingham; Norfolk Under 12,16,19s & 2nds; MCC School of Merit; England Under 17s trial; Vauxhall Mallards; Norfolk Under 25s; Swardeston; Narborough
HS. 11 no v Cumberland June 1994 @ Barrow
BB. 1/20 v Cumberland June 1994 @ Barrow
HS. 33 v Mid Norfolk Sunday Cricket League XI September 1998 @ Lakenham
BB. 4/23 v Western Province Mid Week XI February 1994 @ Cape Town, South Africa
HS. 46 v Suffolk May 1998 @ Framlingham College
111 no for Norfolk Under 16s v Bedfordhire Under 16s 1993
5/60 & 82 no for Norfolk Under 16s v Suffolk Under 16s 1993
87 for Swardeston v Bury St Edmunds August 2000
David Thomas' pen pictures of the members on Norfolk's first overseas tour (1994) said re Paul, "One of the youngsters on the tour, who I am led to believe is a very quiet young man. No doubt the experience of touring will change all that, particularly in the company of Goldie."

RUDD, Nigel Arnold
(b) Norwich 13 December 1943
Lives in Norfolk
Educ. – Norwich GS
Cricket. – Norwich GS; Norwich Wanderers; CEYMS; Norwich Cavaliers; Swardeston
HS. Did not Bat in his one game v Elgin February 1994 @ Elgin, South Africa but had 2 catches and a stumping as a replacement for Steve Crowley who was ill. The oldest ever debutant surpassing SF Charles (q.v).
Nigel gave great service to Norfolk being at various times Chairman (1992-95), Vice Chairman, Treasurer and involvement with Promotions, Sponsorship and Development. The Norwich & Coltishall Wanderers Secretary and their Junior Coaching Co-ordinator.
A Chartered Accountant (FCA) and Fellow of the ICAEW he originally trained and worked for Stoy Centre for Family Business. Nigel is now a Partner of RHP specializing in advising owner-managed and family businesses alongside personal tax and trust cases.

THOMAS, Mark Wynne
(b) Norwich 30 January 1977
Educ. – Norwich School; Nottingham University

Cricket. – Swardeston; Norfolk Under 13-16, 19 & 25s; MCC School of Merit; Norfolk Alliance XI; Leicestershire 2nds; Cambridgeshire; England Under 17 trial

HS. 41 no v Cumberland August 1999 @ Lakenham
BB. 6/31 v Hertfordshire June 1999 @ Tring
HS. 8 no v Essex (2) May 1997 @ Lakenham
BB. 2/40 v MCC Young Cricketers April 1998 @ Lakenham
HS. *31 v Oxfordshire July 1998 @ Challow & Childrey*
BB. *4/27 v Northumberland May 2008 @ Morpeth*
Son of PW (q.v) and Nephew of DR (q.v)
Although 6/31 above was his best figures in the Championship one has to mention his two days at Lakenham against Northumberland in July 1996. Match analysis of 16.1-8-17-7 with figures to die for in the first innings of 6.1-3-6-5 as the opponents slumped from 80-2 to 87-8. Shades of England v Sri Lanka (Cardiff 2011)!
The last time I compiled East Anglian Premier League figures Mark had almost 400 wickets in the competition with a best of 7/49 v Maldon in May 2002. He was also run out on the 59th ball on one occasion after amassing 130 with 12 (4) and 8 (6) – a precocious talent.
F.F. – Lawn Tennis for Norfolk Under 10 & 12s. His Uncle David has gone into print by saying, " So laid back I'm sure that one day he'll fall over." Mark has an Electrical Engineering Degree and is a Qualified Accountant (ACA).

1995

BRADSHAW, Paul John
(b) Chelmsford, Essex 1 May 1978
Lives locally
Educ. – Sprowston High School
Cricket. – Sprowston High School; Sprowston; Norfolk Under 14 & 15s; E.S.C.A; 2nds of Hampshire, Kent & Leicestershire; Norfolk Development Squad; Norfolk Select XI; Minor Counties Under 25s.
HS. 64 no v Northumberland August 2004 @ Horsford – nine years after his debut and beating his previous best from the game before.
BB. 5/13 v Suffolk July 1999 @ Lakenham – Suffolk collapsed to 14 for 7.
HS. 26 no v Alma Marist February 1997 @ Alma, South Africa
BB. 6/20 v Constantia Uitsig February 1997 @ Uitsig, South Africa
HS. *39 v Lincolnshire June 2002 @ Lincoln Lindum*
BB. *7/15 (including a hat-trick) v Hertfordshire July 2005 @ Horsford – a new record for the M.C. KO Cup.*
He hit an incredible 191 for Norfolk Under 15s versus their Suffolk counterparts.
8/39 for Vauxhall Mallards v Horsford June 2008
9-6-7-6 for Vauxhall Mallards v Halstead June 2009

'Bradders' is the undisputed Norfolk bowling King (right arm fast) in Cup ties with 124 dismissals with the nearest being Chris Brown, Steve Goldsmith, and Dave Thomas languishing with 69, 67 and 65 respectively. He invariably took out an opener in his opening burst and more often than not had three wickets per match to his name as well as captaining the side. A North Walsham High School Teacher.

CHILD, Simon Edward Harry
(b) Aldershot 5 October 1974
Lives in S.W. London
Educ. – Gresham's School; Bristol University – studying Politics (BSc)
Cricket. – Gresham's School; Norfolk Under 13-15s; Norfolk 2nds; MCC; Norwich Wanderers; Army CC; Green Jackets CC; Norfolk Young Cricketers; Combined Services; I Zingari
HS. 3 v Lincolnshire July 1995 @ Bourne – a late replacement for the injured Steve Crowley with the 1996 Handbook stating that he could be pleased with his debut.
Simon scored 1,132 runs for Gresham's School to include a ton in 1993 against O.G.S. His finest day was surely for I Zingari versus Sir JP Getty's XI in June 2000. Graham Gooch scored 104 with Simon replying with 73 not out (87 balls, 87 minutes and 10 (4) – and he was facing England Test star John Lever. A Captain in the Royal Green Jackets and now a Research Consultant.

FOSTER, Neil Alan
(b) Colchester, Essex 6 May 1962
Lives in Essex
Educ. – Broomgrove Infant & Junior School; Philip Morant Comprehensive School; University of Salford; Colchester Institute.
Cricket. – Mistley CC; Wivenhoe; Essex Schools, 2nds, Under 25s; Essex; MCC; Norfolk Select XI; Transvaal (S.A); Glenorchy (Tasmania); National Cricketers Association; Northamptonshire 2nds; Duke of Norfolk's XI; Sir JP Getty's XI; MCC; England Young Cricketers; England XI; Rest of the World XI; England – 29 Tests and claiming 88 wickets.
HS. 72 v Hertfordshire June 1995 @ Hitchin – on Championship debut with some fiery hitting and two wickets in his first over.
BB. 4/22 v Bedfordshire July 1995 @ Lakenham – 'Fozzy' on his way to 29 Championship wickets in the season
HS. 5 no v Rest of the World X1 August 1996 @ Lakenham
BB. 2/45 v MCC Young Cricketers April 1995 @ Postwick
HS. *36 v Lancashire June 1995 @ Old Trafford*
BB. *2/55 v Herefordshire June 1995 @ Brockhampton*
8/107 for England v Pakistan July 1987
1st class cricket – 230 matches 4,343 runs 116 catches 908 wickets
He also had 48 One Day Internationals taking 59 wickets.

Summoned from school for a County debut at Ilford versus Kent (the day after his 18th birthday) with his first ball going for 4 wides – he improved leaps and bounds after that by getting out England players Bob Woolmer and Chris Tavare in the match. He hit hard and straight, had an upright bowling action and a strong, low return in the field.

Football – trials with Colchester United and Ipswich Town but his spinal problem put paid to this career.

Plagued by injury with seven knee operations and a stress fracture in two vertebrae near the base of his spine which condition resulted in the insertion of 6 inch metal plates secured by screws.

He graduated June 2003 with an Honours Degree in Physiotherapy awarded by Hertfordshire University. A member of the SCP and OCPPP (both Chartered Societies in Physiotherapy). An Essex CCC Physiotherapist and he runs clinics in East Bergholt, Clacton-on- Sea and Colchester.

POWELL, Mark Geoffrey

(b) Romford, Essex 5 August 1972
Lives in West London
Educ. – St Thomas' Church of England School; Brentwood County High School; Southampton Institute of Higher Education
Cricket. – Brookweald; Leigh-on-Sea; Vauxhall Mallards; Shenfield; Essex Cricket Board XI; Essex 2nds; Leicestershire 2nds; Minor Counties Under 25s and Seniors
HS. 49 no v Hertfordshire August 1996 @ Lakenham
BB. 6/69 v Staffordshire August 1995 @ Lakenham
HS. 4 v Rest of the World X1 August 1996 @ Lakenham
BB. 3/32 v MCC Young Cricketers April 1995 @ Postwick
HS. *37 v Hampshire June 1996 @ Southampton – put on 99 with Neil Fox (q.v) for the sixth wicket.*
BB. *1/43 v Staffordshire May 1996 @ Walsall*
6/67 for Essex (2) v Warwickshire (2) June 1993
His younger brother John has played for Essex and England 'A' and Under 19s. Mark played in the same Essex second eleven as Don Topley (q.v)
A Qualified Chartered Surveyor –BA (Hons) MRICS Dip IPF who has his own Property Consultancy Business in London's West End.

SAGGERS, Martin John

(b) King's Lynn, Norfolk 23 May 1972
Lives in Kent
Educ. – Springwood High School; Huddersfield University - studying Architecture
Cricket. – Runcton; Durham; Kent; MCC; Halifax; Essex; Minor Counties Under 25s; Norfolk 2nds; Leicestershire 2nds; Derbyshire 2nds; Tunbridge Wells; South Northumberland; Beckenham; Bickley Park; Blackheath; Hartley Country Club (S.A.); Randburg (S.A.); England – 3 Tests

HS. 25 v Buckinghamshire July 1995 @ Lakenham
BB. 3/62 v Bedfordshire July 1995 @ Lakenham
BB. 2/29 v Essex (2) May 1996 @ Lakenham
HS. *2 v Staffordshire May 1996 @ Walsall*
BB. *1/31 v Staffordshire May 1996 @ Walsall*
5/29 & 30 for Norfolk (2) v Suffolk (2) July 1995
1st class cricket – 119 matches 1,165 runs 27 catches 415 wickets

The Country's highest first class wicket taker in 2002 with 83 and he once had 5 men out in 6 balls playing for Randburg. He was the forgotten man of England's glorious 2004 summer run. He took a wicket (Mark Richardson) with his first ball in a Test Match in England. A late bloomer as he did not receive any cricket coaching until he was about sixteen – Norfolk have had 16 sixteen year olds play a first team game for them. The life of a fast bowler is invariably about injuries and Martin has had his share with knee, hamstrings, groins and tears disrupting his career. Now a first class Umpire he hopes to be able to travel the world as a Test Match Umpire.

TUFTS, Ian James Peter

(b) Norwich 14 December 1972
Lives in Norfolk but works in London
Educ. – Hingham Primary School; Town Close House School; Wymondham College; Norwich City College; Anglia Ruskin University – studying Business & Economics –BA (Hons)
Cricket. – Town Close House School; Hingham CC; Hardingham; Swardeston; Ingham; Norwich CC; Norfolk Under 25s; Norfolk Young Cricketers
HS. 20 v Cumberland June 2000 @ Kendal – he showed determination against a hostile attack.
HS. 53 no v Constantia Uitsig February 1997 @ Constantia Uitsig, South Africa
HS. *10 v Cambridgeshire June 2000 @ Wisbech*
Amazingly Ian's eleven NCCC's games were all away fixtures. A successful 1992 season for the NYC saw him and Carl Amos dominate proceedings with useful scores culminating in Ian being given the County Award as the player who had most influence on the younger players, and for his fielding and captaincy and he became a heavy scorer in East Anglian Premier League matches. Ian is a Regional Sales Manager for the Insurance Brokers Willis.

WHITE, Shaun Neil

(b) Norwich 15 November 1971
Cricket. – Acle; Barleycorns; Norfolk Young Cricketers; Norfolk Under 25s
HS. 7 v Bedfordshire August 1997 @ Lakenham
BB. 4/65 v Hertfordshire July 1997 @ Radlett
HS. 34 no v Western Province February 1997 @ Impala Park, South Africa

BB. 4/24 v Alma Marist February 1997 @ Cape Town, South Africa

A remarkable debut as he was stuck for 32 off one over 5 (6) and 1 (2) by Hertfordshire's Fletcher who hit 115 with (8 (4) & 7 (6) - at least it was in Hitchin and not at Lakenham. More importantly Shaun and Steve Crowley, as the last wicket pair, then batted out the last nine overs for a draw

He worked for the Ministry of Ag and Fish and he transferred in his job to Yorkshire.

1996

BAILEY, Gary Louis
(b) Norwich 27 July 1966
Lives in Perth, Australia
Educ. –St Williams Primary School; Thorpe St Andrew School; Norwich City College; Edith Cowan University (Western Australia)
Cricket. – Thorpe; Vauxhall Mallards; Norfolk Select XI; Norfolk 2nds; Swanbourne CC (Australia)
HS. 16 v Staffordshire June 1996 @ Cannock
BB. 2/53 v Cumberland June 1996 @ Millom
HS. 10 v Essex XI September 1996 @ Lakenham
BB. 3/22 v MCC Young Cricketers April 1998 @ Lakenham
HS. *2 no v Durham June 1998 @ Lakenham*
A BSc Hons in Business Information Systems and a Diploma in Education gained in Perth.
A Schoolteacher (Head of Years 7and 8) at Emmanuel Catholic College in Perth. A terrific picture appeared recently in a local Norwich paper of his two sons (Sam and Max) with Stan Biss' son Alfie all posing in their Norwich City shirts on Fremantle Beach on Christmas Day.

BLINCOE, Andrew Mark
(b) Norwich 27 July 1977
Lives locally
Educ. – Norwich GS; Nottingham University – studying Law
Cricket. – Norwich GS; Swardeston; Norfolk Young Cricketers; Norfolk 2nds; Minor Counties; Milhillians; Hertfordshire League XI; Constantia Uitsig (S.A) – as a substitute fielder.
HS. 15 no v Koeberg February 1997 @ Koeberg, South Africa
BB. 2/11 v Cape Town February 1997 @ Plumstead, South Africa – he was one of 5 Swardeston players on the tour.
Brother of CP (q.v. Curio Corner)
93 no for Milhillians v Sawbridgeworth June 2004
5/47 for Milhillians v Stevenage July 2004
The Norfolk Young Cricketers 1995 Player-of-the-Year with his best return being 6/75 v Essex YC July 1995 at Old Buckenham bowling his off spinners.
He obtained BA (Hons) PgDL LPC and is a Lawyer Investment

Banker for RBS specializing in the Secured Debts Markets

BOON, Timothy James
(b) Balby, Doncaster 1 November 1961
Educ. – Mill Lane Primary; Edlington Comprehensive School; Doncaster Art School; Peter Van School of Business
Cricket. – Warmsworth; Farsley; MCC Schools; Leicestershire; Old Hararians (Zimbabwe); KwaZulu Natal (S.A); Pirates CC (Durban); England Young Cricketers; Ceylon CC
HS. 116 no v Northumberland July 1996 @ Lakenham
BB. 1/20 v Buckinghamshire july 1995 @ High Wycombe
HS. 68 no v Essex (2) May 1996 @ Lakenham
BB. 3/19 v Rest of the World X1 August 1996 @ Lakenham
HS. *75 v Northumberland June 1997 @ Jesmond*
BB. *1/63 v Hampshire June 1996 @ Southampton*
1st class cricket – 248 matches 11,820 runs 124 catches 11 wickets and another 3,602 runs in 173 One Day games. A fabulous debut season with 902 Championship runs (the sixth highest total by a NCCC man) and the Famous Grouse Trophy was his reward. In 10 matches he plundered 4 (100) and 3 (50). He shared seven century stands in 1996 with three of them coming in the one game v Buckinghamshire. He hit 10 centuries for Leicestershire 2nds with a top score of 170 v Nottinghamshire August 1992. In one spell of fourteen innings for them he scored two tons and nine fifties. In his early days he worked for Leicester Dyers and also sold promotional leisure-wear. 'Ted Moon' (he admits to it) has had cricket coaching appointments with Vauxhall Mallards and Leicestershire CCC (2006-10) . Now the England Under 19 coach and a video analyst.
F.F. – Missed the 1985 season as he suffered a broken leg in a car crash in South Africa. Once had a 16 inch nail removed from his body (don't ask).

BOYDEN, Matthew Kavan Leslie
(b) King's Lynn, Norfolk 24 February 1979
Lives in Victoria, Australia
Educ. – Methwold High School; Downham Market HS
Cricket. – Swardeston; Norfolk Under 13s; English Cricket Board XI; Mornington CC (Australia)
HS. 8 no v Cambridgeshire August 1996 @Lakenham
He holds the NCCC Championship wicket keeping record for dismissals namely 36 (31c 5s) in 1997, eight catches against Suffolk alone to win the Man-of-the- Match Award from Adjudicator Terry Allcock (q.v.).
HS. 32 v Mid Norfolk Cricket League XI September 1998 @ Lakenham
BB. 1/29 v Mid Norfolk Cricket League XI September 1998 @ Lakenham
HS. *8 no v Warwickshire June 1997 @Edgbaston*

116 no for Mornington (3) v Rye February 2004 – in a club record 8th wicket stand of 155

FOWLER, Graeme

(b) Accrington, Lancashire 20 April 1957
Educ. – Accrington GS; Bede College; Durham University
Cricket. – Accrington GS; Accrington; Rawtenshall; MCC Schools; Lancashire Under 25s; England Schools Cricket Association; National Association Young Cricketers; Lancashire; Scarborough (Australia); Perth (Australia); Western Australia; Tasmania (Australia); MCC; Durham; International XI; England Young Cricketers; DB Close's XI; England XI; World XI; Lavinia, Duchess of Norfolk's XI; Norfolk Select XI; England – 21Tests
HS. 5 v Rest of the World X1 August 1996 @ Lakenham- I have classified it as a first team friendly and worthy of mention. The scorecard appeared in the NCCC 1997 Handbook
201 for England v India January 1985 in Madras – with Neil Foster (q.v) having match figures of 11/163.
1st class cricket – 292 matches 16,663 runs 152 catches and 5 stumpings 10 wickets
One Day Internationals – 26 matches 744 runs 4 catches and 2 stumpings
He did not play cricket until he was eleven and when aged fifteen he was the youngest opener in the Lancashire League. The only batter to score two tons in a match with the aid of a runner throughout in a remarkable game for Lancashire against Warwickshire at Southport in July 1982. There were 1,274 runs scored for just 20 wickets with Warwickshire's Alvin Kallicharran (230no) and Geoff Humpage (254) sharing a fourth wicket stand of 470. Graeme and his best friend David Lloyd knocked the runs off in an unbroken first wicket stand of 226. In a contrived game in 1983 against Leicestershire he hit sixes off of ten consecutive balls that he faced as he raced to a century. Gower and Whitaker had bowled 'filth' as their combined 17 overs went for 189 runs.
A neat, jaunty left hander and a fine fielder as befits his profession of PE Teacher. Latterly a Senior Cricket Coach at Durham University and a Coach for Durham Academy. Has also tried radio broadcasting with Henry Blofeld (q.v) with his 1991 Lancashire Benefit Fund reaching £152,885.

LARKINS, Wayne

(b) Roxton, Bedfordshire 22 November 1953
Educ. – Bushmead Primary School; Huntingdon School
Cricket. – Bedford Town; Bedfordshire; Leamington; Bunbury; Huntingdonshire; Northamptonshire; Eastern Province (S.A); MCC; Durham; Young England; Minor Counties; Scarborough Festival Presidents XI; Sydney University; DB Close's XI; England Masters; International XI; DH Robin's XI; TN Pearce's XI; Cricket Association of Bengal

Overseas XI; Norfolk Select XI; Test & County Cricket Board XI; England – 13 Tests
HS. 15 v Rest of the World X1 August 1996 @ Lakenham – I have classified it as a first team friendly and worthy of a mention. The scorecard appeared in the NCCC 1997 Handbook
4/37 (incl a hat trick) for Northamptonshire v Combined Universities May 1980 in the Benson & Hedges Cup.
252 for Northamptonshire v Glamorgan August 1983
1st class cricket – 482 matches 27,142 runs 306 catches 42 wickets plus 13 Tests 493 runs 8 catches.
One Day Internationals 25 matches 591 runs 8 catches
Wayne played on the disapproved-of South African Tour in March 1982 which action induced a three year Test Match ban for him.
Football for Buckingham Town and on Notts County books at one time
F.F. – With Peter Willey, received 2,016 pints of beer (seven barrels) from a Northampton Brewery
as a reward for their efforts in Australia in 1979/80. His Autobiography is entitled 'A False Stroke of Genius'.

NEWMAN, Paul Geoffrey

(b) Evington, Leicester 10 January 1959
Educ. – Alderman Newton's GS
Cricket. – Alderman Newton's GS; Waverly CC; Clarendon Park; Hinckley Town; Cheadle; Staffordshire; English Counties X1; Queensland Cricket Association Colts XI (Australia); Cannock & Rugeley; Minor Counties; Ockbrook & Borrowash; Cannock; Walsall; Wolverhampton; Oldhill; Barleycorns; Norwich CC; Horsford; Acle; Derbyshire; MCC; Leicestershire 2nds; Leicestershire Club & Ground; Durham; Horsford Over 50s; Old Collegians (S.A); Pietermaritzburg (S.A); Test & County Cricket Board XI; Norfolk Select XI; Past Norfolk
HS. 55 no v Bedfordshire July 1999 @ Lakenham
BB. 6/31 v Cumberland June 2000 @ Kendal
HS. 39 v Holland August 1997 @ Lakenham
BB. 7/14 v Suffolk April 2000 @ Lakenham
HS. *46 no v Suffolk May 1998 @ Framlingham College*
BB. *4/23 v Warwickshire June 1997 @ Edgbaston*
1st class cricket – 135 matches 2,160 runs 37 catches 315 wickets with his best being 115 v Leicestershire (1985) and 8/29 v Yorkshire (1988) out performing Michael Holding his new ball partner. The 'Judge' was at Derbyshire with Roger Finney (q.v). He won the Commercial Union Under 23 Bowling Award in 1981 and the Whitbread Scholarship to Brisbane, Australia 1981/82. A NCCC Coach and Manager as well as Captain (1996-2002) winning 4 KO Cups and a Championship. An ECB Level 3 Coach he divided his time between being the Acle CC player/coach; Norwich & Coltishall Wanderers coach plus the Town Close House School coach.

F.F. – The nickname 'Judge' evolved from 'Judge Roy Bean' a western film starring actor Paul Newman. The author associates this cognomen more with Robin Smith (England & Hampshire) so given to him for his crinkly 'judge's wig' hair

ROGERS, Dennis Bruce

(b) Lower Hutt, New Zealand 28 February 1971
Educ. – Eastern Hutt Primary School; Hutt Valley Intermediates; Hutt Valley High School
Came to England in 1991
Cricket. – Dpuni Cambridge (N.Z); Riverside (N.Z); Carrow; Barleycorns; Ingham; Martham; Great Witchingham; Norfolk Alliance League XI; Norfolk 2nds
HS. 33 v Constantia February 1997 @ Constantia, South Africa
BB. 1/26 v Cape Town February 1997 @ Plumstead, South Africa
95 for Great Witchingham v Swardeston (2) August 2004
4/13 for Great Witchingham v Swardeston (2) July 2005
An EDP Production Manager

TUCK, Kieron Spencer Clive

(b) Edgware, London 15 December 1972
Lives in Norfolk
Educ. – Gresham's School; Loughborough University – studying PE/Sports Science (BSc)
Cricket. – Cromer; Swardeston; Norfolk Alliance League XI; Somerset West (S.A); Reigate Priory
HS. Did not Bat nor Bowl in his one match versus Buckinghamshire July 1996 @ High Wycombe – a match in which Norfolk lost just 2 wickets in scoring 390 runs to massacre their opponents by 9 wickets.
Son of EL (qv)
Kieron is the Norfolk Cricket Board Development Manager and has had great success in the last 12 months in among other tasks helping clubs to gain funding for various improvement projects.

WARD, Michael John Paul

(b) Oldham, Lancashire 12 September 1971
Lives in Bolton
Cricket. – Lancashire; Barleycorns
HS. 47 v Staffordshire June 1996 @Lakenham
HS. *0 v Staffordshire May 1996 @ Walsall AND 0 v Hampshire June 1996 @ Southampton*
47 for Lancashire (2) v Derbyshire (2) May 1991 – on as a 2nd day replacement for NJ Speak with day one rained off.
3/38 for Lancashire (2) v Nottinghamshire (2) July 1991 – in the Bain Clarkson Trophy
1st class cricket – 1 match v Oxford University. Did not bat and 2-0-6-0 for his off spin bowling

1997

ADAMS, James Clive

(b) Port Maria, St Mary, Jamaica 9 January 1968
Educ. – Jamaica College (Kingston)
Cricket. – Jamaica Under 19s; Nottinghamshire; MCC; Free State; Berkshire; Wiltshire; West Indies 'A''B' & Under 23s; West Indies Young Cricketers; West Indies Board XI; University of West Indies Chancellor's XI; Scarborough Festival President's XI; Blaydon; Jamaica; Rest of the World XI; CS Cowdrey's XI; Northumberland President's XI; Tesco International XI; Duke of Norfolk's XI; Canada 'A'; TMB Rice's XI; PCA Master's XI; West Indies Masters; Lashing's World XI; Dunstall; Norfolk Select X1; West Indies – 54 Tests
HS. 35 no v International X1 August 1997 @ Lakenham – I have classified it as a first team friendly and worthy of mention. The scorecard appeared in the 1998 NCCC Handbook
5/17 for West Indies v New Zealand April 1996
208 no for West Indies v New Zealand April 1996
1st class cricket – 202 matches 11,234 runs 178 catches 103 wickets.
3,012 runs for his Country with 6 tons. After 12 test matches he had scored 1,132 runs at an average of nearly 87 but fell away as the years passed. A steady left hander, useful spinner, good gully fielder and an occasional wicket keeper the job he undertook for Norfolk in the friendly above.
The 2006 West Indies Under 19 Manager and latterly the President of Federation of International Cricketers' Associations. A frequent Sky Sports Commentator and the Technical Director of the Jamaican Development Programme
F.F. – The son of a pair of Doctors

ADAMS, Nicholas Jack

(b) Bedford 1 March 1967
Educ. – Kimbolton School
Cricket. – Waresley; Huntingdon & District CC; Norfolk Alliance League XI; National Association of Young Cricketers; Horsford; Grasshoppers; Cambridge Granta; Cambridge St Giles; Cambridgeshire; Minor Counties; Essex Club & Ground; Huntingdonshire; 2nds of Leicestershire, Durham & Essex
HS. 16 v Northumberland June 1997 @ Jesmond
HS. 12 no v MCC Young Cricketers April 1997 @ Dereham
BB. 1/7 v Essex (2) May 1997 @ Lakenham
HS. *16 v Wiltshire June 1997 @ Corsham AND 16 v Northumberland June 1997 @ Jesmond*
He played for the Minor Counties against Pakistanis (1992) and Australians (1993).
66 for Durham (2) v Worcestershire (2) September 1992
82 games for Cambridgeshire scoring a healthy 3,347 runs.

HARRIS, Andrew James

(b) Ashton under Lyne, Lancashire 26 June 1963

Educ. – Hadfield Comprehensive School; Glossopdale Community College

Cricket. – Ockbrook & Borrowash; National Association Young Cricketers; Derbyshire; Nottinghamshire; Gloucestershire; Worcestershire; Leicestershire; England 'A'; Victory University (N.Z); Ginninderra West Belconnen (Australia)

HS. Did not Bat v International X1 August 1997 @ Lakenham – with the same comment as that in JC Adams entry.

BB. 1/60 v International X1 August 1997 @ Lakenham
1st class cricket – 147 matches 1,253 runs 38 catches 451 wickets
Only (at the time) the third player to be given out 'timed out' in April 2003 against Durham University.
As the last man in he limped (had a groin strain) to the wicket and the decision meant that Chris Read was left stranded on 94. Part of the Nottinghamshire County Championship winning side in 2005 with 47 wickets which included 6/76 to dismiss Kent to clinch the title.
Appointed Derbyshire's 2nds Coach in January 2011 – over eleven years after he had left the County.

HARRIS, Chris Zinzan

(b) Christchurch, New Zealand 20 November 1969

Cricket. – Canterbury; Gloucestershire; Derbyshire; Southern Rocks; New Zealand Emerging Players; New Zealand Board XI; Southern Conference; South Island; New Zealand 'A'; New Zealand Young Cricketers; New Zealand Academy; Ramsbottom; Rishton; Enfield; Haslingden; Nelson; Bacup; Hyderabad Heroes; ICL World XI; Bromley; M-Net Invitation XI; Rest of the World XI; CS Cowdrey's XI; Tesco International XI; Lashings World XI; World Masters; MCC; Players; Norfolk Select XI; New Zealand – 23 Tests

HS. Did not Bat v International X1 August 1997 @ Lakenham – see JC Adams entry for explanation of this match

BB. 1/38 v International X1 August 1997 @ Lakenham – he had Tom Moody stumped by Jimmy Adams.
He toured the world and played in such diverse places as the Lancashire League, Kent Premier League and the Indian Cricket League.
1st class cricket 131 matches 7,377 runs 14 catches 160 wickets
A staggering 250 One Day Internationals scoring a fine 4,739 runs plus he took 203 wickets and held 96 catches. The New Zealand Cricket Almanack Player-of-the-Year 1997. He resembled a weekend cricketer with his appearance of bald pate and long sideburns and his wobbly seamers but he got wickets. A superb fielder and forever pigeon- holed as a limited-overs specialist. Sanath Jayasuriya once hit 30 off an over of

his but few players mastered his mixture of slow speed and spinners. Became more involved with the indoor version of the game in New Zealand principally coaching Canterbury's Youth team. The father of twins in late 2009 but he found time to appear at Harare Sports Club for Southern Rocks (Brian Lara on board) in the Stanbic Bank Twenty20 Cup for 2010/11.

JEFFERSON, William Ingleby

(b) Derby 25 October 1979

Educ. – Beeston Hall School; Oundle School; Durham University (St Hilda and St Bede Colleges)

Cricket. – Oundle Rovers; Horsford; Norfolk Under 13,14 &15s; Norfolk 2nds; Norfolk Young Cricketers; Essex Club & Ground; Durham University Centre of Cricketing Excellence; British Universities; Young Peoples CC (S.A); South Park (Australia); Papatoetoe (N.Z); Loughton; Essex; Northamptonshire 2nds; Nottinghamshire; Kimberley Institute; Leicestershire

HS. 20 v Holland August 1997 @ Lakenham
Son of RI (q.v) and Grandson of Julian (Army & Combined Services)
222 for Essex v Hampshire August 2004 – up against Shane Warne.
303 no for Essex (2) v MCC Young Cricketers August 2005 – 100 off 145 balls, 200 off 266 and 300 off 376 balls in 449 minutes .Batted on all 3 days being 21 no (Close day 1), 266 no (Close Day2).
1st class cricket (to 06/06/11) – 109 matches 6,623 runs 114 catches 1 wicket
Started playing cricket at about age six with his dad but played seven sports until he was fourteen.
He scored 489 runs in seven innings for Norfolk Under 13s and continued improving in each successive year. Will had a gap year in Cape Town when 20 and had a disc problem which necessitated an operation. His left leg is 14mm longer than his right but a built up shoe has helped alleviate the difficulty. He is 6 feet 10 inches in height (or 2.08 metres).

MOYSER, Robert Alan

(b) Ipswich 24 October 1977
Lives in Leeds

Educ. – Loughborough University

Cricket. – Stowmarket Under 15s; Minor Counties Under 25s; Vauxhall Mallards; Norfolk Young Cricketers; Norfolk XI; Vauxhall Mallards Select XI; Sheffield Collegiate

HS. 75 no v Cambridgeshire August 1998 @ Lakenham
BB. 1/25 v Bedfordshire August 1998 @ Dunstable
HS. 28 v Mid Norfolk Sunday league X1 September 1998 @ Lakenham
HS. *41 v Oxfordshire July 1998 @ Challow and Childrey*
90 no for Norfolk Young Cricketers v Cambridgeshire Young Cricketers August 1995

107 no for Norfolk Young Cricketers v West of Scotland August 1995 – voted Norfolk Young Player-of-the-Year
99 for Norfolk Young Cricketers v Suffolk Young Cricketers August 1996
59 for Sheffield Collegiate v Sheffield United May 2007
In the Vauxhall Mallards side alongside Carl Amos, Gary Bailey, Paul Bradshaw, Steve Goldsmith and Luke Newton

VAN ONSELEN, David
(b) Johannesburg, South Africa 14 October 1975
Lives in Johannesburg
Educ. – Michaelhouse (Balgowan); University of Natal – Bachelor of Social Science and Business Management
Cricket. – Natal Schools; Natal Under 19s; Natal B; Barleycorns; Norfolk Select X1
HS. 23 v An England XI May 1997 @ Swaffham - he replaced Tim Boon in the side
David worked for PruHealth and PruProject (a joint venture with Prudential in the UK). He is now the Franchise Director of Discovery Holdings Pty.

WALKER, James Ross
(b) Norwich 4 March 1981
Educ. – Wymondham College
Cricket.- Norfolk Under 17s; Swardeston; Northamptonshire 2nds; Horsford; Norfolk Cricket Board XI
HS.67 v Cumberland August 2002 @ Horsford
HS. 27 v MCC Young Cricketers April 2003 @ High Wycombe
HS. 76 v Holland August 2001 @ Horsford – in a 2nd wicket stand of 180 with Carl Rogers as Norfolk won by virtue of losing fewer wickets in a tied match
In a friendly match against Holland at Lakenham on 1 August 1997 he had 5 catches, a stumping and involved in a run out as he took the role of occasional wicket keeper for one day games.
148 for Norfolk Under 17s v Holland Under 17s in 1998 at Woodbridge School.

1998

FERLEY, Robert Steven
(b) Norwich 4 February 1982
Lives in Kent
Educ.- King Edward VII High School; Sutton Valence School; Durham University (Grey College) - studying Sports Science
Cricket.- Norfolk Under 12-17s; Norfolk Select XI; Durham University Centre of Excellence; North Runcton; Dersingham; Norwich Wanderers; Kent; Ashford; Folkestone; Bromley; Nottinghamshire; Sir JP Getty's XI; Leicestershire 2nds; England Under 19s; British Universities; Retford; Plumtree; Cranleigh
HS. Did not Bat in his one game v Suffolk August 1998

@ **Mildenhall** – the ninth youngest NCCC Minor Counties debutant with credit for a run out from a direct throw.
1st class cricket – 34 matches 650 runs 10 catches 66 wickets
Son of Tim – Norfolk Over 50s and a career with Hunstanton, Norwich Wanderers and Carrow.
42 no for Norfolk Under 12s v Essex Under 12s in 1994. Rob was praised for his slow left arm bowling for the Under 13s and was the Under 14s captain.
5/62 for Norfolk Cricket Board XI v Essex Under 19s July 1998 – off a marathon 37 overs.
England Under 19s for 2 matches 96 runs 1 catch 5 wickets in India and with the British Universities to South Africa. Norwich & Coltishall Wanderers session coaching (8 -15 year olds) and presently player coach for Cranleigh CC.
F.F. – Founder of My Cricket Professional – a website designed to help cricketers develop their game.

HERR, Kenneth
Cricket. – Barleycorns; Brooke; Vauxhall Mallards; Norfolk Alliance League XI; Norfolk XI
HS. 7 no v Mid Norfolk Sunday Cricket league XI September 1998 @ Lakenham.
The ginger haired wicket keeper (with two catches) was the only non full county player for the match played to commemorate the 100th season of the Mid Sunday Cricket League. The scorecard appears in the NCCC 1999 Handbook.
F.F. – Cannot trace his whereabouts despite almost everyone having a colourful story regarding Ken.

1999

COPPIN, Wendell Ricardo
(b) Barbados 8 August 1966
Educ. – St Michael's Secondary School (Barbados); Wisbech GS
Cricket. – Barbados; YMPC; West Indies Young Cricketers; Hampshire 2nds; Bunbury CC; Colne
HS. 63 v MCC Young Cricketers April 1999 @ Shenley Park – while awaiting confirmation of his qualification for County cricket.
BB. 3/29 v MCC Young Cricketers April 1999 @ Shenley Park
HS. 2 v Surrey Cricket Board May 1999 @ Cheam
BB. 1/36 v Surrey Cricket Board May 1999 @ Cheam – took the wicket of Michael Carberry who would play for England.
6/36 for West Indies Young Cricketers v England Young Cricketers February 1985 – Jimmy Adams (q.v) scored 105 for his side.
59 for Barbados Under 19s v Jamaica Under 19s August 1985
55 for Colne v Rawtenshall September 1992
Initially a Cricket Master at Wisbech GS when he was in the U.K. He became the Barbados Development Manager and he worked for the West Indies National Sports Council and is now

on the West Indies Cricket Board as a Senior Course Instructor.

F.F. – When he was playing for Bunbury CC it was reckoned that Wendell wore the brightest socks in the business.

2000

ALLEN, John Edward
(b) Norwich 13 July 1981
Educ. – Salhouse Primary School; Hillside Avenue School; Wymondham College
Cricket. – Ashmanhaugh; Vauxhall Mallards; Norfolk 2nds
HS. Did not Bat v MCC Young Cricketers April 2000 @ Lakenham - this his one friendly game although he had bowled 6 overs
4/42 for Norfolk (2) v Essex Under 19s July 1999
On a Millfield Sports Academy two week course and he was offered a trial with Somerset but the distance from home was too big a hurdle. John played football for Wroxham and is a Chef by trade.

BORRETT, Christopher Richard
(b) North Walsham, Norfolk 2 December 1979
Educ. – Langley School; Harper Adams University College
Cricket. – Norwich CC; Norfolk 2nds; MCC
HS. 111 v Lincolnshire August 2004 @ Horsford
BB. 4/32 v Northumberland July 2007 @ Horsford
HS. 48 v MCC Young Cricketers April 2011 @ Horsford
BB. 3/30 v MCC Young Cricketers May 2004@ Horsford
HS. *128 no v Dorset June 2004 @ Dean Park*
BB. *4/22 v Leicestershire Cricket Board July 2001 @ Horsford*
Son of PC (q.v), Brother of Andrew (NCCC Scorer), Grandson of Jack (NCCC President 1989/1990)
153 for Norwich CC v Clacton-on-Sea June 2008 and as at 06/06/11 he had plundered 5,736 runs for them.
Shared eight century partnerships in the Norfolk cause and presently holds the 6th & 8th wicket records total for the county at Horsford (Manor Park).The Norwich CC Chairman of Cricket and as a player in 2009 the club were League Runners-Up, won NACO Invitation Cup, won Norfolk 20/20 Cup and were the Carter Cup losing finalists. Rugby Union for North Walsham. He missed NCCCs 2010 pre-season friendlies as he was stuck in Malaga because of the Icelandic Volcano Ash problem with regard to taking plane journeys.
F.F. – Chris undertook a sponsored bike ride in April 2011 from Land's End to John O'Groats to raise money for the Big C Cancer Charity. An Agricultural Merchant.

CLARKE, Andrew Russell
(b) Patcham, Sussex 23 December 1961
Lives in Buckinghamshire
Educ. – Longhill High School
Cricket. – Sussex; Buckinghamshire; Derbyshire 2nds;

Lavinia, Duchess of Norfolk's X1; Bignall End
HS. 3 v Cambridgeshire July 2000 @ Lakenham - I put the month in which the game started. This match was not completed until August!
BB. 5/48 v Cambridgeshire July 2000 @ Lakenham
BB. 3/40 v MCC Young Cricketers April 2000 @ Lakenham
HS. *0 no v Dorset May 2000 @ Bournemouth AND 0 v Cheshire August 2000 @ Lakenham*
BB. *3/25 v Surrey Cricket Board July 2000 @ Lakenham*
1st class cricket – 26 matches 406 runs 7 catches 53 wickets
4/29 & 5/82 for Sussex (2) v Essex (2) September 1987
48 for Sussex (2) v Essex (2) June 1988 – with Rod Bunting a team mate that day.
He took 284 wickets in 62 games for Buckinghamshire as a leg spinner. Andy's dubious claim to fame for NCCC was that he was the last ever wicket to fall at Lakenham on 10th August 2000 against Cheshire.

FREE, Peter John
(b) Norwich 6 December 1971
Educ. – Attleborough Secondary Modern School
Cricket. – Attleborough Secondary Modern School; East Harling; Norwich Union; Norfolk Development Squad; Norwich CC; Norfolk 2nds; Old Buckenham; Vauxhall Mallards; MCC
HS. 64 no v Cambridgeshire August 2000 @ Lakenham
HS. 51 v Cambridgeshire April 2002 @ Horsford
HS. *22 v Nottinghamshire Board X1 June 2002 @ Horsford*
52 for Norfolk (2) v Huntingdonshire (2) July 1997
54 no for Norfolk (2) v Essex Under 19's July 1999
As at 06/06/11 he had scored 3,291 runs for Vauxhall Mallards with a highest score of 156 no v Dereham June 2006. Peter replaced Steve Goldsmith (out after injuring his back putting on his socks) for the last ever game at Lakenham (see Andy Clarke's entry). Peter is in the history books as the last NCCC player to hit a six at the venue plus he took the last catch taken there by a Norfolk player.
F.F. – As we go to press he hammered 100 not out with 7 (4) & 8 (6) in Vauxhall Mallards East Anglian Premier League fixture with Burwell CC. Outside of cricket he is a Marketing Manager at Aviva.

LLONG, Nigel James
(b) Ashford, Kent 11 February 1969
Lives in Kent but is invariably abroad
Educ. – Newtown Primary School; Ashford North Secondary School
Cricket. – British Rail; Ashford; Association of Kent Cricket Clubs Under 19s; Kent; Lavinia, Duchess of Norfolk's XI; Ashburton (Australia); Green Point (S.A)
HS. 50 v Nothumberland July 2000 @ Lakenham
HS. 7 v Suffolk April 2000 @ Lakenham

BB. 1/22 v Suffolk April 2000 @ Lakenham

HS. *90 v Cambridgeshire June 2000 @ Wisbech – with 7 (4) and 4 (6) – three of the latter rope clearers in succession in two good partnerships of 85 and 99*

BB. *1/17 v Cambridgeshire June 2000 @ Wisbech*

1st class cricket – 68 matches 3,024 runs 59 catches 35 wickets batting left handed and bowling right arm off breaks

A prolific scorer in the Woolwich Kent League for his hometown team Ashford with scores between May 1998 and August 1998 of 84no,104 no, 98, 80 and 88 no.

An Umpire from June 2000 (which was the reason for his few NCCC appearances), an ECB 1st Class Umpire 2002 and on the ICC International Panel as a 3rd Umpire before becoming a full member of the said Panel in 2006. Now a Test Umpire with many First Class, ODI's, Twenty20 and TV stints. Nigel has also Umpired Women's Cricket. In 2011 he officiated in five ICC World Cup One Day Internationals.

NEWTON, Luke Tobias Saville

(b) Cambridge 19 October 1981

Lives in Norfolk

Educ. – Northgate School; King's Lynn College

Cricket. – Vauxhall Mallards; Norfolk Development XI; Norfolk Cricket Board XI; Norfolk Under 21s; Norfolk 2nds; Derbyshire 2nds; Leicestershire 2nds & Trialists 'B'

HS. 73 v Staffordshire July 2006 @ Horsford

HS. 40 v Jersey Cricket Board April 2007 @ Grainville

HS. *60 v Northumberland July 2005 @ Jesmond*

49 no for Derbyshire (2) v Lancashire (2) May 2004

67 for Norfolk Development XI v Huntingdonshire May 2005 – in an opening stand of 181 with Ollie Higenbottam (q.v). The team won the East of England Development Competition Title. Luke is the only double winner (2002 and 2006) of the David Lester King Memorial Shield.

He has snared over 100 wicket keeping victims for both NCCC and Vauxhall Mallards

PURTON, Robert Geoffrey Samuel

(b) Norwich 5 September 1980

Lives locally

Educ. – Sprowston High School; Norwich City College – studying Business Management

Cricket. – Sprowston High School; Sprowston CC; Vauxhall Mallards; Norfolk Under 12 to17 and Under 19s; Norfolk Cricket Board XI; Norfolk 2nds; Albion CC (N.Z); Bracewell Academy XI (N.Z)

HS. 25 v Bedfordshire July 2008 @ Horsford

BB. 1/35 v Bedfordshire July 2008 @ Horsford – he broke the opening partnership of 224.

HS. 9 v Essex (2) April 2009 @ Bishop's Stortford

An eight year time lapse before Rob made his second appearance for the first team.

The 1995 NCCC Handbook stated that he gave the side a solid start as an opener for the Under 13s.

75 for Norfolk (2) v Essex Under 19s July 1999

In 180 Matches for Vauxhall Mallards he has scored 3,888 runs with a top score of 116 v Norwich CC July 2008. He bagged 5/45 against Great Witchingham July 2008 out bowling NCCC men Martin Addison, Paul Bradshaw and Richard Moores. He is a Works Manager for Eco Fence and Doors

WALKER, George William

(b) Norwich 12 May 1984

Educ. – Norwich GS; Loughborough University

Cricket. – Norwich GS; Swardeston; Norfolk 2nds; Loughborough University Centre of Excellence; East of England Development XI; Leicestershire

HS. 53 v Bedfordshire July 2008 @ Horsford

BB. 9/48 v Cambridgeshire August 2009 @ Horsford – and 7/48 in the second innings

HS. 27 no v Essex (2) April 2011 @ Southend

BB. 3/34 v MCC Young Cricketers April 2011 @ Horsford

HS. *57 no v Hertfordshire May 2009 @ Welwyn Garden City*

BB. *4/20 v Hertfordshire May 2009 @ Welwyn Garden City*

74 no & 4/77 for Leicestershire (2) v Essex (2) September 2003

His performance above against Cambridgeshire bring out the statistics. The 27th NCCC player to take eight or more wickets in an innings and more important the 9th time that nine wickets claimed in one innings. The NCCC 2010 Handbook does justice to the Championship perspective but for all matches dating back to 1876 George's 9/48 is the 7th best return for an innings. The First X1 Captain for 2011 as he forms the twin spin bowling threat with Chris Brown. George is the third youngest NCCC Minor Counties Championship player in the clubs history and is destined to break more records in the seasons to come.

2001

AUSTIN, Robert James

(b) Norwich 22 November 1977

Lives in Norfolk

Educ. – Wayland High School; Easton College – studying Agriculture

Cricket. – Wayland High School; Old Buckenham; Norfolk Under 14 - 17s; MCC

HS. 7 no v Cambridgeshire June 2001 @ Saffron Walden

BB. 2/16 v Cambridgeshire June 2001 @ Saffron Walden

HS. 0 no v MCC Young Cricketers May 2004 @ Horsford

BB. 3/28 v MCC Young Cricketers April 2002 @ Horsford

HS. *1 v Minor Counties Wales May 2001 @ Horsford*

BB. *2/22 v Leicestershire Cricket Board July 2001 @ Horsford*

5/7 for Norfolk Under 14s v Suffolk Under 14s 1992

34 wickets at an average of 11.02 for the Under 15s won him a Daily Telegraph Award.

A Farmer and a Farm Business Manager for Openfields Agriculture Ltd

F.F. – The EAPL website said that the first ball of his third spell (O.B. v N. Runcton May 2006) went directly upwards about 20 feet

BROWN, Christopher
(b) Oldham, Lancashire 16 August 1974
Educ. – Failsworth High School; Tameside College of Technology
Cricket. – Lancashire Cricket Federation; Lancashire Schools Under 19s; Wernerth; Horsford; National Association of Young Cricketers; Cheshire; England & Wales Cricket Board XI; ECB XI; Unicorns; Minor Counties Under 25s; Badureliya Sports Club; Minor Counties; 2nds of Derbyshire, Essex, Glamorgan, Lancashire & Somerset; Cape Town (S.A); Fish Hoek CC (S.A); Development of Excellence XI
HS. 118 no v Suffolk August 2003 @ Mildenhall – off 167 balls, one of 17 NCCC players to strike a ton against Suffolk plus he had match figures of 9/163.
BB. 8/65 v Bedfordshire August 2005 @ Horsford – added to 5/53 for the other innings
HS. 46 v Guernsey X1 April 2005 @ King George's Sports Club
BB. 4/28 v Netherlands April 2008 @ VOC Rotterdam
HS. *34 no v Suffolk May 2008 @ Woodbridge School*
BB. *4/15 v Devon September 2001 @ Lord's – to help win the ECB County Championship Cup Final.*
1st class cricket 4 matches 45 runs 2 catches 6 wickets- games were in Sri Lanka.
Chris bowled the most overs and took the most wickets in seven consecutive Championship seasons (2001-07), topping the averages 2002-2005 inclusively.
A good July 2000 playing for Cheshire as in three successive bowls he took 5/79, 5/62 and 5/41.
For Horsford at 06/06/11 he had played 107 matches with a top score of 103 v Norwich CC July 1996, but outmuscled that day by Chris Borrett (q.v) who racked up 141 for the opposition. Far too good a bowler at club level he has taken 276 wickets at 13.17 with a best return of 8/29 against Fakenham June 2007. Fakenham were reduced to 31/7 and Chris had all seven. A qualified Level 4 coach in 2010
he went to the West Indies March 2011 to coach at the ICC Americas High Performance Academy. This added to his role as NCCC player/coach together with his work with the Essex Academy spinners at Chelmsford.

COOPER, Flt Sgt Sean
(b) Weston- Super-Mare, Somerset 11 March 1967
Educ. – Fakenham High School; Sprowston High School; Cheshire Middle School (Germany)

Cricket. – Fakenham; Thetford; Sleaford; Norfolk Under 25s; Norfolk Development XI; RAF; Combined Services; Bears CC
HS. 26 v Staffordshire August 2001 @ Walsall
HS. 0 v Cambridgeshire April 2002 @ Horsford
95 for Fakenham v Great Witchingham July 2007
'Coops 'is serving with the RAF Regiment (3rd Squadron) and has completed tours to Afghanistan, Northern Ireland and Iraq.

WHITNEY, David Andrew
(b) Norwich 19 January 1982
Lives in East London
Educ. – CNS; Sussex University- studying Sociology BA (Hons) PGCE
Cricket. – CNS; Norfolk Under 12s to 19s; Midlands Under 14s; England Schools Development Squad; Horsford; Diss; Sussex University; Swardeston; Norfolk Cricket Board XI; Norfolk 2nds: Norfolk Development XI; Albion CC (N.Z); Bracewell Academy XI (N.Z)
HS. 45 v Cumberland July 2001 @ Barrow – helped Steve Goldsmith put on 91 for the sixth wicket.
134 for Norfolk Under 19s v Huntingdonshire Under 19s August 1999
69 no for Norfolk Development XI v Suffolk Development XI May 2001
98 for Swardeston v Mildenhall September 2001
A Teacher at Haverstock Secondary School in Camden.

2002

HARRISON, Ian
(b) King's Lynn, Norfolk 1 December 1977
Educ. – Methwold High School; Downham Sixth Form; Norwich City College
Cricket. – Mundford; Northwood; Downham; Norfolk Schools Under 11-19s; Norfolk Development Squad XI; Norfolk Young Cricketers; SR Harvey's 'West'XI; Vauxhall Mallards; Old Buckenham
HS. 9 v Cambridgeshire May 2002 @ North Runcton
Up to 2010 Ian had 139 games (Vauxhall and Old Buckenham) scoring 2,813 runs with a top score of 91 for Old Buckenham against North Runcton May 2006
5/14 for Old Buckenham v Swardeston August 2004
Ian is an Accounts Manager with an Engineering Company

PANTER, Robert Graham
(b) Norwich 22 May 1978
Educ. – Taverham High School; Hellesdon Sixth Form
Cricket. – Taverham High School; Sprowston Under 13s & 15s; Norfolk Under 15s; Horsford; Old Buckenham; Brooke; C. Brown's 'East' XI; Norfolk Development Squad XI
HS. 2 v MCC Young Cricketers April 2002 @ Horsford
Nephew of DG Godfrey (q.v)

114 no for Norfolk Development XI v Huntingdonshire Development XI June 2001
139 no for Brooke v Beccles 2003
52 no (off 32 balls) for Brooke v Fakenham 20 May 2011(in Twenty20)
Rob is the present Brooke first team captain and outside of cricket a Structural Engineer (CEng MIStructE)

PARLANE, Michael Edward

(b) Pukekohe, Auckland, New Zealand 22 July 1972
Educ. – Bream Bay College
Cricket. – Bream Bay College; Northland; Wellington; NZ Academy; Northern Conference; Wigan; Swardeston; Northern Districts; New Zealand 'A'; Maungakaramea CC
HS. *9 v Berkshire September 2002 @ Reading* – in an innings of SIX ducks with top scorer Steve Goldsmith (with 35) dropped off his first ball.
1st class cricket – 139 matches 7,354 runs 89 catches 1 wicket with a best of 203 for Wellington v Auckland January 2005.
Swardeston's Player-of-the-Year 2002 with 947 runs (86.09) with 5 tons.He started playing cricket on the drive at home with his dad and was 11/12 before he played organized cricket and has completed 20 seasons in New Zealand cricket. Mike was asked if he was not a cricketer what would he be ? He replied – "retired".

SLEGG, Ian Robert

(b) King's Lynn, Norfolk 13 January 1972
Educ. – Fakenham High School
Cricket. – Fakenham High School; Fakenham; Norfolk 2nds; Glamorgan 2nds; Wales Minor Counties; SR Harvey's 'West' XI; Norfolk Cricket Board XI
HS. 29 v Cambridgeshire July 2006 @ Horsford – setting a NCCC ground record of 73 for the ninth wicket with Chris Brown which stood for 5 years
BB. 4/35 v Cambridgeshire July 2006 @ Horsford
HS. 3 no v MCC Young Cricketers April 2002 @ Horsford
BB. 2/41 v MCC Young Cricketers April 2002 @ Horsford
HS. *12 no v Staffordshire May 2007 @ Leek*
BB. *2/29 v Devon July 2008 @ Horsford*
7/34 for Fakenham v Vauxhall Mallards June 2004 – against a line up of NCCC men namely Addison, Amos, Bradshaw, De Bruyn, Free, Goldsmith, Newton, Purton and Spelman (senior).
7/45 for Fakenham v Lowestoft May 2011
78 for Fakenham v Kirkley & Lowestoft Railway June 2009.
Ian topped the NCCC bowling averages in 2006 with his 24 Championship wickets.
As at 06/06/11 he had taken 230 wickets for Fakenham in 1st, 2nd and Sunday X1 matches (per EAPL website)

SPELMAN, James Mark

(b) Norwich 20 August 1983

Educ. – Reepham High School
Cricket. – Reepham High School; Great Witchingham; Norfolk Development Squad XI; Norfolk Under 19 & 21s; Norfolk 2nds; Vauxhall Mallards; Minor Counties Under 25s; Albion CC (N.Z); Bracewell Academy XI (N.Z)
HS. 158 v Buckinghamshire July 2010 @ Horsford – this was his 3rd ton in successive Championship matches a feat never achieved before in NCCC's history.
BB. 3/68 v Suffolk July 2002 @ Horsford
HS. 70 v Huntingdonshire May 2005 @ Horsford
BB. 2/6 v MCC Young Cricketers April 2011 @ Horsford
HS. *56 v Bedfordshire May 2007 @ Ampthill Town*
BB. *2/51 v Lincolnshire June 2011 @ Bracebridge Heath*
Brother of JO (q.v)
54 for Minor Counties Under 25s v Northamptonshire (2) July 2007.
One of four players to gain their County cap during the Northumberland game at Manor Park in July 2007(Michael Eccles, Luke Newton and Trevor Ward were the others)
'Spellers' has already featured in 18 century partnerships being one behind Trevor Ward and two short of Fred Handley's total of twenty. A very stylish batsman he is destined to break many records.

TAYLOR, Jonathan Paul

(b) Ashby-de-la- Zouch, Leicestershire 5 August 1964
Educ. – Linton Primary School; Battram Road School; Pingle Comprehensive School
Cricket. – Pingle Comprehensive School; Old Netherseal CC; Derbyshire Under 17 & 19s; Derby Parkside (N.Z); Papakura CC (N.Z); Hawke's Bay (N.Z); West Hallam; Napier High School Old Boys (N.Z); Langley Mill; Derbyshire; Checkley CC; Staffordshire; England 'A'; England XI; North Kalgoorie (Australia); Northamptonshire; Great Boulder (Australia); Montrose CC (S.A); TMB Rice's XI; Sir JP Getty's XI; Banbury CC; England – 2 Tests
HS. 25 v Northumberland August 2002 @ Jesmond
BB. 3/37 v Buckinghamshire June 2002 @ Ascott Park
HS. 5 v Cambridgeshire May 2002 @ North Runcton
BB. 3/36 v Cambridgeshire May 2002 @ North Runcton – this was Paul's debut for the County
HS. *10 v Berkshire September 2002 @ Reading*
BB. *3/22 v Leicestershire Board X1 May 2002 @ Hinckley*
1st class cricket – 183 matches 2,253 runs 61 catches 559 wickets
On the 1993 England Tour to India and the 1994 'A' Tour to South Africa. Jon also played a One Day International in Sri Lanka. Slightly splay-footed with an open chested action and stamina to burn.
122 & 6/21 for Banbury v Reading July 2004
6/54 for Banbury v Reading May 2005 – included his first ever hat-trick. Paul was Banbury's Director of Cricket and he is

presently Surrey CCC's Director of Cricket Development.
F.F. – A quote attributed to Paul, "Cricket is about participation as well as excellence."

WATSON, Corporal Ashley Malcolm
(b) Drayton Hospital, Norwich 13 February 1984
Educ. – Taverham St Edmunds School; Taverham Middle School; Reepham High School; Norwich City College – studying Leisure & Recreation and Sports Therapy
Cricket. – Taverham Middle School; Reepham High School; Norfolk Under 13 – 19s; Norfolk Development Squad XI; Norfolk 2nds; Norwich CC; Vauxhall Mallards; Great Witchingham; RAF Under 25s; Combined Services; Bracewell Academy XI (N.Z); Albion CC (N.Z)
HS. 100 no v Hertfordshire August 2009 @ Horsford – his maiden ton after he was dropped first ball
BB. 3/41 v Northumberland June 2011 @ Jesmond
HS. 8 v MCC Young Cricketers May 2004 @ Horsford
BB. 1/41 v MCC Young Cricketers May 2004 @ Horsford
Brother of AA (q.v) – it will be a great day for the family when the brothers play in the same game for the County. *His Championship debut saw the two Carls (Amos & Rogers) plunder 335 in their record breaking stand. Based at RAF Honington he is in the RAF Regiment (2nd Squadron) and as we go to press is on his third tour to Afghanistan. Recently in the RAF Shooting Competition at Bisley with his team of six men coming second overall.*

WILKINSON, Matthew Owen
(b) Norwich 17 December 1980
Educ. – Reepham High School
Cricket. – Reepham High School; Horsford; Norfolk Under 14 & 15s (capt); C. Brown's 'East' XI; Norfolk Development Squad XI; Norfolk 2nds
HS. 82 v Cambridgeshire July 2003 @ Horsford
HS. 65 v Essex (2) April 2007 @ Bishop's Stortford
HS. *45 v Lincolnshire June 2006 @ Lincoln Lindum*
90 no for Norfolk Development XI v Cambridgeshire Development XI June 2001
82 no for Norfolk Development XI v Huntingdonshire Development XI May 2002
As at 06/06/11 Matt had scored 1,686 runs for Horsford with a top score of 80 against Vauxhall Mallards in April 2009 from position eight in the batting order.
F.F. – Matt's Grandfather Wilfred was a small holder in animal husbandry and he helped form Horsford CC in 1947. In 1979 Manor Park was bought by RG Carter Ltd (the present sponsors) and merged with Drayton Farms. A verbal agreement made by the owner Sir Richard Barratt Leonard with Bob Carter that Horsford should be allowed to play at Manor Park for as long as they wish.

2003

DE BRUYN, Pierre
(b) Pretoria, South Africa 31 March 1977
Cricket. – Northern Transvaal; South Africa Academy; Northerns 'B'; Northerns ; Easterns CC; Titans; KwaZulu Natal; Dolphins; Vauxhall Mallards; Netherfield
HS. *9 v Lincolnshire August 2003 @ Horsford*
1st class cricket – as at 06/06/11 91 matches 4,637 runs with a top score of 202 for Northerns 'B' v Griqualand West 'B' in November 1998, as well as 6/56 in the same match.
41 no & 4/40 for Easterns v South Africa February 2003 – with Shahid Afridi and Inzaman-ul- Haq being two of his captures.
147 for Vauxhall Mallards v Swardeston May 2004
In a three month period in 2005 in the Northern Premier League he hit six tons (108, 103 no, 117 no, 113 no, 112 no and 119) for Netherfield. He played for South Africa against All Stars, Bangladesh and Sri Lanka in the 2007 Hong Kong Sixes Tournament. Pierre became the Dolphins (S.A) Head Coach (Level 3) and is heavily involved in No Boundaries Youth Cricket in Centurion, South Africa

ECCLES, Michael Patrick
(b) Norwich 22 March 1980
Educ. – Heartsease High School
Cricket. – Swardeston; Norwich; Norfolk Development Squad XI; Sprowston; Norfolk 2nds; Churchill CC (Australia)
HS. 16 no v Cambridgeshire July 2006 @ Horsford AND 16 v Bedfordshire July 2003 @ Wardown Park
BB. 7/74 v Staffordshire June 2004 @ Longton – match figures of 11/145 as by his bowling the last man it produced NCCC's first tied match since 1980.
HS. 18 v Essex (2) April 2011 @ Southend
BB. 3/33 v MCC Young Cricketers May 2004 @ Horsford
HS. *6 v Northumberland May 2008 @ Morpeth*
BB. *5/34 v Staffordshire July 2009 @ Chester-le-Street – it does not get better than a five wicket haul in the M.C.C.A Knockout Trophy Final. The club had the ball mounted for him.*
As at 06/06/11 he had played 224 matches for Swardeston (per EAPL website) with a top score of 47 no versus Vauxhall Mallards (August 2008) but is known for his right arm fast bowling which has seen him claim 329 wickets with a best return of 6/31 versus Cambridge Granta (June 2004).
He is a County Court Bailiff outside of cricket.

EVANS, Stuart David
(b) Bury St Edmunds 25 April 1972
Educ. – Framlingham Earl High School; Notre Dame School; Norwich City College
Cricket. – Framlingham Earl; Martham; Brooke; Great Witchingham; British Police; Horsford; Norfolk Development Squad XI

HS. 5 v MCC Young Cricketers April 2003 @ High Wycombe
BB. 1/37 v MCC Young Cricketers April 2003 @ High Wycombe
Stuart is a Policeman

GOODRHAM, Matthew David
(b) Bury St Edmunds 25 July 1980
Educ. – Methwold High School
Cricket. – Methwold High School; Mundford; Horsford; Norfolk Development Squad XI
HS. 40 v Suffolk August 2003 @ Mildenhall – on debut as part of 9th wicket stand of 103 with Chris Brown which was only 11 runs short of the County record set in 1935.
HS. 1 v MCC Young Cricketers May 2005 @ Uxbridge
29 for Norfolk Development Squad XI v Huntingdonshire Development Squad XI July 2003 – as part of 7th wicket stand of 59 with James Spelman (q.v) after keeping tidily without conceding a bye.
F.F. – Matt was fast tracked into the County side on the recommendation of Chairman Keith Bray. Skipper Paul Newman had never seen him play.

MARQUET, Joshua Phillip
(b) Melbourne, Victoria, Australia 3 December 1969
Lives in Lancashire
Educ. Melbourne University
Cricket. – Dandenong (Australia); Tasmania University CC; Tasmania; MCC; SP O'Donnell's XI; Victoria 2nds; Norwich CC; Chorley; Whalley; Clitheroe; Astley Bridge; Burwood
HS. *4 v Lincolnshire August 2003 @ Horsford*
BB. *3/55 v Lincolnshire August 2003 @ Horsford*
1st class cricket – 22 matches 28 runs 9 catches 60 wickets
'Josh' (with nicknames also of 'Jose' and 'Super') has a British passport and was going to play again for Norwich CC but he got injured and the chance was lost. His record for Tasmania University CC is 326 wickets at 14.85. Is he the right arm fast bowler that got away considering his record elsewhere ? For Whalley CC he nabbed 65 wickets at 18.08; for Chorley CC he bagged 298 wickets at 15.21 and as at 06/06/11 he has filled his boots with 260 wickets at 14.67 for Clitheroe CC.
Josh is a Massage Therapist

···

2004

···

ARTHURTON, Shaun Stephen
(b) Norwich 27 December 1967
Educ. – Reepham High School
Cricket. – Ingham; Norwich CC; Norfolk Under 16s; Norfolk Young Amateurs; Great Witchingham
HS. 38 v Lincolnshire August 2004 @ Horsford – his debut match and he had five stitches in a right thumb to contend with after a fielding injury

HS. 26 v Essex (2) April 2005 @ Billericay
Father of SS (q.v)
As at 06/06/11 he had reached 135 matches for Great Witchingham scoring 2,803 runs (per EAPL website) with an innings of 109 versus Great Melton CC May 2009 – his talented son Sam was out for a first ball duck that day.
In a 30 year career, and still playing, it is estimated that Shaun has hit about 60 tons to include Norfolk League, Alliance League, Carter Cup etcetera with a top effort of 201 for Great Witchingham versus Ingham in the late 1990s. He is a Site Foreman in the Building Industry.
F.F. – His son has the same initials so, considering that their debuts were only four years apart, confusion could arise in the future for the unwary.

BLAKE, Kieren Philip John
(b) Newport, Monmouthshire 29 May 1974
Lives in Victoria, Australia
Educ. – St Julian's Primary School; Haberdashers' Monmouth School; Sheffield Hallam University – BA in Business Studies; University of North Texas
Cricket. – Monmouthshire; Wales Independent Schools; Newport; Glamorgan 2nds; Wales Minor Counties; Newport & District Under 21s & Firsts; Norwich CC; South Wales Country CC (Australia); Beenleigh CC (Australia); Alberton CC (Australia); Helensvale CC (Australia)
HS. 12 v Cumberland August 2004 @ Carlisle – on a rain sodden pitch
BB. 1/20 v Cumberland August 2004 @ Carlisle
3/20 for Norwich CC v Mildenhall June 2004 – with Ashley Watson (q.v) and Tony Penberthy (q.v) also taking wickets for his side
53 no for Norwich CC v Nottingham CC August 2004 – a month before he emigrated to Australia.
American Football – GB Students; Texas Collegians; Denton RFC (Texas)
Kieren is the Managing Director of Turf Factory in Australia – Manufacturers and Distributors of a full suite of synthetic turf.

HIGENBOTTAM, Oliver Thomas
(b) Norwich 22 January 1981
Educ. – Sprowston High School & Sixth Form College
Cricket. – Norwich CC; Norfolk Development Squad XI; Coltishall
HS. 16 v Cambridgeshire July 2004 @ March
HS. 36 v Essex (2) April 2009 @ Bishop's Stortford – these two games were both away fixtures.
106 for Norfolk Development Squad XIv Huntingdonshire Development Squad XI May 2005 – in a first wicket partnership of 181with Luke Newton.
74 for Norfolk Development Squad XI v Essex Development Squad XI June 2005 – in a first wicket partnership of 108 with

Alex Patmore (q.v)
Olly is the Norwich CC Social Chairman with his father David the Club chairman.
A Qualified Accountant (MAAT)

PENBERTHY, Anthony Leonard
(b) Troon, Cornwall 1 September 1969
Educ. – Troon Primary School; Camborne Comp School
Cricket. – Troon; Northamptonshire; National Association Young Cricketers; England Young Cricketers; MCC; Norwich; Cornwall; Great Houghton CC - club president & coach Under 19s
HS. 9 v Staffordshire June 2004 @ Longton
BB. 1/32 v Staffordshire June 2004 @ Longton
HS. 126 v Essex (2) April 2004 @ Billericay – his debut in this friendly despite a tooth abscess attended to during the interval by Essex's Physio Neil Foster (q.v)
BB. 1/21 v MCC Young Cricketers May 2004 @ Horsford
HS. *1 v Dorset June 2004 @ Bournemouth*
1st class cricket 181 matches 7,212 runs 108 catches 231 wickets. A first class wicket (Australia's Mark Taylor) with his very first ball at that level which balanced against his three ball 'pair'in the game.
83 no for England Young Cricketers v New Zealand Young Cricketers August 1989 – alongside Nick Knight and Mark Ramprakash.
132 no for Northamptonshire v Glamorgan April 2001 – part of a sixth wicket stand of 250.
122 for Norfolk v MCC Young Cricketers May 2004 @ Horsford – he smashed 6 (6) to leave him with a final NCCC Friendly Matches average of 99.66
150 for Cornwall v Cheshire June 2005.
59 for MCC v Ottawa Valley Cricket Council Select XI September 2005 – with his teammate Carl Rogers 54 not out in the match.

WARD, Trevor Robert
(b) Farningham, Kent 18 January 1968
Educ. – Anthony Roper County Primary School; Hextable Comprehensive School
Cricket. – Dartford; National Association of Cricketers; Kent; Leicestershire; MCC Schools; England XI; England 'A'; Lavinia, Duchess of Norfolk's XI; Scarborough CC (Australia); Gosnell's CC (Australia); Vauxhall Mallards; Leicester Ivanhoe
HS. 149 v Bedfordshire July 2008 @ Horsford
BB. 1/35 v Staffordshire August 2007 @ Walsall
HS. 34 no v Essex (2) April 2006 @ Bishop's Stortford
HS. *154 no v Bedfordshire May 2007 @ Ampthill Town*
1st class cricket – 248 matches 13,876 runs 226 catches 9 wickets with a top score of 235 no for Kent versus Middlesex August 1991. He has scored tons against fourteen counties only missing out against Durham, Kent, Leicestershire and Nottinghamshire. Trevor went with NCA to Bermuda and

Young England to Sri Lanka.
He scored two centuries (112 & 105no) v Staffordshire 2010 at Stone – only Bill Edrich (q.v) and Steve Plumb (twice – q.v) had previously achieved this feat.After season 2010 Trevor had an average of over 50 for NCCC in all three types of game ie Championship, Cups and Friendlies so he will be a hard act to follow for any future professional when he retires. Of 22 men to have scored more than 2,500 Championship runs for NCCC only David Walker exceeds his batting average. Ted Witherden, Steve Goldsmith and Steve Plumb run him closest with averages in the forties but to their collective credit they all played more matches.

2005

ADDISON, Martin Andrew
(b) Norwich 28 January 1978
Educ. – Thorpe St Andrew High School
Cricket. – Thorpe St Andrew High School; Norfolk Under 14,15 & 21s; Norfolk Development Squad XI; Thorpe; Barleycorns; Anglians; Vauxhall Mallards
HS. 20 v Lincolnshire July 2006 @ Cleethorpes
BB. 2/29 v Northumberland June 2005 @ Jesmond
HS. 1 no v MCC Young Cricketers May 2005 @ Uxbridge
BB. 3/30 v Essex (2) April 2008 @ Bishop's Stortford
HS. *5 no v Northumberland July 2005 @ Jesmond*
BB. *2/43 v Lincolnshire June 2006 @ Lincoln Lindum*
Martin played in the winning 2005 MCCA Knockout Cup Final team against Wiltshire as the County became the first team to lift the Trophy for the fourth time. Yet another switch player batting right handed and bowling left arm medium fast. He first came to notice as a Barleycorns player who got a hat trick for Norfolk Under 14s against Leicestershire Under 14s. The EAPL website (as at 06/06/11) has his Vauxhall Mallards wicket haul as 236 with a best return of 7/32 in September 2009 against Swardeston (a team laden with NCCC players).
F.F. – Martin manufactures Fire Fighting Equipment for a living.

MOORES, Richard David
(b) Wolverhampton 8 July 1979
Educ. – Bridgnorth Endowed School (Shropshire); University of East Anglia
Cricket. – Vauxhall Mallards; Norfolk Development Squad XI
HS. 72 v Cumberland July 2005 @ Horsford – his debut putting on 96 for the sixth wicket with Luke Newton to rescue the side from a perilous 37 for 5 and deservedly winning the Boswell's Man- of -the- Match award.
HS. 38 no v Essex (2) April 2006 @ Bishop's Stortford
BB. 2/29 v Essex (2) April 2006 @ Bishop's Stortford
HS. *18 v Staffordshire May 2006 @ Horsford*
BB. *1/19 v Staffordshire May 2006 @ Horsford*

88 for Norfolk Development Squad XI v Cambridgeshire Development Squad XI June 2005 @ March Town
74 for Norfolk Development Squad X1 v Suffolk Development Squad X1 July 2005 @ Horsford – this innings and that above alerted the senior selectors' attention to his ability.
Richard has passed 2,000 runs in service with Vauxhall Mallards with a published top score of 89 versus Bury St Edmunds in a knock that included 12 (4) and 4 (6) in July 2009, and to show his versatility he has also snapped up 168 wickets for the club.

PATMORE, Alexander James Douglas

(b) Tokyo, Japan 20 December 1987
Educ. – White Woman Lane School; Sprowston High School; University of Sheffield – BA (Hons) in Philosophy.
Cricket. – Sprowston High School; Sprowston CC; Norfolk Under 11 to 19s; Vauxhall Mallards; Norfolk Development Squad XI; Sheffield Collegiate
HS. 22 v Guernsey April 2005 @ King George's Sports Club, Guernsey
81 no for Norfolk Development Squad XI v Huntingdonshire Development Squad XI August 2004 as Alex topped the batting averages at this level for the season.
100 no for Vauxhall Mallards (2) v Downham Town July 2006
54 for Sheffield Collegiate v Castleford July 2010
A wicket keeper in a good intake as also playing at the time were Ben Harvey and Luke Newton.
He has just taken his 100th victim for Sheffield Collegiate with 26 being stumpings off the bowling of Nadeem Khan.
F.F. – A Teacher of RE in Sheffield

SEAGER, Matthew Leslie

(b) Norwich 19 September 1986
Educ. – Thorpe St Andrew High School; Norwich City College
Cricket. – Thorpe St Andrew High School; Midlands Under 13s; Norfolk Under 12-19s; Trials for Derbyshire, Kent & Northamptonshire; Norfolk Development Squad XI; Vauxhall Mallards
HS. 16 no v Guernsey April 2005 @ King George's Sports Club, Guernsey – undefeated in his one innings
4/36 for Vauxhall Mallards (2) v Swardeston (2) May 2004
5-4-1-3 for Norfolk Development Squad XI v Cambridgeshire Development Squad XI June 2006
83 for Swardeston v Diss 2009
A Team Manager for Aviva in Norwich.

WARNES, Matthew Robert

(b) Norwich 12 February 1986
Educ. – Cromer High School; Sheringham Sixth Form College; UCLan University (University of Central Lancashire).
Cricket. – Norfolk Development Squad X1; Norfolk Under

19s; Bradfield; Horsford
HS. 71 v Northumberland June 2011 @ Jesmond – his Championship debut and to the fore with a 159 run partnership with Carl Rogers for the fifth wicket that ended just a dozen runs short of the 1937 club record.
HS. 24 v Netherlands April 2008 @ ACC Amsterdam
BB. 2/23 v Guernsey April 2005 @ King George's Sports Club, Guernsey
53 no for Norfolk Development Squad XI v Suffolk Development Squad XI June 2008 – in the same side as his younger brother Michael (q.v).
Matt missed a Championship debut at March in 2007 against Cambridgeshire as the game was abandoned without a bowl being bowled due to persistent rain falling. He was re-registered with the ECB 06/06/11 just six days before the Northumberland Championship encounter at Jesmond after NCCC had foolishly cancelled his registration in 2009. They have therefore become the first brothers to play together in a Championship match since David and Peter Thomas in 1986. They are one of 39 sets of brothers to play for NCCC since 1876.

2006

BAILEY, Shaun Peter

(b) Norwich 19 February 1990
Educ. – Hockham School; Wayland Community High School; Norwich City College
Cricket. – Norfolk Under 13,15 & 17s; Midland Under 17s; Norfolk Development Squad XI; Northamptonshire Cricket Academy; ECB Elite Player Development XI; Northamptonshire; Swardeston
HS. Did not Bat nor Bowl v MCC Young Cricketers May 2006 – at 16 years 72 days the third youngest NCCC 1st X1 player behind Sam Arthurton and Neville Jessopp. He had no chance to perform as only 68 balls were bowled due to the inclement weather.
HS. *1 no v Staffordshire May 2007 @ Leek*
BB. *5/40 v Lincolnshire June 2008 @ Grantham*
1st class cricket – 1 match 18 runs 1 catch 3 wickets
'Bud' had a recurring stress fracture of the shin which hampered his chances of further appearances for Northamptonshire and as we go to press he has not signed for another club.

EDE, Matthew Paul

(b) Norwich 10 March 1986
Lives in Wellington, New Zealand
Educ. – Angel Road First & Middle School; Blyth Jex High School; Norwich City College – studying Plumbing
Cricket. – Norfolk Development Squad XI; Norfolk Under 11 -16s; Sprowston; Norwich; Anglians; Vauxhall Mallards; Collegians (N.Z)

HS. 15 v Bedfordshire August 2006 @ Dunstable –
drafted in as Carl Amos was unavailable thereby breaking
up the opening partnership of the two Carls after a six year
run (38 consecutive Championship games). Carl Rogers and
James Spelman promptly put on a stand of 282 runs
*53 for Norfolk Development Squad XI v Essex Development
Squad XI August 2007*
*107 for Norwich CC v Mildenhall June 2006 – with 7 other
NCCC's players in his team.*
Matt is a Plumber and Gas Fitter by profession

RIST, William Henry
(b) Guildford, Surrey 22 March 1987
Educ. – Northgate High School
Cricket. – Norfolk Under 16s & Under 21s; Gressenhall;
Fakenham; Swardeston; The Stoics; Cambridge University
Centre of Excellence; Cambridge University
**HS. 0 v Hertfordshire August 2006 @ Horsford AND
0 v Bedfordshire August 2006 @ Dunstable** – both
dismissals were LBW decisions.
1st class cricket – 3 matches 24 runs 2 catches
93 for Norfolk Under 19s v Essex Under 19s July 2006
97 for Cambridge UCCE v Derbyshire (2) April 2008
*231 no for Swardeston v Great Witchingham May 2009 – in
a Bob Carter Cup landslide win despite scores from Shaun
Arthurton (104), Ben Harvey (51), Sam Arthurton (50) and Tom
Collishaw (49)*

2007

GRAY, Stephen Kevin
(b) Barking, Essex 6 July 1988
Educ. – Canon Palmer School; Fakenham College; Anglia
Ruskin University – studying Sports Science gaining a BSc.
Cricket. – Essex Under 9-17s; Essex Development Squad
XI; Buckhurst Hill; Fakenham; MCC Young Cricketers; MCC;
Cambridge University Centre of Cricket Excellence; MCC
Universities; Loughton; Norfolk Development Squad XI;
Minor Counties; Middlesex 2nds; Essex 2nds
HS. 69 v Suffolk August 2008 @ Horsford – in 8th wicket
stand of 81 with Chris Brown.
HS. 67 v Essex (2) April 2009 @ Bishop's Stortford
HS. *76 v Northumberland May 2008 @ Morpeth*
*Steve's best wicket keeping total for a season is 27 victims (26c
1s) in 2008 embracing Championship, Cups and Friendlies.
Winner of the David Lester King Memorial Shield for 2008.
1st class cricket – 8 matches 190 runs 12 catches & 1 stumping
76 for Essex Under 17s v Dorset Under 17s August 2005
132 for Cambridge UCCE v Loughborough UCCE May 2009
57 for MCC Universities v Surrey (2) August 2009 – conceding
only 8 byes of the 687 runs scored
101 for MCC Universities v Loughborough UCCE May 2010*

*125 for Fakenham Sunday 1sts v Hethersett & Tas Valley August
2010 – in an opening partnership with his brother Phil (121 no)*
F.F. – An Administrator for National Instruction College.

MICKLEBURGH, Jaik Charles
(b) Norwich 30 March 1990
Educ. – Bungay High School
Cricket. – Norfolk Under 13,15, 17 & Development Squad
XI; Horsford; Essex (graduating through their Academy,
Development side and 2nds); ECB South Under 17s;
England Under 19s; Newtown & Chilwell CC (Australia)
HS. 45 no v Lincolnshire August 2007 @ Horsford
BB. 1/11 v Staffordshire August 2007 @ Walsall
HS. 63 v Essex (2) April 2007 @ Bishop's Stortford
HS. *75 v Devon July 2008 @ Horsford – an admirable display
but a lonely furrow with the team innings total only 138
1st class cricket – as at 06/06/11 – 34 matches 1,782 runs 20
catches with his maiden ton being 174 for Essex v Durham
April 2010. He batted with Alastair Cook and had a stand of
339 for the 5th wicket with James Foster - it was at the scene of
Norfolk's MCCA Knockout Trophy success the year before.
81 for Norfolk Under 13s v Lincolnshire Under 13s July 2003
162 for Norfolk Under 17s v Leicestershire & Rutland Under 17s
July 2006
57 for England Under 19s v Bangladesh Under 19s July 2009
The 2007 recipient of the David Lester King Memorial Trophy.
Jaik has already hit a 2011 County Championship ton with 112
v Northamptonshire in a 258 second wicket partnership with
England's Alastair Cook. He is destined to reach greater heights
in the game.*

SPELMAN, Jonathan Oliver
(b) Norwich 19 November 1986
Educ. – Reepham High School
Cricket. – Vauxhall Mallards; Norfolk Under 13s; Norfolk
Development Squad XI; Great Witchingham
HS. 0 v Netherlands April 2008 @ ACC Amsterdam – being
run out
BB. 1/23 v Jersey Cricket Board April 2007 @ Grainville – in
the same side as his elder brother.
Brother of JM (q.v)
*58 for Norfolk Under 13s v Cambridgeshire Under 13s June 2000
92 no for Vauxhall Mallards v Bury St Edmunds June 2004 – in
a 3rd wicket stand of 252 with Carl Rogers (151 no)
7/28 & 71 for Great Witchingham v Great Melton May 2009
One part of a current trio of brothers with Norfolk connections
being the Spelmans, Warnes and Watsons*

2008

ARTHURTON, Samuel Shaun
(b) Norwich 22 July 1992

Educ. – Reepham High School; Easton Sixth Form College

Cricket. – Reepham High School; Norfolk Under 13,15,17s & Development Squad XI; Great Witchingham; ECB XI; Essex 2nds; Northamptonshire Cricket Academy; Newtown & Chilwell CC (Australia)

HS. 133 v Staffordshire August 2010 @ Stone – in a third wicket stand of 204 with Trevor Ward.

BB. 1/10 v Buckinghamshire August 2008 @ Burnham

HS. 39 v MCC Young Professionals April 2010 @ High Wycombe

BB. 0/1 v MCC Young Cricketers April 2011 @ Horsford

HS. *133 no v Lincolnshire June 2011 @ Bracebridge Heath – 114 balls, 10 (4) & 7(6)*

Son of SS (q.v)

Sam was in the Norwich City FC Academy at Under 13 level and he had to decide between the two sports. Two weeks coaching at the High Performance Centre (Bangalore) as part of the Graham Gooch Essex Cricket Academy. Their Director John Childs has been monitoring Sam's progress since 2005.

157 for Norfolk Under 13s v Huntingdonshire Under 13s August 2005.

102 no for Norfolk Under 14s v Cambridgeshire Under 14s May 2007.

119 for Norfolk Under 15s v Northamptonshire Under 15s July 2007

Sam has maintained and progressed his rich early promise (he is the youngest ever NCCC debutant) and if determination and dedication have anything to do with it he will become a First-Class County player.

BROWN, James Christopher

(b) King's Lynn, Norfolk 13 June 1988

Educ. – North Wootton Primary School; King Edwards VII GS; Durham University

Cricket. – King Edward VII GS; North Runcton; Fakenham; Durham University; Norfolk Development Squad XI; Norfolk Under 17s – 19s; Clifton Hill (Australia); Lancaster Park; Woolston CC (N.Z); Fiskerton CC; Rood en Wit (Holland)

HS. 17 v Netherlands 'A' April 2008 @ Rotterdam

156 for North Runcton v Swardeston June 2006

FLOWER, Felix James

(b) Norwich 9 January 1988

Educ. – Gresham's School

Cricket. – Gresham's School; Norwich; Norfolk Under 15,17 & 19s; Norfolk Development Squad XI; Norwich & Coltishall Wanderers; Glamorgan & Wales Academy; Cardiff UCCE

HS. 64 v Bedfordshire July 2008 @ Horsford – in a 3rd wicket stand of 162 with Trevor Ward. He also held six catches in the game.

His brother Hugo played for Norfolk Under 21s. Felix scored 12 hundreds for Gresham's and jointly held the record stands for

the 2nd, 8th and 9th wickets as well as snapping up 7/37 versus Framlingham in 2005.

108 for Norfolk Development Squad XI v Cambridgeshire Under 25s June 2005

100 for Norwich CC v Vauxhall Mallards July 2008 – in Stan Biss Trophy semi-final. Dismissed by two NCCC players as he was stumped by Richard Goodenough off of the bowling of Rob Purton.

GILLIAT, Richard Temple

(b) Doncaster, Yorkshire 24 June 1979

Educ. – Barnby Dun First & Middle School; Hungerhill Comprehensive School; Hall Cross Sixth Form; Staffordshire University – studying Sports Science

Cricket. – Barnby Dun CC; Hungerhill Comprehensive School; Yorkshire Senior Schools; Hall Cross; Doncaster Town; Beccles CC; Norfolk Development Squad XI; Horsford

HS. 19 no v Buckinghamshire August 2008 @ Burnham

BB. 5/110 v Northumberland June 2008 @ Jesmond – as he topped the 2008 Championship bowling averages

7/50 for Horsford v Godmanchester Town July 2007

Richard has moved around the UK but has now married and settled in Bungay. He is a fast bowling option for Norfolk but is presently trying to overcome an elbow problem.

PATSTON, Benjamin John

(b) Norwich 18 June 1985

Lives in Oamaru, New Zealand

Educ. – Wymondham College; Bedford University

Cricket. – Norwich CC; SR Harvey's 'West' XI; Norfolk Development Squad XI; Minor Counties

HS. 107 v Staffordshire June 2009 @ Horsford – with 10 (4) & 6 (6) after 75 in the first innings (his 50 off 37 balls).

HS. 52 v MCC Young Cricketers May 2009 @ Horsford

HS. *76 v Northumberland May 2009 @ Horsford – off 59 balls with 10 (4) and 1 (6).*

His swashbuckling, explosive batting was a joy to watch and he was a cast iron certainty to pick up the 2009 Young Player-of-the-Year Shield. The cherry on top was his brutal 65 with 7(4) & 3 (6) in the winning MCCA Knockout Final game versus Staffordshire. When Norfolk batted first it paid to be at the ground for the start of play. His brilliance is missed as he decided to be an egg chaser as follows -

Rugby Union for Bedford Blues; Northampton Saints; Cambridge Rugby Club; Rugby Lions; Birmingham & Solihull Bees; Otago; North Otago; Oamaru Old Boys.

There is a Ben Patston 2010 Rugby Highlight Reel on You Tube. A fine left footed fly-half who makes awesome line breaks and accurate off loads. His side won the Meads Cup Final October 2010 to include his 55 metre penalty. He is having a whale of a time after leaving a major English city for a quiet laidback lifestyle. Ben says, "It's great not to get a regular mud bath when playing."

ROBINSON, Darren David John

(b) Braintree, Essex 2 March 1973
Educ. – Tabor High School; Chelmsford College
Cricket. – Essex Club & Ground; England Under 17 -19s; Essex; Leicestershire; Hornchurch
HS. *64 v Northumberland May 2008 @ Morpeth – off 79 balls being finally stumped as Norfolk won the cup tie by 5 runs.*
1st class cricket – 189 matches 10,489 runs 156 catches 2 wickets with 7,149 of the runs scored for Essex and centuries against 12 Counties. A solid opening bat who was capped by Essex and Leicestershire. He was released by Leicestershire when they were seeking to develop young talent as stated by their coach Tim Boon (q.v)
124 for England Under 19s v Sri Lanka Under 19s September 1992.
200 for Essex v New Zealand August 1999
81 for Leicestershire v Australia July 2005 – after a first baller in the first innings (LBW to Brett Lee)

ROBINSON, Scott George

(b) Norwich 12 January 1988
Educ. – Town Close House School; Wymondham College; Norwich City College; University of West England (Bristol) - studying Business and Property
Cricket. – Town Close House School; Norfolk Under 11-19s; Wymondham College; Norfolk Development Squad XI; University of West England; Vauxhall Mallards
HS. 13 v Netherlands April 2008 @ ACC Amsterdam
Stepson of Roger Finney (q.v)
101 no for Vauxhall Mallards (2) v Drayton CC Sunday X1 May 2005 – plus 3/45 with his right arm leg spinners

SMART, Benjamin Graham

(b) Huntingdon 26 April 1989
Educ.- Ashill Primary School; Wayland High School; King's Lynn College
Cricket. – Hadenham; Old Buckenham; Cambridgeshire Juniors; Norfolk Under 15,17 & 19s; Norfolk Development Squad XI; Fakenham
HS. Did not Bat in his one friendly match
BB. 1/27 v Netherlands 'A' April 2008 @ ACC Rotterdam – he bowled International One Day player Tom de Grooth on the matting wicket
3/26 for Norfolk Development Squad XI v Lincolnshire Development Squad XI May 2007
5/61 for Fakenham v Cambridge Granta July 2007

SMITH, Darren James

(b) Norwich 11 May 1989
Educ. – Hellesdon High School
Cricket. – Horsford; Norfolk Under 17 & 19s; Norfolk Development Squad XI

HS. 9 v Northumberland July 2010 @ Horsford
HS. 1 no v Netherlands 'A' April 2008 @ VOC Rotterdam
HS. *Did not Bat v Suffolk May 2008 @ Woodbridge – a stumping amongst his two victims.*
A right handed batsman and wicket keeper for the game where George Walker took 16/96.
Darren successfully gloved two of the wickets and conceded just one bye in a match total of 282 runs scored by Cambridgeshire

TODD, Addam James Michael

(b) King's Lynn, Norfolk 29 September 1985 - his birth registered as Adam.
Educ. – Clack Close Primary School; Downham Market High School
Cricket. – Downham Town; Norfolk Under 13-15 & 17s; Norfolk Development Squad XI
HS. 13 no v Essex (2) April 2009 @ Bishop's Stortford
HS. *11 v Staffordshire May 2008 @ Horsford*
6/10 for Downham Town v Castle Acre June 2007
125 no for Downham Town v March Town April 2009

2009

BUSH, Harry

(b) Tarzana, Los Angeles, U.S.A 6 November 1989
Came to England at age 4
Educ. – Town Close House School; Framlingham College
Cricket. – Norwich; Norfolk Under 11-19s; Norfolk Development Squad XI; Minor Counties; AD Wilson's XI; Leeds/Bradford MCCU
HS. 75 no v Cumberland June 2010 @ Barrow-in-Furness
HS. 47 no v Essex (2) April 2010 @ Bishop's Stortford
HS. *50 no v Cambridgeshire May 2011 @ Horsford*
BB. *1/10 v Lincolnshire April 2010 @ Horsford*
131 for Norwich v Bromley Common August 2005
5/35 & 82 no for Norfolk Under 17s v Huntingdonshire Under 17s August 2006
103 for Norfolk Development Squad XI v Essex Development Squad XI August 2009
75 for Minor Counties v Kent (2) July 2010
75 for Leeds/Bradford MCCU v Derbyshire May 2011 – batting at no. 8
F.F. – Harry played Hockey, Tennis and Golf for Norfolk Juniors.

HARVEY, Benjamin Lloyd

(b) King's Lynn, Norfolk 15 September 1988
Educ. – Fakenham High School; Wymondham College; University of Bedfordshire
Cricket. – Fakenham; Great Witchingham; Norfolk Under 15

& 17s; Norfolk Development Squad XI
HS. 11 v Staffordshire June 2009 @ Horsford
HS. *Did no Bat v Lincolnshire June 2009 @ Grantham.*
Son of SR (q.v)
A neat wicket keeper who has conceded, in his two NCCC matches, just 9 byes in 861 runs. That after facing 902 balls of the Brown/Walker spin attack.
102 no for Norfolk Under 15s v Leicestershire & Rutland Under 15s June 2004
76 for Norfolk Development Squad v Lincolnshire Development Squad May 2009
95 for Fakenham v Stow May 2011

THELWELL, Sam James
(b) Norwich 5 December 1989
Educ. – Hethersett High School; City of Norwich School
Cricket. – Hethersett High School; Mulbarton; Old Catton; Swardeston
HS. 0 & 0 no v Bedfordshire July 2009 @ Bedford Modern School AND 0 no v Cambridgeshire August 2009 @ Horsford
BB. 2/48 v Bedfordshire July 2009 @ Bedford Modern School
HS. 0 v MCC Young Cricketers April 2009 @ Horsford
BB. 1/35 v MCC Young Cricketers April 2009 @ Horsford
9.2-7-3-5 for Swardeston Sunday XI v Mattishall May 2009
60 for Swardeston Midweek X1 v Saxlingham July 2009
7/29 for Swardeston v Burwell August 2010 – Mark Thomas (q.v) 3/44 was the other wicket taker.

TROWER, Jonathan
(b) Sheffield 12 June 1979
Educ. – Athelstan Primary School; Handsworth Grange School
Cricket. – Handsworth Grange School; Sheffield United CC; Yorkshire Academy; Cleethorpes; Wickersley Old Village; 2nds of Essex, Middlesex & Worcestershire; Lincolnshire; Berkshire; Norfolk Development Squad XI; Minor Counties Under 25s; Clifton Village; Minor Counties; Townsville
HS. 22 v Staffordshire June 2009 @ Horsford
HS. 34 v MCC Young Cricketers April 2009 @ Horsford
HS. *17 no v Lincolnshire June 2009 @ Grantham* – a sixth wicket partnership with George Walker that saw NCCC win with eight balls to spare.
48 for Lincolnshire v Norfolk June 2002
88 no for Minor Counties Under 25s v Middlesex (2) June 2006 – regularly playing with Paul Bradshaw (q.v) and occasionally with two other NCCC men namely James Spelman and Steve Gray.
F.F. – A Civil Servant attached to the Fraud Squad

WATSON, Aaron Ashley
(b) Norwich 7 June 1982

Educ. – Reepham High School; College of West Anglia; Anglia Ruskin University
Cricket. – Great Witchingham; Vauxhall Mallards; Albion Tauranga (N.Z); Norfolk Development Squad XI; Marist (N.Z); Norwich; C. Brown's 'East' XI; Upper Ferntree Gully (Australia); Northern Brothers (Australia); Bracewell Academy XI (N.Z); Albion CC (N.Z)
HS. 2 no v Staffordshire June 2009 @ Horsford
BB. 3/43 v Staffordshire August 2010 @ Stone
BB. 3/57 v MCC Young Cricketers April 2010 @ High Wycombe
81 for Norwich CC Sunday XI v Mundford Sunday XI April 2011
5/22 for Norwich CC v Fakenham May 2009 – with his brother Ashley (q.v) getting 3/14 .
Aaron is the Norwich CC Youth Coaching Co-ordinator. A UKCC2 coach and he is training to reach Level 3.The advent of aeroplanes broadens the cricketers' experience these days with his career taking in Australia and New Zealand.

WISEMAN, Paul David Edward
(b) Norwich 25 August 1972
Educ. – Hewitt School
Cricket. – Hewitt School; Ingham Under 16s; St Catherines; Cringleford; Ingham; Horsford; MCC; Norwich CC
HS. 1 no v MCC Young Cricketers April 2009 @ Horsford
BB. 1/33 v MCC Young Cricketers April 2009 @ Horsford
3/47 for MCC v Spain October 2010 @ La Manga Club – on a tour of Spain and Gibraltar.
63 for Norwich CC v Nottingham CC August 2004
7/29 for Norwich CC v Fakenham May 2010 – the EAPL website credits 'Bart' with 224 wickets at minimal cost. His NCCC Friendly game was probably in recognition of his outstanding wholehearted displays at club level.

2010

BLAKE, Jason Steven
(b) Norwich 22 April 1985
Educ. – Sparkhawk Infant School; Falcon Infant School; Sprowston High School
Cricket. – Sprowston High School; Anglians; Sprowston CC; Norwich CC; Norfolk Development Squad XI
HS. 10 v Cumberland June 2010 @ Furness
Steve Gray has prevailed as the First team wicket keeper in the face of competition from Jason, Richard Goodenough, Ben Harvey, Luke Newton, Alex Patmore, Will Rist and Darren Smith.
65 no for Norwich v Great Witchingham August 2008 – a match show casing thirteen NCCC players with six on his side. The EAPL website (as at 06/06/11) details 140 victims for him with his best being 5 in an innings against Fakenham May 2010 – a total matched by Ben Harvey for the opposition that day.
F.F. – A British Gas Service Engineer.

CASWELL, Luke William

(b) Great Yarmouth, Norfolk 13 July 1989
Educ. – Benjamin Britten High School; Easton College; East Norfolk Sixth Form College – studying Sports Science
Cricket. – Lowestoft; Beccles Town; Gary's Gropers (Indoor Cricket); Norfolk Under 17 & 19s; Norfolk Development Squad XI; Horsford; Hannah's CC (Australia)
HS. 72 v Hertfordshire July 2011 @ Hertford
BB. 1/9 v Lincolnshire August 2010 @ Horsford
HS. 16 v MCC Young Cricketers April 2011 @ Horsford
BB. 1/28 v MCC Young Cricketers April 2010 @ High Wycombe
HS. *2 v Lincolnshire June 2011 @ Bracebridge Heath*
BB. *2/18 v Lincolnshire June 2011 @ Bracebridge Heath*
Luke is a Level 2 cricket coach – the ECB mission statement is that one has to prepare for, deliver and review coaching sessions

COLLISHAW, Thomas Michael

(b) Nottingham 22 December 1984
Educ. – Bluecoat School; Bedford University
Cricket. – Nottinghamshire Under 11-19s; Nottinghamshire 2nds; Kimberley Institute; Norfolk Development Squad XI; Great Witchingham
HS. 25 v Buckinghamshire July 2010 @ Horsford
HS. 55 v Essex (2) April 2010 @ Bishop's Stortford
HS. *2 v Lincolnshire June 2011 @ Bracebridge Heath*
104 for Kimberley Institute v Treeton in the Cockspur Cup May 2005.
120 no for Great Witchingham Mid Norfolk Sunday XI v Bacton Sunday XI August 2010 – he 'feathered' 11 (4) and 9 (6) in a declaration of 220-1 off 25 overs. Carl Rogers and Shaun Arthurton kept their collective bats in the pavilion that day.
His father Colin and Uncle Stephen were both on Nottinghamshire's books in the 1970s. Tom had a great grounding with Kimberley Institute in the Nottinghamshire Cricket Board Premier League. It was after all good enough fare for Will Jefferson (q.v).
Why run when you can powerfully reach or clear the boundary was the prognosis for his blazing 98 no for the Norfolk Development Squad XI against the Lincolnshire counterparts in May 2010. At better than a run a ball he struck 14 (4) and 3 (6).

GOODENOUGH, Richard John Charles

(b) Bury St Edmunds 27 November 1984
Educ. – Feoffment Community Primary School; St James' Church of England High School; King Edward VI GS; Chichester University – gaining a Sports Therapist Degree
Cricket. – King Edward VI GS; Chichester University; Bury St Edmunds; Suffolk Development Squad XI; Suffolk Under 21s; Essex 2nds; Norfolk Development Squad XI; Clacton-on-Sea; Vauxhall Mallards

HS. 0 v Cambridgeshire June 2010 @ March
HS. *Did not Bat in his one cup match against Berkshire May 2010 @ Horsford – the 2011 NCCC Handbook report of the match gives his name as Goodfellow (a 1990 player)! He held two catches in a competent 'backstop' display conceding no byes.*
71 no for Vauxhall Mallards v Fakenham July 2009 – in a first wicket partnership of 114 with Carl Amos (q.v)
A temporary Teacher at King Edward V1 School before accepting the post of Sports Teacher at Mildenhall Upper School (College of Technology)

LAMBERT, Peter Alan

(b) Great Yarmouth, Norfolk 13 April 1990
Educ. – Langley School; Nottingham Trent University
Cricket. – Nottingham Trent University; Norfolk Under 13, 17 & 19s; Norfolk Club & Ground; Norwich Wanderers; Norfolk Development Squad XI; Unicorns 'A'; Swardeston
HS. 40 v Hertfordshire July 2011 @ Hertford
HS. 24 v Essex (2) April 2011 @ Southend
HS. *44 v Berkshire May 2011 @ Newbury*
66 for Norfolk Under 17s v Cambridgeshire Under 17s August 2007
142 for Swardeston v Norwich CC July 2009.
110 for Nottingham Trent University v University of Leicester May 2010
Peter came to national attention in the Final of the Cockspur 20/20 at the Rose Bowl in May 2010.
He effectively won the game for Swardeston against South Northumberland with a truly stunning 72 no off 52 balls with 2 (4) and 5 (6) in front of the Sky TV Cameras.
F.F. – Football for Gorleston in the Ridgeons League

MILES, Jonathan Samuel

(b) Sutton Coldfield, Warwickshire 21 February 1986
Educ. – Sir William Robertson High School; Sleaford Sixth Form
Cricket. – Sir William Robertson High School; Warwickshire Under 11s; Lincolnshire Under 12s & Development Squad; Sleaford; Bourne; Kidderminster Victoria; Lincolnshire; Minor Counties Under 25s; MCC Young Cricketers; MCC; Unicorns; Barrow; 2nds of Durham, Essex, Nottinghamshire; Surrey & Worcestershire; Oswestry CC
HS.17 v Northumberland July 2010 @ Horsford
BB. 4/57 v Northumberland July 2010 @ Horsford
Presently playing for the Unicorns and a great day recently was getting through the defence of Marcus Trescothick for just one as Jonathan continues to play against County sides .
6/115 for MCC Young Cricketers v Durham (2) May 2010.
A left arm pace bowler who made a fine impression in his one season for NCCC and he is now the Oswestry School cricket coach.

2011

BUNTING, Kieran James
(b) King's Lynn, Norfolk 26 August 1992
Educ. – King Edward VII School (King's Lynn) and their Sixth Form
Cricket. – King Edward VII School; Norfolk Under 15-17s; Norfolk Development Squard XI; North Runcton
Son of SJ (q.v) and Nephew of RA (q.v)
HS. 9 v Buckinghamshire August 2011 @ Slough
BB. 1 /30 v Buckinghamshire August 2011 @ Slough

FINDLAY, Ryan James
(b) Norwich 23 May 1993
Educ. – King's Park School; St Nicholas Junior School; Wymondham College – Sports Leisure Studies
Cricket. – Wymondham College; Norfolk Under 11,13-15, 17 and 19s; Norfolk Development Squad XI; Bradenham; Horsford; Northamptonshire Academy, Under 17s & 2nds
HS. 5 v MCC Young Cricketers April 2011 @ Horsford
58 no for Northamptonshire Cricket Academy v Rushton June 2009
He dismissed Steve Gray (q.v) July 2010 while performing for Northamptonshire 2nds against MCC Universities.
5/61 for Northamptonshire Cricket Academy v Northampton Saints May 2011
Plays cricket for Horsford with his brother Luke with their father Roland having played for Norfolk Over 50s cricket team

SHEARER, Alistair Edward
(b) Reading 2 November 1984
Educ. – Framingham Earl High School; Hewett School Sixth Form; De Montfort University - BSc Sports Science; University of Bedfordshire - PGCE
Cricket. – Framingham Earl High School; Northamptonshire Under 11s; Norfolk Under12s; Norfolk Development Squad XI; Brooke; Richmond CC (Australia); Vauxhall Mallards
HS. – 1 v Buckinghamshire August 2011 @ Slough
219 no for Brooke v Cringleford Lodge 2004.
Ali is a Teacher at Thorpe St Andrew School

STONE, Oliver Peter
(b) Norwich 9 October 1993
Educ. – Thorpe St Andrew High School, Moulton College – studying BTEC National Diploma in Sport
Cricket. – Thorpe St Andrew High School; Moulton College; Norfolk Under 10-15s; Vauxhall Mallards; Northamptonshire Cricket Academy; U17s, 2nds and t20
HS. 36 v Bedfordshire July 2011 @ Horsford – in 104 run partnership for the 9th wicket with Carl Rogers
BB. 3/49 Befordshire July 2011 @ Horsford

He has already been on a tour to India with Northamptonshire and thankfully recovered from a stress fracture of the back.
128 for Norfolk Under 14s v Northamptonshire in June 2007.
A fabulous NCCC debut as he clean bowled 5 of his 6 victims. The rules only allowed him to bowl in 7 over spells as he was under eighteen. Called up for the England Under 19 training squad in August 2011.

WARNES, Michael William
(b) Norwich 25 August 1989
Educ. – Cromer High School; Paston Sixth Form School; York St John University – BA (Hons) Sports Studies
Cricket. – Norfolk Under 15 & 17s; Norfolk Development Squad XI; Cromer; Horsford; Great Boulder CC (Australia); Northamptonshire 2nds
HS. 18 v Bedfordshire August 2011 @ Horsford
BB. 4/36 Bedfordshire August 2011 @ Horsford
HS. *2 no v Lincolnshire June 2011 @ Bracebridge Heath*
BB. *2/70 v Lincolnshire June 2011 @ Bracebridge Heath*
Brother of MR (q.v)

YATES, Patrick
(b) King's Lynn, Norfolk 12 February 1991
Educ. – Methwold High School; Loughborough University – studying Business Management
Cricket. – Methwold High School; Norfolk Under 11,13,15 and 17s; Norfolk Development Squad XI; Mundford; Downham Market; Loughbrough University Squad
HS. 4 v Essex (2) April 2011 @ Southend
His father Robin is the Mundford CC Chairman
98 for Mundford Under 16s v Downham Town Under 16s June 2007
6/14 & 57 no for Mundford v Downham Town May 2010 – with a first wicket stand of 120 with his father

CURIO CORNER

ANDERSON, Matthew Alan
(b) Darwin, Northern Territory, Australia 30 November 1976
Lives in Brisbane, Australia
Cricket. – Northern Territory Under 17 & 19s; Sandgate-Redcliffe CC; Queensland Colts, Academy & Bulls; Australia Under 19s; Queensland Academy of Sport; Queenland Country Origin; Norwich CC
Sub Fielder – August 2001 v Holland @ Horsford in Cheltenham & Gloucester Trophy. He held a catch off the bowling of Paul Newman in a victory for NCCC by virtue of losing fewer wickets in a tied match.
He was at Queensland Bulls with Bichel, Hauritz, Hayden & Symonds and a State Contract player alongside Hopes, Johnson, Kasprowicz and Law.

ARMSTRONG, David John Michael

(b) Thorpe St Andrew, Norwich 24 August 1936
Educ. – King's College School (Cambridge) – a Chorister; St John's School (Leatherhead) – a Music Scholar; Cambridge University (Selwyn College – BA 1960 MA 1964)
Cricket. – Norfolk Club & Ground; Surrey 2nds; West Norfolk; Castle Rising; Buckinghamshire (as a sub fielder); MCC; Cryptics; Coltishall
Brother-in-Law of Bill Thomas (q.v)
Sub Fielder – He undertook the role on a number of occasions with most notable time being against Staffordshire in July 1970 @ Lakenham when he held two catches off the bowling of Billy Rose.
Bill Edrich said that if David had caught a third he would have capped him.
NCCC Secretary 1967-1984 and Minor Counties Secretary 1983-2001. NCCC President 2003-2006.
Also PA to Surrey CCC Secretary 1969-70 and quite rightly a NCCC Honorary Life Member.
104 for Cryptics versus Market Drayton in 1967/68.
I have even seen his name on a printed scorecard as a scorer – every NCCC task undertaken.
A former teacher in Hertfordshire and Norfolk he was taught briefly by George Martin (q.v).
F.F. – My favourite statistic is that it is reckoned that David is the only person to have witnessed all four instances of a Norfolk player scoring a century in each innings (1961, 1986, 1991 and 2010)

BERNERS, Major John Anstruther, OBE JP

(b) Mayfair, London 23 September 1869
(d) Woolverstone Park, Suffolk 2 March 1934
Educ. – Eton College; Cheam School; Sandhurst RMC
Cricket. – Eton College; Eton Ramblers; Middlesex; Gentlemen of England; Incogniti; Suffolk; MCC; Free Foresters; London County.
1st class cricket - 2 matches 59 runs
Sub Fielder – He held a catch for Norfolk off the bowling of Charlie Shore against Cambridgeshire at Lakenham in August 1899.
F.F. – A Major in the 1st Dragoon Guards and Master of Eastern Counties Otter Hounds. In 1903 he played four games against Norfolk for four different teams within a fortnight. The last four teams in his list of clubs above.

BLAKE, Marcus

(b) Worthing, Sussex 12 August 1843
(d) Bury St Edmunds 10 April 1919
Sub Fielder – A catch July 1877 at New Ground, Norwich against Suffolk held as a result of a chance offered by his brother.
His brother was the Suffolk cricketer Augustus Frederick

Blake (b1847- d1884). Their father Joseph was a fund holder and Annuitant and he was born in Madras. Twenty years later his birthplace mysteriously changed to South Carolina? Marcus lived on his own means with a Cook and a Parlour Maid in attendance. The other brother in contention for the catch was Robert (b1849 - d1930) who was a Railway Signalman living in such diverse places as Suffolk, London, Essex and Bournemouth. Never still long enough to hold a catch!

BLATHERWICK

Cricket. – Yarmouth Town; Yarmouth Fifteen
Sub Fielder – He held a catch off the bowling of Charles Shore against Durham in August 1899 at Great Yarmouth. An extensive research has failed to even find his Christian name.

BLINCOE, Christopher Paul

(b) Norwich 19 June 1980
Educ. – Norwich GS; University of East Anglia - BSc MSc
Cricket. – Norwich GS; Swardeston; Saxlingham
Brother of AM (q.v)
Sub Fielder – He was just two weeks older than Sam Arthurton (the all time youngest NCCC debutant) when he caught Steve Plumb off Steve Goldsmith at Lakenham against Lincolnshire in July 1996 in a Minor Counties match. Chris was a Mott MacDonald Limited Environmental Consultant and gained his Masters Degree in Environmental Impact Assessment, Auditing and Management Systems. He is now the UEA Project Manager at the Low Carbon Innovation Centre.
F.F. – His mother Caroline won many Lawn Tennis titles at all levels for Norfolk County.

CLARK, Daniel Keith

(b) Military Base, Munster, Germany 17 September 1987
Educ. – Guston Primary School; Elvington & Eythorpe Primary School; Archers Court Secondary School; Coventry University
Cricket. – Tilmingston CC; Betteshanger CC; Selsted; Dover District 12 to 16s; Kent Youth Under 15s; Folkestone; Horsford; Norfolk Development Squad
Sub Fielder – Came on for an over when George Walker left the field v Hertfordshire July 2011 in Hertford.

de ZOETE, Miles Herman

(b) Braintree, Essex 4 September 1907
(d) East Bergholt, Sussex 9 July 1987
Educ. – Ludgrove School; Eton College; Cambridge University (Magdalen College)
Cricket. – Eton College; Eton Ramblers; Public Schools; Hertfordshire; I Zingari; Free Foresters; Gentlemen of Essex;

Rickling Green CC; British Empire XI

Sub Fielder – He held a Minor Counties catch for Norfolk off the bowling of Walter Eagle against his Hertfordshire side at Watford in August 1930.

His father played for Essex CCC and a member of his past family was the Deputy Chairman of the Stock Exchange in 1866. In the family firm of de Zoete and Gorton (Stockbrokers)

DENMARK, Kevin Robert

(b) Norwich 22 November 1956

Educ. – Blackdale Junior School; City of Norwich School

Cricket. – CEYMS; Norfolk Schools Under 15s; Norfolk Young Amateurs; Carrow; Dereham; Bradenham; Anglians; Norwich Cavaliers;

Sub Fielder – In the Minor Counties Championship Challenge Match of September 1981 away at Durham. Father of LRK (q.v)

The Cricket Development Officer for the Norfolk Cricket Board

DENMARK, Lewis Robert Kevin

(b) Norwich 20 December 1993

Educ. – Northgate High School & Sixth Form

Cricket. – Northgate High School; Dereham St Nicholas; Bradenham Bears; Norfolk Development Squad XI; Bradenham

Sub Fielder – In the Minor Counties fixture at Horsford July 2010 against Buckinghamshire

Son of KR (q.v)

167 for Bradenham Bears v Dersingham Royals July 2011 in Junior Carter Cup

FLANAGAN, Benjamin Alexander

(b) Bury St Edmunds 27 March 1992

Educ. – Sheringham High School & Sixth Form College

Cricket. – Sheringham CC; Norfolk Under 13-17 & 19s; Norfolk Development Squad; Aldborough; Norwich

Sub Fielder – Ben replaced skipper George Walker for a short while on the second day of the Northumberland Minor Counties match at Jesmond in June 2011

GOODALL, John

(b) Westminster, London 19 June 1863

(d) Watford, Hertfordshire 20 May 1942

Cricket. – Derbyshire; Hertfordshire

1st class cricket – 2 matches 38 runs 2 catches

Sub Fielder – He held a catch against his own side Hertfordshire in June 1906 @ West Hertfordshire CC Ground off the bowling of Gibson. They thrashed Norfolk by an innings and 116 runs.

John was one of the most illustrious footballers of the late nineteenth century who did not get the praise lavished at Steve Bloomer.

Football for Kilmarnock; Great Lever; PNE; Derby County; New Brighton Tower; Glossop North End; Watford player / manager to Manager; Mardy; England – 14 caps.

A Football League Championship and FA Cup winner who netted four hat-tricks at Division One (now called the Premiership) level with Derby County. He bettered this with 9 for PNE versus Dundee Strathmore and 16 in the famous 26-0 win over Hyde FC.

F.F. – Son of Scottish parents with a brother Archie also a Footballer. John had a shop in Watford outside of football.

HOWES, Oliver Anthony

(b) Norwich 14 April 1992

Educ. – Avenue Middle School; City of Norwich School; Norwich City College

Cricket. – Brooke; Norfolk Under 19s; Hardingham; Norfolk Development Squad XI

Sub Fielder – He was a substitute for Chris Brown for a short while in the M.C.C.A Knockout Trophy clash against Suffolk at Horsford May 2011

Ollie also plays football for Horsford

HUGHES Jonathan Oliver

(b) Hereford 15 November 1977

Educ. – City of Norwich School; Gresham's School (Tallis House); Cambridge University (Peterhouse College BA 2000 MA 2003) – now an MBA

Cricket. – City of Norwich School; Gresham's School; Eaton CC; Peterhouse College; Norfolk Under16s; Norfolk Young Cricketers; Free Foresters

Rugby Union.- Norwich; England schoolboys

Sub Fielder – The first ever NCCC appearance maker to have played for Eaton CC. His appearance was in the late 90s at Lakenham

He worked for Merrill Lynch in London for ten years and is now the head of Global Equities for UBS.

HYLAND, Frederick James

(b) Sedelscombe, Sussex 16 December 1893

(d) Hartford, Cheshire 27 February 1964

Educ. – Sedelscombe School

Cricket. – Sedelscombe; Hampshire; Dereham

1st class cricket – 1 match. He neither batted nor bowled as only two overs were completed. Possibly the shortest first-class career ever?

Sub Fielder – On for George Stevens (I think the assailant was a ball) against Kent 2nds at Lakenham in a Minor Counties encounter in August 1926.

He was a Gardener on Country Estates in his late teens and

latterly a Nurseryman in Cheshire. Fred was also a Sports ground Curator for the Northwich Chemical Company.

F.F. – In his probated London will he left £2,613 to be shared equally by his Pet Shop Proprietor sons Peter and Philip.

JENKINSON, Shaun David

(b) Stone, Staffordshire 20 April 1983

Educ. – St Michael's Primary School; Walton Middle School; Thomas Alleyne's High School; Stafford College

Cricket. – England Schoolboys at 15; Midlands; Stone; Staffordshire; Cheadle

Sub Fielder – On for Andy Clarke he held (to the delight of the Norfolk men) a steepler off of Chris Carey to get rid of top scorer Graeme Archer (ten first class tons to his name) in June 2000 v Staffordshire @ Stone.

Shaun says that he did not play for Walsall despite this being claimed by Cricket Archive.

He is an Assembler for JCB (Mechanical Engineers).

KINGLSEY, Sir Patrick Graham Toler, KCVO

(b) Calcutta, India 26 May 1908

(d) Yeovil, Somerset 24 August 1899

Lived West Hill Farm, Knowle, Coventry

Educ. – Winchester College; Oxford University (New College)

Cricket. – Winchester College; Rest of Schools; Oxford University – Blue 1928-30; Public Schools; MCC; Gentlemen; England XI; Free Foresters; Minor Counties; Harlequins; WFT Holland's XI; Hertfordshire; Devon

Also an Oxford University soccer Blue.

1st class cricket - 47 matches 2,270 runs 41 catches 4 wickets

Sub Fielder – His was a memorable performance in the NCCC v Hertfordshire Minor Counties clash at Cokenach in July 1929. His first innings 111 was in just over two hours with all the strokes and a model of correctness. He fielded for Walter Dann and held two brilliant catches off Rodney Rought-Rought's bowling. He nearly repeated the feat the following year at Watford in August 1930 – this time a single gully catch off Walter Eagle as a replacement for George Scott-Chad who had muscular trouble.

A Major in the Queen's Royal Regiment during WW2.

F.F. – The Secretary and Keeper of records to the Duchy of Cornwall from 1954-1972 (in effect the Chief Executive of the Prince of Wales Estate). This promotion after serving as the Assistant Secretary from 1930-1954

LECK, James Martin Calder

(b) Croydon 15 June 1989

Educ. – Caterham School; University of East Anglia – studying Politics and International Relations

Cricket. – Caterham School; Caterham CC; Horsford; Claremont-Nedlands CC (Australia)

Sub Fielder – A catch off the off-breaks of Chris Brown in the Minor Counties match versus Northumberland at Horsford July 2010. He was fielding for Trevor Ward who suffered some stiffness after his second innings 107.

LEGGE, Robin Humphrey

(b) Liverpool 28 June 1862

(d) Kensington Nursing Home, London 6 April 1933

Educ. – Birkenhead Prep School ; Cambridge University (Trinity Hall College- reading Law)

Cricket. – CT Studd's XI; MCC

Sub Fielder – He caught MCC Skipper Herbert Pigg to help Charlie Shore take 7/55 @ Lakenham August 1890.

He studied music in Leipzig and Frankfurt and was on the Staff of 'The Times' (1891-1906) as an Assistant Music Critic. He became the Music Critic for 'The Daily Telegraph' (1908-1931).

Robin contributed many biographies to the Dictionary of National Biography and to Grove's Dictionary of Music and Musicians. He also published over 100 Chess problems. Census forms list him as an Author and Music Composer. What was his connection to Norfolk ? He Edited the Norfolk Cricket Annual for ten years.

MOORE, David Sidney

(b) Norwich 7 July 1959

Lives in Toronto, Canada

Educ. – Norwich GS; Bradford University – Business Studies

Cricket. – Norwich GS; Norfolk Schoolboys; Norwich Wanderers

Son of NH (q.v) and Brother of GJ (q.v)

Sub Fielder – Held a catch against Buckinghamshire at Lakenham July 1977 off of Billy Rose's bowling. The game in which Terry Barnes took 8/45.

David trained as an Accountant and he is now a Financial Auditor

MOORE, Gregory John

(b) Norwich 27 April 1961

Educ. – Norwich GS; Reading University – studying Land Management

Cricket. – Norwich GS; Norfolk Schoolboys; Reading University; Norwich Wanderers; Totteridge CC; Royal Institution of Chartered Surveyors CC; Hertfordshire League XI.

Son of NH (q.v) and Brother of DS (q.v)

Sub Fielder – The game(s) are not pinpointed as he did not effect a catch nor a run out but he was one of the Norwich GS twelfth men on a regular basis.

Greg is a Chartered Surveyor - BSc (Hons) FRICS. Works at

Chase & Partners LLP in London as the Partner responsible for the Out of Town Occupational/Agency & Development.

MUSK, Dr Stephen Robert Rolin

(b) West Norwich Hospital 21 May 1961
Educ. – Norwich GS; Cambridge University (Corpus Christi – BA 1983 MA 1987 PhD 1988)
Cricket. – Norwich Huns; Corpus Christi; Cross Keys PH; Nomads; Earlham Lodge; Nelson Ward CC
Sub Fielder – The wife of Bryan Stevens took Stephen home to collect his whites so that he could field in place of Andy Agar on a miserable day weather wise at Lakenham against Suffolk in August 1978.
A doctorate in cell biology he principally worked at the Institute of Food Research in Norwich. He is currently an 'expert by experience' training student social workers and clinical psychologists at the University of East Anglia.
F.F. – An enormous help with this tome bringing to the playing field his vast knowledge as the Norfolk Representative for the ACS Minor Counties Project. I thoroughly recommend his 'Lives in Cricket' book (2010) about the Norfolk legend Michael Falcon

NORMAN, Ronald Collett

(b) Kensington, London 5 November 1873
(d) Much Hadham, Hertfordshire 5 December 1963
Educ. – Eton College; Cambridge University (Trinity College – BA 1894 MA 1902)
Cricket. – Eton College; Eton Ramblers
Sub Fielder – He held a catch against Eton Ramblers at Lakenham July 1892 off the bowling of Vincent Hoare. He had a host of relatives who played cricket to County level. He was the Assistant Private Secretary to Hon. G. Wyndham and then worked for Messrs Martin's Bank. An Alderman and JP (Hertfordshire) he was the Private Secretary to the Lord Chancellor (Earl of Halsbury) and a Municipal Reformer for London County Council. He held a number of chairmanships but is most famously known as the BBC Chairman 1918/19, Vice Chairman 1933-35 and Chairman again 1935-39.

PEARSE, Ryan Steven

(b) Norwich 19 October 1993
Educ. – Kinsale First and Middle School; Taverham HS; Hellesdon Sixth Form
Cricket. – Kinsale Middle School; Taverham HS; Norfolk Under 11-17s; Sprowston
Sub Fielder – Fielded the whole of the second innings v Bedfordshire July 2011 @ Horsford as a replacement for Luke Caswell. A great sprint and dive to turn a certain looking boundary into a three in a one run victory for his county.

PERRY-WARNES, Nathan David

(b) Norwich 15 February 1989
Educ. – Corpusty Primary School; Reepham High School; Easton College - studying Agriculture
Cricket. – Corpusty Kwik Cricket; Reepham; Easton College; Norfolk Under 11-17s; Norfolk Development Squad XI; Fakenham; Horsford
Sub Fielder – He held a catch against Northumberland in June 2008 @ Jesmond to help Richard Gilliatt attain his best bowling analysis.
F.F. – He works for his Farmer father

PLAYER, Benjamin Louis

(b) Coventry 24 April 1981
Educ. – City of Norwich School; Brunel University – BSc Sports Science; University of East Anglia – PGCE
Cricket. – City of Norwich School; Eaton CC; Norfolk Under 21s, 2nd XI and Development Squad XI; Old Buckenham; Vauxhall Mallards
80 no for Norfolk 2nds v Huntingdonshire Under 25s June 2001
Sub Fielder – He was a substitute fielder in one of the last games at Lakenham and also in away matches against Buckinghamshire and Cambridgeshire in the early 2000s.
198 for Cromer Sunday v Rollesby 2009.
Ben is a Teacher at Framlingham Earl High School.

POINTER, O

Educ. – Bedford Grammar School
Cricket. – Bedford Grammar School
Sub Fielder – He held two catches against Bedfordshire in Bedford July 1908 with the beneficiaries being Edward Gibson and Len Leman

POTTER, W E

Educ. – Bracondale School
Cricket. – Bracondale school
Sub Fielder – He took the fielding place of Reverend Arthur Davies who was suffering from a sprain that he had been carrying for a couple of days. The game in question was a friendly in June 1894 against the Quidnuncs.
F.F. – Potter & Quidditch is close (Potter & Quidnuncs) they being a JK Rowling invention.

STONE, David Elleray

(b) Ipswich 30 November 1943
Lives Sydney, New South Wales, Australia
Educ. – Hillside Avenue Primary School; Norwich GS; Cambridge University (Emmanuel College – studying Natural Sciences (MA); College of St Mark & St John (Chelsea); London University –Dip Ed.
Cricket. – Norwich GS; Norfolk Schoolboys; Norfolk Club &

Ground; Barleycorns; Cranbrook School

Sub Fielder – On for Bill Edrich who absented himself on business versus Cambridgeshire August 1962 @ Lakenham. He represented Norfolk Schoolboys in Rugby, Hockey and Cross-country. Played football for Earlham Rangers and Rugby Union for ten years with the Sydney Eastern Suburbs Rugby Club to include a club world tour in 1971 that embraced the UK with a match against Richmond.

David taught at Taverham Hall Prep School and at Cranbrook School (Australia) 1966-2006 becoming Head of Chemistry. Also a boarding Housemaster there for 22 years and for the last eleven years the Director of Admissions.

THOMPSON, William

(b) Lowestoft 12 August 1953
Educ. – Norwich GS
Cricket. – Norwich GS; Norfolk Young Amateurs; Norwich Wanderers; Jesters; Great Melton; Cringleford; Cringleford Lodge
Sub Fielder - Against Staffordsire July 1970 at Lakenham. He was the official 12th man and came on for either Tony Smart (pulled muscle) or Walter Elliott (hand injury). David Armstrong was the other substitute fielder in the same innings that day.
F.F. – His father Colonel Ronald Frank Bliss Thompson (28/10/12 – 03/09/93) was a former NCCC President, Chairman and Honorary Life member. He also ran the Norfolk Young Amateurs. He left £127,464 in his will with his three sons being the Executors.

THREAPLETON, John David

(b) Menston, Yorkshire 6 May 1950
Educ. – Menston County Primary School; Aireborough GS
Cricket. – Aireborough; Guiseley; Kendal; Airedale District; Windermere; Workington; West Cumbria Law Society
Sub Fielder – A Minor Counties appearance for Norfolk v Cumberland @ Kendal in July 1984 as a 'step in' for Fred Handley who fell on the ball and cracked a rib
A Fire Officer with the Westmoreland Fire Brigade.

TRIPP, Mark Millar

(b) Gravesend, Kent 17 July 1990
Educ. – Gravesend Grammar School; University of East Anglia – studying Politics
Cricket. – Gravesend Grammar School; Ash CC; Hartley Country Club; Norwich & Coltishall Wanderers; Horsford
Sub Fielder – Came on for one over on the second day against Cumberland June 2010 at Furness CC as Chris Brown needed the toilet.

TURNER, David John

(b) Norwich 22 September 1992

Educ. – Cromer High School; Paston College; University of East Anglia – studying Physical Education
Cricket. – Cromer High School; Bradfield; Cromer; Vauxhall Mallards
Sub Fielder – On for the injured MW Warnes (q.v) on second day of Norfolk v Cumberland game at Manor Park in July 2011

WALTON, Mark Andrew

(b) Merthyr Tydfil 1 June 1969
Educ. – Pen-y-Drae Secondary School
Cricket. – Hoovers CC; Welsh Schools; Colchester; Wivenhall Town; Swardeston; Sully CC; Aberdare; MCC; Port Melbourne (Australia); Norfolk Alliance XI
Sub Fielder – On for Carl Amos (nursing an injured ankle) he held a superb boundary rope square leg catch high over his head off Steve Plumb. It happened in July 1993 at Lakenham versus Buckinghamshire. He was a Goalkeeper by profession.
Football – Swansea City; Luton Town; Colchester United; Norwich City FC; Wrexham (loan); Trials with St Johnstone, Dundee United and West Ham United; Bolton Wanderers; Wroxham; Gillingham; Fulham; Brighton & Hove Albion; Cardiff City
An ECB Qualified Cricket Coach (the sport was always his first love) going into schools on a daily basis during the summer. Mark has a Mexican Restaurant called Amigo's in Aberdare.

WESTLEY, Stuart Alker

(b) Fishergate, Preston 21 March 1947
Educ. – Colplane Primary School; Lancaster Royal GS; Oxford University (Corpus Christi College – studying Law
Cricket. – Lancaster Royal GS; Preston CC; Lancaster CC; Gloucestershire; Oxford University - Blue 1968/69; Lancashire 2nds; Oxford University Past & Present; Free Foresters; Norfolk & Suffolk; Suffolk Cricket Association; Midlands Club Cricket Conference; Suffolk; Minor Counties.
1st class cricket - 34 matches 577 runs plus 80 dismissals (71c 9s)
Sub Fielder – Came on for the injured Andy Agar in the Suffolk match at Lakenham August 1978.
A fine wicket keeper with 10 catches in one match for Suffolk v Buckinghamshire (1980). He had 236 dismissals for Suffolk and in 1977 he won the Wilfred Rhodes Trophy with a season's batting average of 94.50.
Assistant Master King Edward VII School (Lytham); Housemaster & Director of Sudies Framlingham College; Deputy Head of Bristol Cathedral School; Principal of King William's College (Isle of Man); Headmaster of Haileybury & Imperial Service College (1996.3 – 2009).
From September 2009 Stuart is the General Secretary for the Association Governing Bodies of Independent Schools

WILSON, Robert James

(b) Norwich 27 February 1968

Educ. – Fireside Middle School; Norwich GS

Cricket. – Norwich GS; Horsford; Lincolnshire (sub fielder with one catch); Norwich Union

Sub Fielder – A Minor Counties fixture against Bedfordshire August 1985 as a substitute for broken finger victim John Whitehead.

Robert helped at the two week Lakenham Festival selling scorecards and operating the scoreboard. Sir Charles Mott-Radclyffe (NCCC Chairman) took him home to get his kit at the lunch interval in the Norfolk v Lincolnshire game of July 1984. The Lincolnshire opener Munton broke a finger so Robert fielded for them and he caught Robert Bradford. Skipper Fred Handley asked him to be the official 12th man so throughout 1985/86 he made fleeting appearances covering minor injuries and toilet breaks.

F.F. – In a 1985 game at 10.59 am Steve Plumb sent him out to field for him as he needed a toilet break. The umpires would not allow it as if on the pitch for the first ball it was deemed that he would have to play the rest of the match.

PS – Many players have fielded as substitute fielders namely SS Arthurton jnr (2c), RJ Austin (1c), RJ Belmont, PC Borrett (2c), CSR Boswell, H Bush (2c), NR Cooke (1c), RJ Covill (1c), CA Cresswell (1c), F Cunliffe (1c), EH Edrich (2c), E Gibson (1c), R Goderson (2c), RDP Huggins (1c), WJ Lingwood (1c), HF Low (1c), CA McManus (1c), G Mitchell (1c), PG Newman, LTS Newton, MD Oxbury (1c), CBL Prior (1c), GJ Rye (1c), J Shepperd (1c), T Snelling (1c) SJ Starling (2c) and BGW Stevens (2c)

There are still 17 unnamed substitute catchers dating back to 1876. The author asked to field in a Minor Counties match recently as Skipper Chris Brown left the field to get some sugar intake from the club shop (run by the late Joyce King). He passed my sitting position on the boundary and when asked he replied, " But you are not wearing whites."

Players' Yearly Appearances

Players	Season Appearances
Abbs GR	1936-37
Adams CD	1994
Adams JC	1997
Addison MA	2005-06, 2008
Aitken APH	1924-26, 1932
Allen G	1902-05
Allsopp TC	1907-12
Amos C	1993-2008
Arnold RM	1894, 1896, 1901
Arthurton SS (jnr)	2008-2011
Astley DGL	1895
Atkins JP	1966-68
Austin RJ	2001-04
Backhouse J	1924-25
Bagnall RSV	1912, 1923-26
Bailey GL	1996-98
Baker SE	1910
Bally JH	1927-32
Barker CJ	1877
Barnes TH	1977-82
Barratt L	1890-95, 1897, 1899-1908, 1911
Barrett J	1970, 1976-82
Bartlett DMM	1893, 1901
Barton AW	1932-34
Barton GH	1877
Barton WJ	1904
Bassingthwaighte DN	1983
Bathurst LCV	1896-99, 1904
Battelley IN	1968-72, 1974-77, 1982
Beadsmoore WA	1920-31
Becton F	1885
Bell RV	1967-68
Belton EJ	1947-48
Beresford RM	1929-31, 1933-34, 1937, 1939, 1947-48
Bevan JS	1910
Birkbeck H	1935, 1946-47
Birkbeck WH	1895
Blake JS	2010
Blanchett IN	1994-95
Blincoe AM	1996-97
Blofeld JCC	1957
Blyth AG	1882-84, 1888, 1896
Borrett CR	2000-2011
Borthwick CH	1919, 1922-23
Boswell CSR	1939, 1946-55
Boyden MKL	1996-99
Bradshaw PJ	1995-2005, 2007, 2011

Players	Season Appearances
Abel AG	1929
Adams DJ	1993
Adams NJ	1997
Agar AC	1977-79, 1981-83, 1985
Allcock T	1959-62, 1964-70, 1973-75
Allen JE	2000
Ames SS	1911
Arnold HA	1883
Arthurton SS	2004-05
Ash EP	1877
Atherton DA	1951-52
Atmore EA	1877
Ayres IM	1979
Bacon NHP	1982
Bailey FP	1982, 1985
Bailey SP	2006-08
Ballance TGL	1932-39
Banks CJ	1877
Barnes A	1888-89, 1893
Barratt G	1894
Barratt WP	1899
Barrett LA	1938, 1947-54
Barton AJ	1877-78
Barton CT	1912
Barton MR	1933, 1935-37, 1947
Barwell CSW	1888
Bate JC	1952-58
Battelley BL	1969-72, 1976-80
Beacock GN	1972-75, 1978
Beare JC	1952
Bell FR	1928-30
Belmont RJ	1982-83, 1988, 1991
Beresford RAA	1901, 1903, 1909-10
Berwick TFH	1897
Birkbeck GW	1906-08, 1910-12
Birkbeck H	1876-87
Blake GF	1890-1904
Blake KPJ	2004
Bland TG	1965-68
Blofeld HC	1956-61, 1964, 1965
Blundell MC	1973-75
Boon TJ	1996-97
Borrett PC	1967-76, 1978
Boswell BRD	1967, 1972-74
Bowett TD	1957-58, 1965-66
Bradford RL	1978-82, 1984-88
Brand WG	1956

Players	Season Appearances	Players	Season Appearances
Brayne TL	1948-49, 1956-57, 1959	Brighton NA	1933, 1937
Brown C	2001-2011	Brown HE	1905
Brown JC	2008	Buckle FA	1880
Bunting KJ	2011	Bunting RA	1985-87, 1992-95
Bunting SJ	1991	Burrell HJE	1898, 1900
Burrows JW	1934	Bush H	2009-2011
Buxton AR	1888-99, 1901-06	Buxton B	1907
Buxton EG	1887, 1890-93	Buxton GF	1877, 1879-80
Buxton HG	1889-91	Campbell CA	1894
Campbell D	1877	Campbell GV	1906
Campion-Jones P	1959	Cant RW	1919-20, 1922, 1926, 1928-32, 1937
Carey CS	1992-94, 1998, 2000-01, 2003	Carter DD	1947-56
Carter GT	1913-14	Carter JR	1984-87
Carter RD	1911, 1920-25	Caswell LW	2010-2011
Cator CAM	1906	Cattermoule KM	1927
Chamberlain AC	1876	Chamberlain DH	1953-54
Charles SF	1905-07	Child SE	1995
Church P	1900	Circuitt RWP	1877
Clarke AR	2000	Clarke EWR	1879-83, 1886-88
Clements BA	1938, 1947-52	Clowes FW	1933
Cockburn MK	1895	Coldham JM	1924-32
Cole AP	1993-94	Collinson RW	1901-02, 1910-11
Collishaw TM	2010-11	Collison H	1880
Collyer WR	1880	Colman AR	1924
Colman CS	1919-21	Colman DWJ	1939
Colman GRR	1911, 1914, 1920-30	Colvin EG	1878
Compton JJ	1900, 1904, 1907-08, 1910-11	Cook ND	1971-72, 1974-75, 1977-88
Cooke FBR	1949	Cooke NR	1946-47, 1949-50, 1958
Cookson G	1898	Coomb AG	1956-63
Coomber F	1876-77, 1880-81	Cooper KP	1986-88, 1994
Cooper S	2001-02	Cooper T	1876
Coote P	1988-89	Coppin WR	1999
Corran AJ	1955, 1958-60	Covill RJ	1924, 1926-27
Cowles SRB	1891, 1893, 1895-98, 1900-02	Cozens- Hardy A	1888
Cozens-Hardy B	1902, 1904-06, 1908-11, 1913-14	Cozens-Hardy EW	1891
Cozens-Hardy F	1883-85, 1887	Crawshay FGL	1927-28
Cresswell CA	1877, 1880-81, 1883	Crowley SC	1993-96
Cubitt BB	1911	Cunliffe F	1932-35, 1937-39, 1948
Cunningham AD	1958-59	Currie FA	1880-82, 1885-87, 1901
Currie FA	1880-82, 1885-87, 1901	Currie RG	1880
Curteis TS	1881	Cushion JC	1954
Cuthbertson NW	1894	Daley JV	1930-31
Dann WE	1929, 1934	Darnell AF	1894-95
Davies AC	1876, 1878-79, 1882-95	Davies F	1877-78, 1880, 1884-1900, 1902
Davy JDW	1889	De Bruyn P	2003
De Moleyns FRWE	1885	Denton CS	1982
Dewing AM	1886	Dines E	1883
Dixon SB	1986, 1988-95	Dodds NDP	1975, 1978
Donaldson JA	1962-69, 1971	Dougill H	1919-20, 1922, 1924, 1926, 1928-29

Players	Season Appearances	Players	Season Appearances
Dowson H	1893	Drake D	1955
Drake GC	1891-94	Draper WH	1877-78
Drinkwater WL	1951-55	Duffield K	1954
Duffield PG	1960	Dunell OHC	1905-09
Dunn ATB	1886-89	Dunn MJ	1977-78, 1980
Dunning CE	1905-08, 1910	Durrant CF	1909
Eagle WG	1930-32	Earthy MC	1993
Eccles MP	2003-2011	Ede MP	2006
Edrich EH	1919	Edrich EH	1935-39, 1949-51
Edrich GA	1937-39	Edrich JH	1954, 1979
Edrich PG	1951	Edrich WJ	1932-36, 1959-71
Edwards RO	1920	Elliott WJ	1970-73, 1975-76, 1979-80
Ellis MT	1987-91	Ellison BCA	1991-92
Elwes GP	1881-85	Emonson MR	1960-62
English LM	1920	Evans NG	1923
Evans SD	2003	Everett RAL	1922-26, 1928
Falcon JH	1910-11, 1913-14, 1919-24	Falcon M	1906-08, 1910-14, 1919-39, 1946
Falconer R	1912-14	Farmer GAH	1909
Farrer RJ	1956-58	Farrow RDE	1991-94
Fellowes AE	1881	Fellowes EN	1882-83
Fellowes HC	1880	Fellowes R	1959
Fellowes RA	1904	Fellowes RT	1905
Ferley RS	1998	Ffolkes FAS	1886
Fiddler GG	1956-66	Fielding JL	1952, 1955-56
Finch A	1901	Findlay RJ	2011
Finney RJ	1989-94, 1997	Fisher HW	1898-99
Flower FJ	2008	Flower JE	1971-72
Flynn W	1877-80	Fortescue AT	1879-80
Foster NA	1995-96	Foster NL	1931-32
Fowler G	1996	Fowler RH	1908-09
Fox N	1991-2000	Francis JN	1955
Fraser HB	1901	Frederick TH	1912
Free PJ	2000-04, 2008	Frere LRT	1894-97
Fryer EH	1895	Fryer PA	1890-95, 1897-1903, 1905
Fryer PWJ	1921, 1923-26	Fulcher EJ	1910-14, 1920-22
Fulcher WP	1876, 1878	Garland TO	1920-22
Garner JP	1991, 1993, 1999-2003	Garnett CF	1900-1902
Garnier EHC	1939	Garnier ET	1899-1904, 1907, 1909, 1923
Garnier GR	1904	Gascoigne CCO	1908
Gathergood LS	1926	Gemmell G	1911
Gibson E	1902-14, 1919	Gibson JJC	1958-65
Gillham CJ	1969	Gilliatt RT	2008
Gladden RH	1927-30, 1935, 1937	Goderson R	1922-23
Godfrey DG	1958-61	Goldsmith SC	1993-2003
Goode WF	1897	Goodenough RJC	2010
Goodfellow BJ	1990	Goodliff F	1886
Goodley GW	1963, 1970-74, 1978	Goodrham MD	2003-05
Goodwin R	1965-67	Gorrod MA	1954-55
Grainge CM	1953	Grant CB	1954-56

Players	Season Appearances	Players	Season Appearances
Gray SK	2007-2011	Greatrex EJ	1953, 1957, 1963, 1965, 1967-71, 1973
Green CRF	1994	Green GGB	1967-69
Greenwell JW	1929	Groom AJ	1883
Gurdon C	1876-79, 1885	Gurdon ET	1879
Gurdon F	1879-80	Gurney EH	1889-91
Gurney GB	1879	Gurney H	1889-91
Gurney WS	1876-78, 1882-87, 1889, 1892-93	Gurney WSC	1961
Gwillim JH	1885	Hadley IPS	1914
Hale FW	1914	Halford AJ	1967-70
Hall ER	1961	Hall TA	1956-57
Hancock WD	1949-52, 1954, 1957, 1961	Handley FLQ	1969-90
Hankinson RS	1877	Hansell J	1884-88, 1890
Hansell WE	1881, 1889	Hanworth WR	1951
Harbour	1882	Hare JHM	1876, 1882-90
Hare T	1947-48, 1954	Harris AJ	1997
Harris CZ	1997	Harrison I	2002
Harrison MJ	1950, 1953-54	Hart-Davis SO	1880
Harvey BL	2009	Harvey GEA	1922-23, 1930
Harvey SR	1993-95	Harwood PJ	1994-98
Hastings HF	1888-89	Hawes WG	1880
Hayles BRM	1947	Hayter WLB	1900-05
Heading RB	1919-20	Heasman WG	1890-91
Herr K	1998	Heslop GG	1895-1901
Heywood RJ	1962	Higenbottam OT	2004, 2009
Hildyard C	1885	Hill SD	1912, 1914
Hoare AR	1890-92, 1894-96, 1903-05, 1907	Hoare OVG	1903
Hoare VR	1890, 1892-94, 1897, 1903-05	Hoare WR	1887-92, 1896
Hodson ER	1983-86, 1988	Hoff RHG	1951-56
Holley E	1889-94	Holmes JB	1925-26, 1928-29
Hopkins CL	1893	Horne GL	1889
Horsfall THS	1909-10	Hosken JF	1904
Howlett AE	1900-01	Hudson AR	1913-14, 1922
Hudson RC	1919, 1923	Huggins RDP	1965-68, 1970-89
Humphrey W	1879-80	Innes RF	1979-80, 1982-84
Ireland MW	1900-03, 1905-08, 1911	Jackson GR	1906-07
Jackson J	1876-77, 1881, 1882, 1884	Jackson JB	1937
James	1902	Jarvis AW	1878-85
Jarvis CJE	1878-92	Jarvis FW	1886, 1888-90
Jarvis LK	1877-90	Jee AM	1885-89, 1892
Jefferson RI	1968-71	Jefferson WI	1997
Jervis MM	1985, 1990, 1992-93	Jessopp NA	1914, 1919-20
Johnson EG	1882	Jones	1884-85
Jones AMB	1889	Jory HI	1946, 1948
Kemp KH	1877, 1882-85	Kennaway AL	1904
Kennaway CL	1877-87, 1889, 1891	Kennon NS	1970
Kent EA	1957	Kenyon CM	1959-60
Ketton RW	1877-78, 1880, 1884-87, 1889	Keyworth FM	1903
Kilshaw PJ	1977-79, 1981	Kingshott RA	1987-92
Lake EA	1895	Lambert DC	1954-55

Players	Season Appearances	Players	Season Appearances
Lambert PA	2010-2011	Lambourne IR	1981, 1984
Langdale GR	1939	Larkins W	1996
Law G	1877	Lawes ACH	1971, 1973, 1975
Laws BM	1952, 1954	Lay LC	1949-50
Leatham C	1878	Leggatt O	1878
Leggett R	1939, 1950-51, 1953	Leigh BJ	1973-74, 1980
Leman LH	1900-01, 1904-08	Lewis JCM	1987-92, 1994
Lewis PCM	1986	Lingwood WJ	1930-34, 1936-39
Livermore SJB	1991-92, 1998, 2000-02	Llong NJ	2000
Logan DJC	1993	Lomas H	1896-97
Long EF	1923	Lord A	1927-28
Lord E	1909	Low HF	1926-36
Lucas PM	1884, 1886, 1888	Luddington HT	1879-83
Mace AFA	1946-47	Mack AJ	1989-91
Mack ESP	1884-85, 1893-98	Mack HP	1881
Mackenzie RS	1927	MacLaren AC	1920
Mahon GM	1921, 1923	Mann EJ	1901, 1905
Mansfield JW	1882	Marquet JP	2003
Marsh FT	1946, 1948	Marsh TH	1888-90
Marsh W	1888-89	Marshall LP	1882
Martin GH	1921-22	Mason HD	1901
Mason PL	1952	Massingham EA	1892-95
Master HC	1905-08, 1910-11	Master HH	1887
Mattocks DE	1961-69, 1971-1991	Mayes AR	1908
Mayhew KG	1946, 1948	Maynard JC	1993-94
McCormick JG	1899-1906, 1908-09	McLaren WH	1876
McManus CA	1966-75	Meigh BA	1975, 1977, 1980-83
Mercer IP	1964-72	Meyrick-Jones F	1909
Mickleburgh JC	2007-08	Middleton JP	1884-86
Miles JS	2010	Mills A	1953
Mindham PR	1970-72	Mir PJ	1981-85
Mitchell G	1946, 1949-52, 1956,1958	Mitchell LG	1909-10
Montgomerie CTCM	1878-79	Moore NH	1947, 1950-64
Moore RSL	1877	Moore TI	1959-78
Moores RD	2005-07	Morley T	1886, 1888-1900
Mornement RH	1892-96	Morrell DM	1991-92
Morrice CH	1877-79, 1883-85	Morrice FLH	1878
Morris EJ	1883-86	Morse MH	1952, 1955
Morse SA	1920-21	Morton	1879
Morton CH	1880-81, 1885, 1887-91, 1900	Morton PH	1880-83, 1886
Motum PA	1981-82, 1985	Moulton AF	1934-35
Mower GH	1920, 1923-28	Mower HW	1885
Moyser RA	1997-2000	Neville GER	1919, 1926, 1928
Newby EW	1891-92	Newman PG	1996-2003
Newton LTS	2000-07	Nichols JE	1898, 1921-31
North MK	1891	Nugent TEG	1920
O'Brien JR	1950	Orams E	1889-93, 1899, 1902-03
Ormiston RW	1975-76	Orton JOC	1921
Owens JH	1925, 1928	Oxbury MD	1961-62, 1970, 1972, 1975-76

Players	Season Appearances	Players	Season Appearances
Page AC	1876	Page SD	1892, 1895-1905, 1907-10
Panter RG	2002	Parfitt JH	1955
Parfitt PH	1953-56	Parlane ME	2002
Partridge ERW	1898	Partridge PW	1898-1902
Patey E	1894	Patmore AJD	2005-06
Patston BJ	2008-09	Patteson FE	1879, 1881, 1885, 1889
Patteson JC	1876, 1878	Payne AN	1987-88, 1992
Peachment E	1900-01	Pearse AJ	1923
Pearse C	1898	Pearson JM	1946, 1948-51
Pedder GR	1913-14, 1921-25, 1931	Penberthy AL	2004
Penn EF	1899, 1902-06	Perkins RW	1937-39, 1948-52
Perry	1880	Phipps DD	1956-57
Pierpoint FG	1947-49	Pigot G	1876
Pilch DG	1961-1983	Pilch GE	1935, 1937-38, 1946
Pilch RG	1899-1913, 1921	Platten G	1880, 1884
Plumb SG	1978-1995	Pollard E	1878, 1881
Pontifex A	1878-79, 1885-86	Poole JC	1982
Popham CH	1919, 1921	Popham RF	1910-14, 1919-21, 1924
Powell MG	1995-96	Powell PG	1946, 1949-60, 1962-63
Powell TL	1982-83, 1985	Pretheroe EO	1914, 1921
Prior CBL	1906-7, 1911-12	Prior HC	1911-12, 1914, 1922
Purdy RJ	1935-36	Purton RGS	2000, 2008-09
Radley CT	1961	Raikes EB	1882, 1886-89, 1897, 1901-04, 1909
Raikes GB	1890-97, 1904-06, 1909-13	Raikes TB	1919-23
Raven CO	1900	Rayner GR	1923
Rayner MJ	1987-88, 1990	Read CC	1992, 1995, 1997
Read JA	1927	Relf AE	1898-99
Reynolds R	1955, 1957	Rhodes FW	1876, 1879
Rice D	1946	Rice PC	1985
Rice PWM	1965	Richardson ME	1955
Riley JH	1976-77, 1980, 1982, 1984, 1986	Ringwood PJ	1982-84, 1986-88
Rist WH	2006	Rivett-Carnac GC	1876-77
Rix WA	1888-89, 1896	Roberson F	1898
Roberts GJ	1977	Robertson WK	1901, 1903
Robins GF	1877	Robinson DDJ	2008
Robinson MI	1953	Robinson SG	2008
Roff GM	1986-88, 1991	Rogers CJ	1990-2011
Rogers DB	1996-97	Rogerson WTC	1931
Rolph JB	1969	Rose W	1963-67, 1969-72, 1974, 1976-78
Rossi DM	1959-64	Rought-Rought BW	1926-39, 1946-48
Rought-Rought DC	1931-39, 1946-47	Rought-Rought RC	1926-35, 1937, 1939
Rouse AW	1912, 1922	Rowe JC	1974, 1976
Rowe SA	1992	Rudd A	1883-88, 1890
Rudd NA	1994	Rudd RK	1971-75, 1977-79, 1984
Rudd T	1884	Rushforth T	1948
Rutter AEH	1961-62, 1964-65	Rye GJ	1878-95
Saggers MJ	1995-96	Salisbury WE	1903-04
Sands DW	1987	Sandwith ER	1891
Sandwith WFG	1890-93, 1895-99, 1901	Savage DG	1987-90

Players	Season Appearances	Players	Season Appearances
Saville GJ	1967-69	Schofield R	1955, 1957-59, 1962
Scobell GB	1902	Scott GA	1901
Scott-Chad C	1877-78, 1880, 1883	Scott-Chad GN	1920-21, 1923-24, 1928-32
Seager ML	2005	Self FG	1934-39, 1946, 1948
Sewell AP	1894-95	Sharpe JM	1969
Sharpe Peter J	1963-65	Sharpe Philip J	1977-82
Shearer AE	2011	Shelford PW	1902-03
Shepperd J	1963-68	Shingler A	1902-06, 1908
Shore C	1889-1901	Shreeve CM	1971
Skerrett CP	1882	Skinner TJM	1947
Skrimshire HF	1897	Skrimshire JF	1894-97
Slegg IR	2002, 2005-08	Smart AL	1970, 1973
Smart BG	2008	Smith	1891-92
Smith CB	1909-11	Smith CG	1893-95
Smith DJ	2008-10	Smith EW	1902-09
Smith HJ	1893	Smith JJ	1883, 1893-94
Smith R	1951	Smith R	1897
Snelling T	1894, 1901	Softley PLH	1951
Spelman JM	2002-11	Spelman JO	2007-08
Stafford WFH	1889	Stamp DM	1988-91
Stannard GM	1951-52	Stanton JCC	1946
Staples S	1899	Starling G	1905-07
Starling SJ	1979-81	Stephens V	1907-08
Stephenson EK	1914	Stevens BGW	1937-39, 1950-58
Stevens G	1905-11	Stevens GA	1906-14, 1920-30
Stevens GS	1908-09	Stevens NW	1905, 1909-10
Stewart AL	1884	Stockings DC	1967-68
Stocks EW	1876	Stocks GA	1876
Stone GJ	1923-25, 1927	Stone OP	2011
Sugden A	1890	Swarbrick DL	1962
Tate JS	1985-88	Taylor AP	1910
Taylor CF	1889-91	Taylor JP	2002
Taylor K	1972, 1974	Taylor NS	1989-90
Taylor RF	1909	Taylor SK	1988, 1991-93
Tharp AK	1876	Thaxter DW	1956, 1958
Thelwell SJ	2009	Theobald HE	1930-39, 1946-47
Thistleton-Smith JC	1930-39, 1947-48, 1950-51	Thomas DR	1983-1999
Thomas MW	1994, 1996-2000, 2005, 2008	Thomas PW	1982-83, 1986, 1997
Thomas WO	1952-59	Thomson B	1876
Thompson WS	1932-39, 1946-52, 1955	Thorne DC	1954-55, 1959-62
Thorne GC	1914, 1924-25	Thorne ME	1955, 1957-58
Thornton GG	1952-53	Thurgar RW	1907, 1909-14
Thurgar WA	1881-82, 1886, 1890-92	Thursby MH	1911-12, 1927-28
Thursby W	1910-12, 1922	Tillard C	1876-84, 1886-89, 1894-95
Tillard J	1876	Tilney NJ	1954-57
Tipping MR	1993-95, 1997-2000	Tipple FA	1888, 1895
Todd AJM	2008-09	Tomlinson JJW	1957-58, 1963
Tonge WC	1895-96	Topley TD	1984-85
Trafford SWJ	1913	Treglown CJH	1909-13

Players	Season Appearances
Trevor LG	1889-90
Trower J	2009
Tuck KSC	1996
Tufts IJP	1995, 1997, 2000
Turner JF	1903
Utting AG	1929, 1931-34
Veale FH	1924
Walker DF	1931-39
Walker JR	1997-99, 2001-04
Walsh CH	1903-04, 1906
Ward EE	1947
Ward TR	2004-11
Warnes MW	2011
Watling RG	1906
Watson AC	1906
Watson AM	2002-04, 2009, 2011
Watson H	1910-14, 1919-25, 1927
Waymouth SN	1986-88
Wesley PW	1957-58
Wharton TH	1908-10
White K	1922
Whitehead J	1984-90
Whittaker PK	1983-87, 1989
Wild DK	1970-72, 1975
Willett EH	1876-77
Williams G	1910-12
Wilson BK	1896-98, 1900, 1906-09
Wilson FM	1886-88
Wilson KP	1883-84
Wilson TE	1896
Wiltshire CJ	1886, 1888
Wingfield RA	1913
Witherden EG	1956-62
Wood BJH	1933-38, 1946-48
Woolstencroft ML	1965-66
Worman JN	1897-98, 1903-08
Wright TM	1962-65
Wynne-Willson LF	1912-14
Zaidi SMN	1985-86

Players	Season Appearances
Trevor PCW	1890
Tuck EL	1988
Tufnell NC	1923-25
Turner HW	1876-77, 1879-80, 1882-83, 1889, 1891
Tyler AW	1932-33
Van Onselen D	1997
Wakefield HR	1911
Walker GW	2000, 2005-06, 2008-2011
Walmsley PG	1950-1962
Walter CH	1891, 1895
Ward MJP	1996
Warnes MR	2005, 2007-08, 2011
Waters HW	1966
Watson AA	2009-2011
Watson AK	1903-09
Watson CP	1929-30
Watts IM	1956, 1959-66, 1971-73
Weighell WB	1882-83
Wesley RJ	1960-63, 1965
Whitaker MR	1969
White SN	1995, 1997-98
Whitney DA	2001
Wickham AP	1881-90
Wilkinson MO	2002-07
Wiliams DJ	1987
Williamson EC	1925-27
Wilson CP	1882-84
Wilson JC	1895-96, 1898
Wilson MD	1956, 1960
Wilton GW	1973-76, 1980-81
Wiltshire FHC	1904
Wiseman PDE	2009
Witherden N	1980
Woodhouse JS	1954
Wormald J	1922-23
Wright E	1969-70, 1974-82
Wyllys GH de B	1927-28, 1933-34
Yates P	2011

Career Averages

Name	M	In	No	Runs	Ave	100	50	0	Ov	M	Runs	W	Ave	Balls	OW	5i	10m	Ct	St
Abbs GR	10	9	1	61	7.62			1	121	28	286	13	22.00					3	
	1	2		9	9.00				12	0	41	1	41.00					1	
Abel AG	1	1	0	11	11.00				10	1	42	0						2	
Adams CD	6	6	2	75	18.75													3	
Adams DJ	1	1	1	3					24.3	7	73	4	18.25					1	1
Adams JC	1	1	1	35															
Adams NJ	1	2	0	16	8.00			1										1	
	2	2	1	13	13.00				1.5	0	7	1	7.00					1	
	3	3	0	32	10.66			1	3	0	13	0						7	
Addison MA	9	9	3	52	8.66			1	190	31	663	14	47.35					4	
	6	1	1	1					45.1	8	208	6	34.66					2	
	7	3	3	9					47.1	8	211	4	52.75						
Agar AC	21	27	9	250	13.88			3	174	30	641	19	33.73					8	
	3	4	1	14	4.66			2	27	3	91	5	18.20					3	
	10	7	2	27	5.40			3	47	9	169	3	56.33					3	
Aitken APH	5	7	0	46	6.57			3										2	
Allcock T	46	79	10	1470	21.30		8	10										73	20
	2	3		77	25.66													2	
	2	2		28	14.00													7	
Allen G	10	12	2	134	13.40			1	2	0	13	0						17	4
	6	7		19	2.71			3	6	1	22	0						3	4
Allen JE	1																		
Allsopp TC	27	40	5	512	14.62		2	4	512.2	112	1459	71	20.54			4		21	
	7	13	0	163	12.53		1	1	134.1	24	506	21	24.09					4	
Ames SS	3	5	0	42	8.40				21	3	66	3	22.00					3	
	2	4	0	50	12.50			1	16	0	77	0						2	
Amos C	103	176	15	5737	35.63	10	35	13	12	4	119	1	119.00					60	
	41	40	6	1200	35.29		8	2	4	1	34	0						9	
	58	58	4	1660	30.74	1	13	5										13	
Arnold HA	3	6	1	105	21.00			1	47.3	21	58	8	7.25	4		1		2	
Arnold RM	1	2	0	1	0.50			1										1	
	2	2	0	20	10.00														
Arthurton SS (senior)	4	5	0	69	13.80			1										2	
	3	3	1	50	25.00														
Arthurton SS	13	23	2	707	33.67		3	3	9	4	36	1	36.00					5	
	6	5	0	76	15.20				1	1	0	1						1	
	8	7	1	274	45.66	1	1	1	0.2	0	1	0						3	

Name	M	In	No	Runs	Ave	100	50	0	Ov	M	Runs	W	Ave	Balls	OW	5i	10m	Ct	St
Ash EP	2	3	0	2	0.66			2										1	
Astley DGL	1	1	0	14	14.00														
Atherton DA	1	2	1	5	5.00				9	0	50	0							
	1								5	2	10	1	10.00						
Atkins JP	6	9	1	107	13.37													4	
	1	2	0	0	0.00			3	13	6	15	0		4					
Atmore EA	2	2	2	7					17	4	59	2	29.50					2	
Austin RJ	5	1		0					49	5	181	6	30.16					2	
	5			1	1.00				44	8	141	5	28.20					2	
Ayres IM	4	2	2	0					53	8	185	6	30.83					2	
Backhouse J	3	4	0	29	7.25														
Bacon NHP	1	1	0	12	12.00														
Bagnall RSV	7	12	2	162	16.20			2	41	13	80	5	16.00					1	
	2	3	0	64	21.33				34	3	95	5	19.00						
Bailey FP	2	1	0	0	0.00			1										3	
	1	1	0	0	0.00			1											
Bailey GL	3	3	1	24	12.00				15.3	2	67	2	33.50					1	
	4	1	0	10	10.00				25.1	3	84	5	16.80						
	7	1		2					5	0	25	0							
Bailey SP	1	1		1															
	2	1		7					19	1	89	7	12.71			1			
Baker SE	1	2	0	9	4.50													1	
Ballance TGL	50	63	14	974	19.87	2	4	7	1094.2	284	2642	149	17.73			8	1	32	
									88.7	16	238	19	12.52	8		1			
Bally JH	42	64	10	742	13.74	1	1	7	29	2	111	2	55.50					46	15
	2	3	1	8	4.00			1										1	1
Banks CJ	3	5	0	43	8.60													1	
Barker CJ	1	1	1	0														1	
Barnes A	6	10	1	124	13.77				14	3	51	1	51.00	5				5	
Barnes TH	50	27	14	56	4.30			9	1834.4	610	4510	212	21.27			12	4	19	
	4	2	1	1	1.00			1	58	19	153	6	25.50	4					
									12	4	34	1	34.00						
Barratt G	3	6	0	37	6.16			3	4	2	14	0		5					
Barratt L	58	92	10	1920	23.41	2	8	11	266.4	70	695	31	22.41	5		1		29	
	34	58	0	834	14.37		3	11	83.4	20	246	11	22.36	5				12	

Name	M	In	No	Runs	Ave	100	50	0	Ov	M	Runs	W	Ave	Balls	OW	5i	10m	Ct	St
Barratt WP	2	2	1	12	12.00													3	
Barrett J	40	71	11	1449	24.15		4	2	18	1	82	4	20.50					25	
	9	10	0	283	28.30		1		9	0	35	1	35.00					6	
	1	1	0	7	7.00														
Barrett LA	65	99	9	1613	17.92	1	6	9	21.1	2	77	0						23	
	6	5	2	80	26.66													4	
Bartlett DMM	1	2	0	32	16.00			1											
		2	1	4	4.00														
Barton AJ	7	12	1	181	16.45		1		83.2	?	121	16	7.56	4	9	2		6	
									49.2	14	87	5	17.40	4	2		1		
Barton AW	5	7	2	35	7.00			4	12.3	1	80	3	26.66					4	
		1	0	1	1.00														
Barton CT	1	1	0	2	2.00													2	
Barton GH	1	2	1	23	23.00														
Barton MR	20	31	1	910	30.33	1	6	2										14	
		2	1	98	98.00		1												
Barton WJ	2	2	0	24	12.00				11	4	23	1	23.00					1	
		2	0	25	12.50														
Barwell CSW	1	2	0	3	1.5			1										2	
Bassingthwaighte DN	2	2	1	0	0.00			1	33	4	157	1	157.00					11	
									4	1	17	0							
Bate JC	25	40	0	1047	26.17	1	6	4										1	
	3	4	0	99	24.75														
Bathurst LCV	21	36	1	671	19.17		4	1	408.4	132	872	50	17.44	5		1		19	
									17	6	31	1	31.00	6					
	5	8	1	149	21.28		1		95.1	33	177	21	8.42	5		2		2	
Battelley BL	36	46	13	330	10.00			9	603	138	2016	82	24.58			4		17	
	2	2	0	22	11.00				26	11	110	3	36.66						
Battelley IN	23	43	0	839	19.51		3	4	18	5	42	2	21.00					21	
	5	6	0	112	18.66		1		11	5	18	3	6.00					3	
		1	0	29	29.00														
Beacock GN	25	33	16	297	17.47		1	3	485.3	105	1380	55	25.09			2		10	
Beadsmoore WA	74	102	24	764	9.79			19	1912.4	568	4200	294	14.28			18	3	33	
	4	7	5	34	17.00				109.2	22	295	15	19.66			1		3	
Beare JC	1	1	1	2					10	1	46	2	23.00						
Beeton F	1	2	0	8	4.00			1	11	4	16	1	16.00	4					
Bell FR	3	5	0	114	22.80		1	1	27	10	39	1	39.00					2	
	2	3	0	119	39.66		1		13	2	44	2	22.00						
Bell RV	18	17	6	119	10.81				440.1	141	1076	74	14.54			4		14	

Name	M	In	No	Runs	Ave	100	50	0	Ov	M	Runs	W	Ave	Balls	OW	5i	10m	Ct	St
Belmont RJ	3	4	1	62	20.66				37	7	127	5	25.40					2	
	2	2	0	2	1.00			1	16	2	72	4	18.00					1	1
	4	3	1	40	20.00				12.1	2	57	1	57.00						
Belton EJ	7	11	0	73	6.63			6	26.2	4	99	2	49.50					5	
Beresford RAA	7	9	0	127	14.11		1	3	4	0	12	0						4	
	3	6	0	133	22.16		1		7	1	25	0							
Beresford RM	26	34	3	534	17.22		3	2	0.4	0	6	1	6.00					6	
	2	2	0	76	38.00														
Berwick TFH	1	2	0	39	19.50													1	
Bevan JS	1	2	0	26	13.00													1	
Birkbeck GW	38	61	8	1564	29.50	3	6	5	71.2	6	308	9	34.22					15	
	5	9	2	117	16.71			2	43	0	196	11	17.81					4	
Birkbeck H (post war)	7	11	2	171	19.00				83.5	14	252	9	28.00					4	
Birkbeck H	42	67	3	1042	16.28		4	9										11	
Birkbeck WH	1	2	0	22	11.00			1										1	
Blake GF	41	63	3	684	11.40			10	28	9	82	5	16.40	5				37	25
	41	68	4	613	9.57			14	4	0	22	2	11.00	5				35	16
Blake JS	1	1	0	10	10.00														
Blake KPJ	2	2	0	13	6.50				17	2	68	2	34.00						
Blanchett IN	2	2	1	4	4.00			1	29	2	118	2	59.00					1	
	2								21	2	67	3	22.33						
Bland TG	18	28	6	253	11.50			5	300.4	56	1078	46	23.43					6	
	1	1	0	0	0.00			1	9	1	29	1	29.00						
	1	1	0	7	7.00				12	2	29	1	29.00						
Blincoe AM	8	6	3	36	12.00				48.3	3	187	7	26.71					3	
Blofeld HC	45	79	3	1530	20.13		8	4	10	0	54	1	54.00					54	11
	1	1	0	60	60.00		7												
Blofeld JCC	1	2	0	46	23.00													1	
Blundell MC	12	20	2	283	15.72		1	4										9	
Blyth AG	1	2	0	13	6.50			1										4	
	6	11	1	139	13.90		1												
Boon TJ	14	26	5	1036	49.33	4	4	2	34.2	6	152	1	152.00					11	
	6	6	0	229	45.80		2		19	1	54	5	10.80					1	
	6	6	0	130	21.66		7		15	0	85	1	85.00					3	
Borrett CR	53	89	10	2546	32.22	2	17	12	302.2	48	1127	27	41.74					25	
	18	16	1	225	15.00			1	76	5	294	11	26.72					4	
	45	41	6	1089	31.11	1	6	6	98.5	10	466	20	23.30					18	

Name	M	In	No	Runs	Ave	100	50	0	Ov	M	Runs	W	Ave	Balls	OW	5i	10m	Ct	St
Borrett PC	51	85	6	1123	14.21		1	11	25	1	138	2	69.00					19	
	5	5	1	57	14.25			1										2	
	1	1	0	1	1.00														
Borthwick CH	2	2	1	8	8.00			1								1		3	1
	4	7	2	30	6.00													3	1
Boswell BRD	13	10	4	7	1.16			4	260	71	825	27	30.55			1		4	
Boswell CSR	103	144	32	1921	17.15		3	19	2588.4	642	6425	291	22.07			15	2	40	
									186.5	26	820	38	21.57	8		2			
	5	5	1	44	11.00			1	68	12	223	11	20.27			1			
									17	1	26	0		8					
Bowett TD	14	22	3	199	10.47			5										6	
Boyden MKL	27	13	6	24	3.42			3										63	5
	13	6	4	54	27.00			1	4	0	29	1	29.00					12	4
	14	3	2	9	9.00			7										10	
Bradford RL	39	65	5	1374	22.90	1	5	5								1		20	
	2	2	0	13	6.50														
	3	2	0	16	8.00														
Bradshaw PJ	83	86	32	1017	18.83	1	1	14	1520.3	325	4819	175	27.53			3		57	
	31	15	5	92	9.20			1	228.3	41	769	44	17.47			1		5	
	65	37	14	354	15.39			4	554.3	85	2134	120	17.78			2		13	
Brand WG	1								14.5	0	36	1	36.00						
Brayne TL	21	34	4	468	15.60		1	3	14	0	89	1	89.00					11	
Brighton NA	3	2	0	6	3.00			1	48	11	141	6	23.50						
	1	1	0	6	6.00				13	1	44	2	22.00						
Brown C	63	81	14	1365	20.37	1	3	8	2618	611	7557	328	23.04			15	2	13	
	24	17	5	223	18.58			2	218	18	668	39	17.12					4	
	51	36	11	348	13.92				441.1	97	1697	69	24.59					4	
Brown HE	1	1	0	0	0.00			1	4	2	11	0							
Brown JC	1	1	0	17	17.00														
Buckle FA	6	9	3	153	25.50		1	1	26	7	59	3	19.66	4				3	
Bunting KJ	2	1	0	9	9.00				30	6	85	2	42.50					1	
Bunting RA	58	55	21	463	13.61			8	1335	293	4221	201	21.00			11	1	26	
	4								49.4	2	179	12	14.91					4	
	19	14	7	111	15.85			2	186.2	18	704	31	22.70					5	
Bunting SJ	4	2	2	1					60	14	178	4	44.50						
Burrell HJE	1	2	0	15	7.50														
	1	2	0	7	3.50														
Burrows JW	1	1	0	0	0.00			1											

Name	M	In	No	Runs	Ave	100	50	0	Ov	M	Runs	W	Ave	Balls	OW	5i	10m	Ct	St
Bush H	8	15	1	400	28.57		3		6	0	25	0						11	
	2	2	1	76	76.00				3		24	0							
	6	6	1	105	21.00		1		21.1	2	112	4	28.00					7	
Buxton AR	18	28	0	523	18.67		2	3	3	1	9	0						8	
	53	93	2	1473	16.18		5	8										20	
Buxton B	1	2	1	51	51.00													1	
Buxton EG	9	17	2	80	6.15			4	6	0	22	0		5				5	
Buxton GF	3	5	1	14	3.50			1										1	
Buxton HG	3	6	3	14	4.66														
Campbell CA	1	2	0	28	14.00			1											
Campbell D	1	2	0	4	2.00													1	
Campbell GV	1	2	0	9	4.50				8	2	35	1	35.00						
Campion-Jones P	1	1	0	2	2.00				6	2	26	0							
Cant RW	27	39	7	354	11.06			5	283.1	52	947	32	29.59					11	
	3	5	1	23	5.75			2	41	8	127	4	31.75						
Carey CS	17	23	9	358	25.57		1	1	141.4	26	530	11	48.18			2		14	
	6	4	0	70	17.50				27.4	5	109	2	54.50					2	
	12	9	3	62	10.33				54	8	188	8	23.50					3	
Carter DD	50	75	10	1246	19.16		5	8	454.5	117	1299	50	25.98					33	
	3	5	1	72	18.00				11	1	35	1	35.00						
Carter GT	3	4	0	68	17.00				2	0	5	1	5.00					2	
	1	2	1	46	46.00														
Carter JR	17	32	3	703	24.24	1	3	1										6	
	8	7	0	117	16.71													3	
Carter RD	44	65	5	1197	19.95		8	7										13	
	3	6	0	154	25.66			2										4	
Caswell LW	9	16	5	345	31.36		2	2	62	10	248	3	82.67					10	
	3	3	1	18	9.00				10.4	0	75	2	37.50					3	
Cator CAM	1	1	0	2	2.00														
		1	0	0	0.00			1	3	0	18	2	9.00						
Cattermoule KM	1	2	1	30	30.00		1		1	1	0	0						2	
Chamberlain AC	1	1	0	9	9.00														
Chamberlain DH	8	14	2	221	18.41		1	1	2	0	16	0						6	
	2	2	1	22	22.00														
Charles SF	14	20	1	327	17.21													18	8
	3	4	0	52	13.00													2	2
Child SEH	1	1	0	3	3.00			1										2	
Church P	1	1	0	0	0.00			1	28	13	50	5	10.00			1		1	

Name	M	In	No	Runs	Ave	100	50	0	Ov	M	Runs	W	Ave	Balls	OW	5i	10m	Ct	St
Circuitt RWP	1	2	0	4	2.00			1											
Clarke AR	9	5	3	3	1.50			1	212.2	51	738	27	27.33			1		2	
	1								10	1	40	3	13.33						
	6								59	10	199	11	18.09		2			1	
Clarke EWR	21	34	4	405	13.50			6	23	10	44	5	8.80	4				8	
Clements BA	49	81	7	1749	23.63	1	11	7	971.3	254	2264	96	23.58	4		3	1	30	
		2	0	17	8.50				15.3	1	60	3	20.00						
Clowes FW	1	1	0	5	5.00				6	0	16	0							
Cockburn MK	1	2	0	6	3.00													1	
Coldham JM	52	89	8	1580	19.50	1	4	12	9	0	45	0						56	3
	3	5	0	41	8.20													3	
Cole AP	6	5	1	142	35.50	1		1	101.5	22	346	14	24.71					3	
	8	5	1	19	4.75			2	57	6	212	9	23.55			1		2	
	3	3	1	14	7.00				35	4	188	5	37.60						
Collinson RW	9	16	3	431	33.15	1	1		5	0	9	0						7	
	6	8	0	89	11.12			1	47	11	142	9	15.77	4				2	
Collishaw TM	2	3	0	39	13.00													3	
	4	4	1	134	44.66		1												
	1	7	0	2	2.00														
Collison H	2	3	0	29	9.66				36	12	78	1	78.00						
Collyer WR	1	3	0	11	11.00														
Colman AR	2	2	0	3	1.50														
Colman CS	12	19	0	287	15.10			4	16.1	0	75	6	12.50					1	
	3	6	0	112	18.66			1	6	0	41	0							
Colman DWJ	1	1	0	6	6.00														
Colman GRR	49	86	8	2379	30.50	2	14	7	67.2	2	316	17	18.58			1		28	
	3	6	1	74	14.80			1											
Colvin EG	1	1	0	29	29.00													1	
Compton JJ	9	15	1	153	10.92		1	3	51.3	9	201	5	40.20					7	
	3	6	0	100	16.66			2	44.2	1	212	6	35.33					2	
Cook ND	66	107	18	1718	19.30	1	6	14	3.5	0	37	1	37.00					53	
	8	8	0	153	19.12		1												
	5	5	1	87	21.75			1											
Cooke FBR	3	5	0	35	7.00			1											
Cooke NR	14	22	3	180	9.47			6	13	0	61	1	61.00	5				5	
Cookson G	3	6	0	24	4.00			2	11	2	33	2	16.50						
	1	2	0	8	4.00			1	5	2	13	1	13.00	5					
Coomb AG	42	59	7	952	18.30	1		8	1025.4	255	2965	120	24.70			6	2	32	

Name	M	In	No	Runs	Ave	100	50	0	Ov	M	Runs	W	Ave	Balls	OW	5i	10m	Ct	St
Coomber F	6	8	0	123	15.37		1		18	4	30	2	15.00	4	5			6	
Cooper KP	5	10	2	71	8.87			1	18.5	1	86	4	21.50						
	7	7	3	132	33.00				24	2	106		106.00					2	
	5	4	0	51	12.75				8.4	0	38	2	19.00					1	
Cooper S	1	2	0	27	13.50			1											
	1	1	0	0	0.00														
Cooper T	1	2	0	29	14.50									4	3			2	
Coote P	3	6	1	248	49.60		2	1											
	1	1	0	38	38.00														
Coppin WR	1	1	0	63	63.00		1		8.5	0	29	3	9.66					1	
	7	7	0	2	2.00				10	2	36	1	36.00						
Corran AJ	28	38	5	781	23.66	1	2	2	722.1	207	1869	84	22.25			4	1	21	
Covill RJ	17	26	0	201	7.73			10	307.1	53	924	30	30.80					13	
Cowles SRB	22	34	2	343	10.71		1	7	149	41	345	21	16.42	5		2		16	
	8	13	2	108	10.08			6	173	31	537	25	21.48	6					
									100.2	40	203	10	20.30	5		1			
									22	3	74	0		6					
Cozens-Hardy A	1	2	0	7	3.50			1											
Cozens-Hardy B	19	31	5	529	20.34	1	2	5	33	7	122	3	40.66					18	
	3	6	0	67	11.16				23	4	62	6	10.33					1	
Cozens-Hardy EW	2	3	2	31	31.00														
Cozens-Hardy F	6	7	2	26	5.20			2	63.1	16	135	4	33.75	4				7	
Crawshay FGL	4	4	1	84	28.00				10	1	37	0						1	1
Cresswell CA	12	15	0	96	6.40			4										13	
Crowley SC	27	16	13	49	16.33			2										61	8
	14	5	4	38	38.00													20	4
	9	8	5	9	3.00													11	2
Cubitt BB	1	2	0	16	8.00			1											
Cunliffe F	40	47	6	716	17.46		2	3	10	1	24	0						34	
	2	2	1	68	68.00		1												
Cunningham AD	11	21	1	559	27.95	1	3	1	1	0	5	0						6	2
Currie FA	32	46	2	950	21.59		3	6	27	8	55	1	55.00	4				27	
Currie RG	1	2	1	6	6.00														
Curteis TS	1	1	0	16	16.00														
Cushion JC	1	1	0	16	16.00			1											
Cuthbertson NW	2	3	0	14	4.66														
Daley JV	9	12	3	75	8.33			3	16	0	64	0						5	
Dann WE	2	3	0	10	3.33			1											

Name	M	In	No	Runs	Ave	100	50	0	Ov	M	Runs	W	Ave	Balls	OW	5i	10m	Ct	St
Darnell AF	2	4	1	25	8.33			1	4	0	17	0						**1**	1
Davies AC	5	9	0	85	9.44		2		9	1	28	2	14.00	5					
	1	1	0	**12**	**12.00**	3		14	59.4	11	169	9	18.77	5		2		41	
	55	91	1	1582	17.57				131.1	?	163	23	7.08	4	1	2	1		
									314.4	139	556	29	19.17	4					
Davies F	**14**	**21**	**3**	**452**	**25.11**		2	1	16	?	19	3	6.33	4	3			**10**	
	49	81	6	1318	17.57	1	4	10	76	25	118	10	11.80	4	3			30	
									41	13	87	5	17.40	5					
Davy JDW	2	4	0	64	16.00			2											
de Bruyn P	1	1	0	9	9.00														
de Moleyns FRWE	1	1	0	8	8.00													1	
Denton CS	1	1	1	11											1				
Dewing AM	1	2	0	45	22.50				19	5	47	2	23.50	4		1		1	
Dines E	3	5	1	8	2.00			3	135	53	200	12	16.66					2	
Dixon SB	**43**	**74**	**12**	**1642**	**26.48**		**12**	7	26.3	2	153	**3**	**51.00**					**25**	
	6	7	2	150	30.00		2		2	0	17	0						1	
Dodds NDP	16	14	1	178	13.69				6	2	27	0						2	
	4	5	2	50	16.66													7	
Donaldson JA	**29**	**54**	**2**	**1327**	**25.51**		7	4										**23**	1
	1	1	0	0	0.00			1										1	
	2	2	0	37	18.50														
Dougill H	**16**	**20**	**3**	**212**	**12.47**			4	56	14	186	**5**	**37.20**					**10**	
	2	3	0	42	14.00				3	1	5	0						1	
Dowson H	1	2	1	2	2.00			1										1	
Drake D	**1**	**1**	**0**	**0**	**0.00**			1											
Drake GC	4	7	0	79	11.28			1										3	
Draper WH	3	6	0	60	10.00			2							1			2	
Drinkwater WL	**24**	**40**	**8**	**822**	**25.68**		4	2	272.5	67	643	**24**	**26.79**	4				**5**	
	3	4	1	134	44.66				19	2	64	3	21.33						
									8	2	32	1	32.00						
Duffield K	1	1	0	0	0.00			1											
Duffield PG	**3**	**2**	**1**	**1**	**1.00**			3										**2**	
Dunell OHC	**16**	**28**	**0**	**592**	**21.14**		4		52	15	162	**6**	**27.00**					**9**	
	1	2	0	17	8.50				20.1	5	80	**5**	**16.00**						
Dunn ATB	5	7	0	128	18.28		1	1	19	3	62	1	62.00	4				5	
Dunn MJ	**4**	**5**	**3**	**43**	**21.50**			1										**1**	1
	2	2	0	18	9.00													1	

Name	M	In	No	Runs	Ave	100	50	0	Ov	M	Runs	W	Ave	Balls	OW	5i	10m	Ct	St
Dunning CE	25	40	6	756	22.23		5	3	3	0	13	1	13.00					16	
	4	8	2	235	39.16				4	0	19		19.00					3	
Durrant CE	2	3	0	32	10.66			1	2	0	11	0						2	
Eagle WG	16	23	2	172	8.19			6	415.4	109	922	66	13.96			4		4	
	1	2		18	9.00				29.4	5	63	4	15.75						
Earthy MC	2								26.4	3	87	3	29.00						
Eccles MP	44	44	21	159	6.91			10	1078.5	183	4192	111	37.77			2	1	20	
	14	8	5	47	15.66				122.2	14	581	12	48.41						
	17	7	2	16	3.20			1	126.4	12	615	24	25.62					3	
Ede MP	1	1	0	15	15.00													1	
Edrich Edwin H	1	2		86	86.00		1												
Edrich EH	62	95	12	2531	30.49	4	10	7	236.2	58	574	27	21.25			1		115	34
	2	3	0	62	20.66													3	
Edrich GA	32	45	8	1088	29.40	2	3	2	124.7	30	406	16	25.37			1		22	
									15	0	71	2	35.50	8					
Edrich JH	1	1	0	53	53.00		1		1	0	6	0							
	1	1	0	6	6.00														
Edrich PG	2	4	3	15	15.00				20	5	55								
	1	1	0	4	4.00				12	2	36	3	12.00						
Edrich WJ	172	276	47	8034	35.08	9	49	22	3200.2	856	7956	415	19.17			19	3	151	
	7	9	0	367	40.77	1	2		81	9	275	5	55.00					3	
	4	4	0	48	12.00				11.4	0	76	2	38.00					7	
Edwards RO	2	3	1	20	10.00				3	2	9	0							
Elliott WJ	33	55	5	1009	20.18	1	6	9	311.1	64	998	30	33.26			1		8	
	3	3	0	126	42.00				24	2	127	5	25.40						
Ellis MT	19	12	4	30	3.75			3	321.3	68	1118	31	36.06			1		9	
	1								10	0	28	0						1	
	8	4	2	8	4.00			1	64	10	240	10	24.00					2	
Ellison BCA	3	4	1	26	8.66			2	49	7	174	3	58.00					4	
	1								8	1	66	0							
Elwes GP	13	22	3	190	10.00		1	6	5	1	17	1	17.00	4				4	
Emonson MR	4	2	2	2														7	1
English LM	2	3	1	5	2.50			2											
Evans NG	5	6	1	9	1.80			2											
Evans SD	2	1	0	5	5.00				15	1	90	1	90.00					1	
Everett RAL	14	22	4	114	6.33			7										5	

Name	M	In	No	Runs	Ave	100	50	O	Ov	M	Runs	W	Ave	Balls	OW	5i	10m	Ct	St
Falcon JH	21	32	4	446	15.92	1		4	103	22	311	12	25.91					14	
	2	4	0	21	5.25				16	2	59	2	29.50						
Falcon M	247	379	38	11538	33.83	21	63	27	3981.5	872	11336	688	16.47	6		52	9	112	
									15.6	3	59	2	29.50	8					
	21	36	2	872	25.64	1	4	3	285.4	59	895	51	17.54	6		4	1	5	
Falconer R	24	33	14	259	13.63		1	5	621.5	211	1407	125	11.25			14	3	11	
	2	2	1	3	3.00				40	15	79	5	15.80						
Farmer GAH	1	2	0	1	0.50			1	4	1	10	0						1	
	1	2	0	26	13.00			1	4.3	0	21	2	10.50					1	
Farrer RJ	7	9	1	51	6.37			3	112.1	32	335	3	111.66					3	
	1								17	3	72	5	14.40			1			
Farrow RDE	21	32	4	773	27.60		3	3	1.1	0	9	0						6	
	5	5	1	334	83.50	1	2												
	6	6	0	76	15.20														
Fellowes AE	3	3	0	5	1.67			1										1	
Fellowes EN	3	6	1	82	16.40			1										2	
Fellowes HC	3	4	0	36	9.00			1										2	2
Fellowes R	2	3	1	18	9.00														
Fellowes RA	1	2	0	5	2.50			1											
	1	2	1	24	24.00														
Fellowes RT	1	2	0	51	25.50														
Ferley RS	1								5	0	29	0							
Ffolkes FAS	1	2	0	18	9.00														
Fiddler GG	98	164	20	2996	20.81		15	16	154	27	471	11	42.81			1		42	
	2	3	1	56	28.00			1										2	
Fielding JL	10	13	4	98	10.88			1	103.2	8	427	11	38.81					3	
	2	1	1	8					4	0	26	0							
Finch A	1								3	0	16	0							
Findlay RJ	1	1	0	5	5.00				3	0	22	0							
Finney RJ	54	94	15	2855	36.13	4	15	4	14	0	114	7	16.28			1		29	
	13	12	0	260	21.66			1										2	
	17	16	0	370	23.12			7											
Fisher HW	5	8	1	128	18.28			1	15	5	35	0				1		1	
	1	2	1	28	28.00				4	0	14	0							
Flower FJ	2	3	0	94	31.33		1	1										7	
Flower JE	9	11	4	6	0.85			6	194.4	29	806	14	57.57		5	1		1	
Flynn W	6	10	2	42	5.25			2	66.1	?	78	8	9.75	4		1		2	
Fortescue AT	2	3	0	29	9.66				3.1	2	3	3	1.00	4					

Name	M	In	No	Runs	Ave	100	50	0	Ov	M	Runs	W	Ave	Balls	OW	5i	10m	Ct	St
Foster NA	8	13	1	273	22.75		3	1	203	48	637	29	21.96					5	
	2	2	1	6	6.00				18	3	53	3	17.66					1	
	2	2	0	52	26.00				17	3	92	2	46.00						
Foster NL	1	2	0	5	2.50			1											5
Fowler G	2	4	0	36	9.00													1	
	1	1	0	5	5.00													1	
Fowler RH	4	8	0	91	11.37		1	1										1	
Fox N	77	99	23	1540	20.26		6	14	443.4	60	1975	53	37.26			2		27	5
	23	19	4	350	23.33			1	84.3	5	474	17	27.88					4	
	31	27	8	407	21.42		1		29.1	1	183	5	36.60					10	
Francis JN	1	1	0	14	14.00														
Fraser HB	2	4	0	45	11.25			2	4	0	9	0							
Frederick TH	1	2	1	9	9.00														
Free PJ	9	12	1	206	18.72		2	2	8	0	39	0						4	
	8	7	1	120	20.00		1	1	4	0	30	0						3	
	14	12	1	89	8.09			1										4	
Frere LRT	3	5	0	39	7.80			1										5	4
	6	11	3	46	5.75			2										6	5
Fryer EH	1	1	1	32					1	0	2	0							
Fryer PA	26	42	3	1006	25.79	2	4	2										11	5
	26	46	3	747	17.37		3	5										18	2
Fryer PWJ	14	24	3	271	12.90			3	107	19	390	15	26.00					7	
	2	4	0	25	6.25				27	3	136	4	34.00						
Fulcher EJ	71	114	8	2057	19.40	1	10	18	544.4	121	1685	64	26.32			1		63	
	8	15	0	424	28.26		1	2	106.4	24	366	25	14.64			1		8	
Fulcher WP	3	5	0	40	8.00													1	
Garland TO	5	7	5	22	11.00													5	
	2	3	0	36	12.00			1										1	
Garner JP	19	19	4	371	24.73		2	3										31	9
	4	3	0	24	8.00			1										8	1
	23	15	1	196	14.00													17	9
Garnett CF	8	11	1	143	14.3		1	4	45.2	17	118	5	23.60					1	
	4	5	0	26	5.20			2	21	4	78	3	26.00						
Garnier EHC	3	2	1	0	0.00			1	16	1	108	1	108.00	8					
Garnier ET	20	34	5	814	28.06		3	4	7	0	21	1	21.00	5				8	
	11	18	0	245	13.61			6	8	1	21	0		6					
Garnier GR	2	3	0	58	19.33			1	2	0	6	0						11	

Name	M	In	No	Runs	Ave	100	50	0	Ov	M	Runs	W	Ave	Balls	OW	5i	10m	Ct	St
Gascoigne CCO	1	1	0	0	0.00			1											
		1	0	5	5.00														
Gathergood LS	1	1	0	14	14.00				3	0	13	0							
Gemmell G	3	6	0	60	10.00														
	1	2	0	40	20.00														
Gibson E	90	125	36	743	8.34			28	2114.5	593	5164	307	16.82			25	5	58	
	30	46	6	370	8.04			6	825.4	213	2126	123	17.28			10	1	20	
Gibson JJC	48	65	19	923	20.06		4	6	961.2	295	2579	84	30.70			3		26	
Gillham CJ	2	4	0	43	10.75			1										1	
Gilliatt RT	4	5	1	37	9.25			2	83.1	17	271	10	27.10			1			
Gladden RH	22	37	4	588	17.81		3	3										12	
	3	6	0	93	15.50		1											2	
Goderson R	2	4	0	33	8.25			1										1	
Godfrey DG	14	9	1	33	4.12			1	225.1	35	793	25	31.72			2		7	
Goldsmith SC	90	157	20	6063	44.25	10	39	7	1550	332	4856	181	26.82			4		49	
	36	32	2	1077	35.90		9	2	180.4	32	652	36	18.11			1		13	
	50	50	2	1538	32.04	1	13	1	424.4	40	1687	67	25.17			1		14	
Goode WF	1	2	2	10				1										1	1
Goodenough RJC	1	1	0	0	0														
Goodfellow BJ	2	2	2	0	0				31	5	98	3	32.66					2	
	1	1	0						13	4	34	0						2	
Goodley GW	34	53	4	882	18.00		1	3										15	
	3	5	0	49	9.80			1											
Goodliff F	6								2	1	10	0							
	2								3	0	11	0							
Goodham MD	6	6	2	67	16.75			1										14	3
	2	1	0	1	1.00													1	2
Goodwin R	12	12	9	27	9.00			1	136	22	544	15	36.26					6	
Gorrod MA	8	10	4	40	6.66			2	108	16	352	11	32.00					3	
	1	1	1	1					14	4	21	4	5.25					1	
Grainge CM	1	1	1	1															
Grant CB	15	26	6	174	8.70			4	216.2	38	683	19	35.94					4	
	1	2	0	60	30.00				18	2	57	1	57.00					2	
Gray SK	15	24	3	418	19.90		2	3										32	5
	8	7	1	203	33.83		2											11	1
	17	15	3	510	42.50		3											19	1
Greatrex EJ	44	48	16	400	12.50			8										54	18
	2	1	0	10	10.00													1	1
	1	1	0	12	12.00													1	1

Name	M	In	No	Runs	Ave	100	50	0	Ov	M	Runs	W	Ave	Balls	OW	5i	10m	Ct	St
Green CRF	5	3	2	38	38.00			3	68	16	201	4	50.25					7	
Green GBG	12	21	3	238	13.22		1		1	0	8	0						5	
Greenwell JW	5	8	3	20	4.00				20	3	54	0						5	
Groom AJ	1	2	0	6	3.00														
Gurdon C	7	10	0	101	10.10			2										5	2
Gurdon ET	1	2	0	3	1.50														
Gurdon F	2	3	0	7	2.33			2											
Gurney EH	3	5	1	39	9.75			1										3	
Gurney GB	2	3	0	53	17.66														
Gurney H	3	6	0	102	17.00			1										1	
Gurney WS	37	63	3	926	15.43		4	16	19	9	43	0		4				23	
Gurney WSC	1	2	0	16	8.00			1											
Gwillim JH	1	2	0	10	5.00			1											
Hadley IPS	1	2	0	4	2.00			1	5	0	25	1	25.00					2	
Hale FW	4	6	1	32	6.40			2											
Halford AJ	18	23	3	223	11.15			5	253.2	74	721	32	22.53			1		16	
		1	0	24	24.00				10	2	34	2	17.00						
		2	0	5	2.50			1	24	4	107	2	53.50					2	
Hall ER	11	20	1	459	24.15		3	1	21	3	74	3	24.66					9	
		2	0	54	27.00			1											
Hall TA	2	4	0	4	1.00			3	65	7	225	6	37.50					6	
Hancock WD	30	38	10	264	9.42			8	558.3	80	2013	57	35.31			1		6	
	2	2	1	3	3.00				21	6	118	5	23.60					1	
Handley FLQ	162	295	6	7800	26.99	10	47	22	6.2	0	53	0						121	
	12	13	1	356	29.66		1	1										3	
	23	22	0	499	22.68		1	2										11	
Hankinson RS	1	2	0	4	2.00			1											
Hansell J	34	61	4	1248	21.89	2	4	5	960.3	369	1693	99	17.10	4		7	3	26	
Hansell WE	3	5	3	10	5.00				18	5	32	1	32.00	5					
Hanworth WR	1	1	0	27	27.00				4	1	7	0		4					
Harbour	1	2	0	2	1.00			1	15	8	18	1	18.00	4					
Hare JHM	23	38	5	504	15.27		1	5	14	3	44	1	44.00	4				9	
Hare T	7	11	1	92	9.20			1	45	6	164	2	82.00					2	
Harris AJ	1	1							9	1	60	1	60.00						
Harris CZ									8	0	38	1	38.00						
Harrison I	1	1	0	9	9.00				2	0	14	0							
Harrison MJ	12	14	5	86	9.55			2	241	47	739	26	28.42					1	

Name	M	In	No	Runs	Ave	100	50	0	Ov	M	Runs	W	Ave	Balls	OW	5i	10m	Ct	St
Hart-Davis SO	1	2	0	31	15.50				5	1	15	0						1	
Harvey BL	1	2	0	12	6.00													1	
	1																		1
Harvey GEA	3	3	0	47	15.66													1	
	1	2	0	43	21.50														
Harvey SR	5	9	0	110	12.22			1										2	
	5	4	0	107	26.75			1										4	
	2	3	1	52	52.00														
Harwood PJ	2	2	1	18	18.00				10	1	52	1	52.00						
	16	10	3	145	20.71			2	95	11	394	25	15.76					7	
	5	5	0	76	15.20													3	
Hastings HF	3	6	0	57	9.50														
Hawes WG	2	2	0	7	3.50			2	3	0	18	0		4	3			2	
Hayles BRM	1	2	0	3	1.50														
Hayter WLB	11	20	2	335	18.61		1	4	22	5	82	2	41.00					8	
	13	22	0	220	10.00			5	5	0	29	0						4	
Heading RB	3	4	0	51	12.75													1	
	1	2	0	40	20.00														
Heasman WG	5	9	0	173	19.22		1	1	35	14	83	2	41.50	5				2	
Herr K	1	1	1	7														2	
Heslop GG	22	35	3	462	14.43		1	4	54.1	17	135	9	15.00	5		1		9	
									96.4	21	292	11	26.54	6					
	7	13	1	381	31.75	2		3	11	0	41	0		5					
									32	3	116	5	23.20	6				4	
Heywood RJ	2	4	1	31	10.33			2										1	
Higenbottam OT	1	1	0	16	16.00													2	
	1	1	0	36	36.00														
Hildyard C	1	2	0	23	11.50													1	
Hill SD	2	3	0	54	18.00			1										1	
	1	2	0	13	6.50													1	
Hoare AR	19	27	1	690	26.53		4		9	0	29	1	29.00	5				1	
									178.1	43	531	34	15.61	6		4		10	
	20	34	2	731	22.84		3	1	257	76	848	34	24.94	5		4			
									27	6	83	2	41.50	6		(3)		13	
Hoare OVG	2	2	1	21	21.00														

Name	M	In	No	Runs	Ave	100	50	0	Ov	M	Runs	W	Ave	Balls	OW	5i	10m	Ct	St
Hoare VR	**3**	**6**	**0**	**48**	**8.00**			**1**	**5**	**1**	**16**	**1**	**16.00**	**5**				**6**	
	16	29	2	568	21.03		2	2	25	7	63	2	31.50	6					
									129.3	44	235	14	16.78	5				4	
									51.4	10	178	12	14.83	6					
Hoare WR	**1**	**2**	**0**	**10**	**5.00**				**4**	**1**	**17**	**1**	**17.00**	**5**					
	28	51	3	605	12.60		1	7	9	3	19	0		4				23	
									102	27	258	5	51.60	5					
Hodson ER	**26**	**42**	**4**	**369**	**9.71**			**5**	**17**	**1**	**92**	**2**	**46.00**					**9**	
	11	9	2	163	23.28													3	
Hoff RHG	**16**	**24**	**1**	**442**	**19.21**	**1**		**1**										**13**	
	5	5	0	76	15.20			1										1	1
Holley E	17	31	8	194	8.43			5	247	67	564	29	19.44	5	7	2		8	
Holmes JB	**14**	**23**	**1**	**150**	**6.81**			**6**	**4**	**0**	**13**	**0**						**1**	
Hopkins CL	1	2	0	0	0.00			2											
Horne GL	1	1	0	0	0.00			1											
Horsfall THS	**1**	**2**	**0**	**12**	**6.00**				**8**	**2**	**23**	**1**	**23.00**						
	2	4	1	33	11.00			1	3	0	15	1	15.00						
Hosken JF	**1**	**2**	**1**	**5**	**5.00**				**4**	**1**	**7**	**0**							
Howlett AE	**4**	**7**	**3**	**16**	**4.00**			**3**	**96.5**	**28**	**262**	**12**	**21.83**			**1**		**1**	
Hudson AR	**15**	**21**	**3**	**246**	**13.66**			**2**	**36**	**8**	**112**	**7**	**16.00**					**5**	
	2	4	1	84	28.00				3	1	11	0							
Hudson RC	**3**	**6**	**0**	**48**	**8.00**			**1**	**1**	**1**	**0**	**0**						**3**	
Huggins RDP	**157**	**282**	**33**	**6883**	**27.64**	**2**	**38**	**26**										**82**	
	2	2	0	48	24.00													3	
	21	21	3	532	29.55		3											5	
Humphrey W	4	6	1	73	14.60				20	8	48	2	24.00	4	5				
Innes RF	**23**	**24**	**8**	**196**	**12.25**			**6**	**350.5**	**74**	**1146**	**28**	**40.92**					**10**	
	3	3	0	21	7.00			7	38	10	85	3	28.33					1	
	3	3	2	3	3.00				33	4	90	2	45.00					2	
Ireland MW	**15**	**26**	**2**	**275**	**11.45**			**5**	**127.5**	**31**	**412**	**22**	**18.72**			**1**		**15**	
	12	21	4	355	20.88		1		74.1	15	220	16	13.75			1		7	
Jackson GR	**2**	**2**	**0**	**17**	**8.50**			**1**										**1**	
	2	2	0	4	2.00														
Jackson J	6	9	1	71					108	57	114	11			6	1		2	
Jackson JB	**1**	**2**	**0**	**15**	**7.50**														
James	1	1	0	2	2.00														
Jarvis AW	14	21	5	149	9.31			2										8	1

Name	M	In	No	Runs	Ave	100	50	0	Ov	M	Runs	W	Ave	Balls	OW	5i	10m	Ct	St
Jarvis CJE	**84**	**140**	**8**	**2125**	**16.09**	**1**	**8**	**21**	**1501.3**	**558**	**2694**	**162**	**16.62**	**4**	**3**	**1C**	**3**	**55**	**3**
									162.4	57	339	19	17.84	5	3			5	
Jarvis FW	18	33	1	344	10.75			8	5	1	15	0						5	
Jarvis LK	75	125	9	3662	31.56	6	17	8	118	37	238	16	14.87	4	3	1		51	
Jee AM	12	18	0	110	6.11			5	62	15	160	4	40.00	4	5	1		4	
Jefferson RI	**15**	**22**	**2**	**305**	**15.25**				**522.3**	**199**	**970**	**101**	**9.60**			**11**	**4**	**10**	
	1	1	0	39	39.00				7	0	17	3	5.66					1	
	3	3	0	70	23.33		1		33	6	98	4	24.50					3	
Jefferson WI	1	1	0	20	20.00														
Jervis MM	**8**	**9**	**2**	**78**	**11.14**			**3**										**10**	**1**
Jessopp NA	**6**	**8**	**1**	**147**	**21.00**	**1**		**1**	**94**	**23**	**238**	**9**	**26.44**					**2**	**9**
	2	3	2	22	22.00				43.1	13	90	7	12.85						
Johnson EG	1	2	0	0	0.00			1	2	1	6	0		4					
Jones	4	6	2	13	3.25			2	45	13	80	3	26.66	4				2	
Jones AMB	1	2	0	1	0.50			1										1	
Jory HI	**9**	**14**	**1**	**209**	**16.07**		**1**											**4**	**1**
Kemp KH	19	31	4	369	13.66			4										8	
Kennaway AL	**4**	**6**	**0**	**15**	**2.50**			**2**										**2**	
Kennaway CL	39	61	3	909	15.67	1	2	10	12	2	31	1	31.00	4				11	
Kennon NS	**3**	**5**	**0**	**82**	**16.40**			**1**										**1**	
Kent EA	**2**							**1**	**25**	**3**	**81**	**2**	**40.50**	**4**				**1**	
Kenyon CM	**5**	**9**	**3**	**74**	**12.33**			**1**										**10**	**1**
Ketton RW	12	19	0	159	8.36			2	20	?	28	2	14.00	4				7	
Keyworth FM	2	2	0	17	8.50													1	
Kilshaw PJ	**12**	**19**	**5**	**310**	**22.14**		**1**	**3**	**50**	**2**	**246**	**1**	**246.00**					**5**	
Kingshott RA	**50**	**53**	**15**	**500**	**13.15**		**1**	**11**	**1430.3**	**358**	**4419**	**174**	**25.39**			**7**	**3**	**17**	
	8	3							91	13	388	10	38.80					1	
Lake EA	13	7	3	36	18.00				121	14	415	7	59.28					8	
	3	3	0	10	10.00				23	5	46	2	23.00	5				1	
Lambert DC	3	3		1	0.33														
Lambert PA	**6**	**11**	**0**	**202**	**18.36**			**2**	**14.3**	**6**	**24**	**2**	**12.00**					**10**	
	1	1	0	24	24.00													1	
Lambourne IR	**11**	**5**	**2**	**7**	**2.33**			**3**	**94.2**	**14**	**380**	**16**	**23.75**					**7**	
	4	4	0	62	15.50														

Name	M	In	No	Runs	Ave	100	50	0	Ov	M	Runs	W	Ave	Balls	OW	5i	10m	Ct	St
Langdale GR	10	11	1	172	17.20			2	108.4	15	375	22	17.04	8				6	
Larkins W	1	1	0	15	15.00													1	
Law G	1	1	0	4	4.00														
Lawes ACH	2	4	0	17	4.25			1										5	
(italic)	2	2	0	3	15.50														
Laws BM	3	4	0	16	4.00				7	0	37	0						1	
(italic)	1	1	0	46	46.00														
Lay LC	2	4	0	16	4.00														
Leatham C	1	2	0	4	2.00			1										2	
Leggatt O	1	1	0	3	3.00													2	
Leggatt R	13	21	2	202	10.63			5	8	1	33	0	61.00	8				9	
(italic)									58	12	183	3		6					
Leigh BJ	18	33	7	476	18.30		1	5										7	
Leman LH	17	27	7	480	24.00		2	2	101	16	330	9	36.66					14	
(italic)	3	4	0	53	13.25			1	9	1	19	1	19.00					2	
Lewis JCM	35	40	11	512	17.65		1	2	708.1	157	2329	76	30.64			2		11	
(italic)	7	7	1	86	14.33				61.3	4	253	13	19.46			1		1	
(italic)	11	7	2	48	9.60				111.4	15	448	18	24.88					7	
Lewis PCM *(italic)*	1								11	0	52	1	52.00					7	
Lingwood WJ	50	50	21	284	9.79			12	1057.1	316	2343	127	18.44	6		6	1	27	
(italic)									104	16	388	15	25.86	8				1	
(italic)									122	26	243	7	34.71	6				2	
Livermore SJB	10	15	4	303	27.54		1	1	1	0	5	0						7	
(italic)	4	5	2	8	2.66			1										1	
(italic)	2	1	0	9	9.00													6	
Llong NJ	2	4	0	93	23.25		1	1	10	0	22	1	22.00					1	
(italic)	27	26	6	535	26.75		2	2										7	
(italic)	1	1	0	7	7.00														
(italic)	6	5	0	117	23.40		1		27	2	139	3	46.33						
Logan DJC	3	3	3	17				1	29	3	175	4	43.75					1	
Lomas H	2	3	0	34	11.33														
(italic)	1	2	0	7	3.50														
Long EF	5	10	1	140	15.55		1	2	53.4	4	157	9	17.44					2	
(italic)	1	2	0	22	11.00				7	0	34	0							
Lord A	2	3	0	15	5.00				3	0	21	0							
Lord E	1	1	1	3					5	1	15	1	15.00						
Low HF	67	113	6	1744	16.29		6	17	32	2	158	1	158.00					46	1
(italic)	5	7	0	139	19.85			1	30	4	125	3	41.66						
Lucas PM *(italic)*	5	10	0	71	7.10			3										2	

Name	M	In	No	Runs	Ave	100	50	0	Ov	M	Runs	W	Ave	Balls	OW	5i	10m	Ct	St
Luddington HT	11	16	6	83	8.30			2	310	111	496	37	13.40	4	7	4	1	5	
Mace AFA	7	11	0	186	16.90		1		7	2	7	1	7.00					2	
Mack AJ	9	5	3	9	4.50			1	258.1	76	644	43	14.97			3		8	
	1	1	1	7					10	2	22	0							
Mack ESP	11	16	2	89	6.35			3	183	50	417	30	13.90	5		1		6	
	13	23	1	166	7.54			7	15	4	43	2	21.50	4				8	
Mack HP	1	1	0	0	0.00				210.1	66	476	30	15.86	5					
Mackenzie RS	2	2	1	15	15.00			1	50	16	88	7	12.57	4				1	
MacLaren AC	1	2	2	33															
Mahon GM	4	8	2	92	15.33			1										1	
	1	2	0	46	23.00			1											
Mann EJ	3	4	0	27	6.75			1											
Mansfield JW	1	1	0	2	2.00														
Marquet JP	1	1	0	4	4.00				10	0	55	3	18.33						
Marsh FT	3	3	2	5	5.00			1	45	17	56	3	18.66						
Marsh TH	5	8	1	95	13.57			1	34.2	10	85	6	14.16	4		1		1	
									52	11	132	6	22.00	5					
Marsh WH	2	3	1	7	3.50			1	18	7	35	3	11.66	4					
									11	2	43	0		5					
Marshall LP	2	3	0	3	1.00			1										1	
Martin GH	9	15	0	222	14.8		2	2										3	
Mason HD	1	2	0	26	13.00													2	
Mason PL	3	3	0	27	9.00													2	
Massingham EA	2	4	0	6	1.50			3	11	6	17	1	17.00	5					
	11	20	3	254	14.94		2	2	46.2	14	101	5	20.20	5				9	
Master HC	4	8	1	26	3.71			3										2	
	6	10	1	206	22.88													10	
Master HH	1	1	0	5	5.00				5	1	17	0						1	
Mattocks DE	212	279	78	3482	17.32	1	9	41										399	60
	4	3	1	4	2.00			1										4	1
	28	27	8	160	12.30			2										33	3
Mayes AR	1	2	0	34	17.00				21	5	47	0							
Mayhew KG	4	6	1	22	4.40			1	12	0	52	1	52.00					2	
Maynard JC	2	1	0	0	0.00			1										1	
McCormick JG	29	50	1	1239	25.28	4	3	5	3	0	13	1	13.00					23	
	11	18	0	392	21.77		1	2										7	

Name	M	In	No	Runs	Ave	100	50	0	Ov	M	Runs	W	Ave	Balls	OW	5i	10m	Ct	St
McLaren WH	1	1	0	4	4.00				38	?	52	7	7.42	4		1		1	
McManus CA	56	100	10	1725	19.16	1	6	6										30	
	1	1	0	19	19.00													1	
	2	2	0	26	13.00													2	
Meigh BA	27	12	10	34	17.00			1	435	77	1516	50	30.32			1		18	
	4	2	2	9					75.4	11	256	10	25.60					2	
Mercer IP	74	132	16	3688	31.79	2	23	11	11.5	0	53	1	53.00					60	
	2	2	0	2*	10.50				9	1	81	1	81.00						
	4	4	0	8*	20.25				2	0	16	0						1	
Meyrick-Jones F	1	2	1	78	78.00			1										1	
Mickleburgh JC	4	8	1	153	21.85				2	0	11	1	11.00					3	
	5	5	0	176	35.20		2		2	0	18	0						3	
	8	8	0	179	22.37		2	1										5	
Middleton JP	3	5	1	25	6.25			1	16	7	34	2	17.00	4				2	
Miles JS	4	5	1	25	6.25			1	118	17	410	14	29.28					3	
Mills A	5	9	2	115	16.42			2	2	0	23	0						1	
Mindham PR	21	29	8	439	20.90		1	4										12	
Mir PJ	42	75	16	2458	41.66	3	11	3	1554.3	437	3540	167	21.19			5		32	
	2	2	0	200	100.00	1	1		19	5	56	5	11.20					1	
	11	11	3	356	44.50		3		107.5	18	353	14	25.21					3	
Mitchell G	32	55	2	949	17.90	1	3	7	182.2	38	462	19	24.31					11	
Mitchell LG	1																		
	1	2	0	14	7.00				5	1	11	1	11.00						
Montgomerie CTCM	2	4	0	45	11.25													1	
Moore NH	95	162	13	476*	31.95	7	28	14	599.3	110	1867	74	25.23			3		39	
	3	3	0	6*	20.33				13	2	44	2	22.00						
Moore RSL	1	2	1	18	18.00													1	
Moore TI	169	192	67	1582	12.65		2	33	4000.5	925	12001	474	25.28			17	2	88	
	10	11	2	38	4.22			3	76.5	8	346	5	69.20					3	
	4	4	2	4	2.00				47.4	8	171	10	17.10			1			
Moores RD	4	6	0	136	22.66		1	1	19	4	101	0						2	
	6	4	3	47	47.00				38	4	208	6	34.66					1	
	6	4	1	49	16.33				17	1	90	1	90.00					2	
Morley T	34	51	4	661	14.06		2	8	767.2	256	1616	115	14.05	5		7		43	
									12	2	34	0		6					
	55	96	3	1255	13.49		1	13	33	10	82	0		4		3		50	4
									1095.3	395	2153	132	16.31	5			1		

183

Name	M	In	No	Runs	Ave	100	50	0	Ov	M	Runs	W	Ave	Balls	OW	5i	10m	Ct	St
Mornement RH	2	4	1	30	10.00			1	12	3	34	1	34.00	5					
	3	6	0	35	5.83				15	4	43	3	14.33	5				2	
Morrell DM	8	2	0	9	4.50													10	2
	1	1	0	6	6.00														
Morrice CH	12	23	4	359	18.89	1	1	4	15	6	27	1	27.00	4	2			2	
Morrice FLH	1	1	0	26	26.00													1	
Morris EJ	13	22	5	245	14.41			7	6	1	15	0						5	
Morse MH	1	2	0	5	2.50				2	1	2	0							
	2	3	0	52	17.33														
Morse SA	1	1	0	10	10.00													2	
	1	2	0	1	0.50													1	
Morton	2	4	1	53	17.66													2	
Morton CH	1	1	0	0	0.00			1	10	1	46	0						1	
	14	24	1	173	7.52			3	127.1	48	288	19	15.15	4		1		11	
Morton PH	15	22	0	279	12.68				192.3	44	456	37	12.32	5		6	2	22	
Motum PA	12	16	2	239	17.07			3	618	274	906	107	8.46			15	5	7	
	2	2	0	10	5.00			1	18	3	78	5	15.60	4				1	
Moulton AF	3	3	2	25	25.00													6	
Mower GH	38	55	7	323	6.72			19	621.3	116	1941	68	28.54					23	
	3	6	1	46	9.20			1	36	5	127	1	127.00					1	
Mower HW	1	1	0	6	6.00														
Moyser RA	21	30	6	714	29.75		5	3	3	0	25	1	25.00					11	
	1	1	0	28	28.00				4	0	24	0						1	
	5	5	1	101	25.25													2	
Neville GER	2	3	0	18	6.00			1	9	1	30	2	15.00					2	
	2	4	2	43	21.50				28	4	72	6	12.00						
Newby EW	3	5	0	17	3.40													3	
Newman PG	57	61	19	714	17.00		1	9	1226.1	352	3337	127	26.27			3		32	
	17	10	2	224	28.00			1	129.2	28	343	21	16.33			1		8	
	43	32	15	376	22.11			2	350.1	54	1182	43	27.48					24	
Newton LTS	34	44	10	632	18.58		1	12										79	15
	9	7	0	98	14.00			2	62	15	165	5	33.00	5				7	3
	15	10	2	119	14.87													16	2
Nichols JE	100	157	23	3263	24.35	1	14	16	1537.3	359	4215	219	19.24	6		9	1	72	1
	4	7	0	114	16.28				60.5	13	187	5	37.40	6				2	

Name	M	In	No	Runs	Ave	100	50	0	Ov	M	Runs	W	Ave	Balls	OW	5i	10m	Ct	St
North MK	1	2	0	15	7.50			1											
Nugent TEG	1																		
O'Brien JR	3	5	1	163	40.75		1		10	0	48	0							1
Orams E	1	1	1	20					3	1	2	0							
	22	*36*	*0*	*548*	*15.65*	*1*	*1*	*8*										*15*	
Ormiston RW	19	38	1	882	23.83		6	2	176.5	37	593	23	25.78					19	
	3	*3*	*0*	*83*	*27.66*		*1*		*15*	*2*	*54*	*1*	*54.00*						
Orton JOC	1	2	0	3	1.50			1											
Owens JH	4	8	0	64	8.00													2	
Oxbury MD	16	18	7	51	4.63			5	393.3	94	1136	44	25.81			1		10	
	5	*2*	*0*	*11*	*5.50*			*1*	*42.3*	*5*	*185*	*2*	*97.50*					*1*	
Page AC	2	3	1	52	26.00													5	
Page SD	58	91	9	1199	14.62		2	19	1	0	6	1	6.00	5				47	12
	17	*30*	*4*	*312*	*12.00*			*7*										*17*	*3*
Panter RG	1	1	0	2	2.00														
Parfitt JH	2	4	1	37	12.33			1											
	2	*3*	*0*	*15*	*5.00*			*1*											
Parfitt PH	13	17	4	424	32.61	1	2	2	133.4	19	431	18	23.94			1		4	
	2	*2*	*0*	*10*	*5.00*													*3*	
Partridge ERW	1	1	0	18	18.00														
Partridge PW	19	30	4	541	20.80		1	2	4	0	11	0						9	
	8	*14*	*2*	*156*	*13.00*			*1*										*2*	
Patey E	1	2	1	13	13.00													3	
Patmore AJD	2	1	0	22	22.00													4	
Patston BJ	4	7	0	322	46.00	1	2											3	
	1	*1*	*0*	*52*	*52.00*		*1*												
	7	*7*	*0*	*216*	*30.85*		*2*	*1*											
Patteson FE	17	27	1	431	16.57		1	6										10	
Patteson JC	3	5	1	47	11.75														
Payne AN	11	6	4	1	0.50			1										20	5
	1	*1*	*1*	*0*														*1*	
Peachment E	4	7	2	27	5.40			1	85.4	16	231	10	23.10					2	
Pearse AJ	2	3	0	24	8.00			1											
	1	*2*	*0*	*61*	*30.50*		*1*	*1*											
Pearse C	3	5	1	13	3.25			1										3	2
	2	*3*	*0*	*24*	*8.00*													*2*	*2*
Pearson JM	17	26	3	280	12.17		1	6	361.2	106	836	32	26.12					11	

Name	M	In	No	Runs	Ave	100	50	0	Ov	M	Runs	W	Ave	Balls	OW	5i	10m	Ct	St
Pedder GR	30	47	11	453	12.58			4										39	16
	2	4	0	46	11.50													2	
Penberthy AL	1	2	0	13	6.50				23	2	80	1	80.00					1	
	3	3	0	299	99.66	2	1		18	2	81	1	81.00					2	
	1	1	0	1	1.00				9.5	0	53	0							
Penn EF	10	17	2	409	27.26	2		5	67	14	195	5	39.00	5				10	
									99	17	329	14	23.50	6					
	7	9	0	201	22.33		1	1	113.1	21	306	24	12.75	6		3	1		
Perkins RW	19	31	4	516	19.11		2	3	106	3	584	13	44.92					4	
	1	1	0	0	0.00				4	0	39	0		8					
Perry	1	1	0	1	1.00														
Phipps DD	10	11	2	22	2.44			6	156	34	492	15	32.80					4	
Pierpoint FG	26	40	18	207	9.40			4	531.3	123	1386	68	20.38			4		6	
Pigot G	1	2	0	28	14.00														
Pilch DG	225	365	55	6333	20.42	1	27	40	1637	280	5610	222	25.27			1	1	145	
	11	11	2	138	15.33				91	18	316	9	35.11					4	
	6	6	0	27	4.50				34	3	180	9	20.00					2	
Pilch GE	18	21	5	141	8.81			4	386	89	1078	38	28.36					6	
	1	2	1	13	13.00				16.3	3	42	1	42.00						
Pilch RG	34	56	5	432	8.47		1	13	47.2	17	106	2	53.00	5				17	
									306	51	1043	27	38.63	6					
Platten G	14	21	3	267	14.83		1	5	76.1	16	191	5	38.20	6				12	
	4	5	2	10	3.33			2	118	52	147	23	6.39	4	7			2	
Plumb SG	146	265	35	10067	43.77	17	67	14	2854.2	696	8728	283	30.84			5	1	75	
	15	16	0	389	24.31		3	2	141.1	16	450	16	28.12					2	
	39	38	2	1108	30.77	2	4	3	380.4	70	1114	42	26.52					13	
Pollard E	2	3	1	61	30.50				4	3	4	0						1	
Pontifex A	4	7	1	68	11.33			2										1	
Poole JC	1																		
Popham CH	1	2	0	1	0.50			1											
	1	1	0	0	0.00			1	7	1	29	4	7.25					1	
Popham RF	29	43	1	1083	25.78	2	5	2										18	
	5	9	0	104	11.55			1										2	
Powell MG	17	26	5	339	16.14			1	362.2	80	1269	38	33.39			1		9	
	5	4	1	7	2.33				48.4	4	170	6	28.33					2	
	4	4	0	65	16.25				38	0	193	2	96.50					1	
Powell PG	140	247	16	5459	23.63	5	22	18	158.5	22	565	18	31.38			1		100	
	5	6	0	176	29.33		1											4	

Name	M	In	No	Runs	Ave	100	50	0	Ov	M	Runs	W	Ave	Balls	OW	5i	10m	Ct	St
Powell TL	7	10	2	242	30.25	1		2										6	
Pretheroe EO	2	4	0	13	3.25			1										1	
Prior CBL	4	6	1	31	6.20			1	19	2	82	1	82.00					2	2
Prior HC	5	4	0	75	18.75		1	1										6	
	2	4	0	29	7.25													5	2
Purdy RJ	3	3	0	22	7.33													1	
Purton RGS	4	5	0	47	9.40			1	15	3	48	1	48.00					1	
	1	1	0	9	9.00														
Radley CT	9	12	1	225	20.45		1	4	20	4	77	2	38.50	5		1		5	
Raikes EB	11	18	8	105	10.50			6	116.3	40	234	19	12.31	6				6	
									58	5	216	5	43.20						
	29	45	6	255	6.71			14	1146.3	393	2135	143	14.93	4	7	11	5	7	
									238	78	469	33	14.21	5		4	1		
Raikes GB	51	81	4	2466	32.02	5	9	5	271.4	91	572	27	21.18	5		14		42	
									838.2	103	3030	197	15.38	6		6	6		
	21	37	2	945	27.00	1	7	6	219.4	60	465	29	16.03	5		2		13	
									60	9	230	14	16.42	6		2	1		
Raikes TB	24	36	5	467	15.06		1	7	309.5	90	950	42	22.61			1		15	
	1	2	0	4	2.00			1											
Raven CO	2	3	1	163	81.5	1			4	1	4	1	4.00					1	
	1	2	0	3	1.50			1	2	0	12	0							
Rayner GR	3	3	0	8	2.66			1											
Rayner MJ	3	5	1	31	7.75				67.4	15	186	12	15.50			1		4	2
	1								2	0	19	7	19.00						
Read CC	3	4	0	14	3.50			1	7	1	72	0						1	
	6	2	0	17	8.50				35	0	160	2	80.00					2	
Read JA	2	3	0	6	2.00			1										1	
Relf AE	14	22	2	769	38.45	3	4	1	532.4	200	1040	53	19.62	5		4		18	
	3	5	0	87	17.40			1	91	38	195	12	16.25	5				3	
Reynolds R	15	27	1	496	19.07		3	3	10	2	46	0						5	
	1	1	0	15	15.00				8	0	28	1							
Rhodes FW	2	2	0	9	4.50														
Rice D	1	1	0	12	12.00				13	5	23	0						2	
Rice PC	5	8	2	88	14.66			1										2	
Rice PWM	1	2	0	15	7.50				2	0	4	0							
Richardson ME								5	6	2	15	1	15.00						
Riley JH	10	9	3	7	1.16			5										9	4
	7	6	2	9	2.25			3										5	5

Name	M	In	No	Runs	Ave	100	50	0	Ov	M	Runs	W	Ave	Balls	OW	5i	10m	Ct	St
Ringwood PJ	22	36	6	616	20.53		3	5	8	0	22	0						17	
		1	0	28	28.00			1										1	
	5	4	0	48	12.00			1											
Rist WH	2	2	0	0	0.00			2										1	
Rivett-Carnac GC	2	3	1	14	7.00			1	64.3	21	90	5	18.00	4	4				
Rix WA	1	2	1	3	3.00				4	0	17	1	17.00	5					
	3	6	1	21	4.20				18.1	9	23	4	5.75	4					
Roberson F	1	2	0	2	1.00			1										1	
	1	2	0	0	0.00			2											
Roberts GJ	5	10	1	69	7.66			2										3	
	2	2	0	99	49.50		1												
Robertson WK	2	3	0	22	7.33				24	7	52	3	17.33						
	2	4	0	11	2.75				8	1	34	0							
Robins GF	1	1	0	13	13.00														
Robinson DDJ	1	1	0	64	64.00		1												
Robinson MI	4	5	1	35	8.75				5	0	39	0						1	
Robinson SG	1	1	0	13	13.00														
		1	0	13	13.00														
Roff GM	10	11	2	97	10.77			2	127.5	28	497	21	23.66					6	
	5	2	0	0	0.00			2	47	7	179	9	19.88					1	
Rogers CJ	153	282	25	10026	39.01	19	61	14	636.4	132	2155	54	39.91			1		148	
	42	42	5	1393	37.64	2	9	2	95.1	6	397	9	44.11					13	
	90	90	7	2574	31.01	4	16	11	361.3	15	1639	57	28.75			1		41	
Rogers DB	9	10	2	135	16.87				4	0	26	1	26.00					1	
Rogerson WTC	1	1	0	13	13.00													1	
Rolph JB	3	2	2	3	13.00				47	10	140	4	35.00					1	
Rose W	96	139	32	1431	13.37			11	2152.2	675	5770	287	20.10			17	4	42	
	3	3	0	27	9.00			7	27	4	84	2	42.00					1	
	2	2	0	2	1.00			1	12	1	35	0							
Rossi DM	19	28	3	599	23.96		3	1										9	
	1	2	0	6	3.00														
Rought-Rought BW	140	215	18	4665	23.68	6	18	19	132	21	552	21	26.28	8		1		53	
	8	13	0	188	14.46		1											2	
Rought-Rought DC	89	121	10	2948	26.55	4	14	12	1650.5	396	4613	221	20.87	6		8	1	41	
									17	0	72	0	72.00	8					
	7	10	0	84	8.40				63.4	7	224	10	22.40	6				3	

Name	M	In	No	Runs	Ave	100	50	0	Ov	M	Runs	W	Ave	Balls	OW	5i	10m	Ct	St
Rought-Rought RC	**105**	**148**	**21**	**2039**	**16.05**		**9**	**22**	**2810.2**	**782**	**6256**	**408**	**15.33**	**8**		**25**	**4**	**57**	
	9	13	2	109	9.90			1	153.4	26	497	30	16.56	6		3		2	1
									197.5	39	606	28	21.64	8		2			
									17.3	2	75	1	75.00	6					
Rouse AW	2	3	0	8	2.66			2	15	5	33	0		6				1	
Rowe JC	**3**	**6**	**0**	**11**	**1.83**			**4**										**1**	
	3	3	1	82	41.00														
Rowe SA	**4**	**5**	**0**	**39**	**7.80**			**1**	**60**	**17**	**166**	**4**	**41.50**	**4**				**2**	
Rudd A	29	46	18	148	5.28			6	1118.2	440	1887	126	14.97	5		12	3	6	
Rudd NA	1	1	0	7	7.00				14	6	26	1	26.00					2	
Rudd RK	**40**	**43**	**16**	**353**	**13.07**			**5**	**801**	**146**	**2402**	**89**	**26.98**					**12**	
	4	3	2	29	29.00				38	3	147	3	49.00						
Rudd T	2	3	1	32	16.00				5	1	25	1	25.00					1	
Rushforth T	**1**	**2**	**0**	**8**	**4.00**														
Rutter AEH	**17**	**33**	**2**	**613**	**19.77**		**2**	**2**										**8**	
	1	1	0	7	7.00														
Rye GJ	95	157	38	1144	9.61		2	25	40	?	55	2	27.50	4				66	
									1573	711	2273	151	15.05	4	1	11	2		
									1257.4	463	2252	119	18.92	5		5	2		
Saggers MJ	**7**	**3**	**0**	**48**	**16.00**			**5**	**113.5**	**28**	**407**	**11**	**37.00**					**3**	
	1	2	0	2	1.00				8	1	29	2	14.50					1	
	2	2	1					1	19	1	87	1	87.00						
Salisbury WE	**1**	**2**	**0**	**13**	**6.50**													**1**	
	2	2	1	4	4.00														
Sands DW	**1**	**2**	**0**	**16**	**8.00**														
Sandwith ER	1	1	0	2	2.00														
Sandwith WFG	**32**	**53**	**3**	**990**	**19.80**		**5**	**4**										**18**	
	26	46	4	700	16.66	1	1	3										15	
Savage DG	**12**	**18**	**1**	**185**	**10.88**			**4**	**70**	**20**	**240**	**2**	**120.00**					**8**	
	1	1	0	48	48.00				5	0	33	1	33.00						
	1	1	0	1	1.00														
Saville GJ	**32**	**56**	**5**	**2275**	**44.60**	**5**	**10**	**3**	**47.2**	**8**	**197**	**2**	**98.50**					**42**	
	1	1	0	46	46.00														
	2	2	0	81	40.50		1												
Schofield R	**31**	**27**	**11**	**125**	**7.81**			**4**	**580.5**	**87**	**2089**	**66**	**31.65**			**3**		**10**	
Scobell GB	1	1	0	1	1.00														

Name	M	In	No	Runs	Ave	100	50	0	Ov	M	Runs	W	Ave	Balls	OW	5i	10m	Ct	St
Scott GA	1	2	0	11	5.50				20	1	58	2	29.00					2	
	12	20	2	198	11.00			2	15	?	27	1	27.00	4				5	
Scott-Chad C									24	4	48	3	16.00	4					
Scott-Chad GN	40	58	6	977	18.78		4	5	325.2	62	845	36	23.47					10	
	4	7	0	30	4.28			2	38	6	90	4	22.50					2	
Seager ML	2	1	1	16					7	1	35	0							
	2	3	0	63	21.00														
Self FG	31	44	5	635	16.28		3	5										13	
Sewell AP	3	3	1	0	0.00			2	25	9	48	4	12.00	5				2	
	4	6	1	34	6.80				52.2	27	81	10	8.10	5				4	
Sharpe JM	3	1	0	5	5.00		1		51.4	22	98	3	32.66					4	
Sharpe PJ	22	38	2	472	13.11		1	3	38	10	93	3	31.00					11	
	1	1	0	0	0.00			1	13	1	38	1	38.00						
Sharpe Phil J	50	84	18	2038	30.87	1	12	8	12	4	45	1	45.00					70	
	1	1	0	0	0.00			1											
Shearer AE	1	1	0	1	1.00														
Shelford PW	3	5	1	91	22.75			1	4	0	16	1	16.00					2	
									9	2	38		38.00						
Shepperd J	66	91	21	1159	16.55		1	11	1413.1	384	3847	163	23.60			7		59	
	1	1	0	8	8.00														
	2	2	0	6	3.00				25	4	108	4	27.00					4	
Shingler A	7	12	0	190	15.83		1	1	61.5	16	212	7	30.28					5	
	6	9	1	151	18.87	1		1	67	14	212	6	35.33					3	
Shore C	50	72	19	378	7.13			18	1337.2	439	2826	207	13.65	5		21	6	31	
	50	80	28	281	5.40			18	320.5	77	870	44	19.77	6		2	1		
									1960.2	632	3704	312	11.87	5		32	14	22	
									113.5	31	276	19	14.52	6					
Shreeve CM	3	5	0	41	8.20			9	16.2	2	94	1	94.00					2	
Skerrett CP	2	4	0	16	4.00			2										2	
Skinner TJM	2	4	0	33	8.25			1											
Skrimshire HF	1	2	0	10	5.00														
Skrimshire JF	16	28	1	439	16.25		3	9	37.4	10	90	10	9.00	5				12	
	6	9	0	150	16.66			3	6	1	19	0		5					
Slegg IR	17	20	7	122	9.38			4	467.5	102	1358	54	25.14	5				6	
	3	2	2	4					18	3	59	3	19.66						
	10	4	2	13	6.50			1	64.4	7	242	10	24.20						
Smart AL	9	9	1	81	10.12			3	184	52	540	22	24.54					1	
Smart BG	1								8	1	27	1	27.00						
Smith	5	7	1	38	6.33			1										6	4

Cricket club batting & bowling averages — surnames Smith CB to Stephenson EK. Bold rows are the primary (main) figures; italic rows are the secondary figures.

Name	M	In	No	Runs	Ave	100	50	0	Ov	M	Runs	W	Ave	Balls	OW	5i	10m	Ct	St
Smith CB	4	6	0	61	10.16			1										1	1
	2	*4*	*0*	*21*	*5.25*			*1*											
Smith CG	1	2	1	2	2.00			1	11	4	28	3	9.33	5				1	
	5	*10*	*2*	*45*	*5.62*			*1*	*52.1*	*12*	*156*	*8*	*19.50*	*5*				*2*	
Smith DJ	5	6	2	17	4.25			2										8	3
	2	*2*	*2*	*3*														*1*	
	1	*2*																*1*	*1*
Smith EW	48	65	28	276	7.45			14	1412	356	3658	226	16.18			18	6	23	
	25	*35*	*22*	*108*	*8.31*			*3*	*651.1*	*149*	*1857*	*121*	*15.34*			*10*	*2*	*8*	
Smith HJ	1	1		5	5.00				21.1	3	76	3	25.33	5					
Smith JJ	1	2	1	8	8.00				2	0	6	0		5					
	3	*5*	*1*	*81*	*20.25*									*4*					
Smith Ray	1	1	0	46	46.00				8	2	13	0						1	
Smith Reginald	2	3	0	17	5.66				18	3	50	2	25.00	5				4	
Snelling T	1	1	1	3					17	2	61	0		5				1	
	2	*2*	*2*	*11*					*6*	*1*	*20*	*1*	*20.00*						
Softley PLH	1	1	1	3					13	1	59	1	59.00						
Spelman JM	53	94	15	2814	35.62	1	9	8	164.5	25	653	12	54.41					50	
	17	*17*	*2*	*316*	*21.06*		*2*	*4*	*15.1*	*1*	*84*	*5*	*16.80*					*4*	
	36	*28*	*4*	*632*	*26.33*		*3*	*1*	*29.2*	*4*	*137*	*3*	*45.66*					*18*	
Spelman JO	2	1	0	0	0.00				12	0	66	2	33.00					2	
Stafford WFH	2	3	0	76	25.33														
Stamp DM	28	54	6	1317	27.43		6	1	15.5	3	42	1	42.00					27	1
	1	*2*	*1*	*31*	*31.00*													*1*	
	7	*7*	*1*	*205*	*34.33*		*2*		*2*	*0*	*13*	*0*						*2*	
Stannard GM	1	2	0	6	3.00			1											
	1	*1*	*0*	*5*	*5.00*														
Stanton JCC	1	2	0	3	1.50			1											
Staples S	4	5	1	70	17.50		1	1	54	23	121	6	20.16	5				7	
	1	*1*	*0*	*3*	*3.00*													*1*	
Starling G	11	20	2	284	15.77		2	5	61.2	8	234	9	26.00			1		6	
	1	*1*	*0*	*1*	*1.00*				*7*	*1*	*24*	*2*	*12.00*						
Starling SJ	15	11	3	31	3.87			2	174.2	36	577	18	32.05					9	
	2	*2*	*1*	*13*	*13.00*				*27*	*10*	*69*	*7*	*9.85*			*1*			
Stephens V	1	2	0	26	13.00													1	
	1	*2*	*0*	*14*	*7.00*			*1*											
Stephenson EK	1	2	0	80	40.00		1											1	

Name	M	In	No	Runs	Ave	100	50	0	Ov	M	Runs	W	Ave	Balls	OW	5i	10m	Ct	St
Stevens BGW	66	94	16	1068	13.69		3	17										83	30
	6	4	0	51	12.75													4	
Stevens G	12	19	2	189	11.11		1	2	149.3	30	478	24	19.91					3	
	4	5	0	68	10.20			1	32	3	130	3	43.33			1		1	
Stevens GA	158	262	17	8122	33.15	15	44	21	7	2	21	1	21.00					137	1
	15	28	1	501	18.55		3	3										9	
Stevens GS	2	4	0	32	8.00			1											
	1	2	0	25	12.50													1	
Stevens NW	11	20	0	239	11.95		1	4	3	0	14	0						8	
	2	4	0	7	1.75			1											
Stewart AL	2	2	0	11	5.50			1	45	18	80	4	20.00	4					
Stockings DC	16	28	2	570	21.92		2											7	
	1	1	0	9	9.00													7	
	1	1	1	3	3.00														
Stocks EW	2	4	0	18	4.50			2	56	?	112	5	22.40	4	2				
Stocks GA	1	1	1	1															
Stone GJ	9	12	6	73	12.16			2	38	12	107	6	17.83					17	7
Stone OP	1	2	0	58	29.00													1	
Sugden A	1	2	0	14	7.00			1											
Swarbrick DL	3	6	3	91	30.33													2	
Tate JS	11	10	5	30	6.00			3	265	79	716	23	31.13					2	
	3	2	1	1	1.00				25	4	84	2	42.00					1	
Taylor AP	1	2	2	0	0.00			2											
	1	1	0	19	19.00														
Taylor CF	10	17	2	120	8.00			4										5	5
Taylor JP	5	7	2	44	8.80			1	131.3	24	438	14	31.28					1	
	1	1	0	5	5.00				9.5	0	36	3	12.00						
	5	4	1	20	6.66				41.1	3	174	9	19.33					2	
Taylor K	12	20	5	957	63.80	4	5	1	18	5	60	1	60.0					10	
Taylor NS	4	6	0	121	20.16				56	12	181	9	20.11					2	
	3	3	0	63	21.00		1	1	17	0	102	3	34.00					1	
Taylor RF	3	4	1	21	7.00			1											
Taylor SK	4	7	3	126	31.50		1	1											
	2	2	0	7	3.50														
	1	1	1	0	0.00			1											
Tharp AK	2	4	0	80	20.00		1											1	
Thaxter DW	13	20	3	190	11.17			4										4	
	1	1	0	2	2.00														

Name	M	In	No	Runs	Ave	100	50	0	Ov	M	Runs	W	Ave	Balls	OW	5i	10m	Ct	St
Thelwell ST	4	3	2	0	0.00			2	79	16	250	6	41.66						
	1	1	0	0	0.00			1	6	0	35	1	35.00						
Theobald HE	55	84	10	1650	22.29	3	5	10	1	0	12	0		8				26	
	4	6	0	175	29.16		2	1											
Thistleton-Smith JC	67	101	5	2208	23.00	1	12	7	2	0	4	0						14	
	6	11	1	164	16.40													2	
Thomas DR	122	161	53	3002	27.79		14	17	1507.1	357	4302	198	21.72			4		84	
	28	25	10	478	31.86		2		120	24	531	27	19.66					6	
	52	42	8	1036	30.47		5		343	28	1551	65	23.86					22	
Thomas MW	36	32	12	365	18.25			4	543.2	132	1608	80	20.10			2		10	
	8	4	1	22	7.33				50	4	217	3	72.33					5	
	24	16	2	99	7.07			4	199.4	9	933	15	62.20					5	
Thomas PW	7	9	3	37	6.16			2	111.2	25	320	11	29.09					5	
	2	1	0	16	16.00				11	3	42	0						1	
	3	3	1	9	4.50			1	19	1	72	2	36.00					1	
Thomas WO	62	101	6	2259	23.77	3	12	8	188	25	728	19	38.31					16	
	3	3	1	217	108.50	1	1		2	0	11	1	11.00					1	
Thompson B	1	2	1	25	25.00			1										1	
Thompson WS	78	121	10	2323	20.92		14	13	1244.4	252	3953	185	21.36	6		11	1	54	
									80.3	12	295	18	16.38	8		2			
	5	7	1	143	23.83				78.5	8	306	14	21.85	6					
									15	1	78	3	26.00	8					
Thorne DC	22	26	4	220	10.00			3	483.1	137	1310	48	27.29			4		9	
	1	2	0	24	12.00			1	22	1	126	2	63.00						
Thorne GC	6	11	0	130	11.81		1	1	1	0	3	0							
Thorne ME	16	25	5	506	25.30		3		6	1	23	0						5	
Thornton GG	3	5	2	33	11.00				37	6	129	1	129.00	5				1	
Thurgar RW	48	74	3	1108	15.60	1	2	12										64	31
	8	15	1	246	17.57			2										2	1
Thurgar WA	8	11	2	110	12.22			2	4	2	9	0		4				2	
									3	0	12	1	12.00	5					
Thursby MH	9	14	0	222	15.85		1	2										7	
	2	3	0	24	8.00			1											
Thursby W	12	21	1	311	15.55		2	3	19	3	60	1	60.00	5				5	
									10	6	15	1	15.00	4	21				
Tillard C	2	4	0	53	13.25		1		284.2	?	424	48	8.83	4		6	2	31	
	40	66	4	810	13.06			11	984.2	445	1571	127	12.37	4		6	2		
									34.4	9	72	4	18.00	5					

Name	M	In	No	Runs	Ave	100	50	0	Ov	M	Runs	W	Ave	Balls	OW	5i	10m	Ct	St
Tillard J	1	2	0	0	0.00			2											
Tilney NJ	13	18	2	129	8.06			4	218	50	646	20	32.30					6	
Tilney NJ	*4*	*3*	*0*	*47*	*15.66*			*1*	*57.1*	*12*	*147*	*5*	*29.40*						
Tipping MR	25	34	5	605	20.86		2	4										8	
Tipping MR	*5*	*4*	*0*	*39*	*9.75*													*2*	
Tipping MR	*9*	*7*	*0*	*114*	*16.28*			*1*										*5*	
Tipple FA	1	2	1	5	5.00			1	8.2	5	12	1	12.00	5				3	
Tipple FA	*1*	*2*	*0*	*14*	*7.00*				*39*	*18*	*59*	*1*	*59.00*	*4*				*1*	
Todd AJM	3	2	2	14					20.4	1	92	0						1	
Todd AJM	*4*	*2*	*0*	*11*	*5.50*			*1*	*19*	*1*	*99*	*0*						*1*	
Tomlinson JJW	8	9	5	40	10.00				36	2	154	5	30.80					2	
Tonge WC	1	2	0	19	9.50														
Tonge WC	*3*	*5*	*0*	*46*	*9.20*			*1*											
Topley TD	7	7	3	47	11.75			1	190.5	44	655	27	24.25			1		3	
Topley TD	*7*	*6*	*0*	*23*	*3.83*				*61.1*	*6*	*222*	*9*	*24.66*					*1*	
Trafford SWJ	3	5	1	23	5.75			1	10	0	31	0						2	
Treglown CJH	20	34	6	422	15.07		1	4										14	
Treglown CJH	*3*	*6*	*1*	*66*	*13.20*			*2*											
Trevor LG	5	9	0	36	4.00			4	38.2	7	110	10	11.00			1		1	
Trevor PCW	*1*	*2*	*0*	*0*	*0.00*			*2*						*5*				*1*	
Trower J	2	4	0	60	15.00													1	
Trower J	*1*	*1*	*0*	*34*	*34.00*													*1*	
Trower J	*4*	*3*	*1*	*34*	*17.00*													*1*	
Tuck EL	2	3	0	0	0.00			3	46	13	149	3	49.66						
Tuck KSC	1																		
Tufnell NC	9	15	1	190	13.57			1										4	6
Tufnell NC	*1*	*2*	*0*	*9*	*4.50*			*1*										*1*	
Tufts IJP	4	6	1	69	13.80		1											1	
Tufts IJP	*6*	*6*	*3*	*82*	*27.33*														
Tufts IJP	*7*	*1*	*0*	*10*	*10.00*			*1*											
Turner HW	11	19	5	108	7.71			3	10.1	?	18	2	9.00	4				2	
Turner HW									*85.3*	*41*	*119*	*6*	*19.83*	*4*	*1*				
Turner JF	1	2	0	12	6.00													1	
Turner JF	*1*																		
Tyler AW	1	2	0	11	5.50													1	1
Tyler AW	*2*	*3*	*0*	*11*	*3.66*			*1*											*1*
Utting AG	11	17	6	47	4.27			6	215.1	79	416	35	11.88			1		5	
Utting AG	*1*	*2*	*1*	*2*	*2.00*				*63*	*18*	*95*	*8*	*11.87*						
Van Onselen D	1	1	0	23	23.00				3	0	28	0						2	

Name	M	In	No	Runs	Ave	100	50	0	Ov	M	Runs	W	Ave	Balls	OW	5i	10m	Ct	St
Veale FH	1	1	0	18	18.00														
Wakefield HR	4	8	0	186	23.25		2		70	12	307	7	43.85					2	
Walker DF	49	72	9	3997	63.44	13	19	1	55.5	6	192	7	27.42					46	1
	2	*3*	*1*	*37*	*18.50*			*1*	*2*	*0*	*12*	*0*							
Walker GW	28	38	7	402	12.96		1	2	1136.1	249	3510	120	29.25			9	2	12	
	8	*7*	*2*	*73*	*14.60*			*1*	*67*	*8*	*356*	*13*	*27.38*					*3*	
	19	*15*	*5*	*238*	*23.80*		*1*		*160*	*11*	*718*	*28*	*25.64*					*4*	
Walker JR	23	39	2	893	24.13		6	5	10	1	114	0						19	
	6	*5*	*0*	*76*	*15.20*			*3*										*6*	
	21	*20*	*4*	*386*	*24.12*		*2*											*10*	
Walmsley PG	109	99	30	299	4.39			35	2706.4	760	6972	329	21.19			13	3	24	
	7	*6*	*3*	*9*	*3.00*			*2*	*113*	*23*	*339*	*17*	*19.84*			*1*			
Walsh CH	6	11	1	100	10.00			3	10.3	2	24	2	12.00					2	
	2	*6*	*0*	*34*	*5.66*			*2*										*1*	
Walter CH	3	4	1	11	3.66			2											
Ward EE	4	6	0	115	19.16		1		2	0	5	0						1	
Ward MJP	2	3	1	66	33.00				7	0	63	0						1	
	2	*2*	*0*	*0*	*0.00*			*2*											
Ward TR	41	72	10	2892	46.65	8	15	1	7	0	55	1	55.00					40	
	2	*2*	*1*	*65*	*65.00*			*1*											
	28	*26*	*3*	*1285*	*55.87*	*3*	*8*	*7*										*9*	
Warnes MR	4	8	0	199	24.87		1	1	16	0	81	3	27.00						
	5	*3*	*0*	*48*	*16.00*				*9*										
Warnes MW	4	8	5	59	19.66				84.5	14	292	8	36.50					1	
									9	*0*	*61*	*0*							
									19	*1*	*121*	*2*	*60.50*						
Waters HW	2	2	2	2														2	
Watling RG	1	2	0	10	5.00														
	2	*4*	*0*	*47*	*11.75*														
	1	*2*	*0*	*20*	*10.00*			*1*											
Watson AA	7	6	2	3	0.75			2	97.2	18	350	7	50.00					3	
	3								*26*	*3*	*153*	*3*	*51.00*						
Watson AC	1	2	0	127	63.50		2		5	1	18	0							
Watson AK	23	34	2	1045	32.65	1	8	5	4	0	20	0						8	
	4	*8*	*0*	*104*	*13.00*			*3*										*2*	
Watson AM	11	14	2	251	20.91	1		1	157.5	34	523	9	58.11					5	
	1	*1*	*0*	*8*	*8.00*				*7*	*0*	*41*	*1*	*41.00*						
Watson CP	4	6	0	50	8.33			2										3	

Name	M	In	No	Runs	Ave	100	50	0	Ov	M	Runs	W	Ave	Balls	OW	5i	10m	Ct	St
Watson H	95	130	28	1403	13.81		2	19	2176.1	489	5878	341	17.23			15	1	54	
(sub)	*13*	*23*	*8*	*209*	*13.93*			*4*	*318.1*	*54*	*1176*	*52*	*22.61*			*4*		*4*	
Watts IM	46	73	3	997	14.24		3	9										24	
(sub)	*2*	*3*	*1*	*8*	*4.00*														
Waymouth SN	16	19	6	152	11.69			1	185	39	619	17	36.41					8	
(sub)	*3*	*5*	*0*	*36*	*7.20*			*2*	*95*	*40*	*140*	*8*	*17.50*	*4*				*4*	
Weighell WB	4	8	1	93	13.28													1	
Wesley PW	4								5	0	22	0							
Wesley RJ	23	36	2	538	15.82		1	5	72	10	234	6	39.00					20	
Wharton TH	8	13	1	113	9.41			1	20	1	91	3	30.33					1	
Whitaker MR	1	2	0	19	9.50				7	2	20	0							
White K	1	2	0	82	41.00		1											3	
White SN	12	7	3	12	3.00			3	169.3	26	649	20	32.45					2	
(sub)	*9*	*2*	*1*	*34*	*34.00*			*1*	*66*	*6*	*272*	*15*	*18.13*						
Whitehead J	31	51	9	959	22.83		2	4										24	
(sub)	*2*	*3*	*1*	*70*	*35.00*													*2*	
(sub)	*10*	*9*	*0*	*35*	*3.88*			*5*										*3*	
Whitney DA	4	6	2	98	24.50				1.1	0	8	0						4	
Whittaker PK	27	20	9	108	9.81			5	432.2	65	1529	38	40.23			1		17	
(sub)	*15*	*6*	*3*	*24*	*8.00*			*17*	*140*	*28*	*373*	*21*	*17.76*					*5*	
Wickham AP	67	106	24	1005	12.25		1											80	61
(sub)																		*9*	*2*
Wild DK	5	9	4	22	4.40			3										9	
(sub)	*2*	*1*	*1*	*1*														*1*	*1*
Wilkinson MO	20	32	7	762	30.48		5	1	1	1	0	0						20	
(sub)	*13*	*11*	*2*	*198*	*22.00*		*1*	*1*						*4*				*2*	
(sub)	*15*	*12*	*2*	*123*	*12.30*			*4*						*4*				*7*	
Willett EH	7	12	4	78	9.75			2	25		46	4	11.50		3			3	
(sub)									*7.2*	*3*	*23*	*1*	*23.00*						
Williams DJ	4	7	1	107	17.83			1						4					
Williams G	5	8	1	101	14.42			1	27	4	66	1	66.00					2	
(sub)	*2*	*4*	*0*	*25*	*6.25*				*25*	*3*	*92*	*8*	*11.50*						
Williamson EC	24	32	14	172	9.55			6										38	3
(sub)	*1*	*2*	*1*	*6*	*6.00*														
Wilson BK	24	36	2	500	14.70		1	5	17	6	32	3	10.66	5				5	
(sub)	*8*	*16*	*2*	*321*	*22.92*		*2*	*1*	*5*	*1*	*22*	*0*		*6*					
(sub)									*3*	*1*	*9*	*1*	*9.00*	*6*					
(sub)									*9*	*2*	*30*	*1*	*30.00*	*5*					
Wilson CP	12	20	1	440	23.15		4	3	540.2	253	693	70	9.90	4		8	1	15	

196

Name	M	In	No	Runs	Ave	100	50	0	Ov	M	Runs	W	Ave	Balls	OW	5i	10m	Ct	St
Wilson FM	3	6	0	45	7.50			2										2	
Wilson JC	5	10	2	92	11.50			1	5	0	11	0						3	
	1	2	0	5	2.50			1	3	0	7	0						1	
Wilson KP	3	4	0	39	9.75														
Wilson MD	2	3	0	10	3.33				2	0	15	0							
	1	1	0	5	5.00														
Wilson TE	1	1	1	4														1	
Wilton GW	33	57	14	722	16.79		3	5	328.4	68	1128	23	49.04					17	
	6	5	0	48	9.60				82	14	334	8	41.75					1	
Wiltshire CJ	2	3	0	5	1.66			1											
Wiltshire FHC	1	2	0	1	0.50			1	5	1	12	0							
Wingfield RA	3	4	0	16	4.00			1											
Wiseman PDE	1	1	1	1					7	1	33	1	33.00						
Witherden EG	72	128	23	4794	45.65	13	22	4	974.1	310	2200	104	21.15			3		49	
	2	3	0	91	30.33				10	0	46	0						2	
Witherden N	1	1	1	53					10	3	33	0							
Wood BJH	68	82	21	854	14.00		1	7										122	21
	3	3		6	3.00													3	1
Woodhouse JS	2	4	2	20	10.00													2	
Woolstencroft ML	5	9	0	97	10.77													2	
Wormald J	11	17	1	295	18.43		2	4										3	
	1	2	0	3	1.50			1											
Worman JN	29	40	3	504	13.62		2	7	116.3	46	159	10	15.90	5		1		22	
	14	24	1	336	14.60		1	2	776.5	224	1832	117	15.65	6		9	3	10	
									11	4	27	1	27.00	5					
									263.2	79	591	38	15.55	6					
Wright E	72	61	29	302	9.43			10	1621.4	316	5460	215	25.39			9		28	
	6	4	0	12	3.00				69	10	252	11	22.90					1	
	7								9	2	19	0							
Wright TM	23	23	9	124	8.86			5	510.1	101	1769	69	25.64			4	1	7	
Wyllys GHDeB	4	4	0	30	7.50			2											
	1	1	0	12	12.00														
Wynne-Willson LF	10	14	2	192	16.00			1	7	2	16	1	16.00					1	
Yates P	1	0	4	4	4.00				12	1	66	2	33.00					1	
Zaidi ZMN	11	11	3	58	7.25			1	112.1	29	372	14	26.57			1		3	
	2	1	0	4	4.00				18	2	97	2	48.50						

Subscribers as of 14th September 2011

Mr M Davage	32 Norman Drive, Old Catton, Norwich, Norfolk, NR6 7HN
Mr. J Creasy	Flat 28, Bradbury Court, Clifton Park Avenue, London SW20 8BF
Nikita & Terry Delgaty	37 Beambridge Place, Chalvedon, Pitsea, Essex SS13 3LN
Corrinne Davage	13 Drayton Wood Road, Hellesdon, Norwich NR6 5BX
Marc Davage	19 Wright Drive, Scarning, Norwich NR19 2TS
Mrs P Webb	31 Landsear Road, Shloing, Southampton SO19 !EF
Karen Matthews	26 Hunters Close, Chatteris, Cambridgeshire PE16 6BD
Dr. S Musk	87 Newmarket Street, Norwich NR2 2DP
Tony Webb	59c Mount Avenue, Ealing, London W5 1PN
Colin Munford	5 Penhurst Road, Ipswich, Suffolk IP3 8QZ
Mr C Bowling	1 Three Corner Drive, Old Catton, Norwich, Norfolk, NR6 7HA
G.C. Ward	39 Catton Chase, Old Catton, Norwich, Norfolk, NR6 7AS
Mr A E Otway	12 Dixon Road, Norwich, Norfolk, NR7 8QJ
Mrs B I Finch	24 Woodham Leas, Old Catton, Norwich, Norfolk, NR6 7EE
Mr D Armstrong	Thorpe Cottage, Mill Common, Ridlington, Norfolk NR28 9TY
Mr K Bray	160 Cavendish Court, Recorder Road, Norwich NR1 1HX
Mr F Wright	38 Norman Drive, Old Catton, Norwich, Norfolk, NR6 7HN
Mr E Hall	23 Browick Road, Wymondham, Norfolk, NR18 0QN
Mr S Skinner	Old Baddock Barn, 7 West Lane, Horsham St Faith, Norwich, NR10 3JH
Mr P Moore	93 Drayton High Road, Drayton, Norwich, Norfolk, NR8 6AL
Mr R.Innes	Wrangham,3 Cants Close, Barford, Norwich, NRG 4BP
D.C.Stockings	40 Breeze Avenue, Aylsham, Norwich, NR11 6WF
A.G.Coomb	2 Treventow Road, Portscatho, Truro
Mr Eric.A.Kent	33 The Vale, Swainsthorpe, Norwich,NR14 8PL
R.H.G.Hoff	Church Farm, Shouldham Thorpe, Kings Lynn, PE33 0ED
Mr.Michael Eccles	24 Whistlefish Court, Norwich, NR5 8QR
Mr Robert Fellowes	64 Cottesmore Court, Stanford Road, London, W8 5QW
I.Lambourne	13 Heath Court, Baughurst, Tadley, Hants
Mrs J.Hayles	16 Northfield Court, Alderborough, Suffolk, IP15LU
Mrs V.Stevens	2 Gilbert Way, Cringleford, Norwich, NR4 7RN
R.Blower	26 Morello Close, Norwich, NR4 7NF
Mrs J.Borrett	Westfield, Stubb Road, Hickling, Norwich, NR12 0BN
B.G.Drake	26 Lodge Breck, Norwich, NR8 6AR
N.J.Tilney	Greenacres Farm, Newton Road, Hainford, Norwich, NR10 3LZ
B.Taylor	46 Brabazon Road, Hellesdon, Norwich, NR6 6SZ
David Wild	17 Indigo Tard, Norwich, NR3 3QZ
K.Hounsome	27 The Avenues, Norwich, NR2 3PH
J.Belmont	62 Cecil Road, Norwich, NR12 2QN
Mr J Gurney	Sherwood', Chapel Lane, Hempstead Next Holt, Norfolk, NR25 6TH
Mr C Kenyon	8 Glenlairn Park Road, Cheltenham, GL50 2NA
Mrs J Perry-Warnes	Hill Farm House, Saxthorpe, Norwich, Norfolk, NR11 7BX
Mrs K Tuck	26 Cowslip Lane, Sheringham, Norfolk, NR26 8LX
Mrs P Cook	124 Hercules Road, Helesdon, Norwich, NR6 5HJ
Mr M Thorne	Yew Tree House, Alue Road Tollerton, York, YO62 1QA
Mr E Witherden	38 Northend Road, Quainton, Nr Aylesbury, Bucks, HP22 4BE
Mr G Littlewood	Blackwater Lodge, Blackwater Lane, Gt Witchingham, Norwich, NR9 5PH
Mr F Foley	43 Linacre Avenue, Sprowston, Norwich, Norfolk, NR7 8JZ
Mr K P Cooper	404 Unthank Road, Norwich, Norfolk, NR4 7QH

A D Cunningham	Dalbruach, Dall, Rannoch, Perthshire, PH17 2QH
Mr D & Mrs P Tooley	35 Berrington Road, Norwich, Norfolk, NR6 6PH
Mr B.Amos	20 Brook Road, Dersingham, Kings Lynn, PE31 6LG
Andrew Payne	London House, 9 Dereham Road, Mattishall, NR20 3QB
Mr M.Riches	9 Rowan Way, Gorleston on sea, Gt Yarmouth, NR31 8EP
Mr M.C.Sills	7 Beech Lawns, Torrington Park, London, N12 9PP
J.Brackenbury	18 Lea View, Ryhall Stamford, Lincs, PE9 4HZ
Mrs BM Pardon	14 Cherry Tree Lane, North Walsham, NR28 0HR
John Shepperd	30 Thor Road, Thorpe St Andrew, Norwich
Michael Oxbury	3 The Chase, Blofield, Norwich, NR13 4LZ
Mr RS King	16 Westerley Way, Caister on sea, Gt Yarmouth, NR30 5AJ
S.E.Child	84 Wandle Road, Upper Tooting, London, SW17 7DW
P.W.M.Rice	Vine Cottage, Butchers Hill, Ickleton, Saffron Walden, CB10 1SR
Ian Ayres	1 Down End Road, Portsmouth, PO6 1HH
Alan Futter	98 Dean Way, Storrington, West Sussex, RH20 4QS
Mr P.Yaxley	Polperro, Silfield Road, Wymondham, NR18 9AU
Mr Colin Shreeve	Rose Cottage, 8 Pound Road, North Walsham, Norfolk, NR28 9HE
Mr Lenny Mason	22 Jawnys Close, Aylsham, Norwich, Norfolk, NR11 6DL
M P L Smith	Tredegar, Ashmanhaugh, Norwich, Norfolk, NR12 8YN
Mr Andy Agar	5 Albion Close, Crawley, West Sussex, RH10 7WJ
Mr B Dickinson	54 Morston Road, Blakeney, Holt, Norfolk, NR25 7BE
Mrs P Belton	1 New Lane, Stibbington, Cambs, PE8 6LW
Mr A J Barrett	1 Stratford Drive, Norwich, Norfolk, NR1 2EV
Neville R Cooke	16 Sunningdale, Eaton, Norwich, Norfolk, NR4 6AQ
Nigel Dodds	Talgarth. Winch Road, Gayton, King's Lynn, PE32 1QP
R L M Feast	15a Victoria Road, Diss, Norfolk, IP22 4HW
Mr M T Dunn	Brambles, Vicarage Road, Great Hockham, Thetford, Norfolk, IP24 1PE
Dr B M Laws	Cheyne House, Chelmondiston, Ipswich, Suffolk, IP9 1JA
Mr M Pim	99 Cawston Road, Aylsham, Norfolk, NR11 6NB
Mrs C Osborn	246 Wingrove Road North, Fenham, Newcastle-Upon-Tyne, NE4 9EJ
F D Bottomley	Austin's Hill, Brafferton, Helperby, North Yorkshire, YO61 2QB
Mr N F Epps	18 Vine Place, Brighton, East Sussex, BN1 3HE
Mrs M Chilvers	230 Bluebell Road, Norwich, Norfolk, NR4 7LW
Mr R Bonnington	29 Norton Road, Ingatestone, Essex, CM4 0AB
Mr T Ferley	4 Raven Yard, King Street, Norwich, Norfolk, NR1 1PQ
Mr A Fowler	19 Regency Court, Brunswick Road, Sutton, Surrey, SM1 4EH
Mr M Hammond	12 Astley Crescent, Hunstanton, Norfolk, PE36 6HA
Rev A Rutter	Home Farm, Chilson, South Chard, Somerset, TA20 2NX
Mr J Poole	31 Heron Close, Salthouse, Norwich, Norfolk, NR13 6SB
Mrs M Batts	Daleview, The Street, Lyng, Norwich, NR9 5QZ
Mr G Moore	Old Seven Stars, Sandpit Lane, Bledlow, Bucks, HP27 9QQ
Mr P Sykes	12 Potters Drive, Hopton-on-Sea, Great Yarmouth, Norfolk, NR31 9RW
Mr R Roe	The Old Rectory, Cromer Road, Hevingham, Norwich, Norfolk, NR10 5QU
Mr P Defriez	134 Victoria Street, St Albans, Hertfordshire, AL1 3TG
Mr A B Percival	31 Covert Rise, Tattenhall, Chester, CH3 9HA
Andy Porter	32A Aberdour Road, Goodmayes, Ilford, IG3 9SB
Mr N Hill	Red House, Swardeston, Norwich, Norfolk, NR14 8DN
Mr R Woods	13 Ella Road, Thorpe Hamlet, Norwich, Norfolk, NR1 4BP
J.C.C. Stanton	7 Cleaves House, Walsingham, Norfolk, NR22 6DJ
Mrs C Blincoe	Lime Kiln Farm, Norwich Road, Stoke Holy Cross, Norwich, Norfolk, NR14 8AB

Mr R Middleton	19 Seafield Road North, Caister-on-Sea, Norfolk, NR30 5LE
Mrs L Barnard	6 Andrew Goodall Close, Toftwood, Dereham, Norfolk, NR19 1SR
Mr M Calvert	Studio House, Mile End Close, Norwich, Norfolk, NR4 7QV
Air CDRE D A Atherton	11 Northcroft, The Park, Cheltenham, Gloucester, GL50 2NL
Mr S H Back	5 Christchurch Road, Norwich, Norfolk, NR2 2AD
Mr P Rogers	63 Fakenham Road, Lenwade, Norwich, Norfolk, NR9 5AE
Mr J C Rowe	41A Shore Road, Hesketh Bank, Preston, Lancashire, PR4 6RD
Mr B Sutherland	63 Netton Close, Elburton, Plymouth, Devon, PL9 8UL
D.Tubby	88 East Anglian Way, Gorleston, Norfolk, NR31 6QY
W Wyllys	Bay Farm, Tarrant Monkton, Blandford Forum, Dorset, DT11 8RX
Mr A Halford	12 North Dene Park, Chadderton, Oldham, OL9 9JN
J Halford	23 Wenton Close, Cottesmore, Oakham, LE15
K Sharpe	38 Stamford Road, Easton on the Hill, Stamford, Lincs, PE9 3NU
N Stock	77 Eastlands Road, Rugby, Warwickshire, CV21 3RR
J Lee	5 High Street, Blakeney, Holt, Norfolk, NR15 7NA
P Bailey	28 St Johns Road, Orpington, Kent, BR5 1HX
D Sneesby	15 Swanton Grove, Dereham, Norfolk, NR19 2HN
M Ramm	2 West End, Saxlingham Thorpe, Norwich, Norfolk, NR15 1UE
R Claxton	7 Indigo Yard, Norwich, Norfolk, NR3 3QZ
S Waymouth	47 Ancaster Crescent, Motspur Park, New Malden, Surrey, KT3 6BD
Peter Tuck	188a St James Road, Croydon, Surrey, CR0 2BW
Mr PJ Wright	33 Wood View Road, Hellesdon, Norwich, NR6 5QD
Mr J Atkins	Kingstanding House. Westfield Road, Cholsey, Wallingford, OX10 9JW
J Tomlinson	20, Clement Drive, Peterborough, PE29 9RQ
T Pyle	Pyle-Inn, 30 Mill Lane, Horsford, Norwich, Norfolk, NR10 3EX
I Whitney	70 College Road, Norwich, Norfolk, NR2 3JL
T Bland	13 Armitage Close, Cringleford, Norwich, Norfolk, NR4 6XZ
P Walmsley	Tryddyn, Horning Road West, Hoveton, Norwich, Norfolk, NR12 8QJ
G Saville	261 Notley Road, Braintree, Essex, CM7 1HR
B Harvey	76 Spinney Road, Thorpe St Andrew, Norwich, Norfolk, NR7 0PJ
N Rudd	RHP Partnership, Lancaster House, 87 Yarmouth Road, Norwich, Norfolk, NR7 0HF
A.Debenham	4 Vere Gardens, The Grove, Henley Road, Ipswich, Suffolk IP1 4NZ
Mr M.Mann	72 The Street, Rockland All Saints, Attleborough, Norfolk, NR17 1TP
K Flood	45 The Street, Hindringham, Fakenham, Norfolk, NR21 0PR
M Todd	44 Beech Road, Downham Market, Norfolk, PE38 9PH
D Bassingthwaighte	6 Chapel Avenue, Long Stratton, Norfolk, NR15 2TE